THE OXFORD HANDBOOK OF

EXPERTISE
AND
DEMOCRATIC
POLITICS

THE OXFORD HANDBOOK OF

EXPERTISE

AND

DEMOCRATIC

POLITICS

Edited by

GIL EYAL *and* THOMAS MEDVETZ

OXFORD

UNIVERSITY PRESS

Oxford University Press is a department of the University of Oxford. It furthers
the University's objective of excellence in research, scholarship, and education
by publishing worldwide. Oxford is a registered trade mark of Oxford University
Press in the UK and certain other countries.

Published in the United States of America by Oxford University Press
198 Madison Avenue, New York, NY 10016, United States of America.

Library of Congress Cataloging-in-Publication Data
Names: Eyal, Gil, editor. | Medvetz, Thomas, editor.
Title: The Oxford handbook of expertise and democratic politics /
edited by Gil Eyal, Thomas Medvetz.
Other titles: Handbook of expertise and democratic politics
Description: New York : Oxford University Press, 2023. |
Series: Oxford handbooks series |
Includes bibliographical references and index.
Identifiers: LCCN 2022030824 (print) | LCCN 2022030825 (ebook) |
ISBN 9780190848927 (hardback) | ISBN 9780190848941 (epub) |
ISBN 9780190848958
Subjects: LCSH: Information society—Political aspects. | Knowledge,
Theory of—Political aspects. | Expertise—Political aspects. |
Objectivity—Political aspects. | Democracy. | Democratization. | Populism.
Classification: LCC HM851 .O977 2023 (print) | LCC HM851 (ebook) |
DDC 303.48/33—dc23/eng/20221018
LC record available at https://lccn.loc.gov/2022030824
LC ebook record available at https://lccn.loc.gov/2022030825

DOI: 10.1093/oxfordhb/9780190848927.001.0001

Printed by Integrated Books International, United States of America

Contents

PART III. OBJECTIVITY

PART IV. JURISDICTIONAL STRUGGLES

PART V. MAKING THE FUTURE PRESENT

PART VI. THE TRANSFORMATION AND PERSISTENCE OF PROFESSIONS

PART VII. NEW MEDIA AND EXPERTISE

Contributors

Madeleine Akrich
Mines Paris, PSL University, Centre for the Sociology of Innovation (CSI), i3 UMR CNRS

Jenny Andersson
Sciences Po, Centre for European Studies and Comparative Politics

Jakob Arnoldi
Department of Management, Aarhus University

Maria J. Azocar
College of the Sequoias

E. Summerson Carr
Department of Anthropology and Crown Family School of Social Work, Policy, and Practice, University of Chicago

Harry Collins
School of Social Sciences, Cardiff University

Robert P. Crease
Stony Brook University

David Demortain
Laboratoire Interdisciplinaire Sciences Innovations Sociétés (LISIS), French National Institute for Research for Agriculture, Food and the Environment (INRAE)

Darrin Durant
School of Historical and Philosophical Studies, University of Melbourne

Steven Epstein
Department of Sociology, Northwestern University

Wendy Nelson Espeland
Northwestern University

Robert Evans
School of Social Sciences, Cardiff University

Gil Eyal
Department of Sociology, Columbia University

Denis Fischbacher-Smith
University of Glasgow Business School

Tal Golan
Department of History, University of California, San Diego

Zachary Griffen
University of California, Los Angeles

Ruthanne Huising
Emlyon Business School

Andrew Lakoff
Department of Sociology, University of Southern California

Brice Laurent
Mines Paris, PSL University, Center for the Sociology of Innovation (CSI), i3 UMR CNRS

Thomas Medvetz
Department of Sociology, University of California, San Diego

Daniel Navon
Department of Sociology, University of California, San Diego

Aaron Panofsky
University of California, Los Angeles

Frank Pasquale
Brooklyn Law School

Theodore M. Porter
Department of History, University of California, Los Angeles

Vololona Rabeharisoa
Mines Paris, PSL University, Centre for the Sociology of Innovation (CSI), i3 UMR CNRS

Alexander Ruser
University of Agder

Paul Starr
Princeton University

Nico Stehr
Zeppelin University

Eleanor Townsley
Department of Sociology and Anthropology, Mt. Holyoke College

Stephen Turner
Department of Philosophy, University of South Florida

Martin Weinel
School of Social Sciences, Cardiff University

Peter Weingart
Bielefeld University

INTRODUCTION

GIL EYAL AND THOMAS MEDVETZ

WHEN the idea for this handbook was first conceived, back in 2017, we knew that the topic was important. We just didn't know *how* important, or how quickly it would come to dominate politics. If anybody thought that the role of experts in democratic politics is a sideshow to the more important distributional or ideological politics, the Coronavirus pandemic should have disabused them of this notion. There is hardly a variable currently more predictive of the distinctive fortunes of countries (and thus, of the life chances of millions of people) than the way in which the relations between experts, decision-makers, and the public are configured. Where these relations seem to be in deep crisis, further exacerbated by the pandemic, as in the United States and United Kingdom, the death toll is still climbing. Where there was no such crisis to begin with, as in China, Thailand, and South Korea, the response has been decisive and the recovery relatively swift. We venture, therefore, the immodest claim that this handbook is dealing with *the most important challenge facing democratic politics in our era*. Period.

THE CRISIS OF EXPERTISE

What is this challenge? What has gone wrong in the relations between experts and democratic politics? A headline run by the *New York Times* in August 2020 can serve as our way into this labyrinth: "Scientists worry about political influence over Coronavirus vaccine project." (LaFraniere 2020) The article quotes Paul Offit, a member of the FDA's vaccine advisory committee, who warns: "There are a lot of people on the inside of this process who are very nervous about whether the administration is going to reach their hand into the Warp Speed bucket, pull out one or two or three vaccines, and say, 'We've tested it on a few thousand people, it looks safe, and now we are going to roll it out.'" At first sight, this seems fairly straightforward. There is a scientific process of developing and testing vaccines to make sure they are safe and efficacious. Impinging upon it from without, however, is political pressure—with the vivid image of a hand reaching "in" and pulling "out." The White House wanted to develop a vaccine at "warp speed" to boost Trump's re-election chances. The scientists worried that this could lead to "cutting corners," resulting in a vaccine that was neither safe nor efficacious. When you are dealing with a vaccine that will be administered to hundreds of millions of people, even the smallest error or the rarest of side effects could have potentially catastrophic consequences.

But things are not so simple. The White House wanted to short-circuit the three-phase sequence of clinical trials. This sequence itself was established by a *political* process culminating in the celebrated Kefauver-Harris legislation in reaction to another politically charged public health crisis of global dimensions (the Thalidomide affair; Carpenter 2010, 228–297). The considerations that went into crafting the sequence were *both* scientific and political. The aptly named "confidence levels" designed by the statisticians had as much to do with the need to shore up public *trust* in the administrative process, as they did with the methods of statistical inference. Accordingly, perhaps even more than they were worried about the actual risks of fast-tracked vaccines, the scientists were worried about the *appearance* of haste and undue influence and its impact on trust. A failed effort, or merely the appearance that the process had been rushed and rife with conflicts of interest, would play directly into the hands of vaccine skeptics and "fuel public distrust of vaccines."

Or, at least, this is what they said out loud. As Andrew Lakoff argues convincingly in this handbook, "While trust in the safety of technical objects such as vaccines is often seen as depending on the autonomy of regulatory agencies and the objectivity of experts, here the converse was the case: experts and regulatory officials used the construct of public trust—or rather, mistrust—as a means to preserve their autonomy." What the experts discovered is that the bureaucratic device of the Emergency Use Authorization (EUA), put in place in 2004 as part of a new logic of "preparedness," could potentially undermine their autonomy, especially with an executive determined to use it to score political points. In the bureaucratic struggle that ensued, the danger of losing the public's "trust" was mobilized as a resource in the scientists' hands.

And so, once more, the tables turned. The vaccines' skeptic-in-chief in the White House suddenly became their biggest booster, staking his political future on their expeditious rollout; and the champions of vaccination, including the much-maligned big pharmaceuticals standing to make a profit from a universal vaccination campaign, began sounding the alarm, worried about their "reputational risk." The very mechanisms developed to generate trust, themselves became mistrusted. The three-phase structure and deliberate pace of clinical trials were meant to give them the appearance of mechanical objectivity (Carpenter 2010; Daston and Galison 1992; Porter 1995). The religiously followed protocol was meant to draw a boundary between science and politics, between means and ends. Now the protocol, too, was dragged into the struggle. It no longer appeared as an umpire, but as a contestant. To cut corners would be unethical. It could endanger the public or its trust in vaccines or both. To *not* cut corners, however, "would also be unethical," according to a White House official, because it would entail withholding "an effective vaccine for an extra three or four months while more people died just to check the boxes of a more routine trial process." Cynical political ploy? No doubt. But it is exactly the same argument that ACT UP activists made during the AIDS epidemic decades earlier (Carpenter 2010; Epstein 1995), and that other patients' advocates have been making ever since. The protocol is not innocent, they argued; its objectivity is not objective. Its "mechanical" application is murderous and must be tempered with "compassionate use" exemptions. And so, they dance, round and round, changing places and exchanging costumes, the vaccine skeptic-in-chief rehearsing the arguments of the radical activists of ACT UP, and the champions of vaccines being forced to explain the risks they entail and to warn that short-circuiting the process would lead to loss of trust. The predictable result of this dance can only be further erosion of the public's trust in vaccines.

The sense of crisis hovers over practically all the contributions to this handbook. The relationship between expertise and democratic politics, which has always been full of friction, as E. Summerson Carr points out in her contribution, has now reached an impasse. This is not because experts are somehow less relevant or less needed in liberal democratic polities. On the contrary. The crisis is characterized by what Peter Weingart in his contribution calls the "paradox of expertise": Experts are needed more than ever, and experts are less credible than ever. The two relations—dependence and distrust—feed off and amplify one another (see also Eyal 2019). Increasing dependence on experts leads to warnings about technocracy and undemocratic rule by experts. This was already a staple of New Left critiques in the 1960s (Habermas 1970) and of neoconservative analyses of the "new class" in the 1970s (Bruce-Briggs 1979). In the pandemic, it has taken the form of warnings from Supreme Court Justice Alito about "rule by experts" encroaching on constitutionally guaranteed liberties (Wehle 2020). This consciousness of a tension between democratic ideals and the authority of expertise can infuse not only academic discussions of politics with a capital P, but also how ordinary people perceive their interactions with a more mundane sort of expert, as Carr demonstrates in her analysis of Motivational Interviewing (MI), a form of nondirective therapy. But the obverse is also true. The increasing distrust and pluralization of expertise leads to even greater reliance on experts of some sort. This is happening today in dramatic fashion with the Extinction Rebellion movement, as Alexander Ruscher and Nico Stehr recount in their chapter. In his contribution to this handbook, Jakob Arnoldi calls it a "tragic paradox . . . at the heart of modern technological society": The more there are different and conflicting types of knowledge, creating uncertainty about expertise, the greater the demand for authoritative syntheses provided by experts, though these syntheses may no longer be the official ones. As epidemiologists disagree with one another, people turn to "Coronavirus influencers" to sort out the mess (Broderick 2020). Even MI therapists, committed to being nondirective and to treating the patient as expert, find that they need to exert authority, however tacitly. So dependence breeds distrust, but distrust breeds further dependence, and the dance continues.

WHAT IS EXPERTISE?

A book about expertise and democratic politics could have begun with a definition of its subject matter—namely, expertise. We chose to start, instead, where there is agreement among our contributors—namely, the shared sense that expertise is in crisis. There is no similar agreement, however, about what expertise is and where (or whether) to draw the boundaries of the phenomenon. In fact, the broad outlines of the dance we have just described are replicated in the debates about the notion of expertise itself. Scholars concerned with this topic have often conceptualized expertise, in keeping with the term's everyday use, as the knowledge or skill needed to perform a particular task in a particular area (Dreyfus and Dreyfus 2003; Collins and Evans 2007). But there are problems with this way of defining expertise for analytic purposes. These problems run parallel to the dilemmas of trust and credibility sketched above. In the first place, we cannot reduce expertise to knowledge or skill, even if we define both broadly to include both abstract and practical knowledge (i.e., explicit rules and ideas, on the one hand, and embodied mastery and tacit knowhow, on the other). To explain the successful performance of a task, after all, requires more than identifying the knowledge or skill mobilized by an expert. There are also tools, instruments, concepts, measures, and institutional and spatial settings that are all mobilized in the successful and speedy performance of a task, as well as, perhaps, the know-how of other participants who are not typically recognized as experts (Eyal 2013, 2019). By the same token, certain forms of complex knowledge and skill are not ordinarily seen as "expertise," which suggests that something is left out by the innocent phrase "in a particular area." Becoming a competent speaker of a language, for example, requires the mobilization of an enormously complex skillset. Collins and Evans (2007) are certainly correct to call this a "ubiquitous" form of expertise. Yet it is also clear that this is not the meaning of expertise indexed in the title of this book; nor would it be ordinary usage, for that matter, to call a child who becomes proficient in her native language an "expert."

Recognizing these problems, other scholars have taken the alternate approach of defining expertise as an "attribution," or a quality that attaches to someone by virtue of recognition granted by significant others (Friedson 1986; Abbott 1988). Experts, on this view, are those who succeed in earning and maintaining the designation of expert, particularly in their relationships with established authorities. This approach gets around the problem of having to define expertise in terms of substantive qualities, but it, too, is unsatisfying. Above all, it tends to trivialize the phenomenon by implying that expertise is a kind of fiction, a matter of attracting the right forms of approval, as opposed to a real and substantive skill (Fuller 2006).

We will probably not settle this debate here. It is perhaps better seen as an enduring feature of the phenomenon of expertise itself (namely, that its scope and nature are essentially contested). Instead, we would like to offer a maximally flexible analytical framework that does not prejudge the answers to these contested questions yet is attuned to the specific subject matter of this volume. This can be done, we argue, by thinking of expertise as a *historically specific type of performance aimed at linking scientific knowledge with matters of public concern*. This approach has the immediate benefit of recognizing that expertise—say, the performance of a concert pianist—invariably requires advanced knowledge and skill to carry off. At the same time, it accounts for the fact that other ingredients are needed to perform expert tasks. Like the concert performance, expertise requires the proper tools and instruments; typically, it also depends on the contributions of various "backstage" figures (e.g., mentors, intermediaries), who are not, strictly speaking, performers themselves. And if we are concerned with how the performance becomes an authoritative intervention in public affairs, then we must include relevant features of the surrounding context in our conception, such as the venue in which the performance takes place and the response it elicits from audiences and critics, who must recognize the authority claim that the performance enacts. All these points speak to the historical variability of what counts as "expertise." Indeed, it may even appear as its opposite, as "(in)expertise," as Carr shows. But the second part of this definition is equally important: Expertise is a phenomenon of the *interface* between specialized (professional, technical, scientific, bureaucratic, or even "experience-based") knowledge and (political, legal) decision-making. This means that studies of expertise train their attention on the modalities of speech and action, and the types of statements and performances, that are capable of enacting authority in this interface.

One virtue of thinking about expertise in this way, we argue, is that it encourages scholars to set aside the search for an immutable essence or substance in favor of a relational understanding of expertise. The value of a relational approach becomes visible, for example, in Dan Navon's contribution to this volume, which focuses on the role of experts in the classification of human differences. Surveying recent research on this topic, Navon finds that thinking about expertise in relational terms reveals an aspect of the phenomenon that tended to elude scholars of the past. Whereas scholars once depicted categories of human difference as straightforward "outputs" of expert work, classification is better seen as a complex, historically contingent give-and-take between the experts and the "targets" of their classification. Factoring centrally into this account is Ian Hacking's notion of "looping," whereby a classification changes the people being classified in ways that ultimately require a change in the classification. The looping relationship has been observed most extensively in medical and psychiatric contexts, where classifications elicit organized responses among patients and stakeholders. The use of a new diagnostic category, for example, may "lead to the formation of support groups, foundations, social clubs, [and] activist organizations," which may in turn increase public awareness of the condition. The loop is completed when this growing awareness leads to a change in the classification, as when an expanded pool of those seeking diagnosis and treatment leads doctors to identify new types and subtypes of the condition.

THE FRAUGHT RELATIONS BETWEEN EXPERTISE AND DEMOCRACY

The recognition that expertise is bound up with the dilemmas of political decision-making helps explain why the current crisis of expertise has given new urgency to the question of *who may participate* in expert debates. Among citizens, activists, and scholars who are engaged with this question, a broad opposition has intensified. On the one side, the critique of technocracy has fueled campaigns for democratizing expertise, or efforts to extend participation in expert debates to those who are not ordinarily described as "experts." Prominent among these campaigns are the environmental and patients' rights movements. Two contributions to this handbook—by Steven Epstein and by Madeleine Akrich and Vololona Rabeharisoa—eloquently argue that this has been a genuine, though still limited, democratization. Lay experts, they show, are typically *collectives*. The type of expertise they develop is a hybrid of quasi-scientific practices and socially innovative forms of organizing. The combination challenges technocratic frames and, instead, creates a space where the experiences and values of the affected parties—patients and their families, communities suffering environmental degradation—are taken into account and often have priority. Although the authors recognize that the political consequences of lay expertise can sometimes be less than salutary—patients' groups have sometimes been co-opted by pharmaceuticals (Abraham and Davis 2011); their focus can be quite narrow, to the detriment of other, less well-organized, affected parties; and there is likely to be conflict with scientists who consider them to have distorted research priorities—they assess their overall impact to have been an enhancement of what Callon et al. (2009) called "technical democracy."

On the other side of the debate, however, are Harry Collins and his coauthors, Darrin Durant, Robert Evans and Martin Weinel, who worry that there is an elective affinity between lay expertise—and the science studies scholars who champion it—and populism. Lay expertise has undermined the distinction between laypeople and experts, failing to recognize that this distinction, when institutionalized, is one of the "checks and balances" necessary for the functioning of liberal democracies. Expertise is a check and balance because it makes it more difficult for a government to do whatever it wants to do (like distribute a vaccine that has not yet been fully vetted, as Russia did in the summer of 2020), and then justify it as "the will of the people." Expert calculations—however dry and seemingly neutral they may be—can contest the political elites' monopoly over the ability to represent "the will of the people," because they can demonstrate that it is not in the people's interest to take a particular step. The risk will be too high. This was demonstrated with particular force in the Thalidomide affair. The FDA emerged from the affair with new powers because it was able to present itself as a bulwark, defending the American public even as national politicians and national corporate champions had failed it (Carpenter 2010). The more it is possible, therefore, for self-appointed "alternative" experts to present their viewpoints as being equal in value to those of the scientific establishment, the weaker this check and balance is and the more vulnerable the polity is to populism, understood as "a discursive and stylistic repertoire, a set of tropes, gestures, and stances" (Brubaker 2017, 2021) that makes an invidious distinction between the "real people" and the others, who do not really belong (be they "elites," ethnic minorities, or the "undeserving poor"; Müller 2016).

An extreme version of this diagnosis is currently articulated by some in the environmentalist movement, especially activists and scientists affiliated with the Extinction Rebellion. The problem of climate change, they argue, is symptomatic of a crisis of representative democracy, its inability to act decisively because alternative experts (some of whom are funded by corporations, and some of whom articulate a populist position) have weakened the check and balance represented by climate scientists. As Ruscher and Stehr recount in this handbook, some of these activists feel that the urgency of the crisis justifies exceptions to democratic politics, a sort of "expertocracy" defending the true interests of the people. In the language of Collins et al., they feel that this check and balance has been so weakened that a radical counterweight must be introduced to restore equilibrium. It is deeply ironic—and symptomatic of the crisis of expertise—that the demand for an expertocracy is being made from within the very same circles that formulated the critique of technocracy. Dependency led to distrust. Distrust, however, led to uncertainty and the heterogeneity of expertise, and these provoke the most extreme demand for an "authoritative synthesis," as Arnoldi argues. Ruscher and Stehr reject this proposal, saying that it reflects a simplistic understanding of the relations between science and democracy. They concur with Collins et al. about the need to redraw the line between the technical and the political. But they also note that, in this matter, there are distinct differences depending on how the relations between experts and decision-makers are institutionalized. The crisis is more acute, they argue, where these relations are organized in a competitive and adversarial fashion, as they are in the United States. Experts become identified with partisan positions and issue advocacy organizations. Their public clashes undermine trust in experts. In Germany, on the other hand, the relations between experts and decision-makers are organized as a "closed shop." There is a relatively small network of academics who collaborate with the ministries, and alternative experts are excluded. The differences, however, are a matter of degree, not essence.

Collins et al. draw mostly on Durkheim in explicating their thesis, but theirs is an eminently Weberian theme: the process of democratization, by increasing inclusion, undermines itself. It weakens the mechanisms by which the governed can hold the governing accountable, expertise being one of those mechanisms (Weber 1978, 956–1005). For Weber, this was an irreconcilable antinomy. It is arguable that with the current crisis of expertise, we are still in its tentacles. After all, lay expertise, too—as described by Steven Epstein, Madeleine Akrich, and Vololona Rabeharisoa—is a way of making the authorities more accountable to ordinary people. Administrative agencies cannot hide behind "what the experts say," but must explicate the hybrid technopolitical calculus behind their decisions and regulations (as in the three-phase structure of clinical trials). Yet if Collins et al. are right, this salutary democratization has the unsavory effect of weakening the very institutions that hold the other authorities accountable. If scientists are worried that politicians can simply "reach in" and "pull out" vaccines before they are fully tested, this is partly because the FDA of today is a pale shadow of its former formidable self. Its authority and actual powers were undermined by a confluence of opponents, not only by lay experts. Not by a long shot. Yet all these opponents claimed that they were making the FDA "more accountable."

THE PROBLEM OF TRUST

In theory, making official experts more accountable does not necessarily weaken them. To understand why this is an irreconcilable dilemma, or at the very least the trickiest of tightrope acts, one must delve into the nether realms of *trust* and *mistrust*, as Robert Crease does in his contribution. Collins et al. end their chapter with a plea for democratic education. There is a deficit, they claim, in the public's understanding, not of the substance of science, but of the process of science and science's role in a democracy. Yet, as Crease notes, the very qualities of science that they want people to understand—its collective nature, its fallibility, and its long-termism—are precisely what make it vulnerable to *mistrust*. Instead of an "architectural model," concerned with how the boundary between the technical and the political can be redrawn, he suggests an "acoustical model" attuned to the hermeneutics of mistrust. Unlike the spatial imagery of boundaries, acoustics is something that takes place in *time*, and so does trust. Duration, sequence, tempo, resonance, and repetition are of the essence. A note, having been struck, shapes a context in which another note can appear as in harmony with it, or as a "false note." It can continue a melodic line, or it can appear discordant because it is played too early or too late. Collins et al. want people to understand that science is "craftwork with integrity," driven by "a search for truth rather than profit." Yet they hasten to acknowledge that this "imposes a serious responsibility on scientists that has a clear moral dimension"—namely, that "the activity be [actually] done with the utmost integrity." They know full well that the public is aware of many instances in which scientists did not conduct themselves with the utmost integrity, as well as the routine ways in which science is conducted precisely with the search for profit in mind. It does not help to "educate" citizens about how science "should" be conducted, or even to point out that "most" of it is conducted with integrity, because the mysterious quality of trust, as everyone knows, is that it is "typically created rather slowly, but it can be destroyed in an instant—by a single mishap or mistake" (Slovic 1999). A beautiful melody can be destroyed by a single discordant note. The *dis*chord transforms the "acoustical environment" in which both the preceding and following "notes" are heard. Trust is lost and can be regained only slowly and with difficulty.

Several contributions to the handbook analyze how this "acoustical environment" has changed over the last few decades, leading to the present crisis of trust. Peter Weingart provides the most comprehensive account, describing a threefold process in which science has been socialized, politicized, and mediatized. For reasons probably having to do with the present manifestation of the crisis, as well as with the composition of the contributors, most of the chapters in the handbook dwell on the politicization of science. Hence, our discussion of politicization is longer than our discussion of socialization and mediatization. We should also acknowledge that the framework itself is partial because an important dimension—the commercialization of science (Mirowski 2011)—is absent. A different combination of contributors, no doubt, would have brought this dimension much more to the fore.

SCIENCE SOCIALIZED

The *socialization* of science means the end of its "exceptionalism," its status as a realm set apart, due to two partially interrelated, partially independent processes. One of these entails the rise of lay experts and expansion of public participation in science. The other is the subjection of science, especially in universities, to forms of public accountability such as new public management (NPM) rankings (Espeland and Porter, this volume), performance measures, citation counts, and other attempts to quantify and promote innovation. It is important to emphasize that one impetus for these forms of accountability was the increasing dependence on science and expertise, the recognition that both are essential to economic growth and require increasing levels of public investment (Berman 2012). The hen laying the golden eggs could no longer remain cage-free. The two processes of socialization—lay expertise and NPM rankings, if you will—though they are distinct and often originate from opposing political perspectives, share a set of elective affinities. Both articulate mistrust and demystify the halo that used to surround scientists (Shapin 2008)—public accountability was often demanded after incidents of scientific misconduct, for example. Both replace trust in science with a demand for transparency—that is, the NPM or rankings make science transparent by quantifying it, replacing trust in experts with trust in numbers (Porter 1995). And both lead in the direction of a pluralization of expertise.

In the Bourdieusian language Arnoldi has introduced in this volume, this process of socialization of science means that universities and scientific institutions have lost their monopoly over the production and dissemination of *symbolic capital*—that is, over scientific capital that can be parlayed as expertise outside one's field. This symbolic capital is now produced in a much more plural and competitive field that includes new types of knowledge-generating organizations, such as think tanks (Medvetz 2012), R&D-intensive private corporations, consultancies, NGOs, and social movements. We can include here also the lay expert collectives and hybrid forums analyzed by Epstein and by Akrich and Rabeharisoa. The acoustical environment, if you will, is characterized by a certain tendency toward cacophony or, at least, competing melodies developed in parallel.

SCIENCE POLITICIZED

The *politicization* of science is due to the processes that we analyzed earlier in reference to the debate about Covid-19 vaccines. To put it in a formula used by Weingart: the scientization of politics leads to the politicization of science. Governmental reliance on expertise, especially in the form of regulatory science, means that technical questions—How long is an adequate clinical trial for vaccines? What is the "acceptable level" of a pollutant? How can we measure the quantifiable benefits of convalescent plasma? What is the positivity rate in a neighborhood?—are ipso facto political questions, and multiple factors make it impossible to draw the bright line between the technical and the political. In the first place, the questions posed to experts are usually "trans-scientific" questions incorporating matters of value (e.g., what level of protection should be provided to the population?) and requiring expert judgment to supplement calculation. Moreover, the same questions often cut across the jurisdictions of multiple groups of experts, prompting intense jurisdictional struggles over their "ownership" (Weinberg 1972; Beck 1992; Eyal 2019; Abbott 1988). Finally, because even the most technical questions entail decisions with profound redistributive consequences, the government requires input from experts not just to supply answers but to legitimate its decisions. Every aspect of expert judgment, therefore, including the choice of the experts themselves, inevitably becomes politicized. As Crease says: "It is too late to choose the experts after understanding the controversy. They are then no longer experts; they have been determined by the debate itself instead of helping to carry it forward; they are pieces of evidence in an agonistic situation rather than a part of meaning-formation."

The dominant response to this politicization of science and the crisis of mistrust it has provoked has been to conjure "objectivity" as the source of trust. Numerous contributions to the handbook—by Brice Laurent, David Demortain, Tal Golan, Stephen Turner, Frank Pasquale, Wendy Espeland, and Ted Porter—discuss this response, but cast grave doubts about its ability to put the political genie back into the bottle and re-establish trust. One factor behind this doubt is that "objectivity," as Daston and Galison (1992) argue, is a profoundly negative concept—its meaning being variable and deriving from whatever facet of subjectivity is problematized as dangerous or misleading. As they write evocatively: "Objectivity is related to subjectivity as wax to seal, as hollow imprint to the bolder and more solid features of subjectivity." Accordingly, the *objectivity campaigns* that have been waged in response to the politicization of expertise generally contribute to, rather than resolve, the crisis of trust. Inevitably, they proceed by constructing some aspect of expert judgment as problematic, subjective, and untrustworthy; then they build upon this construction a particular meaning of objectivity. But the problematization of subjectivity on which the campaign rests is likely to be self-defeating, since an element of judgment informs every calculation, procedure, or algorithm, however mechanical seeming. By the same token, there is hardly any form of expert judgment that does not rely on some prior measurement or protocol. The real questions, says Brice Laurent, are how different institutions articulate objectivity with judgment; whether they dramatize an opposition between them or, on the contrary, seek to reconcile the tension between them; and by what means.

It is important to recognize, too, that objectivity campaigns are often intertwined with jurisdictional struggles, as one group of experts seeks to capture the jurisdiction of another. Accordingly, the specific forms of objectivity these campaigns uphold reflect how the different groups of experts involved negotiate their jurisdictional settlements (Abbott 1988). The chapters in this volume that deal with this response to the politicization of expertise uncover at least three different meanings and organizational formats of objectivity.

Objectivity as the "View from Nowhere"

Objectivity, perforce, is constructed as "the view from nowhere," a consensus view attributable to no single expert. This is accomplished by means of a theatrical division that hides the differences, negotiations, and jurisdictional struggles between experts backstage and foregrounds the consensus view that is placed frontstage (Bijker et al 2009; Hilgartner 2000). Expert advisory organizations such as the American National Academy of Sciences or the Dutch *Gezondheidsraad* (Health Council), for example, begin by problematizing the subjectivity inherent in the fact that experts *differ* in their judgments. But this is a tricky tightrope act, and one that has become far trickier as the mediatization of science collapses the buffer between backstage and frontstage—think about the now common practice of making preprints widely available.

Moreover, conjuring objectivity as the "view from nowhere" has the unintended effect of undermining trust in expert judgment whenever a disagreement between experts erupts into public view. This becomes clear in Tal Golan's chapter about the history of expert scientific testimony in Anglo-American law. The spectacle of experts clashing in court and reaching opposite conclusions with the same degree of confidence is not new. Nor is it obvious why it should cause moral panic. The adversarial setup of Anglo-American law expects and encourages this phenomenon. Legal truth should emerge out of a robust adversarial contestation. Moreover, when scientists are questioned about this, they often point out that this is how science, too, works. Science proceeds by means of disagreement and critique. Why, then, are judges so exasperated when experts clash in court, so much so that in recent decades they have arrogated to themselves ever-greater gatekeeping powers and taken on "the difficult task of weighing the merit of highly specialized scientific claims"? Golan's answer is that this is not caused by declining trust in science. On the contrary, it is judges' *faith* in science, he says, that leads them to see clashing experts as sign of some moral corruption necessitating the intervention of the judge "in an attempt to . . . differentiate between good and bad science." One should slightly revise Golan's formulation and say that it is the judges' faith in *regulatory* science that leads them to suspect the clashing experts of moral failure. It is regulatory science, as we saw, that is compelled to hide differences backstage and to present objectivity as "the view from nowhere." The unintended consequence is that judges problematize the (legally and scientifically unexceptional) fact that experts differ in their judgments.

This bears out nuclear physicist Alvin Weinberg's fears about regulatory science, as David Demortain recounts in his chapter. An inferior, mongrel kind of science, from Weinberg's point of view, regulatory science pretends to be able to provide policymakers with clear answers to problems that are shot through with insurmountable uncertainties. In return, it is validated when policymakers use the answers as the basis for their regulatory decisions.

The same type of exchange marks the rise of macroeconomic expertise as a policymaking tool since World War II. As Maria Azocar describes in her chapter, and as other scholars have shown (Babb 2001; Fourcade 2009), economists have positioned themselves as indispensable figures in the governance of the world's economies. But a pernicious feedback loop underpins this process. Azocar argues that although they are presented in the guise of objectivity, economists' constructions of the economy embed sexist and androcentric assumptions. When used by politicians, they provide intellectual cover for policies that harm or hinder women, especially in the global South. For example, Azocar points out that by separating housework and childcare from "real" economic activity, economists have lent tacit support to policies that denigrate the domestic sphere as a "realm of dependency, need, and biological vulnerability." In some cases, the effect of these policies has been to intensify women's care work responsibilities (as in the case of the austerity measures implemented in the global South during the 1980s) or to cast women's labor-market nonparticipation as a moral failing (as in the Chilean pension reform debates of the 1980s). Thus, Azocar suggests that the particular "view from nowhere" conjured by economists is based on an unreflexive and highly gendered view of the world.

Epistemic Subsidiarity

But the "view from nowhere" invoked by regulatory science is only one of the guises that objectivity can take. Other organizations—and Laurent claims that this is more characteristic of European institutions and the Intergovernmental Panel on Climate Change (IPCC)—do not hide the differences between experts behind a wall of secrecy. On the contrary, they are either compelled by their very nature or have reached this point by trial-and-error to leverage differences as the basis for what Laurent calls "epistemic subsidiarity." The memberships of European expert bodies, for example, are selected to represent the relevant stakeholders (countries, sectors, publics). Under pressure from critics, the IPCC has taken similar steps to diversify the membership of its expert panels and peer reviewers to include dissenting voices and a broad range of stakeholders from governments, industries, and NGOs. The wager is that objectivity will emerge out of the aggregation and mutual relativization of different perspectives and interests, and that perhaps the stakeholders will provide a check on the *groupthink* of the experts, and the experts will provide a check the biases of the stakeholders.

Stephen Turner in his chapter shows how such organizational arrangements were supposed to guarantee optimal decision-making at the International Monetary Fund, and how it fell dramatically short of this goal during the Greek default crisis. Epistemic subsidiarity may draw on forms of mechanizing expert judgment such as models or algorithms, but even then, legitimacy will presumably flow, not from their supposed neutrality, but precisely from the prior process of negotiation between experts from different countries and sectors. The experts open the black boxes of the models and reshuffle them to create a device that coordinates the interests of the different stakeholders (or, unfortunately, encodes the assumptions of the dominant actor, as Turner shows happened with IMF models that were tailored to support the German position). The result is a paradoxical or oxymoronic form of "interested objectivity" that emerges from negotiation and institutional coordination between all the relevant parties. Laurent thinks that this model is preferable to the "view from nowhere," but he is also clear that it is highly unstable and vulnerable. The oxymoron can easily fall apart. Inclusion can be a token gesture when there are significant imbalances of power. Regulated industries tend to dominate the proceedings. Transparency is always partial because of the need to sort out differences and reach compromise. When failure happens, such as the "mad cow" disease crisis, or when the backstage is exposed, as in the "Climategate" affair, the matter quickly becomes a scandal and critics hasten to point out the proximity of the regulators to industry or the collusion among experts to exclude competing interpretations.

Epistemic subsidiarity is exceptionally vulnerable to the accusation of "capture." The fact that this type of arrangement is increasingly the norm in regulatory science therefore exacerbates the crisis of mistrust in expertise. In his chapter, David Demortain develops a more balanced and nuanced approach to how regulatory knowledge is formed. The concepts, tools, and measures of regulatory science, he argues, do not simply reflect the interests of industry, as the theory of capture suggests. They are "hinges" (Abbott 1995) linking at least four different fields—academic science, the administrative state, industry, and environmental activism (i.e., social movements and lay experts) with varying levels of input into their makeup. Regulatory science is an interstitial field "between" these adjacent fields (see Medvetz 2012), and the production of regulatory knowledge reflects the interactions of all the actors. If we have heard more concerns about "capture" in recent years, Demortain thinks it is due to a globalization of regulatory science. Increasingly, standard setting is done by transnational communities of specialists in product evaluation, operating in international fora such as the Organization for Economic Cooperation and Development (OECD) or the International Conference on Harmonization for pharmaceuticals. In the absence of a strong international regulator, industry influence is perhaps stronger in these fora, but Demortain thinks that, overall, the diagnosis of capture is overblown, ignoring diversity in both the forms and outcomes of regulation.

MECHANICAL OBJECTIVITY

Up till now, we have discussed organizational responses to the politicization of science and the problems posed by the diversity and biases of expert judgment. But Turner makes the more general point that *there is no fail-safe organizational solution* to these problems. As he puts it forcefully:

> There is no God's eye truth to resolve these conflicts. There are only socially organized procedures. We can validate these procedures only partially, by reference to past decisions that are regarded as successful. And these judgments of success refer to "normal" past results. And "success" is relative to interests. If we ignore the possibility of a God's eye view as a nonstarter, we are left with partial views, with different perspectives, knowledge, risk assessments, uncertainties, and interests. From any of these partial points of view, a given procedure of aggregation will appear to be "biased." (chap 11, this volume)

The intractability of expert "bias" and partiality has often given impetus to a different type of objectivity campaign. It problematizes this partiality—the ways in which experts' judgments are biased by their interests, ideologies, entanglements, limited perspectives, and human cognitive equipment—and conjures objectivity as a "mechanical" process unfolding without human intervention and with no need to rely on fallible, biased judgment. You just need to find a good measure, and then let the measure itself drive the process. To quote Bill Gates (2013): "You can achieve amazing progress if you set a clear goal and find a measure that will drive progress toward that goal in a feedback loop." This is the declared intention of the forms of measurement, high-stakes testing, and ranking that Espeland and Porter discuss in their chapter. High-stakes testing, which was originally meant to select the students who were best prepared to succeed, has been transformed in the American context into a tool for supervising teachers and (presumably) reforming education. Clearly, high-stakes testing became a tool by which the jurisdiction of teachers was subordinated to another group of experts. You can't leave it to teachers themselves, they argued, to judge whether one of their own is doing a good job preparing her students and improving their performance over time. Repeated testing will provide an objective assessment and can be used to reward successful teachers and punish ineffective ones. Similarly, the rankings of US law schools published by *US News & World Report* are meant to help applicants make informed choices among relatively opaque goods. Once again, you cannot trust the judgment of law school deans—interested as they are in results biased in their favor—about the quality of the good on offer. Over time, the rankings will presumably drive law schools to improve, the goods will be standardized, and the consumers will benefit.

Espeland and Porter clarify, however, that this problematization, wherein expert judgment is opposed and subordinated to a mechanical form of objectivity, is a matter of jurisdictional struggle, a function of the relative power or weakness of the groups of experts involved. Yet the factors that make for relative vulnerability to an objectivity campaign waged by powerful others (be they another group of experts, public authorities, or social movements) are not always obvious and are dependent on the overall institutional context. The authors demonstrate this by comparing the cases of American and French teachers who were subjected to high-stakes testing. In the American case, because of the decentralized nature of US public education, testing became a mechanism by which teachers are evaluated, their "value-added" measured, and their expertise downgraded ("teaching to the test"). It goes without saying that to achieve this, the objectivity campaign encouraged mistrust of expert judgment. Yet in France, under a different set of institutional conditions in a centralized educational system wherein teachers control the curriculum on which students were tested, French teachers were able to exploit the high-stakes testing to their advantage. Measurement does take place, but it is not seen as a substitute for teachers' expertise; nor does it foster a mistrust of their judgment. Similarly, US law schools—presumably strong and well-endowed organizations—proved to be quite vulnerable to *US News & World Report* rankings, while dentistry schools, precisely because they are relatively small and less numerous, were able to close ranks and mount a successful boycott that blunted the power of the rankings. Most importantly, Espeland and Porter use the case of the *US News & World Report* rankings to show that mechanical objectivity does not eliminate judgment. It merely drives it underground. Underneath the seeming monologue of mechanical objectivity there is a submerged dialogue that can lead to unintended consequences. Rankings unleash dynamics of "reactivity" as the ranked attempt to "game" the measurement and improve their ranking. In response, the ranking agency attempts to anticipate and control reactivity, and it also uses the measurements as a way of punishing recalcitrant law schools.

Jurisdictional struggles are conducted by means of abstraction (Abbott 1988; but see Huising, this volume, for a critique). Pasquale proposes the idea of "meta-expertise" to describe the specific form of abstraction by which objectivity campaigns are conducted. *Meta-expertise* is the expertise to evaluate, measure, and rank the expertise of others. It is the expertise claimed by test developers and those who create metrics and ranking systems, especially economists. And increasingly, it is the expertise claimed by computer scientists who develop AI substitutes for experts.

Once again, there are specific institutional conditions that render certain groups of experts more or less vulnerable to this type of jurisdictional grab, but there is also a clear link to the crisis of expertise. The crisis of expertise, as we saw, is partly fueled by jurisdictional struggle. As jurisdictional struggles intensify, and as new problems emerge over which no group of experts has clear jurisdiction, the professional and disciplinary division of labor becomes destabilized, and at least in the United States, this has meant a resort to the courts as arbiters. Neoliberal courts in the United States, however, have increasingly construed professional privileges as restrictions on market competition and so delegated to state officials the authority to supervise professions. The relative weakness of these officials means that they would rather rely on objective metrics to do the job for them (Porter 1995). Pasquale analyzes how this leads to an alliance between state officials, hi-tech libertarians, and managers who empower meta-experts (computer scientists and economists) that aims to subordinate the jurisdictions of other professions. There is also a normative vision behind this, one of algorithmic account-ability and governmentality. Yet, as we saw earlier, metrics have unintended and per-nicious effects. They can be gamed in ways that ultimately distort the social practice they purport to measure and regulate. Because metrics can seem arbitrary because of their reliance on weights, and hence judgments, there is an attempt to bundle them into algorithms and thus hide the judgments that were employed. The results are "weapons of math destruction" that operate without accountability (O'Neil 2016; Pasquale 2015; Zuboff 2019) and, increasingly, undermine trust in human experts.

The modern field of risk analysis is another site where these "weapons of math de-struction" are deployed, yet with unintended and often deeply ironic consequences. Since the 1970s, practitioners of risk analysis have become "go-to" advisers to decision-makers in politics and industry. They have come to occupy this position by deploying sophisticated tools aimed at identifying threats and assessing their potential consequences. But as Denis Fischbacher-Smith points out in his chapter, prediction is not the only function of the calculative tools risk analysts use. Like other experts, risk analysts inevitably face questions about their objectivity and the role played by powerful interests in shaping their advice. The task of demonstrating neutrality then "invariably… becomes manifested in a move toward the quantification of uncertainty through cal-culative practices." The result is a deep-seated tension in the risk analyst's use of cal-culative tools. As instruments for assessing threat, such tools provide real assistance to decision-makers who lack the ability to evaluate uncertainty in high-stakes situations. But as instruments for foreclosing doubt or warding off mistrust, they do not so much measure uncertainty as conceal it, thereby producing sheer ignorance (Wynne 1992). By masking the working assumptions, imprecise estimates, and rough judgments that enter into the risk analyst's practice, calculative practices blur the line between—to borrow Donald Rumsfeld's phrase—"known-unknowns" and "unknown-unknowns." Thus, the "paradox at the core of risk assessment," Fischbacher-Smith argues, is that the "calcula-tive practices that seek to provide certainty and clarity in judgments around uncertainty may themselves prove to contribute to the generation of the very uncertainty that they are seeking to address."

This paradox is especially pronounced in the case of "extreme events," or high-uncertainty situations "for which there is little, if any, prior experience that would allow for effective predictions." Great Britain's withdrawal from the European Union is a re-cent example, since the most unimpeachable stance a risk analyst could take—namely, acknowledging Brexit's inherent unknowability, along with the fact that any reliable prediction about its effects would require constant revision as new information became available—would risk losing the confidence of decision-makers and the general public. Hence, the type of prediction that was expected of the forecaster was one that obscured the presuppositions that made the prediction possible in the first place. The lesson offered by Brexit reaches into the realm of highly institutionalized, seemingly repeatable events. Take the established category of "presidential elections," which has lately been the site of its own jurisdictional struggle among forecasters. Before the 2016 election, the representatives of a new data science of political polling—personified by Nate Silver—seemed to have supplanted political pundits as the most authoritative predictors of US election results. But the dismal failure of both pollsters and pundits to predict the outcome of the 2016 presidential election, and their serious underestimation of Republican strength in 2020, threw this struggle back into the "toss-up" category. The lesson is that the predictive tools used by forecasters rest on acts of construction—in this case, one that placed an election held in 2016 in the same category of event as one held in, say, 1960—that renders the event amenable to comparison with others of its "type."

The emergent theme across these chapters is that mechanical objectivity cannot resolve the problem of "bias" and partiality once and for all. Having been displaced onto an impersonal device or procedure, the problem is bound to reappear in a different form as the "mechanism" itself becomes a locus of new tensions and uncertainties, or a source of new dilemmas. The political genie refuses to get back in the bottle.

SCIENCE MEDIATIZED

Finally, there is the mediatization of science, to which Weingart dedicates a significant part of his chapter. Here again, there are two distinct processes that intertwine and amplify one another. First, there was a deeply ironic and self-defeating development in which the concern about declining levels of trust in science has led to the creation and globalization of the new profession of "science communication," which had its own distinctive interests that did not always coincide with the original intentions, and that has become a sort of "Trojan horse" within academic science. Under a mandate to foster the "public understanding of science" (PUS), communication and public relations specialists created and staffed new academic programs in "science communication." PUS, however, came under criticism from various quarters—science studies, lay experts, the profession itself—for its patronizing assumption that the distrust of science is due to the public's ignorance of science, a "deficit" that PUS should aim to repair. The focus of science communication was then changed—as a result of the critique, but also in accordance with the interests and professional worldviews of communication specialists—to "public engagement with science and technology" (PEST). PEST was supposed to be a dialogue, in contrast to the monologue of PUS, with a "public" that was now to be taken seriously as an equal party. Yet in the hands of public relations specialists, PEST became an effort to capture maximum media attention. Instead of the genuine dialogue with specific stakeholder publics envisioned by the sociologists of lay expertise, PEST has a public relations orientation to create "visibility."

At the same time, profound transformations in the media field have amplified the mediatization of science represented by PEST. Two contributors to the handbook focus on these transformations. In her chapter on the rise of media metacommentary, Eleanor Townsley traces the development of an increasingly complex news and commentary environment in which traditional performances of expertise have lost much of their authority. In the United States, this development was enabled by the deregulation of the news media and the abolition of the Fairness Doctrine during the 1980s, which then gave rise to a proliferation of cable news and opinion programs. Townsley draws our attention to a raft of "postmodern" political satire shows—in particular HBO's *Last Week Tonight with John Oliver*. Oliver's popularity is symptomatic of a media ecosystem that has become saturated with expert claims, and in which the guise of "detached objectivity," once cultivated by the likes of Walter Cronkite, now seems "inauthentic, self-interested and out of touch."

In parallel, Arnoldi argues that the rise of new social media has meant that the traditional media, especially editors and science journalists, have lost their monopoly on the *symbolic metacapital* that can bestow recognition and legitimacy on claims of expertise. It now shares this metacapital with a broad range of actors, who are active in the new media forums. In the absence of gatekeepers, public recognition as experts is happening in more diverse forums than the traditional news media and is controlled and granted by more diverse actors than those of the journalistic profession, such as social media influencers and even celebrities. The antivaccination movement is a good example: celebrities like Jenny McCarthy are not "lay experts"—that is, they are not recognized as experts, but they now have the power through their blogs and Twitter accounts to recognize others as alternative experts and grant them legitimacy. On the academic side, as Weingart emphasizes, PEST and the increasing circulation of preprints eliminate or at least attenuate the gatekeeping function of peer review. This has been evident throughout the Coronavirus crisis, as media reports and even public policy are driven by a constant churning of preprints justified by the extraordinary emergency of the moment.

Weingart, Townsley, and Arnoldi thus describe a profoundly fragmented media landscape, in which the gatekeeping powers exercised by both the traditional media and academic institutions are considerably weakened, and the distinction between trustworthy and untrustworthy research, credible and noncredible research—as in the case of antivaccination—is increasingly blurry. Instead of gatekeeping, there is an intensification of the self-reference of symbolic capital. Being cited in the media as an expert leads to more citations and more solicitations. Increasingly, being a commentator or a media pundit is conflated with being an expert. Ultimately, the social media actors themselves, the influencers, begin to act and to be recognized as experts. These developments shape an "acoustical environment" wherein mistrust can thrive: the cacophony is amplified because the category of public expert, of those who can speak as experts in public fora, has become so heterogenous and so indistinct that it takes sheer virtuosity to untangle it, as Townsley's chapter on the rise of media metacommentary demonstrates.

New Dynamics of Expertise

As the foregoing discussion has made clear, the last few decades have seen significant changes in the "acoustical environment" in which experts operate. As the old professional and disciplinary orders that once shaped the performance of expertise have been destabilized, new contenders for expert status have emerged, leading to intensified jurisdictional struggles. As a result, the prevailing forms of expertise—not just the styles experts adopt or the resources they deploy, but the default conception of an "expert"— are in flux. A key task for social scientists, then, is to chart the major directions of change in the performance of expertise. Although any conclusions we reach about this issue must be taken as provisional, two general themes emerge from the contributions in this volume.

From Closure to "Flexibility"

First, several chapters in the handbook suggest that there has been a pluralization of the performance of expertise in public life, such that many of the values and practices once associated with experts—first and foremost, the tendency to pursue social closure— increasingly coexist with new values and practices centered on the theme of "flexibility." To be sure, processes of social closure, whereby experts gain status by restricting access to their ranks, remain closely tied to the performance of expertise, just as the model of jurisdictional control described by Abbott (1988) is still the chief guarantor of market advantage for professionals. It remains true, for example, that only a doctor can perform an appendectomy, and only a certified engineer can sign off on a building project, and that in both cases the power of the expert rests on a relationship of exclusion from "nonexperts." But it is also true that as new competitors, including the "lay experts" discussed earlier, have encroached on the territory of traditional experts, some of the lines of demarcation on which expert performances once depended have become blurred. In some cases, too, experts have embraced new tactics and values in response to what Carr characterizes as the paradox of democratic expertise.

Nowhere are these tendencies more apparent than in the system of professions. In her chapter, Ruthanne Huising argues that changes in the landscape of expertise have led to a broad shift in the "means and ends" by which professionals secure authority. Whereas professional groups once sought exclusive control over a particular jurisdiction, more recently they have come to see the benefits of interdependence with other professionals. Relatedly, while the knowledge to which they once laid claim was abstract, principled, and putatively universal, professionals are now more likely to tout local, situated, and contextual knowledge, or knowledge "generated in interaction with clients," as bases of their authority. Professionals may also draw more visibly on their emotions and intuitions, rather than maintain the guise of objectivity. Huising offers as examples therapists, who use their personal familiarity with patients to gain insights into their situations; lawyers, who deploy their knowledge of "how courts work: their procedures, spaces, rituals, and routines" to create value for clients; and army doctors, whose authority depends as much on their ability to "gain the consent and trust of commanding officers" as it does on their command of medical knowledge. While these tactics have been used to a certain extent by professionals and experts in preceding eras, Huising argues that they are more prevalent in an increasingly competitive professional environment, such as our own era characterized by the destabilization of jurisdictional arrangements. As jurisdictional struggles intensify, Huising argues, professionals place unprecedented emphasis on the ethos or moral character of their work and their "dedication to patient or client service." The general result of these changes, Huising finds, has been a shift in the "dominant value" of professional achievement, so that competence, "efficiency and effectiveness" now supersede "the rationality of science and logic" as the ultimate source of professional authority.

What do these changes within and among the professions mean for the study of professionalization? One implication, argues Paul Starr in his chapter, is that we can no longer assume "that members of an occupation [will] seek occupational closure as a route to collective mobility." Nor can we rely uncritically on the model that depicts professionalization as a fixed progression through various "barriers" to group closure. Instead, what is needed is a complementary theory of *non-professionalization* to explain why "some institutional fields see little professionalization even though they demand levels of expertise comparable to fields where professional institutions have been established." Focusing on the case of information technology (IT) workers, Starr identifies two reasons why the distinctive culture of the knowledge economy industries might push highly skilled workers toward non-professionalization. First, because high-tech firms occupy a market in which "flexibility and adaptability are highly prized, while licensed jurisdictions are anathema," they often mount resistance to professionalization by their employees. A second reason IT specialists may defy the traditional model of professionalization is that the employees themselves have "adopted an individualistic, entrepreneurial, market-oriented ideology." In some cases, then, non-professionalization may reflect the efforts of workers to "preserve flexibility for themselves as agents in the market."

At the extreme end of this tendency toward non-professionalization and the blurring of boundaries, one finds the claim to expertise mutating into its opposite, the performance of (in)expertise. Motivational Interviewing therapists, as Carr shows, disavow their own authority and display a willingness to be instructed by lay people. MI training warns therapists against the "expert trap"—namely, against believing and performing as if they know better than the patient how to help her. Carr argues that MI has evolved toward this position in response to the way in which therapy, in the American context, has modeled itself on distinct conceptions of democratic practice. The stance of (in)expertise is thus a particular reaction to the problematic position of expertise in democracies as a form of authority that can appear to encroach on the autonomy and freedom of citizens. MI specifically, and therapy more generally, is political, ethical practice. It is centrally concerned with questions of freedom, autonomy, and democracy, and with the dilemmas that arise in relation to the authority of experts. MI presents itself as a dyadic form of participatory democracy. In reality, of course, it can never be entirely nondirective, hence the characteristic tension in the question of "how to (non)authoritatively direct subjects recognized to be self-governing, who feel they participate on their own terms." To paraphrase, the dilemma of MI therapists, which is also the dilemma of experts in liberal democracies whose publics are increasingly distrustful of their authority claims, is how to be goal directed (i.e., pragmatic) without being directive (i.e., authoritarian), yet remain transparent and non-manipulative. How do we get people to wear masks, for example, without the expert advice appearing to encroach on their personal autonomy? If MI manages, at the moment, to thread the needle, mostly because of its founder's ability to charismatically embody this tension, it is also the case that other responses to the same dilemma, for example, the "paternalist libertarianism" espoused by the theorists and practitioners of nudging (Thaler and Sunstein 2008), veer much more clearly toward "rhetorically masking rather than abolishing expert authority and disguising rather than avoiding professional direction, alerting us that expertise in democracies, more generally, may rely on subterfuge."

Together Huising, Starr, and Carr depict an increasingly complex system of professions in which new, semiprofessionalized groupings have emerged in the spaces between the old, canonical professions, pushing the latter, in some cases, to embrace new values and tactics. It is worth noting, too, that a parallel shift has taken place in the twenty-first-century research university, where the familiar grid of academic departments has been overlaid by a network of "not-departments," or interdisciplinary studies units that secure legitimacy through alternative means (Stevens, Miller-Idriss, and Shami 2018). The result is an arrangement marked by interdependence and stylistic difference, where conventional departments continue to exercise near-monopolistic control over valued academic resources, such as tenure-track appointments, and the not-departments embrace the benefits of hybridity and flexibility. Unbound by the constraints of the established disciplines, the latter are generally freer to enter into joint ventures and short-term projects and better equipped to pursue novel lines of inquiry. Thus, like the evolving system of professions, a terrain that was once marked by a clear separation of tasks has become more complexly organized and typified by a pluralization of values and tactics.

In light of these developments, how should scholars depict the structural environments in which expert work is performed? The spatial language of fields and jurisdictions has long been the default framework for describing how expert *groups* coalesce and establish control over a set of tasks. But as the preceding discussion illustrates, expertise is not just a phenomenon of well-defined groups. As Zach Griffen and Aaron Panofsky note in their chapter, scholars of expertise have increasingly looked beyond the canonical fields analyzed by Bourdieu and other field theorists and toward "fields that are liminal or interstitial in nature" and "not organized to facilitate . . . social closure." But if the privileged sites for studying expertise are "lesser" or secondary fields, then should scholars dispense with the language of fields altogether in favor of a different imagery, such as Crease's acoustical model? Arguing in defense of field theory, Griffen and Panofsky suggest that the problem can be traced to a pair of deeply buried tensions in field theory itself. First, is field theory best understood as "a substantive theory about the organization of modern societies" or as "a heuristic approach for researching and explaining social action" in relational terms? Second, what is field theory's role in normative debates about the proper role of experts? Why, in particular, have so many "scholars with strong normative concerns about expertise" recently made use of "field-like accounts"? Both issues can be addressed, Griffen and Panofsky argue, by situating field theory within a wider "political economy of contemporary capitalist social relations," or a historical framework that seeks to relate all fields, autonomous and interstitial alike, to the workings of the economy. Not only does this framework place all fields on the same analytic plane, it also helps to explain the recent profusion of normative interventions by scholars of expertise. Echoing Bourdieu, Griffen and Panofsky argue that these interventions should be seen as attempts by representatives of the scientific field to defend the field's autonomy and integrity in the face of growing incursions from market forces.

The Rise of "Meta-Expertise"

Alongside the transition from closure to flexibility, many of the institutional settings in which experts operate have become saturated with competing claims to expertise. This saturation, in turn, supplies the context for a second theme: the rise of "meta-expertise." Indeed, no fewer than three of the chapters in this volume propose a variant of this notion to describe recent tendencies in the way specialized knowledge and public concerns are linked. As noted above, the idea of meta-expertise informs Frank Pasquale's contribution, in which the term refers to the expertise claimed by test developers and creators of metrics and ranking systems to evaluate, measure, and rank the expertise of others. A similar notion underpins Eleanor Townsley's chapter on "media metacommentary," which takes the satirist John Oliver as an exemplar of a new type of expert who aims to navigate, contextualize, and interpret the claims made by other contenders for expert status. By switching back and forth between the role of journalist and entertainer, Townsley argues, Oliver cultivates a peculiar type of authority that "relies on and borrows the expert authority of other media performances in the same moment that [it] destabilizes the authority of these other expert media performances."

Finally, the idea of meta-expertise informs Jenny Andersson's chapter on the "synthetic, encompassing" mode of analysis known as forecasting. By drawing knowledge from different fields and merging disparate kinds of data (and "oftentimes combining [these] with elements of subjectivity, imagination and narrative"), the forecaster provides a series of vivid "expectations and projections" about the future. However, forecasting's true social and political effects come into focus, Andersson argues, only when the practice is viewed historically and in relation to other modes of public intervention. Having grown in response to earlier failures of governmental planning, forecasting is a "new means of planning," albeit one that reflects diminished confidence in the nation-state's ability to manage populations, territories, and economies. Operating in a series of "transnational arenas," the forecaster conjures global categories (such as "the climate" and "the environment") tied to the problems of a "planetary world system." But despite its ostensible problem-solving focus, forecasting "serves a deeply conservative function," in Andersson's view. For example, a municipality might address the problem of resource sustainability not by inaugurating a radical systemic change, but by drawing on future forecasting to declare the goal of "zero waste by 2040." This approach serves ultimately to "preserve capitalist structures and management logics" by pushing the problem into the future and prescribing solutions, such as recycling and sustainable consumption, that place the burden of action on individuals. Andersson thus concludes that forecasting's essential purpose is "not to provide future knowledge, but . . . to manage expectations and solve social struggles over temporality by displacing them from the present, to coming time."

* * *

These new dynamics of expertise bring this discussion full circle by recalling the crisis of expertise with which we began the chapter. The essence of this crisis, we argued, can be expressed in terms of a paradox: Experts face unprecedented levels of mistrust, but this mistrust has not in any way diminished our reliance on experts. When considered in tandem, the two tendencies described above—the move from professional closure to flexibility and the rise of "meta-expertise"—help to clarify the nature of this paradox. They also render it somewhat less mysterious by showing that if there has been an uptick in mistrust, it is not *despite* our continued reliance on experts but partly a result of factors tied to their ongoing indispensability (and sometimes the specter of this mistrust can even be a resource in the hands of experts seeking to defend their autonomy and indispensability, as Lakoff shows). As we have seen, the problem of trust is amplified by increases in the number and variety of contenders for expert status; but even the uncertainty resulting from competing expert claims may give rise to new experts and new forms of expertise. Hence the conundrum at the heart of democratic politics today: Reliance on experts may create the conditions for mistrust, even as mistrust begets more reliance. The contributions to this volume represent the "state of the art" of current scholarly efforts to understand this problem.

References

Abbott, Andrew. 1988. *The System of Professions: An Essay on the Division of Expert Labor*. Chicago: University of Chicago Press.

Abbott, Andrew. 2005. "Linked Ecologies: States and Universities as Environments of Professions." *Sociological Theory* 23, no. 3 (September): 245–274.

Abraham, John, and Courtney Davis. 2011. "Rethinking Innovation Accounting in Pharmaceutical Regulation: A Case Study in the Deconstruction of Therapeutic Advance and Therapeutic Breakthrough." *Science, Technology and Human Values* 36 (6): 791–815.

Babb, Sarah. 2001. *Managing Mexico: Economists from Nationalism to Neo-liberalism*. Princeton, NJ: Princeton University Press.

Beck, Ulrich. 1992. *Risk Society: Towards a New Modernity*. London: Sage.

Berman, Elizabeth Popp. 2012. *Creating the Market University.* Princeton, NJ: Princeton University Press.

Bjiker, Weibe E., Roland Bal, and Ruud Hendriks. 2009. *The Paradox of Scientific Authority.* Cambridge, MA: MIT Press.

Broderick, Ryan. 2020. "I'm Not an Epidemiologist but . . .": The Rise of the Coronavirus Influencers." Buzzfeed News, March 18. https://www.buzzfeednews.com/article/ryanhatest his/im-not-an-epidemiologist-but-the-rise-of-the-corona.

Brubaker, Rogers. 2017. "Why Populism?" *Theory and Society* 46:357–385.

Brubaker, Rogers. 2021. "Paradoxes of Populism during the Pandemic." *Thesis 11* 164(1):73–87.

Bruce-Briggs, B., ed. 1979. *The New Class?* New Brunswick, NJ: Transaction Books.

Callon, Michel, Pierre Lascoumes, and Yannick Barthe. 2009. *Acting in an Uncertain World: An Essay on Technical Democracy.* Cambridge, MA: MIT Press.

Carpenter, Daniel. 2010. *Reputation and Power: Organizational Image and Pharmaceutical Regulation at the FDA.* Princeton, NJ: Princeton University Press.

Collins, Harry, and Robert Evans. 2007. *Rethinking Expertise.* Chicago: University of Chicago Press.

Daston, Lorraine, and Peter Galison. 1992. "The Image of Objectivity." *Representations* 40:81–128.

Dreyfus, Hubert, and Stuart E. Dreyfus. 2005. "Peripheral Vision: Expertise in Real World Contexts." *Organization Studies* 26 (5): 779–792.

Epstein, Steven. 1995. "The Construction of Lay Expertise: AIDS Activism and the Forging of Credibility in the Reform of Clinical Trials." *Science, Technology and Human Values* 20, no. 4 (Autumn): 408–437.

Eyal, Gil. 2013. "For a Sociology of Expertise: The Social Origins of the Autism Epidemic." *American Journal of Sociology* 118, no. 4 (January): 863–907.

Eyal, Gil. 2019. *The Crisis of Expertise.* London: Polity.

Fourcade, Marion. 2009. *Economists and Societies.* Princeton, NJ: Princeton University Press.

Friedson, Elliott. 1986. *Professional Powers.* Chicago: University of Chicago Press.

Fuller, Steve. 2006. "The Constitutively Social Character of Expertise." In *The Philosophy of Expertise*, edited by Evan Selinger and Robert P. Crease, 342–356. New York: Columbia University Press.

Gates Foundation. 2013. Grants Database and Biannual Letter 2013. Accessed October 12, 2016. http://www.gatesfoundation.org.

Habermas, Jurgen. 1970. "Technology and Science as Ideology." In *Towards a Rational Society*, 81–127. Boston: Beacon Press.

Hilgartner, Stephen. 2000. *Science on Stage: Expert Advice as Public Drama.* Stanford, CA: Stanford University Press.

LaFraniere, Sharon, Katie Thomas, Noah Weiland, Peter Baker, and Annie Karni. 2020. "Scientists Worry about Political Influence over Coronavirus Vaccine Project." *New York Times,* August 2. https://www.nytimes.com/2020/08/02/us/politics/coronavirus-vacc ine.html.

Medvetz, Thomas. 2012. *Think Tanks in America.* Chicago: University of Chicago Press.

Mirowski, Philip. 2011. *Science Mart: Privatizing American Science.* Cambridge, MA: Harvard University Press.

Müller, Jan-Werner. 2016. *What Is Populism?* London: Penguin Books.

O'Neill, Kathy. 2016. *Weapons of Math Destruction.* New York: Crown Books.

Pasquale, Frank. 2015. *The Black Box Society.* Cambridge, MA: Harvard University Press.

Porter, Theodore. 1995. *Trust in Numbers: The Pursuit of Objectivity in Science and Public Life.* Princeton, NJ: Princeton University Press.

Shapin, Steven. 2008. *The Scientific Life: A Moral History of a Late Modern Vocation.* Chicago: Chicago University Press.

Slovic, Paul. 1999. "Trust, Emotion, Sex, Politics, and Science: Surveying the Risk Assessment Battlefield." *Risk Analysis* 19 (4): 689–701.

Stevens, Mitchell L., Cynthia Miller-Idriss, and Seteney Shami. 2018. *Seeing the World: How U.S. Universities Make Knowledge in a Global Era.* Princeton, NJ: Princeton University Press.

Thaler, Richard H., and Cass R. Sunstein. 2008. *Nudge: Improving Decisions About Health, Wealth, and Happiness.* New Haven, CT: Yale University Press.

Weber, Max. 1978. *Economy and Society.* Berkeley: University of California Press.

Wehle, Kimberley. 2020. "COVID-19: Justice Alito Overstepped Judicial Boundaries." The Hill, November 19. https://thehill.com/opinion/judiciary/526674-covid-19-justice-alito-overstepped-judicial-boundaries.

Weinberg, Alvin. 1972. "Science and Trans-science." *Minerva* 10 (2): 209–222.

Wynne, Brian. 1992. "Uncertainty and Environmental Learning: Reconceiving Science and Policy in the Preventive Paradigm." *Global Environmental Change* 2 (2): 111–127.

Zuboff, Shoshana. 2019. *The Age of Surveillance Capitalism.* New York: Hachette.

PART I

THE FRAUGHT RELATIONS BETWEEN EXPERTISE AND DEMOCRACY

2

TRUST AND DISTRUST OF SCIENTIFIC EXPERTS AND THE CHALLENGES OF THE DEMOCRATIZATION OF SCIENCE

PETER WEINGART

INTRODUCTION

UNTIL the 1970s, experts, when appearing on TV or when being interviewed by print media enjoyed general public reverence. Their statements on scientific issues largely represented a textbook state of (certified) knowledge, and the aloofness of their social status added to their authority. Experts were generally believed by their audiences. This changed dramatically in some European countries and the United States during the nuclear-power debates. Before the accident at Three Mile Island, in 1979, physicists and nuclear-energy experts could declare that reactors were safe and that accidents would occur perhaps once in 10,000 years, and their statements were widely taken to be true. After the accident, when the hitherto unimaginable nuclear meltdown had scarcely been averted, this changed dramatically. Two weeks later, *Newsweek* wrote that one of the first casualties of the accident was scientific credibility, and it reported to its readers on the politicization of science as an institution and of scientific experts as individuals.[1] The failure of the pronouncements of certainty (reactor safety) and the contradictory statements by experts became issues of public debate. Scientific experts and the knowledge they represent suddenly met with incredulity.

This pattern has continued since then, going through an unending series of debates on topics ranging from the BSE (bovine spongiform encephalopathy; or "mad cow disease") controversy to genetically modified food, stem cell research, ozone layer depletion, climate change, and vaccination as a cause of autism. Others are sure to follow. The fact that these issues have attracted so much public and media attention is a defining aspect of the place of science in society in general and in politics in particular. The debates over each of these issues have revealed their political nature or relevance, making them contentious not only among politicians and the general public but also among the experts themselves. A striking characteristic of expert communication now is that it has shifted from expressions of certitude to expressions of probabilities and, more and more often, admissions of ignorance. The homogeneity of the expert community has given way to scientists whose dissenting views can be and are identified with political positions or commercial interests. This signals a change in the place of science (and experts) in society, from a hitherto distanced and unquestioned role to being part of and in the center of society, involved in political controversies and observed by the media. Under these circumstances trust in science and, especially, of experts is conditional at best.

I argue here that the perceived loss of trust in experts is one aspect of a complex development that has affected the place of science as an institution in society. It may be characterized as the "socialization" of science. It has also been termed the "end of exceptionalism," and it is part of a general expansion of public participation. I treat various elements of this development separately: the shift from trust in the institution to the institution's subjection to public accountability; the democratization of expertise and, at least to some extent, of research proper (e.g., in the form of "citizen science"); an orientation within science toward the general public (in the diverse efforts of "science communication") and, in particular, to the media, exemplified by an opening out, from the self-referential internal communication among peers to the communication to outside "publics." These processes leave scientific experts in a precarious constellation of forces in which their credibility based on claims to certified knowledge is challenged by claims to public legitimacy. Rather than assume a linear causal chain, the chapter will show that these developments are interrelated and mutually reinforcing.

Trust and Distrust of Science and Scientists

Modern societies are characterized by a complex division of labor and, connected with this, by an equally complex network of communication. Personal acquaintance plays only a limited role, and most communication relies on sources other than people's own experience. Trust reduces this complexity. It allows taking risks in decision-making. Trust is a product and a requisite of modern, functionally differentiated societies in which familiarity has been replaced by a commitment to institutions (Luhmann 1988, 103–105; [1968] 2014).[2]

Compared to other institutions, science has sustained a comparatively high level of trust for decades. Yet doubts about the stability and continuity of that trust and fears of its decline began to haunt the scientific community and policymakers in the early 1970s (Royal Society 1985, 14). Since then, trust in experts and the scientific knowledge they represent has been an ongoing concern. Surveys of the public's trust in and appreciation of science are regularly taken in both the United States and Europe, and the results are contradictory.[3] We may cite a few examples: The market research company Ipsos MORI found in 2014 that trust in scientists ("to tell the truth" or "to follow rules and regulations") had increased since 2011 (Castell et al. 2014, 87). The company found in 2015 that trust of scientists to tell the truth had declined (by 4 percentage points) since 2014.[4] In the company's Veracity Index of 2017, scientists had again gained (3 percentage points) over 2016.[5] To what extent these changes reflect actual variations in attitudes or are artefacts arising from survey methodology is an open question. Despite these imponderabilia, some of the findings seem to be stable enough. In probing trust of scientists, for example, how they are framed creates assumptions about vested interests, so that trust will differ if they are introduced as climate scientists, scientists who work for a university, or scientists who work for private company (Castell et al. 2014, 87). Trust of scientists is evidently connected to the institutions they are associated with, and the level of trust is higher for institutions that are perceived as independent of vested interests. Just as science as an institution has a higher level of trust than the economy or government, this is reflected in scientists' institutional affiliations. As Hans Peter Peters has noted, "Power and profit are thus seen as being related to partial interests—of companies, labour unions or political parties, for example—rather than to the common good." And as he concludes: "The main difference in public perception (of institutions—PW) is pertaining to their orientation towards the common good. There is thus an apparent contradiction between wide-spread *scepticism of scientists as public experts* and *positive evaluation of science as an institution.* This calls for a clear distinction between general trust in scientific institutions and context-specific trust in scientific actors in concrete situations" (my italics; Peters 2015; Peters et al. 2007). Communication that is identified with a particular interest, political or commercial, is deemed less credible and trustworthy than communication that is considered independent of such interests. Thus, insofar as surveys can be considered reliable, there seems to be a clear sense among the public of the "neutrality" of scientific knowledge as the quality that engenders trust. The identification of the institution of science with the common good appears to be the basis of trust in science. Conversely, trust is jeopardized whenever science gets involved in political debates, when its diagnoses are uncertain, or when it appears to favor particular interests. Likewise, scientists in the role of experts enjoy trust if they demonstrate competence, integrity, and benevolence (Hendriks, Kienhues, and Bromme 2015, 3).

When speaking of scientists in the role of expert, there is one caveat to consider. The scientist acting as an expert in his or her field is not the same as the scientist acting as an expert in a decision-making context, such as on a government commission or an advisory council. The former is considered an expert because of his or her command of specialized knowledge. The latter, besides being an expert in a field of specialized knowledge, has to apply that knowledge to a specific problem in a decision-making situation. Thus, the role of expert adviser is based, on the one hand, on academic knowledge; on the other, it is bound to a specific decision-making context. Often, the advice in demand cannot just be retrieved directly from the scientist's store of knowledge; he or she has to interpret that knowledge to fit the context. The specific type of knowledge produced and conveyed in this interaction is termed "expertise" (Weingart, Carrier, and Krohn 2007, chap. 5). In commercial advisory contexts it is also labeled "client orientation." Knowledge is often incomplete, uncertain, and probabilistic in nature. The translation to a particular decision-making problem adds to this uncertainty and, at the same time, makes it vulnerable to critique by the parties that are adversely affected by the decision.

THE END OF EXCEPTIONALISM OF SCIENCE

The comparatively high levels of trust that science as an institution and scientists as a profession enjoy in most societies is underscored by the fact that until the 1980s and 1990s, Don Price's (1967) characterization applied—namely, that science is the only institution that receives public funds without having to account for them. The highly specialized nature of scientific knowledge and the arcane language and methods of its production, which are mostly inaccessible to a lay audience, are an obstacle to political and bureaucratic control from the outside and consequently require trust on the part of the general public and its political representatives. This arrangement has been called the "social contract" of science, and it characterizes the "exceptionalism" of science as an institution (Guston and Keniston 1994). The trust rests on belief that the self-regulating mechanisms of science ensure that it will operate for the public good—that is, that the public expenditures for science will, owing to the responsible decisions of the scientists, be returned to society in the form of useful knowledge that improves living conditions or can be made commercially profitable or both. In this arrangement, science policymakers and lawmakers are dependent on the public's expectations and perceptions of science.

This trust has been gradually revoked and replaced by "monitoring and incentives" (Guston 2000; Demeritt 2000). The reasons are manifold. Public expenditures for science have risen steadily, reaching levels that call for parliamentary accountability (Ziman 1993).[6] In 1980, research misconduct became an issue in the United States and, subsequently, in Europe, first in the area of medical research. This ultimately led to the establishment of the Office of Research Integrity in the United States and, later, to similar organizations in Denmark and other European countries; and now the European Network of Research Integrity Offices (ENRIO) has been established.[7] The attention to both the maintenance of good scientific practice and ethical standards of research that spawned intensified self-regulation in science and political intervention signaled an increased violation of the respective norms in science as well as public concern about their apparent erosion.

Due to temporary economic stagnation but also an intensified international competition in the context of globalization the pressure on scientists to come up with research results that would lead more directly to innovation increased. Universities were encouraged by their national legislatures to cooperate with industry to accelerate technology transfer. The Bayh Dole Act was passed by the US Congress in 1980 (Berman 2012; Slaughter Rhoades 2009). In conjunction with the liberalization of national economies and public administrations, a new control regime, known as new public management (NPM), was established. Institutions like science that function self-referentially were affected because they appeared to be elitist and opaque in their operations.

Thus trust was largely replaced with control by numbers (quantitative indicators; cf. Porter 1995; Wilsdon et al. 2015). In essence, scientists' activities, which include publishing articles, obtaining research grants, and impacting other researchers' work (documented by number of citations) are reflected by quantitative indicators, which are then turned into publicly available performance measures. Having access to this these measures supposedly allow policymakers to make better-informed judgments and enable research councils, as well as university administrations, to manage their organizations more efficiently. Because they are public, the media have picked up on them. One popular use of them is to construct rankings, mostly of universities, which creates artificial markets and builds competitive pressure.[8] This means that the formerly hidden operations of science, such as quality control through peer review and the attribution of reputation, are being quantified and made transparent to the public. The replacement of self-regulation with external control via such indicators marks the end of exceptionalism of science as an institution.

Early on, quantitative performance measures were welcomed precisely because they promised to create transparency. In the 1970s, this dovetailed with a zeitgeist shaped by the protest movements in the United States and many European countries. Campaigns to democratize societies, in general, and science, in particular, as well as critiques of technocratic experts, established democratic transparency as a core value in the political discourse. These developments ushered in a new era for science. Accountability to the public became the order of the day. Trust was no longer a given but had to be gained. How this would be done was not clear, nor were the unintended consequences apparent at the time.

In the meantime, the use of indicators has also suffused the publishing industry, which has turned the digitizing of scientific journals into a data-producing and data-using business model. The construction of indicators has also been extended to the social media communications of scientists. The original focus on citations (by peers) as signs of recognition (and thus reputation-building) has been expanded to include various signs of *attention*, such as the numbers of communications "read," "liked," or "re-tweeted." These measures no longer distinguish between the *internal* assessments by knowledgeable peers and the *external* attention of the public. In other words, the lay public has become a relevant audience for scientists because attention via social media builds social capital that contributes to reputation and is a currency that can be exchanged for political support (Costas et al. 2017; Diaz-Faes et al. 2019).

The end of the exceptionalism of science has an effect on two levels: science as an institution loses the traditional trust it once had and is subjected to bureaucratic mechanisms of control; and scientists react by "playing the game," by turning to the public and soliciting its attention to grow their reputations.

THE PARADOXES OF SCIENTIFIC EXPERTISE AND DEMOCRATIC ACCOUNTABILITY

Since the end of the Second World War, scientific experts have become formally institutionalized in governments as advisers. The presence of expert advisers in the corridors of political power is not new, but before the war, their advice was sought out irregularly, and the advisers were chosen ad hoc. Some countries (e.g., the United States and the United Kingdom) established an office of chief science adviser.[9] In others (e.g., Germany), a ministry of research is represented in the cabinet, and a plethora of advisory bodies are attached to every ministry (Lentsch and Weingart 2011).

The number of scientific advisory bodies in modern governments has been increasing for decades, following the expansion of the regulatory functions of governments that took place throughout the twentieth century. As the complexity of the tasks grew, so did the engagement of scientific experts. In democratic political systems, the increased presence of scientific experts raises a fundamental problem: if more and more decisions are de facto made by experts who do not have political legitimacy because they are not elected, then the electorate becomes disenfranchised. Democratic rule risks becoming technocratic rule. This ambivalence—that is, governments being, on the one hand, dependent on scientific expertise and, on the other hand, having to represent the public—has shaped the various institutional arrangements for applying scientific advice to policymaking.

Despite recurring attempts on the part of populist politicians to push back the influence of scientific advisers, it can be assumed that such efforts are ultimately bound to fail. While the institution of the scientific adviser as a single individual may have its problematic aspects—taking on a political role and thus ceasing to be an "honest broker" being the most ominous—the importance of scientific advice to governments will remain.[10] Scientific knowledge and, by implication, the experts who have the competence to generate and communicate it, have a legitimating (and, likewise, a delegitimating) function in modern democracies. The primary legitimacy of democratic systems derives from the electoral vote by which the interests and values of the electorate are represented. However, democratically elected governments cannot act in defiance of scientific knowledge where it is relevant for political decisions. If they do so, they risk making costly mistakes, which could lead to public protests. To the extent that notions of "evidence-based" or "science-based" policies are present and respected in public discourse, and as long as science is the ultimate reference for judgments of ' "true" or "false," political claims will be scrutinized according to those criteria. Regulatory procedural rules usually refer to the "state of the art of science and technology" or to the scientific consensus that must be taken into account as a standard to be observed. Compliance with these regulations is governed by law.[11]

Scientific knowledge is a political resource because of its functional importance in conjunction with its legitimating and delegitimating potential. Political positions that are supported by knowledge have more legitimacy; knowledge that contradicts political positions potentially delegitimizes them. This legitimating relevance of scientific knowledge, and of the experts representing it in their capacity as advisers, accounts for the potential to become politicized. The politicization of science is part of a mutually reinforcing dynamic: policymakers call on scientific experts for advice on solutions to their problems; but, at the same time, they attempt to legitimate their own positions in order to retain and secure power.

Most governments' regulatory activities that rely on scientific expertise happen outside the public's awareness. Only a selection of problems comes under public scrutiny and is then politicized. First, these are issues that are related to strong economic or ideological interests. If scientific expertise comes into conflict with these interests, their proponents may question the science or try to discredit the experts who stand for it.[12] Problems involving threats to human health or ethical issues are also likely to become politicized. Examples range from the risks of using nuclear energy and genetically modified plants; the reaction to the BSE, bird flu, and Coronavirus pandemics; the use of stem cells and, more recently, genome editing (the CRISPR-Cas method); and coping with climate change—to name just these few. In these cases, the politicization is intensified because the requisite evidence is often incomplete and expressed in probabilities of risk so that it is open to interpretation. These and similar problems also receive intense media attention. The potential for political delegitimation is therefore high. Finally, dealing with the increased complexity of the problems addressed by politics calls for reliable knowledge if political risks are to be avoided. But the very quest for certainty in solving complex problems reveals the probabilistic nature of much or even most of the knowledge produced or already available to address these problems. In the examples just mentioned, science typically did or does not have the final, unambiguous answers that policymakers want (Weingart 2003b).

The relation between science and politics is paradoxical in several respects. First, the supposed technocratic threat from scientific experts in democratic governments has turned into the opposite, a democratization of expertise in the sense that experts engage in political disputes to legitimate conflicting positions (as experts and counterexperts). Second, the use of scientific expertise as a political resource has led to competition among political actors for scientific experts. But instead of political decisions becoming better founded, more certain, and more consensual, the controversies around them have often intensified. Third, experts lose credibility because of their involvement in politics, and yet the recourse to scientific expertise by politicians continues (Weingart 2003b, 56).

"DEMOCRATIZATION" OF SCIENCE AND SCIENTIFIC EXPERTISE

Another aspect of the end of the exceptionalism of science with significant implications for the recognition of scientific experts is the "democratization" of science. The term "democratization of science" refers to many differently motivated endeavors.[13] The democratization of science was raised as the quest for science to open up to demands from civil society. The rationale was the supposed complexity of ecological problems in the broad sense, from biodiversity to biosafety to climate change, and so on. Research on these problems is fraught with uncertainties, methodological problems, and the conflation of facts and values. Thus the argument is that scientific research has to open up to engaged citizens to tap their expertise (Carolan 2006; Bäckstrand 2003).

The "participatory turn," as it came to be called (Jasanoff 2003), affected the relationship between government and civil society. It was initiated, not surprisingly, by the environmental movement. The US Environmental Protection Agency was founded in December 1970 with a mandate to increase community involvement (Longhurst 2010).[14] Given the political leverage the green movement gained during the 1980s, governments, especially in Denmark, Sweden, Switzerland, and the Netherlands, reacted by developing new forms of involving the public in decision-making processes through "consensus conferences" or "citizens' conferences," as they were called.

This marked a significant shift both on the level of science and with respect to the role of experts. On the level of science, the concerns about the effects of nuclear radiation had triggered the establishment of technology assessment (TA), whose primary tool was "risk analysis."[15] In the subsequent years, TA was applied to a host of technologies and became an expert-based instrument used in providing scientific advice to policymakers. With its focus on risk analysis and determining risks based on probability estimates, TA was already a departure from the previous type of science, which was oriented to the diagnosis of unequivocal facts. With the shift from questions of "what is" to questions of "what should be done" with respect to policy decisions and regulatory measures, values issues inevitably come into play (Carolan 2006, 665). Questions about risky technologies and environmental sustainability belong to the category of what Weinberg (1972) called the "trans-scientific." Such questions can be asked by science, but they cannot be answered by science. Thus, the traditional role of the expert as adviser to policymaking was challenged. The more prominent the discussions of technological and environmental risks became in the political discourse, the more politicians' reliance on traditional experts was questioned. In its place, reference to the expertise of the general public and the inclusion of representatives of the public in deliberations, such as at consensus conferences, has become normal practice. In the meantime, the rhetoric of science policy (and, to some extent, the practice) has moved further in the direction of participatory formats, ranging from conducting surveys of the public's research priorities to its engagement with "citizen science" projects.[16] The elitist hierarchical model of the politician taking advice exclusively from the expert has been transformed—at least, rhetorically—into an egalitarian arrangement in which the public's knowledge is respected. Unlike the previous one, this arrangement can be democratically legitimated.

It has been observed for some time that advisory arrangements have undergone a transition—from legitimation through knowledge to legitimation through participation. But given the growing specialization of knowledge and diversification of the distinction between expert and layman, there are limits to what can be democratized. We can identify several levels of democratization: access to expert knowledge, access to experts, choice of experts and areas of knowledge, and production of knowledge. *Access to expert knowledge* has been granted in many countries that have followed the US example of the Freedom of Information Act (first passed in 1967, and then reformed in 1974), which is designed to guarantee the transparency of government decision-making processes, thereby creating trust and legitimacy. *Access to experts* is no longer an issue since the breakup of governments' monopoly on expert advice. Now nongovernmental organizations have their own advisory bodies, or they tap into the scientific brain power available at universities and research organizations to mobilize "counterexpertise." This choosing of experts according to their political leanings may be understood as a democratization of expertise, but it has also contributed to the politicization of expert advice.

The *choice of experts* is an issue at the government level. High-level advisory bodies and ad hoc committees with a specified mandate often have an expected impact on policy decisions, so that the choice of experts is already politically charged. This is illustrated by the procedure of the German Parliament's Enquête Commissions for choosing their expert members based on proportional party representation. Different mechanisms have been developed for choosing experts according to "relevant" criteria that go beyond their respective disciplines. The United States' Federal Advisory Committee Act of 1972 regulates federal advisory committees to ensure that experts are also being chosen on the basis of gender and geographical region.

Finally, the democratization of *knowledge production* is the most radical form of the democratization of expertise. Governments propagate this under the rubric of "participatory research" or "citizen science." A successful and often-cited example is the impact that AIDS activists in the United States had in convincing researchers to better adapt the protocols of clinical tests of AIDS drugs to the needs of the HIV community (Epstein 1995). In a sense, this was not really a democratization of expertise but, rather, a broadening of the meaning of expert knowledge to include knowledge that is experiential and contextual to specific cases. But since then, the political support for citizen science both in the United States and the European Union has intensified; the number of such projects has grown considerably, and so has the diversity of their formats and motives. Citizen-science projects range from crowdsourcing for large-scale data collection, especially in the environmental sciences (e.g., biodiversity), all the way to community projects whose topics are also defined by nonspecialists (Schrögel and Kolleck 2019; Cooper and Lewenstein 2016).

The reference to the public serves to increase political legitimacy—in this case, of the experts but, more generally, of science. This explains, at least partly, the spread of participatory formats in science policy throughout the industrialized world, following a pattern that has been observed for science policies in general (Drori et al. 2002). It is also another indication of the end of the exceptionalism of science as an institution: the self-referentiality of the determination of research objectives has been, if not replaced, then at least complemented by reference to the external public and its priorities. This development is exacerbated by the role of the media.

THE MEDIALIZATION OF SCIENCE

Having to refer to the general public to make legitimate decisions concerning research funding and priority setting presents the scientific community with a new challenge in seeking support. It now must spend time propagandizing with different publics as the target audiences. One of these publics comprises science policymakers and legislators who make decisions about appropriating public money to fund research councils (i.e., indirectly to scientists), universities, and research laboratories. In this realm, communicating performance and achievements fulfills the function of democratically mandated accountability.

Another public consists of citizens who are more, or less, interested in and more, or less, competent to engage with the information, which is provided mostly by the media, communication organizations, or scientists themselves. The media's communication of scientific results to the general public (the classic task of science journalism) may also be said to serve democratic accountability insofar as it informs the public about the value of science to society—that is, about what it gets for the tax money spent.

Science policymakers themselves are under pressure to legitimate their decisions, which is what triggered the emergence of "science communication"—often referred to as the "public understanding of science" (PUS) or, more recently, as "public engagement with science and technology" (PEST)—in the first place. The global diffusion of science-communication programs and formats has created a new profession. These programs are mostly staffed by communications and public-relations specialists, funded by governments, and appropriated by science organizations and universities. It is estimated that over the past two decades, there has been a roughly tenfold increase in the growth of university press and communication offices (Marcinkowski and Kohring 2014; Kohring et al. 2013). Being a professional group with its own accreditations it obviously has its own interests, but more importantly it operates according to a different logic. Originally, science communication was devoted to increasing public "awareness" and "understanding" of science and its methods, to both gain acceptance for and generate interest in science hoping to recruit potential students to take up STEM subjects as a means to foster a country's innovative capacity (Burns, O'Connor, and Stocklmayr 2003). This paradigm was criticized for proceeding from a "deficit model," from the assumption that the public's knowledge was deficient. The subsequent paradigm called for public's "engagement" with science—that is, for taking the public seriously as an equal party in a dialogue, expressing its own interests (Fischhoff and Scheufele 2013). But having declared the general "public" to be the relevant audience, science communication began to follow the logic of capturing maximum *attention*. This was a departure from the original motives of museums and science centers that were (and still are) supposed to communicate scientific knowledge and thereby inform and educate visitors. The shift in the logic of communication is one from *content* to *form*. The goal is to capture the public's attention, and so formats that employ elements of entertainment and event staging have gained prominence. Outside science, the style (and operation) of (science) communicating is dominated by public relations. One effect is that it has become increasingly difficult to distinguish between institutional communication driven and shaped by the interests of the commissioning organization and factual reporting, such as by science journalists (Carver 2014; Marcinkowski and Kohring 2014; Gioia and Corley 2002; Takahashi and Tandoc 2016; Vogler and Schäfer 2020) or by scientists themselves.

This has serious implications for the public's trust of science, scientific experts, and the knowledge they communicate (Critchley 2008; Weingart and Guenther 2016). The urgently needed balance between democratic accountability and the legitimacy gained from scientific evidence is tipped in favor of the former. The orientation to the general public—selective as it necessarily must be—becomes the frontstage of science policy. "Participation" and "engagement" are now prominent buzzwords in the science-policy rhetoric (Weingart, Joubert and Connoway 2021; Macq et al. 2020). A closer look at the actual practice, however, reveals that it remains very much in line with traditional formats and it has had only limited impact (Felt and Fochler 2010, 236; Smallman 2016, 2017).

Organizations like National academies, scientific societies, universities and research councils support science communication to the general public because they hope to favorably influence the legislators responsible for appropriating public funds to science. In this realm, the job of science communication is to impress the public and gain its acceptance by demonstrating performance. With this, it also fulfills the function of democratically mandated accountability.

For the same reasons, universities and research institutions also communicate with the general public. These efforts—whether in the form of press releases or glossy magazines—are categorized as science communication, but the institutions are primarily motivated by the political mandate to "profile" themselves. Under the NPM régime (and additionally spurred by the rankings published in the media), they have been forced to compete with one another—vying for students, highly productive scientists, and public funds. This explains the spectacular growth of PR departments within these organizations (Kohring et al. 2013).

Finally, this régime has also impacted the communication behavior of scientists, both internally, within their respective fields, and externally. As noted earlier, the introduction of performance measures was initially only intended to allow university administrations and research councils to monitor researchers' publication output and to create the basis for interinstitutional comparisons and the setting of benchmarks. However, scientists are involved in a communication system that has traditionally balanced intense competition for reputation, on the one hand, and co-operation and open professional exchange, on the other. Now the added sanctioning provided by recognition from administrations and/or monetary incentives has tipped this balance.

In seeking recognition by disciplinary peers in terms of quantitative performance measures scientists inadvertently shift to a new "currency": that is, from recognition for scholarly achievement that can only be judged by expert peers to recognition for general attention by an unspecified general public. This public is constituted and represented primarily by the media. By far the largest part of the public are citizens who are more or less interested and more or less competent to engage with the information about science. This information is provided by the media, by science communication organizations or by scientists themselves.[17] Since the mass media is still the most far-reaching medium, the general public has become an important audience with which individual scientists and scientific organizations communicate. It is hardly surprising that this communication adopts techniques for commanding attention. The process whereby the logic of the media ((so-called news values) determines the style and content of the media's science reporting has been dubbed "medialization" (Weingart 2012). The need to get, and sustain, the viewer's or reader's attention often becomes more important than simply communicating the substance of the achievement (Marcinkowski and Kohring 2014). Of course, this does not happen all of a sudden, nor does it capture all of scientific communication. Rather, it becomes apparent in particular instances.[18]

SCIENCE COMMUNICATION AND SOCIAL MEDIA—A CRISIS OF SCIENTIFIC EXPERTISE?

The quest for (public) attention has provided fertile ground for several developments. The most consequential in this context is the digitization of communication. The Internet has revolutionized scholarly communication in several ways. Informal communication has been accelerated, and thereby expanded, dramatically. Formal communications—that is, publications—have been made accessible, at least in principle, to everybody, everywhere, and at any time.[19] This also holds true for the communication of research data (open data). In addition, general information platforms like Google or Google Scholar and specialized platforms targeting medical or legal information, for example, have made it easier to search for information. These technological innovations have had a profound impact on the speed, accessibility, and reach of communication inside science (and, of course, beyond its boundaries).

A fundamental problem with digitization and social media is the loss of gatekeepers. In the mass media, these are the editors and journalists who act as guardians of the veracity and reliability of the news they receive or research themselves and then communicate. The quality of their work determines the reputation of the newspapers or TV programs they shape and, ultimately, the quality of the societal discourse. The communication that pertains specifically to science and science-related issues is executed by a specialized group—that is, science journalists. This branch of media reporting has suffered most from the economic impact of social media on traditional media.[20] At a time when universities are incentivized to use social media, platforms like Facebook and Twitter allow them to communicate directly to the public, avoiding critical intermediaries. Thus, many science journalists who have lost their jobs have moved to the press offices and public relations departments of science organizations and universities (Schäfer 2017). In doing so, they shift from providing and vetting critical information based on observation from the outside to managing institutional communication from the inside. In effect, their role as gatekeepers is lost (Bruns 2005).

Similarly, in science, the gatekeepers of the communication are the scientists themselves. As experts in their respective fields, they serve as reviewers of articles submitted to journals and research proposals submitted to research councils for funding. In principle, every member of the community can be a gatekeeper, deciding on a publication by or the allocation of research funds to his or her peers. In fact, this role is often assigned to the most highly regarded members of the community to assure the quality of judgment. Even though this practice is sometimes criticized as inefficient or biased, the manifest function of gatekeeping in the internal communications of science is quality assurance.

Digitization was initially hailed for "democratizing" science by eliminating gatekeepers.[21] This referred, on the one hand, to the opportunity for "open access" publishing—that is, directly on the Internet, without editors and reviewers intervening—and, on the other hand, to communicating on social media. The latter is particularly relevant here because it affects, above all, the communication of science to the public. Whereas previously, communication within science and communication to the public were separated by clear delineations between the professional audience and the general audience, between expert communication and lay communication, this boundary has now become porous. The disciplinary expert who used to function as a gatekeeper over the scientific information communicated to the outside world was the guarantor of its veracity and reliability. Now, expert and lay communications compete for attention. This may satisfy the expectation of "public engagement" with science propagated by governments and scholars alike. The opportunities offered by the new technology are the general accessibility of communication, its transparency and openness to participation, its directness and emotional appeal, its immediacy and potentially greater reach. These properties have constituted the initial expectations that social media would be instrumental in the democratization of science.[22]

Probably the most important format in this context are the blogs on scientific topics operated either by scientists themselves or by laypersons. At first sight, these appear to be the ideal media for the democratization of science. However, research on bloggers, their motives, and their audiences has shown, not surprisingly, that the differences in the levels of knowledge and the use of specialized language between the "experts"—that is, scientists—and their lay audiences limits the number of people who follow and comment on blogs (Mahrt and Puschmann 2014; Kouper 2010). If blogs have broadened the discourse between science experts and the lay audience, they have eliminated neither the differences between them nor the role of expert as such. This is corroborated by the fact that many if not most science blogs are operated by scientific journals, scientists, or scientific institutions. Meanwhile science communication community's optimistic expectations for blogs have given way to a sober view given their limited impact (Brown and Woolston 2018).[23]

The multilateral communication without gatekeepers on social media has made various forms of manipulation possible. They range from the spread of false information to the intentional misrepresentation of expert discussions and research results (Del Vicario et al. 2015).[24] If nothing else, the social media have multiplied the volume of communication in general and science communication in particular, and they have thereby amplified the occurrence of mistakes, fraud, bias, and misinformation, which makes it harder than ever before to distinguish between evidence-based, verifiable, and trustworthy communication, on the one hand, and pseudo-scientific, propagandistic, institutionally interested communication, on the other (Vosougi et al. 2018).

The providers of the different social media platforms are part of the problem. The market in which they operate is an oligopolistic one in which very few companies (Facebook, Twitter) are dominant. Their business model is based on the sale of data and advertising space, thus their orientation is to the creation of attention, while they renounce any responsibility for content and its quality, claiming that they do not function as traditional media but only provide platforms. The algorithms on which their platforms operate are opaque, and the industry refuses to make them transparent. Their security controls have failed repeatedly, creating a series of scandals involving violations of data protection. As early as 2013, the World Economic Forum warned: "The global risk of *massive digital misinformation* sits at the centre of a constellation of technological and geopolitical risks ranging from *terrorism* to *cyber attacks* and *the failure of global governance*. This risk case examines how hyper-connectivity could enable 'digital wildfires' to wreak havoc in the real world" (World Economic Forum 2013). For all these reasons the providers of social media platforms, first and foremost Facebook and Twitter, have come under regulatory pressure, at least in the European Union. The first regulatory measures that have been put in place are just the beginning of what will be needed in the future because the technology as such will not disappear. The crucial problem for any regulation of the Internet is to find a balance between protecting the freedom of speech and maintaining the many advantages of digital technology, on the one hand, and preventing its abuse in spreading of misinformation and hate speech, on the other. The communication of science via social media has increased its range, speed, and general accessibility. But at the same time, the technology has unleashed an unchecked information overload that makes it difficult, especially for the general public, to distinguish right and wrong and thus to be able to identify the credible and trustworthy information.

Inside the science field the new digital technology has triggered the development of new performance indicators that are entirely attention focused: altmetrics measure "likes" (Facebook), "reads" (on researchgate.net and academia.edu), or re-tweets (Twitter). It is no longer the factual impact in terms of a reference to contents via citation alone that counts; increasingly, it is also the mouse click on a title on the Internet that registers its "having been seen"—that is, having captured attention—that matters. No longer content with receiving feedback on their ideas and research results from their peers, scientists are rivals in a competition for general attention. Not surprisingly, when the desire for attention is coupled with monetary incentives, as is the case now in some national science systems, it invites "gaming" on both sides: on the part of scientists and on the part of the providers of the respective platforms (Wouters and Costas 2012; Espeland and Sauder 2007). Even though the possibility of buying "likes" or "clicks" from the platform providers to promote visibility leads reputation management in the context of this attention economy into absurdity, the impact it will have on the publication culture in science is uncertain. Various tactics to increase publication output have increased the number of publications but only to a much smaller extent substantive knowledge production. If the new indicators of attention, fairly easy to manipulate as they are, assume the function of building reputation inside science, this reputation loses its orienting function for the research community.

The Inevitability, However Precarious, of Scientific Experts and Expertise

In light of all the challenges, the question is whether the secular expansion of participation, which translates into the end of exceptionalism of science, its subjection to accountability, its orientation toward the public and the media, and a movement toward its "democratization" will render the role of the scientific expert obsolete or if these are ancillary phenomena, fads of science policy and social science commentators. Some audacious observers even raise the question if the developments described signal a new epistemological order as is implied with the breakdown of the distinction between certified and non-certified knowledge (Dickel and Franzen 2016, 10).

Instead of thinking in terms of a dichotomy of experts and a lay public, we need to recognize that the answer to this question, and thus the diagnosis of the future of scientific expertise, is more complex. First of all, it is highly unlikely that the production of scientific knowledge will become the business of every citizen or that efforts to certify knowledge will be given up. Instead, the range of epistemologies will diversify. The second half of the twentieth century had already witnessed the shift from physics as the model discipline to biology. Another aspect of this is the shift from laboratory-based research, which controls all relevant variables in an experimental setting, to research of complex natural systems, which cannot be controlled but require distributed data collection through systematic observation and construction of models. The former lead to quite limited but certain and repeatable results; the latter produce statistical models and probability statements. The development of science throughout the last century and a half is one of moving from the study of simple to complex systems.

It is not by accident that most citizen-science projects focus on environmental and biosciences, where citizens participate in observation and data gathering (Hakley 2013, 2017). Such research projects make that kind of participation possible; some are even impossible without "crowdsourcing." Research laboratories with sophisticated equipment whose operation requires highly specialized training are not accessible to amateur researchers. Various analyses of citizen-science projects in different disciplines show that participation and, thus, inclusion vary by degree of intensity (Schrögel and Kolleck 2019).

Secondly, the decision-making contexts and the knowledge they require have diversified and become more complex. This development is a function of both the growth of systematic knowledge and the expansion of government regulatory power. The monarchies of the early nineteenth century regulated only measures and weights. The modern nation-states of the late twentieth and early twenty-first centuries have taken on many more regulatory tasks, which are all based on and call for systematic specialized knowledge. This is reflected in a plethora of advisory bodies attached to government ministries or other administrative organizations. These advisory bodies represent a multitude of different configurations of experts and lay citizens (Lentsch and Weingart 2011, 11).

In addition to formally institutionalized councils, committees, advisory boards etc., which provide advice according to mandates, there is now a virtual advisory industry. Led by reputed think tanks, many organizations and individuals have turned the provision of expert advice to decision-makers into a thriving business. Likewise, scientific academies and research institutes give advice, some on request; others proactively. Given this institutional diversity, it is obvious that the once-elevated social status of the general expert adviser crumbles. The role of the expert becomes inflationary, and the demarcation between disinterested scientific advice and economically or politically interested advice blurs. The greater the leeway in decision-making due to the probabilistic nature of knowledge, the greater the danger that interpretation and the translation of findings into decisions will be conflated with interests and that the advice will become politicized. In the public's perception, the expert often morphs into a lobbyist. The problem is exacerbated if it becomes apparent that scientific experts have given biased advice or have intentionally ignored critical information, as is typically the case when they are attached to a particular industry (Oreskes and Conway 2010).

Thirdly, the same apparently paradoxical constellation can be observed on the level of people's everyday lives. A vast advisory and consultancy market has emerged as all kinds of activities requiring decisions—from the daily nutrition to the raising of children by ordinary citizens to investment decisions by businesses—are the subject of specialized knowledge and its conveyance by expert advisers. Guidebooks and counseling columns in the media give advice on an ever-increasing universe of questions, meeting a seemingly inexhaustible demand, constantly reinforcing the pattern of a lay public appealing to experts for guidance, the increased skepticism toward experts notwithstanding.

The dependence of present-day advanced societies on systematic knowledge is evident both in the plethora of organizations providing expert advice and consultation and in the demand for such advice pertaining to virtually all spheres of life. Not all but most of the advice given is based on academic science provided by academic scientists, and most of the advice requested refers to systematic knowledge produced and communicated by them.

The quest for ever-superior knowledge apparently defines society at large. However, the more instrumental knowledge is for decisions, the more it becomes subject to contention, competing claims, and an undermining skepticism—that is, to politicization in a broad sense of the word. The crisis of expertise is a product of its success, or to put it differently: we are witnessing a self-reinforcing dynamic wherein the continued dependence on knowledge produced and represented by experts, paradoxically triggers growing skepticism of the experts and their knowledge. Conversely, politicized conflicts over certain knowledge claims refer to "better" knowledge—that is, to "sound science." In this way, skepticism leads to renewed dependence on improved knowledge (Eyal 2019, chap. 7).[25]

Various efforts have been made to shield expertise from skepticism and politicization: shielding it institutionally by restoring its exclusivity, providing transparency and opening it to public participation, limiting it to mechanistic procedures or "outsourcing"—that is, distancing it from the client (Eyal 2019, chap. 6).[26] Each of these attempts responds to one cause of the precarious situation of expert knowledge between credibility and legitimacy, but none of them is ultimately successful in the sense that it responds to all of them. There is simply no perfect equilibrium, no middle ground, between legitimacy created by popular consent and expertise based on systematic knowledge.[27] In this sense scientific expertise is inevitable, however contested it may be.

NOTES

1. *Newsweek*, April 23, 1979.
2. Luhmann points to the notorious difficulties of capturing "trust" empirically (Luhmann 1988, 104). This is reflected in the multitude of survey approaches research employs and their contradictory results. Here, we can only mention this as a caveat when interpreting them.
3. The *Edelman Trust Barometer 2018* notes an overall increase in trust, and a section of its report was titled "The Return of the Experts." Trust of technical and academic experts leads the list at more than 60%, having gained as compared to 2017 (Edelman 2018, 11). Cf. Cary Funk (2017).
4. See the Ipsos MORI Veracity Index 2015. Accessed August 17, 2018. https://www.ipsos.com/sites/default/files/migrations/en-uk/files/Assets/Docs/Polls/ipsos-mori-veracity-index-2015-topline.pdf.

5. See Veracity Index 2017, Ipsos MORI Social Research Institute, November. Accessed August 17, 2018. https://www.ipsos.com/sites/default/files/ct/news/documents/2017-11/trust-in-professions-veracity-index-2017-slides.pdf.

6. In many Western industrialized countries R&D expenditures amount to 2.5% to 3% of the gross domestic product. Cf. OECD. "Gross Domestic Spending on R&D." doi:10.1787/d8b068b4-en. https://data.oecd.org/rd/gross-domestic-spending-on-r-d.htm. Accessed August 17, 2019.

7. "Historical Background," US Office of Research Integrity. Accessed October 11, 2018, https://ori.hhs.gov/historical-background. ENRIO has thirty-one member organizations in twenty-three European countries. See "About ENRIO" on their website, http://www.enrio.eu/about-enrio/. Accessed September 13, 2019.

8. Cf. For a critical account of the uses and misuses of indicators, see Hicks et al. (2015).

9. In the US, the President's science advisor is the head of the Office of Science and Technology Policy (OSTP); the UK has the Government Chief Scientific Adviser (GCSA) and Head of the Government Science and Engineering (GSE) profession.

10. Cf. As an indicator of the changing roles of the US president's science adviser under different presidents, see Pielke and Klein (2009). On the role of advisers as "honest brokers" cf. Pielke (2007).

11. Liability law rests, inter alia, on notions of "scientific evidence" and expert verdicts about what is "true" and what is "false."

12. Cf. For a prominent example, see Oreskes and Conway (2010).

13. One of these endeavors was first raised in the 1970s, primarily in European universities, which the student movement had targeted because of their hierarchical structures. Democratization was then achieved by creating new administrative structures that allowed for the representation of students and staff. That is of no concern in this context.

14. Cf. also see "EPA History," Environmental Protection Agency, updated April 19, 2022. https://www.epa.gov/history. Accessed November 1, 2022.

15. The US Office of Technology Assessment (OTA), the first of its kind, was established in 1972 and closed in 1995.

16. While the motives driving the "citizen science" movement are diverse and their realization is more modest, governments, above all the EU, have launched programs to support citizen science (Strasser 2019; Schrögel and Kolleck 2019). Cf. also the EU White Paper on Citizen Science: https://www.ecsite.eu/activities-and-services/resources/white-paper-citizen-science-europe. Accessed November 1, 2022.

17. Organizations typically 'imagine' the publics which they address with their communications. In the case of universities these are science policymakers in legislatures, administrators in science councils, funding organizations or alumni associations (Krücken 2021).

18. One such incident was the premature announcement of the discovery of a blood test for diagnosing breast cancer by the University of Heidelberg in 2019 (Weingart 2019).

19. The limitations of "open access" arise from the business models of publishers and the attribution of costs.

20. With digitization and the advent of social media platforms, many newspapers experienced a crisis as readership shifted to online news sources and they lost advertising revenue, their main source of income. Although this development primarily affected newspapers in the US, where the turn to digital news sources on social media was more dramatic than elsewhere, its impact has been felt around the world.

21. Loader and Mercea (2011) give an account of the shift from early enthusiasm to subsequent skepticism. Similarly, Hindman (2008).
22. Official government documents still convey the enthusiasm in their promotion of citizen science. For the EU, cf. https://www.ecsite.eu/activities-and-services/resources/white-paper-citizen-science-europe. Accessed November 1, 2022.
23. Cf. the many statistics on blogs, e.g., https://blog.feedspot.com/science_blogs/. Accessed October 10, 2018.
24. This was found to be the case with expert discussions on the risks of vaccination, for example. Antivaccination groups distorted the opinions, amplifying minority positions by re-tweeting them (Schalkwyk 2018). Cf. Lazer et al. (2018).
25. Apart from Eyal's example of the conflict over the FDA, another particularly cogent one is the protracted debate over the connection between smoking and cancer, which ultimately led to proof of the link (Oreskes and Conway 2010).
26. Eyal uses slightly different terms: *exclusion, inclusion, objectivity,* and *outsourcing* and gives examples for each of them.
27. Sophie Rosenfeld (2019) provides an illuminating historical perspective on the issue, tracing it back to the first modern democracies in the Age of Enlightenment.

REFERENCES

Bäckstrand, Karin. 2003. "Civic Science for Sustainability: Reframing the Role of Experts, Policy-Makers and Citizens in Environmental Governance." *Global Environmental Politics* 3 (4): 24–41.
Berman, Elizabeth Popp. 2012. *Creating the Market University*. Princeton, NJ: Princeton University Press.
Brown, Eryn, and Chris Woolston. 2018. "Life in the Old Blog Yet." *Nature* 554:135–137.
Bruns, Axel. 2005. *Gatewatching: Collaborative Online News Production*. New York: Peter Lang.
Burns, Terry. W., John D. O'Connor, and Susan M. Stocklmayer. 2003. "Science Communication: A Contemporary Definition." *Public Understanding of Science* 12 (2): 183–202.
Carolan, Michael S. 2006. "Science, Expertise, and the Democratization of the Decision-Making Process." *Society and Natural Resources* 19 (7): 661–668.
Carver, Rebecca B. 2014. "Public Communication from Research Institutes: Is It Science Communication or Public Relations?" *Journal of Science Communication* 13 (3): 1–4.
Castell, Sarah, Anne Charlton, Michael Clemence, Nick Pettigrew, Sarah Pope, Anna Quigley, et al. 2014. *Public Attitudes to Science 2014: Main Report*. Ipsos MORI, London.
Cooper, Caren B., and Bruce V. Lewenstein. 2016. "Two Meanings of Citizen Science." In *The Rightful Place of Science: Citizen Science*, edited by Darlene Cavalier and Eric B. Kennedy, 51–62. Tempe, AZ: Consortium for Science, Policy and Outcomes.
Costas, Rodrigo Antonio, Perianes-Rodriguez, and Javier Ruiz-Castillo. 2017. "On the Quest for Currencies of Science: Field Exchange Rates for Citations and Mendeley Readership." *Aslib Journal of Information Management* 69 (5): 557–575. doi:10.1108/AJIM-01-2017-0023.
Critchley, Christine R. 2008. "Public Opinion and Trust in Scientists: The Role of the Research Context, and the Perceived Motivation of Stem Cell Researchers." *Public Understanding of Science* 17:309–327.
Del Vicario, Michela, Alessandro Bessi, Fabiana Zollo, and Walter Quatrociocchi. 2015. "The Spreading of Misinformation Online." *Proceedings of the National Academy of Sciences* 113 (3): 554–559. http://www.pnas.org/content/113/3/554.

Demeritt, David. 2000. "The New Social Contract for Science: Accountability, Value and Relevance in US and UK Science and Research Policy." *Antipode* 32 (3): 308–329.

Diáz-Faes, Adrian, Timothy D. Bowman, and Rodrigo Costas. 2019. "Towards a Second Generation of 'Social Media Metrics': Characterizing Twitter Communities of Attention around Science." *PLoS One* 14 (5): Article e0216408. https://journals.plos.org/plosone/article?id=10.1371/journal.pone.0216408.

Drori, Gili S., John W. Meyer, and Francisco O. Ramirez. 2002. *Science in the Modern World Polity: Institutionalization and Globalization.* Stanford, CA: Stanford University Press.

Edelman. 2018. *Edelman Trust Barometer 2018 Executive Summary.* Accessed October 10, 2018. https://www.edelman.com/sites/g/files/aatuss191/files/2018-10/2018_Edelman_TrustBarometer_Executive_Summary_Jan.pdf 02/2018_Edelman_TrustBarometer_Executive_Summary_Jan.pdf.

Epstein, Steven. 1995. "The Construction of Lay Expertise: AIDS Activism and the Forging of Credibility in the Reform of Clinical Trials." *Science, Technology and Human Values* 20 (4): 408–437.

Espeland, Wendy N., and Michael Sauder. 2007. "Rankings and Reactivity: How Public Measures Recreate Social Worlds." *American Journal of Sociology* 113 (July): 1–40.

Eyal, Gil. 2019. *The Crisis of Expertise.* Cambridge, UK: Polity Press.

Felt, Ulrike, and Maximilian Fochler. 2010. "Machineries for Making Publics: Inscribing and De-scribing Publics in Public Engagement." *Minerva* 48 (3): 219–238.

Fischhoff, Baruch, and Dietram A. Scheufele. 2013. "The Science of Science Communication." *Proceedings of the National Academy of Sciences* 110 (S3): 14031–14032.

Dickel, Sascha, and Martina Franzen. 2016. The "Problem of Extension" revisited: new modes of digital participation in science. *Journal of Science Communication* 15 (1): 1–15.

Funk, Cary. 2017. "Mixed Messages about Public Trust in Science." *Pew Research Center.* Accessed August 11, 2018. http://www.pewinternet.org/2017/12/08/mixed-messages-about-public-trust-in-science/.

Gioia, Dennis A., and Kevin G. Corley. 2002. "Being Good vs Looking Good: Business School Rankings and the Circean Transformation from Substance to Image." *Academy of Management Learning and Education* 1 (1): 107–120. https://journals.aom.org/doi/10.5465/amle.2002.7373729.

Guston, David. 2000. "Retiring the Social Contract for Science." *Issues in Science and Technology* 16 (4).

Guston, David H., and Kenneth Keniston. 1994. *The Fragile Contract.* Cambridge, MA: MIT Press.

Haklay, Mordechai 2013. "Neogeography and the Delusion of Democratisation." *Environment and Planning A* 45 (1): 55–69. doi:10.1068/a45184.

Haklay, Mordechai 2017. "Volunteered Geographic Information and Citizen Science." In *Understanding Spatial Media,* edited by Rob Kitchin, Tracey P. Lauriault, and MatthewW. Wilson, 127–135. London: Sage.

Hendriks, Friederike, Dorothe Kienhues, and Rainer Bromme. 2015. "Measuring Laypeople's Trust in Experts in a Digital Age: The Muenster Epistemic Trustworthiness Inventory (METI)." *PLoS One* 10 (10): Article e0139309. https://doi.org/10.1371/journal.pone.0139309.

Hicks, Diana, Paul Wouters, Ludo Waltman, Sarah de Rijcke, and Ismael Rafols. 2015. "The Leiden Manifesto for Research Metrics." *Nature* 520 (April): 429–431.

Hindman, Matthew. 2008. *The Myth of Digital Democracy,* Princeton, NJ: Princeton University Press.

Jasanoff, Sheila. 2003. "Technologies of Humility: Citizen Participation in Governing Science." *Minerva* 41: 223–244.

Kohring, Mathias, Frank Marcinkowski, Christian Lindner, and Sarah Karis. 2013. "Media Orientation of German University Decision Makers and the Executive Influence of Public Relations." *Public Relations Review* 39:171–177.

Kouper, Inna. 2010. "Science Blogs and Public Engagement with Science: Practices, Challenges, and Opportunities." *JCOM: Journal of Science Communication* 9 (1): A02.

Krücken, Georg. 2021. Imaginierte Öffentlichkeiten—Zum Strukturwandel von Hochschule und Wissenschaft, *Leviathan* 49 (37): 412–430.

Lazer, David M. J., Matthew A. Baum, Yochai Benkler, Adam J. Berinsky, Kelly M. Greenhill, et al. 2018. "The Science of Fake News: Addressing Fake News Requires a Multidisciplinary Effort." *Science* 359 (6380): 1094–1096.

Lentsch, Justus, and Peter Weingart, eds. 2011. *The Politics of Scientific Advice*. Cambridge, UK: Cambridge University Press.

Loader, Brian D., and Dan Mercea. 2011. "Networking Democracy? Social Media Innovations in Participatory Politics." *Information, Communication and Society* 14 (6): 757–769. doi:10.1080/1369118X.2011.592648.

Longhurst, James. 2010. *Citizen Environmentalists*. Lebanon, NH: Tufts University Press.

Luhmann, Niklas. 1988. "Familiarity, Confidence, Trust: Problems and Alternatives." In *Trust: Making and Breaking Cooperative Relations*, edited by Diego Gambetta, 94–107. Oxford: Basil Blackwell.

Luhmann, Niklas. (1968) 2014. *Vertrauen*. 5th ed. Konstanz: UVK Verlagsgesellschaft.

Mahrt, Merja, and Cornelius Puschmann. 2014. "Science Blogging: An Exploratory Study of Motives, Styles, and Audience Reactions." *JCOM: Journal of Science Communication* 13 (3): 1–17.

Marcinkowski, Frank, and Matthias Kohring. 2014. "The Changing Rationale of Science Communication: A Challenge to Scientific Autonomy." *JCOM: Journal of Science Communication* 13 (3): C04. https://jcom.sissa.it/archive/13/03/JCOM_1303_2014_C01/JCOM_1303_2014_C04.

Macq, Hadrien, Tancoigne, Élise, and Bruno J. Strasser. 2020. From deliberation to production: public participation in science and technology policies of the European Commission (1998–2019). *Minerva*. 58 (4): 489–512.

Oreskes, Naomi, and Erik M. Conway. 2010. *Merchants of Doubt: How a Handful of Scientists Obscured the Truth on Issues from Tobacco Smoke to Global Warming*. London: Bloomsbury Press.

Peters, Hans Peter. 2015. "Science Dilemma: Between Public Trust and Social Relevance." *EuroScientist*. Accessed August 27, 2018. http://www.euroscientist.com/trust-in-science-as-compared-to-trust-in-economics-and-politics.

Peters, Hans Peter, John T. Lang, Magdalena Sawicka, and William K. Hallman. 2007. "Culture and Technological Innovation: Impact of Institutional Trust and Appreciation of Nature on Attitudes towards Food Biotechnology in the USA and Germany." *International Journal of Public Opinion Research* 19 (2): 191–220.

Pielke, Robert A., Jr. 2007. *The Honest Broker: Making Sense of Science in Policy and Politics*. Cambridge, UK: Cambridge University Press.

Pielke, Robert A., Jr., and Roberta Klein. 2009. "The Rise and Fall of the Science Advisor to the President of the United States." *Minerva* 47 (1): 7–29.

Porter, Theodore M. 1995. *Trust in Numbers: The Pursuit of Objectivity in Science and Public Life*. Princeton: Princeton University Press.

Price, Don. 1967. *The Scientific Estate.* Cambridge, MA: Harvard University Press.

Rosenfeld, Sophia 2019. *Democracy and Truth: A Short History.* Philadelphia: University of Pennsylvania Press.

Royal Society. 1985. *The Public Understanding of Science.* Report. London: Royal Society.

Schäfer, Mike S. 2017. "How Changing Media Structures Are Affecting Science News Coverage." In *The Oxford Handbook of the Science of Science Communication*, edited by Kathleen Hall Jamieson, Dan Kahan, and Dietram A. Scheufele, 51–59. New York: Oxford University Press.

Schalkwyk, Francois van. 2018. "New Potentials in the Communication of Open Science with Non-scientific Publics: The Case of the Anti-vaccination Movement." Unpublished diss. PhD Stellenbosch University.

Schrögel, Philipp, and Alma Kolleck. 2019. "The Many Faces of Participation in Science: Literature Review and Proposal for a Three-Dimensional Framework." *Science & Technology Studies* 32 (2): 77–99.

Slaughter, Sheila, and Gary Rhoades. 2009. *Academic Capitalism and the New Economy: Markets, State, and Higher Education.* Baltimore, MD: Johns Hopkins University Press.

Smallman, Melanie. 2016. "*Public Understanding of Science* in Turbulent Times III: Deficit to Dialogue, Champions to Critics." *Public Understanding of Science* 25 (2): 186–197.

Smallman, Melanie. 2017. "Science to the Rescue or Contingent Progress? Comparing 10 Years of Public, Expert and Policy Discourses on New and Emerging Science and Technology in the United Kingdom." *Public Understanding of Science* 27 (6): 655–673.

Strasser, Bruno, Jérôme Baudry, Dana Mahr, and Gabriela Sachnet. 2019. "'Citizen Science'? Rethinking Science and Public Participation." *Science & Technology Studies* 32 (2): 52–76.

Takahashi, Bruno, and Edson C. Tandoc Jr. 2016. "Media Sources, Credibility, and Perceptions of Science: Learning about How People Learn about Science." *Public Understanding of Science* 25 (6): 674–690.

Vogler, Daniel, and Mike S. Schäfer. 2020. "Growing Influence of University PR on Science News Coverage? A Longitudinal Automated Content Analysis of University Media Releases and Newspaper Coverage in Switzerland, 2003-2017." *International Journal of Communication* 14: 3143–3164.

Vosoughi, Soroush, Deb Roy, and Sinan Aral. 2018. "The Spread of True and False News Online." *Science* 359, no. 6380 (March 9): 1146–1151.

Weinberg, Alvin. 1972. "Science and Trans-Science." *Minerva* 10:209–222.

Weingart, Peter. 2003a. "Growth, Differentiation, Expansion and Change of Identity—the Future of Science." In *Social Studies of Science and Technology: Looking Back Ahead*, edited by Bernward Joerges and Helda Nowotny, 183–200. Sociology of the Sciences Yearbook 23. Dordrecht: Kluwer Academic.

Weingart, Peter. 2003b. "Paradox of Scientific Advising." In *Expertise and Its Interfaces: The Tense Relationship of Science and Politics*, edited by Gotthard Bechmann and Imre Hronszky, 53–89. Berlin: Edition Sigma.

Weingart, Peter. 2010. "A Short History of Knowledge Formations." In *The Oxford Handbook of Interdisciplinarity*, edited by Robert Frodemann, Julie Thomson Klein, and Carl Mitcham, 3–14. Oxford: Oxford University Press.

Weingart, Peter. 2012. "The Lure of the Mass Media and Its Repercussions on Science: Theoretical Considerations on the 'Medialization of Science.'" In *The Sciences' Media Connection: Public Communication and Its Repercussions*, edited by Simone Rödder, Martina Franzen, and Peter Weingart, 17–32. Sociology of the Sciences Yearbook 28. Dordrecht: Springer. doi:10.1007/978-94-007-2085-5_2.

Weingart, Peter. 2019. "Dizzying Effect of Spin." *Times Higher Education*, July 18, 38.

Weingart, Peter, Martin Carrier, and Wolfgang Krohn, eds. 2007. *Nachrichten aus der Wissensgesellschaft: Analysen zur Veränderung der Wissenschaft*. Weilerswist: Velbrück Wissenschaft.

Weingart, Peter, and Lars Günther. 2016. "Science Communication and the Issue of Trust." *JCOM: Journal of Science Communication* 15 (5): C01.

Weingart, Peter, Marina Joubert, and Karien Connoway. 2021. "Public Engagement with Science—Origins, Motives and Impact in Academic Literature and Science Policy." PLoS One 16(7): e0254201. https://doi.org/10.1371/journal.pone.0254201.

Wilensky, Harold L. 1964. "The Professionalization of Everyone?" *American Journal of Sociology* 70 (2): 137–158.

Wilsdon, James, Liz Allen, Eleonora Belfiore, Philip Campbell, Stephen Curry et al. 2015. *The Metric Tide: Report of the Independent Review of the Role of Metrics in Research Assessment and Management*. HFCE. doi:10.13140/RG.2.1.4929.1363.

World Economic Forum. 2013. "Digital Wildfires in a Hyperconnected World." In *Global Risks 2013 Eighth Edition*, sec. 2. http://reports.weforum.org/global-risks-2013/risk-case-1/digital-wildfires-in-a-hyperconnected-world/. Accessed June 6, 2017.

Wouters, Paul, and Rodrigo Costas. 2012. *Users, Narcissism and Control—Tracking the Impact of Scholarly Publications in the 21st Century*. Report. SURF Foundation. Utrecht. http://scholar.cci.utk.edu/beyond-downloads/publications/users-narcissism-and-control-%E2%80%93-tracking-impact-scholarly-publications. Accessed December 3, 2022.

Ziman, John. 1993. *Prometheus Bound: Science in a Dynamic 'Steady State'*. Cambridge, UK: Cambridge University Press.

3

THE THIRD WAVE AND POPULISM: SCIENTIFIC EXPERTISE AS A CHECK AND BALANCE

HARRY COLLINS, ROBERT EVANS, DARRIN DURANT, AND MARTIN WEINEL

INTRODUCTION: POLITICS GOES FROM BENIGN TO MALIGN

HERE we present the contribution of what is known variously as "the third wave of science studies" or "studies of expertise and experience" (SEE) to understanding the role of science and other forms of expertise in democratic politics. This approach to science studies, or science and technology studies (STS), can be dated to a 2002 paper by Collins and Evans entitled, "The Third Wave of Science Studies: Studies of Expertise and Experience." The paper defines a First Wave, which was dominant in the decades following World War II, when the self-evident superiority of science as a form of knowledge was explained "logically" by philosophers of science and by an idealistic form of sociology. The Second Wave overturned this view with new kinds of philosophy and "naturalistic" case studies of how scientific knowledge was made in practice; it showed that the interpretation of scientific data was more a matter of social agreement than of logical necessity. The Third Wave was intended to find ways to clarify the interpretation of the Second Wave's consequences for the role of scientific expertise in society and to show that they were not as radical as some would claim. Subsequent books following the Third Wave trajectory by the same two authors include *Rethinking Expertise* and *Why Democracies Need Science*, published in 2007 and 2017, respectively. This handbook chapter also draws on *Experts and the Will of the*

People: Society, Populism and Science, published in 2019, which included Durant and Weinel as coauthors.[1]

The intellectual and political context that forms the background to the debate started by the 2002 paper is the wider erosion of the ideas of expertise and democracy.[2] Although it is important to challenge expertise to ensure accountability and legitimacy, in the last decades expertise has been steadily undermined in Western democracies to the point that, under some interpretations, everyone is counted as an expert.[3] It is now commonplace to assert that the view of traditional experts is fatally narrowed by disciplinary, economic, or political blinkers.[4] At the same time, democracy has been subjected to a continual "authoritarian retrogression" in which the erosion of democratic procedures, for example, the undermining of courts and the media, partisan control of state institutions such as regulatory bodies, and harassment of opposition, leads to ever more monopoly power, with occasional more visible ruptures, such as the events in 1930s Germany or in Chile in 1973.[5] But Third Wave concerns have gained a new urgency with the confluence of the growth of populism in "Western" democracies and the intellectual attacks on science and expertise.[6] The dissolution of the idea that scientific expertise gives rise to a special kind of authority in technological decision-making in the public domain is part and parcel of the erosion of democracy itself.

The actions of former US president Donald Trump are an iconic example of the confluence. His actions while in office were, in effect, "breaching experiments," forcing us to think much harder about what democracy means and revealing things that we did not realize we already knew.[7] For example, we can now see that, before Trump, there was an unwritten constitution underlying the written Constitution of the United States. The unwritten constitution included the expectation that presidents will disclose their tax returns, divest themselves of their private business interests, and not appoint unqualified members of their families as senior advisers. It also assumed that they will refrain from attacking scientific expertise by denying its efficacy and shamelessly proclaiming the existence of an alternative set of truths, authorized by the government and its supporters, which better align with their preferred policies.[8] The Trump presidency and its aftermath have shown us, anew, how democracy works, or used to work, and where scientific expertise fits within it.

STS enters the scene because, as most analysts would agree, the 1970s marked the start of a revolution in the social analysis of science. The abstract descriptions of how science works, or must work, produced by scientists, philosophers, or sociologists (Wave One) were replaced with detailed empirical observations of scientific practice (Wave Two).[9] This move was inspired by earlier analyses of science, such as those by Fleck and Kuhn, and also by less science-focused philosophical work, such as that of Wittgenstein. The unifying theme was to see science not as a logical or mechanical enterprise that can automatically deliver certainty, but as a social activity from which ideas of truth emerged via social agreement among scientists, often influenced by wider social forces.[10] Terms associated with the start of this revolution in "the sociology of scientific knowledge" (widely known as SSK), were "relativism" and "social construction." There was a backlash against SSK by some scientists and philosophers, who feared that the dissolution of the idea of objective truth that is independent of society could lead toward a "dark age" and the end of "reason" itself. The most vocal and outspoken of these critics became known as "science warriors."[11]

In the main, practitioners of the post-1970 social analysis of science ignored the fears of the science warriors, and argued instead that supposedly independent scientific findings could not help but be influenced by social and political forces, and showed how, in particular cases, they were indeed so influenced. This paved the way for the portrayal of professional science as a political actor, operating beyond the scrutiny of democratic institutions and unwittingly captured by social elites: scientific knowledge and methods were being used to discount the wisdom and experience of those outside the scientific community, even when it could be shown to be directly relevant to the issues at stake. This led to arguments for more inclusive approaches to technological decision-making, which can be summed up as a movement to "democratize science." The ultimate expression of this movement was the idea of "lay expertise"—the notion that ordinary people had as much right as scientists to make technical judgments, based on their everyday experiences.

The problems hidden in this framing were not immediately apparent in many of the early case studies, where citizen groups often did have the necessary experience to make valuable, but ignored, contributions to debates over the use of science in public practice. The tensions are clear, however, in cases such as the controversy over the MMR vaccine against measles, mumps, and rubella, when advocates of democratizing science became defenders of parents who chose to refuse MMR vaccinations based on their "lay" observations of the onset of autism in their own children subsequent to the MMR jab. This observation was treated as equally or more valid than the epidemiological evidence showing that there was no association between the introduction of the MMR vaccine in a country and an increased incidence of autism.[12]

The Third Wave paper recognized the "problem of legitimacy"—the extent to which both the general public and nonscientists with relevant experience needed to be brought into technological decision-making if it was to remain politically legitimate—but it raised "the problem of extension," which was that if technological decision-making rights were extended without limit, then the distinction between experts and nonexperts would disappear, giving the "dark age" fears of the science warriors a new salience.[13] Unlike the science warriors, however, the Third Wave paper argued that the clock could not be turned back to the First Wave—the findings of the Second Wave had to be accepted. It was suggested, therefore, that for the purposes of resolving the problem, STS should shift its gaze from the analysis of the generation of scientific truth to the analysis of expertise, something that could be treated as real and identified in real-time, even if the nature of truth was far more difficult to resolve than had been thought under Wave One; this is the program known as Studies of Expertise and Experience, or SEE.

To make this shift in gaze do the work required of it, the way that expertise was thought about had to be changed. Typical philosophical and psychological treatments of expertise took it to be defined by verity or efficacy—an expert knew more true things than a nonexpert or knew how to make better judgments than a nonexpert. But this "veritist" approach creates the same kind of trouble for expertise that sociology of knowledge creates for truth. Thus philosophers working with the view that experts know more true things than others struggle with the fact that experts often disagree and that what we count as true changes over time and sometimes place. SEE replaces veritism with the idea that experts are people who have been socialized into an expert domain—for example, they can pass as experts when questioned by existing members of that domain in an "Imitation Game" but there is no assumption that the expertise in question is efficacious or bears on the truth. [14] Under the SEE approach, astronomy is an expertise and so is astrology—both are real expertises, and there are identifiable expert astronomers and identifiable expert astrologers; if one wants to choose astronomy over astrology, one needs reasons that do not turn on declaring only astronomers to be genuine experts. This is vital because many of the scientific expertises on which we rely in the public domain do not give rise to consensual agreement, so other justifications for their role in policy have to be found.

Incidentally, expert groups can be big or small: native English-speaking is an expertise, and so is gravitational wave physics (and so is tea-leaf reading). To repeat, the experts in each field can be readily identified—it is not a matter of attributing expertise to them but of testing for it. This indifference to scale also means that expertise is no longer necessarily esoteric—there are esoteric expertises and "ubiquitous" expertises, which can be complex and difficult despite their ubiquity. Native language-speaking is a rich and difficult ubiquitous expertise, as artificial intelligence enthusiasts continually discover when their efforts to make computers use native language with complete fluency fail.[15]

RETHINK OR EMBRACE

Before we return to SEE's view of expertise and democratic politics, let us situate what has been said in a more detailed way within contemporary STS. The Third Wave and SEE were spurred by the worry that science studies were monotonically and mistakenly moving toward the dissolution of the distinction between experts and lay persons. A way to recapture that distinction was sought without reverting to pre–Wave Two claims of science's superiority in terms of its success. But the Third Wave was heavily resisted by those who preferred to pursue the further democratization of science to the extent that they attempted to exclude this kind of analysis from the purview of STS, even trying to establish this position in a recent *handbook* of STS; their position remains unchanged despite the startling changes we have seen taking place in the wider world.[16]

Notwithstanding the obvious dangers of the dissolution of the idea of expertise to social life as we know it, even the Third Wave definition of expertise seemed to critics to be fundamentally undemocratic when it came to representation in political decision-making.[17] We can summarize two positions available to those who accepted the fundamental correctness of Wave Two. One, the Third Wave approach, was to try to *rethink* the justification of science even though Wave Two had undermined the traditional demarcation criteria. This approach built on Wave Two to go forward in the justification of science (not backward, as the science warriors did). The other approach was to continue on the existing path and *embrace* and celebrate the most obvious and immediate political consequences of the Second Wave—to continue the leveling down and democratization of science and technology rather than develop new forms of justification for them.[18]

Malign Political Regimes

In 2002, when Wave Three was first mooted, and even when *Rethinking Expertise* was published and the idea of "elective modernism" (see the section "Elective Modernism" below), which underlies *Why Democracies Need Science*, was first being worked out (also around 2008, though the book was not published until 2017), there did not seem to be any immediate urgency about the topic. Nowadays, however, with the rise of populism in Europe and the United States, the homology between the new, malign political movements and the idea that technical expertise is the property of ordinary people and their leadership rather than experts, the issue is ever more pressing.[19] Populist and other authoritarian politics champion fake news and alternative facts because scientific expertise can be constraining. Many of those adhering to the embrace persuasion, being unwilling to find themselves aligned with the new populists, claim, first, that the new populism is not really anything new since politicians have always lied and, second, that STS has not contributed to it and is not homologous with it. Therefore, STS has nothing new to consider even in the manifestly changed political climate.[20] Given the continuing influence of Donald Trump in the US, and the electoral success of populist politicians in Europe and elsewhere, this defense has an air of desperation.

Populism

Democracy and populism are both "rule by the people," but they are different, and the difference between them can be understood sociologically.[21] All societies and all social groups have two faces. One face—the organic face—is made up of the uniform, or nearly uniform, actions that give a culture or group its identity. These uniform actions include the language spoken by its members, including local dialects and practice languages" when we come to small groups; the way its members behave in their public spaces; their standards of clean and dirty, and so on.[22] The other face—the enumerative face—consists of the varying opinions about less uniformly agreed matters expressed by individuals with the ability to disagree. There is agreement about the institutions that should handle disagreements, which are part and parcel of the shared organic aspects of their society. The sociological insight is that both the organic and the enumerative aspects of the social group are essential: the organic face sets the boundaries of what counts as "normal"; the enumerative face determines how the choices that exist within these boundaries are distributed. Neither the organic nor the enumerative aspects of any society or social group are ever totally fixed, and both can, and do, change over time, but the organic face will generally change much more slowly than the enumerative face; the organic feels fixed and societally uniform when compared to the enumerative, which feels changeable and always in tension and with the potential to fragment society. Revolutions, wars, or natural catastrophes can, however, result in rapid changes even to the normally sluggish organic face.

In any genuinely democratic society, the idea that citizens should play a role in determining how they are governed is constitutive of that society's organic face. For these democratic ideals to be put into practice, however, "the people" must be treated in the enumerative way; that is, they must be treated as a set of individuals whose preferences on other issues are divided, varied, and changeable. More or less frequent enumerative exercises reveal the changing distribution of these preferences, with the conflicting views aggregated according to agreed procedures to produce a government or other form of decision that represents "the majority," or something defined as the majority. Crucially, the principles of what we call "pluralist democracy" require that minority views continue to be respected, and any majority party or coalition is expected to operate in a way that takes minority concerns into account even though the ruling party has been chosen by the majority. Some "democracies," such as so-called one-party democracies, are not pluralist democracies, but we consider that all the democracies we would choose to live in are pluralist in the sense we mean. Readers who do not share this view of democracy will find the rest of the argument unconvincing.

Under populism, in contrast to pluralist democracy, "the people" that the government claims to represent are no longer all citizens but only the subset that expressed a particular view—usually the majority view (though this is often substantially less than 50% of the electorate). Crucially, once expressed, this view is treated as a fixed, uniform, and collective view that encapsulates the legitimate aspirations and concerns of the entire society and can be understood and represented by a single leader or party, possibly in perpetuity. Minorities, or others who oppose this vision, are treated as deviants, and their refusal to accept the legitimacy of the populist claim is denounced as a betrayal of what is now defined as the organic view of the people. Under populism, the pluralist democratic principles of freedom and equality that uphold respect for minorities are set aside, and the diversity that pluralist democratic societies permit and even celebrate is seen as a sign of failure or danger.[23]

Given that populism almost always builds on views held by at least some of the people, and usually a large number of the people, the rise of populism is a constant risk in any democratic society. All that has to happen is for those in power to give too much weight to their supporters and to ignore (or worse, actively suppress) those who disagree with them, and the outcome will be an increasingly populist regime. One of the ways in which pluralist democracies seek to protect themselves against such outcomes is to institutionalize a system of checks and balances—with opposition parties, bi- or multicameral systems, a free press, an independent judiciary, and so on. These safeguard minority views and maintain the mechanisms that allow the changing distribution of preferences to be reflected in the policies or actions of that society.[24] In contrast, when democracy slides into populism, these checks and balances are lost as the government confirms, reinforces, and maintains one fixed and eternal *will of the people.*

ELECTIVE MODERNISM

It was Robert Merton who, among others, argued that the values of science and democracy were aligned; the Third Wave analysis develops this point in *Why Democracies Need Science.*[25] Merton, arguing in the malign political atmosphere of the European fascism that led to World War II, defended democracy because the values of democratic societies would nurture science, and science was efficacious; the argument was convincing after the contributions of radar, nuclear weapons, and so forth, to the victory of the democratic powers in 1945 became clear.[26] But, under Wave Two of science studies, the idea of science as intrinsically efficacious can no longer be used as an argumentative lever. Instead, Collins and Evans argue that the values of science and democracy are simply good in themselves and require no further justification. This alternative approach, which Collins and Evans call "elective modernism", is compatible with the constructivist approach of Wave Two but also allows science to be distinguished from other institutions. Focusing on values squares the circle of how to make technically informed decisions once one can no longer draw on objective truth as a criterion; elective modernism claims that it is simply "better" to give more weight to the views of those who have substantial experience of the domain in question and whose way of life, and the constitutive values of their professional institutions, turns on assiduous seeking for the truth of the matter through empirical experience. It is better still when, as in the case of science, that search is informed by values such as universality, organized skepticism, and what philosophers once called the "logic" of scientific discovery but is now better seen as set of professional guidelines that include corroboration and falsification. In *Why Democracies Need Science*, Collins and Evans develop a list of fourteen such values and guidelines, including the four Mertonian norms; the more general values of honesty, integrity, and clarity; and the ex-"logical rules," which, as mentioned, include corroboration and falsification. To repeat, under elective modernism it is taken as self-evident that technological decisions informed by this approach are "better" in some absolute sense than decisions about such things based on power, wealth, celebrity, the contents of ancient books, tea-leaf reading, astrology, and so forth. The approach does not guarantee that the decisions will be right, or even that they are more likely to be right than decisions made in other ways, but given that what is going to turn out to be right is unknowable, they will be, simply, *better* decisions.[27] Thus, while SEE does not try to evaluate the difference between astronomy and astrology, elective modernism does, not via a difference in efficaciousness but in the desirability of the values that inform the practice of the expertises. This may seem a strange philosophy when it comes to the difference between astrology and astronomy, but it is vital if we are to choose between, say, astrology and long-term weather forecasting or any of the other policy-relevant sciences, such as predictive economics or predictive epidemiology, where deep contestation between expert predictions is expected. The slogan of elective modernism is that the test of one's love of science is one's love of unsuccessful science.

Identifying Fringe Science

One more thing that must be accomplished if a common-sense notion of the special nature of science is to be maintained is to distinguish between mainstream science and "fringe" science. Science would cease to exist if all the claims made by fringe scientists were taken seriously, even though large numbers of fringe scientists are undoubtedly experts and many of them adhere to the norms of science that have been discussed so far. The solution to this is, once more, sociological—to compare the forms of life of fringe science and mainstream science and find the ways in which they differ sociologically. The most revealing difference is, perhaps, that which concerns the interpretation of what Kuhn called "the essential tension"—the tension between adherence to the authority of a paradigm and work within certain limits versus the imperative to be creative and question everything; both of these are necessary in science, but they are in tension.[28] We find that fringe scientists value originality and invention above adherence to a paradigm far more than mainstream scientists do. The scales are sufficiently tipped for there to be little coherence even within specialist fringe meetings. This provides one among a number of other sociological demarcation criteria, all based on the notion of the form of life rather than any logic of science.[29]

SCIENCE VERSUS POPULISM

So far, we have tried to identify the sociologically salient aspects of democracy, populism, and science and then to justify giving scientific expertise a special status or role in democracies. We have, we believe, found ways of talking about science as a special contributor to Western democratic culture without referring to its epistemological preeminence or its efficaciousness. Released from the Wave One model of science, where truth and efficacy define science and justify its special status, we argue that the crucial distinguishing features of science are its "formative aspirations"—the norms and values that make up its organic face—and that its contribution to democratic societies is found in the resonance between these norms and core democratic values such as freedom and equality.[30]

We now want to argue that this particular aspect of science—its potential to provide leadership in the realm of values—emerges with particular clarity when democracy is contrasted with populism. We can do this for two reasons. First, under the post–Wave Two model of science we do not need to first establish that a science we wish to defend is true or efficacious. This is important given that experts disagree and that both the policy significance and the political significance of science have to be understood long before disagreements can be resolved and before what is true and efficacious has been established—even if we believe that it will be established in the long term.[31] Second, recent developments in democratic societies have, as already mentioned, provided something close to a breaching experiment in which previously taken-for-granted norms of civic epistemology have been overturned, revealing the tacit assumptions and understandings on which democratic institutions rest.

The role of scientific expertise in democracy, we can now see, is to contribute to the network of checks and balances needed to resist slipping, under the pressure of events, into more authoritarian styles of rule. Science, we claim, fulfills the same kind of role as a "loyal opposition," a second chamber, a free press, and an independent judiciary. Scientific expertise, when it is working properly, and when it is understood properly, makes it more difficult for a government to do just what it wants. Those with a tendency toward populism understand this, which is why they are likely to be dismissive of scientific expertise and to try find ways of undermining its credibility, for example, by suggesting it is driven by the interests of particular social groups or emphasizing its uncertain and provisional nature; claims that are at least superficially similar to ideas developed within the social constructivist analysis of science.[32]

Populism distrusts and discards the idea that a consensual or agreed truth might emerge from disinterested research and analysis. Instead, truth is that which is created by the leader's interpretation of the will of the people, and other models of truth can only weaken the state. Politicians in democratic societies may lie, dissemble, and cherry-pick the evidence they use to support their policies, but they try to hide and deny these activities, and that very hypocrisy reconfirms the basic legitimacy of the values they violate—"hypocrisy is a tribute vice pays to virtue." Under populism, by contrast, there are no lies, no selection of evidence and no corruption, only the organic will of the people interpreted by the leadership. The concepts "mistake" and "lie" disappear from public life—the process being reinforced by the proud proclamation of evident untruths, the more evident the better.

All this was revealed with particular clarity by former president Trump. Consider, for example, Trump's claim immediately after his inauguration speech that a larger crowd had attended his inauguration than had attended Obama's. The claim was backed up by his counselor Kellyanne Conway, who, notwithstanding the consensus among experts that the photographic evidence showed the claim to be untrue, remarked that their version of the event was an "alternative fact." Her statement should be understood as an attempt to relocate the "locus of legitimate interpretation" of facts away from bodies of experts, in this case, those who take and interpret photographs, and give it to the political elite who understand the will of the people.[33]

It cannot be stressed enough that the blatantly preposterous nature of the claim should not be dismissed as foolishness; the lack of any attempt to hide the evidence is not an error but part of the strategy. The idea of "alternative facts" is intended to redefine the balance of power between political leaders and independent experts when it comes to the production of truth. It is an attempt to establish the basis for more portentous claims, such as Trump's denial of climate change, in which expert evidence will again be dismissed because it does not fit with the interpreted will of the people. The attack on experts is part of the aggregation of power to the center that is justified, under populism, by the leadership being the embodiment of the will of the people, and the will of the people being the ultimate authority even on technical matters, irrespective of the views of independent experts.[34]

Defending Democracy, Defending Science

How can democracy be stopped from sliding down this slippery slope? There are fascinating analyses of the way the Trump regime came to power that explain it in terms of the increasing polarization of party politics in the United States and the determination of the Republican Party to win victory at all costs, including the destruction of the procedures of an orderly, pluralist democracy.[35] We want to add to this a new suggestion that is analogous with the second law of thermodynamics and, in particular, the conservation of energy; it is called the "law of conservation of democracy." It states that democracy cannot take out of political society more than it puts in. In other words, if democracy is to last, citizens must understand the meaning of democracy, and because, at the collective level, understanding and practice are two sides of the same coin, the majority of citizens must actively and continually put that understanding into practice, not least in their spoken discourse, reinforcing the idea of democracy through talk and action and refreshing its role in the organic face of society.[36]

We are not arguing that democracy *will necessarily last* if citizens understand it—there are many ways democracy can be destroyed—but we are arguing that it *will not* last if citizens do not understand it. Preserving democracies requires citizens who are willing to call to account a government's, or a leader's, nondemocratic statements and actions, either by voting in elections or via more direct means should democracy break down. We do not intend to engage here in the long-running debate in political science over whether democracy is best served by increasing the role of the citizenry versus setting pluralist institutions in place. It should be clear that we stress the importance of the right kind of representative institutions, including expert institutions, as opposed to giving ever wider responsibility to citizens. Broadly, we favor Walter Lippman's views over John Dewey's and elected representatives over continual referendums. But we modify the usual polarity by claiming that the right kind of representative institutions will not be maintained if the people do not know what they want from them. In other words, citizens have to understand, and that means live out, representative, pluralist democracy if representative, pluralist democracy is to endure. To reiterate, we take the

Wittgensteinian approach to the meaning of "understand." Democracy, not least pluralist democracy, is a set of concepts and a set of practices, including discursive ones: the meaning of democracy is revealed through the actions and talk through which it is enacted. How much of this understanding is explicit and how much is implicit, or tacit, is not something we need to settle, but both aspects are always present. One thing that citizens will have to understand in this rich way is that there is nothing elitist about choosing to have their elected representatives appoint experts to help them make decisions: they already understand this about, say, the judiciary and the civil service.

Of course, the law of the conservation of democracy is in some sense a truism because the argument is that for democracy to survive, democratic "instincts" must be part of the organic face of society, so that the citizens know when something is going wrong; in other words, "societies must be democratic if democracy is to survive." But something follows that is not truistic. This is an understanding of how hard it is to create democracies where there is no organic democratic face in the first place: democracies cannot be created simply by changing the procedures used to choose the government. And the law of conservation of democracy also shows that the erosion of a society's existing democratic organic face is likely to lead to the demise of the democracy, which will be hard to reverse. "The Law" tells us we are right to be frightened about what we see happening in today's Western democracies.

The empirical evidence for the importance of understanding democracy as a form of life in which ideas and actions reinforce each other includes the fragility and short duration of democratic regimes in societies that do not have a tradition of democracy or any substitute for it in the form of intense programs of civic education. We have in recent decades seen many examples of newly formed democratic societies that soon fall victim to authoritarian regimes.[37] Frighteningly, even in the United States, the continuing popularity of a populist leader despite a series of actions that, not long ago, would have been thought to be impossible in a democratic state, opens up the possibility that there might always have been a deficit in the understanding of democracy among a substantial proportion of the population of that supposed icon of democracy, the United States of America.[38] The more likely alternatives are that American citizens once understood democracy and no longer understand it, or that a large proportion of American citizens who understand democracy very well no longer want it—perhaps their long-standing sense of being neglected in an "elitist" pluralist democracy has led them to think things will only get better after a revolution whose leader is ready to cast democracy aside. Both of the latter possibilities comport with the persistent veneration of cultural icons of the Confederacy in the Civil War, the widespread belief that citizens need to own guns so that they can defend themselves and their communities against "big government" and its elected representatives, and the long history of electoral near-success of non-democrats such as Henry Ford, Charles Coughlin, Huey Long, Joseph McCarthy, Charles Lindbergh, and George Wallace.[39] The United Kingdom, in comparison, does not seem beset by these kinds of undemocratic indicators, or at least, not to such a great and regular extent. It is true that the will-of-the-people rhetoric and the success of populists such as Nigel Farage were noticeable features of the United Kingdom's Brexit debate, but equally true that 'following the science' was the main motif of the response to the COVID-19 pandemic.[40] What we have seen in both countries, however, is determined politicians trying to erode the peoples' understanding of what democracy is.

Public Understanding of Science

A proper understanding of the role of science in democratic societies is part of the understanding citizens need. As far as the contribution of science to democracy is concerned, the crucial element is recognizing that the role of scientists and other independent experts is a legitimate constraint on the convenient preferences of politicians. This, in turn, means a radically new approach to the aims and methods associated with the public understanding of science that reflects what SSK (sociology of scientific knowledge), and other social constructivist approaches, taught us about the nature of science but which does not reduce everything to demands for more public engagement.

Again, the three-wave model is helpful in summarizing the main dimensions of the debate. Starting in the 1970s and 1980s, fears that science was losing respect in Western societies gave rise to a concern about the "public understanding of science."[41] Some scientists, drawing on what we would now call a Wave One model of science, took the view that the public would respect science more if they understood it better; this gave rise to what became known as the "deficit model" of scientific understanding and to calls to build public support for science through programs of popular education. Quite rightly, the deficit model became the whipping boy of the social analysts of science: on the one hand, it assumed that the scientists' framing of a problem was correct and rendered illegitimate or irrelevant any of the other concerns the public might have; on the other, there was the problem that, if the science was controversial—as it mostly is in cases that cause public concern—then scientists themselves would disagree about the value of this or that initiative, making it unclear what more public education about the contested facts could achieve.[42]

In each case, the mistake being made was to think that the important deficit was in the public understanding of the substance of science; whereas, actually, the deficit was in the public understanding of the process of science, a deficit encouraged by scientists' own Wave One models of the science. The public are encouraged by overly-simplistic models of science to expect perfection from experts, whereas, like the social analysts of science, the public need to understand that science is a craft practice with the failures and uncertainties associated with all craft practices; the danger is that expecting science to have a kind of "magic" infallibility encourages a reaction when the magic fails—as it inevitably sometimes will.[43] This deficit is still being encouraged by the traditional way scientists have presented their results and the impact of this on the way the public understands what science should be able to deliver.[44] A simple exercise can reveal the problem: imagine you want to convince someone of the importance of science to the understanding of climate change, and you want to find an iconic representation of science to bolster the argument. Type "science" into a Google search and hit the "images" tab.

Then look for an image of science that represents what we need from climate science. There is nothing there (up to the time of writing in late-2022). To find the kind of icon that represents the imperfect science of Wave Two that can, nevertheless, be valued as in Wave Three for its integrity and other values, one must combine images that come up in searches on "craftsperson" and "committee."

A better way to understand the role of science in society is with a more sociological model of the citizen. Citizens cannot live in society without the ubiquitous expertise that is needed to know that one should go to a garage when one's car is broken and to a hospital when one's limb is broken, and to know that taxis are a generally reliable means of transport even though the drivers are complete strangers, and so on, and so on. To conserve democracy, we argue, citizens must understand that the judiciary should be independent; that the press and other media should be free to criticize the government without fear of reprisal; that elections should offer a genuine choice between candidates, preferably offering alternative policies; and that newly elected leaders should divest themselves of their businesses so they cannot make choices to benefit their own financial interests; that they should not favor their own families when making political appointments, and so on. We argue that citizens, as part of their ubiquitous meta-expertise, should also understand that scientific experts (not policymakers) are the *best* advisers when it comes to technical matters, and that their views on the degree and content of any consensus should be established as well as they can be, and made public, before policy decisions are made.[45]

Another way of saying this is that democratic societies require a particular civic epistemology that defines their normative expectations about the networks and institutions that are granted the privilege of making authoritative knowledge.[46] This is not the same as saying that citizens should understand the contents of science or be capable of recognizing which of a set of competing scientific ideas is the true one; nor does it mean that they should understand more about the scientific process than that science is an institution driven by the search for truth rather than search for profit. This last provision imposes a serious responsibility on scientists that has a clear moral dimension. Our argument is that one necessary condition for granting science institutions this role, now that we understand science so much better than we did before the 1970s, is that they strive to endorse and enact the values we have associated with the scientific community, and not fall into the trap of presenting themselves as entertainment or the drivers of capitalism. Science is under a continual threat of erosion due to the attack on its values coming from the demand to prove itself useful in one way or another. But too much "short termism" will eventually destroy the formative aspirations of science, and we will have no science left. To repeat, the responsibility associated with making truth demands that the activity be done with the utmost integrity. This is what adhering to scientific values brings about.

Finally, there are two things we are *not* saying when we argue that independent experts are a necessary element of a truly democratic society. First, we are not saying that scientists are the only experts: on technical questions related to decision-making in the public domain, there will be many other experience-based experts who also have knowledge that will need to be considered and, beyond these technical matters, there are many other important domains and institutions that do not depend on science at all. Second, even when the problem does concern technical decision-making in the public domain, the role of experts in it is, in principle, only ever advisory; to give them more power than this is to replace democracy with technocracy.[47] Instead, our plea is that democratic institutions do not ignore, distort, or deny the advice of scientific experts. If these institutions want to overrule a strong consensus among scientists, that is their choice, but they should be clear it is their choice. Likewise, if, as often seems to be the case in economic policy, politicians want to take a big gamble on what may be very uncertain and contested evidence, they should at least be clear that there is an alternative, and not deny the legitimacy of the alternative view.[48]

SUMMARY

By drawing on Wittgenstein's idea of a form of life, we have argued that any social group can be characterized as a balance between two opposing elements: the organic aspect that defines what the group has in common and thus gives the group its identity as a group, and the enumerative aspect that describes the differing ways in which the organic core can be displayed and enacted.

We have further argued that the organic aspects of democracy and science share similar values and commitments, particularly notions such as disinterestedness, universalism, and honesty, and that these values are best defended on absolute, not utilitarian, grounds. Democratic societies are just better than authoritarian ones, and science is just a better way of making knowledge than divine revelation or oracular pronouncement by the leader. One consequence of this overlap of values is that it creates the possibility for science to provide moral leadership in democratic societies because, to the extent that scientists and other experts succeed in acting scientifically, they reproduce the values needed for both science and democracy to thrive.

Science with integrity contributes to the maintenance of democracy through its role in the system of checks and balances that is needed to prevent the capture of democratic institutions by a single interest group. Science cannot do this alone, and neither can the press, the judiciary, or additional tiers of government. Instead, democratic societies survive by ensuring that the institutional ecosystem that includes all these different functions and cultures remains healthy. Failures of democracy occur when the balance and health of the ecosystem is damaged—too much science leads to technocracy, but too little helps create the conditions for populism.

Finally, we have argued that preserving and extending democratic societies is a practical, not an ideological, task. By this we mean that democracies thrive only when citizens are both able to put democratic practices into action and take the opportunity to do so. Taking part in elections is a part of this, but only a part. Other actions include endorsing an independent judiciary and other institutions of state even when they prevent the government from enacting policies of which they might approve. Most importantly of all in this context, one necessary element of democratic societies is the recognition that independent experts, of which science may be the exemplar, are part of this network of checks and balances, providing an important form of constraint in addition to that provided by the other institutions. Insofar as citizens' understanding of democracy is deficient, either because it always was or because it has been distorted by the pronouncements and actions of contemporary politicians, it needs to be remedied. We believe that formal civic education should also be revived if we are to preserve a lasting pluralist democracy.[49] Education is not just the delivery of information; it is a process of socialization. The very fact that something is being taught is an expression of its value; the very discussion of why practical activities such as voting or participating in civic life matter is an encouragement to engage in actions that are the counterpart of the concepts being advanced. Our specific aim would be to see this education-socialization include, among other things, the role of science in society. In our conception, the dangers of the dishonest application of expertise and of technocracy would have a vital but subsidiary role in the new civic education, whose main emphasis would be explaining the positive role of scientific experts as a check and balance in democracy and the preeminent former of opinions with respect to the properties of the natural and social world. A sociological understanding of science as *craftwork with integrity*, driven by a search for truth rather than profit, should be part of civic education.

NOTES

1. Collins and Evans (2017b) are the authors of *Why Democracies Need Science*. The contents list in *Experts and the Will of the People* (Collins et al. 2019) is available on the Springer website at https://www.palgrave.com/gp/book/9783030269821. Recent contributions develop the concept of expertise in general (Collins 2010, 2011, 2013), as well as particular types of expertise, such as "interactional expertise" (Collins and Evans 2015; Collins, Evans, and Weinel 2017), contributory expertise (Collins, Evans, and Weinel 2016), primary source knowledge (Weinel 2007; Collins and Weinel 2011), and referred expertise (Collins and Sanders 2007), but also focus on the political implications of the SEE approach (Collins, Weinel, and Evans 2010; Collins, Evans and Weinel 2017; Collins, Bartlett and Reyes-Galindo 2017; Durant 2008, 2010, 2011, 2019).

2. Whilst the response to the COVID-19 pandemic in many countries was characterized by a clear reliance on scientific expertise, there was also considerable variation between countries and it remains unclear whether these longer term trends have been changed.

3. Evans and Collins (2007) offer a critical analysis of approaches to expertise that consider expertise as purely attributed or ascribed. Moore (2017) discusses the dual social goods of contestation and collective action. We should resist identifying contestation with democracy tout court, argues Moore, because collective judgment is the flipside to contestation and democracy requires both.

4. Some appear to accept the delegitimation of expertise. Sarewitz (2000) describes the use of expertise in politics as akin to an "excess of objectivity," whereby "science is sufficiently rich, diverse, and balkanized to provide comfort and support for a range of subjective, political

positions on complex issues" (90). Sarewitz suggests that the role of science is to enact plans arrived at by end users (cf. Sarewitz 2016). But there are commercially malignant or politically illiberal end users, so this notion can lead to the politicization of science. Others push back against politicized expertise. Nichols (2017) worries about the incomprehension and rejection of the professionalism that underlies communities of expert practice; Durant (2019) shows that most general arguments against expertise—for example, that experts are like robots or that experts are dangerous per se—fail to hold. The broadest explanatory accounts of the predicaments faced by contemporary experts often coalesce around the idea that expertise has been co-opted by the organs of democratic and social legitimation and inherited their troubles. Eyal (2019) suggests that "the post-war recruitment of scientists and experts into state agencies served to harness science and technology as auxiliary means of legitimation and control" (94). Shapin (2019) depicts a more linear process of legitimation crisis, but also suggests that "by the middle of the 20th century [science] had been woven into the fabric of ordinary social, economic and political life. . . . The entanglement of science with business and statecraft [meant] [that w]hen science [became] so extensively bonded with power and profit, its conditions of credibility look[ed] more and more like those of the institutions in which it ha[d] been enfolded. Its problems are their problems."

5. Ginsburg and Hug (2018, 17). See Przeworski (2019, 172–191) for a discussion of the theory of democratic backsliding, including multiple examples.

6. Przeworski (2019, 188–191) suggests that if the democratic transgression is by stealth, then only citizens who can see where the long-term outcomes lead will turn against the transgressing government. Populist political movements can help conceal the "direction" by enticing social groups with short-term rewards and cultural gains.

7. The classic text on breaching experiments is Garfinkel (1967).

8. Students of philosophy, sociology, and social studies of science should already know that the written constitution is supported by an unwritten constitution because, as the philosopher Wittgenstein (1953) explained, "Rules do not contain the rules for their own application," something that is also evident in sociological studies of bureaucracy (Gouldner 1954). For unwritten norms of American democratic institutions, see Levitsky and Ziblatt (2018, chap. 6).

9. There was a simultaneous movement for "social responsibility in science" that remained relatively independent. For a brief overview of the various activities of the British Society for Social Responsibility in Science (BSSRS), see Bell (2013). For an overview of other alternative approaches to science and technology, see Webster (1991, chap. 6).

10. Ludwik Fleck's (2008) contribution was originally published in the 1930s in German but only gained influence after its translation into English in the 1970s. His idea of "thought styles" (*Denkstile*) is homologous to Kuhn's (1962) influential concept of "paradigm shifts." See also Wittgenstein (1953) and Winch (1958).

11. See, for example, Gross and Levitt (1994); Koertge (2000); and Sokal and Bricmont (1998) for typical attacks by natural scientists on relativist and constructivist social science accounts of scientific practices. See Labinger and Collins (2001) for an extensive dialogue between key participants in the science wars.

12. See Boyce (2007) and Weinel (2019) for analyses; and Leach (2005) and Poltorak et al. (2005) for advocacy.

13. Within STS, these debates echo those between John Dewey and Walter Lippmann in the early 20th Century (Lippman 1927; Dewey 1954). Lippmann was concerned about the extent to which ordinary citizens could be sufficiently knowledgeable to make informed

judgments about the wide and disparate range of issues that affect modern democracies. As a result, Lippman argued that some delegation of decision-making to experts is inevitable, with the role of democratic institutions being to select and manage those experts. In contrast, Dewey offered a more optimistic vision in which members of the public are able to reach informed views by virtue of their active engagement with social and political issues. The argument works because Dewey is talking about particular groups or members of the public—experience-based experts in the language of SEE—rather than the public as a whole. Given what has already been said about the ways in which Wave Two STS seeks to democratize science, it is unsurprising to see that scholars in this tradition are often sympathetic to Dewey's position whilst Wave Three can be seen as echoing the concerns of Lippmann. Collins and Evans (2007, 112–115) set out this argument in more detail, while Mirowski provides a comprehensive overview of the debates within STS in his draft article "Democracy, Expertise and the Post-Truth Era: An Inquiry into the Contemporary Politics of STS," available at academia.edu.

14. The Imitation Game is a new social science research method that affords the exploration and measurement of interactional expertise. See, for example, Collins et al. (2006); Collins and Evans (2014); Collins et al. (2017); Kubiak and Weinel (2016); Collins et al. (2019); Arminen, Segersven, and Simonen (2019).

15. See Levesque et al. (2012) for the total failure of the best deep-learning language computers to cope with Turing Tests involving Winograd schemas. Collins (2018, chap. 10) explains all this in accessible way.

16. Our editors thought it particularly important that we justify the claim that there was fierce resistance to the Third Wave paper, especially given its reception in terms of immediate and continuing very large numbers of citations. In terms of published resistance, published responses to the 2002 Third Wave paper (Collins and Evans, 2002) presented it as out of step with STS as a whole: Wynne (2003) said the Third Wave was "scientistic"; and Jasanoff (2003), that the Third Wave was swimming unjustly against the tide of more public participation as the democratic cure-all. Fourteen years later, Jasanoff (2017) wrote in the STS handbook that the Third Wave is a "turn away from the field's orthodoxies" (275). Given our profession, it does not seem unreasonable to also report on some involuntary participatory fieldwork, including concerns expressed about the effect associated with the Third Wave approach would have on tenure. Also, subsequent submissions of Third Wave–inspired papers to the journal *Social Studies of Science* have been rejected several times by anonymous referees supported by the editor on grounds having to do with the Third Wave's incompatibility with current STS or the Third Wave not really existing. On one occasion, when rejecting the paper, the editor refused to release the referee's comments even in anonymized form. Collins, author of about thirty-six contributions to the journal since 1974, subsequently resigned as an editorial adviser. But perhaps this is how science *ought* to work under the "embrace" interpretation!

17. Durant (2011) showed that the critics of the Third Wave operated with a parochial conception of democracy and that democracy is broader than the critics allowed. More generally, what has been called by Rosanvallon (2011, 129) "the generality of multiplication" is the idea that democracy is about multiplying all the partial expressions of "the good" in any given plural polity; that diversity and dissent are multiplied into a greater whole. Democracy becomes conflated with contestation and critique; much of the work in science studies and the public understanding of science thus displays an "agonistic bias" in which only the opening up and contesting of issues counts as democracy, and the flipside,

the closing down and peaceful resolution of issues, is neglected. Moore (2017, esp. chap. 5 on contestation) makes the case that STS displays an agonistic bias, and Durant (2018) argues that getting the balance right between using without being dominated by experts requires seeing that democracy has two sides (the opening up and the closing down issues). Critics of the Third Wave seem to have inherited (the French Enlightenment philosopher) Montesquieu's hope in 1748 that people power was forever redemptive and corrective. Montesquieu is credited with articulating the principle of the separation of powers, and in *De l'Esprit des Lois* (The Spirit of the Laws), he opined that if the reigning powers abused their power, the citizens would rise up to reset the proper "constitutional" course rather than "revolutionize" the form of government. But while critics of the Third Wave were animated by flagrant acts of hubris by experts, democracy was being eroded by stealth, and expertise along with it. Przeworski (2019, 188–191) discusses the idea that transgressions against democracy could be resolved by citizen power alone and concludes such ideas are "sadly unfounded" (189).

18. The distinction between "rethink" and "embrace" persuasions is developed in Collins et al. (2019). Philip Mirowski wrote a draft paper in April 2020 that sets out the same binary division of reactions to the Third Wave initiative, under the heading "The Levellers vs. the Diggers or the 'Third Science War.'" See "Democracy, Expertise and the Post-Truth Era: An Inquiry into the Contemporary Politics of STS," academia.edu, https://www.academia.edu/42682483/Democracy_Expertise_and_the_Post-Truth_Era_An_Inquiry_into_the_Contemporary_Politics_of_STS?fs=rwbcr-h-2093071274.

19. Heather Douglas (e.g., 2009), argues that natural scientists should take on the values of the society in which they are embedded. This idea works well when the society is benign but is troubling when the society is malign—Nazi Germany being the obvious example and Trump's America providing immediacy. The "rethink" approach ("Digger" in Mirowski's language), takes the formative values of science as the moral baseline so that malign regimes can be resisted by scientific thinking rather than scientific thinking having to follow the values of society, including those of malign regimes.

20. Papers arguing for the lack of responsibility and homology between STS and populist politics include Sismondo (2017) and Jasanoff and Simmett (2017); a response to the former by Collins et al. (2017) is entitled "STS as Science or Politics."

21. Our jumping off point for understanding populism is Jan Werner-Müller's (2017) book, *What Is Populism?* But we develop the idea in slightly different ways—notably, the "two faces of society" starting point and our stress on the abandonment of hypocrisy in populism. There is no shortage of other, often different, accounts of populism, such as Arditi (2003); Judis (2016); Mouffe (2018); Mounk (2018); Mudde and Kaltwasser (2018); and Weale (2018).

22. For more on the idea of uniformity as it applies to social groups, see Collins and Evans (2017a).

23. In the United Kingdom, for example, political debate that followed the referendum on leaving the European Union often had this quality; those who favored leaving frequently described the 52% majority as representing "the will of the people," and pro-Brexit newspapers regularly chastised the judiciary and politicians who did not subscribe to this view as "traitors" or "enemies of the people."

24. For a review of the many different ways in which democratic societies and institutions can be organized, see Held (2006).

25. Collins and Evans (2017b).

26. See, for example, Merton (1973).
27. Elective modernism is first set out in Collins and Evans (2017b).
28. See Kuhn (1977) for an extended discussion of this concept.
29. This analysis is found in Collins, Bartlett, and Reyes-Galindo (2017).
30. See Collins and Evans (2017b) for an extended version of this argument.
31. The importance of separating the evaluation of science from the efficacy of science has been particularly salient during the COVID-19 pandemic. Scientists have struggled to find cures and disagreed about how to minimize deaths, but there is a widely felt certainty that we still prefer to listen to scientists than to populist dictators. Whether this sentiment will be enduring remains to be seen.
32. Similar tactics, though not driven by a populist desire to undermine democracy, have been used to thwart action by the US government on climate change and other issues (Oreskes and Conway 2010).
33. The "locus of legitimate interpretation" is described in more detail in Collins and Evans (2007). In summary, it refers to the idea that cultural practices can be distinguished by the social networks that are able to evaluate their legitimacy. With art, for example, almost all audience members can have a legitimate view or interpretation of a piece, in which case we would say the locus of legitimate interpretation has moved a long way from the producers of the art. In contrast, one characteristic of science is that the locus of legitimate interpretation remains close to the producers in the sense that scientific research must be seen as credible by other experts in the same field if it is to have any wider legitimacy.
34. We might note in passing the resonance between this view and the democratization of science favored by many salient academics in contemporary science and technology studies.
35. This is argument is detailed in Levitsky and Ziblatt (2018).
36. It is crucial to note that individuals can learn to understand practices through immersion in spoken discourse alone—this is known as "interactional expertise" (e.g., Collins and Evans 2015). Acquiring interactional expertise means acquiring a "practice language" pertaining to a domain of practice, but nothing more in the way of practice is required except insofar as to become fluent in a language is to learn a linguistic practice. But without the more concrete actions being practiced at the collective level, the practice language will not develop in the first place. The distinction between collective and individual level is often overlooked. For an example, see John (2018), who develops a critique about the need for honesty and similar virtues in science without taking into account the nature of science *as an institution* as opposed to the logic of demands on individuals in specific circumstances.
37. The fate of democracy in Russia following what in the West at least was a period of post-Glasnost optimism illustrates the pattern with particular clarity. That no lessons were learned from this is revealed by the naive optimism that greeted the so-called Arab spring. In Europe, the increasingly populist and/or authoritarian regimes found in Poland and Hungary show how democratic norms can wither even in what appears to be a very supportive context.
38. Arguably, there was also a failure on the part of the mainstream politicians to recognize the concerns of these groups. In other words, Trump's success is due, at least in part, to an alienation that the majority class had allowed to develop over a period of time. The same could also be said of the Brexit referendum in the UK, when it became clear that those defending the status quo were seen as part of the problem by those they needed to persuade to support them.

39. This list supplied by Levitsky and Ziblatt (2018), who argue that the political success of these non-democrats was foiled only by political parties refusing to nominate them for office.

40. For a discussion of the United Kingdom's initial response to the COVID-19 pandemic, see Evans (2022) and Pearce (2020).

41. In the UK, the creation of the Committee for the Public Understanding of Science (COPUS) and the Bodmer report were the key responses. Miller (2001) provides a summary of these developments.

42. The collection edited by Irwin and Wynne (2003) provides a representative selection of the concerns raised by scholars working in what we have called the Wave Two tradition.

43. The Golem series can be seen as an attempt to promote this more sociological understanding of scientific work. See Collins and Pinch (1993, 2005, 2010).

44. For example, the way in which the detection of gravitational radiation was announced: the attempt was made to keep the 5 months of checking secret until the assured discovery was pulled like a rabbit from a hat. See Collins (2017).

45. The problems are evident in the case of vaccination advice. "Meta-expertise" is expertise about expertise; the term is introduced in Collins and Evans (2007).

46. The term "civic epistemology" is drawn from Sheila Jasanoff's work (e.g., Jasanoff, 2007) and refers to the culturally specific ways in which legitimate knowledge is projected in the public sphere. Jasanoff uses the concept in a descriptive way to highlight how the "same" task is performed differently in different societies; we use it more normatively to argue that this particular task should be performed in a particular way.

47. There are "exceptions that prove the rule," such as delegating interest-rate decisions to the Bank of England.

48. In other publications, this view has been called the "minimal default position"; see Weinel (2010).

49. Robert Putnam is a champion of the need for civic education (e.g., see his 1993). He writes,

> In the aftermath of the collapse of Weimar and the rise of Nazism in a highly educated, advanced nation, much of political science in the *1940s–1960s was devoted to asking "Why Weimar?"... The relevant* literature is huge ... Education in civics was one important substrand of that work. But all that literature tended to die out in the late 1960s, [and] By the 1970s it ... was dead, alongside civic education itself ... in the late 1990s ... the question of the preconditions for stable democracy began to attract more attention, a trend that has for obvious reasons sharply accelerated in the last 5–10 years. (pers. comm. to Collins, March 10, 2018)

REFERENCES

Arditi, Benjamin. 2003. "Populism or Politics at the Edges of Democracy." *Contemporary Politics* 9 (1): 17–31.

Arminen, Ilkka., Otto E. A. Segersven, and Mika Simonen. 2019. "Active and Latent Social Groups and Their Interactional Expertise." *Acta Sociologica* 62 (4): 391–405. doi:10.1177/0001699318786361.

Bell, Alice. 2013. "Beneath the White Coat: The Radical Science Movement." *The Guardian*, July 18. https://www.theguardian.com/science/political-science/2013/jul/18/beneath-white-coat-radical-science-movement.

Boyce, Tammy. 2007. *Health, Risk and News: The MMR Vaccine and the Media.* Media and Culture 9. New York: Peter Lang.

Collins, Harry. 2010. *Tacit and Explicit Knowledge.* Chicago: University of Chicago Press.

Collins, Harry. 2011. "Language and Practice." *Social Studies of Science* 41 (2): 271–300. https://doi.org/10.1177/0306312711399665.

Collins, Harry. 2013. "Three Dimensions of Expertise." *Phenomenology and the Cognitive Sciences* 12 (2): 253–273. doi: 10.1007/s11097-011-9203-5.

Collins, Harry. 2017. *Gravity's Kiss: The Detection of Gravitational Waves.* Cambridge, MA: MIT Press.

Collins, Harry. 2018. *Artifictional Intelligence: Against Humanity's Surrender to Computers.* Cambridge, UK: Polity Press.

Collins, Harry, Andrew Bartlett, and Luis Reyes-Galindo. 2017. "The Ecology of Fringe Science and Its Bearing on Policy." *Perspectives on Science* 25 (4): 411–438. doi: 10.1162/POSC_a_00248.

Collins, Harry, and Robert Evans. 2002. "The Third Wave of Science Studies: Studies of Expertise and Experience." *Social Studies of Science* 32 (2): 235–296. doi:10.1177/0306312702032002003.

Collins, Harry, and Robert Evans. 2007. *Rethinking Expertise.* Chicago: University of Chicago Press.

Collins, Harry, and Robert Evans. 2014. "Quantifying the Tacit: The Imitation Game and Social Fluency." *Sociology* 48 (1): 3–19. https://doi.org/10.1177/0038038512455735.

Collins, Harry, and Robert Evans. 2015. "Expertise Revisited, Part I: Interactional Expertise." *Studies in History and Philosophy of Science Part A* 54 (December): 113–123. doi:10.1016/j.shpsa.2015.07.004.

Collins, Harry, and Robert Evans. 2017a. "Probes, Surveys, and the Ontology of the Social." *Journal of Mixed Methods Research* 11 (3): 328–341. doi:10.1177/1558689815619825.

Collins, Harry, and Robert Evans. 2017b. *Why Democracies Need Science.* Cambridge, UK: Polity Press.

Collins, Harry, Robert Evans, Darrin Durant, and Martin Weinel. 2019. *Experts and the Will of the People: Society, Populism and Science.* Basingstoke, UK: Palgrave Macmillan.

Collins, Harry, Robert Evans, Martin Hall, Hannah O'Mahoney, and Martin Weinel. 2019. "Bonfire Night and Burns Night: Using the Imitation Game to Research English and Scottish Identities." In *The Third Wave in Science and Technology Studies: Future Research Directions on Expertise and Experience,* edited by David Caudill, Shannon N. Connolly, Michael E. Gorman, and Martin Weinel, 109–131. New York: Palgrave Macmillan.

Collins, Harry, Robert Evans, Rodrigo Ribeiro, and Martin Hall. 2006. "Experiments with Interactional Expertise." *Studies in History and Philosophy of Science Part A* 37 (4): 656–674. https://doi.org/10.1016/j.shpsa.2006.09.005.

Collins, Harry, Robert Evans, and Martin Weinel. 2016. "Expertise Revisited, Part II: Contributory Expertise." *Studies in History and Philosophy of Science Part A* 56 (April): 103–110. https://doi.org/10.1016/j.shpsa.2015.07.003.

Collins, Harry, Robert Evans, and Martin Weinel. 2017. "STS as Science or Politics?" *Social Studies of Science* 47 (4): 580–586. https://doi.org/10.1177/0306312717710131.

Collins Harry, Robert Evans, Martin Weinel, Jennifer Lyttleton-Smith, Andrew Bartlett, and Martin Hall. 2017. "The Imitation Game and the Nature of Mixed Methods." *Journal of Mixed Methods Research* 11 (4): 510–527. https://doi.org/10.1177/1558689815619824.

Collins, Harry, and Trevor J. Pinch. 1993. *The Golem: What Everyone Should Know about Science.* Cambridge, UK: Cambridge University Press.

Collins, Harry, and Trevor J. Pinch. 2005. *Dr. Golem: How to Think about Medicine*. Chicago: University of Chicago Press.

Collins, Harry, and Trevor J. Pinch. 2010. *The Golem at Large: What You Should Know about Technology*. Cambridge, UK: Cambridge University Press.

Collins, Harry, and Martin Weinel. 2011. "Transmuted Expertise: How Technical Non-experts Can Assess Experts and Expertise." *Argumentation* 25:401–413. doi: 10.1007/s10503-011-9217-8.

Collins, Harry, Martin Weinel, and Robert Evans. 2010. "The Politics and Policy of the Third Wave: New Technologies and Society." *Critical Policy Studies* 4 (2): 185–201. doi:10.1080/19460171.2010.490642.

Dewey, John. 1954. *The Public and Its Problems*. Athens, OH: Swallow Press. (Original work published 1927).

Douglas, Heather E. 2009. *Science, Policy, and the Value-Free Ideal*. Pittsburgh, PA: University of Pittsburgh Press.

Durant, Darrin. 2008. "Accounting for Expertise: Wynne and the Autonomy of the Lay Public Actor." *Public Understanding of Science* 17 (1): 5–20. doi: 10.1177/0963662506076138.

Durant, Darrin. 2010. "Public Participation in the Making of Science Policy." *Perspectives on Science* 18 (2): 189–225. doi: 10.1162/posc.2010.18.2.189.

Durant, Darrin. 2011. "Models of Democracy in Social Studies of Science." *Social Studies of Science* 41 (5): 691–714. doi:10.1177/0306312711414759.

Durant, Darrin. 2018. "Servant or Partner? The Role of Expertise and Knowledge in Democracy." *The Conversation*, March 9. https://theconversation.com/servant-or-partner-the-role-of-expertise-and-knowledge-in-democracy-92026.

Durant, Darrin. 2019. "Ignoring Experts." In *The Third Wave in Science and Technology Studies: Future Research Directions on Expertise and Experience*, edited by David Caudill, Shannon N. Connolly, Michael E. Gorman, and Martin Weinel, 33–52. New York: Palgrave Macmillan.

Eyal, Gil. 2019. *The Crisis of Expertise*. Cambridge, UK: Polity Press.

Evans, Robert. 2022. "SAGE Advice and Political Decision-Making: 'Following the Science' in Times of Epistemic Uncertainty." *Social Studies of Science* 52(1):53–78. doi: 10.1177/03063127211062586.

Evans, Robert, and Harry Collins. 2007. "Expertise: From Attribute to Attribution and Back Again?" In *The Handbook of Science and Technology Studies*, edited by Edward J. Hackett, Olga Amsterdamska, Michael Lynch, and Judy Wajcman, 609–630. Cambridge, MA: MIT Press.

Fleck, Ludwik. 2008. *Genesis and Development of a Scientific Fact*. Chicago: University of Chicago Press. (Original German edition published in 1935).

Garfinkel, Harold. 1967. *Studies in Ethnomethodology*. Englewood Cliffs, NJ: Prentice-Hall.

Ginsburg, Tom, and Aziz Z. Huq. 2018. "How to Lose a Constitutional Democracy." *UCLA Law Review* 65 (1): 78–169. doi: 10.2139/ssrn.2901776.

Gouldner, Alvin. 1954. *Patterns of Industrial Bureaucracy*. New York: Free Press.

Gross Paul R., and Norman Levitt. 1994. *Higher Superstition: The Academic Left and Its Quarrels with Science*. Baltimore, MD: Johns Hopkins University Press.

Held, David. 2006. *Models of Democracy*. 3rd ed. Stanford, CA: Stanford University Press.

Irwin Alan, and Brian Wynne, eds. 2003. *Misunderstanding Science? The Public Reconstruction of Science and Technology*. Cambridge, UK: Cambridge University Press.

Jasanoff, Sheila. 2003. "Breaking the Waves in Science Studies: Comment on H.M. Collins and Robert Evans, 'The Third Wave of Science Studies.'" *Social Studies of Science* 33 (3): 389–400. doi:10.1177/03063127030333004.

Jasanoff, Sheila. 2007. *Designs on Nature Science and Democracy in Europe and the United States*. Princeton, NJ: Princeton University Press.

Jasanoff, Sheila. 2017. "Science and Democracy." In *The Handbook of Science and Technology Studies*, 4th ed., edited by Ulrike Felt, Rayvon Fouche, Clark A. Miller, and Laurel Smith-Doerr, 259–287. Cambridge, MA: MIT Press.

Jasanoff, Sheila, and Hilton Simmet. 2017. "No Funeral Bells: Public Reason in a Post-Truth Age." *Social Studies of Science* 47 (5): 751–770. doi: 10.1177/0306312717731936.

John, Stephen. 2018. "Epistemic Trust and the Ethics of Science Communication: Against Transparency, Openness, Sincerity and Honesty." *Social Epistemology* 32 (2): 75–87. doi:10.1080/02691728.2017.1410864.

Judis, John B. 2016. *The Populist Explosion: How the Great Recession Transformed American and European Politics*. New York: Columbia Global Reports.

Koertge, Noretta, ed. 2000. *A House Built on Sand: Exposing Postmodernist Myths about Science*. New York: Oxford University Press.

Kubiak, Daniel, and Martin Weinel. 2016. "DDR-Generationen revisited—Gibt es einen Generationszusammenhang der 'Wendekinder'?" In *Die Generation der Wendekinder: Elaboration eines Forschungsfeldes*, edited by Adriana. Lettrari, Christian Nestler, and Nadja Troi-Boeck, 107–129. Wiesbaden: Springer.

Kuhn, Thomas S. 1962. *The Structure of Scientific Revolutions*. Chicago: University of Chicago Press.

Kuhn, Thomas S. 1977. *The Essential Tension: Selected Studies in Scientific Tradition and Change*. London: University of Chicago Press.

Labinger Jay A., and Harry Collins, eds. 2001. *The One Culture?* Chicago: University of Chicago Press.

Leach, Melissa. 2005. "MMR Mobilisation: Citizens and Science in a British Vaccine Controversy." IDS Working Paper 247. Institute for Development Studies, Brighton, UK. http://www.ids.ac.uk/publication/mmr-mobilisation-citizens-and-science-in-a-british-vaccine-controversy.

Levesque, Hector, Ernest Davis, and Leora Morgenstern. 2012. "The Winograd Schema Challenge." *Proceedings of Principles of Knowledge Representation and Reasoning*. http://www.aaai.org/ocs/index.php/KR/KR12/paper/download/4492/4924

Levitsky, Steven, and Daniel Ziblatt. 2018. *How Democracies Die*. New York: Crown.

Lippmann, Walter. 1927. *The Phantom Public*. New Brunswick, NJ: Transaction Publishers.

Merton, Robert K. 1973. *The Sociology of Science: Theoretical and Empirical Investigations*. Chicago: University of Chicago Press.

Miller, Steven. 2001. "Public Understanding of Science at the Crossroads." *Public Understanding of Science* 10 (1): 115–120. doi:10.1088/0963-6625/10/1/308.

Moore, Alfred. 2017. *Critical Elitism: Deliberation, Democracy and the Problem of Expertise*. Cambridge, UK: Cambridge University Press.

Mouffe, Chantal. 2018. *For a Left Populism*. London: Verso.

Mounk, Yascha. 2018. *The People vs. Democracy: Why Our Freedom Is in Danger and How to Save It*. Cambridge, MA: Harvard University Press.

Mudde, Cas and Cristóbal R. Kaltwasser. "Studying Populism in Comparative Perspective: Reflections on the Contemporary and Future Research Agenda." *Comparative Political Studies* 51 (2018): 1667–1693. doi: 10.1177/0010414018789490.

Müller, Jan-Werner. 2017. *What Is Populism?* London: Penguin Books.

Nichols, Tom. 2017. *The Death of Expertise: The Campaign against Established Knowledge and Why It Matters.* New York: Oxford University Press.

Oreskes, Naomi, and Erik. M. Conway. 2010. *Merchants of Doubt: How a Handful of Scientists Obscured the Truth on Issues from Tobacco Smoke to Global Warming.* New York: Bloomsbury Press.

Pearce, Warren. 2020. "Trouble in the Trough: How Uncertainties Were Downplayed in the UK's Science Advice on Covid-19." *Humanities and Social Sciences Communications* 7(1):1–6. doi: 10.1057/s41599-020-00612-w.

Poltorak Mike, Melissa Leach, James Fairhead, and Jackie Cassell. 2005. "'MMR Talk' and Vaccination Choices: An Ethnographic Study in Brighton." *Social Science & Medicine* 61 (3): 709–719. https://doi.org/10.1016/j.socscimed.2004.12.014.

Przeworski, Adam. 2019. *Crisis of Democracy.* Cambridge, UK: Cambridge University Press.

Putnam, Robert. 1993. *Making Democracy Work.* Princeton, NJ: Princeton University Press.

Rosanvallon, Pierre (translated by Arthur Goldhammer). 2011. *Democratic Legitimacy: Impartiality, Reflexivity, Proximity.* Princeton University Press, 2011. JSTOR, http://www.jstor.org/stable/j.ctt7stdc. Accessed 1 November 2022.

Sarewitz, Daniel. 2000. "Science and Environmental Policy: An Excess of Objectivity." In *Earth Matters: The Earth Sciences, Philosophy, and the Claims of Community*, edited by Robert Frodeman, 79–98. Upper Saddle River, NJ: Prentice Hall.

Sarewitz, Daniel. 2016. "Saving Science." *New Atlantis* 49 (Spring/Summer): 5–40. https://www.thenewatlantis.com/publications/saving-science.

Shapin, Steven. 2019. "Is There a Crisis of Truth?" *Los Angeles Review of Books*, December 2. https://lareviewofbooks.org/article/is-there-a-crisis-of-truth/.

Sismondo, Sergio. 2017. "Post-truth?" *Social Studies of Science* 47 (1): 3–6. doi: 10.1177/0306312717692076.

Sokal, Alan, and Jean Bricmont. 1998. *Intellectual Impostures: Postmodern Philosophers' Abuse of Science.* London: Profile Books.

Weale, Albert. 2018. *The Will of the People: A Modern Myth.* Cambridge, UK: Polity Press.

Webster, Andrew. 1991. *Science, Technology and Society: New Directions.* Basingstoke, UK: Macmillan.

Weinel, Martin. 2007. "Primary Source Knowledge and Technical Decision-Making: Mbeki and the AZT Debate." *Studies in History and Philosophy of Science Part A* 38 (4): 748–760. doi:10.1016/j.shpsa.2007.09.010.

Weinel, Martin. 2010. "Technological Decision-Making under Scientific Uncertainty: Preventing Mother-to-Child Transmission of HIV in South Africa." PhD thesis. Cardiff University. http://orca.cf.ac.uk/55502/.

Weinel, Martin. 2019. "Recognizing Counterfeit Scientific Controversies in Science Policy Contexts: A Criteria-Based Approach." In Caudill et al., *Third Wave in Science and Technology Studies*, 53–70. doi:10.1007/978-3-030-14335-0_4.

Winch, Peter. 1958. *The Idea of a Social Science.* London: Routledge and Kegan Paul.

Wittgenstein, Ludwig. 1953. *Philosophical Investigations.* Translated by G. E. M Anscombe. Oxford: Blackwell.

Wynne, Brian. 2003. "Seasick on the Third Wave? Subverting the Hegemony of Propositionalism: Response to Collins & Evans (2002)." *Social Studies of Science* 33 (3): 401–417. doi:10.1177/03063127030333005.

4

THE MEANING AND SIGNIFICANCE OF LAY EXPERTISE

STEVEN EPSTEIN

In his parting words as he prepared to step down from his position as editor of the journal *Public Understanding of Science* in 2003, Bruce Lewenstein, a professor of science communication, called on his readers to embrace "lay expertise"—not just to study it, but also to valorize it. "It is clear that we need to understand the meanings and information that nonscientists bring to technical decisions," wrote Lewenstein (2003, 357). "We need to give authority to those perspectives, acknowledging a 'lay knowledge' or 'lay expertise' model that deeply challenges the idea of a monolithic scientific knowledge that stands alone as 'truth' or the closest that we have to truth." Lewenstein's remarks align with a widespread appreciation, among scholars in science and technology studies (STS) and well beyond, of certain key aspects of the politics of expertise in contemporary societies: his comments resonate with understandings that expertise is exercised not only by the formally credentialed; that pathways to the development of expertise may not always follow the familiar routes; and that an analysis of expertise "from below" is a prerequisite for making sense of the distribution and effects of authority, the assessment of technological risks, and the production and dissemination of knowledge in contemporary societies.

Since the mid-1990s and into the present, many scholars have sought to locate and trace the manifestations of what they call lay expertise, and they have found it operating in remarkably diverse social settings. Though often used with reference to mobilization by sufferers of illness, "lay expertise" has been invoked to characterize bodybuilders' accounts of synthol use (Hall et al. 2016), drug users' harm-reduction practices (Jauffret-Roustide 2009), runners' self-care practices (Campbell 2016), and the contributions to innovation made by technological "visioneers" (Gudowky and Sotoudeh 2017). Scholars have found it at play in early modern antecedents of crowdsourcing (Delbourgo 2012), waste governance in the United Kingdom and China (Hacking and Flynn 2018), local ecological knowledge in urban land-use planning in Finland (Yli-Pelkonen and Kohl 2005), and online public participation in regional transportation decision-making in the state of Washington (Nyerges and Aguirre 2011). Commentators on the broader dynamics of expertise have underscored the significance of this new formulation. According to Holger Strassheim, writing in 2015:

> Along with "citizen science" and "participatory action research," an ambiguous figure has appeared: the "lay expert" seems to cross a threshold, transforming expertise into a hybrid creature situated in the no-man's-land between science and politics. . . . Finally, one may argue, laity strikes back. (326)

What is lay expertise? What are the social problems for which lay expertise might serve as the solution? How is it put to use, and with what effects? Is the term "lay expertise" an oxymoron, and if so, should we care? In this chapter, I argue for the utility of the concept in describing key aspects of present-day social relations surrounding knowledge production, technological development, civic engagement, and struggles for democratization. I begin by providing context for understanding lay expertise by tracing the term's entry into discourse and subsequent spread. I consider how the concept has become embedded in two parallel discussions, one having to do with various forms of "participation" (or engagement, or citizenship) in relation to the promise and dangers of contemporary science and technology, and the other concerning formal knowledge and its various "others" (vernacular, tacit, embodied, local, subjugated, etc.). Taking into account some of the critiques of the concept, and building on the existing scholarly literature, I then attempt a sharper characterization of lay expertise, one that locates the concept in relation to recent reworkings of the notion of expertise more generally. I emphasize not only the kinds of participants and the knowledge and values they bring to their work, but also the fundamentally collective character of lay expertise in its prototypical form. Finally, and with an eye toward an agenda for future research, I outline the gaps in our understanding of two important topics: What are the pathways through which lay expertise develops? And what are the political dilemmas and complications to which its deployment gives rise?

A DISCURSIVE HISTORY OF "LAY EXPERTISE"

In the pages of the *Wall Street Journal* in 1913, an editor introduced an op-ed by vouching for its author as "probably the ablest English lay expert on railroad affairs" ("An Expert Opinion," 1913). Twelve years later, an article in the *New York Times* was headlined "Lay Expert Urged for School Board" (1928). In recent decades as well, such locutions are not uncommon. For example, in 1990, a columnist in the *Chicago Tribune* profiled a citizen whose mother-in-law used a wheelchair: "While crusading on her behalf, he become a lay expert on parking rights for the disabled and testified at state legislative hearings"

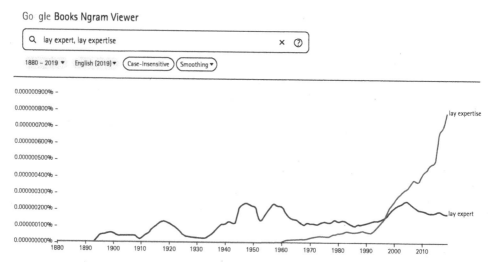

FIGURE 4.1. Usage over time of the terms *lay expert* and *lay expertise* in Google Books, 1880–2019.

Generated using the Google Ngram Viewer (https://books.google.com/ngrams; see note 1), January 13, 2022.

(Zorn 1990). And in 2005, an obituary in the *Reno Gazette* characterized the deceased as "an accomplished artist, photographer, licensed pilot, scuba diver, expert marksman, avid fisherman, and a lay expert in Native American art and culture" ("Obituary: Albert Andre Galli," 2005). In none of these examples, or in any others I found by searching an online newspaper database, did the writers using the term "lay expert" feel obliged to define or explain it, apparently taking the meaning to be self-evident. Indeed, while some academics, as I will describe, have sought to brand "lay expert" as a self-contradictory neologism, the phrase has been used nonetheless (albeit occasionally) in routine communication with a mass public over the course of at least a century, and without any evident concern that ambiguity or confusion might result.

A graph of appearances of the phrases "lay expert" and "lay expertise" in the pages of digitized books in the Google Books database tells an interesting story (Figure 4.1).[1] Of course, neither phrase is especially common. Yet while the phrase "lay expert" has seen a gradual increase, with various ups and downs, from the 1890s onward, "lay expertise" emerged much later, in the 1960s. However, the latter term then experienced such a sharp growth spurt beginning around 1990 that by the mid-1990s, it had surpassed "lay expert" in frequency of use, and by 2019 it was appearing in books more than four times as often. If we think of "lay expertise" as the abstract concept and "lay expert" as a more ordinary descriptor of a kind of person, then we might expect that the recent linguistic success of "lay expertise" roughly corresponds with its entry into formal academic discourse.

This conclusion is supported by a search for "lay expertise" in the Sociological Abstracts database. As shown in Figure 4.2, the phrase first appeared in a scholarly journal indexed in that database in 1995, and it has been employed in a total of 148

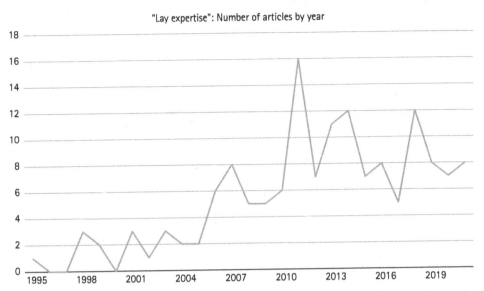

FIGURE 4.2. Number of scholarly journal articles indexed in Sociological Abstracts that use the phrase *lay expertise*.

Source: Sociological Abstracts, online database, accessed January 13, 2022. Scholarly journal articles only.

articles through 2021.[2] While this is an undercount of the scholarly impact—for example, scholars have also used the phrase in numerous articles in the journal *Public Understanding of Science*, which Sociological Abstracts does not catalog[3]—it suggests the arrival of "lay expertise" in social science discourse in recent decades.[4] Of course, the *ideas* reflected by the term have deeper roots; and a proper genealogy, not the terminological history I provide here, would first have to trace the historical emergence of the expert–lay divide and reconstruct the pathways by which we have come to believe we know "where science ends and where other forms of culture begin" (Shapin 1990, 990). Such a genealogy might then consider the range of attempts to bridge that divide (see Prior 2003, 45). For example, the STS scholar Brian Wynne (1992) had investigated, in his study of Cumbrian sheep farmers, how "laypeople [may be] capable of extensive informal reflection upon their social relationships towards scientific experts and on the epistemological status of their own 'local' knowledge in relation to 'outside' knowledge" (281).

Returning, however, to my terminological history: it now takes an autobiographical turn. The 1995 article in which the phrase "lay expertise" first shows up in Sociological Abstracts was my own, entitled "The Construction of Lay Expertise: AIDS Activism and the Forging of Credibility in the Reform of Clinical Trials," published in the journal *Science, Technology, & Human Values* (Epstein 1995).[5] The article title seemed apt in describing how AIDS treatment activists in the late 1980s and early 1990s pushed their way into the rarefied domains of clinical research and drug testing—indeed, how they became so proficient in technical matters that their work informed the scientific research process:

> This case demonstrates that activist movements, through amassing different forms of credibility, can in certain circumstances become genuine participants in the construction of scientific knowledge—that they can (within definite limits) effect changes both in the epistemic practices of biomedical research and in the therapeutic techniques of medical care. This surprising result is, of course, at variance with the popular notion of science as a relatively autonomous arena with high barriers to entry. It is a result that illustrates the danger of understanding the role of laypeople in scientific controversies solely in passive terms—as a resource available for use, or an ally available for enrollment, by an entrepreneurial scientist who is conceived of as the true motive force in the process of knowledge making. (409)

In retrospect, I don't believe I gave the actual term "lay expertise" a great deal of thought. A check of my hard drive reveals that early versions of the article bore alternative titles that lacked the term, and the phrase did not appear anywhere in the long 1993 doctoral dissertation from which the article derived. In the published version of the article, I used the term only once in the main text, without a specific definition, and once more in the endnotes.[6] Specifically, in the article text, I invoked a doctoral dissertation by Gilbert Elbaz about the AIDS activist organization ACT UP/New York. I noted that Elbaz at one point referenced a social divide that developed inside the organization between the lay expert activists and the "lay lay" activists (the latter being those who did *not* come to acquire expertise about the science around HIV/AIDS; Elbaz 1992, 488; Epstein 1995, 429). Yet curiously, I now find, upon returning to Elbaz's work, that while he indeed used the phrase "lay lay," the paired term "lay expert" nowhere appears and is therefore only implied.

In my book *Impure Science*, a revision of my dissertation that I published in 1996, I described at greater length how activists challenged the social, cultural, and epistemic authority of doctors, clinical researchers, government health officials, and the pharmaceutical industry. I attributed their establishment of their own credibility and practical successes to the capacity to weave together their moral authority, local knowledge of the epidemic and its impact, and successful appropriation of many esoteric details of virology, immunology, and biostatistics (Epstein 1996). I referred explicitly to lay expertise on several occasions in both the book's introduction and its conclusion—but almost always containing the term within scare quotes, and consistently failing to provide a definition. (The book also lacks an index entry for the term.) For example, I noted that as individual patients banded together, the collaboration enhanced the breadth and durability of their lay expertise (9). I also identified various tensions embedded in the lay expertise found in health movements, such as that the imperatives of becoming more expert may run at cross-purposes with other movement priorities or commitments (342–343).

In addition to again citing Elbaz, as well as Phil Brown's (1992) work on a parallel concept that has attracted much attention, that of "popular epidemiology" (Epstein 1996, 488, 13), I was also clearly influenced by Hilary Arksey (1994; see also Arksey 1998): I cited her work on the epistemic interventions of a lay advocacy group in the United Kingdom, the Repetitive Strain Injury Association (Epstein 1996, 463). Yet I failed to note in my text that Arksey, in describing "an opening for persons commonly assumed to be technically incompetent to acquire (lay) medical power with regard to the construction of scientific facts," had referred explicitly to what she called "lay 'experts'" (1994, 464). In short, in my early work, which proved influential in introducing the idea of lay expertise to an academic audience (and which continues to be cited in reference to the concept), I placed no great weight on the term, and I was vague and inconsistent in reflecting on its provenance and meaning.

Neither has subsequent scholarship on lay expertise in STS and other fields done much specifically to define the concept. Instead, the idea of lay expertise has become embedded within at least two larger conversations that have distributed the concept across wide-ranging webs of semantic associations. First, the notion of lay expertise has become central to many discussions that are broadly concerned with the question of how lay citizens can or should "participate" in decision-making concerning modern scientific and technological possibilities and risks. Of course, lay participation (in the sense of playing a role in decision-making) and lay expertise are not quite the same and do not necessarily coincide; but they are often treated as closely related and as perhaps implying one another. For example, an article in the *American Journal of Public Health* on "community involvement" in the policymaking around genetic testing cited the examples of AIDS and breast cancer to note "the critical role that members of affected community groups can play in developing health policy." The authors then add: "Similarly, the expertise of individuals who have genetic conditions can provide critical contributions to genetics-related policies" (Gollust et al. 2005, 36).

To be sure, lay "participation" can itself mean many different things—Christopher Kelty and coauthors disentangle seven dimensions of the term as used in contemporary discourse around science and technology (Kelty et al. 2015; see also Chilvers and Kearnes 2016)—and the intersection of lay participation with lay expertise invokes a range of practical and theoretical concerns. These include ideas about the virtues of alternative "ways of knowing" (Grundy and Smith 2007; Pols 2014); the distinctive technologies that laypeople may bring to bear when engaging with credentialed experts (Callon and Rabeharisoa 2003; Murphy 2004, 2012); the agency, reflexivity, and self-management of the modern patient (Armstrong 2014); the forms of sociability and affective ties that enable advocacy groups to advance knowledge claims (Panofsky 2011; Buchbinder and Timmermans 2014; Lappé 2014; Maslen and Lupton 2019); the relation between participation, expertise, and democracy (Callon et al. 2009; Fischer 2009; Jasanoff 2017); and the link between participation and new modes of scientific or biological "citizenship" (Irwin 1995, 2001; Petryna 2002; Allen 2003; Elam and Bertilsson 2003; Heath et al. 2004; Nguyen 2005; Rose and Novas 2005; Gibbon 2007; Jauffret-Roustide 2009; Wentzell 2015).

In addition to this thick bundle of associations, the idea of lay expertise has also become enmeshed in a different semantic web, one that concerns various forms of knowledge seen as alternative, subordinated, or contrarian that stand (explicitly or implicitly) in contrast to forms of knowledge deemed official, standard, universal, or authoritative. The former grouping includes informal knowledge, local knowledge (Geertz 1983; Wynne 1992), tacit knowledge (Polanyi 1958; Mukerji 2006), vernacular knowledge (Escoffier 1999), subjugated knowledges (Foucault 1980, 83–85; Epstein 1996, 357–358), standpoint epistemologies (Harding 1986; Wylie 2003), situated knowledges (Haraway 1988), and so on.[7] These various "others" to official knowledge are by no means identical to one another. Yet each of them perhaps suggests possible characteristics of knowledge as deployed by lay experts—that it might, for example, be less systematic, more situationally specific, more rooted in everyday experiences (perhaps especially experiences of oppression or injustice), more embodied and ineffable, less prestigious, and more oppositional. However, as I will discuss, most of the empirical work on lay expertise speaks to its hybrid character and indicates that lay expertise in practice traverses the boundary between official knowledge and its multiple "others," rather than being located purely on the "alternative" side of the divide.

The Critique of "Lay Expertise"

As it has gradually gained currency among academics since the mid-1990s, the term and concept of "lay expertise" has also acquired critics.[8] Two lines of critique are noteworthy. First, Lindsay Prior (2003) observed that "those who talk of lay expertise often fail to specify how exactly lay people might be expert," and whether such expertise derives from experience, training, or various sorts of immersive experiences (45). Furthermore, taking up the example of the modern patient, Prior correctly pointed out that while patients may be "experts by virtue of 'having experience,'" such experience comes with clear limits and "on its own is rarely sufficient to understand the technical complexities of disease causation, its consequences or its management" (53).

These observations merit discussion, and I will return to them. However, Prior's (2003) primary claim appears to be "that, for the most part, lay people are not experts. They are, for example, rarely skilled in matters of (medical) fact gathering, or in the business of diagnosis. What is more they can often be plain wrong about the causes, course and management of common forms of disease and illness" (45). These latter points strike me as straw arguments, efficacious only in response to those who might claim that all laypeople are always expert, or that laypeople are never wrong. The validity of the contention that laypeople may become lay experts does not depend on whether many or most of them accomplish this transition, and the fact that a patient (or doctor!) may sometimes be wrong does not seem to me to disqualify the prospect of lay (or professional!) expertise. (Nor does Prior explain by what route he stands privileged to judge lay beliefs as being "right" or "wrong." Despite selecting examples such as resistance to vaccination that are meant to be read as self-evidently wrongheaded, he ducks the question—both epistemological and political—of the grounds of his own expertise to evaluate the expertise of others.)

The STS scholars Harry Collins and Robert Evans (and their occasional coauthors) have put forward additional key criticisms of lay expertise as part of a larger theoretical, empirical, and normative project of rethinking the nature and social significance of expertise.[9] While calling for deference to experts, Collins and Evans also open up membership in the category by granting legitimacy to some of those who lack formal credentials—for example, activists and other noncredentialed actors who acquire the capacity to speak about and evaluate scientific developments in a knowledgeable way (Collins and Evans 2002, 2007). Indeed, Collins and Evans refer frequently to "Epstein's AIDS activists," treating them as emblematic of successful nontraditional experts.[10]

Collins and Evans also usefully propose a typology of different varieties of expertise—to which I will return, because I believe it offers resources for understanding aspects of lay expertise. Yet at the end of the day, in their view, people at any given moment are either expert or they are not. Collins and Evans have no truck with hybridity, liminality, or in-betweenness, and therefore they make clear: "Though we are going to talk about widening participation in technical decision-making, we will abandon the oxymoron 'lay expertise'" (Collins and Evans 2002, 238). Indeed, "it is necessary to replace the language of 'lay expertise' with a more systematic and rigorous treatment of the expertise or its absence that characterizes different participants" in the decision-making surrounding science and technology (Evans and Plows 2007, 827). To retain the language of "lay expertise" is to risk a "leveling of the epistemological playing field" and a "collapse of the concept of expertise," in their view. Like Prior, they worry about opening the door to the suggestion "that the knowledge of any set of ordinary people [is] as good as that of the supposed specialists" (Collins et al. 2010, 186–187).

With these critiques, Collins and Evans have raised important issues that I will try to explore further. Yet I will dispute the idea of a slippery slope leading ineluctably from "lay expertise" to what they call "technological populism," which would undermine the very idea of expertise (Collins et al. 2010, 187). I will also seek to muddy the sharp distinctions they have sought to draw between those who are experts and those who are simply not. Thus, I will seek to defend an oxymoron. As the history of many of the oxymorons in common use—for example, "virtual reality"—makes clear, good oxymorons (like other figures of speech) are generative terms that call attention to distinctive but complex characteristics of contemporary social life; they should not be shunned on principle. "Lay expertise," I will argue, is a case in point.

RETHINKING LAY EXPERTISE

A proper reconsideration of the concept of "lay expertise" requires scrutiny of both of the words that make up the compound term. We can begin with the concept of "layness," which is not as straightforward as it may seem. Of course, the use of "lay" in the context of discussions of expertise constitutes a repurposing of a term taken from the domain of organized religion. The metaphor proposes a parallelism between two elites—clerical and technical—in their hierarchical relationship to nonelites, yet the two cases are in many respects quite different. But the fundamental problem with this new conception of the laity, as noted by Ian Shaw (2002), is that a genuine, absolute layperson—if understood to be someone who possesses "lay knowledge" or "lay beliefs" that are altogether untainted by exposure to expert knowledge—is simply not to be found anywhere. Although the idea of lay knowledge may serve as an abstract counterfactual, Shaw argued, "there is no one in western society who is unaware of professional explanations. . . . Common-sense understandings are imbued with professional rationalizations, and even resistance to medical treatments are oriented around medical rationality" (293).

In my view, the implication of acknowledging this important point is that "lay expertise" is by no means the oddity that some have considered it. Rather, if actually existing "lay knowledge" is already a hybrid concoction that partially incorporates modes of understanding we might typically think of as professional or expert—and if, as seems equally certain, "expert" knowledge is also infused with bits and pieces of lay or nonexpert understanding—then we ought not be surprised to encounter a range of real-world cases located somewhere "in-between," where the mixtures of knowledge are even more thoroughly hybrid and impure.

Are there any distinctions, then, to be drawn between "lay," "lay expert," and "expert"? Following the lead of other scholars of expertise (Collins and Evans 2007; Callon et al. 2009; Akrich 2010; Carr 2010; Raz et al. 2018, 102), I will argue that one solution to this puzzle lies in shifting the discussion from "knowing" to "doing." The focus ought not to be solely on who possesses what sort of knowledge but should also be on the assembly of distinctive orientations toward action in relation to knowledge of whatever sort. To develop this point, I combine two recent general perspectives on expertise. First, I adopt Reiner Grundmann's (2017) "relational concept of expertise," which he has concisely summarized as follows: "Experts mediate between the production of knowledge and its application; they define and interpret situations; and they set priorities for action" (27). Therefore, expertise is not a possession (whether of knowledge or of skills), but rather a way of marshaling knowledge and skills to provide interpretive frames that will motivate action. Second, I follow Gil Eyal's approach to expertise as the emergent property of a heterogeneous assemblage of people, tools, and techniques. By this account, expertise is (once again) not a possession but, rather, the orchestrated product of "networks that link together objects, actors, techniques, devices, and institutional and spatial arrangements" (Eyal 2013a, 863; see also Cambrosio et al. 1992; Eyal et al. 2010; Brady 2018). Moreover, such expertise can be found operating not only within conventional fields of social practice, such as the institutional settings where professionals work, but also in the hybrid and interstitial "spaces between fields" (Eyal 2013b), where various "credentialed" and "noncredentialed" experts may bump up against one another. I believe the approaches of Grundmann and Eyal, though distinctive in their origins, can be made congruent. Taken together, they usefully characterize expertise as a heterogeneous assemblage of people, objects, tools, and techniques that operates to provide a bridge between knowing and acting. In this sense, as Holger Strassheim (2015) has observed, "experts are always already boundary workers," involved not only in the validation and justification of knowledge claims but also in making such claims "relevant for collectively ordering and evaluating society" (326).[11]

That brings me, finally, to lay expertise. My suggestion is that we understand lay expertise, not as wholly different from other sorts of expertise, yet as characterized by a particular kind of orientation toward action that also depends on the assemblage of distinctive components. There are four aspects to my characterization: personnel, knowledge, values, and collective mobilization.

(1) Lay expertise is developed or deployed by people not normally or previously deemed legitimate expert participants in the relevant social domain—whether due to their lack of credentials or formal training or some other "discredited" attribute, or as a result of a social process of disqualification, or "othering."

(2) What typifies lay expertise is partly (but only partly) the hybridity of the knowledge, tools, and techniques that it fuses together: formal, experiential, embodied, evidence-based, and so on. Although the knowledge, tools, and techniques deployed by those people conventionally understood as being either "laypeople" or "experts" are, as I have suggested, also hybrid and boundary-spanning, in the case of lay experts, that fusion may simply be more visible, potent, and developed—though also, perhaps, more unstable. (I expand on the hybrid character of lay-expert knowledge in the next section, "Varieties and Components of Lay Expertise".)

(3) Beyond the question of the composition of the knowledge base, what characterizes lay experts is that they marshal their knowledge to take action to advance pragmatic and expressive goals defined by criteria and values drawn substantially from *outside* the domains of routine bureaucratic activity where professionals go about their work. This orientation locates lay experts as a specific variety of a broader category of "counter-experts" (Williams and Moore 2019, 259–261). In pursuing this epistemic pragmatism, lay experts often play a pivotal role in addressing social problems by developing elements of expertise that are otherwise sorely lacking, and that credentialed experts cannot provide. In Michel Callon's (2005) words, lay experts thereby "transform their incompetence into strength": it is "their initial ignorance that enables them to dare to explore new paths and to develop original competencies" (313).

Of course, lay experts and professional experts inhabit overlapping worlds, and their goals and values are likely not altogether distinct. Yet even when commitments to certain overriding values—such as "health," or "security"—nominally underpin the actions of both groups, the interpretation of those abstractions and their translation into concrete advice, demands, or action plans may often differ significantly.[12] Scientists and activists alike may believe sincerely that they are fighting to promote health, yet, as AIDS activists discovered, the moral imperative of health means something different to the basic scientist working on HIV in the laboratory, who has never met a person with AIDS, than it does to someone living in a community under siege (Epstein 1996, 321). It follows, therefore, that lay expertise is not merely an epistemic concern but also, frequently, a matter of *mobilized affect* (Gould 2009; Panofsky 2011; Buchbinder and Timmermans 2014; Lappé 2014; Maslen and Lupton 2019).

(4) Viewed in these terms, examples of the marshaling of lay expertise should be seen as political and cultural projects of *collective mobilization*, and not, in the first instance, as individual activities. It has become common to understand the application of "external" goals and criteria to questions of science and technology policy as a marker of modern scientific citizenship. But, in practice, such work is the product not of abstract, isolated "citizens" but, rather, specific and located collective actors: "concerned groups" (Callon 2003; Callon and Rabeharisoa 2003), social movements (Brown and Zavestoski 2004; Brown et al. 2004; Hess 2004; Landzelius and Dumit 2006; Epstein 2008, 2016; Brown et al. 2011), "online forums" (Barker and Galardi 2011), "lay epistemic communities" (Akrich 2010), and other groupings of various sorts.

Of course, collective action can take many different forms and may not necessarily resemble a traditional social movement. Joanna Kempner and John Bailey's (2019) analysis of online communities of patients engaged in "collective self-experimentation" offers an instructive example of how individual actions may become collectively articulated in ways that generate lay expertise, but without taking the form of conventional political activism. Furthermore, we should not presuppose based on commonly held ideas about activism that lay expertise necessarily stands opposed to established authority. It is important to point out that those adopting this collective-action orientation may position themselves as more or less conciliatory or more or less hostile to conventional expert advice or prescriptions (Elam and Bertilsson 2003). However, this epistemic, affective, and political formation is prototypically "demonstrative" in the double sense described by Brice Laurent (2016): it "points both to the practices of constructing public proofs and of displaying them in public" (774). And it may often distinguish itself by its temporal orientation—a perception of urgency in response to pressing concerns that demand instrumental and expressive action.

To be sure, in stressing the collective and interactive dimensions of engagement as constituent elements of lay expertise, I am breaking with a tendency in the extant literature to emphasize and valorize the roles of (more or less) isolated individuals who may alter the politics of knowledge through their epistemic contributions. We certainly know, from much work in the sociology of health and illness, that medical meanings—including diagnoses and prognoses—are jointly constructed through the encounters of individual patients with individual providers (Heritage and Maynard 2006). This role of patients is also a form of "participation," to use a word that, as I have indicated, has come to acquire many (perhaps too many) shades of meaning. Yet I would prefer to consider the epistemic contributions of those individual patients as being both a building block and a consequence of lay expertise, which is then understood prototypically as a form of collective action. The collective character of lay expertise provides it with its most distinctive features, as well as its epistemic, affective, and political efficacy.

VARIETIES AND COMPONENTS OF LAY EXPERTISE

Existing scholarship helps to flesh out the forms and makeup of lay expertise. For example, lay experts may cultivate and deploy what Collins and Evans (2007), in their typology of expertise, describe as "interactional expertise": the level of expertise necessary to engage with the core participants in expert work and communicate with them intelligently about what they are up to (28–35). At times, though, lay experts go further, to exercise "contributory expertise": a higher level of expertise, in which outsiders make actual contributions to the conduct of scientific and technical processes (24–27, 136–137). Lay experts may also demonstrate what Collins and Evans call "referred expertise"—a kind of "meta-expertise," in their terms, by which the expertise acquired in one domain may prove useful and applicable in a different domain (15, 64–66). That is, lay experts may draw on a range of skills from their other life experiences and involvements—including, for example, an ability to read critically or to analyze statistics—and bring them to bear on scientific and technical processes.[13]

In addition, existing scholarship clearly suggests a point I have already made about the composition of lay expertise: it typically manifests as a fusion of "experiential" or "embodied" knowledge or tools with those that are more "formal," "traditional," or "professional." (Of course, the balance in the mix will vary.) Research on lay experts' assemblages of knowledge, tools, and techniques has called attention to this hybrid character. For example, Callon and Rabeharisoa (2003) have reconstructed the accumulation of knowledge by members of a French muscular dystrophy association who used "proto-instruments" that included "cameras, camcorders for taking films and photos, accounts written by patients or their parents in the form of books for the general public, requested testimonies, spontaneous letters, and lectures given by patients or their relatives"—all of which led to the production of knowledge that was "formal, transportable, cumulative, and debatable" (197–198). We can distinguish this sort of hybridity found *within* lay expertise from the "hybrid forums" described by Callon, Lascoumes, and Barthe (2009)—those actual and proposed spaces in which experts, politicians, and citizen nonexperts come together in order to resolve technoscientific controversies. In fact, lay experts may constitute an already-hybrid element within such hybrid forums.

Both "sides" of the hybrid composition of lay expertise merit discussion. On the one hand, scholars have described how both the moral urgency of lay experts and their strategies for transforming knowledge into action stem from their particular lived experiences—with illness (Pols 2014; Sharma et al. 2017), with environmental exposures (Murphy 2006; MacKendrick 2010; Kuchinskaya 2011), with embodied activities of various sorts (Jauffret-Roustide 2009; Campbell 2016; Hall et al. 2016). Once again, I think it is important to distinguish, at least conceptually, between this dimension of lay expertise—which, as I have suggested, is generated through collective action and geared to mobilizing knowledge toward practical ends—and the (also important) idea that individuals, simply by virtue of having worldly experiences, possess important knowledge resources that may stand in contrast to official knowledge (Williams and Popay 1994; Segal 2005, 147; Shim 2005; Pols 2014). Fundamentally and most significantly, it is through organized forms of social interaction that lay experts hone experiential knowledge derived from multiple sources (their "referred expertise," in Collins and Evans's terms) and turn it into actionable insights (Akrich 2010; Raz et al. 2018, 102).

Even so, experience has its limits, to return to one of Prior's observations. As I have noted elsewhere (Epstein 2008, 517), it is important not to romanticize lived experience as a basis for reliable knowledge or treat it as bedrock resistant to critical interpretation (Scott 1991). Michelle Murphy (2004) put it well in a study of occupational health: " 'Experience' is a category of knowledge that is just as historical as other forms of knowledge. . . . It is only through particular methods rooted historically in time and space that experience becomes a kind of evidence imbued with certain truth-telling qualities" (202).[14]

On the other hand, lay experts do not *only* draw on experience: they also appropriate the official and esoteric knowledge of their credentialed interlocutors. They learn to "talk the talk," and thereby establish their credibility to take what AIDS treatment activists called a "seat at the table." (In Collins and Evans's terms, their interactional expertise provides a springboard for the development of contributory expertise.) This was the dimension of lay expertise that I underscored in my early work: I emphasized how AIDS treatment activists acquired cultural competence in the worlds of biomedicine, and I explored the consequences, both on the research process and on the activists themselves. But in retrospect, I may have underplayed the extent to which they simultaneously hung onto their local and experiential knowledge (not to mention their moral fervor and political commitments—and their willingness to "act up" in the form of disruptive protest) so as to generate a thick stew of ingredients for lay expertise. My failure sufficiently to stress the hybridity of their resulting expertise—and the liminality of their status as lay experts—permitted Collins and Evans to misread my work as suggesting that AIDS activists had simply crossed over: once upon a time, they were lay; then they became expert. I should have done more with such examples as activist Mark Harrington's presentation to a lecture hall full of AIDS researchers at the International AIDS Conference in Amsterdam in 1992: "Using slides of his own lymph tissue as backdrop, Harrington had demanded that scientists attend to 'what is going on in our bodies, rather than exclusively in elegant and often artificial laboratory and animal models.' With representational strategies such as these, activists could hope to bring the 'politics of the body' to bear on the remotest regions of laboratory science" (Epstein 1996, 319).

Subsequently, two lines of research on health activism and patient organizations have called attention to just this kind of hybridity. First, a group of STS scholars that includes Madeleine Akrich, Vololona Rabeharisoa, and Tiago Moreira has described forms of what they term "evidence-based activism" that successfully merge "the experience of a specific condition" with "medical-scientific expertise":

On the one hand, [patient organizations] collect, shape, analyze their members' testimonies, conduct surveys and produce statistics; on the other hand, they provide a scientific watch, synthesize the academic literature, publish documents for the public or organize conferences. This two-fold expertise is mobilized in actions directed both at empowering of the individual patient as well as at shaping health policies. (Akrich and Rabeharisoa 2012, 69)[15]

In this way, lay experts "articulate credentialed knowledge with experiential knowledge in order to make the latter politically relevant." They thereby "reframe what is at stake, destabilising existing understandings of conditions and problems" (Rabeharisoa et al. 2014, 115; see also Moreira et al. 2014).

The second line of research that has painted a somewhat similar picture of hybrid expertise is that conducted by Phil Brown and his students and collaborators, who have written of what they term "embodied health movements" (Brown et al. 2004; Zavestoski et al. 2004; Morello-Frosch et al. 2006).[16] These movements "introduce the biological body to social movements in central ways, especially in terms of the embodied experience of people who have the disease" (Brown et al. 2004, 54). At the same time, even as they are posing challenges to existing medical and scientific frameworks, embodied health movements also "often involve activists collaborating with scientists and health professionals in pursuing treatment, prevention, research and expanded funding" (Brown et al. 2004, 54–55). Consequently, embodied health movements are "boundary-spanning" movements, forcing the analyst "to abandon traditional dichotomies between movement insiders and outsiders, and between lay and expert forms of knowledge" (Brown et al. 2004, 64; see also McCormick et al. 2003). This depiction of boundary transgression also recalls Eyal and coauthors' analysis of the remaking of the network of expertise brought about, in the case of autism research, by the interventions of parents, organized as the National Society for Autistic Children: "It was not a mere teaming up of adjacent groups, parents on one hand and practitioners on the other. Rather, it involved the hybridization of identities, blurring of boundaries between expert and layman, and crucially, 'co-production' of common objects of inquiry and treatment (Eyal et al. 2010, 170).[17]

KEY QUESTIONS AND FUTURE DIRECTIONS IN THE STUDY OF LAY EXPERTISE

Lay expertise has the potential to "[bring] into question the established moral and epistemic authority" of conventional experts and "[open] up epistemic norms and moral criteria to negotiation" (Elam and Bertilsson 2003, 245). It therefore holds significant implications, not merely for knowledge production and the development of technologies, but also for contemporary modes of governance, practices of citizenship, and political struggles of all sorts. I close this critical review of the concept by considering two key sets of issues, both of which point toward gaps in our current understanding and an agenda for future research: the pathways to the development of lay expertise, and the political complications associated with its deployment.

In the scholarly literature, much attention has been devoted to specific mechanisms in the articulation of lay expertise—especially, the role of the Internet and digital tools in facilitating communication, exchange, and knowledge generation (Akrich 2010; Barker and Galardi 2011; Sosnowy 2014; Raz et al. 2018), though also in changing the nature of activism (Petersen et al. 2018). We know far less about the underlying background conditions and broad social and cultural changes that have given rise to the dispositions, competences, and forms of collective identity that have enabled the rise of lay expertise.[18] This deeper history calls out for investigation—ideally of a comparative sort, including cross-national comparisons but also, ideally, attuned to the dynamics of globalization as it affects the politics of knowledge (Leach et al. 2005). We also know relatively little about the loci for the germination of lay expertise beyond the well-studied examples related to health advocacy. What, for example, are the differences in how lay expertise is manifested when it is organized around the space of a cannabis dispensary (Penn 2014), among dieticians (Brady 2018) or in a community of amateur radio operators (Croidieu and Kim 2018), in "copwatching" accountability projects (Grace 2019), in the form of sex advice (Epstein 2022: 181–205), or among LGBT rights activists who advise immigration courts on asylum claims (Vogler 2021)?

In addition, surprisingly little research has examined precisely how lay experts succeed in overcoming what Shobita Parthasarathy (2010; 2017, 16) has called "expertise barriers" to successfully establish their legitimacy. How do they win a "seat at the table"? The question signals the importance of the presence or absence of basic resources, including access to education (Castilhos and Almeida 2018), but it also points to a wide range of possible pathways. My early article on lay expertise identified "four key mechanisms or tactics that [AIDS treatment] activists have pursued in constructing their credibility within biomedicine: the acquisition of cultural competence, the establishment of political representation, the yoking together of epistemological and ethical claims making, and the taking of sides in pre-existing methodological disputes" (Epstein 1995, 410). But I was vague on the question of how necessary or sufficient these mechanisms might be, let alone how generalizable they might be to other cases. A recent article by Croidieu and Kim (2018) is one of the few to take a similar approach in identifying credibility mechanisms for the construction of lay expertise. In their historical case study of amateur radio, they identify four conditions and argue that only when all four were present did the lay expertise of the amateurs come to be recognized as legitimate.

Further research might usefully investigate variations in the "intellectual opportunity structure"—defined by Tom Waidzunas (2013, 4; see also Frickel and Gross 2005) as "those aspects of a multi-institutional field of knowledge production that render it more or less vulnerable to the activity of social movements and [scientific/intellectual movements]." Which configurations best dispose lay experts to success?[19] For example, when credentialed experts suffer from a "credibility gap" because of a widespread perception that they have failed to solve an important social problem, lay experts might find their own authority enhanced (Epstein 1995, 411). Somewhat similarly, lay experts might find it easier to stage an intervention when they can convincingly attribute responsibility for a social problem to a specific group of credentialed experts. By contrast, when causes seem murkier and responsibility seems more widely diffused—an example might be cases of financial crisis—an inability to point the finger of blame in a compelling way might leave lay experts with a weaker epistemic foothold.[20] These examples suggest (*contra* Collins and Evans's (2002, 261–262) attempt to distinguish between a "political" and "technical" phase of scientific controversies) that the ongoing political framing of technical issues inevitably structures the pathways by which different groups assert their expertise and offer epistemic contributions.

Finally, relatively little research to date has considered how lay experts might seek to institutionalize their practices to ensure continuity over time (Myhre 2002, 19), or whether lay expertise tends, over time, toward formalization, professionalization, or bureaucratization (Thompson et al. 2012). All of the above aspects of the rise and trajectory of lay expertise would benefit from further investigation.

A different set of questions for future research concerns the various political and cultural effects, intended or otherwise, of the deployment of lay expertise. The following issues—which intersect in a variety of ways—all raise significant and, in some ways, troubling questions about the limits of lay expertise or its possible downstream consequences.

First, it has been suggested that lay expertise may be prone to a kind of narrow particularism that stands in the way of social action to promote the common good. For example, debates about illness-specific activism—especially in the United States—tend to position the various distinct patient groups as engaged in competition that is inevitably zero-sum (Kaiser 2015). Such activism, it would seem, almost necessarily pits different "disease constituencies" against one another as they vie for attention and their "piece of the pie" in the form of funding allocations from Congress and research grants from the National Institutes of Health (Best 2012). Thus the disease-based model of mobilization seems immediately to raise legitimate doubts about the prospects for opening up broader conversations, not only among those who confront different health challenges, but also between those who are healthy and those who are well. Yet I have argued elsewhere that on-the-ground examination of health advocacy reveals multiple points and pathways of linkage, "sometimes broadening the outlook of patient groups, bridging the gaps between them, and/or connecting them with other sorts of health movements" (Epstein 2016, 247). More generally, there is an important opportunity to study the circumstances under which different groups of lay experts, working on different problems, might find common cause; to identify the mechanisms that facilitate their collaboration; and to consider the consequences (both political and epistemic) of such cooperation.

Second, there is much yet to be learned about the degree to which lay expertise contributes to genuine innovation and radical change. As Eyal and coauthors have asked: When and why do lay experts proceed to "[plug] into existing networks," and when and why do they "[take] the existing network of expertise apart and [weave] a wholly new and alternative network of knowledge production and dissemination" (Eyal et al. 2010, 170)? Interestingly, the same examples may lead different scholars to different conclusions. For example, although I think they have posed an excellent question, I believe Eyal and coauthors inaccurately associated AIDS activists solely with the former approach: plugging into existing networks. I would agree with Jennifer Brady, who recently observed in a discussion of my work and theirs: "the network of biomedicine and the network to which AIDS activists belonged were both transformed and stabilized in new ways as they were induced into being with a newly assembled network" (Brady 2018, 130).

Third, it is worth worrying about the prospect that the rise of lay expertise—even while challenging old hierarchies—may nonetheless place us further under the sway of systems of expert knowledge and technologies, ultimately expanding their reach (Epstein 1991; Eyal 2013a, 876). For example, lay experts may sometimes challenge specific medical facts or explanations even while strengthening the presupposition that a given problem is best viewed and addressed in medical terms to begin with. Yet, lay experts do sometimes succeed in adopting conventional frameworks in a provisional and strategic way, while resisting closure or reification. Further research can help identify the situations that promote or restrict epistemic openness of this sort.

Fourth, yet another concern is that the development of lay expertise may, in effect, feed into the neoliberal state's devolution of responsibility to individuals, who are now expected to fend for themselves by seeking out and assessing information (Sosnowy 2014). Such developments raise the prospect of a democratization of expertise in the absence of genuine empowerment, and with diminished possibilities of holding traditional experts or governments to account. Further study might seek to distinguish between situations that leave lay experts to their own devices and those that entangle lay experts in productive relationships with scientific and political authorities.

Fifth, much concern has rightly been expressed about the cooptation or hijacking of lay expertise by corporate interests (Barker 2011; Davis and Abraham 2011; Segal 2018). Scholars have pointed to instances of outright manipulation of patients in order to coopt them, for example through the creation by pharmaceutical companies of "front groups" masquerading as patient advocacy groups that are intended to build demand for a company's products or garner support for drug approval (Zavestoski et al. 2004, 274; Segal 2018). However, this extreme case is one end of a continuum of relations to pharmaceutical companies, described by Orla O'Donovan (2007), that also includes many other instances in which patient groups receive pharmaceutical industry financing. Indeed, Alan Petersen and coauthors (2018, 11) cite research published in the *New England Journal of Medicine* in 2017 that "found that among 104 of the largest patient activist organisations based in the United States, over 83 per cent received financial support from drug, device and biotechnology companies, and at least 39 per cent had a current or previous industry executive on the governing board." Such figures are sobering. Still, O'Donovan (2007) rightly has cautioned against any automatic assumptions of a creeping "corporate colonisation," calling for detailed study of whether corporations indeed have increased their influence over the "cultures of action" of patient groups. It is important to ask whether symbiotic relationships between lay expert groups and industry may sometimes usefully magnify lay voices and extend the impact of their message—but also whether the authenticity of the lay expert perspective can be maintained in such situations. It is also worth noting that lay experts have themselves been among the sharpest critics of both pharmaceutical industry influence on drug approvals and an undue deference to the anecdotal reports of individual patients who presume that their own positive experiences with therapies are generalizable.[21]

A final issue concerns the sharp dilemmas posed in the current political moment, sometimes inaccurately characterized as one of "post-truth," when it seems that facts and expertise are under attack to an unprecedented and dangerous degree. As Eyal (2019) has observed, this crisis of expertise has been long in development, and it reflects the paradoxical coincidence of a sharp suspicion of experts and a simultaneous profound dependence on expertise. In such a climate of doubt, it is reasonable to worry that the promotion of lay expertise may add fuel to the fire by further encouraging the widespread suspicion and distrust of expert authority (Epstein and Timmermans 2021). Although the concern is legitimate, I suspect that pinning the blame for the spread of antiscience attitudes on the proliferation of lay expertise is both unfair and an inaccurate diagnosis. Moreover, as Parthasarathy (2018) has argued, if the past exclusion of marginalized voices has contributed to citizens' distrust of experts, then the successful development of lay expertise via the incorporation of outsiders may in the long run actually help shore up the general faith in expertise. Here again, we need to resist easy conclusions and undertake more research.

These are critical questions raised by the impressive rise to prominence of the hybrid and collective forms of epistemic action reviewed in this chapter. In my view, it is precisely the significance of these broadly political questions that makes it imperative to continue studying the potently oxymoronic phenomenon called lay expertise.

ACKNOWLEDGMENTS

I am grateful to Gil Eyal for insightful comments and suggestions on a previous draft.

NOTES

1. I generated this graph using the Google Ngram Viewer (https://books.google.com/ngrams) on January 13, 2022. Ngrams are produced through an algorithm that searches the extensive collection of books digitized in Google Books (through the publication year 2019, as of the date of my search). Each Ngram takes the form of a graph over time of occurrences of phrases, expressed as a percentage of all phrases of the same word length

catalogued in the Google Books database, with results normalized by the total number of such books published each year. See https://books.google.com/ngrams/info (accessed January 13, 2022). While Ngrams have become a popular illustrative tool, I believe that scholars should use them with some caution, not only because of potential pitfalls (Zhang, 2015), but also because Google does not make the details of their proprietary algorithm available for scrutiny.

2. By contrast, "lay expert" appears in fewer of the scholarly journal articles indexed in Sociological Abstracts.

3. I obtained this figure by performing a search at the website of SAGE, the journal's publisher, at https://journals.sagepub.com/search/advanced?SeriesKey=pusa (accessed January 13, 2022).

4. Lay expertise has also been discussed in foreign language journals—see, for example, Akrich and Rabeharisoa (2012) on "l'expertise profane" and Castilhos and Almeida (2018) on "expertise leiga"—but I have not attempted to track such literature systematically.

5. However, the phrase "lay expert" had appeared in academic articles earlier.

6. My endnote suggested that the reader should "see also Di Chiro (1992) on lay expertise in the environmental justice movement" (Epstein 1995, 431). However, I now see that Di Chiro herself did not use the term "lay expertise."

7. For reflections on these issues, I am indebted to Chandra Mukerji and the students in a graduate seminar I co-taught with her in 2002 on the topic of formal and informal knowledge.

8. On this point, see also Horlick-Jones (2004, 110).

9. My discussion of Collins and Evans borrows from but also extends beyond my views as presented in Epstein (2011). Here, I mostly leave aside the normative dimensions of their project, which have been subject to much discussion and critique (see Jasanoff 2003; Wynne 2003).

10. As I have noted elsewhere, "the shorthand phrase 'Epstein's AIDS activists' employs the grammatical possessive in a way that, I confess, makes me somewhat uncomfortable, [and] I would certainly want to disavow any claims to 'ownership' of the AIDS treatment activists I studied in the late 1980s and early 1990s" (Epstein 2011, 324).

11. Thus, in Strassheim's (2015, 326) terms, the "epistemic authority" of experts is inextricably tied to their "political authority." This view contrasts sharply with that of Collins and Evans (2002, 2007), who seek to shore up the boundaries between the epistemic and political dimensions of decision-making in relation to technoscientific controversies.

12. On the different valences of "security," see Lakoff and Collier (2008).

13. I am grateful to Gil Eyal for this suggestion and for discussion of this issue.

14. Of course, the rise of modern science was itself marked by much debate about the reliance on experience and the relation between experience and other methods for knowing the natural world. See Shapin (1990, 995–996); Dear (1995).

15. This article was published in French, but I am quoting from the published English translation of the abstract.

16. I do not mean entirely to equate "evidence-based activism" with "embodied health movements." For one view of how they may differ, by proponents of the former term, see Rabeharisoa et al. (2014, 122).

17. On the boundary-crossing character of health movements, see also Archibald (2010); Epstein (2008, 506; 2010; 2016, 251); Wolfson (2001).

18. For some reflections on relevant background changes in the biomedical domain, see Epstein (2008, 500–504).
19. On "timing and opportunities" as a key dimension of the enactment of expertise, see also Strassheim (2015, 327).
20. I am grateful to the PhD students in my Politics of Knowledge seminar (Spring 2019) for helping me think through these issues and for suggesting some of these points.
21. See, for example, http://www.treatmentactiongroup.org/content/false-hope-right-to-try, dated March 5, 2018 (accessed August 21, 2019).

REFERENCES

Akrich, Madeleine. 2010. "From Communities of Practice to Epistemic Communities: Health Mobilizations on the Internet." *Sociological Research Online* 15 (2). https://www.socresonline.org.uk/15/2/10.html.

Akrich, Madeleine, and Vololona Rabeharisoa. 2012. "L'expertise profane dans les associations de patients, un outil de démocratie sanitaire." *Santé Publique* 24 (1): 69–74.

Allen, Barbara L. 2003. *Uneasy Alchemy: Citizens and Experts in Louisiana's Chemical Corridor Disputes*. Cambridge, MA: MIT Press.

Archibald, Matthew E. 2010. "Sources of Self-Help Movement Legitimation." In *Social Movements and the Transformation of American Health Care*, edited by Jane Banaszak-Holl, Sandra Levitsky, and Mayer N. Zald, 227–245. Oxford: Oxford University Press.

Arksey, Hilary 1994. "Expert and Lay Participation in the Construction of Medical Knowledge." *Sociology of Health & Illness* 16 (4): 448–468.

Arksey, Hilary. 1998. *RSI and the Experts: The Construction of Medical Knowledge*. London: UCL Press.

Armstrong, David. 2014. "Actors, Patients and Agency: A Recent History." *Sociology of Health & Illness* 36 (2): 163–174.

Barker, Kristin. 2011. "Listening to Lyrica: Contested Illnesses and Pharmaceutical Determinism." *Social Science & Medicine* 73:833–842.

Barker, Kristin K., and Tasha R. Galardi. 2011. "Dead by 50: Lay Expertise and Breast Cancer Screening." *Social Science & Medicine* 72:1351–1358.

Best, Rachel Kahn. 2012. "Disease Politics and Medical Research Funding: Three Ways Advocacy Shapes Policy." *American Sociological Review* 77 (5): 780–803.

Brady, Jennifer. 2018. "Toward a Critical, Feminist Sociology of Expertise." *Journal of Professions and Organizations* 5:123–138.

Brown, Phil. 1992. "Popular Epidemiology and Toxic Waste Contamination: Lay and Professional Ways of Knowing." *Journal of Health and Social Behavior* 33:267–281.

Brown, Phil, Rachel Morello-Frosch, Stephen Zavestoski, Laura Senier, Rebecca Gasior Altman, Elizabeth Hoover, et al. 2011. "Health Social Movements: Advancing Traditional Medical Sociology Concepts." In *Handbook of the Sociology of Health, Illness, and Healing*, edited by Bernice A. Pescosolido, Jack K. Martin, Jane D. McLeod, and Anne Rogers, 117–137. New York: Springer.

Brown, Phil, and Stephen Zavestoski. 2004. "Social Movements in Health: An Introduction." *Sociology of Health & Illness* 26 (6): 679–694.

Brown, Phil, Stephen Zavestoski, Sabrina McCormick, Brian Mayer, Rachel Morello-Frosch, and Rebecca Gasior Altman. 2004. "Embodied Health Movements: New Approaches to Social Movements in Health." *Sociology of Health & Illness* 26 (1): 50–80.

Buchbinder, Mara, and Stefan Timmermans. 2014. "Affective Economies and the Politics of Saving Babies' Lives." *Public Culture* 26 (1): 101–126.

Callon, Michel. 2003. "The Increasing Involvement of Concerned Groups in R&D Policies: What Lessons for Public Powers?" In *Science and Innovation: Rethinking the Rationales for Funding and Governance*, edited by Aldo Geuna, Ammon J. Salter, and W. Edward Steinmueller, 30–68. Cheltenham, UK: Edward Elgar.

Callon, Michel. 2005. "Disabled Persons of All Countries, Unite!" In *Making Things Public: Atmospheres of Democracy*, edited by Bruno Latour and Peter Weibel, 308–313. Cambridge, MA: MIT Press.

Callon, Michel, Pierre Lascoumes, and Yannick Barthe. 2009. *Acting in an Uncertain World: An Essay on Technical Democracy*. Cambridge, MA: MIT Press.

Callon, Michel, and Vololona Rabeharisoa. 2003. "Research 'in the Wild' and the Shaping of New Social Identities." *Technology in Society* 25 (2): 193–204.

Cambrosio, Alberto, Camille Limoges, and Eric Hoffman. 1992. "Expertise as a Network: A Case Study of the Controversy over the Environmental Release of Genetically Engineered Organisms." In *The Culture and Power of Knowledge: Inquiries into Contemporary Societies*, edited by Nico Stehr and Richard V. Ericson, 341–361. Berlin: Walter de Gruyter.

Campbell, Patricia Ann. 2016. "Public Participation, Mediated Expertise, and Reflexivity: How Multiple Medical Realities Are Negotiated in Runners' Self(Care) Practices." PhD diss., University of Calgary.

Carr, E. Summerson. 2010. "Enactments of Expertise." *Annual Review of Anthropology* 39:17–32.

Castilhos, Washington L. C., and Carla S. Almeida. 2018. "A expertise leiga vale para todos? O lugar das mulheres afetadas no debate sobre zika-microcefalia-aborto na imprensa brasileira." *Journal of Science Communication - América Latina* 1 (1): Y02. https://doi.org/10.22323/3.01010402.

Chilvers, Jason, and Matthew Kearnes. 2016. *Remaking Participation: Science, Environment and Emergent Publics*. London: Routledge.

Collins, Harry, Martin Weinel, and Robert Evans. 2010. "The Politics and Policy of the Third Wave: New Technologies and Society." *Critical Policy Studies* 4 (2): 185–201.

Collins, Harry M., and Robert Evans. 2002. "The Third Wave of Science Studies: Studies of Expertise and Experience." *Social Studies of Science* 32 (2): 235–296.

Collins, Harry M., and Robert Evans. 2007. *Rethinking Expertise*. Chicago: University of Chicago Press.

Croidieu, Grégoire, and Phillip H. Kim. 2018. "Labor of Love: Amateurs and Lay-Expertise Legitimation in the Early U.S. Radio Field." *Administrative Science Quarterly* 63 (1): 1–42.

Davis, Courtney, and John Abraham. 2011. "Rethinking Innovation Accounting in Pharmaceutical Regulation: A Case Study in the Deconstruction of Therapeutic Advance and Therapeutic Breakthrough." *Science, Technology, & Human Values* 36 (6): 791–815.

Dear, Peter. 1995. *Discipline and Experience: The Mathematical Way in the Scientific Revolution*. Chicago: University of Chicago Press.

Delbourgo, James. 2012. "Listing People." *Isis* 103 (4): 735–742.

Di Chiro, Giovanna. 1992. "Defining Environmental Justice: Women's Voices and Grassroots Politics." *Socialist Review*, Oct–Dec, 93–130.

Elam, Mark, and Margareta Bertilsson. 2003. "Consuming, Engaging and Confronting Science: The Emerging Dimensions of Scientific Citizenship." *European Journal of Social Theory* 6 (2): 233–251.

Elbaz, Gilbert. 1992. "The Sociology of AIDS Activism, the Case of ACT UP/New York, 1987–1992. PhD diss., City University of New York.

Epstein, Steven. 1991. "Democratic Science? AIDS Activism and the Contested Construction of Knowledge." *Socialist Review* 91 (2): 35–64.

Epstein, Steven. 1995. "The Construction of Lay Expertise: AIDS Activism and the Forging of Credibility in the Reform of Clinical Trials." *Science, Technology & Human Values* 20 (4): 408–437.

Epstein, Steven. 1996. *Impure Science: AIDS, Activism, and the Politics of Knowledge.* Berkeley: University of California Press.

Epstein, Steven. 2008. "Patient Groups and Health Movements." In *The Handbook of Science and Technology Studies,* edited by Edward. J. Hackett, Olga Amsterdamska, Michael Lynch, and Judy Wajcman, 499–539. Cambridge, MA: MIT Press.

Epstein, Steven. 2010. "The Strength of Diverse Ties: Multiple Hybridity in the Politics of Inclusion and Difference in U.S. Biomedical Research." In *Social Movements and the Transformation of American Health Care,* edited by Jane Banaszak-Holl, Sandra Levitsky, and Mayer N. Zald, 79–95. Oxford: Oxford University Press.

Epstein, Steven. 2011. "Misguided Boundary Work in Studies of Expertise: Time to Return to the Evidence. " *Critical Policy Studies* 5 (3): 324–329.

Epstein, Steven. 2016. "The Politics of Health Mobilization in the United States: The Promise and Pitfalls of 'Disease Constituencies.' " *Social Science & Medicine* 165:246–254.

Epstein, Steven. 2022. *The Quest for Sexual Health: How an Elusive Ideal Has Transformed Science, Politics, and Everyday Life.* Chicago: University of Chicago Press.

Epstein, Steven, and Stefan Timmermans. 2021. "From Medicine to Health: The Proliferation and Diversification of Cultural Authority." *Journal of Health and Social Behavior* 62:240–254.

Escoffier, Jeffrey. 1999. "The Invention of Safer Sex: Vernacular Knowledge, Gay Politics, and HIV Prevention." *Berkeley Journal of Sociology* 43:1–30.

Evans, Robert, and Alexandra Plows. 2007. "Listening without Prejudice? Re-discovering the Value of the Disinterested Citizen." *Social Studies of Science* 37 (6): 827–853.

"An Expert Opinion." 1913. *Wall Street Journal,* p. 1.

Eyal, Gil. 2013a. "For a Sociology of Expertise: The Social Origins of the Autism Epidemic." *American Journal of Sociology* 118 (4): 863–907.

Eyal, Gil. 2013b. "Spaces between Fields." In *Pierre Bourdieu and Historical Analysis,* edited by Philip S. Gorski, 158–182. Durham, NC: Duke University Press.

Eyal, Gil. 2019. *The Crisis of Expertise.* Cambridge, UK: Polity.

Eyal, Gil, Brendan Hart, Emin Onculer, Neta Oren, and Natasha Rossi. 2010. *The Autism Matrix: The Social Origins of the Autism Epidemic.* Cambridge, UK: Polity.

Fischer, Frank. 2009. *Democracy and Expertise: Reorienting Policy Inquiry.* Oxford: Oxford University Press.

Foucault, Michel. 1980. *Power/Knowledge.* New York: Pantheon.

Frickel, Scott, and Neil Gross. 2005. "A General Theory of Scientific/Intellectual Movements." *American Sociological Review* 70 (2): 204–232.

Geertz, Clifford. 1983. *Local Knowledge: Further Essays in Interpretive Anthropology.* New York: Basic Books.

Gibbon, Sahra. 2007. *Breast Cancer Genes and the Gendering of Knowledge: Science and Citizenship in the Cultural Context of the "New" Genetics*. Basingstoke, UK: Palgrave MacMillan.

Gollust, Sara E., Kira Apse, Barbara. P. Fuller, Paul Steven Miller, and Barbara B. Biesecker. 2005. "Community Involvement in Developing Policies for Genetic Testing: Assessing the Interests and Experiences of Individuals Affected by Genetic Conditions." *American Journal of Public Health* 95 (1): 35–41.

Grace, Prince. 2019. "The People's Facts: Community-Based Monitoring and the Politics of Public Knowledge." Unpublished manuscript.

Gould, Deborah B. 2009. *Moving Politics: Emotion and ACT UP's Fight against AIDS*. Chicago: University of Chicago Press.

Grundmann, Reiner. 2017. "The Problem of Expertise in Knowledge Societies." *Minerva* 55 (1): 25–48.

Grundy, John, and Miriam Smith. 2007. "Activist Knowledges in Queer Politics." *Economy and Society* 36 (2): 294–317.

Gudowky, Niklas, and Mahshid Sotoudeh. 2017. "Into Blue Skies—a Transdisciplinary Foresight and Co-creation Method for Adding Robustness to Visioneering." *Nanoethics* 11:93–106.

Hacking, Nick, and Andrew Flynn. 2018. "Protesting against Neoliberal and Illiberal Governmentalities: A Comparative Analysis of Waste Governance in the UK and China." *Political Geography* 63: 31–42.

Hall, Matthew, Sarah Grogan, and Brendan Gough. 2016. "Bodybuilders' Accounts of Synthol Use: The Construction of Lay Expertise Online." *Journal of Health Psychology* 21 (9): 1939–1948.

Haraway, Donna. 1988. "Situated Knowledges: The Science Question in Feminism and the Privilege of Partial Perspective." *Feminist Studies* 14 (3): 575–599.

Harding, Sandra. 1986. *The Science Question in Feminism*. Ithaca, NY: Cornell University Press.

Heath, Deborah, Rayna Rapp, and Karen-Sue. Taussig. 2004. "Genetic Citizenship." In *A Companion to the Anthropology of Politics*, edited by David Nugent and Joan Vincent, 152–167. London: Blackwell.

Heritage, John, and Douglas W. Maynard. 2006. "Problems and Prospects in the Study of Physician-Patient Interaction: 30 Years of Research." *Annual Review of Sociology* 32:351–374.

Hess, David J. 2004. "Guest Editorial: Health, the Environment and Social Movements." *Science as Culture* 13 (4): 421–427.

Horlick-Jones, Tom. 2004. "Experts in Risk? . . . Do They Exist?" Editorial. *Health, Risk & Society* 6 (2): 107–114.

Irwin, Alan. 1995. *Citizen Science: A Study of People, Expertise and Sustainable Development*. London: Routledge.

Irwin, Alan. 2001. "Constructing the Scientific Citizen: Science and Democracy in the Biosciences." *Public Understanding of Science* 10 (1): 1–18.

Jasanoff, Sheila. 2003. "Breaking the Waves in Science Studies: Comment on H. M. Collins and Robert Evans, 'The Third Wave of Science Studies.'" *Social Studies of Science* 33 (3): 389–400.

Jasanoff, Sheila. 2017. "Science and Democracy." In *The Handbook of Science and Technology Studies*, edited by Ulrike Felt, Rayvon Fouché, Clark A. Miller, and Laurel Smith-Doerr, 259–287. Cambridge, MA: MIT Press.

Jauffret-Roustide, Marie 2009. "Self-Support for Drug Users in the Context of Harm Reduction Policy: A Lay Expertise Defined by Drug Users' Life Skills and Citizenship." *Health Sociology Review* 18 (2): 159–172.

Kaiser, Jocelyn. 2015. "What Does a Disease Deserve?" *Science* 350 (6263): 900–902.

Kelty, Christopher, Aaron Panofsky, Morgan Currie, Roderic Crooks, Seth Erickson, Patricia Garcia, et al. 2015. "Seven Dimensions of Contemporary Participation Disentangled." *Journal for the Association of Information Science and Technology* 66 (3): 474–488.

Kempner, Joanna, and John Bailey. 2019. "Collective Self-Experimentation in Patient-Led Research: How Online Health Communities Foster Innovation." *Social Science & Medicine*. Epub, June 12. https://doi.org/10.1016/j.socscimed.2019.112366.

Kuchinskaya, Olga. 2011. "Articulating the Signs of Danger: Lay Experiences of Post-Chernobyl Radiation Risks and Effects." *Public Understanding of Science* 20 (3): 405–421.

Lakoff, Andrew, and Stephen J. Collier. 2008. *Biosecurity Interventions: Global Health and Security in Question*. New York: Columbia University Press.

Landzelius, Kyra, and Joe Dumit. 2006. "Patient Organization Movements." Special issue. *Social Science & Medicine* 62 (3): 529–792.

Lappé, Martine D. 2014. "Taking Care: Anticipation, Extraction and the Politics of Temporality in Autism Science." *BioSocieties* 9:304–328.

Laurent, Brice. 2016. "Political Experiments That Matter: Ordering Democracy from Experimental Sites." *Social Studies of Science* 46 (5): 773–794.

"Lay Expert Urged for School Board." 1928. *New York Times*, p. 33.

Leach, Melissa, Ian Scoones, and Brian Wynne. 2005. *Science and Citizens: Globalization and the Challenge of Engagement*. London: Zed Books.

Lewenstein, Bruce. 2003. Editorial. *Public Understanding of Science* 12:357–358.

MacKendrick, Norah A. 2010. "Media Framing of Body Burdens: Precautionary Consumption and the Individualization of Risk." *Sociological Inquiry* 80 (1): 126–149.

Maslen, Sarah, and Deborah Lupton. 2019. "'Keeping It Real': Women's Enactments of Lay Health Knowledges and Expertise on Facebook." *Sociology of Health & Illness* 41:1637–1651.

McCormick, Sandra, Phil Brown, and Stephen Zavestoski. 2003. "The Personal Is Scientific, the Scientific Is Political: The Public Paradigm of the Environmental Breast Cancer Movement." *Sociological Forum* 18 (4): 545–576.

Moreira, Tiago, Orla O'Donovan, and Etaoine Howlett. 2014. "Assembling Dementia Care: Patient Organisations and Social Research." *BioSocieties* 9 (2): 173–193.

Morello-Frosch, Rachel, Stephen Zavestoski, Phil Brown, Rebecca Gasior Altman, Sabrina McCormick, and Brian Mayer. 2006. "Embodied Health Movements: Response to a 'Scientized' World." In *The New Political Sociology of Science: Institutions, Networks, and Power*, edited by Scott Frickel and Kelly Moore, 244–271. Madison: University of Wisconsin Press.

Mukerji, Chandra. 2006. "Tacit Knowledge and Classical Technique in Seventeenth-Century France: Hydraulic Cement as a Living Practice among Masons and Military Engineers." *Technology and Culture* 47 (4): 713–733.

Murphy, Michelle. 2004. "Occupational Health from Below: The Women's Office Workers' Movement and the Hazardous Office." In *Emerging Illnesses and Society: Negotiating the Public Health*, edited by Randall M. Packard, Peter J. Brown, Ruth L. Berkelman, and Howard Frumkin, 191–223. Baltimore, MD: Johns Hopkins University Press.

Murphy, Michelle. 2006. *Sick Building Syndrome and the Problem of Uncertainty: Environmental Politics, Technoscience, and Women Workers*. Durham, NC: Duke University Press.

Murphy, Michelle. 2012. *Seizing the Means of Reproduction: Entanglements of Feminism, Health, and Technoscience*. Durham, NC: Duke University Press.

Myhre, Jennifer Reid. 2002. "Medical Mavens: Gender, Science, and the Consensus Politics of Breast Cancer Activism." PhD diss., University of California, Davis.

Nguyen, Vinh-Kim. 2005. "Antiretroviral Globalism, Biopolitics, and Therapeutic Citizenship." In *Global Assemblages: Technology, Politics, and Ethics as Anthropological Problems*, edited by Aihwa Ong and Stephen J. Collier, 124–144. Malden, MA: Blackwell.

Nyerges, Timothy, and Robert W. Aguirre. 2011. "Public Participation in Analytic-Deliberative Decision Making: Evaluating a Large-Group Online Field Experiment." *Annals of the Association of American Geographers* 101 (3): 561–586.

O'Donovan, Orla. 2007. "Corporate Colonization of Health Activism? Irish Health Advocacy Organizations' Modes of Engagement with the Pharmaceutical Industry." *International Journal of Health Services* 37 (4): 711–733.

Obituary: Albert Andre Galli. 2005. *Reno Gazette*, p. C13.

Panofsky, Aaron. 2011. "Generating Sociability to Drive Science: Patient Advocacy Organizations and Genetics Research." *Social Studies of Science* 41 (1): 31–57.

Parthasarathy, Shobita. 2010. "Breaking the Expertise Barrier: Understanding Activist Strategies in Science and Technology Policy Domains." *Science and Public Policy* 37 (5): 355–367.

Parthasarathy, Shobita. 2017. *Patent Politics: Life Forms, Markets, and the Public Interest in the United States and Europe*. Chicago: University of Chicago Press.

Parthasarathy, Shobita. 2018. "Public Trust and the Politics of Knowledge in the 'Post-Truth' Era." Conference presentation, annual Meeting of the American Sociological Association. Philadelphia, PA, August 14.

Penn, Rebecca A. 2014. "Establishing Expertise: Canadian Community-Based Medical Cannabis Dispensaries as embodied Health Movement Organisations." *International Journal of Drug Policy* 25:372–377.

Petersen, Alan, Allegra Clare Schermuly, and Alison Anderson. 2018. "The Shifting Politics of Patient Activism: From Bio-sociality to Bio-digital Citizenship." *Health*. Epub, December 7. https://doi.org/10.1177/1363459318815944.

Petryna, Adriana. 2002. *Life Exposed: Biological Citizens after Chernobyl*. Princeton NJ: Princeton University Press.

Polanyi, Michael. 1958. *Personal Knowledge: Towards a Post-critical Philosophy*. Chicago: University of Chicago Press.

Pols, Jeannette. 2014. "Knowing Patients: Turning Patient Knowledge into Science." *Science, Technology & Human Values* 39 (1): 73–97.

Prior, Lindsay. 2003. "Belief, Knowledge and Expertise: The Emergence of the Lay Expert in Medical Sociology." *Sociology of Health & Illness* 25 (3): 41–57.

Rabeharisoa, Vololona, Tiago Moreira, and Madeleine Akrich. 2014. "Evidence-based Activism: Patients', Users' and Activists' Groups in Knowledge Society." *BioSocieties* 9 (2): 111–128.

Raz, Aviad, Yael Amano, and Stefan Timmermans. 2018. "Parents like Me: Biosociality and Lay Expertise in Self-Help Groups of Parents of Screen-Positive Newborns." *New Genetics and Society* 37 (2): 97–116.

Rose, Nikolas, and Carlos Novas. 2005. "Biological Citizenship." In *Global Assemblages: Technology, Politics, and Ethics as Anthropological Problems*, edited by Aihwa Ong and Stephen J. Collier, 439–463. Malden, MA: Blackwell.

Scott, Joan. 1991. "The Evidence of Experience." *Critical Inquiry* 17 (4): 773–797.

Segal, Judy Z. 2005. *Health and the Rhetoric of Medicine.* Carbondale: Southern Illinois University Press.

Segal, Judy Z. 2018. "Sex, Drugs, and Rhetoric: The Case of Flibanserin for 'Female Sexual Dysfunction.'" *Social Studies of Science* 48 (4): 459–482.

Shapin, Steven. 1990. "Science and the Public." In *Companion to the History of Modern Science,* edited by R.C. Olby, G.N. Cantor, J.R.R. Christie, and M.J.S. Hodge, 990–1007. London: Routledge.

Sharma, Ratika, Britta Wigginton, Carla Meurk, Pauline Ford, and Coral E. Gartner. 2017. "Motivations and Limitations Associated with Vaping among People with Mental Illness: A Qualitative Analysis of Reddit Discussions." *International Journal of Environmental Research and Public Health* 14 (7): 1–15.

Shaw, Ian. 2002. "How Lay Are Lay Beliefs?" *Health* 6 (3): 287–299.

Shim, Janet K. 2005. "Constructing 'Race' across the Science-Lay Divide: Racial Formation in the Epidemiology and Experience of Cardiovascular Disease." *Social Studies of Science* 35 (3): 405–436.

Sosnowy, Collette. 2014. "Practicing Patienthood Online: Social Media, Chronic Illness, and Lay Expertise." *Societies* 4:316–329.

Strassheim, Holger. 2015. "Politics and Policy Expertise: Towards a Political Epistemology." In *Handbook of Critical Policy Studies,* edited by Frank Fischer, Douglas Torgerson, Anna Durnová, and Michael Orsini, 319–340. Cheltenham, UK: Edward Elgar.

Thompson, Jill, Paul Bissell, Cindy Cooper, Chris J. Armitage, and Rosemary Barber. 2012. "Credibility and the 'Professionalized' Lay Expert: Reflections on the Dilemmas and Opportunities of Public Involvement in Health Research." *Health* 16 (6): 602–618.

Vogler, Stefan. 2021. *Sorting Sexualities: Expertise and the Politics of Legal Classification.* Chicago: University of Chicago Press.

Waidzunas, Tom J. 2013. "Intellectual Opportunity Structures and Science-Targeted Activism: Influence of the Ex-gay Movement on the Science of Sexual Orientation." *Mobilization* 18 (1): 1–18.

Wentzell, Emily. 2015. "Medical Research Participation as Citizenship: Modeling Modern Masculinity and Marriage in a Mexican Sexual Health Study." *American Anthropologist* 117 (4): 652–664.

Williams, Gareth, and Jennie Popay. 1994. "Lay Knowledge and the Privilege of Experience." In *Challenging Medicine,* edited by Jonathan Gabe, David Kelleher, and Gareth Williams, 118–139. London: Routledge.

Williams, Logan D. A., and Sharlissa Moore. 2019. "Guest Editorial: Conceptualizing Justice and Counter-Expertise." *Science as Culture* 28 (3): 251–276.

Wolfson, Mark. 2001. *The Fight against Big Tobacco: The Movement, the State, and the Public's Health.* New York: Aldine de Gruyter.

Wylie, Alison. 2003. "Why Standpoint Matters." In *Science and Other Cultures,* edited by R. Figueroa and S. Harding, 26–48. New York: Routledge.

Wynne, Brian. 1992. "Misunderstood Misunderstanding: Social Identities and Public Uptake of Science." *Public Understanding of Science* 1 (3): 281–304.

Wynne, Brian. 2003. "Seasick on the Third Wave? Subverting the Hegemony of Propositionalism: Response to Collins and Evans (2002)." *Social Studies of Science* 33 (3): 401–417.

Yli-Pelkonen, Vesa, and Johanna Kohl. 2005. "The Role of Local Ecological Knowledge in Sustainable Urban Planning: Perspectives from Finland." *Sustainability: Science, Practice, and Policy* 1 (1): 3–14.

Zavestoski, Stephen, Rachel Morello-Frosch, Phil Brown, Brian Mayer, Sabrina McCormick, and Rebecca Gasior Altman. 2004. "Embodied Health Movements and Challenges to the Dominant Epidemiological Paradigm." In *Authority in Contention: Research in Social Movements, Conflicts and Change*, vol. 25, edited by Daniel J. Myers and Daniel M. Cress, 253–278. Amsterdam: Elsevier.

Zhang, Sarah. 2015. "The Pitfalls of Using Google Ngram to Study Language." Wired. https://www.wired.com/2015/10/pitfalls-of-studying-language-with-google-ngram/.

Zorn, Eric. 1990. "Crusader Wields Just the Ticket: Hometowns." *Chicago Tribune*, p. D1B.

5

ON THE MULTIPLICITY OF LAY EXPERTISE: AN EMPIRICAL AND ANALYTICAL OVERVIEW OF PATIENT ASSOCIATIONS' ACHIEVEMENTS AND CHALLENGES

MADELEINE AKRICH AND
VOLOLONA RABEHARISOA

INTRODUCTION

THE notion of the "expert patient" has become quite prominent in recent years. In many countries, patients are invited to sit on committees with biomedical specialists and to share their expertise on diseases and health problems with various institutions. This stands in stark contrast with the medical paternalism that prevailed not so long ago. How did this come to pass? What is the nature of the patient expertise that is being solicited? How have health policies changed as a result? These are the questions we examine in this chapter. In light of previous and recent fieldwork that we have done, and a selection of case studies reported in the literature, our objective is to revisit a constellation of notions such as "expert patient," "lay expert," "lay expertise," "experiential knowledge," and "expert of experience" that are not only analytical tools for science and technology studies (STS) scholars and social scientists, but also part and parcel of today's institutional parlance.

Our focus is on patient expertise in the context of actions undertaken by patient associations. It was, indeed, in this context that the notion of "patient expertise" emerged. We define a patient association as a nonprofit organization that brings together individuals with concerns related to a specific disease, disability, or health problem (i.e., those who are directly affected and the people close to them, such as relatives and friends). A few points should be stressed here:

- Saying that a patient association is an organization implies that its functioning is formally defined and that it obeys rules, although these can differ across countries; informal groups that emerge through social networks, for example, are not patient associations. It also means that a patient association explicitly endorses specific missions that play an important role in the orientation of its actions, and that can evolve over time. The missions of a patient association can range from providing mutual support to defending its members' rights and interests to waging war on a disease, which involves seeking not only a cure but also appropriate care and sound medical practices.
- Saying that it is a *patient* organization implies that concerned people as just defined (patients, relatives and friends) play a major role in the organization, in contrast to certain patient groups that have been created and run by professionals. We consider a genuine patient association to have internal decision-making power, even if it has a scientific and medical advisory board or occasionally seeks advice from professionals.

In what follows, we will draw upon empirical studies that we have accumulated over the last fifteen years, mainly, though not exclusively, in France, concerning patient associations as we have just defined them. In these studies, we have deployed different methodologies: questionnaires filled in by representatives from several hundreds of patient associations, interviews with key members of patient associations, participation in events or activities involving these organizations, document analysis, and focus groups. We focus here on a limited number of organizations that nevertheless are quite varied in their sizes, ages, resources, and the types of health issues they are concerned with. Later, we discuss the general lessons from our research findings.

Analyzing patient expertise implies examining how patients become experts. Experts have the experience and knowledge necessary to assess a specific situation and to propose ways to improve it. By extension, expertise is also what experts produce in the form of assessments and propositions. Expertise is intended for specific audiences (e.g., institutions that commission the expertise, actors who must be convinced of the relevance of a proposition, etc.), and is oriented toward action. One question immediately arises: How can one be sure that an individual has the experience and knowledge necessary to make him or her an expert? Recognition of expert status can be more formal or less formal, but it is often based on professional credentials that provide evidence that the candidate expert has mastered a recognized body of knowledge and has significant experience relevant to the issues at stake. How, then, can patients be considered experts, when they often have no professional credentials in the medical and health sciences? The main point that we would like to document is that in order to be regarded as capable and legitimate experts, patients engage in intensive work to acquire competences and build specific bodies of knowledge.

In the 1990s, Steven Epstein's (1995) groundbreaking work on HIV/AIDS activists in the United States paved the way for novel inquiries into how lay people become experts. He coined the term "lay experts" to describe HIV/AIDS activists, who sought to arm themselves with as much knowledge as possible to help patients gain access to experimental treatments. Epstein showed that to be recognized by scientific experts and drug-regulation agencies as competent and legitimate interlocutors, these activists (a) familiarized themselves with the language and content of the biomedical literature; (b) wove together moral and epistemic arguments; and (c) took sides in controversies among opposing scientists on how clinical research should be conducted. Epstein used the term "therapeutic activism" to describe the actions of groups of "lay" people who decided to interfere with debates that were usually confined to the scientific and medical milieu. Janine Barbot (1998, 2002) and Nicolas Dodier (2003) described similar dynamics with regard to HIV/AIDS activism in France. Being acquainted with the scientific literature, these "lay experts" did not function merely as "interactional experts" (Collins and Evans 2002) discussing issues with scientists; more importantly, they managed to transform clinical practices and to involve activists as stakeholders in the design and monitoring of these practices.

Together with HIV/AIDS activist groups, rare-disease patient associations are considered a major source of inspiration for the development of contemporary health activism. As we described in our own work (Rabeharisoa and Callon 1999b) on the French Muscular Dystrophy Association (Association Française contre les Myopathies; AFM), the situation was a bit different from the one described in the case of HIV/AIDS: the AFM's involvement in research was aimed at mobilizing researchers to investigate diseases that nobody knew about in France in the 1980s. As with the HIV/AIDS activists, members of the AFM became acquainted with medical research through contacts with biologists and clinicians, visits to laboratories and medical consultations, and engagement with the scientific literature. Their conclusion was clear: research on muscular dystrophy was almost nonexistent, and very few clinicians were aware of myopathies. To elicit interest in the medical and scientific milieu, the AFM was obliged to produce the first corpus of knowledge on myopathies. The AFM collected testimonies from parents of children with myopathies, made films, conducted surveys to produce the first clinical descriptions of these diseases, and assembled facts to be discussed with clinicians and researchers (Rabeharisoa and Callon 1998). Not only did the AFM families became "lay experts" in the sense given to this notion by Steven Epstein (1996), they also became "experts of experience," able to bring about new knowledge based on their experiences with the disease. By effecting a confrontation between concerned people's experiential knowledge (Borkman 1976) with medical and scientific knowledge, the AFM raised new research questions, identified "zones of undone science" to be investigated (Frickel et al. 2010; Hess 2009), and eventually brought about paradigmatic changes in the understanding of myopathies. For example, a group of parents of children suffering from SMA (spinal muscular atrophy) regularly met to exchange their experiences and realized that the body temperature of their children was lower than the normal (36.5°C, or 97.7°F, on average instead of 37.2°C, or 98.96°F). They alerted clinicians and asked them to figure out the potential causes of this phenomenon. After a series of clinical investigations, it turned out that the low body temperature was related to cardiac problems, though myopathies were not supposed to affect the cardiac muscle. This finding prompted the exploration of comorbidities and contributed crucial knowledge about a category of diseases called "cardiomyopathies" (Rabeharisoa and Callon 2004).

We can therefore say that the notion of "lay expertise" aptly captures a phenomenon that emerged in Western Europe and the United States in the 1980s and 1990s: the mobilization of biomedical research by groups of people concerned about specific diseases or health problems and the recognition of these groups as competent and legitimate interlocutors by scientific experts, at least to a certain extent. Since then, "lay expertise" and "lay experts" have become topical issues in STS and different social science domains.

That said, the notion of "lay expertise" sparks many debates in academia and beyond. Although the term *lay expertise* initially referred to the acculturation of lay people to the biomedical world, today it often reduces lay expertise to lay people's experiential knowledge. This reductionist view is consistent with the long-standing state of medical paternalism. Some observers argue that if lay people develop expertise at all, it can only mirror their own subjective experiences of a disease. The notion that *lay expertise* could denote lay people's command of scientific knowledge is considered to derive from analytical confusion between the social roles and competences of experts and nonexperts, of professionals and patients.

It is this alleged confusion that we would like to revisit in this chapter. Indeed, the debates over the definition of *lay expertise* indicate an ongoing controversy about the role patient associations should play as much as they point to disputes over the role of credentialed experts in the decision-making process. Our approach consists not of discussing notions and concepts *in abstracto*, but of analyzing actual practices developed by patient associations to provide some points of reference in the debate. Drawing on our empirical studies, we show that (a) the expertise deployed by patient associations in their attempts to influence health policies and care practices very often results from a back-and-forth between scientific and experiential knowledge, and that (b) what we mean by the term *experiential knowledge* should be pluralized. Experiential knowledge does not exclusively stem from subjective introspection; it also comes from observations, accumulated day after day, of the evolution of the disease, through practices that resemble scientific practices. It is through the mobilization and hybridization of different forms of knowledge that patient associations put themselves in a position to produce expertise—that is, to make propositions about the nature of issues at stake and how these issues should be addressed.

This chapter is divided into four sections. In the first section, we focus on the production of experiential knowledge by patient associations. In the second section, we show

how they also strive to transform the content of credentialed expertise to better align this expertise with their concerns. The third section illustrates "lay expertise in action" and addresses the following questions: What changes do patient associations bring to health policymaking? How do they achieve these changes? In the fourth, we examine the institutionalization of the "expert patient," which manifests not only in legislation that mandates patient participation, but also in a variety of initiatives implemented by institutions to mobilize patient participation in medical research and health programs. In the conclusion, we suggest a few avenues for future research on aspects that thus far remain less investigated that may complement the corpus of knowledge on lay expertise.

Producing and Articulating Experiential Knowledge to Confront Medical Knowledge: The Construction of "Lay Expertise"

As mentioned previously, the capacity of patient associations and activist groups to influence the course of medical research and clinical trials resulted from an intense acculturation to scientific research. These groups did not involve themselves in scientific debates and activities for the sake of science (Arksey 1994; Barker 2005; Brown et al. 2004; Dumit 2006; Epstein 1995; Landzelius 2006; Rabeharisoa and Callon 2002); they did it because existing scientific knowledge and medical interventions failed to account for patients' experiences and concerns. Their main motive was to realign the content and methods of scientific and medical research with patients' concerns. For their expertise to be acknowledged, they had to speak the language of the communities they targeted.

However, this engagement with scientific research is only one part of the story. In addition to mastering the scientific literature, patient associations must identify the problems they deem important to tackle on behalf of the patients they claim to represent. To do this, they engage in a twofold endeavor: (a) the production of "experiential knowledge" (i.e., knowledge based on concerned people's experiences; Borkman 1976); and (b) the confrontation of experiential knowledge with scientific and medical knowledge. The aim is to reveal potential gaps between these two bodies of knowledge that, from a patient association's point of view, hinder the recognition of problems that patients encounter in their daily lives.

Interestingly, this form of patient activism is an inversion of the so-called deficit model (Callon 1999), which supposes that disagreements between experts and the public arise from the public's lack of information. When correctly informed by the experts, the public cannot but agree with them. Not only do patient associations consider themselves to be "knowledge-able actors" (Felt 2015), but they publicly claim to be experts about their own experiences; they also highlight credentialed experts' lack of understanding or deliberate ignorance, or both, of patients' situations. Therefore, the first role of patient associations as "lay" experts is to problematize those situations, with the goal of making them relevant and legitimate objects of inquiry. But how exactly do they proceed, and what are the nature and scope of the epistemic transformations they produce?

Incorporating Experiential Knowledge into the Medical Understanding of Diseases

Our first example is Génération 22, a small French patient association created in 1997 by families concerned with a rare chromosomal syndrome, the 22q11 deletion syndrome (or 22q11 DS) just a few years after the deletion was identified (Rabeharisoa et al. 2014). Today there is an international consensus on the complexity of this syndrome, which is characterized by multiple organic, cognitive, and psychiatric disorders. However, the mother who founded the association recalled that clinicians she visited in the late 1980s and early 1990s argued that her daughter's various disorders were in no way related to one another. It took her years to assemble facts on the complexity of the condition, and to collect and confront scientific and medical knowledge with the experiences of families. Even after the deletion was identified, different specialists continued to work in isolation. Notably, a few families alerted the association about the incidence of schizophrenia in adolescent patients, a fact that some French medical practitioners viewed with much doubt at the time.[1] The mother who created the association approached a psychiatrist, and together, they conducted a survey that concluded that the prevalence of schizophrenia was indeed higher among those with the syndrome than among the general population. This prompted the launch of a psychiatric genetics research program on 22q11 DS and schizophrenia, in which the association participated. In this case, experiential knowledge not only contributed original observations, but also initiated a paradigmatic change in the understanding of the syndrome, which previously had been scattered among different and unrelated corpuses of scientific and medical knowledge.

Génération 22 then made contact and engaged with French collectives of patient associations and experts that began to emerge in the 2000s to explore connections between chromosomal syndromes and psychiatric symptoms. Génération 22 and sister associations' demands for a multidisciplinary approach to these syndromes were taken into consideration by the French National Plan for Rare Diseases, a policy initiative of the French government in response to a patient organizations' demand: one of its core missions is to establish referral centers that provide diagnosis, care, and research services for patients with specific health conditions. A few of these centers were categorized as specializing in "developmental disorders and deformity syndromes," an ad hoc category comprising different conditions that present significant similarities, despite having different traditional disease classifications.[2]

This case is emblematic of the struggles of French rare-disease associations that had to advocate for patients in the absence of robust corpuses of scientific and medical knowledge about their diseases, and that were in a unique position to refresh medical knowledge and paradigms by drawing on patients' experiences (Rabeharisoa et al. 2014).

Ensuring That Patients' Experiences Count in Medico-Economic Evaluations of Drugs and Disease Burden

Our second example illustrates how patient associations revisit the politics of cure and care by proposing experience-based assessments of the effects of drugs on patients and of disease burden for patients and society at large. This is the case of the AKU Society, a small British nonprofit created in 2002 that is dedicated to supporting patients and families affected by a rare disease called alkaptonuria (Rabeharisoa and Doganova 2021). Alkaptonuria is a genetic disease that results in the accumulation of homogentisic acid in the body due to the lack of an enzyme that breaks it down. This metabolic dysfunction causes a degradation of cartilage that damages joints. In the mid-2000s, the AKU Society identified a drug called nitisinone as a potential treatment for alkaptonuria: nitinisone is prescribed for another rare metabolic disease that presents similarities with alkaptonuria. Previous clinical research conducted in the United States had suggested that nitisinone could reduce homogentisic acid levels. Although patients who took nitisinone reported that they felt better, the clinical trials were inconclusive. But the CEO of the AKU Society hypothesized that the clinical endpoint then used—improved functioning in the hip joint—did not capture the whole story. Indeed, the clinical picture of alkaptonuria is heterogeneous. This prompted the charity to launch a consortium called DevelopAKUre, which designed a totally different trial: instead of the clinical endpoint tested in the American trial, DevelopAKUre targeted a "surrogate endpoint": the reduction of homogentisic acid levels in the body.

Had the second trial been successful, the British National Health Services (NHS) would have been reluctant to pay for the treatment, however. The cost per quality-adjusted life-year (QALY), the main criterion for the pricing of drugs in the United Kingdom, would have been too high. Thus, in parallel with the clinical trial, the AKU Society UK commissioned an independent consultant to study the "real costs" of alkaptonuria for patients and families and, by extension, the NHS. The consultant conducted a survey on a small sample of "real patients" to collect "real life"[3] data on the costs of the disease—notably, the costs of the multiple surgeries that patients had undergone, the costs related to inaccurate diagnoses and inappropriate care (multiple medical consultations and medications, including painkillers, anti-inflammatory drugs, and antidepressants), and other indirect costs (e.g., lost wages and productivity). The study concluded that a "conservative approximation" of the total costs of alkaptonuria in the United Kingdom ranges from £1.4 million to 2.0 million per year, a figure comparable to the expected price of nitisinone, which may cost a few hundred thousand pounds per patient per year.[4] By comparing the disease burden to the potential benefits of the drug from the vantage point of patients, the AKU Society uncovered "missing variables" in the pricing of orphan drugs that the UK National Institute for Health and Care Excellence (NICE)[5] began to acknowledge.[6]

This case demonstrates how a patient association can translate what it is like to live with a complex disease for which there is no appropriate treatment into medico-economic language, with the goal of convincing clinicians and health administrators of the value of considering patients' experiences when evaluating a potential drug, to the benefit not only patients but also the health system.

Confronting the Rationale for Medical Interventions with Concerned People's Experiences

The third case concerns the Collectif Interassociatif Autour de la Naissance (CIANE), the main French organization dedicated to issues related to childbirth. CIANE was created in 2003 from a network of various groups: local associations devoted to supporting parents and defending maternity wards threatened with closure; national associations concerned with specific topics (caesarean section, postpartum depression, breastfeeding, etc.); and Internet-based support groups. Among the latter, one of the most discussed issues was episiotomy. Many women complained about the impacts of this procedure and questioned its relevance; they compared episiotomy to sexual mutilation, and some contended that episiotomy should be considered a manifestation of obstetrical patriarchy. Members of these groups reviewed the literature on episiotomy, which revealed a growing academic contestation of its utility. After the National College of Obstetricians elaborated guidelines on this topic, it sent them to CIANE for feedback prior to publication.

CIANE was quite upset by the new guidelines, which established a 30 percent episiotomy rate as a goal to reach for practitioners. Indeed, CIANE had found no robust evidence to support this rate and assumed it had been a political compromise designed to avoid antagonizing practitioners. To prepare its reply, CIANE formed a working group and conducted informal surveys with members of its network. It then responded with a fifteen-page report that contained a number of criticisms. One crucial criticism was that the document produced by the College of Obstetricians was purely technical and failed to incorporate women's points of view. CIANE pointed out a number of issues the college had ignored, including informed consent, medical complications, and impacts on everyday life such as pain and sexual problems, and argued that those issues pointed to the need for a restrictive episiotomy policy, considering that in most cases, the benefits of the procedure were not scientifically demonstrated.

Moreover, CIANE reconceptualized the prevention of perineal lacerations (the primary justification for episiotomy used by many obstetricians) by pointing out that they were likely caused by other medical practices, and that other strategies (e.g., different positioning during labor) might help prevent them. Drawing on women's complaints, on the one hand, and on the analysis of medical interventions, on the other, CIANE formulated a series of propositions for women's consent, professional training, and modification of medical protocols for the management of labor. For CIANE, episiotomy was only the tip of an iceberg of bad practices rooted in a lack of respect for women, whereas for the College of Obstetricians, it was just a matter of adjusting a rate of intervention. This case epitomizes how concerned people's nonmedical experiences, once they are translated into medical language, can lead to the questioning of the professional conceptions of medical practices.

* * *

These are but a few illustrations, echoing numerous others reported in the literature of how patient associations come to intervene in the orientation of biomedical research, the organization of care, or the evaluation of treatments by contributing new forms of expertise that challenged existing frameworks. The specificity of the forms of expertise developed by patient associations resides in a production of knowledge that begins with inquiries into patients' experiences. Three main characteristics of the fabric of experiential knowledge are worth highlighting here.

First, experiential knowledge is deployed in a variety of domains. The understanding of the disease is one of them. Patient associations regularly collect and synthesize concerned people's accounts of their experiences of a disease, and then confront corpuses of scientific and medical knowledge about its etiology, the clinical picture, and its manifestations with their own narratives. The list of conditions on which patient associations are working has expanded in recent years because they have deemed it necessary to consider potential causes of certain diseases (e.g., environmental causes of certain cancers; Brown et al. 2006; Wynne 1996), or because patients suffer from conditions that biomedical communities and public authorities ignore (Barker 2005; Dumit 2006) or are not documented in the scientific and medical literature. Experiential knowledge is also concerned with the rationale for medical interventions and practices, organization of care, assessment of patients' quality of life, evaluation of disease burden, and more recently, calculation of the costs and efficiency of drugs; in other words, it encompasses all aspects of the functioning of medical and health systems. The possibilities offered by the Internet have been central to this development (Akrich 2010). Internet communication has allowed geographically dispersed people to exchange knowledge about their health problems and has led to the formation of many patient organizations, especially in the domain of rare diseases; it also makes it possible to develop surveys at a low technical and economic cost.

Second, experiential knowledge has a transformative effect on the content of scientific and medical knowledge. Although not all patient associations produce the kinds of paradigmatic changes as Génération 22, they do introduce problems that concerned people actually experience and reshuffle our knowledge about diseases and their consequences. Moreover, patient associations often rearticulate bodies of knowledge that are otherwise separated along disciplinary lines. We can therefore say that experiential knowledge contributes new research questions and novel elaborations of the problems encountered by concerned people and thus enlarges the scope of knowledge and issues to be addressed.

Third, patient associations collect and synthesize patients' narratives, conduct surveys, and produce statistics that transform concerned people's experiences into genuine knowledge. The tools patient associations use to produce and visualize experiential knowledge are not completely alien to those used by the scientific and medical communities. That said, patient associations do not concern themselves with the alleged scientific rigor that governs the production of scientific knowledge because they are adamant that patients' experiences are meaningful whether or not they are consistent with scientific facts. For instance, instead of suppressing an observation that seems extreme compared to others, they categorize it as "anecdotal evidence" (Moore and Stilgoe 2009) to illustrate the severity of a particular situation. In their publications, patient associations often place figures from quantitative analyses of surveys next to patients' qualitative narratives both to ensure representativeness and to value the singularity of each patient's experience (Akrich et al. 2014). Moreover, patient associations sometimes adapt scientific methodologies and even improve upon them when investigating phenomena that are beyond the reach of classic scientific tools. For example, in the United Kingdom, when the Alzheimer's Society decided to include patients, and not only caregivers, as contributors, it decided to call on social scientists for help (Moreira et al. 2014). Because traditional interviews would not always be possible with people suffering from cognitive impairments, the researchers mobilized and invented new methodologies, such as the use of pictograms to capture patients' answers to questions about their experiences and expectations. In doing so, the society empowered patients by giving them the capacity to express themselves—a capacity that would not have emerged otherwise. Patient associations can be quite inventive when it comes to tools and methodologies for exploring, visualizing, and circulating patients' experiences.

BUILDING EPISTEMIC COMMUNITIES: BUILDING NETWORKS OF EXPERTISE, BUILDING EXPERTISE AS A NETWORK

To confront experiential knowledge with scientific and medical knowledge, patient associations engage in a lengthy and demanding learning process that includes identifying and contacting scientists and clinicians, visiting laboratories, reading scientific and medical articles, attending academic conferences, and regularly updating their knowledge when new information becomes available on the Web. Some activists are scientists and clinicians working on diseases that run in their families, for example Nancy Wexler and Huntington's disease (Wexler 1996) and the founding members of the National Society for Autistic Children in the United States (Eyal 2010). Others decide to complement their educations: for instance, the president of HyperSupers (the French association for attention deficit/hyperactivity disorder, ADHD) returned to the university to deepen her knowledge of psychology, and certain members of French rare-disease patient associations have followed a curriculum on bioethics to address issues related to prenatal and pre-implantation diagnosis. Collectively, these examples show that "lay expert" is not an oxymoron (Prior 2003) but refers to a "knowledge-able" person (Felt 2015) who can master knowledge of different facets of a disease without being a specialist in a scientific discipline such as neurology, immunology, psychiatry, pediatrics, endocrinology.

This hybridization process comes with a risk that lay experts may eventually lose sight of their activist identities and turn into experts among experts. This happened with certain HIV/AIDS lay experts, who were fiercely criticized by "lay lay" activists (Epstein 1996). This is where patient associations' engagement with scientific knowledge *and* experiential knowledge plays a decisive role: as both "lay experts" and "experts on their experiences," patient activists are positioned close to and at a distance from the scientific and medical milieu. More importantly, this positioning helps patient associations structure epistemic communities (Haas 1992). These communities comprises networks of actors who share policy orientations (i.e., definitions of the problems at stake and possible solutions) and have relevant expertise on which these policy orientations are based. Epistemic communities therefore expand traditional biomedical communities to include representatives of concerned people. This does not happen without conflict. But first, we must examine how patient associations come to occupy this position.

Patient Associations as Research Coordinators: Supporting the Creation and Maintenance of Patient-Centered Epistemic Communities

Many French rare-disease patient associations provide (modest) financial support to research teams. And over the years, they have learned not to be content with merely providing funding and have also begun to identify specific research targets and monitor the research activities they fund. Patient associations choose the teams they are willing to help, as well as the research policy instruments that they deem consistent with their missions. One remarkable example is that numerous rare-disease patient associations in France support doctoral students and postdocs, with the goal of establishing and maintaining research communities to study specific diseases. For instance, VLM (Vaincre la Mucoviscidose), the French patient association focused on cystic fibrosis, issues an annual call for PhD research proposals on a series of topics selected by its board of administrators (all patients or family members); and it convenes the students it supports once a year to take stock of their research findings. As a consequence, an epistemic community of young researchers now exists in France, and VLM plays an instrumental role in that community, not only as a research payer, but also as a research coordinator.

The existence of such patient-centered epistemic communities sometimes creates turmoil within scientific communities. The case of the AFM is quite telling in this respect. Some of the scientists and clinicians we interviewed had made the decision to leave the epistemic community organized by the AFM because they felt that they no longer had the flexibility to pursue their own research agendas. Some of them even expressed concerns that their fellow scientists and clinicians who continued to collaborate with the AFM were patronized by the association and had given up their personal research objectives. The criticism is interesting because it opposes two conceptions of patient associations held by scientists: (a) that patient associations are research foundations that should be governed by scientists, and (b) that patient associations provide funding for projects that correspond to their research interests.

Let us highlight two points at this stage. First, cooperation between scientists and patient associations does not always go smoothly. Quite the contrary: scientists do not invariably share their prerogatives and are not always ready to acknowledge patient associations' expertise. Moreover, the decision to take or not take patient associations' expertise into account sometimes triggers disputes among the scientists, as the example of the AFM shows. These disputes are about the role that patient associations should play as much as normative views about what credentialed expertise should be. Secondly, most associations are quite different from the AFM or a handful of large associations; they have very few resources and cannot pretend to have much clout on research programs. However, a survey of 215 French patient associations (Rabeharisoa et al. 2008) revealed that many of them play an active role in research, helping to constitute patient cohorts, collect biological samples, prepare clinical trials, or raise money. Beyond these direct interventions, patient associations also use subtler methods to push the production of knowledge in the directions they consider relevant.

Patient Associations as Mediators and Specialists' Partners in Networks of Expertise

The AFM is a large and wealthy association with the ability to provide significant funding for research projects and sustain a community of experts. Money, however, is just one part of the equation. Other patient associations have been able to provide forums that bring together scientists and clinicians to discuss conditions that are much less publicized than rare diseases, and to raise awareness of the need for research and treatment. This is the case with HyperSupers, the French ADHD association. ADHD has long been an unsettled condition, whose the etiology, mechanisms, and manifestations have been mired in uncertainty (Bergey et al. 2017). When HyperSupers formed in 2000, it entered an environment characterized by fragmented scientific and medical expertise and heated controversies between different specialists, particularly between neuropediatricians and child psychiatrists with backgrounds in psychodynamics. Rather than take sides in the controversies, the association began to collect data on patients' and families' experiences and compare them against evidence presented in scientific and medical articles. It realized that different interventions, sometimes in combination, may benefit different children, and that what was needed was a "multimodal approach," implying that one single discipline could not capture the multidimensional nature of the condition. HyperSupers decided to establish a multidisciplinary network dedicated to synthesizing expertise on ADHD and related issues (Edwards et al. 2014).

Historically, HyperSupers has established tight bonds with a few specialists who are sympathetic to its cause. It regularly organizes scientific symposia, and even awards scientific prizes, to gather specialists who typically do not dialogue with each other from disciplines as diverse as neurobiology, cognitive science, child psychiatry, psychology, pharmacology, nutrition, epidemiology, education sciences, disability studies, and even psychodynamics. During these symposia, HyperSupers presents the results of various surveys it conducts on patients' and families' experiences of diagnosis and care, and fosters exchange among specialists about patients' and families' needs and expectations. These specialists form an epistemic community whose members the association regularly invites to make presentations to families at its general assemblies. HyperSupers is not unique in this respect. Many patient associations organize similar arenas, which resemble what Callon et al. (2009) called "hybrid fora," and act as mediators between concerned people and specialists and among different specialists. In doing so, they help raise the scientific, social, and political profiles of diseases to inspire the scientific and medical communities to design research projects and treatment programs.

The example of the National Society for Autistic Children (NSAC) in the United States, described by Gil Eyal (2010), is even more radical. When the organization was established in 1965, a number of members simultaneously belonged to the world of patients and the world of scientists. Bernard Rimland, father of an autistic child and a psychologist who had not initially specialized in autism, and Lorna Wing, psychiatrist and mother of an autistic child, are the most famous examples, but many others also adopted the hybrid identity of "parent-activist-therapist-researcher." They all understood the daily life experience of autism, felt deep dissatisfaction with the way their children were regarded and treated, and possessed intellectual and professional tools that gave them the credibility to articulate other models of autism. Eric Schopler, a psychologist who had been working with the society since the 1970s, developed a research model in which parents served as coresearchers and cotherapists, thereby enabling novel expertise to emerge out of parents' and specialists' engagement in a process of collective inquiry (Dewey 1927).

Enlarging Communities of Knowledge beyond Biomedicine

The examples we have presented so far have shown the role of patient associations in structuring and sustaining biomedical communities for specific diseases. Biomedicine, however, is not the only sphere of knowledge that patient associations are willing to mobilize. The DingDingDong association was established by a young woman whose mother has Huntington's disease. The daughter underwent genetic testing herself, which revealed that she carries the gene for the disease. This news was certainly a shock to her, but she was even more outraged by the medical doctor she consulted, who described a terrible and inescapable fate that she was not prepared to accept. This prompted her to form DingDingDong, with the goal of demonstrating that there exists, *hic et nunc*, a rich and meaningful life with the gene and the disease, a life that the medical doctor she visited wrote off. DingDingDong seeks explores the ordinary lives of people with the gene and the disease, a terra incognita that it says biomedicine largely ignores. DingDingDong-Institute for the Coproduction of Knowledge on Huntington's Disease connects social scientists and artists (writers, filmmakers, photographs); its mission is to inform professionals and the public about the lives of those affected by the condition. In contrast to many rare-disease patient associations that focus on seeking cures and whose epistemic communities are mostly biomedicine oriented, DingDingDong focuses on the lived experiences of those affected by the disease, and privileges collaboration with social scientists and artists to convey an alternative vision of what it means to have the gene and the disease.

* * *

In the first part of the chapter, we showed how patient associations are engaged in a two-way translation process between patients' experiences and scientific and medical expertise that enables patient associations to make patients' concerns understandable to researchers, practitioners, and decision-makers. We also shed light on a related, though slightly different, process by observing how patient associations enroll specialists in networks they coordinate and sustain, turning them into concerned allies, who produce new forms of expertise in close collaboration with patients' representatives. Several characteristics of this process are notable.

First, patient associations identify and familiarize themselves with the networks of scientists and clinicians who study and treat their diseases, read their contributions, and make strategic decisions about whom to involve in their epistemic communities. Because of the fragmented nature of expertise and the conflicts that can traverse scientific and medical communities, patient associations have to make strategic decisions about whom to ally with. As a former president of the AFM once told us: "Scientists are not friends. They are allies we carefully select according to our own objectives." The AFM is not unique in this way. Stuart Blume's (2010) groundbreaking work on deaf communities revealed that deaf people made a decision not to ally with the medical milieu, which promoted cochlear implantation as a solution to deafness. They made this choice not only because they consider that the evidence that cochlear implantation improves quality of life is disputable but also—and most importantly—because they considered deafness a nonnegotiable element of their collective identity. Instead, they turned to sociolinguistics, which has shown that sign language is a language in and of itself and constitutes the core of deaf culture. Groups like DingDingDong or the deaf community are sometimes portrayed as "antiscientific." Our analysis brings a different perspective: these groups do not reject Science with a capital S. Rather, these groups select scientific disciplines and perspectives that resonate with their expectations and thus shape specific forms of expertise. Even in the case of the "antivaccination movement," scholars have shown that this "movement," as a unitary antiscience one, is a construction of pro-vaccination groups (Blume 2006; Ward 2016; Ward et al. 2019) that do not reject vaccination altogether but rather question the undesirable side effects and individual and collective benefits. That lay discourses may either oppose scientific rationality or develop pseudo-scientific arguments is worth being empirically documented: what exactly is this scientific rationality that some lay people contest, and what are those pseudo-scientific arguments they supposedly put together? These questions are core STS inquiries. Our empirical investigation suggests that formal patient associations have learned that science is diverse, that scientific evidence is not self-evident, and that credentialed expertise is a delicate balance between scientific facts and political orientations whose relevance is constitutively open to scrutiny.

Second, the activities involved in shaping and maintaining epistemic communities rely on a range of instruments that contribute to the organization of academic realms, such as scientific conferences, calls for research projects, scientific and medical committees, and biomedical platforms. Many associations have learned not to leave the governance of these instruments up to the scientists. They position themselves as (co-)organizers of scientific workshops, selecting the speakers and delineating the issues to be addressed; the same goes for calls for research projects. Many patient associations today also have scientific or medical committees, or both, which they mobilize in advisory rather than decision-making roles, limiting their power. As numerous examples (Larédo et al. 1996; Rabeharisoa and Callon 1999) have shown, the tensions that emerge as a result are related to a larger question about the status and role of scientific experts. Finally, patient associations are increasingly becoming involved in the management of biomedical platforms and infrastructures; some associations even own collections of biological samples; AFM, for example, created its own DNA bank. Such infrastructures become assets that cement the epistemic communities formed by patient associations.

Third, the constitution of such epistemic communities often entails mutual learning between patients and credentialed experts. It manifests in the publication of white papers on diseases and their consequences that are cowritten by concerned people and professionals, and even in the publication of cowritten articles in academic journals. For instance, Christine Gétin, the president of HyperSupers, published an article in *European Psychiatry* together with a psychiatrist; Yvanie Caillé, the president of Renaloo, an association concerned with kidney disease, cosigned an article with sociologists in *Population*.[7] Mutual learning entails a process through which experiential knowledge and scientific and medical knowledge intermingle, and which transforms patients' experiences and identities. For example, certain people with Asperger syndrome have enhanced their lived experiences by learning neuroscientific facts about the plasticity of the brain, eventually self-describing not as "patients" but as "neuro-diverse" individuals (Chamak 2008). We thus can say that patient-centered epistemic communities partake not only in a politics of knowledge, but also in an identity politics (Epstein 1987), with transformative effects on patienthood that may well be unexpected.

LAY EXPERTISE IN ACTION: PATIENT ASSOCIATIONS' RESHAPING OF HEALTH ISSUES

We have examined how patient associations engage in the production of experiential knowledge and in the discussion of this knowledge within the epistemic communities they assemble to address patients' problems. This shows that knowledges, including experiential knowledges, are not existing resources that patient associations merely mobilize to ground pre-given causes, but a set of statements that patient associations elaborate with the goal of proposing and testing the definitions of conditions and consequences that suit them, and shaping solutions they deem appropriate. In previous work, we suggested calling this entire process "evidence-based activism" (Rabeharisoa et al. 2014).

To discover solutions, patient associations must confront institutional actors and policymakers. In recent years, a number of European countries have promulgated legislation mandating patient representation on institutional committees in the fields of medicine and health, such as France's 2002 Act on Health Democracy. We now explore how patient organizations navigate these institutional arenas and give shape to health issues in unexpected ways.

The Conjoint Texturing of Lay Expertise and Unfolding of Unexpected Novel Health Issues

The case of Renaloo offers an example of a completely new framing of health issues emerging jointly with the production of lay expertise. This patient association grew out of the exchange at a forum created by a young woman blogger who was narrating her life with kidney disease and describing the benefits of the transplanted kidney she had received from her mother. From the outset, patients' experiences were the core of Renaloo's mode of action.

Soon after its creation, Renaloo organized États Généraux du Rein, a large meeting where patients were asked to collectively produce a description of their situation. Three years later, Renaloo launched a large survey on patients' quality of life which showed that transplant recipients live higher-quality lives than patients on dialysis. The survey revealed, for example, that 50 percent of transplant recipients have access to the job market, compared to just 18 percent of patients on dialysis. The survey also revealed that access to kidney transplantation in France is lower than in other European countries, and demonstrated that in the long run, transplantation costs significantly less than dialysis. Renaloo then investigated the reasons for the poor access and the possible ways to increase it. The investigation showed that one major explanation of poor access was the paucity of living donors, which prompted Renaloo to fight for improved access to information about transplantation and for the law to be modified to extend the circle of potential donors beyond close family members to friends. As a result, the number of living-donor transplants in France increased by 60 percent between 2012 and 2016, and accounted for 16 percent of all transplants in 2016, compared to just 11 percent in 2012.

Another unexpected finding from Renaloo's survey was that people with poor educational backgrounds are less likely to benefit from a transplant. This observation triggered heated debates in the media. A close examination revealed the complexity of the issue. Because of their living conditions, disadvantaged people tend to develop cardiovascular diseases, diabetes, or obesity, which are associated with kidney disease and are contraindications to transplantation; moreover, educated people have much easier access to the "right" interlocutors, who may advise them on the best options. Renaloo's intervention illustrates how patient associations can reveal unexpected problems, reflect on the underlying causes, and collect facts and figures through independent inquiry. They can then use this evidence to justify adding those problems to the political agenda and to develop appropriate solutions.

Exploring Medico-Administrative Categories and Confronting Health Authorities Using Their Own Logic

Reshaping health issues they deem important sometimes requires patient associations to extend their expertise into domains that are alien to the core concerns of patients and their relatives. VLM, the French association dedicated to fighting cystic fibrosis, which was studied by Pierre-André Juven (2019), is a case in point. In the 1970s, VLM played a pioneering role in the creation of referral centers for cystic fibrosis, decades before similar centers were established for other rare diseases in France. But the existence of these centers has been threatened by recent changes to the tariff system that regulates the budget allocated by the French public health insurance fund to public and private hospitals. The tariff system is based on the average cost of care for patients with a given disease or condition; for each patient, hospitals receive an amount of money corresponding to this average cost. For hospital budgets to be balanced, this money must cover all aspects of the care they provide to patients.

VLM noticed that the cystic fibrosis referral centers were showing a big deficit and suspected that the tariff for patients with this disease was based on an inaccurate appraisal of the centers' care activities were. With the help of a retired management studies researcher, the association began to collect extensive data on the range of the centers' activities. They discovered that some of the activities performed with patients, such as therapeutic education, had not been taken into consideration by health authorities. The same was true for a series of activities performed when patients were not present, such as coordinating personalized home care. These activities, which VLM considered essential for patients and their families, represented 62 percent of the time spent by professionals.

This analysis opened a new space for negotiation and debate between VLM and the French health authorities, who were reluctant to revise the tariff for cystic fibrosis because they feared a snowball effect for other rare conditions.[8]

Interestingly, VLM developed a strategy that was perpendicular to the one adopted by other opponents of the French hospital tariff. Indeed, for many years, professionals and citizens have contested this tariff, mainly on ideological grounds, denouncing the commodification of health or the perversion of the logic of care by an accounting logic. Rather than engage in these debates, VLM chose to become a "super-expert" and to confront public authorities using their own logic.

Ongoing Inquiry and the Accumulation of Small Changes in the Shaping of Health Issues

The previous examples might lead one to think that for patient associations reshaping the list of issues that they deem important to address, or at least putting certain questions on the political agenda, is merely a matter of producing the relevant evidence and choosing the right strategy. Such a view contradicts the usual skepticism about the power and influence of patient associations. Health systems are often depicted as ocean liners whose trajectories are extremely difficult to modify. In this context, the interventions of patient associations are seen as ineffective at best; at worst, they are seen as legitimizing decisions made by public authorities, with only a semblance of democracy. We cite another example from CIANE, the French childbirth organization, to illustrate how the accumulation of small changes can eventually modify the trajectories of health and medical systems.

In 2004, CIANE was invited by the ANAES (National Agency for Health Accreditation and Evaluation) to review guidelines they elaborated with the CNGOF (National College of French Gynecologists and Obstetricians) on the prevention of postpartum hemorrhage. The guidelines incorporated recent research findings and promoted the practice of injecting mothers with oxytocin, the drug used to induce labor, immediately after delivery to provoke strong uterine contractions that would close the blood vessels. CIANE criticized the way the guidelines defined "prevention," restricting it to drug administration and not considering other factors that contribute to postpartum hemorrhage. France is a particular case because the proportion of maternal deaths due to hemorrhage is significantly higher than in other countries. The proportion of women receiving oxytocin to accelerate labor is also very high. CIANE was especially concerned by this medical intervention, for it appears to increase the pain of labor and to lead to medicalization, which is not the delivery experience all women want. After oxytocin is administered, women often need epidural analgesia and careful monitoring. Putting these observations together, CIANE began to wonder whether administering oxytocin during labor could increase postpartum hemorrhage, their intuition being that the drug might saturate receptors that inhibit the natural release of oxytocin after birth. They eventually obtained funding for a research project on this topic, which ended in 2011. The evidence revealed that CIANE's intuition had been correct.

In 2014, following its strategy of initiating collective discussion about all issues related to obstetrical practices, CIANE proposed that the French High Authority of Health (Haute Autorité de Santé, HAS) develop guidelines for "normal/non-pathological childbirth." The guidelines published in December 2017 state: "It is recommended not to administer oxytocin in the absence of stagnation of dilatation, even if the frequency of uterine contractions is less than three per ten minutes," and stipulate that the use of oxytocin must be restricted to specific clinical situations and moments during the birth process. These guidelines have accompanied tangible changes to previous practices: in 2010, nearly two-thirds of pregnant women received oxytocin injections, a figure that dropped to 52.5 percent in 2016. Between the 2004 guidelines and the 2017 ones, numerous related events, some initiated by CIANE, collectively contributed to the decrease in the use of oxytocin before the 2017 guidelines were released. It is fair to say that the 2017 guidelines were the collective result of intersecting events; the changes are not solely the result of CIANE's actions. That said, CIANE, like many patient associations, made a specific contribution to the changes by translating people's concerns into terms that were understandable to the actors it wanted to convince and mobilize. Ultimately, some cumulative transformations resulted from this lengthy, nonlinear process involving multiple actors.

* * *

Today, patient associations are broadly recognized as stakeholders in the governance of health policies. The cases we have presented enable us to flesh out what it takes and means for patient associations to fulfill this role.

First, patient associations embrace this role by deciding what issues need to be addressed and setting priorities that differ from those of the institutional actors that are typically involved in health policymaking activities. Being atypical experts gives patient associations an advantage in terms of innovativeness (Hounshell 1975); their unique perspective allows them to question taken-for-granted facts and routines, deviate from established frameworks, and make new connections. Patient associations are not content to echo patients' complaints or claims and wait for others to propose solutions; they actively identify issues and help formulate solutions by articulating experiential knowledge in the language of credentialed experts and policymakers. Although their "invasion" of others' territory does not occur without friction, it can also produce changes.

Second, converting a patient-centered perspective into elements that can influence policymaking requires the production of evidence. In areas other than health, influence can be exerted by other means, such as demonstrations, but in domains with strongly constituted expertise, and which concern specific segments of the population, the building of counterexpertise is critical. To do so, patient associations must familiarize themselves with the functioning and parlance of institutions so they can identify the right interlocutors and knock on the right doors. This know-how is not documented in textbooks; it is acquired through a long process of learning by doing.

Third, the capacity of patient associations to bring about change is facilitated by the existence of procedures that accommodate patient expression. Without the 2002 Act on Health Democracy, which mandates the presence of patient representatives on institutional committees, French patient associations would probably have been less influential. Very often though, their influence is not immediate, nor does it result in major paradigmatic change; instead, they tend to adopt a light-touch approach that leads to incremental changes over time that progressively open a space of possibilities.

TOWARDS AN INSTITUTIONALIZATION OF PATIENTS' EXPERTISE . . . BUT WHICH EXPERTISE?

HIV/AIDS activist groups, as well as rare-disease patient associations, have greatly contributed to the public recognition of patients as stakeholders in health-related policies. In France, for example, the Téléthon (a TV fundraising initiative launched by the AFM in 1987) solidified the AFM's public identity as an organization that is governed by patients and serves patients, yet is capable of managing big research programs. This identity sharply contrasts with that of the charities devoted to supporting research and led by researchers that prevailed before the creation of patient associations like the AFM. The French group AIDES, which is concerned with issues related to HIV/AIDS, built an improbable partnership with an umbrella organization of family associations; in 1996, it formed a national collective of patient and user associations, the Collectif Interassociatif sur la Santé (CISS), which had a dozen members at its inception (Lascoumes and Bouchard 2017). The CISS was a pioneer in promoting the participation of patient associations in the governance of health; in fact, the 2002 French Act on Health Democracy was a direct outcome of its relentless political mobilization. In many other countries, the role of patient associations is acknowledged, but within different organizational and legal frameworks (Baggott and Forster 2008; Keizer and Bless 2010).

There is general agreement that involving patients in all aspects of medical and health policies may improve the quality of healthcare services and strengthen democracy in the process. The notion that care should be centered on patients and that their needs, expectations, preferences, and real-life conditions should be taken into consideration, has become indisputable. Some actors argue that taking into account the experiential knowledge of those directly affected by a disease or health problem may help prevent unnecessary medical examinations and treatments (as well as irrelevant research projects), enabling better care and reducing healthcare costs to render health systems more sustainable.

This general trend toward the valuation of patients' perspectives manifests not only in the increasing role of patient associations in the governance of health issues, but also in the proliferation of initiatives being implemented in a variety of institutions. We offer a few examples of these initiatives. We want to argue that the definition of lay expertise and the role of lay experts are at stake in these initiatives but that they are not really discussed. We are still in a relative state of confusion where, depending on the case, the term *lay expertise* can refer either to experiential knowledge or to scientific knowledge and can be the property of individuals, the result of the aggregation of individual experiences, or the outcome of collective reflection. This confusion has political implications we want to highlight.

In countries like Canada and France, the recent development of the "patient-as-partner approach" (Karazivan et al. 2015) is one of these initiatives. At the University of Montréal, for instance, patients are recruited as staff members and contribute to the health sciences curriculum; they also participate as members of healthcare teams and coresearchers in research programs. Some French universities develop special training programs for patients who are willing to be acknowledged as "expert patients," either as patient representatives on health committees or as instructors in patient therapeutic education programs. All such initiatives are rooted in the idea that patients have expert knowledge of their experiences and that their expertise is highly valuable when it comes to developing a truly patient-centered approach to care. Very often, though not always, these expert patients are members of patient associations. That said, the very term *expert patient* places the focus on the individual expertise of the patient rather than the collective expertise that she or he may have gained as a member of a patient association.

Other initiatives are related to the rapid development of patient-reported data and of outcome measures based upon these data (Greenhalgh 2009; Refolo et al. 2012). Interestingly, some initiatives originated in non profit organizations, as illustrated by the creation of the Patient Centered Outcome Research Institute (PCORI), an American funding institution that, since its authorization by Congress in 2010 to 2022 has spent USD $3 billion (Frank et al. 2014). Others are private-sector initiatives, especially through the creation of platforms such as CureTogether or PatientsLikeMe (PLM), and more recently, the Open Research Exchange platform, described by PLM, its founder, as the "first Open-Participation Research Platform for Patient-Centered Health Outcome Measures." The main objective of these platforms is to measure the quality of care in ways that are "relevant and meaningful to patients" and "to help patients, caregivers, clinicians, employers, insurers, and policy makers make better-informed health decisions." They do this by developing questionnaires to gather data on patients' health status, feelings about their diseases, impacts of treatments on their lives, and the things in life that they value most and are eager to preserve. Typically, free expression is not accommodated, the objective being to give researchers "robust tools" that they can exploit and use in a variety of contexts. In this case, professionals and researchers produce expertise about patients' experiences by pre-shaping experiences to produce data they can aggregate and interpret. The professionals and researchers remain the experts, whereas patients are data providers. Once this expertise is produced, it is shared with patients and professionals to help them make care-related decisions.

Scientific institutions also are receptive to the notion of the "expert patient." In 2003, INSERM, the main French health research institution, launched a working group composed of representatives of patient associations and INSERM researchers with the goal of strengthening partnerships. In 2013, *BMJ*, a leading medical journal, launched a "patient revolution" (Richards et al. 2013; Richards and Godlee 2014), taking a series of actions, such as asking the authors of research papers to document how they involved patients in the research process, asking patients to review articles, and inviting patients and patient advocates to join its editorial board and even to write articles. In 2015, *Research Involvement and Engagement (RIE)*, a journal that is entirely devoted to analyzing patient involvement in all types of research, was launched. Despite apparent similarities, *BMJ* and *RIE* rely on different patient participation models. *BMJ* seeks to engage patients as experts of experience; these patients must be talented individuals, although they need not possess health sciences knowledge. In contrast, many researchers who publish in *RIE* favor a statistical model of representation and emphasize the need to gather samples that represent the diversity of the targeted population, mediating lay expertise through research methodologies and analytical frameworks.

These diverse initiatives reveal two main trends related to the institutionalization of patients' participation. First, when institutions call upon "expert patients," they sometimes refer to representatives of patient associations but more often to individual patients. Second, and consequently, institutional conceptions of "expert patients" result in multiple appraisals of lay expertise, even though lay expertise is said to relate to patients' experiences. In some cases, the production of knowledge and expertise remains the domain of the competences and prerogatives of researchers, and patients are regarded only as data providers; this vision is associated with a statistical conception of representational capacity. In other cases, individual patients are supposed to be able to transform their experiential knowledge into expertise that is useful to specific communities (policymakers, health professionals, students, etc.), which can be considered a "symbolic" form of representativeness. In yet other cases, "expert patients" are members of patient associations, which entails a political conception of representativeness; their expertise, which is rooted in their individual experiences as much as it is a collective elaboration of issues by the patient associations they belong to, is what makes them patient representatives.

* * *

To conclude, the notion of the "expert patient" is not expanded without potential backlash; as the saying goes, the road to hell is paved with good intentions. Each format of representation may have its own advantages and bring interesting data to the discussion; but when it comes to the fabrication of expertise, privileging individual patients over patients who are members of patient associations introduces the risk of undermining the work those associations have accomplished and reintroducing medical paternalism by excluding the experiential knowledge and expertise elaborated by groups of concerned people from the public debate.

This is especially pernicious because a common justification for dismissing patient associations is that they are "militant" groups of activists who lack "scientific objectivity" (Blease et al. 2018). This argument misses the point that knowledge and expertise, including scientific knowledge and expertise, are always situated (Haraway 1988), meaning that they are the products of highly political perspectives on the "relevant" questions to be tackled and the "appropriate" factors and "legitimate" actors to be taken into consideration—in other words, the framing of issues that are deemed important at the individual and collective levels. By re-evaluating existing framings from their own perspectives, patient associations renew the fabric of and debates on issues of collective concern: the role of oxytocin in postpartum hemorrhage, the definition of endpoints in clinical trials of nitisinone for alkaptonuria, or what it entails to organize care for cystic fibrosis patients would probably not have been studied and discussed without the intervention of patient associations. It is this potentiality that the institutionalization of the "expert patient" may threaten in the long run: there is a wide gap between expertise as the property of one knowledgeable and experienced individual and expertise as the collective capacity to articulate policy recommendations that draws from a variety of knowledges and experiences; any initiative that views concerned people as data providers and places the elaboration of recommendations in the hands of professionals widens that gap and strongly bends the notion of "lay expertise" that we have highlighted in the examples here.

CONCLUSION

In this chapter, we have presented empirical observations and analyses of lay expertise and a constellation of notions—such as the "expert patient," "patient participation," the "patient-as-partner approach," and "multistakeholder governance"—that have become part of the vocabulary of medical researchers and health institutions. Following in the footsteps of Steven Epstein, we have shown how lay expertise is a political concept that captures a form of patient activism grounded in patient associations' involvement in the production and confrontation of experiential knowledge with scientific and medical knowledge, the building of epistemic communities assembled around patients' concerns, and the (re)shaping of issues that the patient associations deem relevant and legitimate to best help patients. We have also reflected on how lay expertise is mobilized in today's institutional settings and is sometimes reconfigured therein. Moreover, we have emphasized the multiplicity of lay expertise and the complex paths it follows to enter policymaking arenas.

At this point, one may wonder about the extent to which what we described in our examples is specific to the French context or even to the small group of studied cases. Surveys we conducted in 2006 and 2010 (Rabeharisoa et al., 2008, 2011) on, respectively, 215 and 293 patient associations revealed that most of them invest quite a lot of energy in explaining and disseminating medical knowledge, organizing conferences, and supporting research in various ways. Contemporary patient associations do not believe that their options are limited to mutual aid, quite the contrary. Some of the empirical material we relied on was produced in the context of a European project that revealed similar phenomena in different countries (Akrich et al. 2012). Let us recall that the articulation of experiential knowledge with scientific knowledge has also been central in environmental health movements (Akrich et al. 2010; Allen 2004; Brown 1997; McCormick et al. 2003), emergent diseases (Arksey 1994; Dumit 2006; Loriol 2003), and at the intersection of the two (Capek 2000; Kroll-Smith et al. 2000).

Another concern related to the issue of generalization is that we may have missed cases where patient activism merely contributed to the medicalization or biologization of certain problems, or where certain patient groups used the language of biomedicine only to push forward some claims that are contested by health professionals (Barker 2008; Barthe et al. 2010; Conrad 2005; Fair 2010; Graham 2007; Spandler 2018). If this phenomenon is indisputable, it bears saying that medicalization and biologization are not a wrong in and of themselves when patient associations have to fight to get their diseases recognized by biomedical practitioners and health authorities and to enroll them in the war on diseases. In doing so, some patient associations may succeed in transforming something that is rooted in people's experience into an object of inquiry and, eventually, into a medical concept, whereas others may fail. In this chapter, we reported on patient associations that eventually managed to demonstrate the soundness of their expertise and propositions, often after long and tense discussions with professionals. If one is to sort out successes and failures, however, one should remember the principle of symmetry brought to the fore by the early sociologists of science (Bloor 1976)—the success or the failure of a scientific proposition should be analyzed with the same kind of arguments. There are no criteria for setting apart successes from failures a priori, and that should be considered the normal functioning of a form of scientific democracy.

This raises an additional question about the conditions that favor the development of lay expertise, the role of contexts in the integration of lay expertise into the making of health policies, and the global impacts of patient participation on the governance of health. At the very least, we may say that lay expertise requires an atmosphere of democracy to blossom and consolidate and that it impacts the democratization of health in a variety of ways. That said, there is no grand narrative to unveil here. Rather, what we have witnessed are complex dynamics at the intersection of a variety initiatives and events with transformative effects on the politics of knowledge and of care that are continually debated and developed. Among the most debated topics, three warrant further investigation.

The first topic is the alleged destabilization of scientific communities due to the increasing role of patient associations in the orientation, financial support, and monitoring of research programs. At stake here is a fundamental disagreement about whether researchers should collaborate with patient associations. A recent survey conducted by the working group formed by INSERM (Institut national de la santé et de la recherche médicale, the French institution dedicated to health research), composed of representatives of patient associations and researchers, shows that scientists and clinicians who have collaborated with patient associations have progressively conformed their research interests to patients' concerns, which other scientists consider to be a breach of the academic ethos and quest for objectivity.

We think that it would be interesting to explore the scope of this phenomenon and to figure out whether it brings about novel orderings of scientific communities and trajectories. Such an exploration would extend analyses of what Callon et al. (2009) called "technical democracy," for example, the ongoing reshuffling of the modes of production of knowledge as a democratic imperative.

The second topic relates to issues of justice. Notably, HIV/AIDS, rare diseases, Alzheimer's disease, autism, and cancers rank at the top of the list of conditions that benefit from patient activism. This activism has influenced medical research and the health policies on those conditions in many countries in Western Europe and North America. This raises questions about uneven access to public resources among patients with different diseases and health conditions due to the power of certain patient associations. These questions are being addressed not only by academics (Best 2012; Dresser 2001), but also by some patient associations: some worry that certain collective interests may supersede others and eventually threaten the democratic outreach of patient activism.

This issue warrants inquiry into how patient associations, though they are clearly and legitimately self-centered organizations, contribute knowledge, questions, ideas, and solutions that may benefit others. Some patient associations claim that their achievements for their diseases can help other patient associations; for instance, rare-disease patient associations often say that rare diseases can serve as "disease models" that can be used to study and combat common diseases that have similar characteristics. But what it means to be a "disease model," from not only a scientific but also a social point of view, remains an open question. We may also look at umbrella organizations within which different patient associations coalesce with an aim of achieving broader impact. More importantly, it would be interesting to explore how the politics of singularization that support the production of experiential knowledge and lay expertise may transform the traditional politics of numbers based largely on statistical reasoning— that is, the logic in which public policies are grounded.

The third topic that might be worth exploring is the circulation of certain models of patient activism developed mainly in Western Europe and North America to other regions of the world. Studies on transnational activism show how coalitions of patient associations or activist groups engage in the production and discussion of knowledge and expertise in different condition areas (Krikorian 2017; Rabeharisoa and O'Donovan 2014). It might be interesting to extend studies on how these coalitions situate themselves vis-à-vis large nongovernmental and philanthropic organizations that are active in certain regions, and how these coalitions give shape to expertise drawn from concerned people's experiences (if they do). There is much to learn from global health studies, with significant opportunities to extend them by looking at certain regions of the world where multiple international institutions and private foundations take hold and introduce their own modes of action that may contradict groups of concerned people and even prevent them from organizing in a meaningful way.

ACKNOWLEDGMENTS

We acknowledge European funding for the project EPOKS (European Patient Organizations in Knowledge Society, 2009–2012) that we coordinated, and from which we have extensively drawn in this chapter. We are grateful to our colleagues on this project for the rich discussions they contributed. We warmly thank Gil Eyal and Thomas Medvetz for their careful reading of the first version of this chapter and for their valuable comments. We also thank Kara Gehman for editing this chapter.

NOTES

1. Notably, because these medical practitioners approached the 22q11 deletion syndrome from the perspectives of their own specialties.
2. For more details on the intersection of genomic and psychiatric classification, see Navon and Shwed (2012).
3. The expressions "real patients" and "real life" are those of the CEO of the AKU Society, whom we interviewed.
4. AKU Society has estimated the prevalence of alkaptonuria to be one out of every 250,000 people worldwide (https://akusociety.org). At the time of the cost assessment, the AKU Society had identified sixty-two patients in the United Kingdom and three in Scotland.
5. NICE is the UK health technology assessment agency.
6. "Decisions about whether to recommend interventions should not be based on evidence of their relative costs and benefits alone. NICE must consider other factors when developing its guidance, including the need to distribute health resources in the fairest way within society as a whole." NICE (2009), *Patients, the Public and Priorities in HealthCare* (Boca Raton, FL: CRC Press).
7. M. Lecendreux, Christine Gétin, and K. Keddad (2011), "P01-318 —Family Healthcare and ADHD in France," *European Psychiatry* 26: 320; C. Baudelot, Yvanie Caillé, O. Godechot, and S. Mercier (2016), "Maladies rénales et inégalités sociales d'accès à la greffe en France," *Population* 71 (1): 23–51.
8. When Pierre-André Juven did his fieldwork, negotiations were still underway between VLM and the French public health insurance fund.

REFERENCES

Akrich, Madeleine. 2010. "From Communities of Practice to Epistemic Communities: Health Mobilizations on the Internet." *Sociological Research Online* 15:2.

Akrich, Madeleine, Yannick Barthe, and Catherine Rémy. 2010. "Les enquêtes profanes et la dynamique des controverses en santé environnementale." In *Sur la piste environnementale:*

Menaces sanitaires et mobilisations profanes, edited by Madeleine Akrich, Yannick Barthe, and Catherine Rémy, 7–52. Paris: Presses des Mines.

Akrich, Madeleine, Máire Leane, Celia Roberts, and João Arriscado Nunes. 2014. "Practising Childbirth Activism: A Politics of Evidence." *BioSocieties* 9 (2): 129–152.

Akrich, Madeleine, and Vololona Rabeharisoa. 2012. *European Patient Organizations in Knowledge Society*. Final Report. Project n° SIS-CT-2009-230307 funded by the European Commission. https://cordis.europa.eu/project/id/230307/reporting

Akrich, Madeleine, and Vololona Rabeharisoa. 2018. "The French ADHD Landscape: Maintaining and Dealing with Multiple Uncertainties." In *Global Perspectives on ADHD: Social Dimensions of Diagnosis and Treatment in Sixteen Countries*, edited by Meredith R. Bergey, Angela M. Filipe, Peter Conrad, and Ilina Singh, 233–260. Baltimore, MD: Johns Hopkins University Press.

Allen, Barbara L. 2004. "Shifting Boundary Work: Issues and Tensions in Environmental Health Science in the Case of Grand Bois, Louisiana." *Science as Culture* 13: 429 –448.

Arksey, Hilary. 1994. "Expert and Lay Participation in the Construction of Medical Knowledge." *Sociology of Health & Illness* 16: 448–468.

Baggott, Rob, and Rudolf Forster. 2008. "Health Consumer and Patients' Organizations in Europe: toward a Comparative Analysis." *Health Expectations: An International Journal of Public Participation in Health Care and Health Policy* 11(1): 85–94.

Barbot, Janine. 1998. "Science, marché et compassion: L'Intervention des associations de lutte contre le sida dans la circulation des nouvelles molécules." *Sciences Sociales et Santé* 16: 67–95.

Barbot, Janine. 2002. *Les malades en mouvements: La médecine et la science à l'épreuve du sida.* Paris: Balland.

Barker, Kristin K. 2005. *The Fibromyalgia Story*. Philadelphia: Temple University Press.

Barker, Kristin K. 2008. "Electronic Support Groups, Patient-Consumers, and Medicalization: The Case of Contested Illness." *Journal of Health and Social Behavior* 49: 20–36.

Barthe, Yannick, and Catherine Rémy. 2010. "Les aventures du 'syndrome du bâtiment malsain.'" *Santé Publique* 22: 303–311.

Bergey, Meredith R., Angela M. Filipe, Peter Conrad, and Ilina Singh, eds. 2017. *Global Perspectives on ADHD*. Baltimore, MD: Johns Hopkins University Press.

Best, Rachel Kahn. 2012. "Disease Politics and Medical Research Funding: Three Ways Advocacy Shapes Policy." *American Sociological Review* 77 (5): 780–803.

Blease, Charlotte, and Keith J. Geraghty. 2018. "Are ME/CFS Patient Organizations 'Militant'?" *Journal of Bioethical Inquiry* 15(3): 393–401.

Bloor, David. 1976. *Knowledge and Social Imagery*. London: Routledge and Kegan Paul.

Blume, Stuart. 2006. "Anti-vaccination Movements and Their Interpretations." *Social Science and Medicine* 62(3): 628–642.

Blume, Stuart. 2010. *The Artificial Ear: Cochlear Implants and the Culture of Deafness*. New Brunswick, NJ: Rutgers University Press.

Borkman, Thomasina. 1976. "Experiential Knowledge: A New Concept for the Analysis of Self-Help Groups." *Social Service Review* 50(3): 445–456.

Brown, Phil. 1997. "Popular Epidemiology Revisited." *Current Sociology* 45:137–156.

Brown, Phil, Sabrina McCormick, Brian Mayer, Stephen Zavestoski, Rachel Morello-Frosch, Rebecca Gasior Altman, et al. 2006. "'A Lab of Our Own': Environmental Causation of Breast Cancer and Challenges to the Dominant Epidemiological Paradigm." *Science, Technology, & Human Values* 31: 499–536.

Brown, Phil, Stephen Zavestoski, Sabrina McCormick, Brian Mayer, Rachel Morello-Frosch, and Rebecca Gasior Altman. 2004. "Embodied Health Movements: New Approaches to Social Movements in Health." *Sociology of Health & Illness* 26: 50–80.

Callon, Michel. 1999. "The Role of Lay People in the Production and Dissemination of Scientific Knowledge." *Science, Technology and Society* 4(1): 81–94.

Callon, Michel, Pierre Lascoumes, and Yannick Barthe. 2009. *Acting in an Uncertain World: An Essay on Technical Democracy*. Cambridge, MA: MIT Press.

Capek, Stella M. 2000. "Reframing Endometriosis: From 'Career Woman's Disease' to Environment/Body Connections." In *Illness and the Environment: A Reader in Contested Medicine*, edited by SteveKroll-Smith, Phil Brown, and Valerie J. Gunter, 72–91. New York: New York University Press.

Chamak, Brigitte. 2008. "Autism and Social Movements: French Parents' Associations and International Autistic Individuals' Organisations." *Sociology of Health & Illness* 30(1): 76–96.

Collins, Harry M., and Robert Evans. 2002. "The Third Wave of Science Studies: Studies of Expertise and Experience." *Social Studies of Science* 32: 235–296.

Conrad, Peter. 2005. "The Shifting Engines of Medicalization." *Journal of Health and Social Behavior* 46: 3–14.

Dewey, John. 1927. *The Public and Its Problems*. New York: Henry Holt.

Dodier, Nicolas. 2003. *Leçons politiques de l'épidémie de sida*. Paris: EHESS.

Dresser, Rebecca. S. 2001. *When Science Offers Salvation: Patient Advocacy and Research Ethics*. Oxford: Oxford University Press.

Dumit, Joseph. 2006. "Illnesses You Have to Fight to Get: Facts as Forces in Uncertain, Emergent Illnesses." *Social Science & Medicine* 62: 577–590.

Edwards, Claire., Etaoine Howlett, Madeleine Akrich, and Vololona Rabeharisoa. 2014. "Attention Deficit Hyperactivity Disorder in France and Ireland: Parents' Groups' Scientific and Political Framing of an Unsettled Condition." *BioSocieties* 9(2): 153–172.

Epstein, Steven. 1987. "Gay Politics, Ethnic Identity: The Limits of Social Constructionism." In *Social Perspectives in Lesbian and Gay Studies: A Reader*, edited by Peter M. Nardi and Beth E. Schneider, 134–159. London: Routledge.

Epstein, Steven. 1995. "The Construction of Lay Expertise: AIDS Activism and the Forging of Credibility in the Reform of Clinical Trials." *Science, Technology, & Human Values* 20: 408–437.

Epstein, Steven. 1996. *Impure Science: AIDS, Activism, and the Politics of Knowledge*. Berkeley: University Press of California.

Eyal, Gil. 2010. *The Autism Matrix*. Cambridge, UK: Polity.

Fair, Brian. 2010. "Morgellons: Contested Illness, Diagnostic Compromise and Medicalisation." *Sociology of Health and Illness* 32(4): 597–612.

Felt, Ulrike. 2015. "Keeping Technologies Out: Sociotechnical Imaginaries and the Formation of Austria's Technopolitical Identity." In *Dreamscapes of Modernity: Sociotechnical Imaginaries and the Fabrication of Power*, edited by Sheila Jasanoff and Kim Sang-Hyun, 103–125. Chicago: University of Chicago Press.

Frank, Lori, Ethan Basch, and Joe V. Selby. 2014. "The PCORI Perspective on Patient-Centered Outcomes Research." *JAMA* 312 (15): 1513–1514.

Frickel, Scott, Sahra Gibbon, Jeff H. Howard, Joanna Kempner, Gwen Ottinger, and David J. Hess. 2010. "Undone Science: Charting Social Movement and Civil Society Challenges to Research Agenda Setting." *Science, Technology, & Human Values* 35(4): 444–473.

Graham, Linda J. 2007. "Out of Sight, Out of Mind / Out of Mind, Out of Site: Schooling and Attention Deficit Hyperactivity Disorder." *International Journal of Qualitative Studies in Education* 20: 585–602.

Greenhalgh, Joanne 2009. "The Applications of PROs in Clinical Practice: What Are They, Do They Work, and Why?" *Quality of Life Research* 18(1): 115–123.

Haas, Peter. M. 1992. "Introduction: Epistemic Communities and International Policy Coordination." *International Organization* 46:1–35.

Haraway, Donna. 1988. "Situated Knowledges: The Science Question in Feminism and the Privilege of Partial Perspective." *Feminist Studies* 14 (3): 575–599.

Hess, David J. 2009. "The Potentials and Limitations of Civil Society Research: Getting Undone Science Done." *Sociological Inquiry* 79(3): 306–327.

Hounshell, David. A. 1975. "Elisha Gray and the Telephone: On the Disadvantages of Being an Expert." *Technology and Culture* 16(2): 133–161.

Juven, Pierre-André. 2019. "Calculative Infrastructure for Hospitals: Governing Medical Practices and Health Expenditures through a Pricing Payment System." In *Thinking Infrastructures* edited by Martin Kornberger, Geoffrey C. Bowker, Julia Elyachar, Andrea Mennicken, Peter Miller, Joanne Randa Nucho, and Neil Pollock. *Research in Sociology of Organizations* 62, 69–84.

Karazivan, Philippe, Vincent Dumez, Luigi Flora, Marie-Pascale Pomey, Claudio Del Grande, Djahanchah Philip Ghadiri, et al. 2015. "The Patient-as-Partner Approach in Health Care: A Conceptual Framework for a Necessary Transition." *Academic Medicine: Journal of the Association of American Medical Colleges* 90(4): 437–441.

Keizer, Bob, and Ruud Bless. 2010. *Pilot Study on the Position of Health Consumer and Patients' Associations in Seven EU Countries.* The Hague: ZonMW.

Krikorian, Gaëlle P. 2017. "From AIDS to Free Trade Agreements: Knowledge Activism in Thailand's Movement for Access to Medicines." *Engaging Science, Technology, and Society* 3:154–179.

Kroll-Smith, Steve, and H. Hugh Floyd. 2000. "Environmental Illness as a Practical Epistemology and a Source of Professional Confusion." In *Illness and the Environment: A Reader in Contested Medicine*, edited by Steve Kroll-Smith, Phil Brown, and Valerie J. Gunter, 72–91. New York: New York University Press.

Landzelius, Kyra. 2006. "Introduction: Patient Organization Movements and New Metamorphoses in Patienthood." In "Patient Organisation Movements." Special issue. *Social Science & Medicine* 62: 529–537.

Larédo, Philippe, Michel Callon, Bernard Kahane, and Robert Triendl. 1996. *La Recherche à l'AFLM, Etat des lieux et proposition d'évolution.* Paris: Centre de sociologie de l'innovation, Mines Paris PSL.

Lascoumes, Pierre, and Julie Bouchard. 2017. "Le patient, objet de mobilisation." *Politiques de Communication* 9:17–35.

Loriol, Marc. 2003. "Faire exister une maladie controversée: Les associations de malades du syndrome de fatigue chronique et Internet." *Sciences Sociales et Sante* 21: 5–33.

McCormick, Sabrina., Phil Brown, and Stephen Zavestoski. 2003. "The Personal Is Scientific, the Scientific Is Political: The Public Paradigm of the Environmental Breast Cancer Movement." *Sociological Forum* 18: 545–576.

Moore, Alfred., and Jack Stilgoe. 2009. "Experts and Anecdotes: The Role of 'Anecdotal Evidence' in Public Scientific Controversies." *Science, Technology, & Human Values* 34(5): 654–677.

Moreira, Tiago, Orla O'Donovan, and Eatoine Howlett. 2014. "Assembling Dementia Care: Patient Organisations and Social Research." *BioSocieties* 9(2): 173–193.

Navon, Daniel, and Uri Shwed. 2012. "The Chromosome 22q11.2 Deletion: From the Unification of Biomedical Fields to a New Kind of Genetic Condition." *Social Science & Medicine* 75(9): 1633–1641.

Prior, Lindsay. 2003. "Belief, Knowledge and Expertise: The Emergence of the Lay Expert in Medical Sociology." *Sociology of Health & Illness* 25: 41–57.

Rabeharisoa, Vololona, and Michel Callon. 1998. "L'Implication des malades dans les activités de recherche soutenues par l'Association française contre les myopathies." *Sciences Sociales et Santé* 16: 41–65.

Rabeharisoa, Vololona, and Michel Callon. 1999a. La gestion de la recherche par les malades: Le cas de l'Association Française contre les Myopathies. *Les Annales de l'École de Paris du management* VI: 177–184.

Rabeharisoa, Vololona, and Michel Callon. 1999b. *Le pouvoir des malades: L'Association française contre les myopathies et la Recherche*. Paris: Presses des Mines.

Rabeharisoa, Vololona, and Michel Callon. 2002. "The Involvement of Patients' Associations in Research." *International Social Science Journal* 54(171): 57–63.

Rabeharisoa, Vololona, and Michel Callon. 2004. "Patients and Scientists in French Muscular Dystrophy Research." In *States of Knowledge: The Co-production of Science and Social Order*, edited by Sheila Jasanoff, 142–160. London: Routledge.

Rabeharisoa, Vololona, and Michel Callon. 2011. *Report on Rare Diseases Organizations (France)*, Report 5-WP1(P1)—European Commission Project n° SIS-CT-2009-230307 (unpublished report).

Rabeharisoa, Vololona, Michel Callon, Florence Paterson, and Frédéric Vergnaud. 2008. *Mapping and Analyzing Patient Organization Movements on Rare Diseases*. Research report. Convention Agence Nationale de la Rercherche-05-061-01. Agence Nationale de la Recherche, Paris. https://anr.fr

Rabeharisoa, Vololona, and Liliana Doganova. 2021. "War on Diseases: Patient Organizations' Problematization and Exploration of Market Issues." In *Healthcare Activism: Markets, Morals, and the Collective Good Geiger*, edited by Susi Geiger, 55–85. Oxford University Press.

Rabeharisoa, Vololona, Tiago Moreira, and Madeleine Akrich. 2014. "Evidence-based Activism: Patients', Users' and Activists' Groups in Knowledge Society." *BioSocieties* 9(2): 111–128.

Rabeharisoa, Vololona, and Orla O'Donovan. 2014. "From Europeanization to European Construction: The Role of European Patients' Organizations in the Shaping of Health-Care Policies." *European Societies* 16(5): 717–741.

Refolo, Pietro, Roberta Minacori, Vincenza Mele, Dario Sacchini, and Antonio G. Spagnolo. 2012. "Patient-Reported Outcomes (PROs): The Significance of Using Humanistic Measures in Clinical Trial and Clinical Practice." *European Review for Medical and Pharmacological Sciences* 16 (10): 1319–1323.

Richards, Tessa, and Fiona Godlee. 2014. "The *BMJ*'s Own Patient Journey." *BMJ* 348 (June). doi:10.1136/bmj.g3726.

Richards, Tessa, Victor M. Montori, Fiona Godlee, Peter Lapsley, and Dave Paul. 2013. "Let the Patient Revolution Begin." *BMJ* 346 (May 14): f2614–f2614. doi:10.1136/bmj.f2614.

Spandler, Helen, and Meg Allen. 2018. "Contesting the Psychiatric Framing of ME/CFS." *Social Theory & Health* 16 (2): 127–141.

Ward, Jeremy K. 2016. "Rethinking the Antivaccine Movement Concept: A Case Study of Public Criticism of the Swine Flu Vaccine's Safety in France." *Social Science & Medicine* 159: 48–57.

Ward, Jeremy K., Paul Guille-Escuret, and Clément Alapetite. 2019. "Les 'antivaccins': Figure de l'anti-Science." *Deviance et Societe* 43(2): 221–251.

Wexler, Alice. 1996. *Mapping Fate: A Memoir of Family, Risks and Genetic Research*. Berkeley: University of California Press.

Wynne, Brian. 1996. "May the Sheep Safely Graze? A Reflexive View of the Expert-Lay Knowledge Divide." In *Risk, Environment and Modernity: Towards A New Ecology*, edited by Scott M. Lash, Bronislaw Szerszymski, and Brian Wynne, 44–83. London: SAGE.

6

THE POLITICAL CLIMATE AND CLIMATE POLITICS— EXPERT KNOWLEDGE AND DEMOCRACY

NICO STEHR AND ALEXANDER RUSER

It comes down to trust. Global warming deniers ask us to trust them and to distrust scientist individually and collectively. But the American public has always trusted scientists, and for good reasons. Should it stop doing so now, when we need science more than ever?

—James L. Powell (2011, 188)

THE rhetorical question James L. Powell posed in *The Inquisition of Climate Science* is not only of relevance to the United States. Democracies throughout the world expect to draw on scientific advice. This development is particularly visible in the field of climate change. With human-made climate change posing a major, perhaps unparalleled risk to the well-being of people, should not societies turn to climate scientists to enlighten them about the seriousness of the problem and give them expert advice on how to cope?

Despite the fact that climate science is said to have reached a "gold standard of certainty" (Sherman 2019), it is under attack by climate skeptics, and "even among those who accept the science and recognize the size of the challenge, key questions are hotly debated" (Dryzek, Norgaard, and Schlosberg 2013, 2). Indeed, (neo)liberal democracies have a paltry record of being unable to acknowledge ecological scarcity and deal with future environmental challenges. Writing in the early 1980s, a mere decade after the Club of Rome had sparked the "limits of growth" debate, Bruce Jennings (1983) observed: "The normal agenda of the political economy of liberalism has been reestablished with remarkable ease and virtually without any commentary on the implications that this extraordinary failure of political nerve may have for the future" (376).

For climate scientists and activists eager to "get their message through," democracy, with its long agenda of competing political goals, many instances of extensive public deliberation, and countless opportunities to influence public opinion, may indeed become an inconvenience (Stevenson and Dryzek 2014, 3). Likewise, as recent climate protests, show, constituents themselves are feeling alienated from political representatives apparently unable or unwilling to tackle the issue.

James Hansen (2009), for example, renowned climate scientist and former director of the NASA Goddard Space Institute, is increasingly irritated with politicians' inability to deal with scientific findings: "Politicians think that if matters look difficult, compromise is a good approach. Unfortunately, nature and the laws of physics cannot compromise—they are what they are" (Hansen 2009: xi). In a recent interview with the English newspaper *The Guardian*, he argues that the Paris Accord of December 2015 acknowledges that there is a problem, but "the world is failing 'miserably' with the worsening dangers."[1]

Some concerned scientists and activists argue that traditional modes of governance and policymaking have failed to deal with the challenge of climate change. On their UK website, the activist group Extinction Rebellion, for instance, laments the lack of progress in global and national climate politics:

> Extinction Rebellion believes that part of the problem is the way that government operates. The UK's parliamentary democracy is a form of representative government: power is in the hands of a few representatives (Members of Parliament or MPs) who are elected by the people. This form of government has proved itself incapable of making the radical long-term policy decisions needed to deal effectively with the climate and ecological crisis. (Extinctoin Rebellion 2022 "Our Demands")

Their preferred solution, forming a citizens assembly—the Citizens Assembly on Climate and Ecological Justice—is based on the underlying assumption that having knowledge of the science of climate change would allow citizens to come to a consensus on what to do about human-made climate change. Citizen assemblies would discuss the implementation of advice, not its trustworthiness: "The science is clear: It is understood that we are facing an unprecedented global emergency. We are in a life or death situation of our own making. We must act now." (Emily Grossman, "Emergency on Planet Earth," Extinction Rebellion, n.d. https://rebellion.earth/the-truth/the-emergency/)

Effectively, this constitutes a call for the de-politicization of climate expertise and refocus on a political process that presupposes a universal acceptance of climate science. However, such a presupposition is highly unlikely. Even if the scientific facts on climate change were universally "accepted," we couldn't conclude that there would be an "automatic" agreement on specific climate policies and politics. Given the fact that the proposed citizen assemblies would still have to be implemented in national context, a likely outcome of this proposal would be the reproduction of international disagreement and dispute over necessary steps in global climate politics. For there is no reason to assume that the respective national citizen assemblies (even if universal agreement on the scientific facts could be established) would agree on common or even compatible policy solutions beyond the respective national contexts.

The recent demands by activists (e.g., the Extinction Rebellion, but also the Friday's for Future movement) to leave political debate and "political games" behind come as a somewhat strange reversal of attempts to depoliticize climate science. Historically, it was climate scientists who were surprised and made uneasy by the "political use" of their expertise, though activists and other nonscientists seemed well-aware of its political value. As Harry Otway (1987) observed, "Lay people began to realize (and, strangely, more acutely so than scientists themselves) that what counts as fact is conditioned by political, organizational, and peer pressures" (1245).The very fact hat "scientific facts" are not immediately performative but can be used and abused to serve different political agendas might explain activists' disenchantment of with democratic processes that are apparently incapable living up to the task defined by climate scientists. This political use of scientific information can be depicted as an essential feature or a pathology of democracies. Proponents of the first interpretation can argue that neither the most robust nor the most startling scientific finding mandates immediate action. Scientific knowledge, regardless how "certain" and regardless how "urgent," needs to be put in the hands of elected representatives, who then compete for support of their political proposals based on that knowledge. However, proponents of the latter interpretation criticize exactly that. In this view, the urgency of the "climate crisis" justifies making exceptions of democratic practices:

The "we must act now" statement above implies that the unprecedented "climate crisis" renders democratic disagreement and competition irrelevant by somehow establishing a universal "we." Moreover, the urgency of the challenge, the need to act "now," might justify the suspension of democratic processes for some. The frustration with slow, unpredictable democratic procedures might be understandable. Likewise, the inability of democratic institutions to pursue a "decisive" political agenda to reduce greenhouse gas emissions and protect the climate seems kind of obvious. "Dramatic" political turnarounds, such as the United States' withdrawal from the Paris Climate Agreement in 2017 (Ruser 2018a, 11) may further nurture the impression that politicians are not comprehending the urgency of the task. It might therefore be understandable that, for instance, Extinction Rebellion activists wish to put "political manoeuvring" aside. In their view, "the facts are there,"[2] and so the next "logical" step to brake the political gridlock and put climate politics out of reach of "short-sighted" elected representatives "is to embrace 'expertocracy' in the name of the people." This view, however, rests upon a simple and problematic conception of scientific expertise. Scientific experts are conceived of as mere providers of impartial and objective knowledge ("the truth"). Moreover, this approach fails to acknowledge that even undisputed scientific knowledge claims can be invoked to support very different policy proposals. Even if the scientific fact that greenhouse gas emissions contribute to climate change were universally accepted, one would not be able to derive a single "best" policy solution for emission reduction. Some (including economic experts) might argue for large-scale emission trading schemes; others (including other experts) suggest comprehensive regulation.

Which experts should "we" trust then? And how is it that experts can give us contradictory advice?

We will argue here that social problems, including climate change, cannot be dissolved into purely "scientific or technological [issues], but remain social, political, and cultural" (Lowe, 1971, 569). Even if scientific findings are accepted as the basis for policy solutions, such policies emerge in specific, often highly contested political contexts. Policies cannot simply be "read off" scientific knowledge; they inevitably involve political debate, yet science is nevertheless crucial in policymaking. We first turn to some conceptional problems of relating science and democracy (see "Intersections between Science and Decision-Making") before addressing the problem of climate science in polarized discursive environments ("What I'm Saying Is the Planet Is on Fucking Fire"). In the main sections of this contribution, we will outline three different conceptualizations of the relation between science and decision-making ("Science as informative," "Science as communicative" and "Science as competitive") before we sum up the particularities and difficulties of relying on expertise in climate politics ("Voting on climate change").

Intersections between Science and Decision-Making

Given the impression of essentially "gridlocked" or "failing" climate politics this paper focuses on the specific problems of the intersection between science and decision- making. By drawing on aspects of Robert K. Merton's 1942 *Normative Structure of Science* and other perspectives we discuss some key differences between attributes of scientific knowledge and *democratic* decision-making.

To begin with, a cardinal difference between science and democracy can be derived from Merton focus on "disinterestedness." For him disinterestedness is a basic normative element of the ethos of the scientific community. Disinterestedness points to a distinctive structure of control exercised over the individual motives of scientists. Scientist don't "prefer" one outcome of an experiment over another, nor should they choose their research topics for personal gain. These normative elements or "imperatives" separate science from democracy and the scientists form the politicians. The latter has to be interested in and personally engaged with topics, displays an interest in shaping rather than understanding the world, and is seeking personal gain (e.g., electoral success).

Moreover, the moral imperatives of science are more than mere moral principles. They are linked in distinct ways to the cognitive development of science further separating science from politics. For Merton ([1942] 1973, 270) notes, "The mores of science possess a methodologic rationale, but they are binding, not only because they are procedurally efficient, but because they are believed right and good. They are moral as well as technical prescriptions." Are the norms actually prescriptive? The question of the extent to which the scientific ethos actually determines or influences social and cognitive processes in science is a contested issue and has been addressed in two different ways. Some critics relativize or limit the importance of the ethos of science. Others seek to determine the extent to which the norms of science operate empirically in different scientific communities. But there is sufficient evidence that the norm of disinterestedness does play a role in the self-understanding of many scientists *as* scientists (cf. Stehr 1978; Keller 2017, 119).

Moreover, in his 1966 paper *Dilemmas of Democracy* Merton had pointed out the essential tension and potential conflict between "appropriate" and "legitimate" political action: Scientific expertise sometimes struggles with the gap between the two. Unlike in the realm of science, where the correct execution of scientific principles leads to appropriate, justifiable conclusions, policy initiatives may fail to get legitimization (despite being based in the "best available knowledge") or be legitimate despite being based in a "flawed" depiction of a given situation. Drawing on his insights allows for examining the reasons for the "disenchantment with democracy," especially among scientists if what they perceive to be appropriate and perhaps urgent action fails is not democratically legitimized.

Merton was particularly concerned with uncovering the "utopian" myth that [democratic] theory simply "took for granted that every man was just as competent as every other man" (Merton 1966, 1056) thus assuming that [e]very individual would make the effort to learn what she should know and would use the information in reasonable and instructed ways. Merton in contrast thought that "the people" are not necessarily engaged with scientific findings and expert advice, draw "correct" conclusions in line with scientific reasoning or generally display the capacity to formulate a clear and uniform public "will." Merton's conviction was that, in democratic theory individual "competence was assumed, not assessed" (ibid. 1056).

What I'm Saying Is the Planet Is on Fucking Fire

What I'm saying is the planet is on fucking fire! . . . There are a lot of things we could do to put it out. Are any of them free? No, of course not. Nothing's free, you idiots. Grow the fuck up. Bill Nye cited after O'Neil 2019)

The somewhat staged rant by Bill Nye,[3] renowned TV personality and self-declared "science guy" highlights the view common among scientists and climate believers that "individually assumed competence" is lacking. Instead of counting on the competence of citizens, Mr. Nye struck an emotional and unscientific tone. The swearing and ranting is the opposite of the controlled, impassionate, and disinterested passing on of relevant information that Merton envisioned.

And yet, the sense of urgency and frustration with politicians who are not up to the task of protecting the climate expressed by "the science guy" is echoed by pro-climate activists of the Extinction Rebellion movement and the international Fridays for Future protests. In an invited speech at the 2018 Conference of Parties Summit in Katowice the then fifteen-year-old activist leader Greta Thunberg sharply criticized the political elites for their inaction and playing political games:

> Until you start focusing on what needs to be done rather than what is politically possible, there is no hope. We can't solve a crisis without treating it as a crisis. We need to keep the fossil fuels in the ground, and we need to focus on equity. And if solutions within the system are so impossible to find, maybe we should change the system itself. We have not come here to beg world leaders to care. You have ignored us in the past and you will ignore us again. We have run out of excuses and we are running out of time. We have come here to let you know that change is coming, whether you like it or not. The real power belongs to the people (quoted in Rigitano 2018).

The "coming change" and dawning of a new system presented here presuppose a unified will of the people that could be exercised once power is given back to them. But there is no reason to assume that "the people" will inevitably agree on climate politics—not even if we agree with Evelyn Fox Keller (2011) that "there is no escaping our dependence on experts: we have no choice but to call on those (in this case, our climate scientists) who have the necessary expertise" (107), and not even when "the experts" are as explicit the authors of a 2019 policy report by the Breakthrough National Centre for Climate Restoration in Australia, who wrote: "Climate change now represents a near- to mid-term existential threat to human civilization" (Spratt and Dunlop 2019), adding that to "reduce such risks and to sustain human civilization, it is essential to build a zero-emission industrial system very quickly" (4).

The fact that climate scientists and activists feel they have to use drastic language and invoke images of "existential threats" to make themselves heard has some writers wondering whether democratic structures can survive the climate crisis. To Mark Beeson (2010), writing on the rise of environmental authoritarianism in Asia, the "central question that emerges . . . is whether democracy can be sustained in the region—*or anywhere else for that matter*—given the unprecedented and unforgiving nature of the challenges we collectively face" (289; emphasis added).

Given the magnitude of the challenges "we" are facing—the cleavages and political disagreements that are central to democracies seem to become irrelevant. The question is rather whether such dramatic circumstances will give birth to a form of "good authoritarianism" (Beeson 2010, 289) or strengthen a more radical variant of democracy, such the one demanded by the Extinction Rebellion activists (https://rebellion.earth/the-truth/demands/).

If climate change indeed poses an "existential threat," how can scientific expertise contribute to increasing the individual competence to judge knowledge about climate change? In the following sections we will explore the question of whether scientific expertise should be restricted to be mere sources of information or whether scientific knowledge should be conceived of as a source that shapes communication about climate change and, in consequence, enables climate policies.

Science as Informative: Scientific Literacy and Expertise

Probably the quintessential prerequisites for the individual competence to judge climate change knowledge are the availability and an understanding of crucial information. So, perhaps science should focus on simply "informing" decision-makers and the public.

Contemporary theories of science communication stress that the "informing" itself might itself be a tricky task: "One-way, top-down communication of packaged scientific information does not work," writes Brian Trench (2008, 119), adding that "science communication [requires] for the public to talk back, and scientists need to listen, so that understandings can be developed together" (119). The ability to "talk back" has two different aspects. First, it highlights demands to "democratize science" (Kleinman et al. 2007)—that is, granting citizens and "laypeople" the right to take part in debates about scientific findings. Second, the ability to talk back points to the duty of citizens to equip themselves with the necessary knowledge and skills to take part in deliberations on scientific advice, turning scientific literacy into a civic duty. As Jon Miller (1996) pointed out in the late 1990s:

> Looking ahead to the early decades of the twenty-first century, it is clear that national, state, and political agendas will include an increasing number of important scientific and controversies.... The *preservation* of the democratic process demands that there be a sufficient number of citizens able to understand the issues, deliberate the alternatives, and adopt public policy. (186; emphasis added)

To guarantee the proper functioning of democracies in modern knowledge-based societies citizens *have to* acquire the relevant knowledge in order to make informed decisions and to choose, for example, between alternatives pathways presented to them by the scientific community.

However, democracies should take on board divergent interests, different dispositions, and distinctive ideological convictions, even knowledge-based democracies (Stehr and Ruser 2017). And so decision-making processes may run counter to the "impartial" knowledge claims made by the scientific community, thus raising the question of whether science is (still) owed a "special deference precisely because it liberates the truths of nature from particular social and cultural settings" (Robert Merton, quoted in Jasanoff 2010, 236). However, this doesn't mean that science can arrive at (or is even aiming at) universal and eternal truth. Scientific methods, though universal, produce preliminary and falsifiable knowledge claims. Nonetheless, as Evelyn Fox Keller (2011) has pointed out, the "absence of a methodology for guaranteeing absolute truth, certainty and proof" (21) doesn't imply that there is no way of distinguishing between trustworthy and untrustworthy information or that one interpretation of available data is as good as any other (23). In other words, even if scientific knowledge claims are not representing an "absolute truth," they may still express the "best available knowledge" and might therefore preferred over personal beliefs or time-honored traditions. However, there are a plurality of "ways" to distinguish between trustworthy and untrustworthy information. Moreover, these ways might reflect specific cultural and historic backgrounds (e.g., academic traditions).

However, the provisional nature of scientific knowledge may be less of a problem because political decisions in democracies don't require absolute certainty or undeniable proof.[4] According to David Held and Angus Hervey (2011), climate politics are often hampered, not by insufficient scientific knowledge, but by inherently political problems, such as "short termism," "self-referring decision making," and the influence of "interest groups" (90).

However, according to Michael Zimmerman (1997) "the public" not only struggles with making sense of scientific information but often displays an "inability to differentiate science from pseudoscience" (xi), making it hard to distinguish between scientific expertise and charlatanerie. Scientific "illiteracy" therefore does *not* refer to a simple lack of information but to a, more or less, fundamental *misunderstanding* of science. Science is often falsely depicted as "a collection of facts rather than an ongoing investigative process that permits us to gain insights and understanding in the way the world works" (Zimmerman 1997, 14). "The popular conception of the scientist patiently collecting observations, unprejudiced by any theory, until finally he succeeds in establishing a great new generalization, is quite false" stresses Michael Polanyi (1964, 28), highlighting the gap between "observation and interpretation" (Keller 2017, 112) that tends to influence the very construction of a scientific fact. What to observe and how interpret the observed data normally depend on theoretical preconceptions that guide the research process, determine the research design, and separate "relevant" from "irrelevant" aspects. "Finding out" something about the world therefore involves finding plausible explanations of observed data deemed relevant from a given theoretical perspective.

Presumably, these apparent limitations of science as a means to inform the public can only be overcome if science education itself changes: "The public understanding of science' seems to concentrate on trying to help people know more science, and there is much too little effort to help people know more *about* science, about the way it is done and its limits" (Fischer 1996, 110). But according to Fischer (1996), such an undertaking would face huge obstacles: "Nobody knows what the public is," he writes, adding:

> There are several layers or agencies between science and the public. The public hardly ever meets science directly, it is mostly informed by journalists, and this special group of people are . . . much more influenced by social scientists than by physicists, chemists, biologists, or the like . . . . I believe also that no-one knows what the public knows. We know only what the public is getting to see or read, and we all know that a journal or a magazine is not primarily interested in scientific correctness but in the number of copies that are sold of each issue at the newsstand. (112)

To play the role of informing society properly, experts would have to be very clear about their message. At the same time, "the people"—that is, a heterogeneous conglomerate of individuals, groups, and subgroups—would somehow have to commit themselves to learning about science (not just about an isolated bit of information), and simultaneously, the neutrality of the respective "channels" used for disseminating scientific knowledge should somehow also be ensured. Certainly, this is not an easy task.

And not a new one either: John Stuart Mill affirmed that democracies depend on constituents who possess some basic skills. "I regard it as wholly inadmissible that any person should participate in the suffrage without being able to read, write, and, I will add, perform the common operations of arithmetic," he wrote in his *Consideration on Representative Government* (chap. 8), adding that literacy is a necessary prerequisite for "pursuing intelligently their own interests."

This old idea of giving more weight to the suffrage of the better educated aged well with scholars concerned with the interplay of ecology and democracy. William Ophuls (2011), a prolific writer on environmental challenges and governance, warned of the consequences of ignoring (or being ignorant of) environmental problems because the "long-term effect of unleashed passions . . . has been to violate nature's laws and limits and provoke an ecological crisis" (19). To him, the way out is obeying "natural law," understood as "right reason in agreement with Nature" (20). But what does it take to "reason in agreement with nature"? Apparently, the passive "reception" of scientific information isn't enough. What follows from such a conception for the citizens of "knowledge democracies"? As we have seen, they could have the duty to become scientifically literate to understand the information given to them by "experts," and vice versa. One might also conceive of experts as being responsible for making their specialized knowledge *accessible*. From this perspective, the scientific experts need to acquire the relevant communicative skills to explain their findings to laypeople.

Science as Communicative: Experts as Bearers, Translators, and Distorters of Knowledge

Whether one favors democratic approaches or envisions policies imposed by well-meaning autocrats (Ophuls 1973), one thing disenchanted scientists, disillusioned citizens, and rebellious activists can agree on is that climate politics need to be based on expertise.

Theoretical conceptions that attempt to systematize and typecast experts and their means of translating knowledge (thus explaining how politics could be based on expertise) often focus on outlining *preferable* roles. Jürgen Habermas, for instance, argued that the perfect place for scientific experts is somewhere between a technocratic perspective, where experts actually *make* the decision, and a decisionist perspective, where they are reduced to the role of pundit whose expertise is requested as long as it fits with political preferences and agendas. He envisions a *pragmatic model* in which "the relationship between science and politics is reciprocal and non-hierarchical and discursive" (Ruser 2018b, 772).

However, in many countries, most notably, the United States, the production and dissemination of knowledge has increasingly been relocated, from publicly funded research centers and universities to private or corporate research institutes and think tanks (Rich 2004; Medvetz 2012). This makes it harder to locate the expert "between" the roles of technocrat and mere "informant" because experts have ever more sides to choose.

Trusting "experts" thus becomes ever more difficult, when all experts seem become "someone's experts." The consequences of this blurring of the line between "distanced investigation and active promotion" (Rich 2004, 29) is, again, particularly visible in highly polarized political systems like that of the United States (Kuo and McCarthy 2015). Here, "issue advocates," partisan, and/or profit-oriented experts find abundant opportunities to side with political camps and tailor their advice to the preexisting ideological preferences of clients and specific target audiences (Dunlap and Jacques 2013; Dunlap and McCright 2015).

Other countries, in contrast, have developed other contexts for advice giving and thus for distinguishing between trustworthy from untrustworthy knowledge (see Keller 2017 above). Germany, for instance, has a complex political system that relies quite heavily on climate experts and environmental think tanks. In contrast to the United States, however, "issue advocates" and, especially, partisan organizations in Germany are marginalized and do not maintain ties to either mainstream political parties or important news outlets. The reason is not the somehow "higher" scientific literacy of German citizens, who are thus immune to partisan expertise. The explanation lies in the institutional environment in Germany, which resembles a "closed shop" (Ruser 2018a, 114), where a small number of scientific experts and academic think tanks form a close network with ministries and elected representatives. Advocacy think tanks and partisan experts are (by and large) effectively excluded from public funding and, more importantly, political debate. This is not to say that political debate about climate change in Germany is more "rational" than in other countries and free from the influence of special interests. Economic interests and powerful business associations have had and continue to have an impact on political debate and policymaking. However, they use strategies that resemble classical "lobbying tactics" instead of invoking public "counterexpertise" to climate science, and they limit their attacks to specific policies rather against the "fact" of climate change (Eberlein and Matten 2009, 249).

The question of whether putting faith in "our" experts can reduce political dispute and disagreement over scientific matters therefore depends on the institutionalized interplay between experts and decision-makers in the first place.

Accordingly, demands like Extinction Rebellion's call for the strengthening of direct democracy and the implementation of "citizen assemblies" will likely fail to move climate issues "beyond politics" when and where invoking expertise (and counterexpertise) is an accepted strategy in political disputes. For instance, excluding "climate deniers" from such citizen assemblies would require labeling their experts "untrustworthy" and "illegitimate." In Germany (and other European countries), this might be possible by pointing out their lack of academic credentials or their overall marginalized position. In the United States, however, the same strategy would most certainly backfire, earning the hypothetical citizen assembly the criticism of being biased, "liberal," and "leftist."

Moreover, because of the complexity of climate science, distinguishing "scientifically sound" expertise from politically motivated expertise is difficult, if it is even possible (Machin and Ruser 2019), which means that "pure" scientists face obstacles in telling the facts. Because experts operate in sometimes polarized media landscapes and political systems, the question of "how" to communicate their findings challenges the idea of "our" neutral experts. As early as 1988, renowned climate scientist Stephen Schneider warned of the difficulties of competing for attention in media contexts that require dramatization and emotionalism:

> To [reduce the risk of global warming], we need to get some broad-based support, to capture the public's imagination. That, of course, means getting loads of media coverage. So, we have to offer up *scary scenarios, make simplified, dramatic statements,* and make *little mention of any doubt we might have.* Each of us has to decide what the right balance is between being effective and being honest. (quoted in Pool 1990, 672; emphasis added)

Although the need to capture attention is understandable, the adoption of "successful" communication strategies by experts carries the risk of contributing to "the abuse of expert authority and the creation of pseudo-sciences" that Merton ([1942] 1973) identified as a major challenge for the use of scientific knowledge in democracies. Moreover, when both sides are willing to exaggerate, dramatize, and weigh effectiveness against honesty, how can even the most dedicated citizen hope to learn "what he should know" to be able to "use the information in reasonable and instructed ways" (Merton 1966, 1056)? If "our" experts adopt the strategies of "their" experts, how can we hope to rely on expertise to put climate change beyond politics?

Climate change and climate politics thus clearly highlight a dilemma for modern democracies. Catching up with complex findings of climate science is itself a challenge. Moreover, since "scientific facts" can't always be clearly separated from norms, values, or simply preferred ways of living, any acquisition of knowledge inevitably involves a normative decision. Preexisting normative convictions, in turn, can render some scientific knowledge claims "unacceptable" and therefore unbelievable. Although such normatively "filtered" knowledge is "wrong" from the perspective of science, it still allows people to set something in motion (e.g., prolonging the status quo or opposing regulatory overreach by environmentalists). The failure to use "information in reasonable and instructed ways," which for Merton, identified as a dilemma for democracy is, at the same time, a dilemma for modern science. If scientific experts refrain from technocratic temptation and want people to engage with their expertise, they can't count on any preexisting scientific literacy among the public or willingness to become scientifically literate. Moreover, since any expert knowledge might have to compete for attention and might be challenged (for whatever reason) by rival knowledge claims in the political arena, experts have to decide whether and to what a degree they want to engage in political debates, political infighting, and the "battle" of ideas (Schneider 2009).

Science as Competitive: Knowledge and Climate Expertise

Since scientific knowledge isn't immediately performative, we have to turn to the question of what it means to "have" knowledge, in general, and about climate change, in particular. Moreover, we have to consider that (scientific) knowledge may well support different political positions.

A *sociological* conception of knowledge has to differentiate between "between what is known, the content of knowledge, and knowing itself" (Stehr and Ruser 2017). This means pointing out the complicated relation of and sometimes subtle differences between "information" and "knowledge." As we have seen, debates on scientific literacy and "understanding" expert advice focus on "information." Although the term "information" is itself ambiguous and can refer to both "codified knowledge" and "indirect knowledge" (Adolf and Stehr 2017, 26), overall, "the substance of information primarily [is] concern[ed] with the properties of *products and outcomes*. Information is exactly what can be passed on and 'deciphered' and owned by the (scientifically) literate. Knowledge in contrast is not so much something you 'have' but something you can 'use' ":

> We suggest defining knowledge as the capacity to act (or capability of taking action), as the possibility of "setting something in motion." Knowledge is a model for reality. Thus, for example, social statistics are not necessarily (only) a reflection of social reality, but rather an explication of its problems; they refer to that which could be, and in this sense, they confer the capability of taking action. (Stehr and Grundmann 2012, 32)

In consequence, knowledgeability shouldn't be confused with a passive understanding or acceptance of facts presented by experts. If "the social significance of scientific discoveries, . . . lies primarily in the capacity to make use of knowledge as the ability to act," and if "knowledge gains in distinction on the basis of its ability to change reality," as Stehr and Grundmann (2012, 33) describe, then, accordingly, knowledge claims *about* reality (such as scientific knowledge claims) demand special attention:

> In this sense of our definition of knowledge, *scientific and technical* [emphasis in the original] knowledge clearly represents "capacities for action or capacities to intervene." But this does not mean that it is not subject to interpretation; a resource that is incontestable; that it travels without serious impediments . . . ; that it can be reproduced at will; or that it is accessible to all—nor [does it mean] that scientific and technical knowledge primarily conveys unique and generally effective capacities for action. (Stehr 2016, 30–31)

This being said, the crucial aspect of "knowing about climate change" is not so much "understanding" the complex interplay between, say, the emission of some aerosols and their interaction with incoming solar radiation (as simple models of scientific literacy would assume) as it is understanding what can be *done* with such knowledge (e.g., labeling the burning of fossil fuels "dangerous" or "irresponsible"). Moreover, when knowledge is understood this way, the role experts can possibly play changes. Rather than simply informing a scientifically literate public and "rationalizing" decision-making, expert knowledge is always introduced in specific contexts, where it has to compete with rival knowledge claims, and where it can be contested and tested in a variety of political controversies. As noted above, trust in expert knowledge (Stehr 2003, 647), expert authority, and specific experts is established in concrete social settings; rather than stemming from the "obvious" persuasiveness of expert knowledge (Adolf and Stehr 2017, 44–45).

Given the magnitude and "seriousness of the implications" (Keller 2017, 113), it might be surprising that climate knowledge *isn't* set apart from other controversies that circle around the "use" of scientific knowledge in public and political debates. This is all the more astonishing because climate politics is a field that was established exclusively by scientific knowledge. In fact, the term "climate" itself refers to a scientific condition that—unlike the local weather—cannot be "experienced" directly, as the definition given by the Intergovernmental Panel on Climate Change (IPCC) clearly shows:

> Climate in a narrow sense is usually defined as the "average weather," or more rigorously, as the statistical description in terms of the mean and variability of relevant quantities over a period of time ranging from months to thousands of years. The classical period is 3 decades, as defined by the World Meteorological Organization (WMO). These quantities are most often surface variables such as temperature, precipitation, and wind. Climate in a wider sense is the state, including a statistical description, of the climate system.[5]

Climate science is concerned with the collection and analysis of complex and diverse data, the constructing of time-series data sets, and the development of sophisticated "scenarios" (Ruser 2015; 2018a, 18–19) to estimate the likely impact of changes in the "average" weather on the global, regional, and local stages. None of this is easily accessible. The use of complicated scientific methods and the inevitability of the use of computer models[6] further increases the need for explanation. Finally, since climate science aims at predicting the outcomes of changes in the average weather, these explanations often include several options (e.g., "best vs. worst case scenarios") meaning that the trustworthiness of not only the underlying science but also the individual expert might be particularly important for convincing any audience.

In short: giving scientific expertise is going beyond convincing potentially multiple audiences that their respective knowledge claims are *true* (e.g., that an invisible gas is in fact altering atmospheric chemistry in a way that traps outgoing solar radiation inside the atmosphere and is slowly leading to an increase in average surface temperature).

Moreover, the trustworthiness of experts seems to be rather loosely coupled with the content of their knowledge claims and their methods for arriving at certain discoveries. As the very fact that the same knowledge claim (for instance, about the impact of human emission on atmospheric chemistry) that is convincing to some people in some circumstances and rejected by others points toward the significance of the respective social context in which the expert advice is given. In some environments, such as in the partisan system of the United States, even the "best available knowledge" might not be good enough.

Demands by political activists, however understandable, to put the urgent challenge of climate change beyond politics and take the warnings of scientific experts seriously are, for these reasons, unlikely to be successful. Scientific experts cannot be depicted as impartial providers of information. Nor can the process of advice giving be reduced to the passing on of sound knowledge. In the highly contested field of climate politics, scientific expertise is inevitably "politicized." Moreover, as scientific knowledge enters the political arena, experts may have to use the same techniques to get attention as their opponents: dramatize, emotionalize, and simplify the message (see Antonio and Brulle 2011, 196). The trustworthiness of experts therefore might differ in different countries and different political constellations.

VOTING ON CLIMATE CHANGE? CONCLUSION AND OUTLOOK

Can people vote on climate change and what to do about it? No, they can't. Can people vote on climate politics? Sure, they can. The plausibility of scientific knowledge claims and subsequently of expert advice based on such claims cannot be democratically decided. Scientific findings do not conform to the preferences of a majority but are the product of careful, "disinterested" (Merton [1942] 1973) observation, experimentation, measurement, and testing. Opening the research process for democratic voting would not increase its legitimacy, but it would damage its epistemological status. This is why we can't vote on the soundness of climate science. Anything but a scientific debate about the rigor of the research, the quality of data, and the drawing of conclusions can't challenge climate science *as* science. However, debates on the quality of scientific research can't replace political debates about its use either. Even the "best available knowledge" has no immediate democratic legitimacy. Therefore, neither "replacing" democratic deliberation nor "basing" it on scientific research is likely to end political dispute.

To avoid this dilemma, some suggest turning the question of whether scientific knowledge should trump democratic processes and institutions into a less fundamental one. Following Friedrich Hayek's remark that "it is sensible *temporarily* to sacrifice freedom in order to make it more secure in the future" (emphasis added; Hayek, 1944, 189) it seems reasonable to support giving experts greater expert power if it is narrowed to climate politics and granted only until the crisis is over.

But is that possible? How would such a restriction to "climate politics" be organized when the climate is affected by economic activity, as well as personal activities around individual mobility, maintaining a high and convenient standard of living, dietary habits, and in general population growth?

Scientific experts would inevitably have to interfere with personal liberties. Nothing but a fundamental lifestyle change (in Western countries) wouldn't be sufficient to guarantee lasting emission reductions, individual willingness to adopt more "sustainable" ways of producing and consuming is key for climate protection. However, this willingness, can't be "commanded" by experts but is more likely to be a consequence of an emotional attachment.

This implies that any "empowering" of experts could lead to a conflict not only about political preferences or feasible economic strategies, but about individual liberties. Unlike in democracies, where any restriction of personal liberties should be democratically legitimized, experts' rule carries the danger of curtailing these liberties without deliberation and without public consent, paving the way for "authoritarian environmentalism."

Therefore, climate politics, like any other "science-based" question cannot be relegated to "the experts." Scientific discoveries haven´t ended racial prejudice or gender discrimination. From the perspective of modern science, the claim that one "race" is superior to another doesn't hold, and yet racist politics prevails. Likewise, it is unlikely that a new discovery by climate scientists will end the political dispute about climate politics. The confidence of scientific experts in their research cannot replace political debates about climate politics. Even if the demands by global climate activists to strengthen democracy would be met and citizen assemblies would impact the ways how expert advice could be turned into policies the question whose expertise should count and what political action should follow, remains.

This means that the essential tension between the "appropriate" and "legitimate" highlighted by Robert K. Merton remains with us too. Climate experts can only tell us what is—according to the standards of scientific research—"appropriate." Legitimizing expert advice is an essential political task. The current disenchantment with democratic processes, visible in critical statements of climate scientists and the demands of (global) activist movements should not be confused with a general disillusion with science or with democracy in general.

NOTES

1. See Oliver Milman (2018), "Ex-Nasa Scientist: 30 Years on, World Is Failing 'Miserably' to Address Climate Change," *The Guardian*, June 19. https://www.theguardian.com/environment/2018/jun/19/james-hansen-nasa-scientist-climate-change-warning.
2. As becomes visible on the Extinction Rebellion website, which tells "the truth."

3. Nye said this on a late-night television show; he was speaking to an audience that is most likely to believe in climate change.

4. This fact is emphasized by Keller (2011), who points out that "military policy, economic, health and welfare policy, cannot afford to wait for 'proof,' but must be arrived at on the basis of best information available" (24). Economic and welfare politics are particularly prone to "fashions" in economic theorizing, with large-scale policies being implemented on the basis of scientific "models" and projections (Mirowski 2014), an approach that is otherwise fiercely attacked by climate skeptics.

5. IPCC Fifth Assessment Synthesis Report 2014. http://www.ipcc.ch/ipccreports/tar/wg2/index.php?idp=689.

6. Advanced computer modeling is key for the advancement of climate science, not only because it makes it possible to include and analyze large quantities of data, but also, and mainly, because it makes it possible to construct "controlled environments." Computer models provide researchers with artificial "control Earths," which enables them to test for the likely impact of single parameters. For a more detailed evaluation, see Ruser (2018, 19ff).

REFERENCES

Adolf, Marian, and Nico Stehr. 2017. *Knowledge: Is Knowledge Power?* 2nd ed. London: Routledge.

Antonio, Robert J., and Robert J. Brulle. 2011. "The Unbearable Lightness of Politics: Climate Change Denial and Political Polarization." *Sociological Quarterly* 52 (2): 195–202.

Beeson, Mark. 2010. "The Coming of Environmental Authoritarianism." *Environmental Politics* 19 (2): 276–294.

Dunlap, Riley, and Peter Jacques. 2013. "Climate Change Denial Books and Conservative Think Tanks: Exploring the Connection." *American Behavioral Scientist* 57 (6): 699–731.

Dunlap, Riley, and Aaron McCright. 2015. "Challenging Climate Change: The Denial Countermovement." In *Climate Change and Society: Sociological Perspectives*, edited by Riley E. Dunlap and Robert Brulle, 300–332. New York: Oxford University Press.

Dryzek, John S., Richard B. Norgaard, and David Schlosberg. 2013. *Climate Challenged Society*. Oxford: Oxford University Press.

Eberlein, Burkard, and Dirk Matten. 2009. "Business Responses to Climate Change Regulation in Canada and Germany: Lessons for MNCs from Emerging Economies." *Journal of Business Ethics* 86: 241–255.

Extinction Rebelloion. 2022. "Our Demands" https://rebellion.earth/the-truth/demands

Fischer, Ernst P. 1996. "The Public Misunderstanding of Science." *Interdisciplinary Science Reviews* 21 (2): 110–116.

Grundmann, Reiner, and Nico Stehr. 2012. *The Power of Scientific Knowledge: From Research to Public Policy*. Cambridge, UK: Cambridge University Press.

Hansen, James. 2009. *Storms of My Grandchildren: The Truth about the Coming Climate Catastrophe and Our Last Chance to Save Humanity*. London: Bloomsbury.

Hayek, Friedrich. A. v. 1. 1944. *The Road to Serfdom*. Chicago, University of Chicago Press.

International Panel on *Climate Change (IPCC). 2014. Climate Change 2014: Synthesis Report. Contribution of Working Groups I, II and III to the Fifth Assessment Report of the Inter- governmental Panel on Climate Change*. Edited by Core Writing Team, R.K. Pachauri and L.A. Meyer. IPCC: Geneva, Switzerland.

International Panel on Climate Change (IPCC). 2018. *Global Warming of 1.5 °C (SR15)*. Special report. International Panel on Climate Change. Geneva, Switzerland. http://www.ipcc.ch/.

Jasanoff, Sheila. 2010. "A New Climate for Society." *Theory, Culture & Society* 27:233–253.

Jennings, Bruce. 1983. "Liberal Democracy and the Problem of Scarcity." *International Political Science Review* 4 (3): 375–383.

Keller, Evelyn Fox. 2011. "What Are Climate Scientists to Do?" *Spontaneous Generations: A Journal for the History and Philosophy of Science* 5 (1): 19–26.

Keller, Evelyn Fox. 2017. "Climate Science, Truth, and Democracy." *Studies in History and Philosophy of Biological and Biomedical Sciences* 64: 106–122.

Kleinman, Daniel Lee, Maria Powell, Joshua Grice, Judith Adrian, and Carol Lobes. 2007. "A Toolkit for Democratizing Science and Technology Policy: The Practical Mechanics of Organizing a Consensus Conference." *Bulletin of Science, Technology & Society* 27, no. 2 (April): 154–169.

Kuo, Didi, and Nolan McCarthy. 2015. "Democracy in America, 2015." *Global Policy* 6: 49–55.

Lowe, Adolph. 1971. "Is Present-Day Higher Education Learning 'Relevant'?" *Social Research* 38: 563–580.

Medvetz, Thomas. 2012. *Think Tanks in America*. Chicago: Chicago University Press.

Merton, Robert K. (1942) 1973. "The Normative Structure of Science." In *The Sociology of Science: Theoretical and Empirical Investigations*, edited by Robert K. Merton and Norman W. Storer, 267–278. Chicago: University of Chicago Press.

Merton, Robert K. 1966. "Dilemmas of Democracy in the Volunatry Association." *American Journal of Nursing* 66(5): 1055–1061.

Miller, Jon D. 1996. "Scientific Literacy for Effective Citizenship." In *Science/Technology/Society as Reform in Science Education*, edited by Robert E. Yager, 185–202. Albany: State University of New York Press.

Milman, Oliver. 2018, "Ex-Nasa Scientist: 30 Years on, World Is Failing 'Miserably' to Address Climate Change," *The Guardian*, June 19. https://www.theguardian.com/environment/2018/jun/19/james-hansen-nasa-scientist-climate-change-warning.

Mirowski, Philip. 2014. *Never Let a Serious Crisis Go to Waste: How Neoliberalism Survived the Financial Meltdown*. London: Verso.

O'Neil, Luke. 2019 "The planegt is on fire: Bill Nye driven to F-Bomb rant by climate change." *The Guardian* 14 May 2019.

Ophuls, William. 1973. "Leviathan or Oblivion." In *Towards a Steady-State Economy*, edited by Herman E Daly. San Francisco W. H. Freeman.

Ophuls, William. 2011. *Plato´s Revenge: Politics in the Age of Ecology*. Cambridge, MA: MIT Press.

Polanyi, Michael. 1964. *Science, Faith and Society*. Chicago: University of Chicago Press.

Pool, Robert. 1990. "Struggling to Do Science for Society." *Science* 248:672–673.

Powell, James Lawrence. 2011. *The Inquisition of Climate Science*. New York: Columbia University Press.

Rich, Andrew. 2004. *Think Tanks, Public Policy, and the Politics of Expertise*. Cambridge, UK: Cambridge University Press.

Rigitano, Emanuele. 2018. "COP24, the Speech by 15-Year-Old Climate Activist Greta Thunberg Everyone Should Listen To." *Lifegate*, December 17. https://www.lifegate.com/greta-thunberg-speech-cop24

Ruser, Alexander. 2015. "By the Markets, of the Markets, for the Markets? Technocratic Decision-Making and the Hollowing Out of Democracy." *Global Policy* 6 (S1): 83–92.

Ruser, Alexander. 2018a. *Climate Politics and the Impact of Think Tanks: Scientific Expertise in Germany and the US.* Basingstoke, UK: Palgrave.

Ruser, Alexander. 2018b. "Experts and Science and Politics." In *The SAGE Handbook of Political Sociology*, edited by William Outhwaite and Stephen P. Turner, 767–780. Los Angeles: SAGE.

Ruser, Alexander, and Amanda Machin. 2019. "What Counts in the Politics of Climate Change? Science, Scepticism and Emblematic Numbers." In *Science, Numbers and Contemporary Politics*, edited by Markus Prutsch. Basingstoke, UK:203-225, Palgrave Macmillan.

Schneider, Stephen. 2009. *Science as a Contact Sport: Inside the Battle to Save Earth's Climate.* Washington DC: National Geographic.

Sherman, Erik. 2019. "Scientists Say Evidence for Man-Made Climate Change Has Reached a 'Gold Standard' for Certain." *Fortune*, February 26.

Spratt, David, and Ian Dunlop. 2019. "Existential Climate-Related Security Risk: A Scenario Approach." Policy Report. Breakthrough National Centre for Climate Restoration, Melbourne, AUS.

Stehr, Nico. 1978. "The Ethos of Science Revisited." *Sociological Inquiry* 48, no. 3–4 (July): 172–196.

Stehr, Nico. 2003. "The Social and Political Control of Knowledge in Modern Societies." *International Social Science Journal* 55: 643–655.

Stehr, Nico. 2016. *Information, Power, and Democracy: Liberty Is a Daughter of Knowledge.* Cambridge, UK: Cambridge University Press.

Stehr, Nico, and Reiner Grundmann. 2012. "How Does Knowledge Relate to Political Action?" *Innovation: European Journal of Social Science Research* 25: 29–44.

Stehr, Nico, and Alexander Ruser. 2017. "Knowledge Society, Knowledge Economy and Knowledge Democracy." In *Handbook of Cyber-Development, Cyber-Democracy, and Cyber-Defense*, edited by Elias G. Carayannis, David F. J. Campbell, and Marios Panagiotis Efthymiopoulos, Dordrecht: 1–20. Springer.

Stevenson, Hayley, and John S. Dryzek. 2014. *Democratizing Global Climate Governance.* Cambridge, UK: Cambridge University Press.

Trench, Brian. 2008. "Towards an Analytical Framework of Science Communication Models." In *Communicating Science in Social Contexts*, edited by Donghong Cheng, Michel Claessens, Toss Gascoigne, Jenni Metcalfe, Bernard Schiele, and Shunke Shi. Dordrecht: 119-135, Springer.

Zimmerman, Michael. 1997. *Science, Nonscience, and Nonsense: Approaching Environmental Literacy.* Baltimore, MD: Johns Hopkins University Press.

PART II

TRUST

7

MISTRUST OF EXPERTS BY POPULISTS AND POLITICIANS

Robert P. Crease

Introduction

EXPERTS are commonly relied on not only in issues involving a scientific-technological dimension but across the entire landscape of human experience, from art appreciation and architecture to parenting and politics. To the extent that the human world is made possible by reliance on experts, however, it is also made vulnerable to poor, ignored, or absent expertise—as well to the mistrust and denial of experts, of expert advice, and of their associated institutions. Such mistrust threatens democracy itself (Rosenfeld 2019).

Mistrust of experts and their institutions is now an established feature of the political landscape in the United States and elsewhere. The mistrust is frequently not wholesale, but selective. One may mistrust doctors who recommend vaccinations but not other doctors, for instance, or one may mistrust scientists whose findings point to long-term climate changes, but not meteorologists or scientists in other areas. The mistrust, moreover, is generally accompanied not by a rejection of all experts but by an embrace of alternate advice-givers. Furthermore, and needless to say, mistrust may be provoked and productive.

Just as expertise is a complex phenomenon, mistrust of expertise is equally complex, provoked by different aspects and dimensions of the relations of expertise. One can mistrust the expert advice by specific individuals or institutions based on their track records or other behaviors, or one can mistrust expert advice as part of a broader suspicion of the social or bureaucratic infrastructure that produces and maintains it. An example is the skeptical reaction that now greets "Better living through chemistry," the famous slogan derived from the DuPont company's advertising. The skepticism is directed not so much against individual chemists or even specific businesses but against the entire chemical industry.

This chapter reviews the sources of this mistrust of experts, expert advice, and associated institutions in relation to the populist and other groups that mistrust or reject mainstream sources of expertise. It will also focus on mistrust of experts in the scientific-technological domain, though similar issues arise in other domains.

Call-and-Response Expertise

A basic model for approaching the movement of expertise might be termed "call and response." The call-and-response model involves a simple, intentional relationship between a producer and a consumer of expertise. A user experiences a need for information that cannot be obtained by oneself but is required to perform some tasks; this user seeks out the appropriate authority for such information; the authority responds by delivering that information; and the user acts accordingly.

The call-and-response model correctly portrays the movement of expertise as a dynamic process in which advice is sought by and delivered to someone who intends to regard it as authoritative and to act on it. Mistrust of expertise, in this model, must be due to the consumer's being ignorant, dishonest, or having interests that override the desire to act on mainstream authoritative advice; to the consumer's mishearing the information; or to the consumer's perceiving the expert to be phony, deceitful, or not the right kind of authority, after all.

While the call-and-response model can seem intuitive and comfortable to both experts and consumers of expertise, it has limitations and weaknesses. First, it too-innocently portrays expertise as going from a stable, relatively reliable, context-free object to a welcoming, open-minded, responsive subject. Second, it fails to recognize that experts can shape the "call" of the "call-and-response." Government panels and advisory boards, for instance, can "curate"—anticipate, select, and structure—the questions they are asked and how they are solicited for advice (Bijker et al. 2009; Oppenheimer 2019). Third, it overlooks the ways that consumers of expertise might react to the "response," from thoughtful evaluation to programmed embrace to denial. Fourth, the call-and-response model ignores the influence of scientism. Experts, especially those with technical and scientific specialties and credentials, can assume that their expertise entitles them to give advice about how their expertise should be implemented *and* about fields outside their specialty—and this can be naively accepted by consumers of the expertise or be seen as grounds for mistrust.

Finally, the call-and-response model neglects the phenomenology of the vast populist and political mistrust and denial of expertise. In some environments, mainstream expert voices are heard clearly and authoritatively; in others, they are drowned out, or other voices are heard as authoritative. The call-and-response model fails to account for selectivity in the choice of experts, the embrace of alternative experts, the differential amplitude of expert voices, or for the fact that expert denial is more prominent in certain social strata than others; nor does it account for the impact of culture and history on the choice of experts. The call-and-response model, in short, fails to account for the full complexity of how expert voices are heard in changing environments.

THE ACOUSTICAL MODEL OF EXPERTISE

A more nuanced approach is found in what one might call the "acoustical model." The acoustical model also portrays the movement of expertise as a dynamic and ongoing process in which advice is sought and delivered to someone who intends to act on it. But it envisions the movement of expertise as occurring in a hermeneutical (sense-making) space in which voices are heard and interpreted differently. This acoustical space is never neutral, and it works to make some voices clearer and more audible than others. Investigating the acoustics of expertise thus points to a variety of hermeneutical dimensions, both of expertise and of expert denial and mistrust.

The call-and-response situation is, in fact, a special case of the acoustical model, one in which the voice is heard clearly and loudly by someone who sought it out and is prepared to hear and act. In the special condition of the laboratory or classroom, for instance, an expert's voice is readily recognized and carefully considered; in the public arena, it is hard to recognize and easily overwhelmed by other voices clamoring for attention.

The acoustical model offers a more comprehensive approach to understanding mistrust of experts and expertise. It helps to explain why mainstream expert voices can be unheard, misheard, received skeptically, or simply ignored. It explains why this does not leave hearers relying only on their own resources; they still intend to act, and they will find other nontraditional voices to listen to as experts. It also points to the need for empirical research into questions of how consumers of information respond to specific kinds of advice or information (Roulston and Smith 2004). The acoustical model therefore sees distrust of experts and expertise as something other than ignorance, stupidity, selfishness, or mendacity. The acoustical model avoids the mistake of regarding the process of addressing controversies with a scientific-technological dimension as a matter of assembling the right kinds of expertise.

THE TECHNOCRATIC SETUP

Social stratification creates the background environment in which mistrust of mainstream experts and expertise must be understood. The republics established in the United States and Europe in the eighteenth and nineteenth centuries embodied social stratification in their dependence on a governing class whose members claimed to have knowledge and wisdom, and were assumed to be adept at statecraft. This is the thrust of James Madison's words in Federalist 57: "The aim of every political constitution is or ought to be first to obtain for rulers men who possess [the] most wisdom to discern, and [the] most virtue to pursue, the common good of the society" (quoted in Rosenfeld 2019, 51).

The stratification drives the tendency of those who are not in the governing class to reject, in the name of "the people," the decrees issued by the experts of that class as undemocratic and to create a "populist epistemology" that is associated with an oppositional culture (Rosenfeld 2019, 107). Populists "tend to reject science and its methods as a source of directives, embracing in many cases emotional honesty, intuition, and truths of the heart over dry factual veracity and scientific evidence, testing, and credentialing" (102). In the United States, Sophia Rosenfeld (2019) points out, populist epistemology has existed since the birth of the republic. She cites one anti-Federalist, writing in 1788, who denounced the "Machiavellian talents, of those who excel in ingenuity, artifice, sophistry, and the refinements of falsehood, who can assume the pleasing appearance of truth and bewilder the people in all the mazes of error" (108).

Social stratification, and an accompanying suspicion of experts, is consolidated and amplified when it is combined with a society that is dependent on science and technology to produce what might be called the "technocratic setup." The "technocratic setup" refers to an organization of society in which technology plays a leading role in the social structure and inefficiencies and defects are addressed by the application of more technology. An example of the technocratic setup is the arrangement envisioned by Emmanuel G. Mesthene in a sunny report on the social benefits of modern technology issued by Harvard University's Program on Technology and Society in 1968, entitled "The Social Impact of Technological Change" (Scharff and Dusek 2014). Richard Hofstadter (1963), in his book *Anti-intellectualism in American Life*, devoted chapter 8, entitled "The Rise of Experts," to such a development. The oppressive character of this stratification has often been depicted fictionally, such as in Ken Kesey's (1962) novel *One Flew Over the Cuckoo's Nest*, where one of the protagonists, Chief Bromden, regards the hospital as but one part of a vast, repressive social apparatus that he calls "the Combine."

John McDermott starkly depicted the extent of the stratification, and its ominous consequence of social mistrust, in his response to Mesthene's report. Modern technology, McDermott wrote, has seen "the increasing concentration of decision-making power in the hands of larger and larger scientific-technical bureaucracies." The result is "a growing separation between ruling and lower-class culture in America," with the latter ever more removed from social decision-making and the possibility of self-management. The outcome is that "social irrationality becomes the norm, and social paranoia a recurring phenomenon." McDermott dramatized the point via an episode involving US soldiers during the Vietnam War, who, cut off from sources of information and asked to blindly follow orders, concocted wild stories and began believing in conspiracies. When facts ceased "to discipline their opinions," McDermott writes, "fantasy and wild tales [we]re the natural outcome." Indeed, McDermott continues, "it is probably a mark of the GI's intelligence to fantasize, for it means that he has not permitted his intellectual capacity to atrophy. The intelligence of the individual is thus expressed in the irrationality of the group" (McDermott, quoted in Scharff and Dusek 2014, 698).

Some authors do not see the association of social stratification and expertise as inevitably producing populism, mistrust, or setting obstacles to democracy. Collins et al. (2019), for instance, contrast pluralist democracies, in which respect is shown for preferences that do not prevail in voting outcomes, and populist movements, which portray such voting outcomes as representing the will of the people. Scientific and technical expertise, Collins et al. argue, should be seen as a key part of the checks and balances—and are even constitutive—of pluralist democracies, while populists "attack scientific expertise just as they attack other checks and balances." In pluralist democracies, respect for the independence of expertise and its role in providing checks and balances has to be achieved through a socialization process consisting of civic education and various mediating institutions that encourage a "civic epistemology which allows a proper range of experts to give advice to government" (Collins et al. 2019). The aim of this socialization process is to get citizens to simply accept social stratification and the authority of expertise. Yet, as I will show, that would have to be achieved through a reshaping of the acoustical environment rather than through managing an escape from it.

CASE STUDY: THE ANTIVACCINATION MOVEMENT

The nonneutrality of the acoustical environment serves to enable and encourage a variety of forms of populist mistrust.

An example is the antivaccination movement. Several reasons make this a good beginning case study. Like all forms of populist mistrust, its background is the social stratification described above and its byproduct, antistate and antigovernment stances. The antivaccination movement is not necessarily associated with a particular political movement—with the right or the left or with liberals or conservatives. Political interests are not involved, at least, not directly. Nor is the antivaccination movement associated with economic interests; nobody makes much money by refusing to take a vaccine and, in fact, runs the risk of having to spend more of it. Many people who mistrust in such cases have spent time doing research of various kinds—into the ingredients of vaccines, accounts of autism, reports by nonmainstream experts, and so forth. In rejecting mainstream experts' advice to be vaccinated, parents are mainly motivated by the welfare of their children. Despite this, manifold variants of distrusting medical advice occur—and the gap between the status of experts inside the medical establishment that promotes vaccinations and those outside that establishment who resist is a key part of the context needed to understand these variants.

The breadth of the hermeneutical dimensions of expert denial can be gleaned from Jennifer A. Reich's book *Calling the Shots: Why Parents Reject Vaccines*, a study of parents who reject the conventional expert advice about administering vaccines to their children. The book contains numerous accounts of how that advice is either selectively heard, mistrusted, or rejected outright. It characterizes the situation and status of the parents, the experts, and the atmosphere in which both function. Reich (2016) seeks to put the views of the antivaccination parents "in a cultural, historical, and social context" to "paint complex pictures of the meanings of disease, risk, fear, and health that are woven through all disagreements about vaccines" (19). This lays the groundwork for understanding the environments in which parents are prepared to hear certain non-traditional voices or in which mainstream experts have strong, weak, or no voices, and even—though Reich's account does not emphasize this—the conspiracy theory mentality of many antivaxxers, their willingness to put others at risk, and their often using almost any excuse to avoid vaccinating their children.

Parents who refuse to vaccinate their children do not see themselves as ignoring the health of their children but, on the contrary, as committed to protecting it. According to Reich (2016), the parents who are most prone to reject mainstream expert medical advice tend to be privileged, often "white, college-educated mothers" (207). These parents are in a position to do research on disease, vaccines, regulations, and pharmaceutical companies and to seek information from "books, websites, research, peers, providers, or their own intuitions" to make decisions about vaccine safety (20). Some are responding to reports of the failures of the medical establishment; others, to the fear that vaccinations will be harmful to their children. Still others are responding to the empowerment, self-help, and do-it-yourself movements, asserting the right to opt out of mainstream programs. "Parents with resources are most able to demand services, more likely to view providers as contributing advice rather than dictating behaviors, and less likely to be reported to state agencies like child protective services" (16). Reich refers to this as "individualist parenting." Privileged parents, as well, are more able to withstand the hostile reactions and even demonization they often face from peers and from doctors. "Vaccine resistance," Reich says, "then represents an individual sense of entitlement to use public resources without shared responsibility to others" (237).

Experts who prescribe vaccinations, on the other hand, are burdened by two factors: specific instances of breakdown in the mainstream medical infrastructure, and commercialism—the impact of the profit motive of that infrastructure.

Several widely publicized breakdowns in the medical infrastructure have undermined trust in assurances of safety. One of the most dramatic, frequently cited by those in the antivaccination movement, is the so-called Cutter incident. In 1955, the Cutter Laboratories released over a hundred thousand doses of polio vaccine that contained live instead of inactivated polio virus, resulting in over 40,000 children developing some form of the disease. The doses had passed the regulation safety tests, and a government commission found nothing wrong with Cutter's procedures (Offit 2005).

Trust-undermining episodes such as this can lead, in turn, to a suspicion of commercialism—the belief that the pharmaceutical industry is guilty of putting profits over safety and covering up flaws in the system to protect those profits, and that the experts who advise taking vaccines, inadvertently or not, are part of a conspiracy. Pediatrician and infectious disease expert Paul Offit describes himself as a "poster boy" for an alleged conspiracy to promote vaccines, and he has been vilified and received death threats (Offit 2013). The influence of the profit motive can generate suspicion of the medical infrastructure even apart from specific horror stories.

Trust-undermining episodes also have reciprocal impacts on mainstream sources of authority, for mistrust of one expert implies mistrust of the institutions that trained, credentialed, and managed that expert. These episodes, for instance, undermine the authority of regulatory agencies such as the Food and Drug Administration (FDA) and the Centers for Disease Control (CDC), as well as the validity of clinical studies and trials. Such mistrust can have some justification, as when corporate executives cycle in and out of regulatory agencies. Moreover, in what might be called "mistrust creep," mistrust can spread across the distinctions between various kinds of institutions. Mistrust of a hospital, for instance, can become mistrust of the doctors employed by that hospital and of the medical establishment that supports the hospital. Similarly, mistrust of the state or of an industry can lead to mistrust of science sponsored by that state or industry, and vice versa (Hutt 2008; Harris Poll 2015; Attwell et al., 2017; Millstone and van Zwanenberg 2000; Harbers 2004).

Reich also cites factors affecting the dynamics of how expert voices are heard. One is the spread of causes, such as the "back to nature" movement, whose proponents may regard vaccines as being unnatural. Another relevant cause is autonomy and the right of parents to make decisions about their children's health. This is a particularly ambiguous issue because vaccination has from the beginning been presented as offering both individual protection and herd immunity—but achieving the latter can seem to make the former redundant, and therefore seems to justify parents' assertions that their making autonomous antivax decisions is safe. In another manifestation of mistrust creep, controversies about other, nonvaccine issues, such as nuclear power plant safety, contribute to the mistrust of government and industry officials in general and foster the desire to rely on personal research and decisions. Reich also notes that certain diseases—one thinks of polio and HIV/AIDS, for instance—have a symbolic history, whose particular stories matter to how their dangers are socially interpreted.

While Reich's book focuses on privileged and well-educated parents, members of different socioeconomic strata are all too familiar with the trust-undermining, unethical clinical trials and experiments that have been conducted on minority populations. These include the infamous, four-decades-long Tuskegee Study, sponsored by the US Public Health Service, examining the effects of untreated syphilis in African Americans. It is, in short, impossible to treat mistrust of experts and expertise in the antivaccine movement and elsewhere as a purely "medical" issue stripped of the sociopolitical background.

Features of the antivaccination movement that are also found in other areas of distrust of experts include differential mistrust of expert advice. Many parents who reject many vaccines, for instance, nevertheless have their children vaccinated for tetanus without necessarily regarding that decision as irrational, self-contradictory, or unwise.

Such parents also follow many other expert-recommended measures for promoting the health of their children.

Parents also seek out their own alternative experts and may consider themselves lay experts. A favorite of the antivaccination movement is the gastroenterologist Andrew Wakefield, lead author of a 1998 paper, published in the British medical journal *Lancet,* in which he proposed that the measles-mumps-rubella vaccine might cause autism (the study sample size was 12). Although the paper was heavily criticized and withdrawn by *Lancet* six years later, it is still strongly influential in the antivaccination movement, and Wakefield himself continues to be considered a leading, if not the leading, expert—or, at least, spokesperson—on the subject. Ardent celebrities with loud voices also promote the cause, including, most notably, the model Jenny McCarthy, whose son Evan was diagnosed with autism at age two. Reich quotes an episode that McCarthy recounts in her book *Mother Warriors*—the title itself is telling—about an appearance on Oprah Winfrey's program when Winfrey asked McCarthy about the lack of scientific support for the connection between vaccines and autism. McCarthy recalled thinking, "Who needs science when I'm witnessing it every day in my own home?" She said to Winfrey, "At home, Evan is my science" (Reich 2016, 67).

The reaction of mainstream experts to parents who oppose vaccinations, Reich shows, is nearly always to treat vaccinating children simply as a parental decision. Critics of that decision consider parents who make that decision as irrational, foolish, manipulated, or ignorant of how vaccines work, or as being selfish "free riders" who rely on others taking the advice of medical experts, and unaware of the severity of the dangers of not vaccinating. Reich sees the opposition between the proponents and opponents of vaccinations in broader terms, as taking place in a social and cultural environment that raises the amplitude of certain champions of the antivaccination movement and makes their voices more audible. The environment also prepares the parents to hear and respond to such voices.

Reich (2016) characterizes such parents as motivated by the desire to create "gated communities" in which their lifestyles are preserved and their children safe (205). She points out, however, that the children inside the walls of such communities are less safe than those on the outside. To break down the desire to create and live in such communities, Reich suggests trust-building measures for all stakeholders, in effect, strategies to change the acoustics of the entire issue.

Trust-building takes time and is highly vulnerable to disruption. As Elisa Sobo (2015) has pointed out, reactions that brand parents antivaxxers can polarize communities. The same holds true in connection with other opposition movements against, for example, GMOs, nuclear power, fracking, and global warming.

The antivaccination movement, Reich (2016) says, "raises fundamental questions about individual choice, bodily integrity, community responsibility, and individuals' relationship to the state" making the issue "bigger than vaccine choice" (252). The episode also highlights several features of the mistrust of expertise that it is important to disentangle.

COMMON FEATURES OF EPISODES
INVOLVING MISTRUST

Many features of the antivaccination recur in various combinations in other cases of the mistrust of experts, and one or more of these features may be visible than others. To understand the acoustics of expertise it is important to distinguish these features and to understand what motivates them. They include the appearance or cultivation of alternative experts, accusations of corrupt motives, celebrity voices, and the gratifications of solidarity.

Alternative Experts

One feature apparent in the antivaccination movement that recurs in other episodes is the appearance of alternative experts. Mistrust of experts does not mean the rejection of all experts but, rather, the selection of alternative experts. These experts can be contrarian members of the relevant field of science, members of nonrelevant areas of science, or nonscientists. In such situations, the issue is not that the experts are trusted or mistrusted; it is about choosing one's experts—that is, one tends to regard as authoritative either those who advance one's cause or make sense of issues of concern.

In the antivaccination controversy, Wakefield is an example of a contrarian member of the relevant field. Another example of someone in a relevant field being anointed and treated as an expert by outsiders but not by mainstream experts involved the construction of the Golden Gate Bridge in San Francisco, a project that was opposed by the local shipping industry, ferry operators, and landowners. These constituencies sought a credentialed scientist who would declare the bridge unsafe. They found one in Bailey Willis, an emeritus professor of geology and mining at Stanford University. Mainstream geologists repeatedly discredited Willis's claims about the relevant geology. But Willis's advantages included not only that he was a credentialed geologist, but also that he was colorful and articulate. Anointed an expert by opponents of the bridge, he and flourished as a media figure.

Examples of individuals seeking to become, and then seeming to become, experts outside their field include the Nobel laureate in Chemistry Linus Pauling when he claimed that large doses of Vitamin C were effective at preventing and curing the common cold. Examples of someone inadvertently becoming an expert outside their field include the psychiatrist and author Immanuel Velikovsky, who claimed that, millennia ago, the Earth had several catastrophic collisions with other planets, whose effects are described in the Bible and other ancient literature. Velikovsky's rise to expert stature in planetary history among many other catastrophists was less the result of his writing the blockbuster book *Worlds in Collision* than to the fact that there was already an audience of people yearning to hear catastrophic stories about the past; such people naturally embraced him as an expert (Gordin 2012). Similarly, Charles Piazzi Smyth, the Astronomer Royal of Scotland, was not appealing to colleagues when he wrote, in *Our Inheritance in the Great Pyramid*, that the Great Pyramid of Giza was "a Bible in stone" containing divine instructions; rather, he found an existing audience among amateur Egyptologists and opponents of the metric system (Gardner 1957). Physicist Ernest Sternglass's claims that radiation causes everything from high infant mortality and crime rates to low SAT scores have been thoroughly discredited, yet he had an engaging demeanor and was embraced by the antinuclear movement (Boffey 1969; Musolino 1995; Weart 2012, 184–6).

Fascination with catastrophes is often accompanied by trust in alternative experts. Willis is a good example; the claim of his that attracted the most media attention was that the Golden Gate Bridge would collapse and cause a horrific loss of life. A focus on catastrophes can overlap with causes, as when antinuclear activists focus on the potential for nuclear power plant meltdowns or invoke the 1986 Chernobyl accident. But a focus on catastrophes is not necessarily linked with specific social or political causes. The attention given to the predictions—made despite the lack of scientific justification—that heavy-ion accelerators at Brookhaven National Laboratory and at the European Organization for Nuclear Research (CERN) would create black holes or strangelets that would destroy the universe was not associated with any particular cause (Crease 2000).

Prominent figures who have scientific credentials but not in the relevant field can be sought out as experts. Some such individuals have stakes in the industries or causes; others are motivated by personal convictions. Oreskes and Conway (2010) characterized some of the experts in the tobacco industry and elsewhere as "hawkish, superior, technophilic, and communophobic," who "knew how to get press coverage for their views, and how to pressure the media when they didn't. They used their scientific credentials to present themselves as authorities, and they used their authority to try to discredit any science they didn't like" (29, 8).

Mistrust of mainstream experts can involve turning to or seeking out, not only alternative experts, but also alternative research projects. In the case of the antivaccination movement, Reich mentions a study commissioned by the antivaccination institution the National Vaccine Information Center, motivated by a distrust of studies associated with the pharmaceutical industry. According to one of the founders, the study (which had not been released when Reich's book was written) was motivated by a desire for "the people" to take back "vaccine science from the institutions which have failed us" (2016, 143). Another example is the Tooth Fairy Project, where antinuclear activists collect baby teeth from children living around nuclear power plants to measure Sr-90 concentrations, in the belief that they will be higher than normal. Scientific studies do not support this claim (National Research Council 2004). In numerous other cases, however, citizen science has uncovered or brought to the public's attention toxins or sources of pollution that had previously been overlooked or hidden, or exposed deficient practices (Feenberg 1992).

The acoustical environment can help explain how alternative experts appear and the power that they can acquire. Depending on the environment, certain voices can be heard more clearly by this constituency because of their location in the environment, while the other voices blend into an indistinct background or are drowned out.

Corrupt Motives

One element that is less prominent in the antivaccine case, as Reich describes it, than in cases such as global warming, is the presence of substantial political and financial stakes. Global warming, in particular, involves high political and financial stakes, accompanied by accusations and counteraccusations of corruption, conspiracy, disguised motives, and the presence of experts-for-hire on all sides (Oreskes and Conway 2010). These accusations can then come to dominate the acoustical environment.

An example of politically motivated posturing against an authoritative claim, not involving global warming, is the 2010 "Bermdoggle" episode, when Louisiana's Governor Bobby Jindal invested $220 million to build sand berms in an attempt to block the five-million-barrel BP Gulf oil spill. When scientists at the National Oil Spill Commission said the berms were a failure, would harm local ecology, and eventually wash away, Jindal attacked their study as "partisan revisionist history at taxpayer expense" and likened his expert-defying actions to those of Huey Long, a populist predecessor. Seven cases of mistrust involving the financial and political motives of promoters of mistrust are included in Oreskes and Conway (2010) book *Merchants of Doubt*. The book details the reactions to the evidence of the hazards of smoking and of secondhand smoke by the tobacco industry, of global warming by the fossil fuel industry, of the dangers of plans for strategic defense by advocates of military buildup, of the harm posed by acid rain by chemical industry, and of the evidence of the ozone hole by the aerosol industry.

In the ozone case, Oreskes and Conway (2010) quote the physicist Siegfried Singer, who said that some of the voices arguing for urgent action "are socialists, some are technology-hating Luddites; most have a great desire to regulate—on as large a scale as possible," and that environmentalists have a "hidden political agenda" against "business, the free market, and the capitalistic system" (134). The authors describe the backstory to the episodes they recount as "not free speech" but objection to regulations and "free market fundamentalism" (2010, 248, 251). Oreskes and Conway, as have others, documented the tobacco industry's use of experts to claim that smoking was harmless or, at least, to say that the evidence that it was not is controversial. If experts can be tainted here, why not elsewhere?

Globally sponsored organizations with international memberships have also been charged with having hidden agendas. These include the United Nations Scientific Committee on the Effects of Atomic Radiation and the International Panel on Climate Change. Here again, mistrust creep may spread the accusations around, from targeting individual scientists to institutions to supporting agencies.

Even in cases where initial expressions of mistrust are not associated with high financial or political stakes, the acoustics may affect politicians to deploy them as political weapons. The antivaccine movement has given rise to some political posturing (Resnick 2018); the alleged connection between cell-phone use and cancer, to even more.

The dynamics of corrupt motives on the part of those who mistrust experts, or who promote such mistrust, have been captured dramatically and often comically in cartoons, books, films, and plays. Comedians and cartoonists have a license to speak directly and reveal the hidden truth of a situation. In a *Doonesbury* comic strip, cartoonist Gary Trudeau once featured an "honest" science denier being interviewed on a radio talk show. "I don't oppose sound climate policy because it's flawed," he says. "I oppose it because I care *much* more about my short-term economic interests than the future of the damn planet. *Hello*?" Other examples include the movie *Jaws* and the Ibsen play *Enemy of the People*. Each of these works depicts a community that depends on visitors (beachgoers in *Jaws*, spa-goers in *Enemy of the People*), the discovery by experts of a deadly threat to those visitors (a shark, a toxin), and the questioning and ultimate repudiation of the finding by politicians. In both cases, the authenticity of the experts and expert advice and the mendacity of the politicians and their supporters are made clear to the audience. But so is the authenticity of the mistrust among at least some of the other characters. From the perspective of at least some of those who belong in the situation—the residents of the respective towns rather than the tourists—it is not easy to tell the difference between authentic expertise and nonauthentic expertise, between the true scientist and the corrupt politician, businessman, or spineless reporter. These fictionalizations capture situations in which the real experts don't wear halos, and the halo-wearers are not experts.

Another tactic that often arises in populist movements, and in episodes where the political and financial stakes are substantial, is that members do not just seek out alternative experts but often also actively cultivate individuals or agents to undermine trust of mainstream institutions. That is, partisans of causes seek out ways to sow doubt, not so much about experts and expert advice, but about the institutions or research projects behind them or the atmosphere in which they are heard. Oreskes and Conway call this "trust mongering" whose slogan is "doubt is our product," and they provide numerous examples in the tobacco industry and other cases (Oreskes and Conway 2010 34).

Entire organizations are created whose sole purpose is to promote mistrust, again, not in scientific findings themselves, but in the institutions that create such findings. These organizations can be called "social Iagos," after the character in Shakespeare's *Othello* who seeks to advance his career by promoting suspicion (Crease 2007). Those who seek to counter both social Iagos and the causes they serve can face ugly retaliation by watchlists and misinformation machines. Social Iagos can include government representatives. Hamlin (2008) quotes an administrator in the Bush administration: "Should the public come to believe that the scientific issues are settled, their views about global warming will change accordingly. You need to continue to make the lack of scientific certainty a primary issue in the debate" (168). Oreskes and Conway mention an article by someone in the tobacco industry describing an attempt to discredit the scientific evidence linking tobacco to cancer by seeking to "keep the controversy alive." In implementing what the authors call the "Tobacco Strategy," the tobacco industry created the Tobacco Institute and hired a public relations firm (Oreskes and Conway 2010, 5–6).

These organizations, however, are only effective because the environment is pre-prepared and already conducive to their effort. They exploit the difference between the language of risk as scientists speak it, and the public understanding of and discourse around risk. The gap could once be bridged by reference to the authority of mainstream experts, but in the current environment, bridging that gap has become more precarious and problematic (Wynne 1992). Risk calculations and algorithms no longer suffice and can even backfire, as illustrated by the episode in which heavy-ion accelerators made headlines because of the alleged (non-zero, according to scientists) risk that they might create strangelets or black holes to destroy the universe (Crease 2000).

Celebrity Voices

The use of celebrities as experts to promote causes is another example of how the acoustics of a debate may be altered. Celebrities have often been used as amplifying voices in social controversies involving health. Jenny McCarthy served this role in the antivaccination movement; as did the actress Meryl Streep in the Alar contro-versy (Lichter and Rothman 1999, 166) and the best-selling novelist Michael Crichton in the DDT controversy (Oreskes and Conway 2010, 232–233). Celebrities are adept at manipulating the acoustics to make their voices heard, as illustrated by the tireless efforts of attorney and activist Robert F. Kennedy Jr. to promote a connection between vaccination and autism (Helmuth 2013); or, Alec Baldwin's assertion that the connec-tion between low levels of radiation and certain kinds of cancer has been empirically demonstrated (Crease with Bond 2022).

Solidarity

A significant aspect of any "anti-mainstream" movement is the acquisition or ex-pression of a sense of community, support, and solidarity (Benford 2000). An anti-mainstream movement can be the outcome of a shared cultural perspective, according to the "cultural theory of risk perception" (Douglas and Wildawsky 1983; also Tansey and O'Riordan 1999; Schwarz and Thomson 1990). Or, movement participants can see themselves as belonging to a common cause that makes sense of disparate phe-nomena and pursues the common good (Davis 2002). Expressing mistrust alongside others sometimes "functions," as the anthropologists say, by providing mutual support for individuals to pursue their desires and dreams. The musician Lauren Fairweather depicts an ironic and self-conscious form of this in her song "It's Real for Us," about a youngster's love for the magical world of Harry Potter and what is gained from the com-panionship of others with a similar love, companionship that enables it possible to cope in a difficult and alien world.

Consequences of Mistrust

Actively cultivating mistrust of experts or their associated institutions can cause various kinds of damage, including actual harm to individuals and to the reputations of institutions. Most dramatically, cultivating mistrust of vaccinating children can result in childhood illnesses and death. In another form of mistrust creep, asserting mistrust of mainstream institutions also involves denying the competence or legitimacy of the system for selecting experts. It is one thing to distrust a finding or an expert, but this may also entail distrusting the system that issued the finding or credentialed and continues to maintain the expert. When former US president Donald Trump declared that his was the best attended of any inauguration, despite photographs taken by the National Parks Service showing otherwise, it undermined the work of that institution. Those who make public their mistrust of experts whose findings support the safety of vaccines or expose the dangers of smoking, the existence of an ozone hole, or the reality of climate change undermine the legitimacy of the institutions in which those experts work.

JUSTIFICATIONS OFFERED FOR MISTRUST

The justifications offered for mistrust are not the same as the motives. By "motives" I mean the origins of the trust or mistrust, and by "justifications" I mean the reasons, alleged or otherwise, that are offered to defend, explain, or promote the trust or mistrust. Whether these justifications for mistrust are earnestly held or cynically advanced does not matter; the alleged justifications provide at least the appearance of legitimacy.

One can think of professions, especially scientific ones, as giant workshops. These workshops are highly regulated environments that generate, maintain, and rely on experts. These experts create and study phenomena and events that do not appear, or appear crudely and rarely, in the surrounding world. They can then issue findings or develop technologies that affect the world outside the workshop. Several features make these workshops effective, including that they are *collectives*, that their work is *technical and abstract*, that it is regarded even in the workshop as *fallible*, that it can lead to irreversible *changes in the physical world*, and that it can and disrupt important *social values and attitudes*. But these very features that make the workshops effective also make them vulnerable to mistrust (Crease 2019).

Collectives

Every profession is constituted by an infrastructure to produce and supervise experts. Francis Bacon recognized the extensive and multifaceted requirements of a successful and ongoing scientific infrastructure metaphorically in Salomon's house in the *New*

Atlantis; John Ziman characterized it descriptively as a "republic." A scientific infrastructure is, in any case, a *collective*. That scientific infrastructures are collectives means that their findings are not the opinions of individuals but the result of collective checks and cross-checks. There are many different kinds of collectives, some focused on supporting scientific research, and others on promoting, consuming, or applying it. Even those that are primarily focused on specific kinds of research are highly dependent on trust and credibility (Collins 1981).

That scientific research and the experts who report it are associated with collectives also makes it seem legitimate to claim that the findings are products of the elite or disguised interests of institutions and bureaucracies. This can happen even in the case of relatively uncontroversial issues. Pielke (2007) cited the example of the famous "food guide pyramid" to illustrate this. The very social character of facts—that they are produced by a collective—can be used to discount them. This is what politicians and others appeal to when they dispute the findings of, for instance, the United Nations Scientific Committee on the Effects of Atomic Radiation, the International Panel on Climate Change, the World Health Organization, the American Medical Association, and so on, by claiming that the institutions and the scientists in them have their own agendas. When former president Trump declared that "scientists also have a political agenda," he was not wrong (CBS News 2018). But the phrase "having an agenda" is ambiguous and too easily used as a weapon against those who have a different agenda than one's own.

This is a form of mistrust that may be called the "disguised agenda" objection. Embracing the mistrust of mainstream experts is associated with assertions of hidden agendas and conspiracies. I have already mentioned numerous examples: the alleged conspiracy of scientists in claiming the existence of climate change, the safety of vaccines, the dangers of tobacco, and so on. In some cases, the questioning of how a scientific institution operates does indeed expose inadequacies, an example being AIDS activism in the early 1980s and 1990s (Epstein 1995).For, as in the case of other justifications offered for mistrust, it can be difficult to know, except in retrospect, whether questioning the collective manufacture of a fact is constructive or not. That is the point of the justification; it provides a veneer of legitimacy for the questioning.

Technical and Abstract

That the work of these infrastructures is *technical and abstract* means that interpreting the data requires expertise, but it can also make science seem sufficiently remote to provide cover for politicians and other leaders who want to dismiss it. And because science is technical and abstract, a gap arises between the scientific findings and the relevance of these findings to actions. This is a function, not just of science being abstract, but also of scientists' concern to state only the bare conclusions of their work and to protect it from being politicized or influenced by external concerns. This gap can be exploited by critics, who can drive a wedge into the gap to make it seem bigger, implying that the scientific findings are so distant from practical everyday concerns that they do not matter. This can be called the "I am not a scientist" objection. Modern versions are numerous, wide-ranging, and absorbing for the confidence they express. US Supreme Court Chief Justice John Roberts referred to quantitative studies of the impact of gerrymandering as "taking these issues away from democracy" and "sociological gobbledygook" (Roberts 2017). US Senator Mitch McConnell, when asked if greenhouse gas emissions cause global warming, replied, "I am not a scientist. I'm interested in protecting Kentucky's economy" (McConnell 2014). Robert F. Kennedy Jr., in defending his assertion that vaccines cause autism, said, "I'm not a scientist. But I have an expertise, I would say, in reading science and spotting junk science because that's what I do with most of my time" (Kennedy 2017). In 2006, US Supreme Court Justice Antonin Scalia said at a hearing, "I am not a scientist. That's why I don't want to deal with global warming" (quoted in Oreskes and Conway 2010, 2).

Furthermore, the inability of expertise to be fully captured in rules—the way much competent and incompetent know-how, as well as Monday-morning quarterbacking can be—can expose an expert to accusations of misconduct by those who note that they are not following rules. Examples include the David Baltimore case, in which the disclosure that a scientist in Baltimore's laboratory had failed to follow proper procedures led to accusations of fraud, and Baltimore himself was accused of misconduct for failing to take action swiftly enough (Kevles 1998)—even though the soundness of the researcher's results were not questioned. Another example is "Climategate," an episode involving publication of the hacked emails of climate scientists that appeared to show deviations from scientific practice, but which from the point of view of the climatologists, represented business as usual. Experts are expected to be able to "explain themselves," meaning to cite the rules they are following, even when their expertise depends on a sense of things that is less accessible to articulation. Critics can exploit this to amplify mistrust.

Fallible

That the work of the infrastructure is regarded even by its own experts as *fallible* means that findings can be revised on the basis of new information or analysis. But this can also make it possible to say that any result is tentative, and that future information may change it. This objection goes all the way back to Galileo's time, when Pope Urban advised Galileo that he could safely publish his work on heliocentrism only if he stipulated that, because nobody can know the mind of God, any conclusion about the matter was unavoidably tentative. We may call this "The jury is still out" objection or the "Pope Urban" objection. The fallibility of a result, once more, may be a cover for rejection of a finding or a serious concern about it. It is a frequent tactic of opponents of action on global warming, who have claimed that current models of future climate conditions are imperfect and may change in the future, and therefore that taking expensive action may be premature. Oreskes and Conway call it the "we don't know what's causing it" objection, using the words of the head of the Environmental Protection Agency William Ruckelshaus with reference to acid rain (Oreskes and Conway 2010, 101). Another example is found in the words of a later agency head, Scott Pruitt (Grandoni 2018), when he was asked about the urgency of action on global warming: "Do we really know what the ideal surface temperature should be in the year 2100, in the year 2018? That's fairly arrogant for us to think that we know exactly what it should be in 2100."

Potential Frankensteins

The activities of experts can effect irreversible *changes in physical world*. This is, after all, a major reason humans build scientific infrastructures—to discover and disseminate technologies that may improve the human condition. Yet this can also expose the activities of experts to charges that they are engaged in activities that are out of control and should be stopped. This "Frankenstein" objection is often lodged by those who oppose GMOs, nanoparticles, and nuclear power. This objection can have many origins. It may be produced, for instance, by overgeneralizing from instances of the poor application of science, or by confusing scientific expertise with an alleged expertise in the use of it, or by assuming that scientific research by itself is responsible for the production of Frankenstein-like phenomena.

Disruptive Impact on Values

Expert findings can also collide with *social values and attitudes*. The discovery that a bacterium causes syphilis, for instance, collided with, but then slowly eradicated, the belief that it contracting it was due to divine retribution. Yet, that expert advice can affect values also exposes it to rejection by those to whom such values are primary. This objection was even lodged in Galileo's time, in the hypersensitive Counter-Reformation climate after the Council of Trent, when the church judged his work to be heretical. It is also one of the objections frequently raised by modern-day creationists who reject the evidence proffered by evolutionary biologists, or by those who reject the idea that climate change will make human conditions worse. "My views on the environment are rooted in my belief in Creation," claimed the talk-show host Rush Limbaugh (2015). "We couldn't destroy the earth if we wanted to."

This justification is different from the others because it is less about mistrust of expert findings than about outright rejection of them due to prejudices, ideologies, positions of power, and so forth, that are already in place before the appearance of the findings in the first place.

THE ARCHITECTURAL MODEL

Although the acoustical model depicting expertise as a sense-making process of hearing and interpreting voices captures the phenomenology of mistrust better than the call-and-response model does, the acoustical model can still be difficult to accept. If one approaches a situation already thinking that one knows who the experts are, then it is possible to think that no interpretation is necessary, that one need not immerse oneself in the details of the situation to resolve it, and that one can resolve the controversy "from a distance" without paying close attention to the acoustics.

One may approach the solution to a controversial situation, for instance, as requiring drawing a distinction between the technical and political aspects, and then bringing the appropriate experts together to make a decision. From the audience's perspective when watching *Jaws* and *Enemy of the People*, for instance, the predicaments clearly call for the respective communities to find experts to make the relevant findings (whether there is a shark in the water, whether a deadly toxin is leaching into the spa), and then to find other experts to undertake the needed wise, practical action informed by the facts. This reaction springs from the assumption that there is a neat boundary between technical issues and social or political issues. If a border exists, then it is obvious where to begin to look for experts and how to apply them, as well as to recognize who does not need to be listened to and whom to mistrust.

In *Rethinking Expertise* (Collins and Evans 2007), and in other writings, Collins and Evans take this route. They attempt to describe boundaries between technical and polit-ical questions, and thus between the proper domains of the experts and the politicians in a controversy. They called this the "problem of extension," or "who is entitled to con-tribute to the technical component of a technological decision?" Too technocratically narrow an extension leads to mistrust, but too broad an extension risks "technological populism," which results in decisions motivated either purely by politics or by "lifestyle choice." Collins and Evans were responding to the success of the social studies of science of the past half-century in bringing to light the social dimensions of science, arguing that it is possible to make this compatible with the favoring of science. Their efforts to delineate boundaries between technical questions, and to describe types of expertise, was an attempt to describe what kinds of expertise dampen mistrust and ensure the force of scientific-technical information in public controversies without importing the disguised political agendas of one faction or another.

Collins et al. (2019) adopted a similar approach in *Experts and the Will of the People: Society, Populism and Science*, in which the authors depict a "fractal model" of society containing several levels of groups of different sizes, each constituted by distinctive spe-cialist expertises. The expertises are seen as authoritative within each of the groups, but not necessarily by other parts of society. Establishing the authority of these expertises outside the groups requires "civic education" and the cultivation of "the habits and lan-guage that constitute a democratic society's culture" so that they become "taken for granted ways of being in the world." In this model, experts have some autonomy in virtue of their expertise. "In a democracy, when scientific claims are part of the issue, it has to be better to give special weight to the views of those whose profession's central values include disinterestedness, integrity and a commitment to observation and experiment" (Collins et al. 2019, 59). In the case of the antivaccination movement, for example, education plus socialization would be seen as the means to promote recognition that experts are the best source of judgments—"best" meaning "morally best"—to determine the meaning of data concerning the safety of vaccines.

Collins and Evans developed this idea in part by discussing Brian Wynne's classic study of Cumbrian sheep farmers after their exposure to nuclear fallout. The failure of government scientists on the scene to understand the full extent of the threat was one of failing to recognize the presence of two kinds of expertise: that of the nuclear scientists, who knew a great deal about the physics of cesium and the biological processes in which it might be involved, and that of the sheep farmers, who understood more than the government scientists about the local conditions and how the fallout might have been distributed and taken up by the sheep (Wynne 1996). Another term for these cases is an "unrecognized contributor" situation (Whyte and Crease 2010). The inevitable result was mistrust and dismissal by each group of the other.

Collins and Evans responded to the problem of extension by developing a "periodic table of expertises" in an attempt "to classify all the kinds of expertise that might be brought to bear on a technological problem." They found around a dozen kinds. This advantage of this approach is that it recognizes that controversies with scientific-technological dimensions require different kinds and modalities of expertise. Collins and Evans have also proposed the creation of a new kind of institution, the "College of Owls," which would be staffed by social scientists to advise governments about "the strength and substance of scientific consensus in disputed domains . . . as a non-determining element in policy formation" (Collins et al. 2019).

But simply assembling the right kinds of experts and even of institutions—in what might be considered an architectural model—does not guarantee that the "right" kinds of expertise will be recognized. The fact that these problems are pre-labeled "technological" before expertise is even invoked seems to assume that problems are simply lying there out in the world waiting to be solved. How is it possible for an outsider to recognize the "right" kind of expertise in the first place? Some parties to a controversy already think they know who is trustworthy and who not. And many controversies revolve precisely around differences over what the "right" kind of expertise is, making a classification system either unnecessary or unhelpful and meaning that nobody is likely to change their minds because of it. Collins and Evans know that experts disagree, and that calling on experts does not guarantee the resolution of a controversy. Yet a serious obstacle to the project from the beginning arises because one is bound to ask about the standing—and the understanding—of the classifiers, for their perspective grounds their assertion of the "right" kind of expertise. Someone who thinks it is possible to exhaustively classify the expertise in a controversy has already interpreted the situation as one in which the messy details tell us little about the sort of expertise that is needed. An outsider, one might say, approaches a situation with a certain kind of acoustics that has already predetermined how that outsider understands the situation.

THE ACOUSTICAL FOUNDATIONS OF THE ARCHITECTURAL MODEL

I once attended a meeting of experts who had assembled to discuss a volatile controversy about the hazards of low levels of radiation that were coming from a research reactor. At one point, an expert in the audience announced, "I have a solution to this situation, but it's not implementable." There was a short pause. Someone in the back of the room then gave voice to the thought that was dawning on everyone: "If it's not implementable, it's not a solution." This time a lengthy pause ensued.

The episode illustrates that "situation" is an ambiguous term. It warns us against considering a controversy from the viewpoint of enlightened experts who nevertheless sees themselves as having or facing an audience. There is nothing collaborative about such a viewpoint. Rather, there are only viewpoints, all of them determinate, life-concerned, and owned by someone, and none deserves total ontological hegemony over any of the others. Someone seeking to move a controversy forward must start by learning how to give their accounts, critically as well as descriptively, of all of them, without playing ontological favorites. An architectural approach to controversies involving mistrust has an acoustical (hermeneutical) grounding.

In the Cumbrian case, indeed, the scientists seem just as guilty of selectively decontextualizing expertise and the situation as the farmers. If the scientists say, "We have the knowledge you need to apply for this situation," the sheep herders will surely say, "See? Here we go again, with outsiders giving advice when they don't understand the situation." Recognizing two kinds of expertise comes no closer to a solution. What the situation is, and therefore the expertise it requires, depends on the group. What often happens is that the choice of an expert reflects the position of a particular constituency in the acoustical environment. Or more precisely, the constituency partly brings itself into being by designating certain experts as "our experts" (Marres 2005).

The starting point for all groups must be the unsatisfactory present situation, where even a rudimentary attempt to define it as problematic must involve both experts and nonexperts. Hamlin addresses the idea in a critique of Collins and Evans (Hamlin 2008). Expertise, he says, "cannot be reified and abstracted from situations." In the Cumbrian case, for instance, the scientists did not grasp the situation because they understood neither farming practices nor the food uptake of sheep. "The problem with the scientists' approach is not that it privileges their so-called expertise over the layperson's experience, but that it is bad science." The scientists did not understand "the variables that need to be considered in a comprehensive expertise" (178). The variables arise from the situation. Arguing against Collins and Evans, Hamlin said that expertise "cannot be reified and abstracted from situations" and that situations are not puzzles to be solved or areas to be delineated by boundaries. "We cannot, as Collins and Evans suggest, simply add 3 ml of contributory, 2 of interactional, and 1 of refereed expertise," says Hamlin; "instead, expertise is real, embodied, and dependent on the changing levels of trust and credibility" (179). Understanding the situation requires focusing on "the unfolding present with the constant confrontation of problems to be coped with, not on presumably eternal nature." In other words, understanding the right kind of expertise to bring to bear on a situation is not an external, analytic issue but an interpretive one, internal to the situation at hand. The situation comes first, prior to the experts who are brought to bear on it.

This point is in the spirit of others, such as Callon (drawing on Dewey), who argue that many of the pressing problems for which a community might want to rely on expertise are novel matters of concern for which no established expertise exists. The expertise needs to be developed by judging which existing forms of expertise are relevant in a process of collective experimentation (Callon 2005; Callon et al. 2009; Dewey 1916).

To put Hamlin's point another way, you cannot pick the right experts to enable you to understand a controversy before you have finished understanding it. To understand it, moreover, is already to have an understanding of who the experts are; we already have a sense of whom to trust and mistrust. The landscape of the controversy, and therefore knowing which experts to consult, is part and parcel of the controversy itself; how you understand the given situation shapes your understanding of whom you should listen to in order to navigate it. When we consult an expert, it is generally not to get something fixed or even to obtain an item of information. "What we usually want from an expert," says Hamlin, "is an assessment or an authorized solution that permits action" (Hamlin 2008, 173–174). But though Hamlin does not say so, our assessment and understanding of a situation may call on us to seek out alternative experts and discredit mainstream experts. An understanding of a situation is not always purely pragmatic and sensible; it can be motivated by political, economic, religious, or other factors, as many of the cases discussed here have revealed. We use our grip on the situation to seek out experts to give us a better grip on the situation. We use experts to help us understand the situation, but we use our understanding of the situation to choose the experts.

If this seems circular, it is so in the way of all hermeneutical situations—something that we cannot avoid. What has just been described is a meaning-making activity in which we use our grasp of a situation's meaning to choose experts to deepen our grasp of its meaning. We can, indeed, misuse experts—we can become dependent on them, abandon our judgment to theirs, and choose those who will ratify an already-decided position—but these ways of using experts are parasitic. It is too late to choose the experts after understanding the controversy. They are then no longer experts; they have been determined by the debate itself instead of helping to carry it forward; they are pieces of evidence in an agonistic situation rather than a part of meaning-formation. The point is that behind any deciding lies an understanding that guides it.

The fundamental role of the expert is hermeneutical—to help us to get a better grip on a situation rather than deciding or repairing it. But as the situation in Ibsen's fictional Norwegian town illustrates, no one *in the situation* ever experiences the Technical vs. the Political and then asks, "Which one should I give greater weight to?" The Collins-Evans social science perspective is useful and informative, but it is unlikely to be effective in the sort of situations it is meant to clarify. It is our prior commitments and choices— how we are leading our lives, and what these lives depend upon—that determine our reaction to expert findings, not something inherent in the findings themselves. A controversial situation is composed of viewpoints, each of them "owned" by someone, with none deserving special hegemony over others. Experts do not speak from nowhere to just anyone; their acoustics are correlated with an audience which has a particular set of preexisting commitments and connection with the expert.

Furthermore, any predelineation of the experts involved in a decision runs the inevitable risk of mistrust, of accusations that experts were chosen to reach just that decision. We can call these "poisoned-well" cases (Whyte and Crease 2010). This drawback accompanies any attempt to settle controversies via settling the extension. Situations, furthermore, rarely have a single audience, but instead, a plurality of people attempting to make sense of the situation. Hamlin points this out with respect to the Cumbrian case. Whose situation was it: that of the farmers, the consumers of the beef, the British scientists, or the British government? "Are the goals of the parties identical or even comparable?" (Hamlin 2008, 177) The farmers are likely to be concerned with survival of their farms, beef consumers with the edibility of the beef, scientists with British lamb and exports, British politicians with the reputation of the British food producing system, and so forth. Similarly, in Amity—the affected beach community in *Jaws*—and in the Norwegian spa in *Enemy of the People*, the citizens are likely to be more concerned than the marine scientist or the doctor with their own livelihoods, and therefore to listen to a different set of voices. The experts who are trusted and mistrusted will be different in each case, and their role will be more problematic if they are part of the mix that *equally* involves all the other "stakeholders."

Conclusion

Mistrust of expertise is best envisioned in terms of a model of expertise that pictures this mistrust occurring in a hermeneutical (sense-making) space, where voices are heard and interpreted differentially, which is not one situation but many, depending on the position of the hearer. The acoustical space is not neutral. It tends to make some voices more audible than others, and can produce severe controversies, mistrust of expertise, and people who talk past one another. This space may not only have multiple voices, but many of those voices may be neither scientific nor expert.

Moving a controversy involving mistrust forward, then, is not just an matter of giving scientific expertise a better hearing, and the issues certainly cannot be fully laid out from the point of view of experts who understand themselves as the deserving arbiters of how a practice might best be conducted. First, there needs to be a widespread reformation of the idea of a public space as one in which "information," generated by experts, is transmitted and spreads uniformly, and is received without distortion. Rather, the loudest voices can be the best-funded proponents or the biggest celebrities, the experience of social and cultural and political injustice can encourage hostility toward those perceived to be "winning," and even scientists can slide quickly from a general defense of real expertise into special pleading for themselves, for their better-informed perspective, for science, and for those who profit from using their results and thereby sustaining existing structures of social and political power.

Miranda Fricker's notion of "hermeneutic injustice" helps to clarify why these conflicts occur. Hermeneutical injustice, for her, occurs "when a gap in collective interpretive resources puts someone at an unfair disadvantage when it comes to making sense of their social experience"; an example is "suffer[ing] sexual harassment in a culture that still lacks that critical concept." Hermeneutical injustice is caused by "structural prejudice in the economy of collective hermeneutical resources" (Fricker 2007, 1). Hermeneutical injustice is caused by gaps or flaws in our tools of social interpretation, resulting in the production of impoverished social meanings. The experiences of groups "are left inadequately conceptualized and so ill-understood," and are then "not heard as rational owing to their expressive style being inadequately understood," so that they suffer from "a situated hermeneutical inequality." "Their social situation is such that a collective hermeneutical gap prevents them in particular from making sense of an experience which it is strongly in their interests to render intelligible" (7).

Fricker uses the notion of "hermeneutic injustice" with the experiences of women and minorities in mind, but it can be usefully applied to controversies as well as people. For instance, it can help to think about cases where the atmosphere in which a controversial issue—animal experimentation, fracking, genetic modification, global warming, nuclear power, and so forth—fly in the face of the usual understanding of what one should think and do. The atmosphere in which such controversies are discussed comes pre-loaded with potent imagery and associations that clash and seem incommensurable. (For an example of the role of this atmosphere in the discussion of nuclear-related matters, see Weart 2012.) This atmosphere tends to drown out or distort expert testimony and all but thrust a decision about what to do at an audience. Such imagery and associations are often deliberately manipulated by celebrities and social Iagos who actively seek to delegitimize or taint experts to advance their own causes. These can include activists and business executives and even government representatives. The existence of social Iagos is a dark side to the issue of expertise with which almost all scientists involved with science policy are familiar.

Expert advice is now given in contexts where many voices are heard; science is only one voice, and far from the loudest. An important step in understanding trust and mistrust in expertise is to understand the acoustics of such contexts—to investigate the relation between expert counsel and the hermeneutical space that is already in place before the expert findings are presented, as well as the nonneutrality and sometimes deliberate distortions that can affect that space. To fully understand acoustical environments in which mistrust takes place, along with understanding Rosenfeld's "populist episte-mology" and Collins et al.'s "civic epistemology," we also must consider what might be called "hermeneutic epistemology."

ACKNOWLEDGMENTS

Many thanks to Harry Collins, Gil Eyal, and Robert C. Scharff for their extensive suggestions on part or all of the draft.

References

Attwell, Katie, Julie Leask, Samantha B. Meyer, Philippa Rokkas, and Paul Ward. 2017. "Vaccine Rejecting Parents' Engagement With Expert Systems That Inform Vaccination Programs." *Journal of Bioethical Inquiry*, 14: 65–76.

Benford, Robert D. and David A. Snow. 2000. "Framing Processes and Social Movements: An Overview and Assessment." *Annual Review of Sociology* 26:611–639.

Boffey, Philip M. 1969. "Ernest J. Sternglass: Controversial Prophet of Doom." *Science* 166:195–200.

Bijker, Wiebe, Roland Bal, and Ruud Hendriks. 2009. *The Paradox of Scientific Authority: The Role of Scientific Advice in Democracies*. Cambridge: MIT Press.

Callon, Michel. 2005. "Disabled Persons of All Countries, Unite!" In *Making Things Public: Atmospheres of Democracy*, edited by Bruno Latour and Peter Weibel, 308–313. Cambridge, MA: MIT Press.

Callon, Michel, Pierre Lascoumes, and Yannick Barthe. 2009. *Acting in an Uncertain World: An Essay on Technical Democracy*. Cambridge, MA: The MIT Press.

CBS News. 2018. "President Trump: The '60 Minutes' Interview." By Lesley Stahl, October 15. https://www.cbsnews.com/news/donald-trump-full-interview-60-minutes-transcript-les ley-stahl-2018-10-14/.

Collins, Harry M. 1981. "'Son of Seven Sexes': The Social Destruction of a Physical Phenomenon." *Social Studies of Science* 11 (1): 33–62. doi:10.1177/030631278101100103.

Collins, Harry, and Robert Evans. 2007. *Rethinking Expertise*. Chicago: University of Chicago Press.

Collins, Harry, Robert Evans, Darrin Durant, and Martin Weinel. 2019. *Experts and the Will of the People: Society, Populism and Science*. London: Palgrave Macmillan.

Crease, Robert P. 2000. "Case of the Deadly Strangelets." *Physics World* 13:7 July 19.

Crease, Robert P. 2007. "Tale of Two Anniversaries." *Physics World* 20:5 18.

Crease, Robert P. 2010. "Interdisciplinarity in the Natural Sciences." In *The Oxford Handbook of Interdisciplinarity*, edited by Robert Frodeman, 79–102. New York: Oxford University Press.

Crease, Robert P. 2019. *The Workshop and the World: What Ten Thinkers Can Teach Us about Science and Authority*. New York: W. W. Norton.

Crease, Robert with Peter Bond. 2022. *The Leak: Politics, Activism and Loss of Trust at Brookhaven National Laboratory*. Cambridge, MA: MIT Press.

Davis, J. E. 2002. *Stories of Change: Narrative and Social Movements*. Albany: State University of New York Press.

Dewey, John. 1916. *Democracy and Education*. New York: Free Press.

Douglas, Mary, and Aaron Wildawsky. 1983. *Risk and Culture*. Berkeley: University of California Press.

Epstein, Steven. 1995. "The Construction of Lay Expertise: AIDS Activism and the Forging of Credibility in the Reform of Clinical Trials." In "Constructivist Perspectives on Medical Work: Medical Practices and Science and Technology Studies." Special issue. *Science, Technology, & Human Values* 20 (4): 408–437.

Fricker, Miranda. 2007. *Epistemic Injustice: Power and the Ethics of Knowing*. New York: Oxford University Press.

Feenberg, A. 1992. "On Being a Human Subject: Interest and Obligation in the Experimental Treatment of Incurable Disease." *Philosophical Forum* 23:3. https://www.sfu.ca/~andrewf/books/On_being_human_subject_interest_obligation.pdf

Gardner, Martin. 1957. *Fads and Fallacies in the Name of Science*. Mineola, NY: Dover.

Gordin, Michael. 2012. *The Pseudoscience Wars: Immanuel Velikovsky and the Birth of the Modern Fringe*. Chicago: University of Chicago Press.

Grandoni, Dino, Brady Dennis, and Chris Mooney. 2018. "EPA's Scott Pruitt asks whether global warming 'necessarily is a bad thing.'" *Washington Post*, February 8, 2018. https://www.washingtonpost.com/news/energy-environment/wp/2018/02/07/scott-pruitt-asks-if-global-warming-necessarily-is-a-bad-thing/.

Hamlin, C. S. 2008. "Third Wave Science Studies: Toward a History and Philosophy of Expertise." In *The Challenge of the Social and the Pressure of Practice: Science and Values Revisited*, edited by. M. Carrier, D. Howard, and J. Kourany, 160–188. Pittsburgh, PA: University of Pittsburgh Press.

Harbers, Hans. 2004. "Trust in Politics, Science and Technology: Breaching the Modernist Constitution." In *Trust: Cement of Democracy?*, edited by Frank R. Ankersmit and Henk Te Velde, 145–164. Leuven: Peeters.

Harris Poll. 2015. "US Mint and FAA Receive Highest Rating of 17 US Agencies." February 26. https://www.prnewswire.com/news-releases/us-mint--faa-receive-highest-ratings-of-17-government-agencies-fbi-cdc-nih-cia-and-office-of-the-surgeon-general-also-well-regarded-300041476.html. Last accessed October 30, 2022.

Helmuth, L. 2013. "So Robert F. Kennedy Jr. Called Us to Complain . . . " Slate, June 11. http://www.slate.com/articles/health_and_science/medical_examiner/2013/06/robert_f_kennedy_jr_vaccine_conspiracy_theory_scientists_and_journalists.html.

Hofstadter, Richard. 1963. *Anti-intellectualism in American Life*. New York: Vintage Books.

Hutt, Peter Barton. 2008. "The State of Science at the FDA." *Administrative Law Review* 60:2.

Kennedy, Robert F., Jr.. 2017. https://www.sciencemag.org/news/2017/01/exclusive-qa-robert-f-kennedy-jr-trumps-proposed-vaccine-commission?r3f_986=https://www.google.com/.

Kesey, Ken. 1962. *One Flew Over the Cuckoo's Nest*. New York: Viking.

https://www.justice.gov/sites/default/files/civil/legacy/2014/09/11/amended%20opinion_o.pdf

Kevles, D. 1998. *The Baltimore Case: A Trial of Politics, Science, and Character*. New York: W. W. Norton.

Lichter, S. R., and R. Rothman. 1999. *Environmental Cancer—a Political Disease?* New Haven, CT: Yale University Press.

Limbaugh, Rush. 2015. *The Way Things Ought to Be*, 153. New York: Pocket Books.

Marres, Noortje. 2005. "Issues Spark a Public into Being: A Key but Forgotten Point of the Lippmann-Dewey Debate." In Latour and Weibel, *Making Things Public*, 208–217.

McConnell, Mitch. 2014. https://www.courier-journal.com/story/news/politics/elections/kentucky/2014/10/02/mcconnell-climate-change-scientist/16600873/.

Monbiot, George. 2016. *The Guardian*, November 30.

Musolino, Stephen V. 1995. "Comments on 'Breast Cancer: Evidence for a Relation to Fission Products in the Diet.'" *International Journal of Health Services* 25 (3): 475–480.

National Research Council. 2004. "Radiation Protection and the 'Tooth Fairy' Issue." Backgrounder report. https://www.nrc.gov/docs/ML0721/ML072150423.pdf.

Offit, Paul A. 2005. "The Cutter Incident, 50 Years Later." *New England Journal of Medicine* 352: 1411–1412.

Paul A. Offit. 2013. *Do You Believe in Magic?: Vitamins, Supplements, and All Things Natural: A Look Behind the Curtain*. New York: Harper.

Oppenheimer, Michael, Naomi Oreskes, Dale Jamieson, Keynyn Brysse, Jessica O'Reilly, Matthew Shindell, and Milena Wazeck. 2019. Discerning Experts: The Practices of Scientific Assessment for Environmental Policy. Chicago, IL: University of Chicago Press.

Oreskes, Naomi, and Eric Conway. 2010. *Merchants of Doubt*. London: Bloomsbury Press.

Pielke R. A., Jr.. 2007. *The Honest Broker: Making Sense of Science in Policy and Politics*. Cambridge, MA: Cambridge University Press.

Reich, Jennifer A. 2016. *Calling the Shots: Why Parents Reject Vaccines*. New York: New York University Press.

Resnick, Gideon. 2018. "Oregon's GOP Governor Candidate Knute Buehler Wants Weakened Vaccine Laws." *Daily Beast*, October 15. https://www.thedailybeast.com/oregons-gop-governor-candidate-knute-buehler-wants-weakened-vaccine-laws.

Roberts, John. 2017. "Gill v. Whitford." Oyez, www.oyez.org/cases/2017/16-1161. Accessed October 30, 2022.

Rosenfeld, Sophia. 2019. *Democracy and Truth*. Philadelphia: University of Pennsylvania Press.

Roulston, M. S., and L. A. Smith. 2004. "The Boy Who Cried Wolf Revisited: The Impact of False Alarm Intolerance or Cost-Loss Scenarios." *Weather and Forecasting* 19 (2): 391–397. 2004.

Scharff, Robert C., and Val Dusek, eds. 2014. *Philosophy of Technology: The Technological Condition: An Anthology*. Hoboken, NJ: Blackwell.

Schwarz, Michiel, and Michael Thompson. 1990. *Divided We Stand: Redefining Politics, Technology and Social Choice*. New York: Harvester Wheatsheaf.

Sobo, Elisa J. 2015. "Social Cultivation of Vaccine Refusal and Delay among Waldorf (Steiner) School Parents." *Medical Anthropology Quarterly* 29 (3): 381–399.

Tansey, James, and Tim O'Riordan. 1999. "Cultural Theory and Risk: A Review." Health, Risk & Society 1:71.

Wadman, Meredith. 2017. "Robert F. Kennedy Jr. on Trump's proposed vaccine commission." Science Insider, January 10. https://www.science.org/content/article/exclusive-qa-robert-f-kennedy-jr-trumps-proposed-vaccine-commission?r3f_986=https://www.google.com/.

Weart, Spencer R. 2012. *The Rise ofuclear Fear*. Cambridge, MA: Harvard University Press.

Whyte K. P., and Robert P. Crease. 2010. "Trust, Expertise, and the Philosophy of Science." *Synthese* 177:411–425.

Wynne, Brian. 1992. "Uncertainty and Environmental Learning: Reconceiving Science and Policy in the Preventive Paradigm." *Global Environmental Change* 2 (2): 111–127.

Wynne, Brian. 1996. "Misunderstood Misunderstandings: Social Identities in the Public Uptake of Science." In *Misunderstanding Science?*, edited by A. Irwin and Brian Wynne, 19–46. Cambridge, MA: Cambridge University Press.

8

A REGULATORY STATE OF EXCEPTION

ANDREW LAKOFF

In the summer of 2020, the long-simmering crisis in the public role of expert knowledge in the United States seemed to reach a boiling point. The rapid and deadly spread of the novel coronavirus in the previous months had coincided with a bitterly fought presidential campaign. In its response to the pandemic, the Trump administration had thrown into question the very premise that the claims of technical experts should—or could—be considered independently of political calculations. Respected government health institutions, such as the Centers for Disease Control and the National Institutes of Health, were sidelined from the management of the crisis, their experts' recommendations ignored or overruled. Representatives of what the president derisively called the "deep state" were inherently suspect. Urgent health-policy questions remained unsettled and even became sources of public unrest: Should masks be required in public places? How should epidemiological thresholds for the closure of schools and businesses be determined? Should doctors be allowed to prescribe highly touted but unproven medications?

Regulatory science had perhaps never been so explicitly politicized. It was in this fraught context that the question of how soon a vaccine to contain the pandemic would be made available came into public view. As the date of the 2020 presidential election neared, President Trump staked his claim that he had adequately responded to the pandemic on the premise that the government's vaccine development program—Operation Warp Speed—would deliver a technical fix by the fall. Indeed, it seemed possible that the outcome of the election would hinge on the timing of what was ostensibly a technical decision: the regulatory authorization of a COVID vaccine. In the end, the administration's efforts to accelerate the authorization timeline did not succeed; government regulators put guidelines in place that made it impossible to assess a vaccine candidate before the election. This chapter examines how, at this critical moment, key actors defended the autonomy of the regulatory process. An alliance of academic scientists, federal agency staff, and drug-industry leaders presented the specter of vaccine hesitancy to fend off political interference. Although trust of the safety of technical objects such as vaccines is often seen to depend on the autonomy of regulatory agencies and the objectivity of experts, here the converse was the case: the experts and regulatory officials used the construct of public trust—or rather, mistrust—as a means to preserve their autonomy.

RAPID VACCINE DEVELOPMENT

In April 2020, the Trump administration introduced Operation Warp Speed, an ambitious government-led effort to accelerate the development, production, and distribution of vaccines to address the pandemic emergency. Coordinated jointly by the Departments of Health and Human Services and the Defense Department, the program contracted with several pharmaceutical and biotechnology companies to support vaccine research, development and manufacturing, with an initial $10 billion budget. The time frame envisioned by Operation Warp Speed was audacious given the prior history of vaccine development: it sought to deliver 300 million doses of "safe and effective" COVID vaccines by the beginning of 2021.[1] A typical vaccine development process, including R&D, clinical trials, regulatory review, manufacturing, and distribution could take six years or more to complete, but Operation Warp Speed sought to reduce the timeline to roughly one year through a series of efficiency measures, including viral genome sequencing to identify vaccine candidates, large-scale clinical trials that would run in parallel with government-supported manufacturing, and an expedited regulatory evaluation using a device known as an "emergency use authorization." By the summer of 2020, the program seemed to be on the verge of success: several vaccine candidates supported by Operation Warp Speed had already entered Phase III trials, each enrolling between 30,000 and 60,000 research subjects.

Accelerating the regulatory review process was a critical element of the "warp-speed" strategy. Under normal circumstances, a vaccine candidate must go through a lengthy Biologics License Application (BLA) process before the FDA will approve it for entrance onto the market. The lengthy BLA review process involves a benefit-risk analysis conducted by FDA scientists and, in some cases, by an external committee of experts as well, based on comprehensive evaluation of clinical trial data provided by the vaccine developer. This standardized, quantitative procedure provides a form of what Theodore Porter calls "mechanical objectivity" that protects the agency against accusations of bias or mistaken judgment.[2] From the perspective of regulators, strict adherence to these protocols ensures public confidence in the integrity of the agency's decisions.

However, in the context of a deadly pandemic for which no pharmaceutical interventions were available, Operation Warp Speed planners anticipated the need for an alternative to the normal regulatory process. The emergency use authorization (EUA) mechanism enables the temporary use of an unapproved medical product if the secretary of health and human services has declared a "public health emergency" under section 564 of the Food, Drug, and Cosmetic Act. The FDA may issue an EUA for a medical product if the available evidence indicates that it is "reasonable to believe" that the product in question "may be effective" in treating the condition identified by the emergency declaration. The EUA thus provides the federal government with a flexible method for the rapid authorization of an unapproved medicine in the urgent and uncertain circumstances of a public-health emergency. However, the very flexibility of the EUA opens it up to the danger of the perception of external influence: by attenuating the lengthy process used to generate mechanical objectivity, the issuance of an EUA may be seen to compromise the integrity of a regulatory decision.

The EUA procedure inhabits a different form of governmental rationality than the normal procedures of drug regulation. It is a preparedness device: in contrast to the public-health world in which evidence of safety and efficacy is compiled through statistical analysis, the EUA addresses a future incident whose onset is unpredictable and potentially catastrophic. It was first introduced in the context of bioterrorism preparedness initiatives in the late 1990s and early 2000s. Biosecurity specialists had assembled the Strategic National Stockpile to prepare for a potential chemical, biological, radiological, or nuclear (CBRN) attack. The stockpile contained troves of medical countermeasures, such as smallpox and anthrax vaccines, nerve-gas antidote, and antitoxins, many of which did not have FDA approval for their projected uses. This became apparent as a problem in the immediate aftermath of the 2001 anthrax attacks, when the lack of regulatory approval made it difficult to provide postexposure anthrax vaccine to postal workers. Security officials worried that in a future biological emergency—such as a smallpox attack—when there would be an urgent need to provide mass treatment but no approved countermeasure, there would not be enough time for a prospective drug or vaccine to go through the normal regulatory approval process.

The Congress addressed this apparent gap in preparedness in the 2004 Project Bioshield Act, which aimed to provide the government "with the ability to develop, acquire, stockpile and make available the medical countermeasures needed to protect the US population against weapons of mass destruction."[3] Project Bioshield legislation included a provision—the Emergency Use Authorization—that would expedite the use of a potentially life-saving countermeasure in the event of a mass casualty attack.[4] Upon the declaration of a public-health emergency affecting national security, EUA authority allows the FDA to "facilitate availability and unapproved uses of [medical countermeasures] needed to prepare for and respond to CBRN emergencies."[5] The EUA procedure was used for the first time in 2005 by the Department of Defense, to enable the military to immunize soldiers against anthrax using a vaccine that had not received regulatory approval.

In 2006, new legislation enacted in response to the threat of an avian influenza pandemic extended the framework of biological preparedness beyond the scenario of a bioterrorist attack. The Pandemic and All-Hazards Preparedness (PREP) Act expanded the scope of the EUA mechanism to include "emerging diseases such as pandemic influenza." The legislation provided the FDA with a list of criteria for evaluating an EUA application: the disease must be life-threatening; it must be "reasonable to believe the product may be effective" for the specified use; the known and unknown benefits of the medicine must outweigh its known and potential risks; and there must be no available alternative. The EUA mechanism built in flexibility to allow for the exigencies of an as-yet-unknown future situation: the FDA would decide on a "case-by-case" basis what kinds of evidence concerning safety and efficacy would be necessary, and what method would be used to calculate the ratio of benefit to risk. For instance, a vaccine that would be given to millions of healthy individuals would presumably have to reach a different threshold in a benefit-risk analysis than would a potentially lifesaving drug intended for an infected patient.

The EUA was distinct from normal procedures of regulatory assessment in that it participated in the logic of "emergency government."[6] American emergency government, developed in the mid-twentieth-century contexts of wartime mobilization and Cold War nuclear preparedness, involves the use of anticipatory techniques that enable officials to manage a future crisis situation without recourse to extralegal measures. One such technique is scenario-based planning in which officials imaginatively enact the aftermath of a potential future event and then seek to address gaps in response that are revealed by the scenario. Underpinning the EUA was the scenario of an event such as a biological attack or a pandemic in which an alternative to the standard drug-regulatory process would be needed. In such an event, the FDA's statutory requirement for a comprehensive review of clinical trial data could be suspended to enable a response to the exigencies of a rapidly unfolding situation. The EUA establishes a space of regulatory ambiguity: how an authorization for emergency use may be granted will be up for negotiation and contestation. In the case of the COVID vaccine, as we will see, an unintended consequence of this interpretive leeway was to open up the regulatory process to what some observers considered dangerous external pressure.

The COVID-19 Emergency

On February 4, 2020, two weeks after the initial detection of the novel coronavirus in the United States, Health and Human Services secretary Alex Azar declared the event a "public health emergency that has a significant potential to affect national security" under the Food, Drug, and Cosmetic Act. Based on this declaration, the secretary then determined that "circumstances exist justifying the authorization" of medical devices not yet approved by the FDA—specifically, in vitro diagnostics for detecting the novel coronavirus.[7] Over the next several months, the FDA drew on the EUA mechanism to authorize the temporary use of a number of unapproved medical products, including diagnostic tests, protective equipment, and medicines. The issuance of an EUA in late April 2020 to allow clinicians to prescribe hydroxychloroquine for the treatment of COVID-19 proved controversial. The drug's efficacy in treating coronavirus disease was still under investigation at the time, but it had been promoted as a wonder drug by then president Trump, as well as a number of public commentators. After several studies failed to demonstrate its efficacy (and indicated potential harm), the FDA withdrew its EUA in mid-June.

The FDA's use of the EUA mechanism again sparked controversy in late August, when FDA commissioner Stephen Hahn appeared at a press conference alongside President Trump and Secretary Azar to tout the success of convalescent plasma therapy in treating severe cases of COVID-19 and announce that the FDA had issued an emergency authorization for its clinical use. Soon after the announcement, a number of scientists outside government pointed to the published clinical trial results, which were less robust than Hahn had suggested, and sharply criticized the commissioner for making exaggerated claims about the efficacy of the treatment. As Eric Topol, editor-in-chief of *Medscape Medical News*, wrote in an open letter to Commissioner Hahn: "We cannot entrust the health of 330 million Americans to a person who is subservient to President Trump's whims, unprecedented promotion of unproven therapies, outrageous lies, and political motivations."[8]

Even more troubling to many observers was the possibility that the administration would use the EUA mechanism to prematurely authorize the use of a COVID vaccine. Indeed, this was a more-or-less explicit strategy of the Trump campaign, which hoped that a rapid vaccine rollout would aid its reelection effort. As the *New York Times* reported in early August, "Trump campaign advisors privately call a pre-election vaccine 'the holy grail.'"[9] The scenario of an "October surprise vaccine" became more plausible with the confident announcement by the CEO of Pfizer that a "conclusive readout" of clinical trial results for its candidate vaccine would be available by the end of October, after which the company would immediately file an application with the FDA for an EUA.[10]

In this context a number of scientists made public statements questioning the integrity of the EUA process. The editor-in-chief of *Science* magazine published a scathing editorial assailing the Trump administration's health agencies for bowing to political pressure and calling on doctors to refuse to administer any vaccine authorized under questionable circumstances. "We now know that Redfield, Azar, and Hahn are not capable of, or willing to, stand up to President Trump," he wrote. "The medical community must stop this dance as we get closer to rolling out a vaccine for COVID-19 because we now know that we will not get any help from the federal government."[11] Topol, in his open letter, called on Commissioner Hahn to pledge to conduct a rigorous vaccine assessment process or immediately resign. He argued that public confidence in vaccines must be shored up by demonstrating the autonomy of the regulatory process from political influence—an assertion that would be repeated by multiple commentators over the next several weeks. "Any shortcuts will not only jeopardize the vaccine programs," he wrote, addressing Hahn, "but betray the public trust, which is already fragile about vaccines, and has been made more so by your lack of autonomy from the Trump administration and its overt politicization of the FDA."[12]

From inside the government, a group of senior FDA officials also linked the credibility of the agency's regulatory decisions to its insulation from external interference.

"When it comes to decisions to authorize or approve the products we regulate," wrote the group in a *USA Today* op-ed, "we and our career staff do the best by public health when we are the decision makers."[13] The stakes of preserving expert autonomy for public health were high, the officials warned: "If the agency's credibility is lost because of real or perceived interference, people will not rely on the agency's safety warnings."

Biotech executives joined the chorus of opposition to political meddling in regulatory decisions. In an "open letter to the biopharmaceutical industry" members of the Biotechnology Innovation Organization (BIO) wrote that the "FDA should maintain its historic independence as the gold-standard international regulatory body, free from external influence." Again, the preservation of public trust served as the rationale for defending regulatory autonomy: "This will assure the public that the FDA review process will adhere to the highest standards of scientific and political integrity."[14]

Thus an alliance had formed among academic scientists, government regulators, and drug industry leaders to protect the vaccine authorization process from a perception of political interference. The assumption was that the success of a vaccination program would hinge not only on the therapeutic efficacy of the vaccine as demonstrated in clinical trials, but also on public confidence in the integrity of the regulatory process. Here, the specter of vaccine hesitancy loomed: if a significant proportion of the population refused to take the vaccine—especially since there was uncertainty about the degree of therapeutic efficacy that an eventual vaccine would demonstrate—a mass vaccination program might well fail to stem the pandemic. A COVID vaccine was "unlikely to achieve herd immunity unless it has a high rate of effectiveness (> 50%) and wide public acceptance (> 70%)," as one health policy analyst put it. "Perceptions of political interference in regulatory approval generate distrust, while amplifying fears about a future vaccine's safety and effectiveness."[15]

MEASURING PUBLIC TRUST

In parallel to—and in interaction with—experts' defense of regulatory autonomy, a number of surveys reported diminishing public confidence in the regulatory process along with decreasing willingness to take a prospective COVID vaccine. Between May and September 2020, according to a study by the Pew Research Center, the number of respondents who said they would either "definitely" or "probably" take an available vaccine declined from 72% to 51%, and over three-quarters of respondents indicated a belief that a vaccine would likely be approved before its safety and efficacy had been comprehensively assessed.[16] A CNN poll reported a drop from 66% to 51% from May to October in the percentage of those polled who said they would try to get a COVID vaccine once it was available. Similarly, Gallup reported a 16% decline from July to late September in the number of respondents who would be "willing to be vaccinated" if "an FDA-approved vaccine was available right now at no cost." A group of former FDA commissioners cited the finding of an Axios-Ipsos poll that "42 percent of Americans lacked trust in FDA decision-making." The implications of these survey data were "potentially dire," the group argued, for addressing the day's "most urgent" question: "When the FDA approves a Covid-19 vaccine, will Americans accept it?"[17]

Following insights from the sociology of risk and trust, we should be cautious in interpreting the significance of these measures of public trust in a COVID vaccine. Trust in regulatory science, as Gil Eyal notes, is not best understood as "an attitude measured by surveys" but rather should be seen as a byproduct of institutional mechanisms, embedded in social arrangements. Trust can easily swing into distrust, and then back again. It "is a moving target shifting with the winds," he writes, "sensitive to recent events or to how a question is formulated."[18] In this case, political winds were likely shaping public response to survey questions. In the context of a polarizing election campaign in which one's position with respect to the administration's management of vaccine development could well depend on one's political self-identity, survey responses did not necessarily indicate what a given member of the public was likely to actually do when faced with the concrete situation of an available, FDA-authorized vaccine.

For our purposes here, however, the question is not so much whether these surveys accurately measured a coherent entity—public trust—or how to explain an apparent decline in levels of trust. Rather, what is of interest is how such measures of declining public trust were marshaled as a resource by scientists and regulatory officials who sought to insulate the FDA from external political pressure. Under these circumstances, the prospect of vaccine hesitancy changed its normative valence. For over two decades, scientists and public-health specialists have considered vaccine hesitancy to be a problem demonstrating the need for improved "public understanding of science"— that is, as a problem of irrational fear sparked by rumor and misinformation, a deficit requiring correction. The task for experts and officials, in turn, has been to use the tools of "risk communication"—such as transparency, openness, engagement—to assuage irrational public fear. But in late summer and early fall 2020, as the pandemic emergency intensified and the election approached, the relation of scientific authority to public distrust shifted: the specter of vaccine hesitancy became a resource to defend regulatory autonomy rather than a target for correction.

DEFENDING REGULATORY AUTONOMY

In September 2020, two companies with promising vaccine candidates—Pfizer and Moderna—indicated that preliminary results from their clinical trials might be available as early as the following month. Each company had already produced millions of vaccine doses in anticipation of rapid authorization for distribution. To prepare their application for an EUA issuance, the companies requested guidance from the FDA on how the agency planned to make a decision on granting an EUA for a novel vaccine candidate. Meanwhile, a bureaucratic struggle was brewing between FDA career scientists, on the one hand, and White House officials, on the other, over how vaccine candidates would be evaluated as the results of vaccine developers' Phase III trials came in. FDA director Hahn, stung by criticism of the EUA process from respected scientists, insisted that the agency would use stringent criteria for authorization, and would subject all vaccine candidates to assessment by an external body of experts.

FDA staff drew up a set of proposed guidelines for vaccine developers that would help "provide adequate information to assess a vaccine's benefit-risk profile."[19] In a public statement, the FDA's lead vaccine evaluator emphasized that "increasing trust in vaccines" was the rationale for these new requirements.[20] "[B]eing transparent about the data that we will evaluate in support of the safety and effectiveness of these vaccines," he wrote, "is critical to build trust and confidence in their use by the public." The new guidelines sought to emulate, within a circumscribed time frame, the kind of regulatory scrutiny that a normal biologics license application would require. The effort was to at least partially reconstruct the mechanical objectivity of a normal benefit-risk analysis as a means to publicly demonstrate the agency's integrity.

Two of the proposed guidelines were of particular note: First, clinical trial subjects would have to be tracked for at least two months for potential adverse reactions. And second, a minimum number of severe COVID cases would have to be included in the control group numbers. It was not lost on White House officials that the adoption of these guidelines would extend the timeline for a potential authorization of a novel vaccine beyond the date of the election. In response, the White House demanded that the FDA provide "very detailed justification" for the extended timeline required by the proposed guidelines.[21] According to President Trump, the regulatory requirements were "a political move more than anything else."[22] And the president's chief of staff complained about "new guidance that came out just a few weeks before we're hopefully going to have some very good results on three clinical trials from some of these vaccines." By early October, reported the *New York Times*, White House officials were "blocking strict new federal guidelines for the emergency release of a coronavirus vaccine, objecting to a provision that would almost certainly guarantee that no vaccine could be authorized before the election on Nov. 3." The approval of the guidelines was "now seen as highly unlikely."[23]

At this moment of intensifying struggle within the executive branch, a number of external authorities weighed in to support the FDA's autonomy in determining the EUA evaluation procedures, invoking the need to secure public trust in regulatory authority. "If the White House takes the unprecedented step of trying to tip the scales on how safety and benefits will be judged," wrote a group of seven former FDA commissioners in a *Washington Post* editorial, "the impact on public trust will render an effective vaccine much less so."[24] In a letter to HHS Secretary Azar, the president of the Biotechnology Innovation Association insisted that "new FDA guidance should be finalized and communicated with those on the frontlines developing potential vaccines." The guidance must also "be shared more broadly with the American public," she continued, alluding to the fragility of public trust in regulatory science. "We cannot allow a lack of transparency to undermine confidence in the vaccine development process."[25]

At this stage, with a high-stakes meeting of the agency's external advisory committee on vaccines scheduled to meet later in October to discuss the review process, FDA officials performed what the editor of *Science* magazine called "bureaucratic jujitsu." They stealthily inserted the new guidelines into briefing materials that the agency posted online for participants in advance of the advisory committee meeting. As the date of the meeting approached—perhaps due to the collective pressure of the FDA scientists' allies in academia, government and industry—the White House did not, in the end, block the proposed guidelines. With the new guidelines in place, it would be impossible for any of the most advanced vaccine candidates to receive an EUA before the election. FDA scientists celebrated the online appearance of the new guidelines, reported the *New York Times*, which described the event as "a win for career civil servants."[26] Meanwhile, President Trump dismissed the outcome as "another political hit job," making it "more difficult for them to speed up vaccines for approval before election day."[27]

CONCLUSION

The public health emergency of the COVID-19 pandemic generated an experiment in the provisional reconstruction of a regulatory process designed to ensure public trust in governmental expertise. The construct of public trust and the specter of vaccine hesitancy, wielded by an alliance of academic scientists, industry leaders, and government regulators, enabled the FDA to fend off external interference and sustain the perceived integrity of the vaccine authorization process. What occasioned this struggle, we have seen, was the distinctive bureaucratic space in which the evaluation of COVID vaccine candidates took place. In response to the pandemic emergency, the federal government had created a state of regulatory exception, in which "emergency use authorization" was a tool that enabled the FDA to curtail the normal regulatory approval process. As a preparedness device, the EUA had been put in place with a specific scenario in mind, in which there would be no time to perform a normal regulatory evaluation of the safety and efficacy of a novel medical countermeasure to address a public-health emergency. The structure of a future emergency situation had been envisioned in advance; what had not been envisioned was the potential for abuse of the EUA procedure. The emergency use authorization made it possible for external political influence to shape an ad hoc regulatory decision. In this context, US regulatory agencies and medical experts sought to fend off external interference—at a moment of intense political pressure—by invoking the need to preserve public trust as a way to ensure the efficacy of a mass vaccination campaign.

NOTES

1. US Department of Health and Human Services, "Explaining Operation Warp Speed." https://www.nihb.org/covid-19/wp-content/uploads/2020/08/Fact-sheet-operation-warp-speed.pdf
2. See Theodore M. Porter, *Trust in Numbers: The Pursuit of Objectivity in Science and Public Life* (Princeton, NJ: Princeton University Press, 1995).

3. US Department of Health and Human Services, Administration for Strategic Preparedness and Response, "Project Bioshield." https://www.medicalcountermeasures.gov/barda/cbrn/project-bioshield-overview/.

4. Stuart L. Nightingale, Joanna M. Prasher, and Stewart Simonson, "Emergency Use Authorization (EUA) to enable use of needed products in civilian and military emergencies, United States," *Emerging Infectious Diseases* 13:7 (July 2007): 1046–1051.

5. US Food and Drug Administration, "Emergency Use Authorization of Medical Products and Related Authorities: Guidance for Industry and Other Stakeholders." January 2017. https://www.fda.gov/regulatory-information/search-fda-guidance-documents/emergency-use-authorization-medical-products-and-related-authorities.

6. See Stephen J. Collier and Andrew Lakoff, *The Government of Emergency: Vital Systems, Expertise, and the Politics of Security* (Princeton, NJ: Princeton University Press, 2021).

7. *Federal Register*, "Emergency Use Authorization Declaration: A Notice by the US Health and Human Services Department on 3/27/2020." https://www.federalregister.gov/documents/2020/03/27/2020-06541/emergency-use-authorization-declaration.

8. Eric Topol, letter to FDA Commissioner Stephen Hahn, *Medscape*, August 31, 2020.

9. Sharon LaFraniere, Katie Thomas, Noah Wieland, Peter Baker and Annie Karni, "Scientists Worry about Political Influence over Coronavirus Vaccine Project," *New York Times*, August 2, 2020.

10. Katie Thomas, "All Eyes Are on Pfizer as Trump Pushes for Vaccine by October," *New York Times*, September 30, 2020.

11. H. Holden Thorp, "We're on Our Own," Editorial. *Science Translational Medicine* 12, no. 562 (September 23, 2020).

12. Topol, letter to Commissioner Hahn.

13. "Senior FDA Career Executives: We're Following the Science to Protect Public Health in Pandemic." *USA Today*, September 10, 2020.

14. Jeremy M. Levin, Paul J. Hastings, Ted W. Love, Michelle McMurry-Heath, Ron Cohen, Rachel K. King, John Maraganore, and Richard Pops, Open letter to Biopharmaceutical Industry, September 3, 2020. https://www.bio.org/sites/default/files/2020-09/An_Open_Letter_to_the_Biopharmaceutical_Industry.pdf. That pharmaceutical and biotech industry leaders—who might seem to have something to gain from a rapid vaccine authorization—nonetheless defended the FDA's autonomy, is striking testimony to the strength of the alliance around the normal regulatory order.

15. Lawrence O. Gostin, "Science, Leadership, and Public Trust in the COVID-19 Pandemic," *Milbank Quarterly*, September 28, 2020.

16. Alec Tyson, Courtney Johnson, and Cary Funk, "U.S. Public Now Divided over Whether to Get COVID-19 Vaccine," Pew Research Center, September 17, 2020.

17. "Opinion: 7 Former FDA commissioners: The Trump Administration Is Undermining the Credibility of the FDA," *Washington Post*, September 29, 2020.

18. Gil Eyal, *The Crisis of Expertise* (Cambridge, UK: Polity, 2019), 62; 52.

19. US Food and Drug Administration, "Emergency Use Authorization for Vaccines to Prevent COVID-19: Guidance for Industry," October 2020. https://www.regulations.gov/document/FDA-2020-D-1137-0019

20. Peter Marks, "The FDA's Vaccines and Related Biological Products Advisory Committee and its Role in Advising the Agency on COVID-19 Vaccines." https://www.fda.gov/news-events/fda-voices/fdas-vaccines-and-related-biological-products-advisory-committee-and-its-role-advising-agency-covid

21. Laurie McGinley, Yasmeen Abutaleb and Josh Dawsey, "Trump, White House Demand FDA Justify Tough Standards for Coronavirus Vaccine, Raising Concerns of Political Interference." *Washington Post*, September 25, 2020.

22. Sharon LaFraniere and Noah Weiland, "White House Blocks New Coronavirus Vaccine Guidelines." *New York Times*, October 5, 2020.

23. "White House Blocks New Coronavirus Vaccine Guidelines." *New York Times*, October 5, 2020.

24. "Opinion: 7 Former FDA commissioners: The Trump Administration Is Undermining the Credibility of the FDA," *Washington Post*, September 29, 2020.

25. Biotechnology Innovation Organization, Letter to The Honorable Alex Azar, Secretary of US Department of Health and Human Services, October 1, 2020. https://www.bio.org/sites/default/files/2020-10/BIO%20Sends%20Letter%20to%20HHS%20Secretary%20Alex%20Azar_0.pdf.

26. Sheila Kaplan, Sharon LaFraniere, Noah Wieland and Maggie Haberman, "How the F.D.A. Stood Up to the President." *New York Times*, October 20, 2020.

27. Drew Armstrong, Robert Langreth, and Angelica Peebles, "Pre-Election Vaccine Hopes Dim as Regulators Assert Power," *Bloomberg*, October 6, 2020.

PART III

OBJECTIVITY

9

EXPERTS IN LAW

TAL GOLAN

INTRODUCTION

Expertise has long presented a fundamental challenge for the smooth operation of modern democracy.[1] This is because modern democracy demands transparency, but only experts know what they are talking about. Among the many social institutions that have struggled with this problem, none has done so for longer and in more depth than the law.[2] In time, two general solutions emerged. The first solution emphasizes a regulated and standardized market of expertise as the best guarantee for impartial and efficient justice. It endows the expert with the halo of objectivity and secures it with state mechanisms, such as standardized training, official certification, and professional norms. The second solution emphasizes an open and competitive market of expertise as the best protection against the abuse of expertise. It treats experts with suspicion, excludes them from the decision-making processes, isolates them in the witness box, and allows the lay jury to decide whom to believe. The first solution was adopted by most European countries that share the Roman legal tradition. The second solution was adopted by the British common law tradition and spread throughout the British Empire, including the United States.

This chapter addresses the history of the second solution in the British and American legal systems. It describes the efforts by the legal and scientific communities to cooperate in the mutual pursuit of truth and justice within the adversarial framework of the Anglo-American legal tradition. The chapter shows that the difficulties of fitting expertise into the adversarial system have existed ever since the system was introduced in the late eighteenth century. It argues that these difficulties need to be understood in the context of the essential tension generated by the democratic efforts to deploy expert means to public ends. The chapter further shows that efforts to manage this tension have eroded the traditional adversarial commitment to an open market of expertise and propelled growing judicial scrutiny of the proffered experts and their expertise.

The Historical Forms of Expertise in Common Law

Common law had long acknowledged the importance of expert advice in cases where the disputed facts were such that the courts lacked sufficient knowledge to draw from them an informed decision. In 1554, an English judge declared:

> [I]f matters arise in our law which concern other sciences or faculties, we commonly apply for the aid of that science or faculty which it concerns. Which is an honorable and commendable thing in our law. For thereby it appears that we do not despise all other sciences but our own, but we approve of them and encourage them as things worthy of commendation.[3]

By the sixteen century the English legal system had developed three options for using experts in the courtroom. The first option was to call them as jurors. The second was for the court to nominate them as advisers, whose opinion the court and the jury could adopt as they pleased. The third was for the parties to call experts as witnesses, to testify on their behalf in court.

Expert Juries

Summoning to the jury people with special knowledge concerning the disputed facts of the particular case was but a natural extension of the medieval community-based jury. Drawn from the vicinity where the case developed and chosen because of their direct knowledge of the facts of the case, including the reputations and intentions of the parties involved, medieval jurors functioned as witnesses, investigators, and decision-makers, all at once. In cases that required specialized knowledge in order to do justice, expert juries were often assembled, with members who had that knowledge. Trade disputes were probably the most frequent cause for summoning expert juries. Juries of goldsmiths, booksellers, wine merchants, attorneys, and fishmongers, to name but a few, were summoned to investigate and decide whether trade regulations had been violated. All-female juries constituted another class of expert juries. Central among these was the jury of matrons, summoned in cases involving pregnancy, sexual assault, and infanticide.[4]

Court Expert

The second option for deploying experts in the early modern English courtroom was for the judges to summon their own experts. The earliest reference we have is from 1299, when physicians were called to advise the court on the medical value of the flesh of wolves. Medical advice was the most often sought after, typically in cases of malpractice or when the nature of wounds was at issue. Advice of grammarians was in demand in cases where the disputed facts concerned language. In juryless courts, such as the Patent and Admiralty courts, the experts sat alongside the judges, providing them with their advice. In jury trials, too, the experts apparently were often summoned to advise the court rather than to provide evidence to be evaluated by the jury.[5]

Expert Witnesses

Experts also appeared in court as witnesses to testify under oath on behalf of the parties. Thus, physicians and surgeons testified in criminal, insurance, and will cases; surveyors testified in property cases; linguists testified concerning the meaning of Latin phrases used in contracts; merchants, concerning the particular customs and norms of trade; tradesmen, concerning the quality of particular goods; shipbuilders, concerning the state and construction of vessels; other artisans, concerning their respective subjects of mechanical skill, and so on and so forth. However, unlike with the expert juries and expert advisers, there was no formal procedure that would differentiate these testifying experts from other, lay witnesses. Early modern trials were typically quick and short, and evidence was mostly adduced by the judge, who dominated the proceedings and examined the parties and the witnesses himself, or by direct in-court altercation between accuser, accused, and the witnesses. In this environment, testimonial formalities had little meaning, and although the judges made known their preference for testimony based on first-hand experience, lay witnesses were often allowed to testify to their opinion, especially if it was based on their intimate knowledge of the facts of the case.[6]

The differentiation of the expert from the lay witness was part of a wider transformation of the English legal system that came to be known as the Adversarial Revolution. By the start of the eighteenth century, the self-informed, community-based jury had been succeeded by its modern offspring—the tabula rasa jury, whose members were supposed to know nothing about the case and expected to judge it based on the evidence presented before them in open court. By the end of the eighteenth century, the judicial involvement in the evidentiary processes diminished, the litigating parties gained control over the production of the evidence in court, and their lawyers took over the examination of witnesses, established the right to argue points of law, and perfected the techniques of cross-examination.

Still prohibited from speaking directly to the jury, the lawyers fought their battles mainly over the content and presentation of the evidence. By the end of the eighteenth century, these battles had produced two powerful doctrines: the *hearsay doctrine*, which attempted to limit witness testimony to information based solely on personal observation, and the *opinion doctrine*, which sought to control the form in which witnesses communicated their perceptions to the jury, requiring them not to use inferences where the subject matter is susceptible to factual statements. Curtailing the privileges of all other testimonial sources, these two powerful evidentiary doctrines differentiate the role of the expert witness as the last but necessary exception to the rising rules of evidence—a witness who was allowed, indeed invited, to pronounce an opinion on the facts of the case, even if he or she personally knew nothing about the circumstances of the particular case. Thus, the expert witness was conceived from the start as an exception: the only source of information the new system could not rationalize under its evolving doctrines. And such it would stay—an incompatible yet indispensable figure in the modern adversarial courtroom.

The Changing Nature of Expertise

As the practice of deploying partisan experts as witnesses in the adversarial courtroom grew, a second change, equally important, was taking place in the nature of the expertise deployed. For centuries, the experts summoned to advise or testify before the court were men of large and tested experience, who, from their special training and experience, could instruct the judge and the jury about the disputed facts. Their fields of expertise varied widely, but they all were expected provide advice or testimony that was based on empirical observations, readily traceable to their specific training and experience. Distilled through ages of legal experience and immortalized in the early seventeenth-century writings of Lord Chancellor Francis Bacon, this legal epistemology found abstract explanations suspicious and stressed the primacy of direct observational data in the legal processes of proof.

By the late eighteenth century, a new culture of expertise had begun its rise to dominance, which defied this legal epistemology. This was the culture of science, confident in its ability to discern the hidden laws of nature, however subtle their workings. At the start of the eighteenth century, science was still a bookish culture that studied nature in general. As the century progressed, science narrowed its focus to the inanimate world, supplemented books with experiments, borrowed some mathematics, and gave indications of practical utility. Its practitioners, who styled themselves as gentlemen of science (the word "scientist" was yet to be invented), still theorized like philosophers but, increasingly, acted like skilled professionals. They reasoned from first principles but concerned themselves with the observable, the measurable, and the practical. By the end of the eighteenth century, these scientific experts had become central to Britain's booming economy, revolutionizing agriculture; inventing and improving engines, pumps, and other machinery; and designing and overseeing the construction of waterways, bridges, and harbors.

The lawyers, who had been solidifying their control over the production and presentation of evidence in the new adversarial courtroom, took notice of the rising authority of these scientific experts and began to hire them to testify in the courtroom on behalf of their clients. Late eighteenth- and early nineteenth-century rulings show little judicial concern with this expanding practice of calling experts as partisan witnesses. The absence of judicial angst is surprising if we take into account the prevalent judicial dismay at the time about lay testimony. The slightest interest in the result of the trial rendered the late eighteenth-century witness unreliable. People were not allowed to testify in cases in which they had financial interest. Husbands and wives were forbidden from testifying for or against each other. Why, then, the partisan expert witness? Why did the authoritative royal judges not mold a new procedure that would keep the experts out of the adversarial fire? Perhaps it was the aloofness of the eighteenth-century royal judges, who dominated their courtrooms to such an extent that they could not imagine it otherwise, that a time might come when their judicial powers would no longer suffice to control the influence of the partisan expert in their courtrooms. Perhaps, it was a different aloofness of the royal judges, who did not worry about the behavior of their fellow gentlemen, who, by ties of honor and professional code could be counted on to give disinterested opinions on the witness stand. In either case, in retrospect, one can only appreciate the irony in the judicial leniency toward the new partisan role experts were taking as witnesses. Soon, the tremendous expansion of industry and the subsequent rise of the culture of professional expertise turned the scientific expert witness into a pivotal figure in the courtroom, and by the mid-nineteenth century, partisan expert testimony had become a major bone of contention between the prospering legal and scientific professions.

The Growing Problems of Expert Testimony in Nineteenth-Century England

The growth and spread of technology and industry in the nineteenth century, along with the constantly enlarging applications of science to the various wants of society, had inevitably expanded the legal uses of scientific experts. Among the experts allowed into the nineteenth-century courtroom as expert witnesses, we find the growing presence of medical practitioners, chemists, microscopists, geologists, engineers, mechanists, and so on. These experts untangled for the court and the jury the complexities of the rising tide of cases involving science and technology, appraised the disputed claims with their experimental techniques, and, in general, offered their intimate knowledge of the principles of nature, which the jurors then could apply to the facts at issue before them.

Despite this ascent, the scientific experts quickly found that their forays into the courtroom were exceedingly frustrating. Moving across professional and institutional boundaries, from the exclusivity of their lecture theaters, workshops, laboratories, and societies to the public courtroom, they had hoped to represent there laws that were not controlled by human whim. Instead, they found themselves quarantined in the witness box, excluded from the legal decision-making processes, and manipulated as mere tools in the hands of the lawyers. Browbeaten and set against each other, the scientific witnesses quickly found that their standard strategies for generating credibility and agreement did not always withstand the adversarial heat of the courtroom well. Often, the outcome was an embarrassing public display of eminent scientists zealously opposing each other from the witness stand, a spectacle that cast serious doubt on their personal integrity, and on the integrity of their science.[7]

The legal profession and the public were no less frustrated. Science had promised to deliver a superior tool for the resolution of factual disputes. However, as the nineteenth century progressed, the legal profession discovered that the promised scientific ladder to the summit of truth frequently collapsed under the weight of adversarial proceedings, providing the astonished court with a view, not of the hard facts of the case, but of definitions in disarray, conflicting hypotheses, inconsistent experimental results, and contradictory conclusions. As the nineteenth century advanced, the courts and the public became skeptical not only of the opinions of men of science but also of their integrity. Ironically, the increasing derision of scientific expert testimony resulted largely from the overwhelming success of Victorian science in promoting the scientific method as the yardstick of truth, and the impartial man of science as the best keeper of this truth. Once one believed these claims, then the zealous opposition among the scientific witnesses could only be interpreted as a sign of moral decadence.

Most scientific commentators blamed the adversarial proceedings for the troubles of science in court. Even those who were ready to concede that scientific opinions may legitimately differ did not believe that the judges and lay juries could reliably assess such differences. Throughout the second half of the nineteenth century, men of science repeatedly demanded that the legal system reform its procedures related to expert testimony and employ the scientific expert independently of the parties, as either part of a special tribunal or an adviser to the court. However, these reform proposals collided with the fundamental principles of the adversarial system. Instituting expert tribunals to decide the scientific facts at issue goes against the fundamental political right to a trial by a jury of one's peers. The suggestion to allow the court to call in experts who would be independent of the parties went against two other, equally fundamental postulates—the right of the parties to furnish all the evidence and the neutrality of the court. The legal profession therefore rejected the reform suggestions as remedies worse than the disease.

The conflicts over the experts' performances in court brought into focus a major anxiety that had faced the Victorian scientific community: the overwhelming of the ideal of science as a personal calling by the utilitarian passions of the age. Early in the nineteenth century, the correlation of science and utility had been the target of criticism, mainly by romantic thinkers, who conceived of the growing popularity of science as symptomatic of the mechanistic and materialistic values of the middle class, which was interested in the practical benefits that followed from the control of nature. As the nineteenth century progressed, this critique was increasingly shared by conservative gentlemen of science, who were afraid that the attempt to popularize science would lead to its plebification, and by researchers concerned that scientific research would be overpowered by the demand for instantly useful knowledge.[8]

The debate about the application of scientific expertise in the courts became a focal point for the larger Victorian debate about the role of men of science in an increasingly industrialized and professionalized world. Those who bemoaned the eroding of the ethical code of gentlemanly science by the rising culture of professionalism pointed to the embarrassing scientific disagreements aired in courts as a clear example of the moral menace of science for hire. On their part, the quickly growing species of men of science, who earned their living by directing the perpetual flow of new scientific facts and processes to the wants of society, saw little contradiction between the values of the scientific community and expert witnessing. Truth, they argued, is not less true because it was paid for. It was only because they were applying the obsolete code of scientific voluntarism to a free-market situation that the scientific community had persuaded itself otherwise. This laissez faire rhetoric found a sympathetic ear within the legal profession, which objected to the scientific community's to attempts to monopolize expertise by drawing a line between scientific and nonscientific experts and by referring to the students of the exact sciences as the only true representatives of the laws of nature.[9]

With no resolution in sight, the legal and scientific fraternities grew belligerent. The legal profession remained troubled by the scientific partisanship displayed in the courtroom, and the scientific community remained frustrated by the awkward position it occupied in the courtroom. Still, this mutual disenchantment did not stop the increasing deployment of expert testimony in the courts. Indeed, the rising popularity of science and the growing scope of scientific knowledge continually expanded the uses of experts and tended to make the courts more and more dependent upon their advice. But the increasing tendency of lawyers to fortify their cases with expert testimony did not reflect an appreciation of its excellence, but the requirements of the rising culture of Victorian professionalism. The result was an ironic schism that emerged clearly during the second half of the nineteenth century—the same increasingly indispensable expert opinions that were in everyday life treated as safe and reliable under the mere good faith of social and business reputations were considered unsafe and unreliable when given under oath in court.

THE DEVELOPMENT OF SCIENTIFIC EXPERT TESTIMONY DURING THE NINETEENTH CENTURY IN THE UNITED STATES

The sale of expert advice did not become widespread in America until the middle decades of the nineteenth century. Once it did, though, the deployment of expert testimony in American courts of law grew quickly, and with it appeared all the familiar woes. The American legal system observed the same adversarial procedures of the Common Law; and the American scientific community advertised the same high expectations from the scientific method as did its English counterpart. These two features ensured that despite the significant differences in the institutional and social dynamics of the legal and scientific communities between the two countries, the problem of expert testimony would develop in nineteenth-century America following the same basic pattern displayed in England. Thus, as in England, the growing deployment of men of science in divergent areas of litigation turned the American courts into a lucrative arena for scientific activity. And as in England, this arena soon put on public view the curious spectacle of leading scientists contradicting each other from the witness stand, a view that served to cast doubts on the integrity of the experts and their science.

Like their English colleagues, American men of science were much concerned with the damage that the scandals in court were doing to the public image and credibility of their fledgling community. Like their English colleagues, American scientific experts were bitter about the adversarial legal machinery that placed them in the awkward position of partisan witness. And just like in England, the American legal profession rejected the scientific reform bids as remedies worse than the disease itself.[10] However, unlike in England, nineteenth-century American science lacked the organization, status, and political resources needed to challenge the legal system and its adversarial procedures.

Most of the attempts to reform the legal procedures governing the use of expert testimony were initiated by members of the legal and medical professions. Indeed, reform became one of the hottest topics in the meetings of the various bar associations that were mushrooming in late nineteenth-century America, and many bills were drafted to remedy the evils of expert testimony. As for the selection of experts, it was suggested that they be chosen by the court, either reserving or denying the right of the parties to call additional witnesses; that the courts make their selections unassisted or choose from an official list compiled in some other manner; and that the official list be either permanent or tailored for each case. Concerning the examination of witnesses, it was recommended that it be done by the court, with or without the right of the parties to cross-examine, or alternatively, that there be no witness examination at all, and that the expert would submit a written report. In regard to decisions when experts disagree, it was recommended that a jury of experts be selected or that an expert sit with the judge during the trial to advise him. Alas, the American legislature and judiciary seemed even more reluctant than their English counterparts to dissent from the axioms of the adversarial system. Most reforms bills did not get past the legislative stage, and the few that did were promptly held unconstitutional.[11]

Both the English and the American legal systems were aware of the need to protect the credulous jury from charlatans. Still, neither system was able to lay down a precise rule for determining who was and who was not a competent expert. The only legal criterion was many centuries old: the persons qualified to speak as experts are those who possess special training and experience in the subject in question. Everything beyond this point remained purely a matter of discretion with the presiding judge, who often found it hard to satisfy himself as to the qualifications of the proffered experts. Scientific titles and diplomas and professional reputation carried little judicial meaning in the nineteenth century, and preliminary examinations were impossible to make. Because the courts were unable to distinguish with any reasonable degree of accuracy between experts and charlatans, the practice, English and American, came to be to generously admit the proffered experts, leave it for cross-examination to expose quackery, and to let the jury to be the judge of the ensuing battles between expert witnesses and lawyers. No one trusted the jury to be able to do this job properly. Still, the legal profession considered this a fair price to pay for a free market of expertise, which was regarded as the best protection from the abuse of political and executive powers.

Although the English legal system recognized the jury as the final adjudicator on the facts of the case, it nevertheless granted judges the freedom to take part in the questioning of the witnesses, and to advise the counsels in the framing of their questions or the jurors on the credibility of the witnesses and the weight of their evidence. The authoritative royal judges used these instruments to control the use of expert testimony in their courtrooms, and to guide the jury in its assessment of the scientific witnesses and their evidence. During the second part of the nineteenth century, the English courts also began to divert cases involving scientific expertise from jury trials to the juryless Chancery court. At first, these were mainly patent trials, but in 1875, Parliament passed a bill that officially granted trial judges unfettered discretion in all civil actions to order a trial without a jury in any matter requiring scientific evidence that, in their opinion, could not be handled by the jury.[12]

The American legal system had no access to such instruments. The American colonies adapted with added zeal the notion of the institution of the jury as a mainstay of liberty, and the fact that many judges were laymen with no special claim to legal competence only added to the prominence of the jury. The Jacksonian faith in the ability of the common man, and the enduring political philosophy that supported citizen participation and local government, kept this enthusiasm alive throughout the nineteenth century to an extent unfamiliar in England. Consequently, nineteenth-century American juries did pretty much as they pleased. The second half of the century saw a growing pressure by the business community for more predictability and rationality in the operation of the jury. The pressure, however, also bred popular fears of undue judicial influence on the jury. The result was a practical compromise. On the one hand, the power of the jury to determine the law, especially in civil cases, was eroded. On the other hand, fears of undue influence on the jury were addressed by legislative restrictions on the power of the trial judge to charge the jury. By the end of the nineteenth century, in twenty-one of the forty-nine US states and territories, judges were expressly forbidden by constitutional provisions to charge the jury on questions of facts. In about half of the remaining twenty-eight states and territories, the courts had voluntarily adopted the same restriction. Only in federal courts and a minority of state courts were judges allowed to comment on the weight of the evidence in their charge to the jury.[13]

The Failure of the American Law of Evidence to Control the Problem of Expert Testimony

Unable to check either the selection of the experts or the jury's assessment of their evidence, nineteenth-century American courts attempt to check the growing problem concentrated their efforts on the law of evidence by regulating the processes through which the experts communicated their information in court. One major legal doctrine sought to protect the credulous jury from being uncritically influenced by the expert's view by preventing the expert from giving his opinion on the "ultimate issue"—that is, the precise factual issue before the jury. To permit that, it was held, would be to allow the expert to invade the province of the jury. Rational as it may sound, the application of this doctrine created great confusion. In theory, it made irrelevancy a ground for admission, and relevancy for exclusion. In practice, the "ultimate issue" was often what the expert testimony was all about, and the doctrine tended to exclude expert advice exactly where it was most needed. Consequently, the courts developed various ways to bypass the rule and allow the witnesses to give their opinion on the ultimate issue.[14]

One popular practice was to allow an expert to state in general terms whether a certain cause could have produced the result under consideration and leave it to the jury to decide whether it did produce it or not. To enable this, a second evidentiary doctrine came into play—the "hypothetical question" doctrine—which dictated that the expert's testimony be in the form of answers to hypothetically framed questions. These questions specified a set of factual premises, already submitted in evidence, and the expert was asked to draw a conclusion from them, assuming they were true. The use of this cumbersome technique was justified on triple grounds, as a means of (a) enabling the expert to apply his general knowledge to facts that were not within his personal knowledge; (b) allowing the jury to recognize the factual premises on which the expert opinion was based; and (c) allowing the expert to give his opinion on the ultimate issue without "invading" the province of the jury. The court then instructed the jury to credit the opinion given only if it believed these premises. Sound in theory, the doctrine broke down in practice. If counsel was required to recite all the relevant facts, the hypothetical question became intolerably lengthy. If counsel was allowed to select the facts presented, it prompted one-sided hypotheses. Designed and controlled by the interested parties, the hypothetical question became a means to manipulate the facts of the case rather than to clarify them for the jury.[15]

Even the old and powerful hearsay doctrine turned out to be problematic in the context of expert testimony. The courts' caution in admitting opinions not based on firsthand observation of the facts of the case, and the fear of misleading jurors by reading to them scientific statements they were hardly competent to assess, had often led courts to exclude from the evidence what many people considered the most natural resort to scientific information—standard textbooks, reports, and so on. The hearsay doctrine was used to justify excluding these written statements on the premise that they were not made under oath or that their authors were not available for cross-examination. As with other doctrines, the courts slowly devised ways to work around this one. Some courts permitted the use of scientific treatises, but only to discredit an expert. Others allowed experts to "refresh their memory" by reading from standard works. Others even allowed publications of exact science, assuming their statements to be of ascertained facts rather than of opinion, and excluded other treatises, especially medical works. Confusion and inconsistency, again, were rampant.

Thus, though the problem of expert testimony first raised its head in the English courts, it was in America that it reached its fullest expression. The diversion in England of technical litigation away from jury trials and the efforts of the authoritative royal judges seemed to have kept the thriving business of expert testimony relatively in check. The last decades of the nineteenth century saw the bitter English debates concerning the problems of expert testimony subsiding. Across the Atlantic, though, the problem of partisan expert testimony continued to escalate. By the end of the nineteenth century, the judicial feeling was that the problem of expert testimony had reached a nadir. Pressure to find a remedy was mounting. Eventually, something had to give way in the sacred triangulation of the adversarial system: the postulate of the lay jury, the right of the parties to furnish all evidence, or the neutral position of the bench.[16]

The Developments during the Twentieth Century in the United States

In 1905, the state of Michigan made the first legislative attempt to reform the procedures of expert testimony. It passed a statute that embodied the most popular reform suggestion—that of allowing the court to nominate its own experts. The statute contained the mildest possible version of such a reform. It did not preclude the parties from using their own witnesses, but in criminal cases, it stipulated that the court could appoint up to three disinterested persons, whose identities should not be made public, to investigate the issues involving the use expert knowledge and testify to their findings at the trial. Nevertheless, the Michigan Supreme Court considered did not consider it among the duties of the court to select witnesses, and it held the statute to be in violation of both the state constitution's provision for a separation of powers and the accused's fundamental right to a fair and impartial trial.[17]

The Michigan Supreme Court's decision dealt a serious blow to those who had been advocating for expert testimony reform by means of statutory enactment. Instead, twentieth-century American courts turned their attention to improving the standards of admissibility for expert evidence.[18] Their renewed hopes of succeeding where their predecessors had so miserably failed hinged on a clear change in the market for scientific expertise being created by the rising professional culture in America. By the second decade of the twentieth century, the individual expert who developed and marketed his or her own expertise had been replaced by a community of experts who shared, and were defined by, common standards of competence and ethics. A wide range of expertise from the scientific and technological fields of chemists, physicists, and engineers to architects, surveyors, actuaries, realtors, insurers, and accountants came to be dominated by professional associations of practitioners. These associations developed codes of ethics; established standards of education, training, and practice; and defined minimum qualifications of certification, through either their own examinations or those of the various state boards of examiners.[19]

THE FRYE TEST

In 1923, the Court of Appeals of the District of Columbia came up with the first effective formula to take advantage of this standardized market of expertise to check the problem of expert testimony. The appellate intervention was occasioned by an attempt to introduce the results of the newly invented lie-detector test as evidence in a murder trial. The trial judge had excluded the controversial test, and the appellate court justified the exclusion in the following short opinion:

> Just when a scientific principle or discovery crosses the line between the experimental and demonstrable stages is difficult to define. Somewhere in this twilight zone the evidential force of the principle must be recognized, and while courts will go a long way in admitting expert testimony deduced from a well recognized scientific principle or discovery, the thing from which the deduction is made must be sufficiently established to have gained general acceptance in the particular field in which it belongs. We think that the systolic blood pressure deception test has not yet gained such standing scientific recognition among physiological and psychological authorities as would justify the courts in admitting expert testimony deduced from the discovery, development, and experiments thus far made. The judgment is affirmed.[20]

The opinion came to be known as the *general acceptance standard*, or, more simply, the Frye test, after the defendant's name, and it offered a potent departure from the traditional deadlock of scientific expert testimony. The jury was still considered the final trier of facts, and the experts would still be chosen by the parties, but the ruling significantly extended judicial ability to control expert testimony by shifting the focus of the admissibility test from the qualifications of the individual experts to their proffered evidence. The portrayal of scientific knowledge as an evolutionary process, which had to advance from the experimental to a demonstrable stage before it could be accepted in the court, resonated admirably with the American professional culture that conceived of expert knowledge as a communal product that could be objectively evaluated independently from the individual expert. In a similar fashion, the search for general acceptance within the relevant scientific community accorded well with the dominant progressive views of the age, which conceived of law as an organic part of the greater society and emphasized the role of coordinated expertise in the joint attempt to run society efficiently and uniformly.

Still, originating in an extreme case and containing no precedential citations, the Frye opinion remained at first an isolated solution to the radical technology of lie detection. But after World War II, the courts began to apply it to a constantly broadening range of new scientific evidence. The Supreme Court of the United States restricted the acquisition of evidence in criminal cases via traditional interrogation techniques; federally sponsored crime laboratories flooded the courts with innovative scientific technologies;

and criminal trial judges used the Frye test as a ready-made tool to decide the reliability of evidence derived from voice prints, neutron activation analysis, gunshot residue tests, bite mark comparisons, scanning electron microscopic analysis, and numerous other techniques. By the 1970s, Frye had become the sine qua non in practically all criminal courts that considered the admissibility of new scientific evidence. By the late 1980s, the judiciary expanded its use from criminal to civil proceedings, thereby completing its transformation from special judicial device for checking controversial new techniques to general judicial device for pretrial screening of scientific evidence.[21]

The expanding judicial dominion over scientific expert testimony met with increased criticism. The earliest attacks had considered judicial screening of the scientific evidence as an unnecessary procedure that deprived the jurors of their right to decide for themselves what facts are valuable. The general acceptance criterion was criticized for being too narrow or too slow, thus depriving the courts of potentially valuable evidence. Proponents of the Frye test argued that it finally provided the courts with a uniform method for ensuring the reliability of the scientific evidence. But the ambiguities inherent in determining "the thing from which the deduction is made," and in deciding how to measure its "general acceptance," left ample room for judicial discretion. Consequently, as the critics pointed out, the Frye test ended up having not one but many "general acceptance" criteria, which the courts seemed to apply in a selective manner, according to their own views about the reliability of the particular forensic technique before them.[22]

THE FEDERAL RULES OF EVIDENCE

In 1975, the plot thickened with the codification of the rules of evidence that federal judges followed. Ignoring the Frye test and its general acceptance standard, the newly published Federal Rules of Evidence (FRE) did not prescribe any special test to ensure the reliability of scientific evidence, new or old. Instead, casting a wide net, Rule 702 of the FRE provided:

> If scientific, technical, or other specialized knowledge will assist the trier of fact to understand the evidence or to determine a fact in issue, a witness qualified as an expert by knowledge, skill, experience, training, or education, may testify thereto in the form of an opinion or otherwise, if (1) the testimony is based upon sufficient facts or data, (2) the testimony is the product of reliable principles and methods, and (3) the witness has applied the principles and methods reliably to the facts of the case.[23]

Rule 702, because it left open the critical question of how one defines "scientific, technical, or other specialized knowledge," was interpreted by the judiciary as prescribing a flexible hands-off judicial consideration of scientific evidence that would allow more types of scientific evidence to enter the court. But since the FRE did not state an explicit intent to abandon the Frye test, some federal and a majority of state courts remained committed to the general acceptance standard as an absolute prerequisite to the admissibility of scientific evidence, at least in criminal cases.

The debate concerning the proper judicial standard for the admissibility of scientific expert evidence was further fueled by the growing fears of a mass tort litigation explosion. Since the 1970s, technological failures, dangerous drugs, industrial defects, environmental pollutants, and other toxic substances have all been the subject of prolonged litigation with ever-escalating financial stakes. In the great majority of these cases, the central legal questions were ones of risk and causation, which invariably turned on the scientific evidence and, once again, revealed the all-too-familiar sight of leading experts on the witness stand producing conflicting data and contradictory conclusions. The customary complaints soon followed, and the alarm was sounded that America's courts were being swamped by junk science produced by an unholy alliance between unscrupulous experts and opportunistic attorneys aiming to milk the deep pockets of the corporations.[24] The judges were urged to raise the bar and rely on the conservative Frye test to protect the credulous jury from pseudoscientific experts and the corporations from greedy lawyers. Some commentators objected. The Frye test, they argued, sanctions a stifling scientific orthodoxy and prevents the courts from learning of authentic scientific innovations. They urged the court to follow the relaxed admissibility requirements of the FRE.[25]

THE DAUBERT TRILOGY

The debate over the proper legal test for expert testimony came to a head in *Daubert v. Merrell Dow Pharm., Inc.*, a 1993 civil suit entered by a minor named Jason Daubert. The suit was one of approximately 2,000 suits filed against the giant pharmaceutical corporation Merrell Dow Pharmaceuticals asserting that its drug Bendectin caused a wide variety of birth defects, ranging from limb reductions to heart defects to neurological problems. The Bendectin litigation had been gaining steam since the mid-1980s, and the crucial battles of were fought over the scientific evidence. To prove a causal link, the plaintiffs' experts offered animal studies that linked Bendectin to malformations, and chemical analyses that pointed to structural similarities between Bendectin and other substances known to cause birth defects. On the defense side, Merrell Dow based its strategy on the failure of epidemiological studies to demonstrate a statistically significant correlation between Bendectin and birth defects.[26]

By the early 1990s, Merrell Dow was winning the war. Responding, perhaps, to the growing criticism of junk science, the courts began to dismiss Bendectin cases for lack of probative epidemiological evidence. Daubert's legal team was therefore careful to add to the typical mix of in vitro, in vivo, and chemical evidence a new statistical study that analyzed a super data set, pooled from the data sets from several previous epidemiological studies, and detected statistically significant links between the drug and the alleged birth defects. The trial judge was not impressed. The new statistical study, the judge noted, was prepared especially for the trial and had not been subjected to peer review and therefore could not be considered under Frye to be generally accepted by the scientific community. Once the plaintiffs were stripped of the novel epidemiological card, their science was insufficient to prove general causation, and the judge gave a summary judgment for Merrell Dow. Daubert's lawyers appealed all the way to the Supreme Court of the United States. They argued that the trial judge had erred by following Frye instead of the FRE, and that according to the FRE, it was for the jury, not the judge, to determine the weight of their scientific evidence.[27]

The Supreme Court of the United States, which had thus far stayed away from the protracted problem of expert testimony, agreed to review the Daubert case to clarify the proper admissibility standard for scientific evidence. Excited by the historic opportunity, a new crop of experts—historians, sociologists, and philosophers—sent the court amici briefs with their advice on the best way to deploy science in the courtroom. Alas, the advice of the new experts was as contradictory as the expert advice they aimed to regulate. Some stood firm with Merrell Dow and argued that the courts should stick with Frye and admit scientific evidence only in accordance with laws of nature, laid down by scientific authorities and enforced by peer review. Others stood with Daubert, reminding the Supreme Court of the contingencies of scientific knowledge and pleading with it to adopt the liberal stand of the FRE and not reject a scientific opinion only because it lacks consensus.[28]

The Supreme Court's ruling carved a new interpretive space. The Justices agreed with the petitioners that the FRE superseded Frye but rejected the prevalent let-it-all-in interpretation of the FRE. Instead, the Supreme Court read Rule 702 as a directive for federal judges to ensure the reliability of the scientific evidence they admit into their courtroom. With this new reading, the court fashioned a new role for the trial judge as an active gatekeeper. To help the judges in the Sisyphean effort to distinguish between legitimate and junk science, the Supreme Court equipped them with a flexible recipe of four nonexclusive factors that should be considered in determining the quality of the proffered scientific evidence:

1. Testability: whether the suggested theory or technique had been tested
2. Peer review: whether the suggested theory or technique had been subjected to preview
3. Standardization/Error rate: whether standards had been established for controlling the technique's operation and error rate
4. General acceptance (the Frye rule): the degree to which the theory or technique has been generally accepted in the scientific community

The Supreme Court's foray deep into the exotic territories of scientific expertise did not end with *Daubert*. Once the trial judges started exercising their new gatekeeping authority, a confusion emerged about the standard the appellate courts should apply in reviewing the lower courts' decisions to admit or exclude expert evidence. In 1997, the high court found it necessary to step in again to clarify the confusion. The occasion was *Joiner v. General Electric*, a toxic tort case that revolved around the connection between exposure to polychlorinated biphenyls (PCBs) and lung cancer. The district court had excluded the plaintiff's expert testimony for failing the Daubert test and granted a summary judgment for General Electric. The US Court of Appeals for the Seventh Circuit reversed, holding that because the FRE display a clear preference for admissibility, appellate courts were required to apply a stringent standard of review to the trial judge's exclusion of expert testimony. Applying that standard, the court of appeals found that the trial judge had erred in excluding the testimony of Joiner's expert witnesses. Then the Supreme Court reversed once again and ruled that trial judges should not be held to a special standard when deciding on the admissibility of expert testimony. The proper review standard for appellate review, the Supreme Court clarified, was the traditional "abuse of discretion" standard, which defers to the trial judge and reverses only in cases of clear error.[29]

Meanwhile, a second disagreement had developed among the circuit courts over whether the *Daubert* factors applied only to strictly technoscientific expertise that could be readily measured and tested or could be extended to "softer" expertise, such as economics, psychology, and other "technical, or other specialized knowledge" as specified in Rule 702. In 1999, the Supreme Court felt it necessary to visit its *Daubert* decision once more, to clarify its span. The occasion was *Kumho Tire Co. v. Carmichael*, a product liability case in which the plaintiffs sued a tire manufacturer after a tire on their car blew out and caused an accident that killed a passenger and injured others. The district court had excluded the testimony of the plaintiff's leading expert, a tire-failure analyst, for not satisfying the *Daubert* factors. The Eleventh Circuit reversed, holding that the lower court had erred by applying *Daubert* to a nonscientific expert. The Supreme Court reversed again and held that the district judge had been correct in applying the *Daubert* factors to the tire analyst. Finding no relevant distinction between experts who rely on their intimate knowledge of the laws of nature and those who rely on "skill or experienced-based observation," the Supreme Court held that trial judges' gatekeeping responsibility and the *Daubert* test may be applied to all types of expert testimony.[30]

Known as the Daubert trilogy, the three Supreme Court opinions in *Daubert, Joiner,* and *Kumho* shaped a new role for the trial judge, extended the dominion of the courts to all types of expert testimony, and instructed the appellate courts to defer to the trial judge's new authority. Some states followed course and adopted the *Daubert* trilogy in its entirety. Other states have accepted it piecemeal, following only part of the trilogy. And other states continue to use the Frye general acceptance test, or some combination of *Frye* and *Daubert*.[31]

DISCUSSION

Every generation seems to perceive the malaise of scientific expert testimony in the courts as a sign of the times, the result of the growing volume and complexity of modern science. It is therefore important to note that the putative problems of scientific expert testimony in common law courts have all existed ever since science was first introduced into the adversarial courtroom. The difficulties of fitting science within the adversarial procedures; the reluctance of courts to mold a procedure that would shield science from the adversarial fire; the failure of the scientific professions to regulate the market of expertise; the fear of a credulous jury bewitched in the name of science by charlatans and opportunists; the failure of the law of evidence to check the contradictions of partisan expert testimony—all these predicaments had already emerged during the nineteenth century, on both sides of the Atlantic. Conflicting expert testimony is therefore a feature of, and not a bug in, the adversarial system. Underlying it are the normative and epistemic commitments to generate alternative accounts in the courtroom and to the superior ability of the adversarial procedure to shed light on grey areas and interpretive conflicts within the scientific evidence.

Considered in its full arc, the history of experts in the courts tells a dramatic story. Early on, the legal and the scientific fraternities dreamed of establishing an alliance that would bring justice and truth together. However, instead of bringing law and science closer, scientific evidence pulled them further apart. What had seemed early on as a central civil function of science had by the twentieth century turned into a perennial source of discontent. The scientific community was growing increasingly bitter with the adversarial deployment of its services, and the courts were growing increasingly weary and wary of conflicting expert testimony. This growing disenchantment has driven a trend of ever-greater judicial scrutiny of expert evidence. Until the twentieth century, there was no special rule for determining the admissibility of scientific evidence. As with every other type of evidence, the courts evaluated scientific evidence according to the traditional evidentiary criteria: the qualifications of the witness, the relevancy of the evidence, and its helpfulness to the trier of fact. In 1923, the *Frye* court introduced for the first time a special admissibility test for expert evidence—the Frye rule. At first, the courts used it narrowly and only in criminal cases to screen particularly controversial expertise such as lie-detection and truth sera. By the second part of the twentieth century, the practice had been extended to civil cases and to all types of novel scientific evidence. Finally, by the end of the twentieth century, the courts felt it necessary to defer no more to the judgement of the scientific community and to start running their own detailed inquiries into the legitimacy of the proffered expert evidence.[32]

Ironically, this growing judicial scrutiny of scientific evidence has not been occasioned by the loss of faith in science. On the contrary, despite the problematic history of partisan science in the adversarial courtroom, the legal profession has never wavered in its trust in the scientific method. This steadfast belief in the scientific method as the best measure of demonstrable truth has induced the judiciary and the public to interpret conflicting expert testimony, not as legitimate debate, but as a sign of moral corruption—if the experts were true to science, they would have found a way to agree more. Throughout the twentieth century, this conviction pushed and legitimized a growing judicial incursion into scientific territory in an attempt to exorcise charlatanism and differentiate between good and bad science. Consequently, early twenty-first-century judges find themselves venturing deeper than ever in the strange land of biostatistics, confidence levels, meta-analysis, and falsifiability, charged with the diffi-cult task of weighing the merit of highly specialized scientific claims. How well can the lay judges meet these challenges? Will their new gatekeeping role lead to better adjudi-cation? The jury is still out on these questions.

NOTES

1. Stephen Turner, *Liberal Democracy 3.0* (London: Sage, 2003).
2. Tal Golan, *Laws of Men and Laws of Nature: A History of Scientific Expert Testimony* (Cambridge, MA: Harvard University Press, 2004).
3. Buckley v. Rice Thomas, *English Reports* 75 (1554): 182–192.
4. James C. Oldham, "The Origins of the Special Jury," *University of Chicago Law Review* 50 (1983): 173–175.
5. J. H. Beuscher, "The Use of Experts by the Courts," *Harvard Law Review* 54, no. 7 (May 1941): 1108–1110; Learned Hand, "Historical and Practical Considerations Regarding Expert Testimony," *Harvard Law Review* 15 (1902): 40–43; see also Thomas Roger Forbes. *Surgeons at the Bailey. English Forensic Medicine to 1878* (New Haven: Yale University Press, 1985), pp. 26–33..
6. John Henry Wigmore, *A Treatise on the Anglo-American System of Evidence in Trials at Common Law*, 2nd ed. (Boston: Little, Brown, 1923), sec. 1917, pp. 101–103.
7. Tal Golan, "Scientific Expert Testimony in the English Courtroom," *Science in Context* 12, no. 1 (1999): 5–34.
8. Christopher Hamlin, "Scientific Method and Expert Witnessing: Victorian Perspective on a Modern Problem," *Social Studies of Science* 16 (1986): 485–513.
9. Golan, *Laws of Men*, 107–134.
10. Golan, 135–143; Chas. F. Himes, "The Scientific Expert in Forensic Procedure," *Franklin Institute Journal* 135 (June 1893): 407–436.
11. Gustav A. Endlich, "Proposed Changes in the Law of Expert Testimony," *Pennsylvania Bar Proceedings* (1898): 189–221; note, "Appointment of Expert Witnesses by the Court," *Harvard Law Review* 24, no. 6 (April 1911): 483–484.
12. R. M. Jackson, "The Incidence of Jury Trial during the Past Century," *Modern Law Review* 1 (1937): 139–140.
13. "Changing Views of Jury Power: The Nullification Debate, 1787–1988," *Law and Human Behavior* 15, no. 2 (1991): 165–182.
14. Charles T. McCormick, "Expert Testimony as an Invasion of the Province of the Jury," *Iowa Law Review* 26 (1941): 819– 820.
15. John Henry Wigmore, *A Treatise on the System of Evidence in Trials at Common Law*, vol. 2 (Boston: Little, Brown, 1904), secs. 672–686, at 766–781.
16. Gustav Endlich, *Expert Testimony: What Is to Be Done with It?* (Philadelphia, 1896), 5, 12–13.
17. People v. Dickerson 129 N.W. 199, 199-201 (Mich. 1910).
18. A. M. Kidd, "The Proposed Expert Evidence Bill," *California Law Review* 3 (1915): 216–223.
19. Thomas L. Haskell, ed., *The Authority of Experts: Studies in History and Theory* (Bloomington, Indiana: Indiana University Press, 1984), 180–225.
20. Frye v. United States, 293 F. 1013, 1014 (1923).

21. Bert Black, Franscisco J. Ayala, and Carol Saffran-Brinks, "Science and the Law in the Wake of Daubert: A New Search for Scientific Knowledge," *Texas Law Review* 72 (1994): 725–727.

22. Paul C. Giannelli, "The Admissibility of Novel Scientific Evidence: Frye v. United States, a Half-Century Later," *Columbia Law Review* 80, no. 6 (1980): 1197–1250.

23. Federal Rules of Evidence (New York: Federal Judicial Center, 1975), rule 702.

24. Peter W. Huber, *Galileo's Revenge: Junk Science in the Courtroom* (New York: Basic Books, 1991); Kenneth R. Foster, David E. Bernstein, Peter W. Huber, eds., *Phantom Risk: Scientific Inference and the Law* (Cambridge, MA: MIT Press, 1993).

25. Mark McCormick, "Scientific Evidence: Defining a New Approach to Admissibility," *Iowa Law Review* 67, no 5 (July 1982) 879, 908–915.

26. Kenneth R. Foster and Peter W. Huber, *Judging Science: Scientific Knowledge and the Federal Courts* (Cambridge, MA: MIT Press, 1997), 4–16.

27. Daubert v. Merrell Dow Pharm., Inc., 727 F. Supp. 570, 571 (1989), aff'd, 951 F.2d 1128, 1128 (9th Cir. 1991), vacated by 509 U.S. 579 (1993).

28. Daubert v. Merrell Dow Pharmaceutical, Inc., *United States Law Week* 61(1993): 4805–4811.

29. Joiner v. General Electric 522 U.S. 136 (1997).

30. Kumho Tire Co. v. Carmichael, 526 U.S. 137 (1999).

31. David E. Bernstein and Jeffrey D. Jackson, "The Daubert Trilogy in the States," *Jurimetrics* 44, no. 3 (2004): 351–366.

32. Tal Golan, "Revisiting the History of Scientific Expert Testimony," *Brooklyn Law Review* 73, no. 3 (2008): 879–942.

10

INSTITUTIONS OF EXPERT JUDGMENT: THE PRODUCTION AND USE OF OBJECTIVITY IN PUBLIC EXPERTISE

BRICE LAURENT

INTRODUCTION

How to define the appropriate expertise for policymaking? This question traditionally receives an answer in the terms of objectivity. Objective facts are described as the main ingredients of the sound scientific advice required making decisions about complex policy matters. A central issue, then, is to integrate the contribution of individual experts. The judgment of experts is a component of the production of objective knowledge that is both necessary and potentially problematic, as it is tied to the personal experience of the expert as a human being who is bound to be subjected to various limitations and potential bias.

How experts are then expected to behave to produce objective facts for policymaking has thus proven to be controversial. In recent years, the trustfulness of public expertise and its ability to convincingly ground objectivity in the judgment of public experts have been questioned. Events such as Brexit and the 2016 election of Donald Trump as US president have been interpreted as outcomes of a pervasive mistrust of the ability of public experts to provide convincing advice. These events can be (and have been) read as signs of a re-imagination of expert judgment, as the question of whether to reserve them to certain authorized people appears more problematic than ever. The expression "alternative facts," used by Trump adviser Kellyanne Conway, was a clear attack on the uniqueness of the voice of objectivity. It seemed to indicate an opening of the ownership of the production of facts, at the risk of suggesting that any judgment could be considered "expert."

In parallel with a growing mistrust in experts, other actors claim that new ways of producing objective knowledge could insulate the production of claims from subjective interventions and individual bias. "Evidence-based policy" has been used as an umbrella term to point to a range of methods, from cost-benefit analysis to randomized controlled trials, meant to insulate policymaking from the tribulations of politics. The pervasive reference to machine learning can be situated in that context as well, as algorithms are said to be able to finally provide an automated channel toward the objective description of reality. Thus, Facebook's recent claim that artificial intelligence could be used as a tool to identify "fake news" ties together the broadening of the definition of expert judgment with the calls for new mechanical ways of ensuring objectivity.

Kellyanne Conway's and Facebook's interventions are two opposite reactions to the fact that the ability of expert judgment to provide objective knowledge is being questioned. The former points toward the limitless extension of who has the ability to be trusted as experts, and the latter supposes that the automation of expert judgment could eliminate persistent, and necessarily biased, subjective elements. The former is not very satisfactory: if anyone can be an expert, then no one in particular can be trusted as one. But neither is the recourse to an even more technologized version of expertise because that can only exacerbate the democratic issues arising from the restriction of expert advice to a well-defined group of people. The first reaction gets rid of the problem of objectivity by turning to a whole mass of individual subjects. The second one hopes to make the human subject disappear behind automatized tools that are expected to ensure objectivity.

For all their situatedness in the era of the former Trump presidency, Brexit, and the alleged influence of social media in the growing mistrust of expertise, these reactions are not entirely foreign to a long-term debate in science-policy circles about the potential widening of the sources of public expertise. In 1979, a report by the Organisation for Economic Change Co-operation and Development (OECD) discussed public participation in science and technology in the wake of what was already construed as a delegitimation of public expertise, and explored the ways in which such participation could be articulated with the production of objective expertise (OECD 1979). Since then, the issue of the finding the appropriate balance between opening up the circles of expertise and maintaining a control over what counts as objective knowledge has been widely discussed in theoretical and practical terms.

Both these discussions and the current difficult situation that expertise faces are invitations to theorize the relationships between objectivity and expert judgment. This chapter builds on the important body of work in science and technology studies (STS) to discuss some analytical perspectives that can be useful in theorizing these relationships and, eventually, in tackling the current challenges that public expertise faces. Central to the argument here is that objectivity for the sake of expertise is manufactured in public institutions in ways that also determine the type of expert judgment considered acceptable. In that sense, objectivity is not gained *despite* the subjective human component, but relies on operations that actively shape human subjects and social organizations.

The chapter is organized in two sections. The first one reviews the STS works that have analyzed objectivity as a historical and social construct. These works invite us to consider that public expertise always articulates objectivity and expert judgment, yet in ways that differ in various institutional settings. The second section discusses the specific case of European expertise. The European institutions have struggled to stabilize a unique expert voice, at the same time they are accused of being overly technocratic. But instead of considering the European case as an illustration of failed attempts at manufacturing public expertise, I show that it proposes an original, if unstable, articulation of objectivity and expert judgment. As such, the European example offers a magnifying lens on the current difficulties of expertise, and may provide elements for exploring the potential ways forward.

MANUFACTURING OBJECTIVITY, SHAPING SCIENTIFIC SUBJECTS

Objectivity in Historical Perspective

A first step in reflecting on the relationships between objectivity and expert judgment consists in problematizing objectivity itself. History is a powerful resource in this regard because it helps us to situate a version of objectivity that we might consider straightforward. Lorraine Daston and Peter Galison's (1992, 2006) works on the history of scientific images have demonstrated that objectivity has a history. They analyze the historical evolution of scientific atlases in Western countries, covering various scientific fields, including botany, biology, paleontology, and astronomy. They show that the quality of the scientific image as a convincing representation of reality has been diversely evaluated over time. Early scientific images were the product of individual craftsmanship, and the outcome of the ability of an individual to correct direct observations, complement them with additional elements, or combine several of them to produce a fictitious "type." Daston and Galison then document the gradual emergence, in the nineteenth century, of what they call "mechanical objectivity." Whereas the earlier understandings of objectivity associated the production of the scientific image with the personal intervention of the scientist, mechanical objectivity supposes that the individuality of the scientist can be erased, so that scientific representation is only obtained by mechanical means. The emergence of mechanical objectivity, in Daston and Galison's account, is directly linked to the growing importance of technical instruments in scientific practice. It means that scientific images are expected to be unmitigated reflections of a natural reality on which the individuality of the observer is not expected to act. Although mechanical objectivity has been dominant since the nineteenth century, it can be contrasted with contemporary scientific disciplines that require the active intervention of the individual scientist in the production of representations of nature. Nanotechnology, for instance, is a domain where the scientist's manipulation of atoms is a way of both learning about physical laws and making new properties emerge. In this case, objectivity is not only mechanical but also relies on the personal intervention of a scientist who seeks to obtain original physical features for future practical applications, if not economic gain.

The history of objectivity is a crucial element in our reflection on objectivity and expert judgment. First, it shows that defining good practices for objectivity implies a set of expectations about scientific selves. Mechanical objectivity is based on a series of hypotheses about how the scientist is expected to behave. It cannot exist without an understanding of the subjectivity of the individual scientist, defined precisely by his or her ability to disappear behind a neutral instrument that will provide a faithful representation of nature uncorrupted by human intervention. The "moral economy of science" (Daston 1995) that goes with mechanical objectivity is a kind of asceticism, requiring the scientist to make an abstraction of the mundane contingency that might corrupt the work of the instrument. In doing so, it also introduces expectations about the audience for the scientific image, who will then be required to interpret the image based on professional knowledge. Along with a scientific self in charge of producing images go other imaginations of individual scientists, tasked with mustering their own professional abilities to read information that is inaccessible to lay people. What this shows is that objectivity is not produced in spite of expert judgment but requires particular forms of expert judgment.

A second significant contribution of the historical works on objectivity is that they situate an understanding of objectivity that has become dominant in contemporary liberal democracies. Philosopher Thomas Nagel (1989) spoke of the "view from nowhere" that would characterize objectivity. He wrote: "A view or form of thought is more objective than another if it relies less on the specifics of the individual's makeup and position in the world, or on the character of the particular type of creature he is" (5). From there, Nagel could then consider that "the standpoint of morality is more objective than that of private life, but less objective than the standpoint of physics" (5). The "view from nowhere" can then be considered as a condition for a particular kind of objectivity—namely, mechanical objectivity. The historical situatedness of mechanical objectivity also suggests exploring the material conditions under which it is possible to craft it. Daston and Galison's works on scientific instruments can be related to a rich landscape of STS studies of scientific practices that have examined how the circulation and the standardization of instruments result in the production of the view from nowhere. Thus, historian of science Ted Porter (1993) spoke of "a 'kind of objectivity' that is more nearly identical to impersonality, or standardization" (89; see also Latour 1990) and is produced by the construction of standardized instruments. The dominant understanding of objectivity has a history, and requires active work to be produced. How it translates in the world of expert advice is the question we will now examine, by extending these reflections to institutional settings.

Objectivity in Scientific Institutions

The historical and sociological works about objectivity have illuminated the tight connection between the making of objective knowledge and the construction of the scientific self. Thinking about expertise requires adding another dimension, though. The history of science has shown that the production of facts relies not only on material and literary technologies, but also on social technologies. Shapin and Schaffer's (1985) seminal study of the birth of the experimental practice in seventeenth-century England has shown that when Robert Boyle invented a set of material practices around such instruments as the air pump and a type of experimental discourse, he also defined a social organization whereby only certain individuals were able to act as witnesses in charge of attesting experimental results

This historical work has an important consequence for our reflection—namely, that expertise necessarily ties together the problem of scientific objectivity with the social organization of the institutions in charge of delivering knowledge. We can now develop our considerations about mechanical objectivity and the view from nowhere by examining the institutional work they require. What historical studies such as Shapin and Schaffer's suggest is that *boundary work* is one of such techniques. Ever since sociologist Thomas Gieryn (1983) pointed the analytical attention toward the work needed to differentiate "science" from "non-science," empirical studies have illuminated the work of the institutions that are expected to ensure that this boundary is well maintained. Among these institutions are the scientific bodies in charge of regulating scientific publication. Thus, one can consider peer reviewing as a social technology in charge of delimitating what counts as knowledge. This social technology, in the guise of Boyle's process of selecting who can be a witness in charge of evaluating scientific experiments, relies on a definition on who is authorized to say what counts as knowledge.

The recent history of the practice of anonymity in scientific publications is a fascinating lens through which to not only examine the empirical practice of peer reviewing, but also, and more importantly for our concern here, to discuss how the institutions of scientific publishing articulate the production of objectivity with the practices of expert judgment. David Pontille and Didier Torny (2014; 2015) have shown that anonymity, particularly under its "double blind" guise, is a relatively recent invention, marked by pervasive issues about who should be "blind," and under what conditions. Pontille and Torny's works discuss the various approaches used in different scientific journals, as well as recent episodes that mark a reconfiguration of the sources of scientific objectivity and the practice of expert judgment. One of these episodes is the case of Donna Haraway, who chose to reveal her identity as a reviewer for a paper in *Social Studies of Science*, and was then quoted by name in the acknowledgments. Pontille and Torny note that Haraway, the author of "Situated Knowledges: The Science Question in Feminism and the Privilege of Partial Perspective" (Haraway, 1988) and a critic of objectivity as imagined in the terms of a universal category, was, indeed, a perfect advocate for a situated expert judgment, fully embodied in the individual person of the known reviewer. Other telling episodes are provided by academic journals in economics, which publish papers that have already circulated widely as working papers or conference papers, and which use metrics of circulation, readership, and popularity as basis for granting publication. While the Haraway case is one of the resingularization of the universal voice of the blind expert, this latter is one of the extension of the community of peers to a wide and not pre-circumscribed audience.

From Scientific Institutions to Expert Institutions

The scholarly analysis of peer reviewing extends the analysis of objectivity and expert judgment to the institutional organizations expected to manufacture objectivity. It has the interest of explicitly thematizing the role of expert judgment. Here, the "expert" is the reviewer in charge of evaluating the scientific value of the paper. He or she might be anonymous or a known contributor, a member of a delimitated discipline or of an extended community of interested people. His or her works is tied to an institution expected to maintain boundaries between what is scientific and what is not, between who can exercise scientific judgment and who cannot. How these operations are conducted in some cases directly echo a view from nowhere—and one can situate the conditions of anonymity in this framework. In others, the view of the expert is expected to be situated, either in a known individual (as in the Haraway example) or in a broader collective (as in that of the economics journals). In all cases, institutional rules tie together the practices of objectivity and the definition of the appropriate expert judgment.

The operations of boundary-making are remarkably similar in the institutions of expertise that are the main focus of this chapter—namely, that of the public bodies in charge of providing expert advice for decision-making purposes, or "public expertise." These institutions, like those discussed earlier, tie together the production of objectivity with the practices of expert judgment. But they add another crucial element to this already complex mix—namely, the expected legitimacy of the public institutions in charge of providing advice for decision-making purposes.

When we shift our analytical focus from scientific institutions (such as those related to peer reviewing in scientific journals) to policy ones, the issue of political legitimacy becomes crucial. One of the main results of STS in the analysis of public expertise has been to theorize the joint production of scientific objectivity and political legitimacy. Sheila Jasanoff (2005) has written extensively about expert advice in policy settings, and has reflected on what she calls the "three body problem" of expert legitimacy. Jasanoff explains that the legitimacy of expertise, in the eyes of decision-makers and the wider public expected to trust it, relies on three different kinds of "bodies." It needs a consistent "body of knowledge," to be used by the "body of the expert" as a human being. One can understand the view from nowhere in the context of this dual requirement: here, the body of the expert has to disappear for the body of knowledge to be used in acceptable ways. She also underlines the importance of the third dimension—namely, the "public body" of the institutions in charge of providing expert advice. Thus, if the view from nowhere is seen as a desirable basis for public expertise, then it requires corresponding public institutions. The American institutions of public expertise are good illustrations of this position, and its associated tensions (Jasanoff 1990, 2011). They rely on operations of boundary-making between what is expected to be the domain of expert advice (supposedly purely scientific) and what is expected to be the domain of policymaking (Jasanoff 1987). A telling illustration of this process is provided by the case of the public presentations of reports written by the US National Academy of Science. STS scholar Steve Hilgartner (2000) has shown that maintaining a boundary between what scientists do behind closed doors and what is presented to the public is a crucial operation for the academy, seen as a condition for producing objective work and legitimate advice. The diagnostic of the pervasiveness of the view from nowhere in the American regulatory system can be nuanced when considering the practice of expertise in the court system. American courts require each party to summon their experts; these experts are then tied to the interests of the party that brings them in. The confrontation of expertise here is about who can produce facts before the court, which is expected to side with science, can rule (see e.g., Jasanoff 1997). Legal scholars have noted the specificity of American courts, where the adversarial system of expert witnessing is accompanied by "a special penchant for fact finding," as opposed to other legal systems in which "judges are more willing to recognize the limits of fact-finding, using presumptions when necessary to bridge the gaps in the evidence."[1]

A Variety of Institutional Constructs

The American situation provides a telling illustration of how the view from nowhere is institutionalized. It is one particular solution to the three-body problem of expertise, and not necessarily the only one. One can, indeed, compare it to the case of other public institutions of expertise in national and international contexts. Sheila Jasanoff's (2005) comparative study of biotechnology policy has analyzed the British and German cases. In the United Kingdom, a public demonstration conducted by a known professional appears to be an essential condition for claims to credibility. In Germany, collecting representative viewpoints from various social actors proved to be crucial in the production of expert advice. Instead of the desirable view from nowhere, the British and German cases suggest that a view from "somewhere" or a view from "anywhere" might be a basis for public expertise. These examples are useful for our reflections here because they force us to theorize objectivity in other terms than those of the view from nowhere. The British and German public institutions of expertise show that public facts can be grounded in the judgment of a known individual or on the representations of social groups. In both cases, objectivity is manufactured by known and active human subjects. One can then contrast the view from nowhere with other approaches to objectivity in public institutions. The British "view from somewhere" and the German "view from anywhere" are two examples of the other approaches, but there is no reason to limit the landscape of possible articulations between objectivity and expert judgment.

One can extend this analytical thread by examining international organizations. Some of them adopt the discursive and institutional practices of the view from nowhere. The World Trade Organization (WTO) and the OECD, for example, strategically problematize the conditions of legitimacy of the expertise they produce by drawing rigorous boundaries between international scientific expertise and the national regulatory choices of sovereign member countries (Bonneuil and Levidow 2012, on the WTO; Laurent 2016a on the OECD). By contrast, the Intergovernmental Panel on Climate Change (IPPC) is a hybrid institution; it is expected to provide scientific knowledge while serving as an arena for international negotiations. Doing so relies on a complex organization whereby scientific and diplomatic operations are carefully distributed (Beck 2011; Miller 2001). The example of the IPPC shows that international organizations may favor procedural approaches to define the conditions under which objective knowledge can be produced and experts are expected to behave. Alberto Cambrosio and Peter Keating speak of "regulatory objectivity" to refer to situations in which public and private institutions need to agree on the procedures according to which various regulatory entities can be crafted. Regulatory objectivity "consistently results in the production of conventions, sometimes tacit and unintentional but most often arrived at through concerted programs of collective action" (Cambrosio et al. 2006, 190). Describing various standardization and regulatory interventions related to biomedicine, Cambrosio and Keating analyze the ways in which public and private actors coordinate with each other to produce procedural instruments ("conventions" or "protocols") that allow them to stabilize the use of technological tools that might otherwise vary across the local sites where they are applied. The notion of "regulatory objectivity" points to an institutional configuration whereby objectivity and expert judgment are articulated through a set of agreed principles that provide experts with common references to base their actions on.

The diversity of the institutions in charge of providing expert advice is not only about organizational choices. It also points to the plurality of approaches used to define what counts as credible knowledge and legitimate policy. These approaches can be characterized as "institutionalized practices by which members of a given society test and deploy knowledge claims used as a basis for making collective choices," or, in Sheila Jasanoff's (2005) terms, "civic epistemology" (255). The term "civic epistemology" can be read as a proposition for theorizing the articulation between objectivity and expert judgment in public institutions. Examining various civic epistemologies in national or international contexts, then, shows that the role of the public institutions of expertise is less to tame subjective expert judgment for the sake of objectivity (as if the two were opposed) than to solidify practices of defining who the experts should be and how they should behave.

Cracks in the Public Institutions of Expertise

The contrasts I just sketched among several civic epistemologies might point to an overall landscape of geographical zones, neatly distinguished according to how they define the sources of the objectivity and legitimacy of expert advice. The situation, however, is less stable, and the challenges for the institutional production of expert advice are numerous.

Some of these challenges can be situated in the institutional constructs described above. Thus, the American public bodies have often struggled to maintain the boundary between science and policy. As soon as that boundary between risk assessment (i.e., the scientific phase) and risk management (i.e., the policy phase) was affirmed as a necessary basis for producing credible expert advice, particularly in the document that became known as the *Red Book* (National Research Council 1983), it was also nuanced as necessarily porous in practice (Jasanoff 1990). Accordingly, controversies in the American institutional context revolve around the possibilities of producing expert advice seen as detached from political bias. A telling illustration of the dynamics of these controversies, and of their institutional consequences, is that of the Office of Technology Assessment (OTA), as described by political scientist Bruce Bimber (1996). Created in 1972 and closed in 1995, the OTA's short history is marked by pervasive controversies about its alleged political bias. Eager to ensure the office would be seen as a neutral provider of expert advice, successive institutional reforms established a firm boundary between the OTA's contributions and policy decisions. Eventually, in 1995, as the newly elected Republican majority in Congress was looking for ways to cut the budget, it could argue that no policy use could be identified for the OTA. In other institutional contexts, controversies about public expertise might take a different form. In the United Kingdom, for instance, episodes when known professionals fail to convince the public of the value of their knowledge claims can be read as failures to stabilize institutions of public expertise that give so much weight to the intervention of the individual and known public expert (Jasanoff 2005).

Other difficulties arise in sites where different civic epistemologies might clash. This is especially the case in international organizations, where the oppositions between member countries are arbitrated in ways that might favor one civic epistemology over others. That the WTO tends to reason in the terms of the view from nowhere makes it more difficult for European countries to make their position appear to be objective (Jasanoff 2011; Winickoff et al. 2005). The framing of the OECD reports about science policy in terms of international expert advice that is neatly distinguished from national regulatory choices makes it impossible to envision new risk-governance instruments, such as public engagement, in terms that would significantly transform the relationships between science and society (Laurent 2016a).

Less described in the STS literature are current situations where the very terms under which public expertise is expected to be produced are questioned. The French bodies of public expertise provide an illustration of one such situation. Historically marked by the crucial role of the public expert who is able to manipulate technical tools and was trained in state-controlled *grandes écoles* (Porter 1991), French public expertise now faces challenges about its ability to include unruly people and objects (Joly 2009; Laurent 2016b, 2017). Recent debates about technological programs, such as biotechnology, nanotechnology, and synthetic biology, have seen attempts by the French public bodies of expertise to rethink the terms under which public expertise is crafted and deemed legitimate (or, in Jasanoff's terms, its civic epistemology). Public debates have been organized to make dialogue between public experts and various concerned groups possible, and regulatory decisions have been made to allow the public administration to characterize technical and legal uncertainties about objects such as nanomaterials or synthetic organisms. These initiatives are not consensual, and the new missions undertaken by the French public experts are far from clear. Political scientists and practitioners have identified institutional weaknesses in the ability of the French public institutions to manage their stated objectives to govern uncertain risks and ensure public participation (Besançon and Benamouzig 2005; Dab and Salomon 2013). This shows that the integration of new publics and objects on the perimeter of the French public expertise is still very much in transition.

The French transition situation is an illustration of the new instabilities that institutions of public expertise face, and which have accelerated with the help of digital technologies. These instabilities show a current lack of institutions able to stabilize the conditions under which expert knowledge can be considered acceptable. The emergence of individual skepticism channeled by social media is often read as a threat to the existing expertise institutions. In this case, the current unease about the uncontrolled circulation of information on social media shows the consequences when institutions meant to stabilize the criteria for granting credibility are lacking. Symmetrically, digital technologies are often claimed to be resources for crafting new technical tools for ensuring public objectivity. A good illustration is how Facebook refers to artificial intelligence as the solution to eliminate fake news.[2] Here again, a crucial issue, though one not often made explicit, is the absence of institutions that would ensure that what Facebook does is appropriately kept in check.

At this stage in our reflection we cannot pretend that solely a call for objectivity could solve the current problems that public expertise faces. It is not that objectivity is not worth looking after or useful as a common reference point for public discourse. But a simple call for objectivity has little chance of settling the subtle constructs that are necessary to stabilize the public institutions of expertise. Because the terms under which objectivity should be produced are situated in institutional contexts, there is an institutional work to undertake if the production of objective knowledge is to be reimagined.

There is a real-world laboratory in which to explore both the challenges of manufacturing institutions for expert advice and the complexity of the allure of the unproblematized reference to objectivity. This real-world laboratory is that of the European institutions, where the question of the appropriate institutional format for public expertise has been debated for years, and where it is still far from solved.

A Laboratory for Objectivity and Expert Judgment: The European Institutions of Public Expertise

European Expertise: Objectivity and the Representation of Interests

The European project was initially, and still is, an economic one, so much so that legal scholars speak of the unwritten "economic constitution" of the European institutions, whereby the source of political and legal legitimacy is the construction of the common market, and the imagined beneficiary of the European project is an economic agent, either a consumer being offered a variety of choices at reasonable prices, or a producer free to engage in business activities across the member states (Streit and Mussler 1995). The economic constitution of the European Union acquired a new layer of meaning with the addition of the Monetary Union. It should not, then, be a surprise that the European economic expertise produced by the European Central Bank has adopted the view from nowhere (Hall and Franzese 1998; McNamara 2002; Vauchez, 2016).

Scientific expertise is an entirely different story, though. Scientific expertise started to become a European concern when the construction of the single market in the 1980s made the harmonization of consumer goods a central European objective. After the 1986 Single European Act, health and safety matters became part of the scope of the European competences. The 1997 Amsterdam Treaty then asked the European Commission to "take as a base a high level of protection, taking account in particular of any new development based on scientific facts" in domains related to "health, safety, environmental protection and consumer protection."[3] In many respects, scientific expertise is now everywhere in Europe, as the rich scholarly literature on the topic shows. The conduct of European regulation has been characterized by a growing mobilization of scientific advice via committees that are expected to provide technical information and expertise, particularly in the health and safety sectors (Demortain 2009; Vos 1997); and networks of experts based in national institutions routinely exchange information and thereby take part in shaping European regulations (Dehousse 1997). Political scientists have produced detailed analyses of the composition of the European expert groups and the way they operate. They have talked about "technicization" or "depoliticization" to point to the mechanisms whereby large-scale policy issues are turned into matters of expert examination by groups that are, if not entirely secluded from public view, then at least extremely difficult for members of nongovernmental organizations or other civil society groups to access (Robert 2010; Radaelli 1999). As these expert groups strengthen the executive power of the European Commission at the expense, so the analyses show, of political discussions taking place in institutions such as the European Parliament, national parliaments, or in publicly held negotiation arenas, they may well contribute to the Union's democratic deficit and the prevalence of technocracy.

The pervasiveness of scientific expertise in the European institutions can hardly be described in the terms of the view from nowhere, though. In the practice of European expertise, expert judgment is directly tied to the political representation of the interests of the actors involved. A prime reason for this is that the production of European expertise is tightly and explicitly articulated with lobbying activities in Brussels. Many expert groups are also supposed to be platforms for negotiating with stakeholders (Saurugger 2002). If expertise is everywhere in Europe, it does not usually result in a single authoritative voice of the kind that would originate from a well-defined expertise body subsuming the contributions of individual experts under a common reference to objective science. Rather, the production of expertise is distributed in many places, which also serve as sites for collective bargaining.

This articulation between objectivity and the representation of interests has not been fundamentally transformed by the growing importance of the European technical agencies. The independence of the European Central Bank is very peculiar, in fact, when compared with other EU agencies and authorities that have been created since the 1990s to provide independent scientific advice to European institutions, above all, the European Commission. Consider, for instance, the case of pharmaceutical products. This has traditionally been a difficult domain for market harmonization, as already recognized in the 1985 White Paper on *Completing the Internal Market* (European Commission, 1985). Since then, many attempts have been made to harmonize the pharmaceuticals market, including the "multi-state approach," whereby each Member State recognizes the decisions taken elsewhere by virtue of a principle of "mutual recognition," was deemed unsatisfactory for market harmonization (Orzack et al. 1992). As part of this ongoing attempt at harmonization, a European expertise agency about pharmaceuticals, the European Medicines Evaluation Products Agency, was created in 1995, renamed the European Medicines Agency (EMA) in 2004. The EMA has not approached harmonization as requiring the sudden replacement of national expert bodies with a centralized European epistemic authority. Instead, the agency introduced a centralized authorization procedure focused on innovative medicine products that would not replace the whole range of activities undertaken by national expert bodies[4], and the European approach is primarily based on coordination between member states and the European level for deciding on the authorization of medicines (Groenleer 2011; Orzack et al. 1992; Permanand and Mossialos 2005).

The EMA illustrates the European approach to public expertise characterized by a distribution of action among experts tied to their national origins and institutional coordination between European and national expert bodies. One sees this approach in other European agencies, such as the European Chemicals Agency (ECHA). The work of the ECHA has been described, as the EMA's could be, as an illustration of epistemic subsidiarity (Jasanoff 2013; Boullier 2016)—that is, an institutional arrangement whereby the production of expertise is the outcome of carefully orchestrated exchanges between European and national sources of expertise. *Epistemic subsidiarity* is a useful way to characterize the articulation between objectivity and expert judgment that is seen in the European institutions of expertise. Here, objectivity is the outcome of co-ordinated operations, related to both science and politics. Many experts are involved. Some come from national public bodies; others, from private companies or civil society organizations that participate in the Commission's technical working groups. Eventually, the role of the European expert working in agencies such as the EMA or the ECHA is to orchestrate the distribution of roles and the circulation of knowledge. The European expert uses procedural or technical tools to assess knowledge claims (such as those presented by companies wishing to register chemicals at ECHA) but also needs to coordinate with evaluations undertaken at national levels or in private organizations. In that context, attempts to mechanize expert judgment, for instance, by using models, require that European experts reopen technical black-boxes and use their personal experience (Laurent and Thoreau 2019). These attempts do not signal an institutionalization of mechanical objectivity, but rather, an extension of the coordinating role of the European expert.

The Instability of Epistemic Subsidiarity

The landscape of European expertise that appears through the numerous expert committees of the European Commission, and technical agencies such as EMA and ECHA ties the production of objective knowledge to the negotiation between national and European, public and private interests. In this context, expert judgment is not expected to ensure a view from nowhere but, rather, a distributed gaze, itself a product of epistemic and political practices. This European approach to expertise faces pervasive issues, including its problematic legitimacy and a persistent uncertainty about its institutional format.

First, that European expertise relies on the articulation between knowledge production and political negotiation does not imply that anyone can participate in the production of European expertise. Rather than publicly visible deliberative bodies, European expert groups are sites marked by unequal powers of influence, as shown by the numerous studies that have examined lobbying practices in Europe.[5] As such, European expertise is characterized by a pervasive legitimacy issue. This issue relates to the management of the relationships between European regulatory decisions, and the interests of private economic actors, or individual member states. For instance, a regular source of controversy about EMA has been the close relations between the agency and the pharmaceutical industry.[6]

Second, the institutional organization of the European expertise is far from stable. A sign of this instability is the profusion of scholarly works about the institutional nature of European expertise, particularly as it is produced by European agencies. Since the 1990s, scholars of European integration have discussed the form of regulation "by information" that European agencies propose (e.g., Majone 1997), how these agencies are controlled (e.g., Dehousse 2008), the way they appear out of networks of European experts and functioned in conjunction with them (e.g., Borras et al. 2007; Chiti 2000; Levi-Faur 2011), and how certain modes of organization circulate from one agency to the next (e.g., Demortain 2008). The problematic institutional nature of European expertise is not merely an academic issue. It also manifests itself in numerous public controversies about seemingly arcane bureaucratic evolutions inside the European Commission. For instance, the relevance of the "science adviser" of the president of the European Commission, a position created in 2012 by José-Manuel Barroso, was vigorously debated. NGOs argued that the position added a layer of opacity to an already complex decision-making process, which, though allegedly aimed at ensuring that European policy was "evidence-based," gave industrial interests privileged access to the president of the Commission (Parr 2015). Others saw the NGOs' position as merely a reaction against the alleged pro-GMO position of Barroso's science adviser, Anne Glover.[7] Eventually, Jean-Claude Junker scrapped the position, to the dismay of science-policy scholars, who had hoped to turn it into a vehicle for renewed dialogue about the relationships between science and policy in Europe.[8] This episode is revelatory. It shows that if European expertise proposes an original articulation between objectivity and expert judgment, this proposition is not clearly stabilized in institutional terms.

This instability also manifests itself in international settings. A good illustration here is the case of GMOs. The ban of certain GMOs in Europe was contested at the WTO by Argentina, Canada, and the United States (Winickoff et al. 2005). The opponents of the European regulation believed that the evaluation of the risks should be the product of a universal science expected to serve as a judge of international trade conflicts. The ban, for them, was nothing but a political move meant solely to protect the interests of European farmers at the expense of international trade. As STS scholars have shown, the challengers of the European ban imagined objectivity in the terms of the view from nowhere, as the outcome of mechanistic processes able to eliminate uncertainty and stabilize a technical assessment of risks, free of political considerations (Winickoff et al. 2005). By contrast, one could have framed the European ban as an attempt to deal with pervasive uncertainties about both the scientific evaluation of GMOs and the social expectations about them. That Argentina, Canada, and the United States won their case against Europe is a sign that this framing failed to be articulated in convincing ways.[9]

A European View from Nowhere?

The proposition for European expertise based on an original articulation between objectivity and expert judgment is barely stable. In that context, the reference to a form of public expertise based on the uniqueness of the voice of objectivity that is expected to be free of any subjective influence (or, in other words, a variation on the view from nowhere) has often appealed to European actors. Consider, for instance, the case of the European Food Safety Authority (EFSA). EFSA was created in 2002 as an institutional response to the BSE (bovine spongiform encephalopathy) "mad cow" crisis.[10] The crisis had propelled far-ranging reflections about how the European Commission had based its action on scientific facts, and how it had used scientific expertise. The 2000 White Paper on Food Safety (European Commission, 2000) called for the creation of a European expert authority on food safety to prevent another crisis like the mad cow scandal by ensuring that food products were properly assessed before being circulated on the European market. The reorganization of the European expertise about food safety eventually led to the creation of EFSA, a centralized European expert body that would identify the food products that were safe for consumption across Europe (Vos 2000).[11] The new agency would isolate European decision-making from the economic interests of particular member states or private actors. Because member states were said to have influenced the delayed reaction to the BSE crisis,[12] the EFSA would be composed of individual experts, and not based on national representation.[13] EFSA, contrary to propositions that saw a need for the agency to be granted regulatory power, was conceived as a public body whose power would be restricted to "risk assessment"

(Demortain 2009). EFSA, in short, would be the locus of a renewed European objectivity on food safety, based on the ability to independently assess food products. The new agency was to "restore trust" in the European institutions' ability to deal with technical risks. Yet the Authority has been the object of much criticism, pertaining to the quality of the scientific advice it provides, the transparency of its functioning, and its independence from special interests. Criticisms have been voiced by NGOs[14] about EFSA's proximity to industrial interests. The value of EFSA's advice on GMOs has been heavily contested, as the standardized tests it used have themselves been controversial (Demortain 2013). If EFSA's objective was to "restore trust," it fell well short of that goal.

EFSA introduced several changes were at in response to the criticism. EFSA asked its experts to disclose their financial and institutional ties and launched a "glass house" policy of opening scientific meetings to the public in 2012. It introduced a "stakeholder consultative platform" in 2005, tasked to "assist the Authority in developing its overall relations and policy with regard to 'civil society stakeholders'" and launched several "public consultations" (Dreyer and Renn 2013, 332). This evolution is consistent with a growing discourse of the "democratization of expertise" adopted by the European Commission in the 2000s (Moodie and Holst 2014). But it did not free EFSA from public controversies. Endocrine disruptors have been one recent instance of a controversial domain about which EFSA's contributions have been severely criticized by environmental organizations (Bozzini 2017; Horel 2016). Construed as an entity that could adjudicate controversies thanks to expert knowledge based on the view from nowhere, EFSA has itself become a topic of controversies.

The difficult construction of European expertise through agencies such as EFSA is telling. It can be read as yet another example of contested science and policy boundary-making in public institutions (Jasanoff 1987), rendered even more difficult by the dual objective of ensuring that science is purified from political discussion *and* is open to public participation.[15] The EFSA situation might be a reaction to the instability of epistemic subsidiarity by attempting to centralize European expertise. But instead of providing a single authoritative voice that is able to ensure the legitimacy of European decision, EFSA has become perhaps the most visible illustration of the impossibility of basing European expertise on the view from nowhere.

A Path Forward for Public Expertise?

The European situation provides an original and unstable institutional configuration meant to produce public expertise. This configuration is based on epistemic subsidiarity. It does not separate the production of scientific advice from policymaking but ties them together. It has consequences for the definition of objectivity and expert judgment. Here, objectivity is inherently tied to regulatory objectives, on the one hand, and to the concerns and needs of the actors involved in its production, on the other. As such, it can be labeled an "interested objectivity." The expert judgment that participates in manufacturing interested objectivity is explicitly political, in that it serves both to produce technical advice and to represent interested parties, be they member states or concerned stakeholders.

Getting back to the current difficulties that expertise faces, one might want to turn to the European situation to provide theoretical and practical elements for identifying what be a path forward would be. The debates about European expertise, indeed, resonate with the current and more general crisis of expertise. The questions raised today are about who has the ability to be an expert, and what the bases for ensuring objectivity are. These questions underscore the political character of expertise by suggesting that it is either hopelessly biased or in need of being "freed" from politics. In Europe, what I have described here as interested objectivity can be seen as an attempt to define public expertise in explicitly political terms, for the sake of both robust technical advice and legitimate decision-making. Because the European context makes expertise a matter of both epistemic production and political negotiation, the question of how to organize public expertise is bound to receive sophisticated answers. Thus, configurations that are characterized by epistemic subsidiarity are based on an unlimited opening of the possibility for expertise production nor on a tight delimitation of expertise to technical means.

Perhaps because of its originality, this approach faces pervasive instability, and is regularly confronted with the persistent allure of the view from nowhere, as the example of EFSA shows. There are two potential readings of this situation. The first one diagnoses a persistent failure to ensure that a true European expertise can convince member states, and possibly the European public at large, of its value. It sees a need to make yet other attempts to stabilize a centralized body of European expertise, which, at last, would be able to provide a unified voice of science. The second reading also identifies a failure, although not in the same terms (see e.g., Carr and Levidow 2009; Jasanoff 2013; Wickson and Wynne 2012). Often inspired by STS, this second reading sees epistemic subsidiarity as a way of recognizing that the production of expert advice is a scientific process and a political process, which should more explicitly associate the exploration of scientific uncertainties with that of social concerns. In this reading, the specificities of European expertise are not to be erased but further cultivated. If we adopt this second reading, we are to consider that if there is a failure, it is related to the inability to publicly account for European expertise in ways that would convince international audiences (for instance, at the WTO) and European ones that it can be scientifically robust and politically legitimate.

While the mechanism of European expertise suggests that original institutional constructs might produce objective expert advice and sound expert judgment, it also illustrates the amount of work needed to ensure that new propositions such as interested objectivity are both scientifically robust and politically legitimate. In Europe, this work implies correcting the asymmetries of access that make participating in regulatory circles far easier for skilled lobbyists representing corporate interests than for concerned environmental protection groups. But it also implies a more fundamental theoretical and institutional task, which pertains to the mode of scientific and political representation. There are resources in the science studies literature at this point, particularly

Bruno Latour's (2004a, 2004b) discussions of "matters of concerns" as potential entry points for rethinking the sources of scientific objectivity and democratic legitimacy. As their main activities all relate to technical entities, such as energy, chemicals or data, the European expertise institutions are already connected to the main public concerns of contemporary societies. As such, they might provide institutional paths for making interested objectivity a vehicle, if not for renewing the European project, at least for ensuring the scientific quality and the political legitimacy of expert advice.

At this point, the failure of EFSA to provide a European view from nowhere is a forceful reminder of the limited value of calling for an unproblematized "objective expertise" to solve the issues faced by European expertise. By contrast, what the instability of European expertise and its contestations in international settings make visible is the dual necessity of an analytical repertoire and institutional support to ensure the scientific and political robustness of epistemic subsidiarity. Although this situation is specific to the European context, it can also help us understand the current difficulties of public expertise. As public expertise is contested on scientific and political grounds, the call for "objectivity" is tempting. What the European example suggests is that a reimagination of the institutional organization of expertise might be, if theoretically and practically more challenging, also more relevant to ensure the public credibility of expertise.

CONCLUSION

How to define the appropriate expert judgment in institutions that are in charge of producing objective facts for policymaking? This question seems to be particularly problematic as current challenges to the voices of official expertise often prompt public and private actors to call for "objective knowledge" and "trustful experts" without clarifying those terms.

The contemporary issues about objectivity and expert judgment are not qualitatively different from the problem of how public institutions of expertise ought to function, about which STS works offer crucial resources. These works have shown that the production of expert advice necessarily brings together knowledge production and legitimacy building. They have commented on the institutionalized practices whereby particular expert claims are considered trustworthy, or "civic epistemologies." They have illuminated the variety of civic epistemologies, and analyzed various sources of instability in the public institutions of expertise. Europe is a particularly interesting laboratory in which to reflect on these instabilities. How to organize the European public expertise has been a topic of concern for years. On technical committees and in agencies such as EMA or ECHA, it originates from distributed processes whereby the production and use of knowledge is undertaken by member states and at the European level. This "epistemic subsidiarity" also means that negotiations with the involved stakeholders occur in processes that are expected to provide to the European institutions with expert advice. In that context, experts come from national institutions, private organizations, and European bodies, and their judgment is tied to their positions.

The difficulties in stabilizing the institutions of European expertise reveal both that sophisticated institutional constructs are possible and that their stabilization requires significant scientific and political investments. They signal a crucial need for inventing institutional formats, as well as analytical repertoires that are able to account for practices of expertise that attempt to redefine the relationships between science and policy.

NOTES

1. Jasanoff (1990, 45). Jasanoff refers to legal scholar Martin Shapiro (1981), in particular.
2. "AI is 'Part of the Answer' to Fake News, Facebook Scientist Says". *Bloomberg Europe Edition*, May 23, 2018, last accessed October 29, 2022, https://www.bloomberg.com/news/articles/2018-05-23/ai-part-of-the-answer-to-fake-news-facebook-scientist-says.
3. Article 95(3) of the Amsterdam Treaty.
4. See "The Centralized Procedure," European Medicines Agency, February 2010, available at http://www.ema.europa.eu/docs/en_GB/document_library/Presentation/2010/03/WC500074885.pdf, accessed September 22, 2018.
5. See, for instance, among others in a prolific literature, Coen (1998); Coen and Richardson (2009); Laurens (2015, 202–209; 2017).
6. See (Permanand and Mossialos 2005). Two opposite movements have been at stake here, because the agency tried not to exclude experts because of distant industry ties (see "Medicines Regulator Amends Conflict of Interest Rules to Ensure Suitability of Experts," The Pharmaceutical Journal, November 25, 2014, last accessed June 3, 2018, https://www.pharmaceutical-journal.com/news-and-analysis/medicines-regulator-amends-conflict-of-interest-rules-to-ensure-suitability-of-experts/20067248.article, while being criticized for providing confidential yet profitable "advice" to companies to help them produce development plans. See "The EMA's Scientific Advice to Pharma Companies Is a Conflict of Interest, Says Industry Coalition," Thepharmaletter.com, July 15, 2014, last accessed June 3, 2018, https://www.thepharmaletter.com/article/the-ema-s-scientific-advice-to-pharma-companies-undermines-is-a-conflict-of-interest-says-industry-coalition.
7. Chief Greenpeace scientist Doug Parr (2015) opposed this interpretation.
8. See the tribute written by science-policy scholar James Wilsdon: "Juncker axes Europe's chief scientific adviser," *The Guardian*, November 13, 2014, last accessed June 3, 2018, https://www.theguardian.com/science/political-science/2014/nov/13/juncker-axes-europes-chief-scientific-adviser. The debate about the chief scientific adviser position has been presented in a collective volume edited by Wilsdon, Doubleday, and Stirling (2015).
9. In other cases, the European institutions adopt the language expected by the international organization. Thus, the European Commission introduced a moratorium on the use of recombinant bovine growth hormone for reasons related to agricultural price controls; the moratorium was challenged at the WTO, and the European Commission eventually explained it to be "exclusively motivated by reasons of animal welfare and health." These reasons could be described as "ostensibly objective, scientific concerns" (Kinchy and Kleinman 2003, 584).

10. The discussions within the European Commission about the need for a food-safety agency had been ongoing since the mid-1980s (Demortain 2009).

11. Before that, the European regulation of foodstuffs was only partially harmonized, through mutual recognition and comitology systems, and no centralized body existed (Kraphol 2007).

12. See a discussion in Kraphol (2007) about the United Kingdom. The UK also contested the intervention of the European Commission at the European Court of Justice.

13. See Levidow and Carr (2007). The composition of the board, however, became a strategic concern of member states (Demortain 2009).

14. See, for instance, "Can EFSA Ever Cut Ties with Industry," Foodnavigator, May 3, 2017, last accessed June 3, 2018, https://www.foodnavigator.com/Article/2017/05/04/Analysis-Can-EFSA-ever-cut-ties-with-industry. For an account of these criticisms that sees them as impetus for EFSA to maintain its scientific integrity, see Kupferschmidt (2012).

15. Studies of the European attempts at public participation in expertise have shown that the potential contradiction in this tension is often resolved by denying public participation the possibility to challenge the framing of what counts as "science" or what should be discussed in the first place (Wynne 2006). The conflicted institutionalization of expertise at EFSA might also be related to the fact that boundary-making has to be conducted inside the agency, EFSA being in charge of risk assessment *and* risk management (Dreyer and Renn 2013).

References

Beck, Silke. 2011. "Moving beyond the Linear Model of Expertise? IPCC and the Test of Adaptation." *Regional Environmental Change* 11 (2): 297–306.

Benamouzig, Daniel, and Julien Besançon. 2005."Administrer un monde incertain: Les nouvelles bureaucraties techniques. Le cas des agences sanitaires en France." *Sociologie du travail* 47 (3): 301–322.

Bimber, Bruce Allen. 1996. *The Politics of Expertise in Congress: The Rise and Fall of the Office of Technology Assessment*. Albany: State University of New York Press.

Bonneuil, Christophe, and Les Levidow. 2012. "How Does the World Trade Organization Know? The Mobilization and Staging of Scientific Expertise in the GMO Trade Dispute." *Social Studies of Science* 42 (1): 75–100.

Borrás, Susana, Charalampos Koutalakis, and Frank Wendler. 2007. "European Agencies and Input Legitimacy: EFSA, EMEA and EPO in the Post-delegation Phase." *European Integration* 29 (5): 583–600.

Boullier, Henri. 2016. "Autoriser pour interdire: La fabrique des saviors sur les molecules et leurs risques dans le réglement européen REACH." PhD diss., Université Paris Est.

Bozzini, Emanuela. 2017. "Open Controversies: Bees' Health, Glyphosate and Endocrine Disruption." In *Pesticide Policy and Politics in the European Union*, 77–104. Cham, Switzerland: Palgrave Macmillan.

Cambrosio, Alberto, Peter Keating, Thomas Schlich, , and George Weisz. 2006. "Regulatory Objectivity and the Generation and Management of Evidence in Medicine." *Social Science & Medicine* 63 (1): 189–199.

Carr, S., and Les Levidow. 2009. *GM Food on Trial: Testing European Democracy*. London: Routledge.

Chiti, Edoardo. 2000. "Emergence of a Community Administration: The Case of European Agencies." *Common Market Law Review* 37:309.

Coen, David. 1998. "The European Business Interest and the Nation State: Large-Firm Lobbying in the European Union and Member States." *Journal of Public Policy* 18 (1): 75–100.

Coen, David, and Jeremy Richardson, eds. 2009. *Lobbying the European Union: Institutions, Actors, and Issues.* Oxford: Oxford University Press.

Dab, William, and Danielle Salomon. 2013. *Agir face aux risques sanitaires.* Paris: Presses Universitaires de France.

Daston, Lorraine, and Peter Galison. 1992. "The image of objectivity." *Representations* 40: 81–128.

Daston, Lorraine, and Peter Galison. 2006. *Objectivity.* Cambridge: The MIT Press.

Daston, Lorraine. 1995. "The Moral Economy of Science." *Osiris* 10:2–24.

Dehousse, Renaud. 1997. "Regulation by Networks in the European Community: The Role of European Agencies." *Journal of European Public Policy* 4 (2): 246–261.

Dehousse, Renaud. 2008. "Delegation of Powers in the European Union: The Need for a Multi-principals Model." *West European Politics* 31 (4): 789–805.

Demortain, David. 2007. "European Agencies: The European Medicines Agency (EMEAI and the European Food Safety Authority (EFSA)." In *Food and Pharmaceutical Agencies in Europe: Between Bureaucracy and Democracy; Cross-National Perspectives; a Commented Bibliography*, edited by Daniel Benamouzig and Oliver Borraz, 40–77. Grenoble: CNRS—Maison des Sciences de l'Homme-Alpes.

Demortain, David. 2008. "Institutional Polymorphism: The Designing of the European Food Safety Authority with Regard to the European Medicines Agency." Discussion paper no. 50. Centre for Analysis of Risk and Regulation. London School of Economics and Political Science.

Demortain, David. 2009. "Standards of Scientific Advice: Risk Analysis and the Formation of the European Food Safety Authority." In *Scientific Advice to Policy Making: International Comparison*, edited by Justus Lentsch and Peter Weingart, 141–160. Leverkusen, Germany: Verlag Barbara Budrich.

Demortain, David. 2013. "Regulatory Toxicology in Controversy." *Science, Technology, & Human Values* 38 (6): 727–748.

Dreyer, Marion, and Ortwin Renn. 2013. "EFSA's Involvement Policy: Moving towards an Analytic-Deliberative Process in EU Food Safety Governance?" In *Expertise and Democracy*, edited by Cathrine Holst, 323–352. Oslo: Arena.

European Commission. 1985. *Completing the Internal Market.* COM(1985) 310. Luxemburg: Office for Official Publications of the European Communities.

European Commission. 2000. *White Paper on Food Safety in the European Union.* COM(99) 710. Luxemburg: Office for Official Publications of the European Communities.

Gardner, John S. 1996. "The European Agency for the Evaluation of Medicines and European Regulation of Pharmaceuticals." *European Law Journal* 2 (1): 48–82.

Gehring, Thomas, and Sebastian Krapohl. 2007. "Supranational Regulatory Agencies between Independence and Control: The EMEA and the Authorization of Pharmaceuticals in the European Single Market." *Journal of European Public Policy* 14 (2): 208–226.

Gieryn, Thomas F. 1983. "Boundary-Work and the Demarcation of Science from Non-science: Strains and Interests in Professional Ideologies of Scientists." *American Sociological Review* 48(6): 781–795.

Groenleer, Martijn. 2011. "The Actual Practice of Agency Autonomy: Tracing the Developmental Trajectories of the European Medicines Agency and the European Food

Safety Authority." Open forum CES paper no. 5. SSRN (https://papers.ssrn.com/sol3/papers.cfm?abstract_id=1904462).

Hall, Peter A., and Robert J. Franzese. 1998. "Mixed Signals: Central Bank Independence, Coordinated Wage Bargaining, and European Monetary Union." *International Organization* 52 (3): 505–535.

Haraway, Donna. 1988. "Situated Knowledges: The Science Question in Feminism and the Privilege of Partial Perspective." *Feminist Studies* 14 (3): 575–599.

Hilgartner, Stephen. 2000. *Science on Stage: Expert Advice as Public Drama*. Stanford, CA: Stanford University Press.

Jasanoff, Sheila. 1987. "Contested Boundaries in Policy-Relevant Science." *Social Studies of Science* 17 (2): 195–230.

Jasanoff, Sheila. 1990. *The Fifth Branch: Science Advisers as Policymakers*. Cambridge, MA: Harvard University Press.

Jasanoff, Sheila. 1997. "The Eye of Everyman: Witnessing DNA in the Simpson Trial." *Social Studies of Science* 28 (5–6): 713–740.

Jasanoff, Sheila. 2005. "Judgment under Siege: The Three-Body Problem of Expert Legitimacy." In *Democratization of Expertise?*, edited by Sabine Maasen and Peter Weingart, 209–224. Dordrecht: Springer.

Jasanoff, Sheila. 2011. "The practices of objectivity in regulatory science." In *Social Knowledge in the Making*, edited by Charles Camic, Neil Gross, and Michèle Lamont, 307–338. Chicago: University of Chicago Press.

Jasanoff, Sheila. 2013. "Epistemic Subsidiarity: Coexistence, Cosmopolitanism, Constitutionalism." *European Journal of Risk Regulation* 4 (2): 133–141.

Joly, Pierre-Benoît. 2009. "Beyond the French 'Technocratic Regime'? Transformations of the Use of Scientific Expertise for Public Decisions." In *Scientific Advice to Policy Making: International Comparison*, edited by Justus Lentsch and Peter Weingart, 117–140. Leverkusen, Germany: Verlag Barbara Budrich.

Kleinman, Daniel, and Abby Kinchy. 2003. "Boundaries in Science Policy Making: Bovine Growth Hormone in the European Union." *Sociological Quarterly* 44 (4): 577–595.

Krapohl, Sebastian. 2007. "Thalidomide, BSE and the Single Market: An Historical-Institutionalist Approach to Regulatory Regimes in the European Union." *European Journal of Political Research* 46 (1): 25–46.

Kupferschmidt, Kai. 2012. "Amid Europe's Food Fights, EFSA Keeps Its Eyes on the Evidence." *Science* 338 (6111): 1146–1147.

Latour, Bruno. 1990. "Visualisation and Cognition: Drawing Things Together." In *Knowledge and Society: Studies in the Sociology of Culture Past and Present*, vol. 6, edited by Henrika Kuklick, 1–40. Greenwich, CT: Jai Press.

Latour, Bruno. 2004a. *Politics of Nature*. Cambridge, MA: Harvard University Press.

Latour, Bruno. 2004b. "Why Has Critique Run Out of Steam? From Matters of Fact to Matters of Concern." *Critical Inquiry* 30 (2): 225–248.

Laurens, Sylvain. 2015. "Lobby." *Dictionnaire critique de l'expertise*. Presses de Sciences Po (PFNSP).

Laurens, Sylvain. 2017. *Lobbyists and Bureaucrats in Brussels: Capitalism's Brokers*. Routledge.

Laurent, Brice. 2016a. "Boundary-Making in the International Organization: Public Engagement Expertise at the OECD." In *Knowing Governance*, edited by Jan-Peter Voss and Richard Freeman, 217–235. London: Palgrave Macmillan.

Laurent, Brice. 2016b. "Political Experiments That Matter: Ordering Democracy from Experimental Sites." *Social Studies of Science* 46 (5): 773–794.

Laurent, Brice. 2017. *Democratic Experiments: Problematizing Nanotechnology and Democracy in Europe and the United States.* Cambridge, MA: MIT Press.

Laurent, Brice, and François Thoreau. 2019. "A Situated Expert Judgment: QSAR Models and Transparency in the European Regulation of Chemicals." *Science and Technology Studies* 32(4): 158–174.

Levidow, Les, and Karin Boschert. 2008. "Coexistence or Contradiction? GM Crops versus Alternative Agricultures in Europe." *Geoforum* 39 (1): 174–190.

Levi-Faur, David. 2011. "Regulatory Networks and Regulatory Agencification: Towards a Single European Regulatory Space." *Journal of European Public Policy* 18 (6): 810–829.

Majone, Giandomenico. 1997. "The New European Agencies: Regulation by Information." *Journal of European Public Policy* 4 (2): 262–275.

McNamara, Kathleen. 2002. "Rational Fictions: Central Bank Independence and the Social Logic of Delegation." *West European Politics* 25 (1): 47–76.

Miller, Clark. 2001. "Hybrid Management: Boundary Organizations, Science Policy, and Environmental Governance in the Climate Regime." *Science, Technology, & Human Values* 26 (4): 478–500.

Moodie, John R., and Cathrine Holst. 2014. "For the Sake of Democracy? The European Commission's Justifications for Democratising Expertise." In *Expertise and Democracy*, edited by Cathrine Holst, 293–321. Oslo: Arena.

Nagel, Thomas. 1989. *The View from Nowhere.* Oxford: Oxford University Press.

National Research Council. 1983. *Risk Assessment in the Federal Government: Managing the Process.* Washington, DC: National Academies Press.

OECD. 1979. *Technology on Trial.* Paris: Organisation for Economic Co-operation and Development.

Orzack, Louis H., Kenneth I. Kaitin, and Louis Lasagna. 1992. "Pharmaceutical Regulation in the European Community: Barriers to Single Market Integration." *Journal of Health Politics, Policy and Law* 17 (4): 847–868.

Parr, Doug. 2015. "Why It Made Sense to Scrap the Post of Chief Scientific Adviser." In *Future Directions for Scientific Advice in Europe*, edited by James Wilsdon, Robert Doubleday, and Andrew Stirling, 82–89. Cambridge, UK: Centre for Science and Policy.

Permanand, Govin, and Elias Mossialos. 2005. "Constitutional Asymmetry and Pharmaceutical Policy-Making in the European Union." *Journal of European Public Policy* 12 (4): 687–709.

Pontille, David, and Didier Torny. 2014, "The Blind Shall See! The Question of Anonymity in Journal Peer Review." *Ada: A Journal of Gender, New Media, and Technology*, 4.

Pontille, David, and Didier Torny. 2015. "From Manuscript Evaluation to Article Valuation: The Changing Technologies of Journal Peer Review." *Human Studies* 38 (1): 57–79.

Porter, Theodore M. 1991. "Objectivity and Authority: How French Engineers Reduced Public Utility to Numbers." *Poetics Today* 12 (2): 245–265.

Radaelli, Claudio M. 1999. "The Public Policy of the European Union: Whither Politics of Expertise?" *Journal of European Public Policy* 6 (5): 757–774.

Robert, Cécile. 2010. "Les groupes d'experts dans le gouvernement de l'Union européenne." *Politique Européenne*, 32, 7–38.

Saurugger, Sabine. 2002. "L'expertise: Un mode de participation des groupes d'intérêt au processus décisionnel communautaire." *Revue Française de Science Politique* 52 (4): 375–401.

Shapin, Steven, and Simon Schaffer. 1985. *Leviathan and the Air Pump : Hobbes, Boyle, and the experimental life*. Princeton: Princeton University Press.

Shapiro, Martin. 1981. *Courts: A Comparative and Political Analysis*. Chicago: University of Chicago Press.

Streit, Manfred E., and Werner Mussler. 1995. "The Economic Constitution of the European Community: From 'Rome' to 'Maastricht.'" *European Law Journal* 1 (1): 5–30.

Vauchez, Antoine. 2016. *Democratizing Europe*. New York: Palgrave.

Vos, Ellen. 1997. "The Rise of Committees." *European Law Journal* 3 (3): 210–229.

Vos, Ellen. 2000. "EU Food Safety Regulation in the Aftermath of the BSE Crisis." *Journal of Consumer Policy* 23 (3): 227–255.

Wilsdon, James, Robert Doubleday, and Andrew Stirling, eds. 2015. *Future Directions for Scientific Advice in Europe*. Cambridge, UK: Centre for Science and Policy.

Winickoff, David, Sheila Jasanoff, Lawrence Busch, Robin Grove-White, and Brian Wynne. 2005. "Adjudicating the GM Food Wars: Science, Risk, and Democracy in World Trade Law." *Yale Journal of International Law* 30:81.

Wickson, Fern and Brian Wynne. 2012. "The anglerfish deception: The light of proposed reform in the regulation of GM crops hides underlying problems in EU science and governance." *EMBO reports* 13(2): 100–105.

Wynne, Brian. 2006. "Public engagement as a means of restoring public trust in science. Hitting the notes, but missing the music?" *Public Health Genomics* 9(3): 211–220.

11

EXPERTISE AND COMPLEX ORGANIZATIONS

STEPHEN TURNER

INTRODUCTION

SOCIAL organization in the broad sense includes everything from constitutional states and international organizations to complex organizations and the family. But social organization is always also the organization of a distribution of knowledge; and every division of labor is a division of epistemic labor. We can think of an organization as a set of roles in which the different incumbents have access to different kinds of knowledge and different skills, share different bits of knowledge with others, and need to acquire knowledge from others. But the converse is also true: every distribution of knowledge is always also socially organized. Basic facts govern this. People have to be paid or cared for. Decisions need to be made. Authority needs to be exercised. Rules need to be followed and enforced. The knowledge of others needs to be judged, its trustworthiness established, and it must be relied on. And perhaps most important: knowledge is never independent of others, whose teachings, tools, and products are necessary to becoming knowledgeable. All socially organized systems, then, are knowledge systems.

"Expert" systems are knowledge systems whose participants have or claim the social status of expert. Like organizations, knowledge systems are both divisions of labor and distributions of knowledge, with the added feature that experts do not merely define their status as experts within the organized structures in which they participate; they also play an active role in defining their status collectively outside the organization and in enforcing, defending, and developing it, for example, through professional organizations.

We can think of such systems of expert-driven decision-making, abstractly, on analogy with the biases of fast-thinking heuristics as discussed in the experimental literature on the psychology of rational choice (Turner 2014a). Individual experts come to their expertise through thinking that itself depends on such things as heuristics for assessing data, social cognition for the assessment of others, and through heuristics governing selectivity, among other things. These heuristics have biases. They are shortcuts. Organized decision-making works in an analogous way: it is also the product of systems, which themselves have biases and therefore typical patterns of error, and which are designed to deal with and correct for the biases of participants. One can think of these systems as made up of participants, each with their own heuristic biases, which are aggregated through a process that is more or less rule based. Biases are both produced and corrected for by the elements of the system itself—such as the scheme for the selecting participants; the reward structure; the evaluation structure; the particular powers; resources; and the roles and responsibilities of the advice-giving bodies at each stage of the process (Turner 2014d).

We can put such systems in the category of knowledge aggregation, and regard expert systems and expert-involved organizations as cases of knowledge aggregation. Traditionally, social epistemologists have modeled processes of aggregating knowledge on minimally social models, such as averaging guesses about the number of beans in a bottle at the county fair, which is a method of canceling individual biases (Solomon 2006, 34–35; see also Miller 2013). Economists, similarly, use the market as a model for aggregating opinions and extend the model to knowledge generally. This is a start on the problem of aggregation but a potentially misleading one. We tend to think of science as a self-correcting enterprise, like the market, but it, too, is organized, has biases, and needs to incentivize and organize the means of self-correction. These means have their own biases. Complex organizations also incentivize and implement self-correction, and create structures to do so. This, too, is a source of bias, potentially an important one.

"Bias" is of course a problematic concept. Daniel Kahneman (2001) compared the individual heuristics that people unconsciously use in making fast-thinking decisions to formal decision theory. This is a somewhat arbitrary choice as a standard, and not a useful one in this context. Kahneman treats bias as a problem in decision theory. The decisions in question are the kind that can be solved by formal decision theory: they are what Herbert Simon (1973) calls "well-structured problems." But expertise is called upon, indeed is especially called upon, in the face of problems that are ill-structured, for which there are no optimal solutions, differing perspectives, or conflicting considerations or interests. And decision-making in these situations is typically organized in terms of processes of aggregation in which experts have designated and limited roles. Applying the concept of bias to such situations requires something different from a simple comparison to decision theory.

Nevertheless, thinking about expert knowledge systems as means of collectivizing knowledge designed to correct for individual biases and that have their own biases is a start in the problem of understanding the relationship between organization and knowledge. In what follows I will generally proceed from this starting point, and then return to it at the end. I will discuss the background to the problem, the theoretical and disciplinary traditions that have informed it, and then turn to a case: the International Monetary Fund's processes in the 2008 and Greek financial crises. In both cases, the IMF's expert knowledge system failed. But the response reveals some of the complexities of the problem of designing an expert knowledge system, and is a concrete example of the thinking that goes into the ongoing reflection on and reorganization of such systems, a process that is a characteristic feature of these systems.

Expert Failure and the Problem of Organizational Design

Science is sometimes thought to be a self-correcting system: replication and the fact that other scientists must rely on the previous and related research results to perform their own experiments is thought to provide error detection. Sometimes, this works. But as the statistician John Iaonnidis (2005) has shown with respect to medical research, the idea that the system is self-correcting may be an illusion: "Simulations show that for most study designs and settings, it is more likely for a research claim to be false than true. Moreover, for many current scientific fields, claimed research findings may often be simply accurate measures of the prevailing bias" (40). Researchers searching for a particular drug effect, for example, may find it and report it, but they will not report failures to find it, or they will abandon research strategies that fail to find it. And this bias is a result of facts about the social organization of research—namely, the institutional reasons that cause people to look for confirming results, or, as Iaonnidis explains, where there is "financial and other interest and prejudice; and when more teams are involved in a scientific field in chase of statistical significance" (2005, 40).

We can see, sometimes in advance, that particular institutional arrangements, such as highly competitive grant systems, which rely on peer review, are likely to produce a great deal of conformism and far less high-risk innovative thinking. This was a fear of the physicists who produced the A-bomb. They used the risk-reducing device of setting up rival teams, with rival approaches, notably on the 600,000-person Manhattan Project and throughout the postwar period. Lockheed pioneered the use of "skunk works," innovation-oriented units created outside the normal organizational structure, to generate alternative technologies, which, at IBM, produced the personal computer (PC). And there are ongoing efforts in science to create institutional structures to correct for issues that become problematized. In recent years, for example, there have been organizations that publicize misconduct, such as Retraction Watch, and a large structure of research misconduct mechanisms was created over the last generation. Most recently, there have been such innovations as the online postpublication commentary forum on PubMed (Marcus 2013) and funding for replication studies (Iorn 2013).

Institutional design and redesign is thus an ongoing organizational phenomenon. Every one of these arrangements can go wrong, for the simple and nontheoretical reason that the circumstances under which they operate can change, or they can be misjudged from the outset, so that the protections against error that worked in the past no longer work, or because of intrinsic weaknesses, such as the concentration of decision-making that the Manhattan Project physicists thought would come from putting nuclear power under a National Laboratory system.

There are two traditions in the science and technology studies (STS) literature, one that focuses on problems of design, and another, focused on the problem of expert failure. Steve Fuller, in *Social Epistemology*, asked how science could be optimally organized (Fuller [1988] 2002; Turner 2018). Two widely used texts written by Harry Collins and Trevor Pinch, *The Golem* ([1993] 2012) and *The Golem at Large* (1998), dealt with controversies in science and technology that reflected long-term muddles and errors. A "golem" is a large, powerful, but bumbling and therefore dangerous creature of Jewish folklore. Collins and Pinch's golem was science as a community; their emphasis was on the bumbling or error-prone character of science and technology, but the controversies typically had an organizational aspect. Apart from this STS work on science, a literature developed in economics on expertise that dealt with many of the same issues but in different theoretical terms. The economics and STS literatures were brought together by Roger Koppl (2018) in *Expert Failure* (see also Turner 2019b).

Koppl's (2018) basic commitment is to the idea that market-like structures are the best means of correcting expert error, "that there is a market for expert opinions whose structure determines the reliability of experts and the power of non-experts" (37). The key facts about market structure have to do with freedom of entry and barriers to entry. As Koppl (2019) notes, this connects to the sociological tradition in a particular way: the concept of "professions" is about barriers to entry (82). Professionalization is a barrier to entry. It reduces the incentive to challenge rivals (Koppl 2018, 205). And professions tend to ally with and employ state power to restrict rivalry, producing homogenization of expert opinion (206). This produces epistemic risk. And Koppl (2018), notes that many other institutional arrangements, such as what he calls the "entangled state," exemplified by the enclosed intelligence community, limit the kind of redundancy that is needed. The barriers to entry are high, and despite conflicting interests, rival opinion tends to be suppressed to achieve policy consensus (224).

Professions typically operate in markets, which they seek to control. My concern, however, is with nonmarket structures: organizations with authority relations and a division of labor that is also a division of epistemic labor or knowledge. Koppl (2018) makes a key argument that bears on such organizations, as well as on markets. Real markets need competition, but, he argues, that is not enough: without what he calls "rivalry" or "synecological redundancy" competition may be a poor safeguard against error (89). The terms require some explanation. By "synecological" he means characterized by an epistemic division of labor—the example he gives is from a famous essay by Leonard Read (1958) showing that no one knows how to make a pencil; it requires the knowledge of different parts of the process held by different people. Correcting for possible error involves redundancy, for example, someone looking at a decision again, which can be as routine as having a supervisor give approval after looking over paperwork. By synecological redundancy, he means something more than this kind of correction, which he calls "simple redundancy," which involves the same evidence being looked at again, but genuinely diverse "evidence channels" with different structural elements (Koppl 2018, 185).

PROTECTING EXPERTISE

The sheer variety of arrangements for addressing the problem of organizing expertise at the societal and civilizational level is astonishing. All social orders involve institutional arrangements that define a relation between the distribution of knowledge and the distribution of such things as authority. In the case of experts or those claiming expert knowledge, this is typically a two-way relationship, in which the possessors (or claimants) of knowledge create methods of self-protection, and collective identities such as professions allow a degree of discretion that is beyond the control of outsiders and authorities. We can understand this relationship between expertise and protection from a nonorganizational, purely market-based perspective. The classical professions, such as law and medicine, used their collective identity to define good practice in such a way that conforming with it shielded the individual practitioner from liability or control. Many aspects of this model of protection carry over to the role of experts in complex organizations, but it fails to capture the issues that arise between authority and expertise. The point of the market analogy is to describe an ideal situation in which there is no authority. In organizations, the expert has superiors with whom conflict may occur.

There is, however, a way to conceptualize the expert-authority relation that explains the role of protection in organized bodies. The relevant concept is discretion. A professional judgment is a discretionary judgment, within the limits of what counts as "professional." States and authority structures organized as offices also have discretionary powers—that is, powers to make decisions that are not overseen or corrected except in special circumstances. Courts are simple examples of this. Although there are courts of appeal, "systems of redundancy" in Koppl's terms, they limit themselves to errors, look at a different stream of evidence presented in the appealing lawyers' briefs, and grant the subordinate courts a degree of discretion in interpreting the law (Kelsen 2005, 348–356). Administrative law, where it is subject to judicial review, is similarly "deferred to," meaning that if the administrative rules promulgated by a regulator are not egregious violations of the authorizing law, they are valid, thus allowing administrator discretion. The same concept of discretion applies to complex organizations (Sandhu and Kulik 2019). Discretion implies protection: a discretionary act is protected from review by higher authorities and, indeed, any authority. But it is itself an exercise of authority. For an expert in an organization, this may have legal implications. At the same time, the person exercising this authority must be protected. In the case of the state, the administrator is not personally liable for official acts. This is the cornerstone of having officeholder status.

The case of the expert is analogous. But the discretion of the bureaucrat is a creation of law. The expert may be recognized in law, but the claim of expert status—and the nature of the protection—have different origins. Weber gave the classic account of the need for protection in relation to the assertion of special knowledge when he spoke about the "disenchantment of the world," discussing the transition from magic, where the magician could be held personally responsible for the failure of the magical acts, to the priest, who performed the rituals by the book, so to speak, which transferred responsibility from the person of the priest to the doctrine and to the collective body of the church that authorized the doctrine and the powers of the priest (Turner 2015; Weber [1921–1922] 1968, 400–401). Experts generally invoke some version of this kind of collective authorization: they speak *as* an economist, or *for* physics, and submit themselves to the criteria for this collectively sanctioned identity.

"Professionalization" is merely the most familiar strategy for obtaining authority and protection. In its classic Western forms in medicine and the law, professionalization was characterized by oath-taking, secrecy, membership rituals, and self-denying ordinances that served to define and limit responsibility. These limits determined what counted as "professional opinion"—that is, speaking as representative of the profession as distinct from speaking *in propria persona*. But, as we have noted, the model of professionalization is potentially misleading: lawyers and physicians are, in the traditional sense, *independent* professionals competing in a market, though the term has come to apply to and be claimed for people who are employees. The point of claiming the status of "professional" is similar: to assert a zone of authority or professional discretion that provides protection, an assertion backed, in some sense, by epistemic and ethical standards that are specific to the profession and in some fashion enforced collectively, but also protected by professional solidarity in the face of attacks by outsiders. This necessarily creates a zone of potential conflict with the authority of the organization itself.

As we will see, there is a common organizational remedy for issues that arise in connection with discretion. It takes the form of committees or structures that review discretionary decisions, normally not with the intent of replacing them, but with the aim of protecting against the consequences of errors in those decisions. These involve synecological redundancy. An important discussion of collective bodies that serve as correctors is found in *Securities against Misrule: Juries, Assemblies, Elections* by Jon Elster (2013; see also Austen-Smith 2015). Elster makes the point that the function of these bodies is not to produce optimal outcomes, which would require an almost magical amount of expertise, but to produce and understand institutional designs as means of reducing the risks of partiality, passion, self-interest, and so on (12). But they are subject to a regress problem (Turner 2019a). The issue, as becomes clear in Koppl's exposition of the concept, is this: one does not escape from the problem of granting discretion to experts. One simply adds another body that needs to be granted its own discretionary power. This may be the power to veto an expert decision; or the power of decision-making may be vested in the secondary, reviewing body, so that the first body's or person's actions—for example, in the form of an expert recommendation—are "advisory." Or there may be another division of labor, such as the one between fact-finding and law-finding, in which each body is given a different task.

THE IMF AND THE CRISES OF 2008 AND GREEK DEBT CRISIS OF 2010: A CASE STUDY

These arrangements are the product of conscious efforts at organization, and expert systems are constantly subject to reflection and suggestions based on the failures of the past and changes in current circumstances. The case I discuss here is a relatively simple and much discussed one, which happens to have been the subject of two formal inquiries into the problem of expert failure and its organizational causes. It involves International Monetary Fund, which is a body of granting nations that supplies emergency funds on conditions of reform, conditions decided on through a process of aggregation of expert opinion involving bodies—organizational units—with synecological redundancy. The expert failures were two: the failure to anticipate the 2008 financial crisis, and the errors in the decisions made, with the IMF's participation, in responding to the Greek debt crisis.

The two events were interlinked, and the organizational issues revealed in the published reports of the evaluation committees extended to both cases. Those reports are particularly valuable in that the committees had an unusual, though not unfettered, level of access to the organization and its participants. The study of expert failures depends, in large part, on reports of this kind. Researchers usually cannot get access to key players or confidential information. The major technical failures of recent years, such as the BSE (Bovine spongiform encephalopathy) epidemic, the Columbia Shuttle disaster, and the Fukashima nuclear power plant disaster led to reports that relied on enhanced access. These reports need to be read critically, but they are useful as data, and are themselves part of the process of organizational design and redesign.

In the period leading up to 2008, there was a considerable amount of asset inflation in the world economic system, fueled in part by low interest rates. A prominent, and economically hefty factor in this inflation was in the US housing market. Housing prices were rapidly increasing, and buying was made possible by mortgages that treated the increasing market value of houses as real. Banks were not holding the mortgages as assets, but selling them on the market to brokers who then packaged them into large bundles and sold the bundles as assets: they were thus "securitized." These securities could be borrowed against to buy more assets, and the holdings insured against losses by other instruments, called *credit default swaps*. These, too, could be bought and sold, and they were sold by banks, to one another and to the market. This was an "insurance" market. The buyer paid the seller in exchange for a guarantee that the seller of the swap would pay out if the product, a loan, defaulted. This was thought to be a low-risk deal, and easy money for the bank, because the likelihood of default was assumed to be low. These instruments were sold internationally and allowed for leveraging—that is, borrowing on the basis of assets to buy more assets. But much of this market was backed by a single insurer, AIG. This market created the conditions for a banking crisis. But the larger market was for "repo" or repurchase agreements between banks and banks and hedge funds, which allowed for significant leveraging. These agreements worked like this: a bank would purchase and immediately resell an asset, with a promise to repurchase it in the future, which could be a soon as the next day or as long as three months away, with a haircut, for example, a price difference of 2 percent. They could use the proceeds of the sale for a new purchase. This meant that for the 2 percent, they had the money to invest in some other asset. This was fine, as long as these agreements could be rolled over repeatedly. If they could not, the bank or fund would have to pay up immediately. This market involved vast amounts of money and included only very big players.

The crisis began in earnest when the Wall Street investment bank Lehman Brothers was forced into bankruptcy. Lehman had invested heavily in the mortgage and subprime, or risky, mortgage market and effectively become a real estate hedge fund. When the housing bubble began to burst, the underlying real estate assets lost value, and the mortgages no longer generated the necessary income. The market reacted to this, and the mortgage packages became unsalable. Half of its balance sheet was in repo. When it became clear that the firm was in trouble, Lehman was unable to raise the money it needed to keep this game going. The market also sold off shares in AIG. None of the entities committed to mortgage-backed equities could raise funds, which raised the threat of multiple bankruptcies and the collapse of the repo market. The threat extended to the rest of the banking sector, and banks now began to fear loaning money to one another, creating more threats of bank failures. In the United States, the crisis led to massive government intervention—a bailout—to save the financial sector. Aid was extended to European banks as well. Europe was vulnerable because it had invested heavily in these securitized mortgages and had become a largely unregulated market for US assets. The buyers included groups that did not want to be identified to US regulators. These were therefore particularly unstable markets.

What went wrong? Many failures have been identified. The standard econometric model that was used to predict the macroeconomy treated financial markets as separate from the "real" economy, so the model did not predict changes in the real economy, and for the most part the model was right—employment and manufacturing revived quickly. The relevant regulators ignored the collapse in the housing market, which began in 2006, because it was believed that it was separate from other markets. The issue of moral hazard, particularly the fear of setting a precedent of bailing out banks that had profited from reckless and legally dubious mortgage lending, prevented regulators from saving Lehman from bankruptcy. European banking institutions, such as the European Central Bank, were forbidden by their own rules to intervene: unlike the Federal Reserve, the bank had price stability as its only mandated goal.

One of the main assets used in repo agreements was government debt. In 2010, Europe was suffering from multiple problems in the financial system, one of which was related to Greek debt. Although the amounts were not large, and the debt had been inherited from past Greek governments, debt service was a large part of the national budget. The threat of default as a result of the economic slump in tourism and Greece's traditional exports undermined the position of some major European banks, which held Greek public debt, and also forced the Greek government to pay extraordinary rates to sell its own debt. If Greece was shut out of the bond market, the Greek state could not function. The banks, which in Europe played a much larger role in the financial system, already had balance sheets in a weakened condition. On paper, they could afford to write off the debt, but their bond holdings, together with private debt, which had risen, would potentially cause them problems in the highly leveraged repo market. If they could not access these markets, they would collapse.

The story of the Greek debt crisis is complicated, as is the role of the IMF in it. The solutions were simple: the Greek government needed cash; the debt needed to be "restructured," with losses for the debt holders; and someone needed to pay the bill. This would not happen for complex reasons, the most important of which was the desire not to set a precedent that would apply to the much larger economies of Italy and Spain, which faced similar problems, and the desire to protect the banks from losses. This led to a strategy that was labeled "extend and pretend," in which the Greek government received help in exchange for promises that could be fulfilled only through a major reduction in their own economy, which entailing significant suffering and burdens stretching into the distant future. The promises, together with significant deleveraging by the banks, enabled the banks to survive and minimized the losses of the governments that were compelled to lend to Greece. The Greek economy was to be, for a time, governed by a "Troika" of international financial bodies, including the IMF, which invested significant funds into the rescue project. There were national interests, and national experts, involved with all of the members of the Troika, making this an especially complex case of organized expertise, and also one in which political interests and expertise were combined in a complex way, which is precisely what the structures of expert systems are designed both to protect against and to accommodate.

The IMF had not been a welcome participant. It was seen as "American" (the other institutions were purely European), appropriate for the Third World only, and its experts were skeptical of the strategies the Europeans were using to delay facing up to the issues with Greece and imposing the kinds of rescue solutions the IMF itself had repeatedly imposed. Rescue was opposed by the Germans, with the support of the Finns. In the end, a muddled compromise was worked out that had the effect of saving the German and French banks with money loaned to the Greeks to enable them to avoid defaulting on their sovereign debt. The IMF goal of creating a stabilized and reformed Greece with healthy future growth prospects was not achieved.

There was an important role for expertise in this situation. The decisions being made had to be justified in terms of economic models. The IMF supplied these models, and they were, notoriously, both false and tailored to support the political and financial agenda of the German government.[1] They also represented a betrayal of the other countries that contributed to the IMF itself. But the episode shows the importance of expert power: without the models, the "solution" to the Greek debt crisis would not have been implemented. There are, of course, many facets to this situation, which have been inconclusively discussed and are still live issues. My concern here is the response of the IMF, which treated the problem, at least in part, as one of organizational design and used the language of the field of organizational design in the reports it commissioned to examine the failures. These reports provide a limited, but nevertheless very useful window into both the organization of expertise within the IMF and the larger problem of the organization of expertise in complex organizations generally.

THE REPORTS: FOUR ISSUES

The reports on the failures at the IMF assume a great deal about the operations of the IMF that is not explained. The work of the organization was divided into units that dealt with specific countries, and with specific loans. The governance of the organization itself was by committee, and membership was drawn from the donor nations. This was itself a form of expert rule, namely, stakeholder governance. The stakeholders had, or represented, "skin in the game." But they also represented nations with their own, often very considerable, expert resources and relevant information. The internal structure of the IMF involved a hierarchical order in which reports were submitted up the hierarchy in such a way that the ultimate consumers of the reports, the representatives of the stakeholder nations and the governance of the IMF, would accept them.

What went wrong, from the point of view of the IMF reports? In both crises, the IMF had made errors—in the first, by failing to anticipate the problems, and in the second, by agreeing to a bad strategy. The failure to anticipate was blamed, in a now infamous statement in the 2011 Independent Evaluation Office (IEO) of the International Monetary Fund report, on "group-think, intellectual capture, a general mindset that a major financial crisis in large advanced economies was unlikely, and incomplete analytical approaches" (IEO 2011, vii, 1, 17; 2016, 48). These items have an organizational basis. The report cites several: "Weak internal governance, lack of incentives to work across units and raise contrarian views, and a review process that did not 'connect the dots' or ensure follow-up also played an important role, while political constraints may also have had some impact" (IEO 2011, 2).

SILOS

"Weak internal governance, lack of incentives to work across units and raise contrarian views, and a review process that did not 'connect the dots'" are all "organizational" issues: they involve what the report calls "silos." The units reported up a chain of command, involving organizational features that produce consistent and rapid results through classical organizational forms of a strict division of labor, clear hierarchy, and career paths tied to these forms. They are, however, features that make it difficult to "speak truth to power." But it was also understood that the hierarchical structure involved intermediation between the lower-level analysts and the ultimate recipients of the reports. This carried its own tension: between the need to be effective by producing results that would be implemented and concern about the consequences of presenting unvarnished truths that might have been unacceptable to stakeholders. Ironically, the same consideration, of producing an acceptable report, is evident in the IEO reports themselves, which do not name names or even identify the countries involved in interfering with the experts. There were other organizational obstacles to challenging the hierarchy mentioned in the reports. Among the issues within the IMF itself were career paths involving high turn-over and short-term assignments that made newly appointed staff uncomfortable about challenging existing policy or the national experts of subject countries.

The 2016 report mentions but does not pursue an organizational feature that may have produced the phenomenon of silos: delegation (IEO 2016, 41). Because tasks were delegated to units, and in effect to specific unit leaders, there was little communication between units. There was no process that would have connected the results of different units to one another. These units were what were described as "silos." "Silos" is a concept from organizational design consulting and analysis (Bach 2016; Tett 2015), and is usually employed for organizations with a product.

Ever since the publication of Bruno Latour and Steve Woolgar's *Laboratory Life* (1979), we have been used to thinking of science as also having products—in this case, research papers. What was the product in the IMF, and how was it produced? The IMF is a treaty organization, with specific limited goals. It is concerned with national public-debt crises and resolving them in ways that assure that they will not recur, through "structural" reforms in the economy usually known as "austerity." The role of the IMF is to act as a superbanker, with all that entails: creating and assessing the equivalent of a business plan for the ailing country that will satisfy stakeholders, that is, the treaty signatories who govern the IMF and provide the money, and monitoring the state's compliance with the terms of the loan, for example, by seeing that money that might have been provided for a particular infrastructure is actually spent on infrastructure, and not dissipated in bribes. All of this required expertise. But it was expertise used to produce a product.

The product, in the terms of *Laboratory Life*, was reports, documents of various kinds that form a kind of pyramid reaching to the reports that are made to the governing body of stakeholders. It is important to note, and this will be discussed shortly, that the stakeholders were expert stakeholders, and that the governing body itself, apart from the IMF apparatus, was a particular, and common, form of expert organization. The audience for any given report was the person at the next level up in the administrative hierarchy. The hierarchy resolved problems of aggregation—that is, the integration of multiple kinds of information and sources, a topic we will return to in the conclusion. But the endpoint of the IMF process was not a journal article, but the reporting to the stakeholders, who were both technically sophisticated and had their own sources of information, such as their diplomats in the countries in question, and many other sources. And they knew more about their own banks and financial stakes in the process than the IMF did.

The most important technical product was the reporting justifying the loan, which depended on an econometric analysis of the loan's effects given particular assumptions about such things as the reduction of state expenditures and the raising of taxes, as well as the proposed "structural" reforms, for example, to labor markets and contracts. The point of the exercise was to show that the loan would eventually be (usually partially) repaid as a result of the measures, and that the economy would be stabilized and enabled to grow. As a practical matter, growth was the necessary condition for any reasonable prospect for repayment, and also for the government's meeting a reasonable part of its obligations in addition to debt, such as pension obligations and other welfare measures. Only when a quantitative case could be made that the reforms would actually work would a rescue be approved. The goals did not include protecting the investments of private speculators in the country's debt.

As we know from science studies, the process by which the "products" are generated is messy and filled with arbitrary decisions, uncertainty, and matters that get excluded from the pristine presentation of the documents themselves. This is also true of econometric analysis. There are many choices of assumptions, the implications of which are obscured in the final presentation. Quite modest changes in assumptions can produce radically different outcomes in the final presentation. Nor are the models made from scratch. They are based on conventional modeling assumptions about the economy as a whole that may not be true. In the case of the 2008 crisis, which was a product of miscalculations by the Federal Reserve Board, not the IMF, in there were two such errors. The first was that real estate markets were functionally independent from the rest of the economy and were self-regulating in ways that would not affect the rest of the economy—namely, the output of goods and services and wages. In short, it was assumed that a real estate crash would only affect the real estate market. The second was that financial markets were also self-regulating and independent, in more or less the same way. This assumption was based on the experience of past financial crises whose effects on the "real" economy were short-lived, and it was built into the basic models of the economy used by macroeconomists and by the Fed itself. These models were revised as a result of the 2008 crisis.[2] So was the mandate of the IMF, which was expanded "in 2012 to include all macroeconomic and financial sector issues that bear on global stability" (International Monetary Fund 2018).

Modeling, however, does not occur in a vacuum. The modelers are supposed to be expert in another sense: they are supposed to have contextual knowledge and wisdom about the models' appropriateness and applicability. So, the reports are modeling exercises, but only in part. They need to reflect a larger understanding of how economies work and at least some understanding of the particular circumstances in the countries in question, on which they are supposed to become "expert," and to have knowledge that is not shared generally and may include tacit knowledge acquired by interacting with the bankers and bureaucrats of the country itself. The threat of political interference was fully realized in the second crisis, when staff needed to negotiate with the Euro Group, one of the partners in the Greek rescue, and the European Central Bank.

These reports were "legitimating" in a sense: they formally legitimated the proposed actions to the stakeholders, and indirectly legitimated them to the citizens of the affected country, and also indirectly legitimated them to the citizens of the donor countries. But the process by which these reports were developed was opaque, and intentionally so. Knowledge of the potential actions of the IMF would have value for bond speculators, and had to be secret, as with much banking information generally. Moreover, this secrecy seems to have extended to the internal processes of the IMF technical team and its units, and to the IMF's dealings with its European partners, so that many documents were produced, kept secret, and were not even available to the evaluation team. While banking information was, depending on the country, available to the public, the degree of resolution was not great—one could not tell the exact holdings of a bank, and it is probable that much of the banking information on which the evaluations might have relied was available to national authorities, especially in the large economies, but was inaccessible to the IMF staff.

INTELLECTUAL CAPTURE

The second issue cited by the review panel was "intellectual capture" (IEO 2011, 17). This is an interesting but curious charge. The complaint was that the IMF experts were insufficiently independent intellectually from the experts on the staffs of the major central banks. In retrospect this was certainly true, in the sense that had they been less dependent and respectful of the IMF governing body's national central banks, they might have gone against their expert advice and been correct in their alternative analysis. But here again, one sees design features that normally worked well but led to error in the face of a crisis. Nevertheless, in this case again, we find a bug that is also a feature of the situation of the experts. The experts need legitimacy, and part of the legitimacy of experts comes precisely from agreement with other experts. The most relevant experts in the case of country restructuring plans, the main work of the IMF, were going to be the staffers of the central banks of the country in question. They would be the people with the most experience with, access to, and understanding of the data.

The term *intellectual capture* does not have a well-defined meaning. It derives from George Stigler's concept of regulatory capture, which implies the capture of the regulators by the intellectual outlook and values of the regulated (1971; see also Library of Economics and Liberty). But it has also been used to describe Alan Greenspan's adherence to Ayn Randian ideology and central bankers' dependence on Chicago School economics orthodoxies (Mirowski 2013, 77).

What each of these usages implies is a lack of independence of thought by the experts. But here we come to a feature, rather than a bug, of expertise. The origins of expert consensus might be held to be in the coming together of independent minds. But the thing that makes expertise "expert" is its representational character, that is to say, when the expert speaks as an expert, she does so by representing the consensus of experts, rather than *in propria persona*. An expert who speaks against the consensus risks losing the status of expert. And this is grounded in a basic feature of expertise itself: the legitimacy of expertise is closely associated with the legitimation provided by other experts who validate the expertise, the credentials if not the specific views, of the expert in question. So "intellectual capture" in the sense of the mutual dependence of experts on one another for legitimacy is a feature, not a bug, of expertise, and an organization that promotes opinions that fall outside of the range of what other experts treat as genuine expertise risks reputational loss or the loss of expert legitimacy.

Intellectual capture by other experts, experts who are situated in mission-oriented institutions such as national treasuries, finance ministries, or central banks is another matter, but it shares some of the same features. It is rational to defer, at least to some extent, to local expert knowledge; and in the case of the IMF, which must negotiate with local experts, it is essential to be speaking in mutually intelligible ways about the issues, to have some agreement on models, and so forth. So here again, we have a tension that is intrinsic to the organizational role of the IMF expert economist, analogous to what used to be known as "role-conflict," in which the expert is an intermediary between bodies of experts. "Capture" is not simply a risk but also, to some extent, a condition of functioning in the role of intermediary between experts.

GROUPTHINK

As noted, a defining feature of IMF policymaking was the need to "agree" on a policy acceptable to the board's members, often within a short, crisis-dominated, time frame. This in itself forces making decisions in a way that is different from science. Policy, and even the expert advice preceding policy, requires ignoring uncertainties as a condition of action. And this implies some sort of negotiation of the uncertainties to be ignored. The IMF staff was by its nature intellectually dependent: policy staffers are not academics, and are a step lower in the professional hierarchy than academics. They are not expected to be, and normally are not, original thinkers, and they are not, as noted, subject to the slow, not to say endless, process of correction in the professional literature of economics. Their correctors are the parties to the negotiation of policy and recommendations.

The report makes a point of noting that the culture of the IMF and its hierarchical internal structure served to suppress independent thinking and disagreement. It made a point of noting that there were incentives for agreement, but strong, even career ending, disincentives for "contrarian" opinions. The incentives for agreement are not discussed in detail, but they are familiar from all organizational settings: "to get along, go along" is a winning strategy. But there is a cognitive incentive that is even more powerful: to go along with the group on which one is already intellectually dependent in multifarious ways is a form of self-protection for experts. What saves an expert from paying a price for error is the fact that others made the same mistake. It is striking that Oppenheimer, after the success of the Manhattan Project, was motivated by concerns similar to those in the reports—that groupthink would lead to bad decisions—and did what he could to recreate the atmosphere of prewar physics in the changed circumstance of secrecy and the need for vast investments in ideas to test them or make them viable. The main fruit of this effort was the H-bomb, which Oppenheimer himself had believed to be a physical impossibility, but which he allowed a group to work on (Turner 2014c, 287–291). One might ask whether there are analogous solutions in the case of a policy-oriented organization like the IMF. Could one have a "skunk works" that would operate outside the formal system and come up with new ideas that the formal system would have strangled at birth? What would the effect of incentivizing contrarian views be? And what would this look like? As will become clear in a later section, this would not work. Prolonging the discussion led, as it would normally lead, to policy paralysis.

The IMF, however, had a built-in corrective to groupthink. It was not an independent organization, but rather one governed by a board representing stakeholders with their own very considerable body of expertise. This was the organizational form of the synecological redundancy that was built into the system. The lack of independence is a design feature: the IMF is a stakeholder scheme. Put differently, the IMF process involved expertise *and* checks on expertise. The reports themselves were in some very limited sense, as we will see, pure research, but the corrective mechanisms for the research were not academic; they were the responsibility of the stakeholders. The system was thus a hybrid. The IMF has no skin in the game, so to speak, nor do its experts. They are, like banks, intermediaries. But the central banks and the treasury departments of the contributing nations do have skin in the game, even if the actual participants do only indirectly as part of their institutional responsibilities. So, there is a strong check built into the governance system, which constrains both decision-making and research; research is constrained because there is no point in producing research as a base for the policy that will be rejected.

As the evaluation reports make clear, this reality influenced the research process throughout. Moreover, the reports cite the information asymmetry there was between the IMF and the member nation experts. The member nations had data that was not shared with the IMF, a fact the IMF experts would not ignore and had to assume motivated the member nation experts. In normal circumstances, these asymmetries were typical stakeholder correctives to the IMF system of expertise, which was necessarily limited and thus error prone. In exceptional circumstances, the corrective mechanisms failed, but they failed because the member nation experts had been wrong. We have, in short, a system with particular features designed to avoid error, which happened to have failed in this instance.

With this, we come to a fundamental tension, for which there is no organizational solution that does not itself create problems. The specifics of this case are worth considering. If, as I have suggested, the stakeholder model serves as a substitute for open contestation and a corrective to organizational inertia and groupthink, why did the stakeholders fail to correct the errors here? In fact, they made the situation worse. As the IEO evaluation of the IMF response to the Greek crisis indicates, secrecy—so intense that the IEO itself was unable to get many documents, including many that had been prepared and circulated outside channels—played a large role. This was in part understandable: key national players did not want their interests exposed, and information that could be valuable to markets needed to be suppressed. But the effect was to empower the "Euro partners," who blocked what was widely understood and accepted within the IMF as the best solution, "an upfront debt restructuring" (IEO 2016, 150). The means of blocking was the reopening of debate itself.

The tension between the need for analysis and the need for decisions and decisive action was an internal problem within the IMF. Internal debates took too long and thus did not work to produce a conclusion that could be agreed on in time to respond to the crisis.

Debate paralyzed policy (IEO 2016, 28). At the same time, discussion and normal review were curtailed on other matters (48–49) to meet the need for rapid decision-making. Quantitative analysis of spillovers, the effects of decisions on other economic agents, which had become a key motivator in light of the Lehman experience, was not done. The IMF could have operated, as the reports suggest, in a way that allowed for greater dissent and less control of subordinates' opinions. This might have prepared them better for the two crises they faced and performed badly in relation to. But conclusions needed to be arrived at—policies and analyses needed to be completed.

In a policy context, where there is a need for short-term decision-making, and is governed by stakeholder interests and opinions, the question would be whether there are means of improving expert advice without impairing the policy-formation process, which involves negotiation, dealing with member nations, and being credible to outside academic opinion. There are reasons to be skeptical about this possibility. The existence of contrarian opinions, in this case, worked to the advantage of one side of the controversy, because paralysis, which controversy produced, prevented changes in policy direction even in the face of massive evidence that the policy was a failure. The result of open debate was that "an increasingly unworkable policy was maintained for too long" (IEO 2016, 29). The Schmittian dictum that sometimes a bad decision is better than no decision is apropos here.

POLITICAL CONSTRAINTS

The final criticism involved political constraints, though this topic ran through the analysis. Senior staff were quoted as complaining that area departments were unduly captured by the countries they worked on, and that analytical work was driven by the need to justify proposals and "get along well" with the countries' authorities—a combination of intellectual capture and politics. This is another aspect of the stakeholder problem: without the need for agreement with the countries being aided, not only would the correctives provided by local knowledge be limited, but the risk of error and of appearing arrogant and dictatorial would be increased. Getting the right balance between stakeholder opinions and local opinions is an ongoing problem faced by the IMF experts. But replacing this process with a God's eye view without stakeholder correction has its own risks of error.

Overt political constraints had a role in the Greek crisis, indeed dominated it, though the report said that their presence did not figure into the errors made in relation to the 2008 crisis. The report's comments on the Greek crisis are nevertheless interesting. Exempting the United States, which did not interfere, it noted that certain unnamed large countries had been aggressive in demanding that reports be toned down, to the extent that "concluding meetings were just negotiations on the language" of the reports (IEO 2011, 20). It was believed that smaller and emerging countries were more likely to be given hard-hitting reports, while the large countries were able to demand that staff be replaced, and the administration would side with the countries rather than the staff in these situations, leading to self-censorship. In this setting, as noted, groupthink was a protective measure. It protected the various individual participants in the process from being assigned personal responsibility for the outputs. If they could be identified, the donor governments would be in a position to identify them personally, and demand that they be gotten rid of.

The Stakeholders Response

The authorities in the major countries had their own diagnostic complaints, which are curiously at odds with the report. Their complaints provide us with a window into the hidden purposes of the organizational structures themselves. The major countries, apparently with the exception of the United States, which was not at odds with the IMF during the crises, complained about the overall IMF governance: a lack of clarity about the roles of the top administrators, their deputies, and the board and a lack of a clear accountability framework. What is the meaning of these complaints, and what do they tell us about the interests being protected by the organizational structures they are complaining about? And what did the complaining countries have in mind as an alternative? In the first place, the complaints are a sign of the extraordinary pressure that the IMF is under to satisfy the donors. The donors demand more power in the form of "accountability," by which they mean the personal accountability of specific persons in the IMF structure whom they can take action against.[3]

This would suggest a turn to an even stronger version of the command-and-control, strict division-of-labor, style of management that the rest of the report indicts for the failure to "connect the dots" (IEO 2011, 21) that were pointing to the financial crisis of 2008. The complaints by the donor nations, the stakeholders, underscore that protective institutional structures are there for a reason: these suggestions would have made the IMF even less responsive to the crisis, but more responsive to the governments in question. Indeed, the very vagueness of roles that the governments complain of is a way of protecting the IMF staff from the political pressure governments can produce by failing to cooperate or making overt demands, or by promoting their pet priorities. This, and the examples from the report that follow, illustrate a basic feature of the organizational design of expertise. The features that are criticized, and that "failed" during the crises, have a purpose under normal circumstances, and that serve this purpose under normal circumstances, but that under the unexpected and unanticipated circumstances of the crises worked against the organization (IEO 2011, 8, 11, 18, 26, 42).

Are There General Lessons Here?

Discussions of the details of cases easily fall into the category of "this is interesting, but what does it show in general?" In what follows, I will bring out some of the general issues and return to the issues I addressed in the introduction to the case. There is the general problem of knowledge and social organization discussed earlier. The "solutions" to this "problem" present us with a dazzling array of forms. Consensus, even the limited kind of agreement necessary to produce a policy decision through the aggregation of expert knowledge, requires procedures. And as suggested earlier, these are procedures in which the contributions of biased individuals are aggregated in ways that themselves have biases. The point of the procedures, to be sure, is in part to avoid the effects of self-interest, coercion, partiality, and other sources of bias. But the effects of these correctives are inevitably limited and produce their own biases. The corrective procedures, the synecologically redundant bodies, for example, also have biases.

In the case of the Greek crisis, this is one of the major causes of failure. The stakeholders, in their role as IMF corrective and in their different stakeholder roles in the Troika negotiations, including the IMF, ultimately decided on the terms for relief of Greek debt, and each was in a position to correct the biases of their contributing bodies and was staffed by or supported by experts. Their role was both to enact and legitimate an expert solution, not merely to protect their interests—though this is also an important epistemic feature of the stakeholder expertise, since knowing one's interests is also a matter of expert knowledge. The epistemic value of having stakeholders is that they can, and in a successful stakeholder committee should, cancel one another's biases, at least to a significant extent. But the legitimating role of such committees makes them a tempting target for the exercise of power, and in this case, power mattered. It is also important, with respect to the issue of canceling biases, that the committee members are chosen to be diverse in a way that does cancel biases. In this case, the selection of participants actually produced a bias toward an unworkable solution preferred by parties whose stake was overrepresented at the later stages of the process, particularly at the stage of final negotiations.[4]

Why are the biases of decision procedures so difficult to eliminate? The problem is intrinsic to the notion of bias itself. The gap between individual knowledge or opinion and the final product of organized decision-making is large. The difference between "truth" as seen by individuals, who are limited, and policy decisions is also large. Policy decisions typically involve imperfect alternatives which have differential effects on interests or persons. They are decisions made in the face of ill-structured problems with suboptimal solutions, which are more suboptimal from the point of view of particular sets of knowledge or interests than others. There is no God's eye truth to resolve these conflicts. There are only socially organized procedures. We can validate these procedures only partially, by reference to past decisions that are regarded as successful. Of course, these judgments of success refer to "normal" past results. And "success" is relative to interests. If we ignore the possibility of a God's eye view as a nonstarter, we are left with partial views, with different perspectives, knowledge, risk assessments, uncertainties, and interests. From any of these partial points of view, a given procedure of aggregation will appear to be "biased." It will favor some perspective, though not necessarily the expected one.

What we also know from classical science studies is that there are epistemic interests—a desire for one's position to win—that operate within the institutions of science themselves and are indistinguishable from the desire for truth. The decision procedures of science constrain outcomes in ways that introduce their own biases, whose effects are difficult to correct or detect—and whose epistemic effects can only be detected using the biased methods of the scientific community itself. The Matthew effect is one of the most obvious of these. The institutional practices of science may "work," in a pragmatic sense, to produce results accepted by outsiders as "expert" in normal circumstances, but fail in abnormal ones, for example, when undetected biases conjoin (see Turner 2019b).

Social epistemologists sometimes talk about well-ordered epistemic systems, social communities of scientists, or appropriate institutional systems (Winsberg 2018, 213–226). Is this notion helpful here? Perhaps in a small way. Our knowledge of whether a given present system is a well-ordered one is retrospective and is based on a "normal" past. In the case of the 2008 crisis, the problem was that the situation was not "normal." The epistemic system failed in the face of novel and unexpected circumstances. In the case of the IMF and doubtless for other structures, there was little organizational learning from past errors that had resulted from these biases. Organizational and intellectual forms are thus very entrenched. These issues clearly generalize. But constructing lessons is likely to be difficult. Nevertheless, it is instructive that the issues with the IMF in the face of the Greek debt crisis were known in advance, even if they were not dealt with, which suggests that some sort of reform of expert institutions, despite the limits on our predictive powers, would be valuable and in a limited sense possible.

Nevertheless, the idea of creating well-ordered systems, that is to say, designing systems that will work well, is itself a problematic idea. We can look to the past and its normal circumstances to identify flawed systems based on actual errors and biases that those systems produced. But we have no way of saying that these "normally" successful designs of the past, or our present institutions, are optimal. That would require knowledge of what could have been achieved with alternative designs. But we have knowledge, at best, only of what has been achieved with present and past systems. Thus the "well," in well-ordered, is merely an expression of satisfaction with a current or expected epistemic outcome, an outcome which might have been better with a different and unknown system. It is thus itself an expression of bias, not a standard by which to judge bias.

Notes

1. The long story of the disputes over the models, which almost led to a revolt against the president of the IMF, is described by Yanis Varoufakis (2017, 414–440) in his memoir of the events.
2. The combination of errors in a complex, closely linked system of expert analysis is a typical cause of catastrophic expert error (Turner 2014d).

3. The problem of assigning responsibility for expert opinion in settings involving the aggregation of expert knowledge is a significant issue on its own (Turner 2014b, 2014c).

4. For a discussion of another failure of the stakeholder model, in the case of the Hamburg cholera epidemic, see Turner (2014c, 129–136).

REFERENCES

Austen-Smith, David. 2015. "Jon Elster's *Securities against Misrule: Juries, Assemblies, Elections*: A Review Essay." *Journal of Economic Literature* 53 (1): 65–78.

Bach, Olaf. 2016. "Organizational Silos Are a Good Thing except When They Aren't." Management Kits (website). https://www.managementkits.com/blog/2016/4/5/organizatio nal-silos-are-a-good-thing-except-when-they-arent. Accessed October 27, 2022.

Collins, Harry, and Trevor Pinch. [1993] 2012. *The Golem: What Everyone Should Know about Science*. 2nd ed. Cambridge, UK: Cambridge University Press.

Collins, Harry, and Trevor Pinch. 1998. *The Golem at Large: What You Should Know about Technology*. Cambridge, UK: Cambridge University Press.

Elster, Jon. 2013. *Securities against Misrule: Juries, Assemblies, Elections*. Cambridge, UK: Cambridge University Press.

Fuller, Steve. [1988] 2002. *Social Epistemology*. 2nd ed. Bloomington: University of Indiana Press.

Iaonnidis, John. 2005. "Why Most Published Research Findings Are False." *Chance* 18 (4): 40–47. https://doi.org/10.1080/09332480.2005.10722754.

IEO. 2011. *IMF Performance in the Run-Up to the Financial and Economic Crisis: IMF Surveillance in 2004–07*. Evaluation report. Independent Evaluation Office of the International Monetary Fund. Washington, DC: International Monetary Fund.

IEO. 2016. *The IMF and the Crises in Greece, Ireland, and Portugal: An Evaluation by the Independent Evaluation Office*. Evaluation report. Independent Evaluation Office of the International Monetary Fund. Washington, DC: International Monetary Fund.

International Monetary Fund. 2018. "About the IMF." https://www.imf.org/en/About. Accessed October 1, 2018.

Iorn, Elizabeth. 2013. "Reproducibility Initiative Receives $1.3M Grant to Validate 50 Landmark Cancer Studies." Science Exchange, October 16. https://blog.scienceexchange.com/2013/10/reproducibility-initiative-receives-1-3m-grant-to-validate-50-landmark-cancer-studies/. (accessed October 27, 2022.)

Kahneman, Daniel. 2011. *Thinking: Fast and Slow*. New York: Farrar, Straus and Giroux.

Kelsen, Hans. 2005. "Part VIII: Interpretation." In *Pure Theory of Law*. Translated from the second (rev. and enlarged) ed. by Max Knight, 348–356. Union, NJ: Law Book Exchange. (First edition published in 1934 Deuticke, Vienna).

Koppl, Roger. 2018. *Expert Failure*. Cambridge Studies in Economics, Choice, and Society. Cambridge, UK: Cambridge University Press.

Koppl, Roger 2019. "Response Paper." In Book Review. "Symposium on Roger Koppl's *Expert Failure*." Cambridge: Cambridge University Press. *Taxis and Cosmos: Studies in Emergent Order and Organization* 7 (1+2): 73–84. https://cosmosandtaxis.org/current-issue/.

Latour, Bruno, and Steve Woolgar. 1979. *Laboratory Life: The Construction of Scientific Facts*. Beverly Hills, CA: Sage Publications.

Library of Economics and Liberty, n.d. "George J. Stigler." EconLib. Encyclopedia. https://www.econlib.org/library/Enc/bios/Stigler.html. Accessed October 27, 2022.

Marcus, Gary. 2013. "Science and Its Skeptics." *New Yorker*, November 6. https://www.newyorker.com/tech/annals-of-technology/science-and-its-skeptics.

Miller, Boaz. 2013. "When Is Consensus Knowledge Based? Distinguishing Shared Knowledge from Mere Agreement." *Synthese* 190:1293–1316. doi:10.1007/s11229-012-0225-5.

Mirowski, Philip. 2013. *Never Let a Serious Crisis Go to Waste: How Neoliberalism Survived the Financial Meltdown*. New York: Verso.

Sandhu, Sukhbir, and Carol T. Kulik. 2019. "Shaping and Being Shaped: How Organizational Structure and Managerial Discretion Co-evolve in New Managerial Roles." *Administrative Science Quarterly* 64 (3): 619–658.

Simon, Herbert. 1973. "The Structure of Ill-Structured Problems." *Artificial Intelligence* 4:181–201. https://cschan.arch.iastate.edu/235/6_Simon_Ill_defined_problem.pdf. Accessed October 27, 2022.

Solomon, Miriam. 2006. "*Groupthink* versus *The Wisdom of Crowds*: The Social Epistemology of Deliberation and Dissent." *Southern Journal of Philosophy* 44:28–42.

Stigler, George. 1971. "The Theory of Economic Regulation." *Bell Journal of Economics and Management Science* 2 (1): 3–21.

Tett, Gillian. 2015. *The Silo Effect: The Peril of Expertise and the Promise of Breaking Down Barriers*. New York: Simon and Schuster.

Turner, Stephen. 2014a. "Double Heuristics and Collective Knowledge: The Case of Expertise." In *The Politics of Expertise*, 239–256. New York: Routledge. (Original work published in 2012).

Turner, Stephen. 2014b. "Expertise and Political Responsibility: The Columbia Shuttle Catastrophe." In *Politics of Expertise*, 71–92. (Original article published in 2005).

Turner, Stephen. 2014c. "Expertise in Post-Normal Science." In *Politics of Expertise*, 277–295.

Turner, Stephen. 2014d. "Normal Accidents of Expertise." In *Politics of Expertise*, 257–276. (Original article published in 2010).

Turner, Stephen. 2015. "*Entzauberung* and Rationalization in Weber: A Comment on Iván Szelényi, and Incidentally on Habermas." *International Political Anthropology* 8 (1): 37–52.

Turner, Stephen. 2018. "Fuller's roter Faden." *Social Epistemology Review and Reply Collective* 7 (5): 25–29. https://social-epistemology.com/2018/05/17/fullers-roter-faden-stephen-turner/.

Turner, Stephen. 2019a. "Circles or Regresses? The Problem of Genuine Expertise." *Social Epistemology Review and Reply Collective* 8 (4): 24–27.

Turner, Stephen. 2019b. "Massive Error." "Review Symposium: Roger Koppl. Expert Failure." *Taxis and Cosmos: Studies in Emergent Order and Organization* 7 (1+2): 52–56.

Varoufakis, Yanis. 2017. *Adults in the Room: My Battle with the European and American Deep Establishment*. New York: Farrar, Straus and Giroux.

Weber, Max. [1921–1922] 1968. *Economy and Society*. Berkeley: University of California Press.

Winsberg, Eric. 2018. *Philosophy and Climate Science*. Cambridge, UK: Cambridge University Press.

12

DATA AND EXPERTISE: SOME UNANTICIPATED OUTCOMES

THEODORE M. PORTER AND WENDY NELSON ESPELAND

EXPERTISE is a balancing act between knowledge and craft. Once it has been demonstrated and reduced to a formula, it ceases to be expertise. In English and American courts, having recognition as an expert is a license to go beyond eyewitness observations and to offer an opinion about what the evidence means. Expertise may work with general principles, but generalization is not the real work of expertise. Instead, it involves mobilizing diverse kinds of evidence to get a grip on problems and circumstances that remain distinctive. The ideal of case-based reasoning is supported by long traditions of medical and legal expertise. Around 1920, the "case method" was adopted at the new Harvard Business School as an explicit strategy for raising business to the status of a profession. Statistics, though widely valued as a form of expertise, often function as a check on subjectivity. In recent times, the relationship of statistical calculation to professional expertise has become increasingly adversarial. It is rarely possible for any expert to do without a claim of special insight or competence. Data does not speak for itself but through the mouths of more, or less, expert interpreters. Data scientists, too, depend on understandings that fall short of proof, and that in any case are not transparent to nonspecialists. Data work now is routinely called on as a basis for regulating the practices of doctors. They, however, have considerable resources and can fight back. For professionals in more subordinated positions such as schoolteachers, as we argue in the second of our three cases, standardized test data are sometimes treated as transparent and unanswerable.

Our aim here is to explore, historically and sociologically, some of the relations between quantitative ideals and professional and political ones. Social science itself arose in no small measure as a tool of elite administrators and reformers, who sometimes described themselves as physicians to the body politic. Professional ideals of expertise emphasize wisdom and experience that is passed down, perhaps from one generation to the next. Such knowledge may be contrasted to inflexible routines scorned by critics as bureaucratic, which, it is sometimes said, uphold the letter while putting aside the spirit of the rules, and replace intellect with statistical routines (Porter 2011). Few scholars now regard the ways of bureaucracy as so constrained. The work of gathering data for a census is indeed highly repetitive, but serious statistics do not arise effortlessly when legions of lackeys write down whatever their informants tell them. Homogeneous numbers are almost never the outcome of mindless recording. They depend on the consistent application of rules of classification that are often not straightforward (Bowker and Starr 1999; Timmermans and Epstein 2010). Still, these controlled acts of micro-interpretation are performed for the sake of reliable uniformity, not as uncontrolled interpretive takeovers.

Case-based expert reasoning is quite different (Forrester 1996). Etymologically, the *case* stands in opposition to the scientific law. In Latin, Italian, and Spanish, the words for "chance" are cognates of *case*. This sense of the term has survived in such English words as *casual*, which once meant "fortuitous." We still buy casualty insurance to compensate for misfortune. And, with other Europeans, Anglophones have cultivated logic and science for a presumed rigor that gives protection against casuistry, typically characterized as setting aside truth to exploit and manipulate ambiguity. Lawyers in adversarial legal systems are even expected to exploit evidence to make persuasive arguments rather than to seek truth. In other contexts, we may feel confident in looking to professionals for the best available explanation of a case. Professional expertise is valued for judging what eludes demonstration because it cannot be rigorously standardized. The classical professions of law, medicine, and theology were organized to train experts in interpretation. Even priests, claiming access to the revealed Word of God spelled out in authorized ecclesiastical doctrines, face the challenge of determining how it should be applied to a given case or what to do when different passages seem to contradict one another. Professionals are supposed to possess the training and experience in a particular domain that enables them to do their work well and disinterestedly.

Data refers now to relatively unprocessed information, very often quantitative, that can provide the raw ingredients of scientific knowledge. "Data-driven" has resonance that is almost akin to "evidence-based," implying a virtuous reliance on measures and numbers. Data analysis is customarily described, not as a hermeneutic art, but as "letting the numbers speak." The word *data*, though it feels modern, goes back several centuries. In the beginning, it referred to whatever may legitimately be assumed, for example, in a mathematical proof. Although data nowadays is amassed, not postulated, it continues to be treated in many contexts as foundational, a starting point that need not be scrutinized (Chadarevian and Porter 2018; Rosenberg 2008). Statistics in use is sometimes carried out almost blindly, following the directions of a software package. This, to be sure, can create trouble, and is not generally sanctioned by degreed statisticians, who are, on the whole, comfortable with the idea that in their field, too, expertise may entail making hard choices. Still, departing from the recipes in this business is grounds for suspicion. Statistics in use, like accounting, typically works to avoid calling attention to itself. It is safer to appear unoriginal, even boring, especially when something consequential is at stake, such as a drug approval or the acceptance for publication of a research paper. In recent times, data science has become closely associated with algorithms, whose creation (like significance tests) requires expertise but thereafter should proceed mechanically (Porter 1992).

THEMES AND CASES

Metrics are typically designed to reveal and make legible with numbers something that was already out there, on the supposition that it has not been perturbed or distorted by the act of being measured. As numerical assessments of individuals and institutions become increasingly prevalent, this attitude seems more and more naive. Charles Goodhart, Donald Campbell, and others have been credited with different versions of the "law" or rule that relying on measures as the basis for compensation or rewards leads to the corruption of the measures. Even seemingly simple measures such as cartons of eggs or quarts of water depend, ultimately, on complex social practices of regulation and trust. Something really complex, such as teaching effectiveness or business success, presents many more complications, as well as temptations to cheat or distort. Especially in these cases, quantification is not simply a matter of counting or measuring what already clearly exists but depends on the challenging work of standardization. It increasingly appears that metrics and statistics are simultaneously descriptions and interventions.

We highlight the close relationship between quantification and administration in our first example, drawing on social and medical statistics from the nineteenth century. Statisticians had long dreamed of international standardization as a strategy to discover the causes of important problems such as crime and madness. The devout quantifiers were slow to recognize that official numbers could scarcely be standardized when laws and institutions remained different. The push to standardize asylum statistics, which appeared as if it might be achieved about 1869, is especially revealing on questions of quantification and expertise. A prominent Bavarian asylum director, Friedrich Wilhelm Hagen, moved from cautious support of standardization to radical opposition as he came to realize how much expertise was required to prepare the statistics of even his own institution. You couldn't really understand the numbers without knowing the personnel and practices of the institution in question, he concluded. Medical standardization involving legal and bureaucratic categories must always be imperfect, and more so when they reach across national boundaries (Porter 2018, 171–173).

Even within these boundaries, it is serious work to impose categories that facilitate effective quantification. Our second example compares the forms and outcomes of educational testing in France and the United States to clarify how testing can ratify or impose limits on professional authority or can impose limits by promoting a shift to metrics. In France, throughout the nineteenth and early twentieth centuries, national tests came to be based on a centralized curriculum and were mainly used to sort students onto vocational or academic tracks.[1] The expertise of the teachers was not undermined but re-inforced by the examination system. In contrast, schools in the United States took shape as local, decentralized institutions, subject, to be sure, to increasing regulation by the states but scarcely any by the federal government. Standardized tests in the United States were developed mainly as a basis for competitive admissions to private colleges and universities. With that aim in mind, the test designers deliberately set out to circumvent the local and regional peculiarities of American schools. Ironically, what was intended to be a neutral standard for judging students soon began to be applied to public schools themselves, and even to individual teachers, as a basis for judging and comparing their achievement. Standardized testing in the United States thus tended to undermine the expertise of schoolteachers, who found themselves pressured to teach to the test.

As our third example shows, many of the ways in which numbers intervene in institutions are unintentional. That is, metrics produce changes that are not in line with what their creators or users had imagined. We analyze the unintended consequences that devolved from the creation of educational rankings.[2] These rankings—of colleges, universities, and graduate programs—were the brainchild of media whose primary goal was expanding their brand and increasing revenue, as well as informing educational consumers. Despite administrators' low regard for the rankings, they became a powerful tool of administrative reform that imposed on schools a standardized definition of educational excellence and encouraged innovative gaming in the manipulation of rankings criteria.

These three themes of metrics as interventions, as drivers of new forms of expertise, and as producers of unintended consequences overlap, and we will discuss some of the ways they do so. Our overarching theme is the tension that often emerges between professional authority and the ideals of quantitative decision-making.

MADNESS OF NUMBERS: AN ORIGIN STORY OF THE DATA DILEMMA

The modern ideal of reasoning as a form of computation appears as if it were designed to automate knowledge-making. Electronic computers have brought this dream closer to reality, yet it reflects a much older ambition to rely on numbers because of their seeming impartiality. If subtle expertise could be reduced to data work, its all-too-human limitations and distortions might be held in check. The "statistical movement" that took form about 1830 combined a bold push for knowledge grounded in numerical data with skepticism, and sometimes anxiety, regarding the ties of knowledge to personal opinion, however expert. The Statistical Society of London articulated increasingly strict rules to exclude mere opinion from their meetings. It was simultaneously a bold assertion of the power of numbers and a disavowal of responsibility. Their emblem, a sheaf of wheat, and motto, *aliis exterendum* (to be threshed out by others, i.e., for others to interpret), reveals the acute political anxieties of the 1830s, the decade of "the social question," when revolution seemed possible, even in England. The founders of the new British Association for the Advancement of Science feared that any hint of politics in social science might tarnish natural science as well. In fact, the early statisticians were not shy about letting the dross of routine data be silently transmuted into meaningful explanations and solutions. For example, they cherished the hope that the expansion of education offered a remedy for crime, and they did not hesitate to invoke the limitations of routinely gathered data when it had the appearance of undermining the moral necessity of schooling (Porter 1986, 173–174).

Submitting to the facts, letting the data do the driving, did not appeal to everyone. Physicians had long relied in good conscience on a single case that appeared sufficiently similar or adapted their treatments to suit the patient's "constitution." Elite doctors emphasized the importance of personalized treatment, which also was congruent with the economy of individualized payments. Public health, including (in those days) hospital medicine, involved quite different social and economic relations and less individualized treatment. Insane asylums were like this too. By 1840, state mental hospitals had set off on a course of relentless expansion that would continue at least to the 1950s, and they soon became obsessed with data. A well-ordered institution was defined in part by copious recordkeeping, which also was demanded by state legislatures and health ministries. On their own initiative, doctors at these institutions began pushing for a national and then an international standardization of data on patients' characteristics and outcomes. Yet they made no effort to subject medical treatments to any kind of standardized assessment. Perhaps they recognized that this would open the door to statistical oversight and regulation of medicine itself, which could not easily be squared with the ideals of a dignified profession.

France made the first serious move toward a centralized asylum system in 1838. French data templates provided a model of statistical uniformity, and later provided the model for an international plan of standardization, which was initiated in 1867. Such dreams were destined to fail, of course. Heterogeneous institutions, operating under diverse legal regimes and with varying systems of oversight, could never produce uniform data, and no state administration would ever think of overturning its judicial or health regimes for the convenience of international statisticians. Yet the French-led standardization efforts absorbed quite a lot of effort, even enthusiasm, at meetings of asylum doctors in Switzerland and in various German states over the next few years. They were hopeful that a compendium of international statistics of mental illness might allow for minute comparisons and reveal what really was working to prevent and cure insanity. And though many doctors expressed reservations about the push for uniformity, these initially were concerns about details of classification rather than objections of principle.

The dream of a perfect database succumbed to multiple causes of death. The most obvious was the eruption of war and the breakdown of relations between France and Prussia in 1870. By then, the Prussians were introducing a new, more flexible census technology based on individualized data cards. The integration of asylum data into the larger German census was already beginning to seem more important than a harmonization with data from other countries.

In Bavaria, Friedrich Wilhelm Hagen articulated the most profound objection to statistical uniformity when he wondered whether uniform medical statistics were even possible apart from uniform administration. Perhaps it was an illusion to suppose that the inscription of medical information could ever be made routine. The determination of causes, disease forms, onset and duration of illness, and hereditary relations, he now argued, all depended on medical and administrative practices that were specific to each institution. This, he continued, was not to reject statistics, but merely to recognize its institutional specificity. It followed that standardized categories, spurious or not, could never be as effective simply as knowledge. Bureaucratic power was required to produce meaningful statistics, and the knowledge created would inevitably be converted back into bureaucratic power. This was not, for Hagen, a desirable outcome. He joked that the standardization project must lead to a World-Central Commission of Experts in Insanity Statistics, which soon would be comparing all kinds of variables, such as cure rates and durations of stay, and demanding an explanation for any discrepancies.

Such comparisons, he continued, would almost always be spurious. They went beyond the capacity of even a bureaucratic juggernaut. A true harmonization of statistics required subtlety more than power, to go beneath the surface of bureaucratic categories and extend to shared practices of treatment and categorization. The knowledge required to make a classification meaningful depended on a staff that worked together closely within a particular institution and discussed among themselves patients they all knew personally. In such an institution, categorizations could indeed be applied consistently, and could even support conclusions that were meaningful to other experts elsewhere, but there was no prospect of achieving real knowledge by piling up data, no matter how carefully gathered, from disparate institutions. The data accumulated by a centralized administration could not support real scientific knowledge, only the misleading appearance of knowledge, undermining rather than supporting effective medical practice.

In the end, Hagen supposed, the pursuit of routinized knowledge under a central administration would give way to battles of mutual deception, as all parties learned to manipulate classifications to make them work to their own advantage. Soon there would be "deception alliances" among asylum doctors, comparable, he suggested, to the tricks of some notorious Rhinelanders, who had fixed one medical evaluation to avoid the draft and later a contrary one to be accepted for life insurance. This, of course, was not what the champions of unified statistics and numbers-based administration had in mind. Once real power is invested in numbers, there will be too much at stake to leave the statistics to chance. Standardized data, conceived as a resource of medical progress, must instead give rise to doctored accounts (Hagen 1871, 271–279; Porter 2018, 170–173).

TESTING SCHOOLS: NUMBERS IN ACTION

Our comparison of French and American education is also a story of standards, which are indeed very often intrinsic to the subtle power of numbers. We are concerned here once more with bureaucratic power allied to scientific ambitions. Although this has led to cases of flagrant bureaucratic deception, outcomes might differ radically from what the actors intended. That is, the consequences of standardized testing in American schools were largely unanticipated, even if some powerful actors welcomed them. Standardized tests developed for one purpose came to be applied to quite different ones. And the power of American standardized tests to disrupt and reshape educational systems, in a way that never happened in France, does not come down to differences of bureaucratic power.

French teachers had much less power than their American counterparts to deviate from the bureaucratically prescribed curriculum. The real challenge to American teachers in the postwar era was the widening gap between the curriculum they were charged to teach and the testing regimes by which they were beginning to be judged. Increasingly, they felt obliged to "teach to the test" instead of emphasizing what the logic of the curriculum demanded. Interventions by state authorities might, of course, be resented as meddling, but their more fundamental role is to provide direction and specificity, to define the goals of an education, and in this way to define the goals of teaching. Standards are almost indispensable in efforts to enhance the uniformity of these heterogeneous institutions. Teachers everywhere depend on them even if they sometimes challenge them (Rottenburg 2015).

Schoolteachers' command of the curriculum, of course, is only part of the standardization story. Their expertise also arises from their close daily interactions with students, as well as from their professional training. These give them at least some independence from the rules and instructions set forth by their administrative superiors, the principals, superintendents, and boards of education. As Kurt Danziger has emphasized, standardized tests were among the most effective tools deployed by school administrators to get information about student ability and performance that was not filtered through the teachers. The capacity of administrators to act from a distance depended on such sources (Danziger 1990).

In the seventeenth century, German education ministries were already relying on filled-out forms to assess student performance and monitor what was going on in classrooms. William Clark characterizes this paperwork as meddling that was typical of the bureaucratic pursuit of power rather than a response to educational needs (Clark 2004). But by the late nineteenth century, when universal primary education was beginning to become routine in much of Europe and among European settlers abroad, there was clearly more at stake than administrative control. Schools were there to create or reinforce a common language, form patriotic citizens, raise the quality of the labor force, and encourage or regulate religion. Some countries, including France and the

United States, emphasized political equality, but what they achieved was at best a degree of regulation of inequality, along with designs and rationales for sorting and ranking the students (Carson 2007).

France was already famous for its centralizing ambitions, but its system for organizing schooling was broadly like others on the European continent. Apart from a few students who were judged incapable of being educated to a normal level, all children were to have access to primary education. Most, in the early decades, were not expected to advance beyond elementary schedule, but there was room for a few, even among children of poor farmers and factory laborers, to be passed along to secondary schools and to university-level institutions if they showed unexpected talent and diligence in primary school.

In the twentieth century, these practices were systematized in the form of standard examinations, taken at about age 12, which separated children into vocational and university tracks. Although examinations designed to detect innate mental weakness or degrees of intelligence had some role in European educational policies, for the most part, the most crucial examinations of students were based on their classroom studies. In France, the education ministry achieved uniformity to a remarkable degree. Although examinations of various kinds had a critical role in sorting students into different kinds and levels of educational programs, hyperelite grands *écoles* as well as universities, they were mainly based on a prescribed curriculum, and for that reason they tended to reinforce rather than to challenge the forms of expertise managed by schoolteachers and administrators. School promotions to carry out the work of assessing and sorting students did not require specialist forms of measurement.

An American Exception

Already by 1920, American schools appeared to be more receptive to quantitative management and standardized testing. Yet nobody planned the reconfiguration of schooling that was set in motion in 1983 by a Reagan administration report. Its outcomes were in many respects inadvertent and even undesired, yet they demonstrate the puzzling power of numbers to reshape or upend expertise even as it builds on established traditions.

Mass schooling developed differently in the United States. The rural and neighborhood schools, sometimes associated with churches, that became common in the early nineteenth century were perhaps not out of line with European developments. In stark contrast to France, however, the United States never even tried to develop a national system of education or even a shared curriculum. To be sure, it was not simply the Wild West. Departments of education and superintendents of public instruction (under various titles) worked to create more unified curricula at the state level. Their efforts were increasingly persuasive as the states took over the funding of schools from local jurisdictions. The standards of accrediting bodies can also be hard to resist. The public universities of each state have had considerable power to dictate course content.

And certainly, the schools had a tendency to copy one another, apart from bureaucratic requirements.

Yet standardized tests have not merely accommodated curricular decisions; they have had an important role in shaping them. As admission to prestigious private universities became more competitive, and as they began admitting a more dispersed and socially inclusive population of students, the examinations they used could not very well be based on school curricula, which remained heterogeneous. Tests devised by the College Board followed the model of the IQ test, designed and from the outset deployed most extensively in America. The famous Scholastic Aptitude Test (SAT), then, aimed to measure ability or aptitude, not mastery of school subjects. The standardized tests aspired to measure something that was less dependent on specific school curricula, "aptitude." Devised to help pick out scholarship students, they soon took on a key role in the admission of students from less privileged educational backgrounds to elite private colleges (Lemann 1999).

By doing what they could to escape the gravitational pull of classroom subjects, standardized examinations went some way toward undermining them. This undermining of curriculum should not be exaggerated. Even the IQ tests reflected what American students from educated backgrounds were likely to have experienced as children, and it was the same for the aptitude tests. But these tests were never modeled on school curricula. The influence went mainly in the opposite direction. By the 1960s, American high schools were beginning to be judged by their students' performance on these tests. Even before the supposed failure of educational attainment began to be described as a crisis, schools had been modifying their curricula to improve performance on the SATs. In the new millennium, with the introduction of standard national examinations to assess the quality of schools, they had little alternative but to prepare students for these tests.

We should not automatically assume that teaching that has been reconfigured to enhance "aptitude" must be without value. At least, aptitude implied a preference for a skill in reasoning over rote memorization. Still, the rationale for using aptitude in college admissions was based on the supposition that aptitude, like IQ, was not readily teachable. Be that as it may, beginning in the 1960s, a whole industry grew up to prepare students to get high scores on these tests, and middle-class students soon began to regard these expensive courses as an obligatory step in preparing for admission to colleges and to professional schools. Standardized examinations with such high-stakes outcomes led inevitably to specialist instruction based on leaked information about recent or even forthcoming exams. In any case, students learned to focus their attention on the topics and skills that could have a role in getting them desirable jobs. The Victorians already had a word for this, "cram," and almost all the tricks of our own day are, at least, prefigured in the experience of Britain in the nineteenth century (Elwick 2021).

Test design is itself a form of expertise, closely linked to statistics. It was imperative to confine expert judgment to the design of the exam. Whatever choices entered into the design, the exam would at least be uniform, and those who designed it strongly preferred that the grading be automatic. Automatic scoring not only saved labor but provided assurance against arbitrariness. This control of arbitrariness is the defining feature of an "objective" examination. Of course, there was no easy way to exclude bias from the content of the questions, and the exercise of judgment about what sorts of knowledge are relevant and appropriate for making admissions decisions about the content of exams could not possibly be excluded. It was, of course, often convenient to pretend that the technical factors were the ones that really mattered. The experts on the technical, statistical dimensions of the exams seem to have been largely oblivious to the moral dimensions. Like so many public numbers, the test scores were treated as data, and not as foci of interpretive subtlety.

In 1983, a report of the US Department of Education, *A Nation at Risk*, with its warning of a "rising tide of mediocrity that threatens our very existence as a Nation and a people," opened a new era of testing for the evaluation of US schools. High-level mathematical and scientific education for the mass of American students had never been on the agenda until after the Second World War, when it took on an air of great significance related to military security. The shift is often said to have begun with the Soviet Union's launch of the Sputnik I satellite, in 1957, but in fact, US fear of Russian scientific superiority and the effort to raise the standards of scientific education were already in place (Rudolph 2002). In the wake of World War II and the GI Bill (officially, the Serviceman's Readjustment Act of 1944), universities expanded significantly both as research and as teaching institutions. Even elementary-level schools became much more academically ambitious, as the mostly unsuccessful experiment with teaching "the new math" shows (Phillips 2015). At the high-school level, more students were encouraged or compelled to follow curricula that would prepare them for college. Entrance to the top universities became increasingly competitive, and in that context, standardized testing took on ever greater significance.

It was, in a way, a noble dream to suppose that all or most students could achieve competence in school mathematics. The effort did not succeed at the hoped-for level, and the standardized tests provided a measure of its failure. The evidence of budding educational calamity in the 1983 report featured thirteen "indicators of the risk," including illiteracy rates and dissatisfied employers, with the greatest emphasis on scores from the college admissions tests administered by the College Board One. , and The panicked response to the crisis was the creation of a new generation of written examinations that tested students in order to assess their schools (see Mehta 2013). Most of the time, scores on these tests were thought to speak for themselves, and to require no interpretation beyond a quick glance to confirm that scores were declining. In fact, the raw numbers were, easily challenged. Any competent statistician could recognize that the downward trend was based on numbers that were not comparable because far more students than ever before were now taking these tests. What are we to say about a presidential administration and a Department of Education that can foment a crisis based on evidence like this?

Whatever we may think of the quality of argument and evidence and the political ambitions that created this panic, it was the work of recognized experts, whose expertise was mainly quantitative. The 1983 report, it must be added, was unmistakably an affirmation, not a denial, of educational expertise. However, it was a challenge to one important variety of expertise, that of teachers and school officials. The direct experience of classroom teachers, of course, always had its limits. Unlike the data of the statistical analyst, it could not extend over a whole nation. But here again, the uncritical reliance on totemic numbers was by no means a rejection of expertise but a rebalancing, away from knowledge arising from direct classroom experience to a still greater reliance on data work. The statistical conclusions of the 1983 report, derived mainly from standardized test data, were used, not just to assess the quality of schooling at the state and national levels, but also to judge individual schools and individual classrooms. But statisticians and social scientists recognize that students' test scores are not determined by the schools alone, but also by the families and communities in which the students are brought up. Soon they were working out assessment techniques to go beyond simple test outcomes in favor of improving test performance from one year to the next. They adopted a tax idiom, calling the improvement "value added."

There were, of course, other ways of judging the success of teachers, such as classroom visits and school inspectors. (This was how the Victorian poet Matthew Arnold had earned a reliable income, for example.) School principals and senior teachers could be delegated to visit classrooms. And periodic school accreditation exercises were designed to assure educational quality. But this kind of evidence was largely rejected in the evaluations that had the most serious consequences, such as firing teachers for poor classroom results and even closing schools. For decisions like these, high officials preferred the ostensible rigor of statistical work. They did not merely take their methods off the shelf; they developed new ones to address the new challenges presented by the rising tides of mediocrity. We have the elements here of a self-fulfilling prophecy: numbers that had declined mainly because of the academic ambitions that had led so many more students to submit to the tests. The developers of these tests had no idea that tests of individual aptitude would be repurposed as tests of the quality of schools.[3]

Reacting to Rankings

The idea of unintended consequences is an old one. In what Russell Hardin (1991) called one of the "major insights of the Scottish Enlightenment," Hobbes observed that people can create social institutions as an accidental by-product of action that was directed toward other ends). Adam Smith's invisible hand, the unexpected positive result of individuals maximizing their self-interests, is one such institution. But many unintended consequences are less congenial.

As the sociologist Robert Merton (1936) noted, virtually all the major social thinkers describe some form of "unintended consequences." His own analyses popularized the term. Merton gives three reasons for unintended consequences. First, our knowledge may be too meager for us to fully anticipate the effects of our efforts. Second, we may err in our assessment of the results of our actions. Our predictions are often wrong. Third is what Merton terms "the immediacy of our interests," meaning that short-term concerns may interfere with the predictions of later ones.

The gaming of numbers is an especially prominent form of unintended consequences, and it embodies short-term thinking. It involves manipulations that produce the target numbers without regard for what they were designed to measure.[4] If resources, reputations, and power are attached to certain numbers, no one should be surprised that great effort is exerted to game or "juke" the numbers. So, we witness efforts to manipulate crime statistics by police forces (Eterno and Silverman 2012); test scores, by educators (Aviv 2014); Medicare ratings, by nursing homes (Office of the Inspector General 2014; Lowry and Hicks 2014); and share prices and earnings, by executives (Brooks 1978; Zhang et al. 2008). Of course, some numbers are harder to game than others. But even when the link between manipulation and results is unclear, the pressure to game the numbers can be intense. The advent of university rankings offers a clear case.

Surely nobody at *U.S. News and World Report* originally intended their university rankings to change legal education, and the editors were shocked at the amount of gaming that went on. A weekly news magazine back when such magazines mattered, *U.S. News* suffered in the shadows of the more prominent *Time* and *Newsweek*. The editors who conceived of the rankings were hoping to distinguish their product from the others, make their magazine more visible, and, of course, sell more copies and boost advertising revenues. They framed it as a populist project, making insider knowledge available to outsiders and expertise available to educational "consumers." To that end, and in keeping with their new tag line for the magazine, "news you can use," they launched a survey asking some 1,300 university presidents to name the best liberal arts colleges and universities. According to *U.S. News*, more than half of them responded. [5] No doubt many would now consider that to have been a lapse in their expert judgment.

The first published rankings, in 1983, struck a chord with *U.S. News* readers. The rankings issue, especially, proved to be popular with readers, and the results quickly circulated, as the magazine had intended, as "news." The magazine had believed that readers would appreciate clear, comparative information about the quality of different schools, and they were proved correct. It reproduced the survey exercise several times. Then it invested in a more complex rankings formula that included a compilation of weighted statistics and survey results, mostly assembled using the substantial unsubsidized labor of school staff and administrators. It began to publish these evaluations annually. Mel Elfin, the education editor at *U.S. News* at the time, remembers that the "early issues sold very well, far more than average issues of the magazine. When academics dismissed [the] rankings as not serious, as foolish, they created a wave of interest."[6] In other words, the critics helped propel the rankings.

Now, instead of ranking only the top twenty universities or the top twenty-five law schools, the rankings became more exhaustive, including the top 150 universities or, in the case of law schools, every accredited school. But why stop there? In 2014, *U.S. News* began publishing the best global university rankings. It currently ranks the top 2000 schools ranks from ninety-one countries.[7] The scope and form of the ranking operations also grew to include rankings of graduate departments and professional schools, community colleges, and high schools and then extended into different media, with online rankings and rankings blogs; published guidebooks; about rankings; "do-it-yourself rankings" (in which someone can pick which factors to emphasize); and endless new ranking categories, all derived from different ways of aggregating and classifying its data. The U.S. News website boasts of offering "more than 100 different types of numerical rankings and lists to help students narrow their college search." One might, for example, search the "A-Plus Schools for B Students Rankings"—for "students with non-stratospheric transcripts." [8] The criteria? They have "strong ratings"—most are ranked in the second tier (51–100) or the top of the third tier (101–150)—and "accept a significant number of students with non-stratospheric transcripts." This is a recycling of old information into new categories, an option made easier with quantitative data.

U.S. News no longer confines itself to education; it now ranks everything from hospitals to diet plans, even countries. Its ranking machinery continues to expand as new constituencies form, some that find the rankings useful, some that wish to challenge their influence. It's hardly an exaggeration to say that U.S. News is now more a rankings empire than a news magazine. Having spread to many kinds of institutions, each comprising many varieties of professional and technical expertise, its influence is vast. Many of these ranked targets feel compelled to assess their reputational claims and even their most standardized practices in response to U.S. News's version of excellence.

What does this version of excellence look like? For law schools the threats to their expertise were subtle at first. Despite being widely regarded as terrible measures, the U.S. News rankings seemed, at first, to pose little threat to law school administrators, who could safely ignore them.[9] But that luxury ended when they realized that prospective students were using the rankings to decide where to apply and where to attend. Law school classes were thus being shaped by U.S. News metrics, and that demanded attention and action. "Outrage" is not too strong a word to describe how people law schools first reacted to rankings. What was at stake for them? Their professional judgment, their discretion, once a pillar of their authority as educators. Their sense of affront was all the greater because U.S. News—a mediocre news magazine—had no relevant expertise in evaluation, statistics, or education. Indeed, the magazine was not directly challenging educators' authority by forcing schools to change. Instead, the rankings gradually but profoundly changed the status system in which they and their schools were embedded, prompting the many unintended consequences that devolved from rankings (Sauder 2006).[10] U.S. News could and did absolve itself of responsibility for some of the perverse effects of their rankings; law schools, they claimed, were responsible for their own reactions to what the magazine saw as one, scientifically valid measure of the relative value of what would be a big financial investment for many students and their families. And the market demand for the rankings was obvious. The magazine's rankings issues were the biggest sellers by far and generated enormous press.

No one likes to compromise on the parts of their work that matter to them, to feel coerced into doing things they don't believe are in their own or their organization's best interests, not least law school administrators. Of course, not all of them felt this way. Some deans acknowledged that the metrics could be improved, but felt that the rankings did show how schools could better themselves in relation to others, and did offer prospective students and their families helpful guidance. But unquestionably, a vast majority of the law school administrators and faculty we interviewed said that they had lost at least some control over their professional selves and their work.

One broad type of change that the rankings initiated was to shift the discretion of educators. *U.S. News* now defined what excellence meant. Before the rankings, for example, legal administrators used their judgment to admit students they thought would be interesting and make for what they often called "a well-rounded class." True, they cared about test scores and grade averages, but they felt they had much more latitude to include people with other kinds of accomplishments. After the rankings, test scores largely determined admissions, despite schools' public pronouncements that they vetted applicants based on all the information contained in a student's dossier. And high standardized test scores, we know, are not evenly distributed across race, class, age, and gender (Jencks and Phillips 1998; Wightman 1996;1997; 2003; Wilder 2003). As James Chu (2020) has shown, schools on the thresholds of tiers face the most pressure to change admissions procedures, something that can heighten other forms of inequality.

Before rankings, administrators also had more autonomy to set their own organizational and professional goals. They could invest in scholarships for needy students or in other programs rather than "buy high test scores" with scholarship money. They could hire faculty or build more legal clinics. They had more latitude to help determine what the law school or university should be. While accreditation is always a standardizing force in education, administrators and faculty could choose which values to emphasize and how to distribute resources accordingly. Should they serve specific communities, specialize in certain areas of law, appeal to specific types of students? Should they be "regional", uphold religious principles, serve the needs of local communities, or should they aspire to national prominence? Should they promote access or selectivity? Rankings ratchet up the pressures toward homogenization because they are often based on a single algorithm in which is embedded a particular conception of what a law school is for and what excellence means. Rankings constrain those who want to define their organizations in ways that don't mimic the idealized school implicit in rankings. As several of those interviewed reported told us, "We can't all be Yale Law School."

Staff in career-services departments also feel the brunt of the rankings system because placement statistics are an important component of the rankings. These staff are expert at helping students find jobs, which entails services such as counseling, meeting with law firms and trying to convince them to hold on-campus interviews, promoting their students, and helping students negotiate job offers. Having accurate placement statistics might even seem to be a useful enterprise, but few saw it this way. Instead, career-service personnel had to become expert at tracking down graduates who had failed to report their employment status, which is extremely time-consuming and hardly satisfying work.[11] A the director of small career services office explained:

[It] is the most aggravating part of my job . . . It's a huge amount of effort and what is unfortunate is that we spend so much time trying to collect that data that there are two or three weeks straight through that Susan and I would have to block out our calendars and not take any appointments because we had to be focusing on these numbers. And it ultimately affects the efficient running of our office.

One frustrated administrator admitted to considering hiring a private detective.

The expertise of law school educators is more easily challenged because the rankings were designed to be public and simple to use: up is good, down is bad. Anyone with access to the rankings is free to criticize school administrators, including subordinate groups who, before rankings, would never have had the nerve or the wherewithal. Prospective students now query deans about declines in their rankings, and current students demand public meetings and sometimes that staff or even deans be fired if the school's ranking drops. State legislators may also feel emboldened to grill a president or a dean about a rankings drop, which may make the schools claims for resources easier to dismiss. Newspapers report the annual rankings, which adds to the pressure.

But rankings do not simply constrain discretion. They clearly put more limits on what a school can do without risking its reputation, but discretion and expertise emerge elsewhere and take new forms. One such form is becoming expert at managing or manipulating rankings. A prominent mode of this learning, used by nearly every law school we encountered, took the form of reverse-engineering the rankings: working backward from the current ranking to the adjustments that might lead to a desired one, or at least, trying to learn how each metric was built to be able to explain what was happening to their ranking to the growing number of interested parties who were tracking it. This reverse engineering is not as easy as it sounds. After all, it is an expensive expertise, sold by consultants to all sorts of companies.

The reverse engineering of rankings begins with a critical analysis of the ranking's components and how they are defined and measured. Law school rankings assess four main factors—"reputation," "selectivity," "placement success," and "faculty resources."[12] *Reputation* is weighted the most heavily and is measured by two surveys. *Selectivity* is based on the test scores and the undergraduate grade averages of first-year law students, and acceptance rates. *Placement success* is derived from employment rates at graduation and nine months later, and bar passage rates; *Faculty resources* is a mish-mash of measures, such as student-to-faculty ratios, money spent per student, and library books. In every category, as in the rankings, higher is better. The basic algorithm for most of the *U.S. News* university rankings, including law schools, hasn't changed, yet there has been much tinkering with how to define or measure certain factors or how to contain gaming (more on that below). Measures of most factors for many universities and law schools are tightly compressed. Small shifts in small measures can have dramatic effects on an institution's overall rank. This feature, which it did not take schools long to appreciate, invites close scrutiny and encourages the backward logic of deconstructing rankings into each of their components. This, in turn, encourages careful "management" of the numbers. Put another way, it encourages manipulation or gaming. As one faculty member reported, "I think it's ethically shady. So, *U.S. News* is a driving force in what really has come down to gamesmanship in how colleges and law schools and admissions offices are making policy decisions."

Differently ranked schools respond differently to the rankings. Although it no doubt grates on Harvard to lose a student to Yale, Harvard's elite status enables it to attend only infrequently to rankings. The schools that suffer the most are those relegated to the fourth tier, where the stigma is extremely demoralizing, even if the school does a good job serving a mission that varies from those of the more elite schools. Schools on the cusp of tiers also suffer, because they must be constantly mindful of any tiny, statistically meaningless changes that may cause them to plummet a tier (Espeland and Sauder 2007; Chu 2020).

U.S. News characterizes the shifts in methodology as improvements, showing their responsiveness to educators and continual efforts to contain misrepresentation and gaming. Their expertise, in other words, expands. Critics suggest that such small changes are important for introducing volatility and thus keeping the annual rankings newsworthy. Whatever the motive, the result has been an ongoing recursive relationship between changes and reactions to changes, a dynamic that makes reverse engineering a perennial project. All of this is amplified by the fact that rankings are relative measures, so that the fate of one school depends on what all other schools are doing.

After deconstructing the factors making up their own and others' rankings, to the extent the available information plus interpolation permits, schools' next response is to decide which components are the most amenable to improvement. One component over which schools have some control is moving the median test scores. One law school endured the stigma of dropping from the second to the third tier. When the dean was asked whether the school was developing strategies to get back into the second tier, she replied, "Oh, absolutely. Absolutely. We've done a lot of careful studying of the *U.S. News* methodology to figure out what counts the most and what is perhaps the most easily manipulated, because those are not necessarily the same things."

The assumptions about educational excellence behind each factor become, in practice, far less important than what will move the numbers. As we know, standardized test scores have long been used in the United States as a measure of students' potential or even ability. And median test scores have long been used by law schools (and universities) and the accrediting overseers to characterize the status of applicants and matriculated students. So, *U.S. News* reasoned, why not include them in the rankings as a relatively weighty component of selectivity? But if a school feels it is living and dying by its numbers, becoming a better law school is too lofty and ambiguous a response. Instead, the recourse is to fiddle with the numbers. One feature of this is that the admissions process becomes more "mechanical," in the words of one dean. Some schools now create admissions formulas that make the process seem more automated: say, for every applicant below the median test scores they admit, they must admit two who score above it. Many admissions offices keep a running tally of their median test scores and grade averages.[13]

Toward the end of the process, scores are carefully calculated for how they will "move the median." There is still discretion here: the decision to create a more mechanical process or adopt certain target statistics, or even to admit a "risky" applicant. But this discretion is heavily mediated by *U.S. News*'s literally formulaic definition of excellence.

One jaded law professor suggested: "The most innovative thing about law schools now [i]s the invention of new gaming techniques." To improve their test scores, some law schools have radically cut the size of cohorts. Some schools sent encouraging letters to applicants who had no chance of being accepted so they could reject them and lower their acceptance rates. Some forced faculty to take sabbaticals in the spring to be back in time to be included in the fall faculty-to-student ratios. The calculus of how to improve or game rankings rankled. One dean asked a friend at *U.S. News*:

> Do you think it would be a better law school if I cut 30 or 40 of my students from here, lost the revenue, ceased hiring faculty members, but our LSAT would be higher, and therefore [we] rose in the rankings? Are we a better law school doing that than having the 30 students who might be a little bit weaker but bring enough revenue so we can hire better faculty to teach the students that are here? Which of those makes us a better law school? And the answer to that can't possibly be that we're a better law school by robbing the 170 remaining students and by cutting the 30 [of enrollment] than it would be to have 200 students with more resources available to all 200 of them.

Placement statistics are also subject to administrators' manipulations. No one assumes that someone would spend some $150,000 and three years to work for a minimum wage job in the service industry. Yet, some law schools broadened the definition of "employed" and began to count as employed any student with any job. , Schools that didn't follow suit saw their rankings drop. This change in the definition of employment diffused quickly as a result. To improve their placement numbers, schools also hired their own students during the periods when the numbers were collected or paid law firms to hire their students temporarily. Exactly how many schools engage in how much of this behavior is hard to pin down, and *U.S. News* has closed some of these loopholes in a direct response to gaming. Nevertheless, evidence suggests that such gaming behavior remains widespread. Sometimes the practices seem more innocent than unethical. As one dean said:

> There are three kinds of things people might do. There are the "let's look at the data, and what's the most favorable way we can look at the data [to be] consistent with these instructions and outlines." That's fine, I don't have a problem with that. That's like any other behavior, take the data most favorable to yourself. So if you have a rounding upward instead of rounding downward, who's going to care? I mean if you round upward from a LSAT of 150 to 160, that's a problem. But if you go from 150.4 and say, really that's 151; alright, so it's not quite the way you do math, but it's really not off the charts crazy.

Whatever its incidence, gaming is the subject of much gossip and suspicion inside law schools. And though there is a seductive side to it, a sense of trying to outsmart the illegitimate apparatus that is evaluating you, no one feels too good about it.

Resistance to rankings has taken many forms and been notoriously ineffective. A group of a deans crafted a letter denouncing the rankings that was signed by nearly every dean. The letter was then sent to every student who took the LSAT. Special pleading, efforts to develop alternative rankings, public relations campaigns, denunciations of all sorts—all have failed to hamper the rankers. Widespread efforts to boycott *U.S. News*, as Reed College did, could have been a catastrophic problem for the rankings. *U.S. News* responded to the schools that tried it by conservatively "estimating" the requisite data, something that punished the school with much less favorable statistics than it would have had otherwise. These schools saw their rankings drop. Capitulation was quick and almost universal, except at Reed, which plummeted in the rankings and stayed there.[14] Writing in *The Atlantic* magazine, Reed president, Colin Diver (2005) explained the reasons for Reed's decision and why, despite his urgings, other colleges didn't follow suit. One reason, he wrote, is that "rankings create powerful incentives to manipulate data and distort institutional behavior for the sole or primary purpose of inflating one's score. Because the rankings depend heavily on unaudited, self-reported data, there is no way to ensure either the accuracy of the information or the reliability of the resulting rankings."

But when compare the rankings of other schools to those of law schools, we can see some of the conditions that make effective resistance possible. Dental schools, for example mounted a successful boycott of the rankings. Compared to law schools, dental educators are a smaller, more cohesive professional group. Dental schools trusted one another enough to overcome collective action problems and had more sway over their members. Even though law schools are bigger and better resourced than dental schools, in this case, being "smaller and closer" made it easier to enact a boycott.[15] It is also probably relevant that the dental education market for *U.S. News* is much smaller than that for other professional schools so it seems likely that the magazine was less invested in imposing rankings on them. Law schools are *U.S. News*'s biggest graduate market.

One big difference between law schools and business schools is that for business schools, multiple rankings, by *Forbes, Fortune, Financial Times, Business Week,* and the *Wall Street Journal,* are considered credible. Each uses slightly different criteria, and their rankings vary dramatically. The effect of the multiple rankings is that business schools have more latitude to emphasize the areas they rank best in, which lessens the impact of rankings generally. Still, considerable gaming goes on—for example, schools wishing to do well in the *Financial Times* rankings, the most important in Europe, tell their faculty to publish only in the journals that are included in the *FT*'s citation counts.

Other factors that affect how and how much a school can resist the rankings, in addition to where they are ranked, is whether they have the support of upper administration to pursue a mission that is not captured in the rankings. If a university president champions the mission, it offers protection from rankings pressure, which lessens the need to resist. Resources also matter. Poorly funded schools have fewer options to resist.

Law schools without part-time programs (these tend to be more elite schools) success-fully lobbied *U.S. News* to rank part-time programs separately. A familiar gaming tactic had been to admit desirable students with lower test scores into part-time programs, and then to sometimes allow them to switch to a full-time program after the first year, when their numbers don't count. Ranking the part-time programs eliminated this strategy, and a number of schools fell precipitously when this new ranking was added.

The range of gaming strategies prompted by rankings reflects much creative stra-tegic thinking, and one can't help but admire the attention to detail that goes into it. But as is true of many performance measures, the temptation to tinker with numbers that influence money, power, or status is hard to resist. Rankings have now redefined status so thoroughly that schools can no longer make claims about being a top twenty-five school unless *U.S. News* says they are. Outcomes seem unambiguous because all the uncertainty is smuggled into the assumptions behind the numbers and how they are made operational. The new "expertise" embodied in reverse engineering and expressed in gaming is but one of the unintended consequences that rankings unleashed. A new status system that is begrudgingly accommodated is another.

CONCLUSION

The confrontation of academic science with less formalized varieties of expertise has been a familiar theme of the history of science since the mid-nineteenth century. This story takes in the expanding role of school culture and mathematics in engineering, the expanded role of science in the creation and deployment of medical therapies, the di-verse new roles of psychology in education, and the gradual emergence of academic so-cial science as a rival to or a resource for the reformers and administrators who first called on "social science" to make the world run more rationally. The "professionali-zation" of science meant much more than earning a comfortable living at a univer-sity by teaching and doing research. Modern science was about new expert roles in its borderlands with medicine, education, journalism, business, law, and government. Often, the scientist's earnings came from professional or consulting positions bound up with enterprises like these. Data and statistics are ever-more important participants in professional and bureaucratic activities. One key role of quantitative science has been to make professional knowledge more rigorous and less personal, to focus resolutely on neutral data and statistics. For about a century, professional statisticians have been applying mathematical skills regularly and even routinely in such domains as agricul-ture, commerce, development economics, therapeutic medicine, engineering quality control, marketing, finance, polling, policing, courts, prisons, and schools. Their role is simultaneously to provide a basis of professionalism and to challenge the less codified, less self-consciously rigorous standards that were typical of professional reasoning.

The episodes we have presented here provide a broad sense of the historical devel-opment and the increasingly ubiquitous practical applications of numbers. Although data specialists bear some of the responsibility for the failures (and credit for successes), it is important to recognize that the power relations of expertise are complicated. Masters of abstraction are almost never given control over issues that people care about. Certainly, they pose challenges to professionals such as asylum doctors, educators, and law deans, but these stories do not begin with the divine pronouncement, "Let there be statisticians." Numbers already had a role at the outset in our cases. Doctors and school officials had long debated their appropriate presentation and use. Even the push to formalize the use of numbers arose partly from within the professional fields of medicine, law, and education. The emergence, toward the end of the nineteenth century, of statistics as a specialty in its own right intensified these conflicts, which, indeed, did not only pit doctors and educators against statisticians, but also medical professionals against other professionals and statisticians against statisticians. The internecine battles of statisticians have been among the most bitter and sustained found in the whole history of science (MacKenzie 1981). At the same time, warring statisticians have managed to form alliances across professional boundaries with doctors, lawyers, school administrators, and other scientists (Porter 2004, 2018).

The notion of data run amok, which recurs in all three of our cases, suggests that the expertise of the sort claimed by medical and educational professionals can be made less powerful. Hagen imagined a world in which bureaucrats drew up policies and praised or condemned institutions based on numbers that might be virtually meaningless, since the expertise going into the classification was completely unregulated. This is in sharp contrast to the multiple-choice examinations used to evaluate schools, for which rigorous standardization was valued above all else. The relation between test content and the curriculum, however, was largely ignored until teachers and students came to recognize that their fate and that of their schools might hinge on adapting the curriculum to an examination system nominally focused on aptitude rather than achievement. Finally, law schools faced a highly heterogeneous grab bag of measures that were nonetheless procrustean. When these measures were transformed into rankings, it virtually compelled students and schools to alter their behavior in patterned but broadly unintentional ways. The force of these numbers did not depend on expert approval. Rather, they had some capacity to override forms of expertise, including expertise that was not directly reflected in or confronted by the numbers.

Much of the time, numbers function by combining, summing up, or making precise what is encountered in the world. But here, we see how numbers can become unmoored from ordinary experience and from the forms of expertise that aim to interpret it. Numbers make knowledge that is remarkably portable. They travel easily, especially when they are produced and mobilized by the media, and they are adept at traversing what might have once been barriers. However secure one's expertise is, the portability of numbers, their capacity to move into new locations for new uses, is one reason they are hard to police by experts with more conventional kinds of authority.

In our examples, we have numbers whose significance is determined in no small degree by unanticipated (at first) human reactions to other numbers. These can as well be self-negating as self-affirming, and certainly, they can be complex. As we have seen, most compellingly in the case of rankings, they have provided an irresistible stimulus to discover new forms of expertise, arising perhaps in reaction to the failures of expert management by older professions. We catch a scent here, perhaps, of neoliberal decentralizing and of big data manipulations. Expertise that is grounded in the authority of numbers can prove threatening to the authority of other forms and sources of expertise. Whether these are doctors, teachers, or law school deans, trust in other kinds of experts can be tenuous when confronted with the power of numbers that so often simultaneously represent and intervene.

ACKNOWLEDGMENT

We thank Gil Eyal for his excellent comments.

NOTES

1. The entrance exams for top elite *grands écoles* came to be integrated within special preparatory schools.
2. The research on rankings was conducted jointly by Michael Sauder and Wendy Espeland.
3. We should add that extensions like these have been quite common—for example, in the claim, deduced from IQ tests, which had been devised to identify promising officers in World War I, that new immigrant populations were bringing about a decline of American intelligence (see Carson 2007, pt. 3).
4. Although the term "gaming" is usually applied to numbers, we can imagine efforts to game other sorts of expertise. For example, someone might present their medical history to a doctor in ways that make them seem more insurable. Gaming numbers, however, can be especially insidious because we often take numbers at face value and treat them as having universal, objective meanings, characteristics we don't attribute to other forms of expertise or knowledge. Moreover, numbers often impose a relative relationship on entities that can stimulate intense competition. They contain assumptions about what matters most or what excellence means that can threaten the autonomy of administrators.
5. Boyington (2014).
6. Mel Elfin, phone interview with Espeland. the, November 14, 2006. Should be singular for reasons too complicated to explain.
7. U.S. News and World Report. https://www.usnews.com/best-colleges/rankings.
8. U.S. News and World Reports. "A-Plus Schools for B Students." https://www.usnews.com/best-colleges/rankings/regional-universities/a-plus.
9. US law schools were the primary subject of the research on rankings (see Espeland and Sauder 2016), but the analyses included the college rankings, business school rankings, and global rankings more broadly.
10. Some may assume that the elite schools were immune to the pressure to change that the rankings introduced. They were not. The statuses of elite schools were better known and more secure, but they were still vulnerable if they failed to adopt the changes that other schools were implementing. Before the rankings, when law school applicants were

admitted to Harvard and Yale, roughly half attended each school. After the rankings, Yale law school was ranked number one each year. Instead of splitting the pool, most students chose to go to Yale law school over Harvard. The number of these "cross-admits" that chose Yale over Harvard rose to above 90%. As one professor said, "We never lose to Harvard anymore." In response, Harvard invested more energy and money in efforts to seduce students who had also been admitted to Yale. Elite schools react differently than less elite schools, however. For example, they can offer students research funds that many schools could not afford, contact famous alumni to be in touch with applicants or other means of impressing applicants. Because of the nature of their applicant pools, the elite schools were freer to emphasize individual characteristics other than test scores and grades. Lower ranked schools were more focused on test scores in admissions.

11. Espeland and Sauder (2016, 148–152, 151).
12. Espeland and Sauder (2016); for a more detailed description of how rankings are made, see pages 14–15, 218. On reverse engineering, see pages 33–36. See also Espeland (2016).
13. Some schools have made standardized test scores optional, which instantly improves their ranking because students who tested well reported their scores, and those who did poorly did not. Now, some schools do not accept any standardized test scores. The effects of this are not yet clear. In the past, *U.S. News* has "estimated" missing data, often using lower numbers as proxies. If enough schools stop accepting standardized test scores, *U.S. News* will have to alter its selectivity factor.
14. Recently, some Reed students reverse engineered its ranking, which was 90th, or near the bottom of the second tier of liberal arts colleges. One of the ranking factors *U.S. News* had estimated seemed especially off. Financial resources—how much schools spend per student for teaching, research, and services—was ranked very near the bottom, number 169 out of 172 schools. Using publicly available data, the students created models that could accurately predict *U.S. News*'s rankings 94% of the time for all schools, with one exception: Reed. Working backward, they were able to determine that Reed should have been ranked 39th instead of 90th (Lydgate, 2018). https://www.reed.edu/apply/college-rankings.html.
15. Thanks to Gil Eyal for this observation.

REFERENCES

Aviv, Rachael. 2014. "Wrong Answer: In an Era of High Stakes Testing, a Struggling School Made a Shocking Choice." *New Yorker*, July 21.

Boyington, Briana. 2014. "Infographic: 30 Editions of the U.S. News Best Colleges Rankings U.S. News' process for ranking colleges has evolved since the first edition was published in the early 1980s." *U.S. News and World Report*, September 9. https://www.usnews.com/education/best-colleges/articles/2014/09/09/infographic-30-editions-of-the-us-news-best-colleges-rankings.

Bowker, Geoffrey, and Leigh Starr. 1999. *Sorting Things Out: Classification and Its Consequences.* Cambridge, MA: MIT Press.

Brooks, John. 1978. *The Go-Go Years: The Drama and Crashing Finale of Wall Street's Bullish 60s.* New York: Wiley.

Carson, John. 2007. *The Measure of Merit: Talents, Intelligence, and Inequality in the French and American Republics, 1750–1940.* Princeton, NJ: Princeton University Press.

Chadarevian, Soraya de, and Theodore M. Porter. 2018. "Introduction: Scrutinizing the Data World." *Historical Studies in the Natural Sciences* 48: 549–556.

Chu, James. 2021. "Cameras of Merit or Engines of Inequality? College Ranking Systems and the Enrollment of Disadvantaged Students." *American Journal of Sociology* 126: 1307–1346.

Clark, William. 2004. *Academic Charisma ant the Origins of the Research University*. Chicago: University of Chicago Press.

Danziger, Kurt. 1990. *Constructing the Subject: Historical Origins of Psychological Research*. Cambridge, UK: Cambridge University Press.

Diver, Colin. 2005. "Is there Life After Rankings?" *The Atlantic*, November.

Elwick, James. 2021. *Making a Grade: Victorian Examinations and the Rise of Standardized Testing*. Toronto: University of Toronto Press.

Espeland, Wendy. 2016. "Reverse Engineering and Emotional Attachments as Mechanisms Mediating the Effects of Quantification." *Historical Social Research* 41 (2): 280–304.

Espeland, Wendy Nelson, and Michael Sauder. 2007. "Rankings and Reactivity: How Public Measures Recreate Social Worlds." *American Journal of Sociology* 113 (1): 1–40.

Espeland, Wendy, and Michael Sauder. 2016. *Engines of Anxiety: Academic Rankings, Reputation and Accountability*. New York: Russell Sage Press.

Eterno, John A., and Eli B. Silverman. 2012. *The Crime Numbers Game: Management by Manipulation*. Boca Raton, FL: CRC Press.

Forrester, John. 1996. "If p, then What? Reasoning in Cases." *History of the Human Sciences* 9:1–25.

Hagen, F. W. 1871. "Ueber Statistik der Irrenanstalten mit besonderer Beziehung auf das im Auftrage des internationalen Congresses vom Jahre 1867 vorgeschlagene Schema." *Allgemeine Zeitschrift für Psychiatrie und psychisch-gerichtliche Medicin* 27:267–294.

Hardin, Russell. 1991. "Hobbesian Political Order." *Political Theory* 19 (2): 156–180.

Jencks, Christopher, and Meredith Philips. 1998. *The Black-White Test Score Gap*. Washington, DC: Bookings Institution Press.

Lemann, Nicholas. 1999. *The Big Test: The Secret History of the American Meritocracy*. New York: Farrar, Straus and Giroux.

Lydgate, Chris. 2018. "Reed and the Rankings Game," September 12. https://www.reed.edu/apply/college-rankings.html

Lowery, Wesley, and Josh Hicks. 2014. "Troubling Reports Sparks New Wave of Calls for VA Chief's Resignation." *Washington Post*, May 28.

MacKenzie, Donald. 1981. *Statistics in Britain, 1865–1930: The Social Construction of Scientific Knowledge*. Edinburgh: Edinburgh University Press.

Mehta, Jal. 2013. *The Allure of Order: High Hopes, Dashed Expectations and the Troubled Quest to Remake American Schooling*. New York: Oxford University Press.

Merton, Robert K. 1936. "The Unanticipated Consequences of Purposive Action." *American Sociological Review* 1 (6): 894–904.

Office of the Inspector General. 2014. *Occupational Outlook Handbook*. 2014–15 ed. Interim report, May 28. U.S. Department of Veterans' Affairs. http://www.va.gov/oig/pubs/VAOIG-14-02603-178.pdf. Accessed June 19, 2020.

Phillips, Christopher. 2015. *The New Math: A Political History*. Chicago: University of Chicago Press.

Porter, Theodore M. 1986. *The Rise of Statistical Thinking, 1820–1900*. Princeton, NJ: Princeton University Press.

Porter, Theodore M. 1993. "Quantification and the Accounting Ideal in Science." *Social Studies of Science* 22:633–652.

Porter, Theodore M. 1995. *Trust in Numbers: The Pursuit of Objectivity in Science and Public Life*. Princeton, NJ: Princeton University Press.

Porter, Theodore M. 2004. *Karl Pearson: The Scientific Life in a Statistical Age*. Princeton, NJ: Princeton University Press.

Porter, Theodore M. 2011. "Reforming Vision: The Engineer Le Play Learns to Observe Society Sagely." In *Histories of Scientific Observation*, edited by Lorraine Daston and Elizabeth Lunbeck, 281–302. Chicago: University of Chicago Press.

Porter, Theodore M. 2018. *Genetics in the Madhouse: The Unknown History of Human Heredity*. Princeton, NJ: Princeton University Press.

Rosenberg, Daniel. 2018. "Dates as Words." *Historical Studies in the Natural Sciences* 48:557–567.

Rottenburg, Richard, Sally E. Merry, Sung-Joon Park, and Johanna Mugler, eds. 2015. *The World of Indicators: The Making of Governmental Knowledge through Quantification*. Cambridge, UK: Cambridge University Press.

Rudolph, John. 2002. *Scientists in the Classroom: The Cold War Reconstruction of American Science Education*. New York: Palgrave.

Sauder, Michael. 2006. "Third Parties and Status Systems: How the Structures of Status Systems Matter." *Theory and Society* 35 (3): 299–321.

Timmermans, Stefan, and Steven Epstein. 2010. "A World of Standards but Not a Standard World: Toward a Sociology of Standards and Standardization." *Annual Review of Sociology* 36:69–89.

Wightman, Linda. 1996. *Women in Legal Education: A Comparison of the Law School Performance and Law School Experiences of Women and Men*. LSAC Research Report Series. Law School Admission Council, Newtown, PA.

Wightman, Linda. 1997. "The Threat to Diversity in Legal Education: An Empirical Analysis of the Consequences of Abandoning Race as a Factor in Law School UAdmissions Decisions." *New York University Law School Law Review* 72 (1): 1–53.

U.S. News and World Report. A-Plus Schools for B Students. https://www.usnews.com/best-colleges/rankings/regional-universities/a-plus

Wightman, Linda. 2003. "The Consequences of Race-Blindness: Revisiting Prediction Models with Current Law School Data." *Journal of Legal Education* 53 (2): 229–253.

Wilder, Gita. 2003. *The Road to Law School and Beyond: Examining Challenges to Racial and Ethnic in the Legal Profession*. LSAC Research Report 02-01. Law School Admissions Council, Newtown, PA.

Zhang, Xiameng, Kathryn M. Bartol, Ken G. Smith, Michael D. Pfarrer, and Dmitry M. Khanin. 2008. "CEOs on the Edge: Earnings Manipulation and Stock-Based Incentive Misalignment." *Academy of Management Journal* 51 (2): 241–258.

13

EXPERTS IN THE REGULATION OF TECHNOLOGY AND RISK: AN ECOLOGICAL PERSPECTIVE ON REGULATORY SCIENCE

DAVID DEMORTAIN

INTRODUCTION

SCIENTISTS who are active in regulatory settings, whether they are employed by regulatory agencies or are associated with them as scientific advisers, frequently experience the politicization of science and expertise. Like many other scientists who engage in policy and administration, they embrace and claim the ideals of objectivity, transparency, evidence-based decision-making, and keep a professional distance from politics (Gieryn 1983; Jasanoff 1995). Yet this professional demarcation of science from politics is constantly eroded in the concrete performance of expertise. Scientists are an integral part of the political machinery of regulation (Grundmann 2017; Eyal 2019a; Demortain 2020). Their knowledge claims have implications for regulatory decisions. They can hardly hope to remain unaffected by the controversies surrounding technologies and their risks in society, and their regulation.

Indeed, scientists have become objects in the disputes concerning these very acts (Weingart 1999). Scientific experts who are involved in the regulation of technologies and their risks are sometimes accused of mixing science and politics, of unduly distorting data, measurements, and predictions to enact implicit values and policy commitments. At a time when science has become a proxy battleground in policymaking and politics (Brown 2009), these accusations may come from any of the publics of the regulatory acts. Regulated businesses criticize scientific experts, knowing that they sometimes legitimize strong regulatory intervention. Public-interest groups may be critical as well, mindful that the science that is invoked sometimes minimizes the risks and leads to the adoption of insufficiently protective measures. Industries will criticize scientific committees and the scientists at regulatory agencies for exaggerating risks, applying poor standards of scientific evidence, or giving in to the irrational fears of the public. Public-interest groups will accuse scientists of being too cozy with industry, applying outdated testing methods, or excluding large swaths of academic and citizen knowledge from their reviews.

More recently, regulatory science has become the terrain of a broader discourse, fueling the supposed crisis of expertise (Nichols 2017; Eyal 2019): regulated industries have gained control over the standard methods used to test their products, and have captured regulatory science—as the knowledge invoked to establish the risks and benefits of regulated products. The results of multiple investigations by journalists, environmental or public health activists, public-health groups, and pro-transparency groups have been published that document the conflicts of interest of many public experts who collaborate, directly or indirectly, with regulated industries by conducting studies of their products and then advising the regulatory bodies on the hazardousness and benefits of these very products (Rosenbaum 2015; Heath 2016). In multiple regulatory areas (finance, pharmaceuticals, chemicals, nuclear energy, etc.), in the United States and in the European Union, professional scientists seem to go through a revolving door of industry and regulators, which contributes to the fact that expertise, overall, pertains to the former rather than to the latter (Center Watch 2015; Corporate Europe Observatory 2013; Frickel 2011; Katic 2015; McCarty 2014; Piller 2018; Poulain 2018; Prasad and Bien 2019).

My aim in this chapter is to discuss the notion that scientific experts, who, ideally, are impartial mediators or brokers between science and policy (Pielke 2007), are losing autonomy vis-à-vis interests active in the politics of technology and risk regulation. What are the implications of the seemingly rising industrial stakes behind regulatory decisions and regulatory science for the authority and credibility of scientific experts? How should one approach, theoretically, the link between scientific expertise and industry interests, specifically? The understanding behind a lot of the literature on the industry capture of science is that structural industrial power is undermining professional autonomy in scientific practice. I put forward a framework to help analyze the implications of the industry presence in regulatory policy and science for the social and epistemic positioning of scientists. In theoretical terms, I look for a way to put the sociology of scientific expertise and the construction of scientific authority into dialogue, using arguments stemming from the political economy of science concerning the presence of interest groups in regulation.

I first describe the historical origins of the term regulatory science, which is contemporaneous of the adoption of laws, in the United States, requiring dedicated agencies to technically evaluate complex technologies and their intended and unintended, uncertain effects. Second, I outline two ways in which regulatory science was problematized in the then nascent field of science and technology studies (STS), as an uncertain science practiced in the space of regulation, and as a way of knowing risks structured by particular standards of proof. The latter perspective opens to the growing conversation about industrial influence and capture of regulatory science, to which I turn in the fourth section, showing how industries shape ways of knowing. The final section of the chapter goes beyond the narrative of capture to offer a reinterpretation that takes into account both the structural weight of industries and the local construction of knowledge claims and facts in regulatory science, which STS has typically taught us to apprehend. The perspective suggested is that of an ecology of *regulatory knowledge*, whereby this knowledge emerges from interactions between knowledge producers positioned in a variety of adjacent fields—the administrative state, academia, industry, or activism. The notion of *regulatory knowledge*, and its ecology, is deemed useful for embracing the full environment in which regulatory science is performed, and in assessing the importance of the industrial determinants of public expertise. This perspective is used to account for the fact that regulatory knowledge is produced in a variety of social fields and that the authority of experts, and the evidence they value, is best understood if we analyze their positioning in and across these fields. The argument herein is not that the regulated industries systematically capture these public experts, hence, the regulatory agencies. But the themes of capture and of experts' conflicts of interest signal an important, constitutive trait of scientific expertise as it relates to regulation: its embeddedness in a set of relationships organizing the production of regulatory knowledge in which industry plays a variable yet growing role.

REGULATORY SCIENCE AS THE SCIENCE OF ADMINISTRATIVE AGENCIES

The phrase *regulatory science* emerged in the second half of the 1970s in the United States to qualify the science invoked by the agencies that oversaw the authorization or listing of medicines, food additives, pesticides, and chemicals. It seems to have first appeared in a document of the Food and Drug Administration (FDA), when an FDA historian used it in his preface to a 1976 compendium of annual reports on the administration of the Federal Food, Drug, and Cosmetic Act, for which the FDA has responsibility (Janssen 1976). Soon after, the term appeared in documents of the Environmental Protection Agency, whose mandate is to regulate pesticides and industrial chemicals. In a report that reviewed policy activities and the information concerning toxic substances that was available from the federal government, EPA staffers noted that the FDA performed most of the research in regulatory science, implicitly supporting calls for the EPA to embrace a similar effort (Environmental Protection Agency 1979). The term surfaces in the discourse of regulatory agencies to denote the dire problem they faced, of producing more relevant research and fill the knowledge gaps that prevented them from fulfilling their regulatory missions, be they improving air quality, registering safe pesticides, authorizing depollution technologies or defining what a hazardous chemical was (Science Advisory Board 1977).

Jurgen Schmandt (1984), a lawyer and professor of public affairs, picked up the term *regulatory science* in 1984 in his guest editorial in a special issue of the journal *Science, Technology, and Human Values*, on science and regulation. The regulation of technologies and their risks pertained to a new generation of regulatory laws addressing the health and environmental problems linked to industrial products and activities (Wilson 1980). Regulatory policy was at first economic in nature, dedicated to the control of monopolies and the functioning of markets. *Social regulation*, in contrast, is public intervention in the activities of industry, and is legitimized by social, environmental, or health motives. The rise of this so-called social regulation is inseparable from the social movements of the 1960s and 1970s—notably, the environmental movement—and the pressure being exerted on parties and elected politicians to pass new laws to address emerging environmental problems (Vogel 1988; Harris and Milkis 1989). In the United States, this led in the early 1970s to the creation of new regulatory agencies—notably, the Occupational Safety and Health Administration and the EPA—to apply the new statutes, which had been adopted despite the resistance of the industries that were going to be regulated (Wilson 1980). The laws of this new wave of regulatory policy all mandated the scientific measurement and testing of the health and environmental effects of industrial activities. As Schmandt (1984) argues, "This model for regulation [social regulation]—one central in the development of environmental policy during the late 1960s and early 1970s—shifted the focus of regulation from industry's economic behavior to its use of technology. It also prepared the ground-work for using science in regulatory proceedings. [This phase of regulation] further shifted the focus of regulation to risks associated with science-based or high-technology industries" (25).

Because Schmandt had worked at the EPA, where these various forms of knowledge were then slowly being codified and put in practice (Demortain 2020), he was in a position to name the specific scientific activities that constituted regulatory science. He cast a wide net to include, first, the authoritative summary and interpretation of scientific and medical research results (health assessment, exposure assessment, hazard assessment, and risk assessment); second, environmental impact statements and cost-benefit analyses by economists; and third, legal and policy analysis to support the formulation of options for regulatory decisions. Thus, Schmandt wrote, "through the accumulation and interpretation of data, [regulatory science] has the task to link policy concepts to scientific evidence in a responsible and verifiable way. Although regulatory principles begin in social goals that are often quite vaguely stated in legislation, the process must proceed to the development of scientific evidence, which is indispensable to understanding the new issues and to defining and justifying the range of possible solutions" (26).

The term *regulatory science* is intentionally paradoxical. It marks the inherent tensions in the practice of scientific knowledge in the context of regulatory, legal actions against industries and technologies: that is, doing the work to uncover the causes and magnitudes of a risk, not having to pretend to be able to dispel all the uncertainties that surround complex, hard-to-observe, and nearly untestable events. Regulatory science is the scientific practice of determining the adverse effects and benefits of products in the context of technical uncertainty. It is in this precise sense that FDA bureaucrats and scientists initially used the phrase, in fact. In 1977, the then commissioner of the agency was attempting to sensitize members of the House of Representatives to the difficulty of his task, which he described thus: what made his job difficult was having to make decisions and produce answers at a given point in time, without being able to wait for the availability of the pure, fundamental science. Regulatory science, the science of the FDA, meant making decisions in the face of "uncertain, but potentially significant benefits; unproven, but troublesome hazards" (Kennedy 1977a, 79). The commissioner was of the view that his agency's knowledge of products, risks, and benefits—his "regu-latory science base"—needed to be constantly fed and augmented by research centers (Kennedy 1977b, 5). If that link between research and decision-making, between science and administration, was missing, he was bound to fail. With more regulatory science, or "science-for-policy," he could on the contrary hope to use "scientific evidence, data, and insights to illuminate public policy issues that are not primarily scientific, but that are strongly dependent on scientific and technological information" (Brooks 1987, 1).

REGULATORY SCIENCE: PRODUCING KNOWLEDGE IN A SPACE OF POLITICS AND DISPUTES

Alvin Weinberg, a prominent American nuclear physicist, long-time director of the Oak Ridge National Laboratory, and science adviser to Presidents Eisenhower and Kennedy had, a few years before the phrase "regulatory science" appeared in the discourse of regulators, coined the term "trans-science" (Weinberg 1972; Eyal 2019a) to stress the un-resolvable tension inherent in the use of science for administering uncertain hazards: notably, the fact that in policy environments, scientists are often asked to do some-thing that looks like scientific research but, in fact, is in stark contrast with it because of the level of uncertainty and lack of structuration of the issues that are being tackled.[1] Scientific advisers are mandated to provide all sorts of answers to questions that are couched in the language of science, but that cannot be resolved with the knowledge, methods, or paradigms that are, at that particular moment, recognized as valid science.

The problem with the notion of "regulatory science," Weinberg (1985) later argued, was that it continues to promise that scientists will be able to resolve these uncer-tain, intractable issues, with the unfortunate result that an inferior kind of science, producing half-baked answers, and behaving as if things are certain, gets validated in regulatory decisions and endorsed by policymakers. For Weinberg, it was dangerous for democracies to create a separate domain of science and authority—regulatory science—in which we content ourselves with providing half-baked answers, ignoring blatant uncertainties. It would be better if regulators and the public admitted that uncertainties bear on science anyway, and stopped demanding impossible answers from science, just as it would be better if scientists admitted the limits of their knowledge and stayed strictly within the bounds of established scientific knowledge (Weinberg 1985). The problem posed by trans-science, or regulatory science for that matter, is a thorny one politically: zones of ignorance and uncertainty open up spaces for scientific experts, to make and enact assumptions, values and particular policy commitments, often in discreet ways, couched in the language of facts and figures—the early days of the regulation of toxic substances were, for instance, filled with discussions of the assumptions that experts were making about the doses at which a carcinogenic substance would cause cancer (Jasanoff 1982, 1987). If uncertainty fails to be recognized, and if dreams of a positive, science-based determination of public decisions continue to dominate, then the risk is that scientists effectively take more power than a given polity would agree to delegate (Majone 1984). Lack of agreement and common understanding about what scientists know and can help determine, result in endemic disputes and confusion about what science says (Nelkin 1984). And indeed, regulatory agencies and their experts, have from the very beginning of the era of science-based regulation, been accused of wrongly using science and of excessive discretion (Dumanoski 1978; Ashford 1984; Greenwood 1984; Regens et al. 1983).

The main lesson from early, precautionary writings about regulatory science, is therefore that science is intricated with what were called "values" in the controversies of that time (e.g., Kunreuther and Ley 1983). It is a science that can hardly hope to end disputes by establishing definitive proofs of risk or its absence; one that can only fuel, or be a proxy battleground for, the politics of risk and uncertainty. As sociologists have established, uncertainty is a structural problem, linked to the incapacity of Western societies to produce consent and collective knowledge (Wynne 1987; Schwarz and Thompson 1990; Borraz 2007). Uncertainty surges from the more fundamental fact that there is deep disagreement within societies about how and how far risks should be regulated. The uncertainty facing the agencies and decision-makers who have to make decisions about technologies based on the risk-benefit assessments rests in the difficulty of having their decisions accepted when the various publics and interest groups involved have such widely diverging concerns and definitions of what matters (Douglas and Wildavsky 1983). This uncertainty is pervasive in risk societies in general, but national institutional systems may magnify it. The adversarial American institutional system is an example; it magnifies uncertainty in that various interest groups and institutional actors have institutional access to decision-makers, and also have the right to challenge in Courts their choices and the scientific facts they claim as the basis for their decisions (Jasanoff 1990). And so, the rules for restoring the possibility of trust in scientific authority, in societies characterized by political fractures and endemic dispute, necessarily evolve.

In the social sciences, the term *regulatory science* has been conceptualized to denote this intertwining of efforts to calculate or predict risks and the necessarily disputed and politicized handling of uncertainties. Mark Rushefsky (1986), a political scientist studying the development of cancer-risk-assessment methods as applied to industrial chemicals or pesticides, showed how this domain of scientific practice differed from normal science. Regulatory science and normal science share a number of traits (both address uncertainties, search for consensus, and navigate continual change in methods and paradigms), but several things distinguish regulatory science from normal science: the pervasiveness of a three-valued logic (meaning that answers to regulatory-scientific questions cannot be strictly binary, "true" or "false," but often pertain to the "unde-cided"); the direct public-policy implications of its scientific data and claims; the new role scientists are led to play in this setting (advocate, rather than detached expert); and the different atmosphere in which regulatory science is practiced (notably, the institu-tional pressures that bear on the production and interpretation of regulatory studies; Rushefsky 1986, 24–26). Salter (1988), expanding on her notion of "mandated science" and, even more so, Jasanoff (1990) put at the center of the definition of regulatory sci-ence its having to grapple with the tensions emerging from the scientists' practical involvement in policymaking and institutional environments that are marked by un-certainty and dispute. In terms of content, regulatory science aims specifically to fill the knowledge gaps in the process of evaluating technologies and risks, provides knowledge syntheses, and is oriented toward the prediction of risks. In terms of context, Jasanoff notes that regulatory science is characterized by the involvement of government and industry, institutional pressures, accountability demands, and changing criteria for the evaluation and validation of knowledge.

Regulatory science may thus be defined as an intermediary space of production of knowledge, in between the fields of research and spaces of regulatory politics such as agencies and courts; a space characterized by endemic difficulties to construct author-itative facts, because of the value disputes that surround the regulation of technologies and risks, and which actors of regulatory politics translate into conflicting positionings about the quality and appropriateness of scientific knowledge, from data to calculations, through hypotheses, methods and interpretations. Regulatory science is an uncertain science, technically and politically. In this space, knowledge is technically incomplete, facts are mixed with values and thus disputed; the social authority that scientists usually enjoy, is hard to acquire or contested.

For this reason, regulatory science has been a rich terrain for social scientists: one which brought out the ways in which scientists and experts may forge credibility and authority. As Jasanoff (2012) puts it, regulatory science has evolved ways of "making ob-jectivity" and is a useful, instructive field of investigation for sociologists of expertise interested in the ways of enacting authority (Carr 2010). The main practice, as Jasanoff (1987, 1990) showed early on, is for scientists to mobilize a set of resources, rhetorical and institutional, to actively differentiate their work from that of politics and value commitments (Gieryn 1983). Since the early 1980s, an institutional rule for the use of science in political decision-making and regulation has emerged that heeds Weinberg's warning about the risk to science of the loss of authority. Around 1984, the EPA was reorganizing itself and the internal interactions between scientists and the bureaucratic officials in charge of regulatory decisions, along the lines of the creation of a separation between "risk assessment" and "risk management" (Demortain 2020); a protocol that sustained the impression of objectivity and scientific reputation that the leaders of the agency were aiming to forge (Porter 1995). The separation was meant as a kind of institutional recipe for managing the boundaries between fact-finding, the exploration of uncertainties, and policymaking. It was a guide for performing the kind of professional boundary work that is instrumental to preserving the credibility of the claims scientists make in policy contexts, and of their cultural authority more broadly. It barred scientists from entering into discussions of values and policy criteria and from "dictating the policy response" (Schmandt 1984, 26), or to explicate the values and assumptions they apply when producing facts about risks. Boundary work aims to achieve a kind of purification of regulatory science and defense of its "purely-scientific nature," to convince publics and audiences that scientists do not interfere with regulatory responsibilities (Jasanoff 1987; Konopasek et al. 2008).

REGULATORY SCIENCE AS A WAY OF KNOWING RISKS

It is, however, possible to define regulatory science differently than through a comparison with, on the one hand, ordinary normal or research science and, on the other hand, policy- or decision-making. Irwin et al. (1997), showed how we can get trapped by this classification game. Defining the concerns and typical content of a supposedly discrete regulatory science necessarily leads to a claim that it is an inferior science. This way of defining regulatory science is not satisfactory because it has normative implications: "The reification of regulatory science as non-science made more scientific, leaves the methods and results of regulatory science open to challenge on the grounds that they are just policy strategies disguised in scientific language" (19). Stressing the institutional context in which regulatory science is practiced is also unsatisfactory because it leads to a construct, an idealized, indeed, not very realistic view of research science (20). Regulatory science seems to be juxtaposed to a mythical kind of laboratory science that is detached from any institutional environment. While indeed, institutional pressures and modes of accountability may differ between "research" and "regulatory science," it may be more a matter of degree than of type.

Irwin et al. (1997) suggested approaching regulatory science less as a strictly delimited kind of science, and more as a "meeting ground" between science (of various types) and policy, a space in which science and policy mutually construct each other (Rothstein et al. 1999; Shackley and Wynne 1995). This mutual construction takes place through recurrent, increasingly professionalized activities, such as experimental testing, the development of guidelines, joint interpretation of tests results, delivery of scientific advice to regulatory decision-makers, product R&D programs, and so on. These activities bring together "a range of specialty and disciplinary orientations," and "embrace varying levels of scientific uncertainty/indeterminacy (from complex and innovative work on mechanisms through to routine testing). They are, to varying degrees, bureaucratic and rule-based, and incorporate "scientific, economic and political" concerns at once (Hunt and Shackley 1999). In regulatory science, technical data informs the application of more conventional and bureaucratic instruments, such as "cutoffs, thresholds, guidelines, surrogate end points, acceptable risk levels, consensus documents," to produce "regulatory facts" (Eyal 2019a) about uncertain objects.

Stressing these activities, as Irwin et al. suggest we do, makes sense because they manifestly expanded and became institutionalized and, increasingly, standardized during the 1980s and 1990s. In both North America and Europe, mandatory testing and evaluation have come to apply to a wider range of products and industrial technologies. Science is at the heart of what has emerged as "approval regulation" (Carpenter 2010), or "gate-keeping" (Faulkner 2017), "that form of regulation in which the state must confer particular rights upon a producer or a consumer for an economic transaction to take place, where the rights are conferred at the discretion of the state and only upon the completion of a submission process in which the producer may test the product" (Carpenter 2010a). The premarket regulation of technologies has expanded, in both breadth and depth, since the advent of social regulation laws in the 1970s in the United States. Since the first half of the 1980s, more laws have been adopted that include the mandatory testing of technologies, first in the United States and then in the European Union (Vogel 2003, 2012). The capacity to anticipate or predict the effects of technologies ahead of their generalized use or consumption has legitimized the imposition of such ex ante controls for many kinds of products, from medicines, additives, and pesticides (first) to medical devices, pediatric medicines, vaccines, and nearly every new technology that has appeared in the interval—all biotechnology-related products, notably, but nanotechnologies (Laurent 2017; Sainz et al. 2016) or products of synthetic biology (Joly 2016), too.

One will not find the phrase "regulatory science" in such areas as automotive regulation, aviation or financial regulation. However, one can approach the evaluation of these technologies, where it exists, precisely from the perspective of this science-based premarket product testing (Demortain 2008). Recent controversies about the regulation of diesel engines or the introduction of new aviation technologies (Downer 2017) indicate that regulatory science expands as an instrument for governing industries and markets from a distance.[2] More regulatory agencies have been set up, and their staff sizes have grown, notably, there are more people who review regulatory studies and develop options for regulatory standards and rules. Regulatory agencies in the United States and elsewhere, notably in the European Union, have strengthened their ties to and collaborations with research institutions, whose involvement in risk assessment, technology assessment, risk-benefit product assessment and the likes, have also slowly increased.

As the regulation of pharmaceuticals and chemicals has become internationalized, institutions have been established to evaluate product safety. More documents have been written, describing what tests, scientific data, and interpretations are required to let products circulate. Guidelines have been established nationally and internationally, too. More and more frequently, the codification of product evaluation has taken place in international fora, such as the Organisation for Economic Cooperation and Development (OECD) for chemicals and the International Conference on Harmonization (ICH) for pharmaceuticals. Transnational communities of product-evaluation specialists, who in many ways are the owners of regulatory science, have emerged, which forge the standards of regulatory science and lend it its objectivity (Cambrosio et al. 2006; Demortain 2013). Regulatory science, as first, the science of regulators and then as an intermediary branch of science consisting of locally negotiated proofs of risk, has increasingly started to resemble a demarcated, potentially universal body of knowledge, a sort of standard way of knowing products and their risks, that performs the potential public administrative acts applying to these products (Gaudillière and Hess 2012). Beyond purely regulatory areas, in climate science or biodiversity policies, we see a similar phenomenon at play: cadres or colleges of scientists, in close connection with national or transnational authorities in these areas, negotiate and protect the epistemic norms based on which problems are measured and framed. In the process, regulatory sciences solidify, and the groups of experts in question reinforce their expertise and authority, being the guards of international regulatory epistemologies (Winickoff and Bushey, 2010).

Industry Strategies and Regulatory Capture through Science

Now that we have reached the point in the present discussion where regulatory science has actually become the science of regulating products and their risks, we can now move on to underline new controversies about the scientists who participate in public regulatory processes. Those controversies are less about the responsibility and morality of experts to judge the benefits and risks of technologies, their relationships with institutions, and the decision-making actors. They center on the control of knowledge standards and scientists' commitments and interest in elaborating them. Social scientific research has grown increasingly critical on this question, underlining the structural influence of industry organizations on the epistemic content of regulatory science.

John Abraham (1994, 1995) has consistently looked at the effects of industrial involvement on the science that is used in pharmaceutical regulation. Although he initially did not use the notion of regulatory science, he did explore the negotiations surrounding testing methods and standards. He has shown how the "production of risk assessments by industrial scientists and the concomitant processes of negotiation between scientists in government and industry" leads to a form of bias (i.e., inconsistency with commonly accepted standards of communication and reason) that is ultimately favorable to companies' interests. International standards negotiated by industries evince a worrying technical trajectory—namely, the loosening of testing requirements— that is concealed in a "discourse of technological innovation and scientific progress" (Abraham and Reed

2001, 2002). He suggests that "commercial and corporatist interests" bias the risk assessment of medicines by industrial or government institutions (Abraham 1994), and that the regulatory authority depends on the industry it regulates as the nearly sole or monopolistic source of knowledge about its products. The toxicity testing of medicines has been investigated to demonstrate that firms and their scientific representatives dominate in the international negotiations over the protocols and parameters of these tests, and notably, their duration (Abraham 1993; Abraham and Reed 2002; Abraham and Ballinger 2012a, 2012b). The current transformation of the hierarchy of evidence in pharmaceuticals assessments, and the changes affecting the gold standard randomized clinical trial, evinces for some analysts the same kind of industry influence (Abraham 2007; Carpenter 2012 Roseman 2019).

Several recent controversies surrounding the regulation of chemicals and pesticides help to illustrate the point. In the past few years, the science that was used to determine product safety became the subject of heated public debates when various regulators, academic groups, industries, agriculture groups, and environmental activists disputed the safety and regulatory status of the best-selling herbicide worldwide, which contains the active substance glyphosate. The International Agency for Research on Cancer (IARC) disturbed an otherwise smooth reauthorization process of the substance in the European Union by classifying it as a probable carcinogen based on a review of the research on its carcinogenic potential. The classification triggered further review by multiple other regulatory agencies, which selected, reviewed, and interpreted the results of sometimes different sets of studies, or applied different criteria of plausibility and evidence to them.

After the German Federal Institute for Risk Assessment (Bundesinstitut für Risikobewertung, BfR) and, later, the European Food Safety Authority (EFSA) and the European Chemicals Agency (ECHA) did not confirm the IARC classification, various questions emerged, notably, concerning what value to assign human studies—given more weight by the IARC people—but also how much weight to give undisclosed toxicity studies performed or requested by the industry. The IARC did not consider the industry studies in making its determination, whereas the BfR and the European agencies treated them as essential resources to establish the absence of hazard of glyphosate. Journalistic investigations later revealed that the BfR and EFSA had subjected the industry studies to a very low degree of scrutiny, and that this was also true for the data submitted to them by the industrial applicants, the Glyphosate Task Force. Journalists and public integrity groups revealed that the BfR had simply copied and pasted a large amount of the text from industry documents (Neslen 2019; Pigeon 2019) in its own report. The heads of BfR and EFSA both denied irreflexive borrowing and said that if text had been copied, it was because, after verifying the data and claims, their experts were in agreement with the text provided. However, the public perception, by and large, was that there was undue alignment on the part of the public experts with industry-provided science, and that by leaving out the data in the human studies documenting the total exposure of populations to the pesticide, the regulatory agencies had not considered as broad a knowledge base as they should have (Arcuri and Hendlin 2019).

This dispute resonated with others that also suggest too close an alignment between regulatory agency processes and industry objectives. The regulation of chemical products, particularly with respect to their endocrine-disrupting properties, has been the subject of similar disputes concerning the alignment of the criteria regulatory agencies apply when determining which scientific studies of endocrine-disruptors are relevant to demonstrating the risk or absence of risk with what the chemical industry produces or funds (Myers et al. 2009a, 2009b; Vogel 2013). In the past decade, there have also been disputes concerning the safety of genetically modified organisms—and the trust placed in short-term animal studies to establish their risks (Levidow 2007; Demortain 2013) and about the protocols used in testing pesticides (Foucart 2014). There has also been concern about nutritional products and verifying the validity of health claims (Hendrickx 2013; Todt and Lujan 2017) and about food additives (Burgess 2013; Coudray 2017; Millstone and Dawson 2019).

There seems to be a common pattern across these various regulatory areas: the epistemic standards governing the selection of knowledge used in making regulatory decisions favor studies performed or funded by the regulated industries; it is as if they have taken control of the standards of proof of risks and of the absence of risk, often by populating the arenas in which these standards take shape—international ones in particular, as mentioned above. Industry presence seems particularly strong here, too, as the case of the International Life Science Institute—an industry-funded platform for shaping risk-and-benefit product-assessment standards—illustrates (Demortain 2011; Sacks et al. 2018; Steele et al. 2019; Hessari et al. 2019).

These investigations all point to the observation that, as the production of regulatory science becomes the province of the industry, what gets admitted as the right or best regulatory science incorporates only those methods, data, and paradigms that minimize risks. Tests find only the effects that they are designed to reveal. If one finds only minimal effects, then more uncertain, but possibly vast, risks can be systematically overlooked in evaluations of technologies. The pattern seems clear: regulated industries have taken control over the standards applied in product testing and evaluation, and thus they control the production of regulatory science. This has led to an epistemological reduction of this knowledge to a set of agreed-upon forms and criteria, making it more difficult to introduce alternative, plural forms of knowledge into the reservoir of information that regulators consider. In the frequently used terminology, a seemingly conservative *regulatory science* emerged that increasingly appears to be divorced from research science and constitutes a narrow knowledge base in which to root regulatory decisions.

In recent years, social scientists and historians have argued that industry control over regulatory science derives from industry's deployment of strategies directed at science and its political economy (Tyfield et al. 2017). From the beginning, regulatory science was the target of explicit political strategies by corporations. The legitimacy of the wave of new regulatory laws and agencies established in the 1960s and 1970s to protect consumers and workers from health and environmental risks had been ensured by the actions of a coalition of consumer advocates in Congress, civic-issue entrepreneurs like Ralph Nader, organized labor, and advocacy journalists (Wilson 1980; Derthick and

Quirk 1982). But by the end of the 1970s, during the Jimmy Carter presidency, social regulation was being met with political resistance and a powerful opposition movement backed by the affected industries in the form of dedicated think-tanks and front organizations. Both political parties in the United States soon heeded the message. As early as 1977, a movement for regulatory reform took shape under Carter that argued forcefully for regulatory reasonableness and moderate regulatory intervention, to be achieved by instituting a more systematic cost-benefit and regulatory analysis (Sabin 2016; Berman 2017, 2022; Demortain 2020). This movement grew stronger, and under the Reagan administration became one of outright deregulation and regulatory "relief." Science was at the heart of this effort. Industry believed that calculating the risks, costs, and benefits of regulatory rules and standards—two early incarnations of regulatory science—could result in more balanced decisions and less intervention, and would preserve market freedom. Specifically, it would help to block overtly precautionary, restrictive standards. At the very least, by revealing gaps in the data and underscoring the need for further research, it would help diffuse the threat of immediate regulatory intervention. Industry groups have invested huge amounts of money to defend their methods of risk assessment, of chemicals, for instance, and created various organizations and groups to lobby for the use of more predictive, uncertainty-reducing methods—creating what Wagner terms a "science charade"—and forcing regulatory agencies to answer questions scientifically that are effectively impossible to answer in scientific terms (Wagner 1995).

In the past decade, students of agnotology have shed light on those strategies (McGoey 2016). The chemical industry has taken steps to shape the science on which regulatory agencies base their decisions in ways that favor industry interests over the pursuit of more ambitious environmental or public-health protection goals (McGarity and Wagner 2008). The industry push to base regulatory decisions on sound science—when science cannot provide the all the answers to regulatory risk problem—is a strategy to create intractable problems for the regulatory agencies or, to use Wagner's (1995) term, a charade. Emphasizing or manufacturing uncertainties is a second industry strategy. Much of what industries do to try to shape science is to argue that substantial uncertainty remains, and that in the face of such uncertainties no decisions should be made (Michaels 2006, 2008; Freudenburg, Gramling, and Davidson 2008). The invocation of uncertainty is instrumental to regulated companies' efforts to slow down, block, or delegitimize public regulatory intervention.

Industry's capacity to credibly establish uncertainty, and therefore to assert that more scientific research is needed to achieve robust decisions, comes from its multiple links with scientific communities and institutions. Without these relationships, industries would simply not have the credibility to say what is knowledge, what is nonknowledge, and what research should or should not be done. McGarity and Wagner (2008) drew up a list of industry tactics with respect to scientific research that demonstrates the capacity to capture, systemically as it were, scientific research by controlling the channels of its diffusion into public spaces and administrations. Industries hire academics with expertise in a field to argue the existence of these uncertainties in journal articles, on expert committees, or at public congressional hearings. They also hire consultancies specializing in expertise in biochemistry, toxicology, or risk assessment whose scientists have experience in product regulation (and have often worked in regulatory agencies themselves) and develop science-based strategies to counter any efforts to regulate their production. Companies avoid the publication of their studies containing negative results, by invoking intellectual property rights to protect their "regulatory data" and manipulate the interpretation of studies by presenting test results selectively (McGoey and Jackson 2009); they use "rented white coats" to "ghost-write" academic articles for publication (Sismondo 2007, 2018; Heath 2016). They also shape public research by extensively funding research teams that are central in the field (Krimsky 2004; Serodio et al. 2018); they fund counter studies performed by cherry-picked scientists; they control the scientific terms of the public controversies surrounding their products through public relations campaigns using experts to convey supportive messages (Rampton and Sauber 2002); they populate scientific advisory committees with scientists who are likely to moderate attacks on their products and their risks (Michaels 2008; McGarity and Wagner 2008).

The result of these strategies is that many of the scientists governmental bodies employ or consulted with about technologies and their risks have been taken part in industrial collaborations; and they may have developed sympathy with the industry goal of protecting innovation and minimizing data and claims about the risks. This lack of cognitive independence translates into the already mentioned search for higher levels of evidence and the call to apply the standards of evidence that are forged in the circles that industries dominate. Cognitive regulatory capture (Kwak 2014) ensues when regulatory agencies fail to detect industry-sponsored research (Michaels and Wagner 2003) and do not realize that the knowledge they invoke in their (non)decisions was developed in this particular space, and not sufficiently confronted with the knowledge produced outside the industries and university-industry collaborations. Expertise, because it is shaped and produced by the regulated industries, makes the regulator dependent on the industry it regulates (Slayton and Clark-Ginsberg 2018).

Discussing Capture

This broad evolution of the industrialization of regulatory science, and industries' control of the knowledge that is used to regulate them, begs us to revise the kinds of questions we ask about regulatory science and about the scientists who get involved in regulatory standard-setting. This new context sheds a totally different light on the conditions under which scientific experts and scientific advisers operate and defend their science and authority. The question has become precisely what Irwin et al.'s (1997) definition of regulatory science, as a set of activities in large part carried out industrial settings, gets us to look at: what are the relationships, and what is the balance of power, between and among the actors and the sites where product testing and risk calculations take place. Regulatory science and the work of scientific experts who are involved in product regulation or risk regulation cannot be abstracted from the economy that directs the production of knowledge, including the knowledge that is used to review products and technologies. Both are necessarily influenced by the ideologies, structures of interests, and geographies that sustain that economy (Nowotny et al. 2005; Mirowksi and Plewhe 2009; Lave et al. 2010). The challenge of enacting expertise has thus become one of maintaining authority and objectivity in a changing political economy characterized by closer, and constant, relationships with private interests.

For all we have discovered about the manufacturing of doubt and uncertainty, the kind of political economy perspective that this uses has disadvantages. First, stressing the interests, resources, and structures that govern the production of regulatory science ignores the fact that no knowledge is definitively authoritative in this area, and that any effort to legitimize a policy through a specific set of information or scientific claims will cause this information and claims to be attacked—controversy is a near-default condition here.

Second, there exists no knowledge monolith of regulatory science that will systematically produce the same industry-favorable marketing decisions and relaxed safety standards. Although regulatory science is in important ways framed by epistemic standards, the scientists who review and interpret test results and assemble other information to produce overall product risk and benefit assessments for regulators, do not mechanically draw their conclusions from numbers. Regulatory science remains, at least in part, an open and undetermined practice, making use of facts and truths negotiated in local interactions—precisely as the first generation of STS work on regulatory science taught us (see above, section "Regulatory Science: Producing Knowledge in a Space of Politics and Disputes")—and that should not be lost by adopting a more structuralist view about industry weight. As a toxicologist reviewing applications to market genetically modified plants in Europe put it, the scientists advising the regulators don't simply rubber-stamp the applicant companies' studies. Regulatory agencies and the scientists they work with sometimes succeed in casting doubt on the quality of evidence, study results, a test protocol, or the overall value of the method being applied. In a sense, the narrative of industry capture of regulatory science omits the lessons of the first generation of social scientific work on regulatory science, reviewed in the first part of this chapter: it is an area of scientific practice that is full of uncertainties, precluded by conflicts, in which causal claims and methods never fully obtain validation. In Wynne's (1984) terms, it is a field with no clear identity, confusing criteria of scientific epistemology, and a marked incapacity to attain "the mores, authority and independence of conventional science" (3). This structural uncertainty may work against the interest of industries, for it means an incapacity to prove the hazardousness of their technologies.

Third, a structural political economy argument may also risk neglecting the diversity of outcomes in regulatory science controversies, and the variations in the work and positions adopted by the scientific experts (Brint 1990). Here, a connection may be made with the Carpenter and Moss's (2014) critique of capture theory, in particular, their assessment of an overdiagnosis of capture, and an overtly dichotomous, all-or-nothing view of capture, that reflects the opposition, in the United States at least, between equally caricatural public interest and capture theories (Carpenter 2010). It is difficult, given the currently available historical and empirical reservoir of research on regulatory science controversies, to argue that industry always wins, and that the regulatory-scientific expertise articulated by scientists is necessarily influenced by industrial interests. For one thing, this diagnosis is limited because it is based on an integrated notion of "industry" and "interest." Analyzing knowledge processes and controversies involves reinterpreting these notions to account for the fact that interests are diverse, and that this diversity is best understood if we consider interests in a more processual fashion, as materializing in the process of forming identities and objectives in a given set of relationships between an actor, its allies, and its enemies (Cambrosio et al. 1991).

A Reinterpretation: Regulatory Knowledge and its Ecology

What the political economy of science teaches us, however, is that the source of regulatory knowledge, the ways in which it is produced and the norms that are applied in its production, matter much more than they used to.

The implication of these changes, which occur upstream from regulatory agencies, so to speak, is that one should be able to understand how regulatory agencies and their experts are linked to these producers of regulatory knowledge and the fields in which they evolve. The term *regulatory knowledge* is used to avoid the suggestion that there is one fixed, validated science that would serve the interests of the various actors. Regulatory knowledge is a complex and evolving assemblage of techniques and activities. It is not easily reducible to one "science," and a definitive set of methodologies, theories, and claims, or to an epistemic culture. What is more, speaking of a "science" only encourages the confusing ownership claims to this kind of knowledge made by various academic and interest groups to win what have come to be described as "regulatory science wars" (Wagner et al. 2018) and establish themselves as the definitive provider of truth and evidence in particular regulatory arenas. Regulatory knowledge (Demortain 2017) opens our gaze to the ensemble of experiences, information, data, simulations— knowledge claims in general—that constitute something as an object of regulation and qualify it for regulatory intervention. Taking inspiration from both Abbott and Bourdieu, and their theorizing of social environments and interactions (Bourdieu 1976; Abbott 2005; Martin 2003; Liu and Emirbayer 2016), one can construe regulatory knowledge as a production stemming from four adjacent and mutually influencing fields.

The first field is that of the regulatory agencies, their scientists, and their laboratories— the field of the administrative state, emphasized at the beginning of the chapter, on which I do not expand further here. The second, on which I will comment further, is the academic field. Despite the frequent rhetorical rejections of regulatory science as an inferior, box-ticking science one finds there, it remains true that many of the public laboratories doing fundamental research do study regulated substances and products and diffuse knowledge about them, potentially fueling the base of regulatory knowledge. The need for regulatory knowledge means that, though the world of fundamental research in biology and other disciplines has long looked at regulatory science with contempt, regulatory science is increasingly recognized as an area that is worthy of investment. Regulatory agencies and the regulated industries agree that there is a shortage of people trained in these exercises (National Academies of Sciences, Engineering, and Medicine 2016). In 2011, this led the US Food & Drug Administration to develop a strategic plan to advance regulatory science (FDA 2011), which resulted in the funding of dedicated academic centers, for example, at the University of California, Berkeley and Harvard (Hamburg 2011). Scholars in the concerned disciplines have developed dedicated research programs and centers. An online academic journal has been created that is entirely dedicated to the advancement of the "emerging" regulatory science and to the "application of science to the regulatory process" (Hermann 2013, I; Moghissi et al. 2014); and several other important academic journals in pharmaceutical sciences now include the concerns of regulatory science and scientific evidence in regulatory standard setting within their scope (e.g., Frontiers in Medicine; see Leufkens 2019). The push by toxicologists for alternative to animal testing has been a driver of innovation in regulatory science and led to the development of more complex in vitro and in silico methods. Master programs, teaching centers, curricula, and LinkedIn groups have been set up.

This professionalization has meant that the term *regulatory science* now refers to more than risk assessment, economic analysis of regulatory decisions, and legal analysis, as in the days when Schmandt was writing about it. Across the varieties of technologies whose benefits and risks are regulated, one will find mention of in vitro or in vivo toxicity testing, clinical evaluation, methods for the engineering of product quality and safety, and product stewardship. Regulatory science now encompasses a broader range of scientific disciplines. The main evolution since the 1980s has been that not only are policy sciences involved but, depending on the area, the medical, biological, environmental, and engineering sciences are also mobilized. Inseparable from this growth is a belief that science may now provide answers more accurately than it used to. The growth of regulatory science, in other words, is fully intertwined with the evidence-based policy movement and the assumption—or expectation—that science now provides firm answers to the questions about the quality, safety, and benefits of products developed for consumers and patients (Dance 2013). If risk scientists in the 1980s refrained from saying that risk assessment was a *science*, the term is now widely accepted.

A third field has taken shape and is—perhaps—the main producer of regulatory science today, which we may call the *industrial field of regulatory knowledge*. It is a heterogeneous one, comprising industry product development and production, but also the auxiliary testing industry. Probably the most striking development that has been seen since the first characterization of regulatory science in the 1990s concerns regulated industry itself. From the standpoint of the activities that constitute it, regulatory science seems to originate, in great part, from the regulated industries themselves: the firms producing the technology or products being regulated, and the parts of them that are dedicated to developing, testing, measuring, and evaluating their own products according to criteria that are defined in the law or hypotheses that they set for themselves. Regulatory science has industrialized in the sense that industries now have a major stake in it and it is produced within the sphere of private, industrial research and development efforts.

Agrochemical and pharmaceutical firms have large regulatory affairs departments that monitor the development of rules and requirements defined by regulatory authorities, or engage with authorities to discuss the concepts, methodologies, and criteria of regulatory evaluations of products. Their R&D departments perform various product tests that are mandated, formally or informally, by the regulatory agencies. Oftentimes, these tests are organized in various sequences or stages that are directly applied inside companies to structure the development of their product and define the role of the various teams involved. Testing is also increasingly performed by firms in what is a dedicated auxiliary industry. The requirements for testing products, generating technical information about technologies, conducting scientific studies to capture the uncertainties associated with a product before regulatory decisions about it are made is have led to the establishment of many organizations that do this work, including profit-making organizations. This industry includes testing laboratories (specialized scientific service organizations that perform tests for the manufacturing industry, estimated to be a several-billion-euro market annually), regulatory consulting companies (consultancies dedicated to handling regulatory requirements for regulated industries), and the various companies that manufacture and sell the equipment used in testing (also a large, highly concentrated, transnational industry that includes firms that produce biological materials, raise rats for laboratory experiments, or design computational modeling and environmental information-management software). For pharmaceuticals, these contract research organizations represent a several-billion-dollar market, either in toxicity testing or clinical testing—likewise, for other regulated products such as certain categories of foods or chemicals. Industry's expanded investment in regulatory science follows from the growing number of laws and rules that mandate the performance of studies, materializing in the allegedly growing costs of developing the full set of studies and tests required to put a chemical or medicine on the market (Breslau 1997).

The fourth field is that of social movements—that is, of public mobilization around issues of environmental protection and health and consumer safety. This knowledge, to be sure, is different from that found in the other three fields. It is often described as local, embodied, experiential, or communal. But this field counts dozens of organizations in each country, many of which also produce information about products and safety. They have developed scientific expertise and, broadly speaking, have become more technically sophisticated in their modes of action and discourse. The scientization of social movements is something that Ulrich Beck (1992) observed early on. This scientization, the capacity of these movements to engage with expert knowledge and the calculation of risk—to criticize it and re-emphasize the uncertainty—is integral to the rise of a risk society. Research has shown that these organizations generate a large amount of information through processes of inquiry and investigation of health and safety issues. They sometimes test products themselves. They read and review the scientific knowledge produced by others, rearticulating it in their own terms and circulating it to the institutional field. They build alliances with researchers, funding them or helping to promote the findings when they align with their own objectives.[3] In doing so, they manage to influence the standards of science that are applied in product testing, or at the very least, they succeed in opening debates about these standards, their epistemic content and limitations, the risks they document, and those that they may overlook (Arancibia 2016; Brown, Morello-Frosch, and Zavestoski 2011; Brown and Zavestoski 2004; Epstein 1996 Hess 2005; Leach and Scoones 2007).

Extending the language of "fields" and using Andrew Abbot's linked ecologies as inspiration (Abbott 2005),[4] one can say that regulatory knowledge—comprising information, experiences, and data that can potentially inform regulatory standards—is produced in diverse environments, and not just by the regulated industry or in dedicated parts of academia. And so, beyond the questions of interpretation and of translating knowledge into decisions that occupied many of the authors who originally studied regulatory science, the diverse ways in which regulatory knowledge is produced matter. Thinking about this diversity of knowledge production and the use of regulatory knowledge helps in analyzing at least two important dimensions of the controversies briefly recounted here, which the political economy perspective has difficulty identifying.

The first is the interaction between and among fields, and the way the dynamics in one field of knowledge influences the dynamics in the others—that is, how the logics of what counts as science in one field influences the others. In this respect, several key phenomena should be highlighted. First, industry has invested in the production of regulatory knowledge, and developed strategies for doing so, in response to what was happening in the field of regulation itself, and the rise of ex ante, test-based regulation of products and technologies. Second, the fields of industry and academia have gotten closer in the past decades, as researchers who stress the pervasive commercialization and privatization of science have argued (Lave et al. 2010; Mirovski and Sent 2008). Research on biomedical research contract organizations has shown that they are more than a side business that has captured a fraction of the work university-based research used to perform; they represent an entirely new regime of scientific research, a commercialized one, which will colonize more areas than just pharmaceutical testing (Krimsky 2004; Mirovski and Van Horn 2005; Jonvallen et al. 2011). The fields of industry and academia are tied to each other by denser links, sharing a common logic of knowledge production —though this convergence should be subjected to much inquiry and "pertinent qualifications" (Shapin 2008). The literature on university- and industry-research relationships is useful here. The relationships between universities and industries have an effect on the norms and values defended by scientists, as well as on their practices, including their views on the public release of data, materials, and publications. The research indicates that, overall, there remain important differences between academic and industrial scientists—for instance, concerning the use of legal protection mechanisms such as patents—but that collaborations between the two seem to influence academic scientists to embrace more secretive attitudes (Campbell et al.

2002; Walsh & Hong 2003; Evans 2010). In many ways, any conflicts of interest stem from the fact that science-based industries provide large numbers of jobs and research contracts, which is particularly important at a time when government funding of research and teaching is decreasing.[5] The significance of this should be compared with another factor that seems to play a large role in the reluctance of public scientists to leave their laboratories and join expert committees or regulatory agencies themselves: the intensification of professional competition in the academic field and the levels of investment needed to stay competitive throughout a career, lead university-based scientists to consider expert work a distraction and unbeneficial use of their time.[6]

But one should also consider how academia and social movements are linked to each other, and how these links have supported the scientization of the latter and the possibility of criticizing industrial standards of risk and technology assessment (Pandey and Sharma 2019). The knowledge embedded in social movements and citizens groups is frequently developed with the help of scientists, and it can, indeed, become formal, modeled, and circulate outside the social movement itself. And the interactions between scientists or engineers and activists can generate new information and knowledge (e.g., Tesh 2000; Allen 2003; Ottinger and Cohen 2011). Frickel et al.'s (2015) study of the environmental justice movement in the United States showed that there are networks of scientists who traverse the boundaries of activism and professional scientific research. But in any case, there is greater reliance on expertise in social movements and activism, just as there are demands for and the utilization of scientists in industry and in regulation. Whether the knowledge about the environment and the effects of technologies on the environment and health that is produced within the perimeters of social movements travels to mingle with information produced in other fields depends on the mobility of the experts themselves. There is no definitive data on the transmission of this knowledge from the field of activism to other fields, notably regulation, chiefly because the expert activists may themselves be in conflict and thus fail to package and carry the knowledge elsewhere. For Lave (2012), though, "citizen scientists (of the activist persuasion) are now accorded a place at the table in many regulatory decisions" (29), and the forms of knowledge which they carry and circulate enter into dialogue or confrontation with other, industrial, academic of expert forms, to concurrently shape regulatory knowledge (Suryanarayanan and Kleinman 2013).

The second main benefit of an ecological perspective is that it helps in analyzing the full complexity of the environment in which the knowledge that reaches regulatory agencies is produced, most importantly, the various networks of experts though which this knowledge travels (Eyal 2013). The ecological perspective helps to formalize and take into account the fact that the production of regulatory knowledge extends across diverse fields and circulates through networks of scientists that cut across them—of which the regulatory scientist advising an agency is the last fetter. Regulatory science, or validated regulatory knowledge, forms at the interface of these fields via networks of people who are active in their fields of origin—and playing the game in these fields, for example, as academics—but who move beyond their field of origin to establish relationships with people active in other fields. These cross-field dynamics need to be better explored to understand how networks of producers of regulatory knowledge take form, what positions they occupy in each field and, consequently, what sort of episte-mology and way-of-knowing technologies and risks they are most likely to apply. The forms of regulatory knowledge produced in the various fields co-evolve. The ecological perspective helps recognize this, and compensate for the tendency to study industrial knowledge, academic knowledge, citizen science or expertise separately. Indeed, it is striking that these are the objects of separate literatures, which hardly ever come to di-alogue, to be able to capture how various producers and forms of knowledge change in relation to one another.

Such a perspective leads us to think about the implications of the growing interde-pendence of agencies and knowledge industries for researchers acting as scientific advisers to regulatory institutions. In other words, it helps us address what it is to be an expert, and what kind of epistemologies of technologies and risks are applied. An expert—in this case, the scientist who works for or advises a regulatory agency—is a scientist positioned in various fields simultaneously. Existing research on the multi-positioning of experts and on how expert authority derives from the occupation of cer-tain positions in interdependent fields lend credit to this perspective (Medvetz 2012; Demortain 2011).

Different experts or networks of experts occupy suites of positions in the variegated fields that constitute the environment in which regulatory knowledge is produced and regulatory acts are negotiated. Scientific experts forge an interpretation of the know-ledge emerging from these fields, in contact with regulatory agencies. Scientific advisers, in the first instance, are people who cumulate positions in the field of research and in the field of regulatory agencies. The conflict-of-interest question arises from the fact that these scientists, in turn, though they are primarily located in the academic field—positioned in a public university and competing for recognition—collaborate regularly and share knowledge with actors in the industrial field or social movements. Their ex-perience of products and risks, and their perspective on these risks and their regulation, may be informed, to a significant degree, by these collaborations. The norms of know-ledge applied in each field also vary, and there may be alignment or misalignment be-tween them. Each field may be concentrated on different objects of knowledge, but they will sometimes be concerned with the same things.

CONCLUSION

An ecological perspective helps us elaborate answers for the problems with which this chapter began. It shows that people who are considered competent in or expert at product evaluation—or at evaluating studies of a product—and credible experts, at that, are necessarily tied to various fields of knowledge through which they have forged knowledge capacities. This chapter finally leads us to the suggestion that expertise is defined by the fundamentally political process (a) of managing the ties through which the credibility of knowledge is forged, which is a dual process of creating such ties and of erasing traces of them, to both produce and construct the objectivity of knowledge; (b) of being involved, learning in the sites where learning is possible; and (c) of forging a view from nowhere, eliminating the traces of this situatedness so that the knowledge can be carried and applied to new situations. Appearing expert, authoritative, objective involves managing those interdependencies and the visibility of the ties: reinstituting boundaries that the interdependencies on which the production and validation of knowledge rest negate.

This ecological view incorporates scientists' variegated positions in the politics of regulation and defines rules and modes of responsibility. Indeed, accusations of capture focus on certain interdependencies and ties—those between public scientists and industries—without contextualizing them. And they overtly focus on the moment of creation of those ties, and dependencies, overlooking this other movement by which a scientist becomes an expert, that of the institution of distance.

The influence of these ecological conditions on scientists' conduct of regulatory studies and on their participation in advising governmental bodies on science, should at least be conceptualized, and possibly measured, because they vary a great deal. The proportion of scientists affected by these collaborations, and the diversity of ways in which they are affected, remains unknown (Perkmann et al. 2013). It should be included in the reflection about what to do, as well. Institutional responses are already being formed in response to the question of the responsibility of publicly engaged scientists, working with the knowledge that emerges from various fields of regulatory knowledge, and about what they, as expert advisers, do toward industry strategies towards regulatory science, as well as toward the necessarily limited capacity to foresee and anticipate risks. One response consists in codifying what experts' independence means and what situations represent conflicts of interest. Such codification is informed by a formal and material sense of independence, one that is actually difficult to establish and prove. Another, softer institutional response takes the form of frameworks of "responsible research and innovation" (Stilgoe et al. 2013). Through this notion, another figure of the expert takes shape, one that proactively asks "what if" questions; constructs broader imaginaries to subvert or pluralize the promissory discourses surrounding products and to anticipate—meaning imagine, not just predict—risks (Barben et al. 2008). Scientists could sustain the collective examination of concerns and exploration of policy possibilities, instead of taking part in the foreclosure of decisions.

Both movements are limited, however, by the conception of individual responsibility they evince—as if everything hinged on individual morality and relationships of single individuals. The same goes for a whole strand of research on the production of ignorance and on capture that has a decidedly individualistic perspective, emphasizing the wrongdoings and interests of one or another person, whose representativeness remains unclear. In a sense, these responses put the responsibility for correcting the problems of an ecology of knowledge production on the shoulders of individual experts, as if the expert were an abstract entity rather than a social actor holding a position and drawing knowledge from this environment. Metaphorically, the notion of ecology invites us to think about the diversity of knowledge and of scientists taking part in the production and use of science for regulatory purposes. But the notion also crystallizes some of the problems and stakes behind institutional and organizational arrangements for science policy—namely, the capacity to maintain this diversity, while preserving the capacity to decide.

Notes

1. Funtowicz and Ravetz (1993) later suggested that "post-normal science" would be a better label because Weinberg's "trans-science" implied that with enough time and resources, science could eventually solve uncertain issues.
2. One should add: Regulatory science includes not only the ex ante testing of products, but also any information about the product and its properties generated by users, prescribers, and sellers—which one can describe as *monitoring*. This is the cornerstone of what some have called "regulation by information" (Kleindorfer and Orts 1998; Sunstein 1999; Karkkainen 2001), a regime that attempts "to change behavior indirectly, either by changing the structure of incentives of the different policy actors, or by supplying the same actors with suitable information" (Majone 1997, 265). Regulation by information has translated into product-labeling laws and regulations that mandate the computation and disclosure of various types of indicators, from accident rates to toxic chemical emissions, mainly by the regulated companies (Coglianese and Lazer 2003) in the nuclear industry, the consumer products industry, as well as the pharmaceutical, chemical, and pesticide industries.
3. A potential fifth field is that of the media and journalistic coverage of product- and risk-regulation issues and regulatory and judiciary decisions and the related controversies among the scientific groups and experts involved. The extent to which the journalistic field may qualify as a field of knowledge production and use is debatable. But its interaction with other fields, particularly as knowledge production becomes public, should nonetheless be conceptualized and accounted for in empirical studies.
4. With this term, Abbott places the focus on the expansion of professions in adjacent potential spaces of professional practice. Abbott's approach has already been applied to an great variety of domains, from financial auditing (Mennicken 2010) to the discipline of economics (Fourcade and Khurana 2013), by promoters of randomized clinical trials in development policies (Souza Leão and Eyal 2019).
5. Evans (2010) notes: "Scientists in industry, however, now publish some of the most highly cited articles in the biological sciences. Moreover, with the recent slowdown in government funding and the surge of science-based industries, firms furnish less constrained careers and the academy more."
6. A recent survey indicates that, even in public research institutes with a scientific-advice culture (a high degree of participation by scientists in meta-analyses for governmental bodies, frequent involvement in expert committees, strong pressure to seek funding through the research programs of regulatory bodies), the pressure to publish leads scientists to consider expert advisory activities to be too time-consuming and costly. We need to know this more systematically, comparatively also, across disciplines, research fields or industries, and countries or regions.

REFERENCES

Abraham, John, and Rachel Ballinger. 2012a. "Science, Politics, and Health in the Brave New World of Pharmaceutical Carcinogenic Risk Assessment: Technical Progress or Cycle of Regulatory Capture?" *Social Science & Medicine* (1982) 75(8):1433–1440. Doi: 10.1016/j.socscimed.2012.04.043.

Abraham, John, and Rachel Ballinger. 2012b. "The Neoliberal Regulatory State, Industry Interests, and the Ideological Penetration of Scientific Knowledge Deconstructing the Redefinition of Carcinogens in Pharmaceuticals." *Science, Technology, & Human Values* 37 (5): 443–477.

Abraham, John, and Tim Reed. 2001. "Trading Risks for Markets: The International Harmonisation of Pharmaceuticals Regulation." *Health, Risk & Society* 3 (1): 113–128.

Abraham, John, and Tim Reed. 2002. "Progress, Innovation and Regulatory Science in Drug Development. The Politics of International Standard-Setting." *Social Studies of Science* 32 (3): 337–369.

Abraham, John. 2007. "Drug Trials and Evidence Bases in International Regulatory Context." *BioSocieties* 2 (1): 41–56.

Abraham, John. 1993. "Scientific Standards and Institutional Interests: Carcinogenic Risk Assessment of Benoxaprofen in the UK and US." *Social Studies of Science* 23 (3): 387–444.

Abraham, John. 1994. "Distributing the Benefit of the Doubt: Scientists, Regulators, and Drug Safety." *Science, Technology, & Human Values* 19, no. 4 (Autumn): 493–522.

Abraham, John. 1995. *Science, Politics and the Pharmaceutical Industry: Controversy and Bias in Drug Regulation.* London: UCL Press.

Allen, Barbara L. 2003. *Uneasy Alchemy: Citizens and Experts in Louisiana's Chemical Corridor Disputes.* Cambridge, MA: MIT Press.

Arancibia, Florencia. 2016. "Regulatory Science and Social Movements: The Trial Against the Use of Pesticides in Argentina". *Theory in Action* 9(4):1–21.

Arcuri, Alessandra, and Yogi Hale Hendlin. 2019. "The Chemical Anthropocene: Glyphosate as a Case Study of Pesticide Exposures." SSRN Scholarly Paper. ID 3413272. Rochester, NY: Social Science Research Network.

Ashford, Nicholas. 1984. "Advisory Committees in OSHA and EPA: Their Use in Regulatory Decision-Making." *Science, Technology & Human Values* 9 (1): 72–82.

Barben, Daniel, Erik Fisher, Cynthia Lea Selin, and David H. Guston. 2008. "Anticipating Governance of Nanotechnology: Foresight, Engagement, and Integration". P. 979-1000 in *The Handbook of Science and Technology Studies*, edited by E. J. Hackett, O. Amsterdamska, M. Lynch and J. Wajcman. MIT Press.

Beck, Ulrich. 1992. *Risk Society: Towards a New Modernity.* London: Sage Publications.

Berman, Elizabeth Popp. 2017. "From Economic to Social Regulation: How the Deregulatory Moment Strengthened Economists' Policy Position". *History of Political Economy* 49:187–212.

Berman, Elizabeth Popp. 2022. *Thinking Like an Economist: How Efficiency Replaced Equality in U.S. Public Policy.* Princeton University Press.

Borraz, O. 2007. "Risk and public problems". *Journal of Risk Research* 10 (7): 941–957.

Bourdieu, Pierre. 1976. "Le Champ Scientifique." *Actes de La Recherche en Sciences Sociales* 2 (2): 88–104.

Brint, Steven. 1990. "Rethinking the Policy Influence of Experts: From General Characterizations to Analysis of Variation." *Sociological Forum* 5 (3): 361–385.

Brooks, H., and C. L. Cooper. 1987. *Science for Public Policy.* New York: Pergamon Press.

Brown, Mark B. 2009. *Science in Democracy: Expertise, Institutions, and Representation.* Cambridge, MA: MIT Press.

Brown, Phil, Rachel Morello-Frosch, and Stephen Zavestoski. 2011. Contested Illnesses: Citizens, Science, and Health Social Movements. University of California Press.

Brown, Phil, Stephen Zavestoski, Sabrina McCormick, Brian Mayer, Rachel Morello-Frosch, and Rebecca Gasior Altman. 2004. "Embodied Health Movements: New Approaches to Social Movements in Health". *Sociology of Health & Illness* 26 (1): 50–80.

Burgess, Adam. 2013. "Manufacturing Uncertainty out of Manufactured Sweeteners: The Curious Case of Aspartame." *European Journal of Risk Regulation* 4 (3): 377–381.

Cambrosio, Alberto, Camille Limoges, and Denyse Pronovost. 1991. "Analyzing Science Policy-Making: Political Ontology or Ethnography?: A Reply to Kleinman". *Social Studies of Science* 21 (4): 775–781.

Cambrosio, Alberto, Peter Keating, Thomas Schlich, and George Weisz. 2006. "Regulatory Objectivity and the Generation and Management of Evidence in Medicine". *Social Science & Medicine* 63 (1): 189–199.

Cambrosio, Alberto, Peter Keating, Thomas Schlich, and George Weisz. 2006. "Regulatory Objectivity and the Generation and Management of Evidence in Medicine." *Social Science & Medicine* 63 (1): 189–199.

Campbell, Eric G., Brian R. Clarridge, Manjusha Gokhale, Lauren Birenbaum, Stephen Hilgartner, Neil A. Holtzman, and David Blumenthal. 2002. "Data Withholding in Academic Genetics: Evidence From a National Survey". *JAMA* 287 (4): 473–480.

Carpenter, Daniel P. 2010. *Reputation and Power: Organizational Image and Pharmaceutical Regulation at the FDA*. Princeton, NJ: Princeton University Press.

Carpenter, Daniel. 2012. "How Business Power Contests Conceptual Orders: The Political and Strategic Reimagination of the Phased Clinical Trials", Conference "Sites of Regulatory Knowledge", IFRIS, Paris, France.

Carpenter, Daniel, and David Moss, eds. 2014. *Preventing Regulatory Capture: Special Interest Influence and How to Limit It*. Cambridge, UK: Cambridge University Press.

Carr, E. Summerson. 2010. "Enactments of Expertise". *Annual Review of Anthropology* 39 (1): 17–32.

CenterWatch. 2015. "EMA Tightens Rules on 'Revolving Door' for Committee Members and Experts." CenterWatch. Accessed September 18, 2019. https://www.centerwatch.com/news-online/2015/05/07/ema-tightens-rules-on-revolving-door-for-committee-members-and-experts/.

Coglianese, Cary, and David Lazer. 2003. "Management Based Regulation: Prescribing Private Management to Achieve Public Goals." *Law & Society Review* 37 (4): 691–730.

Corporate Europe Observatory. 2013. "Banking on the Revolving Door: Rules Full of Loopholes for Former Finance Officials | Corporate Europe Observatory." Accessed September 18, 2019. https://corporateeurope.org/en/news/banking-revolving-door-rules-full-loopholes-former-finance-officials.

Coudray, Guillaume. 2017. *Cochonneries: Comment la charcuterie est devenue un poison*. Paris: La Découverte.

Daemmrich, Arthur A. 2004. *Pharmacopolitics: Drug Regulation in the United States and Germany*. Durham, NC: University of North Carolina Press.

Dance, Amber. 2013. "Regulatory Science: Researchers in the Pipeline." *Nature* 496 (7445): 387–389.

Souza Leão, Luciana de, and Gil Eyal. 2019. "The Rise of Randomized Controlled Trials (RCTs) in International Development in Historical Perspective." *Theory and Society* 48 (3): 383–418.

Demortain, David. 2008. "Credit rating agencies and the faulty marketing authorisation of toxic products". Risk & Regulation. Magazine of the ESRC Centre for Analysis of Risk and Regulation, London School of Economics and Political Science, London.

Demortain, David. 2011. *Scientists and the Regulation of Risk: Standardising Control.* Cheltenham, UK: Edward Elgar.

Demortain, David. 2013. "Regulatory Toxicology in Controversy." *Science, Technology, & Human Values* 38 (6): 727–748.

Demortain, David. 2017. "Expertise, Regulatory Science and the Evaluation of Technology and Risk: Introduction to the Special Issue". *Minerva* 55 (3): 139–159.

Demortain, David. 2020. *The Science of Bureaucracy: Risk Decision-Making and the US Environmental Protection Agency.* Cambridge MA: MIT Press.

Derthick Martha, and Paul J. Quirk. 1982. *The Politics of Deregulation.* Washington, DC: Brookings Institution Press.

Douglas, Mary, and Aaron Wildavsky. 1983. *Risk and Culture: An Essay on the Selection of Technical and Environmental Dangers.* San Francisco: University of California Press.

Downer, John. 2017. "The Aviation Paradox: Why We Can 'Know' Jetliners But Not Reactors". *Minerva* 55 (2): 229–248.

Dumanoski, Dianne. 1978. "The Politics of Bad Science". *The Boston Phoenix*, August 22, 1978.

Environmental Protection Agency. 1979. *EPA Chemical activities: status report. EPA-560/13/79-003.* Washington D.C.

Epstein, Steven. 1996. *Impure Science: AIDS, Activism, and the Politics of Knowledge.* Berkeley: University of California Press.

Epstein, Steven. 1996. *Impure Science: AIDS, Activism, and the Politics of Knowledge.* Berkeley and Los Angeles: University of California Press.

Evans, James A. 2010. "Industry Induces Academic Science to Know Less about More." *American Journal of Sociology* 116 (2): 389–452.

Eyal, Gil. 2019a. "Trans-science as a Vocation." *Journal of Classical Sociology* 19 (3): 254–274.

Eyal, Gil. 2013. "For a Sociology of Expertise: The Social Origins of the Autism Epidemic." *American Journal of Sociology* 118 (4): 863–907.

Eyal, Gil. 2019. "Trans-Science as a Vocation". *Journal of Classical Sociology* 19 (3): 254–274.

Eyal, Gil. 2019. *The Crisis of Expertise.* Cambridge, UK: Polity.

Faulkner, Alex. 2017. "Special Treatment? Flexibilities in the Politics of Regenerative Medicine's Gatekeeping Regimes in the UK." *Science as Culture* 28 (2): 149–173.

FDA. 2011. *Advancing Regulatory Science at FDA: A Strategic Plan.* US Food and Drug Administration. Department of Health and Human Services, Washington, DC.

Foucart, Stéphane. 2014. *La Fabrique du mensonge: Comment les industriels manipulent la science et nous mettent en danger.* Paris: Editions Gallimard.

Fourcade, Marion, and Rakesh Khurana. 2013. "From social control to financial economics: the linked ecologies of economics and business in twentieth century America". *Theory and Society* 42 (2): 121–159.

Freudenburg W. R., R. Gramling, and D. J. Davidson. 2008. "Scientific Certainty Argumentation Methods (SCAMs): Science and the Politics of Doubt." *Sociological Inquiry* 78 (1): 2–38.

Frickel, Scott, Rebekah Torcasso, and Annika Anderson. 2015. "The Organization of Expert Activism: Shadow Mobilization in Two Social Movements." *Mobilization: An International Quarterly* 20 (3): 305–323.

Frickel, Scott. 2011. "Who Are the Experts of Environmental Health Justice?" In *Technoscience and Environmental Justice: Expert Cultures in a Grassroots Movement*, edited by G. Ottinger and B. R. Cohen, 20–40. Cambridge, MA: MIT Press.

Funtowicz, Silvio O., and Jerome R. Ravetz. 1993. "Science for the Post-normal Age." *Futures* 25 (7): 739–755.

Gaudillière, Jean-Paul, and Volker Hess. 2012. *Ways of Regulating Drugs in the 19th and 20th Centuries*. London: Palgrave Macmillan.

Gieryn, Thomas. 1983. "Boundary-Work and the Demarcation of Science from Non-science: Strains and Interests in Professional Ideologies of Scientists." *American Sociological Review* 48 (6): 781–795.

Greenwood, Ted. 1984. "The Myth of Scientific Incompetence of Regulatory Agencies." *Science, Technology, & Human Values* 9 (1): 83–96.

Grundmann, Reiner. 2017. "The Problem of Expertise in Knowledge Societies." *Minerva* 55 (1): 25–48.

Hamburg, Margaret A. 2011. "Advancing Regulatory Science." *Science* 331 (6020): 987–987.

Heath, David. 2016. "Meet the 'Rented White Coats' Who Defend Toxic Chemicals: How Corporate-Funded Research Is Corrupting America's Courts and Regulatory Agencies." Center for Public Integrity. Accessed September 16, 2019. https://publicintegrity.org/environment/meet-the-rented-white-coats-who-defend-toxic-chemicals/.

Hendrickx, Kim. 2013. "Rivaling Evidence-Bases and Politics in Regulatory Science". *Food Science and Law* 4.

Hermann, Timothy. 2013. "A New Journal for the Emerging Field of Regulatory Science". *Journal of Regulatory Science* 1 (1): i–ii.

Hess, David J. 2005. "Technology- and Product-Oriented Movements: Approximating Social Movement Studies and Science and Technology Studies". *Science, Technology, & Human Values* 30 (4): 515–535.

Hessari, Nason Maani, Gary Ruskin, Martin McKee, and David Stuckler. 2019. "Public Meets Private: Conversations Between Coca-Cola and the CDC". *The Milbank Quarterly* 97 (1): 74–90.

Hunt, Jane, and Simon Shackley. 1999. "Reconceiving Science and Policy: Academic, Fiducial and Bureaucratic Knowledge." *Minerva* 37 (2): 141–164.

Irwin, Alan, Henry Rothstein, Steven Yearley, and Elaine McCarthy. 1997. "Regulatory Science—Towards a Sociological Framework." *Futures* 29 (1): 17–31.

Janssen, Wallace. 1976. "Introduction". In *Annual Reports 1950-1974 on the administration of the Federal Food, Drug and Cosmetic Act and Related Laws*. Washington D.C.: Food and Drug Administration.

Jasanoff, Sheila. 1982. "Science and the Limits of Administrative Rule-Making: Lessons from the OSHA Cancer Policy". *Osgoode Hall Law Journal* 20: 536.

Jasanoff, Sheila. 1987. "Contested Boundaries in Policy-Relevant Science." *Social Studies of Science* 17 (2): 195–230.

Jasanoff, Sheila. 1990. *The Fifth Branch: Science Advisers as Policymakers*. Cambridge, MA: Harvard University Press.

Jasanoff, Sheila. 1995. "Procedural Choices in Regulatory Science." *Technology in Society* 17 (3): 279–293.

Jasanoff, Sheila. 2012. "The Practices of Objectivity in Regulatory Science." In *Social Knowledge in the Making*, edited by C. Camic, N. Gross, and M. Lamont, 307–338. Chicago: University of Chicago Press.

Joly, Pierre-Benoît. 2016. "Science réglementaire: Une internationalisation divergente? L'évaluation des biotechnologies aux Etats-Unis et en Europe." *Revue Française de Sociologie* 57 (3): 443–472.

Jonvallen, Petra, Elisabeth Berg, and Jim Barry. 2011. "The Development of Contract Research Organisations in Sweden: Health Care, Privatisation and Neo-Liberalism". *New Technology, Work and Employment* 26 (3): 196–209.

Karkkainen, Bradley C. 2001. "Information as Environmental Regulation: TRI and Performance Benchmarking, Precursor to a New Paradigm". *Georgetown Law Journal* 89 (2): 257–370.

Katic, Ivana V. 2015. "Antecedents and Consequences of the Revolving Door between U.S. Regulatory Agencies and Regulated Firms." PhD diss., Columbia University, 167 pages.

Kennedy, D. 1977a. "Statement before the Subcommittee of the Committee on Appropriations." In Agriculture and related agencies appropriations for 1978. Hearings before a subcommittee of the Committee on Appropriations, edited by House of Representatives, Ninety-fifth Congress. Washington, DC: U.S. Government Printing Office, 79–80.

Kennedy, D. 1977b. "Statement before the Committee on Agriculture, Nutrition and Forestry." In Food Safety and Quality: Regulation of chemicals in food and agriculture. Hearings before the Subcommittee on Agricultural Research and General Legislation, edited by Committee on Agriculture, Nutrition, and Forestry, US Senate, Ninety-Fifth Congress. Washington, DC: U.S. Government Printing Office, 3–23.

Kleindorfer, Paul R., and Eric W. Orts. 1998. "Informational Regulation of Environmental Risks." *Risk Analysis* 18 (2): 155–170.

Konopasek Z., T. Stockelova, and L. Zamykalova. 2008. "Making Pure Science and Pure Politics: On the Expertise of Bypass and the Bypass of Expertise." *Science, Technology, & Human Values* 33 (4): 529–553.

Krimsky, Sheldon. 2004. *Science in the Private Interest: Has the Lure of Profits Corrupted Biomedical Research?* Lanham, Rowman & Littlefield.

Kunreuther, Howard, and Eryl V. Ley. 1982. *The Risk Analysis Controversy: An Institutional Perspective*. Berlin: Springer-Verlarg.

Kwak, James. 2014. "Cultural Capture and the Financial Crisis." In *Preventing Regulatory Capture: Special Interest Influence and How to Limit It*, edited by Daniel P. Carpenter and David A. Moss, 71–98. Cambridge, UK: Cambridge University Press.

Lanier-Christensen, Colleen. 2018. "Privileged Access: Industry Influence in OECD Chemical Testing Standards." Presented at the Pervasive Powers Conference. Corporate Authority and Public Policy, June 14, Paris.

Laurent, Brice. 2017. *Democratic Experiments: Problematizing Nanotechnology and Democracy in Europe and the United States*. Cambridge, MA: MIT Press.

Lave, Rebecca. 2012. "Neoliberalism and the Production of Environmental Knowledge." *Environment and Society* 3 (1): 19–38.

Lave, Rebecca, P. Mirowski, and S. Randalls. 2010. "Introduction: STS and Neoliberal Science." *Social Studies of Science* 40 (5): 659–675.

Leach, Melissa, and Ian Scoones. 2007. "Mobilising Citizens: Social Movements and the Politics of Knowledge". *IDS Working Paper* 276.

Leufkens, Hubert G. n.d. "Regulatory Science: Regulation Is Too Important to Leave It to the Regulators." *British Journal of Clinical Pharmacology* 86 (12): 2333–2334.

Levidow, Les, Joseph Murphy, and Susan Carr. 2007. "Recasting 'Substantial Equivalence': Transatlantic Governance of GM Food." *Science, Technology, & Human Values* 32 (1): 26–64.

Liu, Sida, and Mustafa Emirbayer. 2016. "Field and Ecology." *Sociological Theory* 34 (1): 62–79.

Majone, G. 1997. "The new European agencies: regulation by information". *Journal of European Public Policy* 4 (2): 262–275.

Majone, Giandomenico. 1984. "Science and Trans-Science in Standard Setting." *Science, Technology, & Human Values* 9 (1): 15–22.

Martin, John Levi. 2003. "What Is Field Theory?" *American Journal of Sociology* 109 (1): 1–49.

McCarty, Nolan. 2014. "Complexity, Capacity and Capture." In Carpenter and Moss *Preventing Regulatory Capture*, 90–123.

McGarity, Thomas O., and Wendy Elizabeth Wagner. 2008. *Bending Science: How Special Interests Corrupt Public Health Research*. Cambridge, MA: Harvard University Press.

McGoey, Lindsey, and Emily Jackson. 2009. "Seroxat and the Suppression of Clinical Trial Data: Regulatory Failure and the Uses of Legal Ambiguity". *Journal of Medical Ethics* 35 (2): 107–112.

McGoey, Linsey. 2016. *An Introduction to the Sociology of Ignorance: Essays on the Limits of Knowing*. Routledge.

Medvetz, Thomas. 2012. *Think Tanks in America*. Chicago: University of Chicago Press.

Michaels, David 2006. "Manufactured Uncertainty: Protecting Public Health in the Age of Contested Science and Product Defense". *Annals of the New York Academy of Sciences* 1076 (1): 149–162.

Michaels, David, and Wendy Wagner. 2003. "Disclosure in Regulatory Science." *Science* 302: 2073.

Michaels, David, ed. 2008. *Doubt Is Their Product: How Industry's Assault on Science Threatens Your Health*. Oxford: Oxford University Press.

Millstone, Erik Paul, and Elisabeth Dawson. 2019. "EFSA's Toxicological Assessment of Aspartame: Was It Even-Handedly Trying to Identify Possible Unreliable Positives and Unreliable Negatives?" *Archives of Public Health* 77 (1): 34.

Mirowski, Philip, and Dieter Plehwe. 2015. *The Road from Mont Pèlerin: The Making of the Neoliberal Thought Collective*. Cambridge, MA: Harvard University Press.

Mirowski, Philip, and Robert Van Horn. 2005. "The Contract Research Organization and the Commercialization of Scientific Research". *Social Studies of Science* 35 (4): 503–548.

Moghissi, A. Alan, Sorin R. Straja, Betty R. Love, Dennis K. Bride, and Roger R. Stough. 2014. "Innovation in Regulatory Science: Evolution of a New Scientific Discipline." *Technology & Innovation* 16 (2): 155–165.

Myers, John Peterson, Frederick S. vom Saal, Benson T. Akingbemi, Koji Arizono, Scott Belcher, Theo Colborn andal. 2009. "Why Public Health Agencies Cannot Depend on Good Laboratory Practices as a Criterion for Selecting Data: The Case of Bisphenol A." *Environmental Health Perspectives* 117 (3): 309–315.

National Academies of Sciences, Engineering, and Medicine. 2016. *Advancing the Discipline of Regulatory Science for Medical Product Development: An Update on Progress and a Forward-Looking Agenda*. Washington, DC: National Academies Press.

Nelkin, D. 1984, *Controversy. The politics of technical decision*, Beverley Hills, CA: Sage.

Neslen, Arthur. 2019. "EU Glyphosate Approval Was Based on Plagiarised Monsanto Text, Report Finds." *The Guardian*, January 15.

Nichols, Tom. 2017. *The Death of Expertise: The Campaign against Established Knowledge and Why It Matters*. Oxford: Oxford University Press.

Nowotny, Helga, Dominique Pestre, Eberhard Schmidt-Aßmann, Helmuth Schulze-Fielitz, and Hans-Heinrich Trute. 2005. *The Public Nature of Science under Assault: Politics, Markets, Science and the Law*. Springer Science & Business Media.

Ottinger, Gwen, and Benjamin Cohen. 2012. "Environmentally Just Transformations of Expert Cultures: Toward the Theory and Practice of a Renewed Science and Engineering". *Environmental Justice* 5 (3): 158–163.

Pandey, Poonam, and Aviram Sharma. 2019. "NGOs, Controversies, and 'Opening Up' of Regulatory Governance of Science in India." *Bulletin of Science, Technology & Society* 37 (4): 199–211.

Perkmann, Markus, Valentina Tartari, Maureen McKelvey, Erkko Autio, Anders Broström, Pablo D'Este, et al. 2013. "Academic Engagement and Commercialisation: A Review of the Literature on University–Industry Relations." *Research Policy* 42 (2): 423–442.

Pielke, Roger A. 2007. *The Honest Broker: Making Sense of Science in Policy and Politics*. Cambridge: Cambridge University Press.

Pigeon, Martin. 2019. "The EU Glyphosate Assessment and the 'Monsanto Papers' When Industry's 'Sound Science' Meets Peer Review." Presentation before the Special Committee on the Union's Authorisation Procedure for Pesticides, European Parliament, 6 September 2018, *Brussels*.

Piller, Charles. 2018. "FDA's Revolving Door: Companies Often Hire Agency Staffers Who Managed Their Successful Drug Reviews." *Science*, July 3, published online, doi: 10.1126/science.aau6841.

Porter, Theodore M. 1995. *Trust in Numbers: The Pursuit of Objectivity in Science and Public Life*. Princeton, N.J: Princeton University Press.

Poulain, Mathilde. 2018. "The Political Economy of Financial Regulation." PhD Dissertation, Université Paris 1 Panthéon-Sorbonne.

Prasad, Viney, and Jeffrey Bien. 2019. "Future Jobs of US Food and Drug Administration's Hematology-Oncology Medical Reviewers." *British Medical Journal* 343:d5147

Rampton, Sheldon, and John Stauber. 2002. *Trust Us, We're Experts PA: How Industry Manipulates Science and Gambles with Your Future*. New York, Penguin.

Regens, James L., Thomas M. Dietz, and Robert W. Rycroft. 1983. "Risk Assessment in the Policy-Making Process: Environmental Health and Safety Protection." *Public Administration Review* 43 (2): 137–145.

Rosemann, Achim. 2019. "Alter-Standardizing Clinical Trials: The Gold Standard in the Crossfire." *Science as Culture* 28 (2): 125–148.

Rosenbaum, Lisa. 2015. "Reconnecting the Dots: Reinterpreting Industry–Physician Relations." *New England Journal of Medicine* 372 (19): 1860–1864.

Rothstein, H., A. Irwin, S. Yearley, and E. McCarthy. 1999. "Regulatory Science, Europeanization, and the Control of Agrochemicals." *Science, Technology, & Human Values* 24 (2): 241–264.

Rushefsky, Mark E. 1986. *Making Cancer Policy*. Albany: State University of New York Press.

Sabin, Paul. 2016. ""Everything Has a Price": Jimmy Carter and the Struggle for Balance in Federal Regulatory Policy". *Journal of Policy History* 28 (1): 1–47.

Sacks, Gary, Boyd A. Swinburn, Adrian J. Cameron, and Gary Ruskin. 2018. "How Food Companies Influence Evidence and Opinion – Straight from the Horse's Mouth". *Critical Public Health* 28 (2): 253–256.

Sainz, Vanessa, João Conniot, Ana I. Matos, Carina Peres, Eva Zupančič, Liane Moura, et al. 2015. "Regulatory Aspects on Nanomedicines." *Biochemical and Biophysical Research Communications* 468 (3): 504–510.

Salter, Liora. 1988. *Mandated Science: Science and Scientists in the Making of Standards.* Dordrecht: Kluwer Academic.

Schmandt, Jurgen. 1984. "Regulation and Science." *Science, Technology, & Human Values* 9 (1): 23–38.

Schwarz, M., and M. Thompson. 1990. *Divided We Stand: Redefining Politics, Technology and Social Choice.* Philadelphia: University of Pennsylvania Press.

Science Advisory Board. 1977. *Report on the Research, Development, Monitoring, and Technical Support System of the US EPA.* Washington DC: US EPA Science Advisory Board, Environmental Measurements Advisory Committee.

Serôdio, Paulo M., Martin McKee, and David Stuckler. 2018. "Coca-Cola – a Model of Transparency in Research Partnerships? A Network Analysis of Coca Cola's Research Funding (2008–2016)". *Public Health Nutrition* 21(9):1594–1607.

Shackley, Simon and Brian Wynne. 1995. "Global climate change: the mutual construction of an emergent science-policy domain". *Science and Public Policy* 22(4):218–230.

Shapin, S. 2008. *The Scientific Life: A Moral History of a Late Modern Vocation.* Chicago: University of Chicago Press.

Sismondo, Sergio. 2007. "Ghost Management: How Much of the Medical Literature Is Shaped Behind the Scenes by the Pharmaceutical Industry?" *PLoS Medicine* 4 (9): e286.

Sismondo, Sergio. 2018. *Ghost-Managed Medicine: Big Pharma's Invisible Hands.* Manchester: Mattering Press.

Slayton, Rebecca, and Aaron Clark-Ginsberg. 2018. "Beyond Regulatory Capture: Coproducing Expertise for Critical Infrastructure Protection." *Regulation & Governance* 12 (1): 115–130.

Steele, Sarah, Gary Ruskin, Lejla Sarcevic, Martin McKee, and David Stuckler. 2019. "Are Industry-Funded Charities Promoting "Advocacy-Led Studies" or "Evidence-Based Science"?: A Case Study of the International Life Sciences Institute". *Globalization and Health* 15 (1): 36.

Stilgoe, Jack, Richard Owen, and Phil Macnaghten. 2013. "Developing a Framework for Responsible Innovation." *Research Policy* 42 (9): 1568–1580.

Sunstein, Cass R. 1999. "Informational Regulation and Informational Standing: Akins and Beyond." *University of Pennsylvania Law Review* 147 (3): 613–675.

Suryanarayanan, Sainath, and Daniel Lee Kleinman. 2013. "Be(e)Coming Experts: The Controversy over Insecticides in the Honey Bee Colony Collapse Disorder." *Social Studies of Science* 43 (2): 215–240.

Tesh, Sylvia Noble. 2000. *Uncertain Hazards: Environmental Activists and Scientific Proof.* Ithaca, NY: Cornell University Press.

Todt, Oliver, and José Luis Luján. 2017. "Health Claims and Methodological Controversy in Nutrition Science." *Risk Analysis* 37 (5): 958–968.

Tyfield, David, Rebecca Lave, Samuel Randalls, and Charles Thorpe. 2017. "Introduction: Beyond Crisis in the Knowledge Economy." In *The Routledge Handbook of the Political Economy of Science*, edited by David Tyfield, Rebecca Lave, Samuel Randalls, and Charles Thorpe, 1–18. London: Routledge.

Vogel, D. 2003. "The Hare and the Tortoise Revisited: The New Politics of Consumer and Environmental Regulation in Europe". *British Journal of Political Science* 33:557-80.

Vogel, David. 1988. "The 'New' Social Regulation in Historical and Comparative Perspective." In *American Law and the Constitutional Order: Historical Perspectives*, edited by L. M. Friedman and H. N. Scheiber, 431–448. Cambridge, MA: Harvard University Press.

Vogel, David. 1998. "The Globalization of Pharmaceutical Regulation." *Governance* 11 (1): 1–22.

Vogel, David. 2012. *The Politics of Precaution: Regulating Health, Safety, and Environmental Risks in Europe and the United States*. Princeton, N.J: Princeton University Press.

Vogel, Sarah A. 2013. *Is It Safe? BPA and the Struggle to Define the Safety of Chemicals*. Berkeley: University of California Press.

Wagner Wendy, Elizabeth Fisher, and Pasky Pascual. 2018. "Whose Science? A New Era in Regulatory 'Science Wars." *Science* 362 (1415): 636–639.

Wagner, Wendy E. 1995. "The Science Charade in Toxic Risk Regulation." *Columbia Law Review* 95 (7): 1613–1723.

Walsh, John P., and Wei Hong. 2003. "Secrecy Is Increasing in Step with Competition". *Nature* 422 (6934): 801–802.

Weinberg, Alvin M. 1972. "Science and Trans-Science." *Minerva* 10 (2): 209–222.

Weinberg, Alvin M. 1985. "Science and Its Limits: The Regulator's Dilemma." *Issues in Science and Technology* 2 (1): 59–72.

Weingart, Peter. 1999. "Scientific Expertise and Political Accountability: Paradoxes of Science in Politics." *Science and Public Policy* 26 (3): 151–161.

Wilson, J. Q. 1980. *The Politics of Regulation*. New York: Basic Books.

Winickoff, David, and Douglas M. Bushey. 2010. "Science and Power in Global Food Regulation: The Rise of the Codex Alimentarius". *Science, Technology & Human Values* 35 (3): 356.

Wynne, Brian. 1984. "'Mandated Science': A Workshop and Project Report Vancouver, Canada, April 1984." *4S Review* 2 (2): 3–4.

Wynne, Brian. 1987. "Uncertainty—Technical and Social". In *Science for Public Policy*, 95–115. Harvey Brooks. Pergamon Press.

14

EXPERT POWER AND THE CLASSIFICATION OF HUMAN DIFFERENCE

DANIEL NAVON

WE can barely even imagine the world around us without invoking categories. Some ways of classifying things seem entirely beyond question—they appear to "carve nature at its joints," as Plato famously put it. The various plant and animal species we find near our home, the distinction between night and day, winter and summer, north and south, edible or poisonous, and so on, may seem totally independent of our minds and our culture. To this day, many philosophers still talk about the "natural kinds" that are given to us by the world. In contrast, other classifications are clearly contingent. When we think about the seven-day week, the Fahrenheit scale, or clothing sizes, for example, it is very easy to imagine other ways of carving up the world. But systems of classification move between those two poles—between seeming wholly natural or beyond dispute and entirely arbitrary or plain wrong. They are always in flux. The power and givenness (or *apodicticity*, to use the philosophical jargon) of a way of classifying things are deeply intertwined: a system of classification is at its most powerful when we cannot conceive of a viable alternative.

Yet classification is always a human activity, even when the categories we create are reified and inscribed in the world around us. This means that classification is almost invariably laden with *uneven* power relations. Whoever has control of classification in a particular domain can shape the very terms of deliberation and contestation over social action. Hence, experts and institutions often derive great power from their ability to monopolize the way things are classified. After all, expert classifications are all around us. We are constantly classified by doctors, marketers, bureaucrats, and many other kinds of experts (increasingly aided by classification algorithms). When we fill out a census form or decide on a book to read, a home to live in, what food to eat, and, of course, what wine to drink (Zhao 2005), our decisions are guided by systems of expert classification that we do not really understand. They are behind the scenes too, undergirding many aspects of modern commerce.[1] What's more, the incessant classification of people and resources is arguably the quintessential function of modern state bureaucracies (Hacking 1990; Scott 1999). Expert authority itself is often grounded in epistemic, normative, and legal claims that one is in a privileged position to classify. This is precisely why classification is such a fecund topic for both history and the social sciences: we have the opportunity to analyze and unpack the way expertise, power, and classification practices intersect and change one another over time. And yet, even though it was central to Durkheim's later work, sociologists have only returned to the systematic study of classification quite recently.

In this chapter, I take stock of the resurgent sociological interest in classification, especially as it relates to the issue of expert power. By and large, I focus on the expert classification of *human difference*. Why? On the one hand, it has been arguably the most productive area of sociological research on expert classification. On the other hand, focusing on the way we distinguish between our fellow humans highlights two essential yet seemingly countervailing aspects of classification: the way it accords immense power to experts even as it tends to unleash social forces they cannot fully control.

From races, nations, and ethnicities to sexes and genders, and through to abilities, disabilities, and diseases, the way we are classified can have far-reaching consequences. Being labeled one way over another can shape the very terms of experience; it can confer enormous privileges or condemn a person to subjugation. Classification is therefore one of the most fateful forms of social relation, and it is even more powerful when it seems like a simple factual statement about a person or a group. When it comes to diagnosing disease or mental illness, for example, sociologists have tended to accord a unidirectional power to experts. Recent work has painted a more dynamic picture. It is more dynamic for two reasons. First, this strain of research pays greater attention to the myriad ways in which classification and diagnosis can truly change the people being classified, sometimes in unexpected ways. Second, this new wave of scholarship accords far more power to the people being diagnosed, their families, and a range of other stakeholders. In this way, as Ian Hacking and others have shown, action by many different actors can "loop" back to reshape experts' theories and practices. Above all, these new approaches to classification take stock of the fact that people are not just passive objects that can be sorted this way or that; they are active participants, whose reactions can force changes in the categories that are applied to them. I will argue that this framework represents the most promising avenue for unpacking the relationship between expertise, the classification of humans, and the people whose lives are shaped by classification.

Finally, I explain how an old ghost is once again rearing its head: the idea that new advances in genetics and biology can point us toward objective systems of medical and racial classification. This confers an enormous amount of power on experts—a power that often goes unquestioned because it is ostensibly based on nature itself. These new moves toward the biological classification of humans are therefore ripe for sociological analysis and critique.

THREE PILLARS FOR A SOCIOLOGY OF CLASSIFICATION

Philosophers have debated the nature of categories for millennia. Beginning in earnest with Aristotle's treatise on classification, *Categories*, they have tried to explain how it is possible to sort and characterize the things we experience in the world around us. Where do categories come from? Are they independent of our experience of them? To this day, "realists" and "nominalists" do battle over the question of whether categories are out there in the world to be discovered or products of our classifying minds. That debate will not detain us here. Instead, we will see how philosophy has repeatedly provided a springboard for social theories of classification. In what follows, I outline three conceptual pillars—each one a departure from philosophical debates about the nature of language and categories—which can support a robust sociology of expert classification.

Pillar One: Unveiling the Social Foundations of Expert Classification

It was Émile Durkheim who, over a century ago, provided a sociological path out of the Sisyphean philosophical debate about the nature of categories. Indeed, we find a sociological theory of classification at the very heart of the later Durkheim's magnum opus, *The Elementary Forms of Religious Life*. His point of departure for a sociology of classification was Immanuel Kant's influential concept of the "transcendental deduction": the anti-skeptical idea that categories like substance and causality are necessary for the very possibility of experience (Kant [1787] 2003). Durkheim lifted this line of argument from ongoing metaphysical debates and repurposed it to undergird a sociological theory of the possibility of knowledge. He laid the foundation for our first conceptual pillar by insisting on, and theorizing, the indelibly *social* nature of categories—a foundation that others would build on to unveil the complex dynamics of power and expertise that are at play in classification practices.

Durkheim famously argued that the categories which allow us to do everything from navigating space to sorting things into coherent groups are, indeed, external to us. However, they are external only because they are given to us by society and its cultural schemas, that is, by *collective representations*. In Durkheim's later work, classification therefore lay at the very foundation of both experience and social life. But he also argued that the categories and distinctions we use to make sense of the world around us are themselves a sort of externalization of the group's social structure and norms (Durkheim 2001; Durkheim and Mauss 1967). Although sociological theorists have mostly rejected this stronger claim (at least in its more simplistic formulation; see e.g., Smith 1984, 238), it remains influential in both cultural sociology and social anthropology (see Douglas 1986 for a highly influential account). In sum, Durkheim helped us to get past metaphysical questions about classification and see that the way we actually classify the world and the people around us is fundamentally grounded in social processes, with sweeping implications for almost every subfield in sociology.

The next important blocks of our first pillar were laid decades later when scholars began to interrogate the mutability of categories, who makes them, and how—all of which pointed to the central role of experts and expert systems. No one looms larger in this area than Michel Foucault. In his earliest works, Foucault outlined the radical convulsions in the way psychiatry had classified madness across the centuries—convulsions that could not be read as part of a coherent "history of ideas" (Foucault 1954,[1961] 1988). We will return to Foucault's work on medical and psychiatric classification later. But beginning with *The Order of Things* and, especially, *The Archaeology of Knowledge* (Foucault 1982, 2001), Foucault developed a more general account of how certain forms of depth knowledge (*savoir*), or *epistemes*, govern what is thinkable and knowable in different historical periods. These shifting "discursive formations" are visible in the statements or truth claims one encounters in a given time and place. They are not hidden per se, nor are they confined to the interiors of our minds as subjects. Nevertheless, they make discourse possible and therefore set parameters for what even *could* count as true. Foucault explained how there are certain authoritative groups and "grids of specification . . . the systems according to which," to take psychiatry as an example, "the different "kinds of madness" are divided, contrasted, related, regrouped, classified, derived from one another as objects of psychiatric discourse" (1982, 41–42). Crucially, these grids did not specify objects that were already out there and waiting to be classified: "It would be quite wrong," Foucault argued, "to see discourse as a place where previously established objects are laid one after another like words on a page" (42–43). Experts and other actors do have considerable leeway in formulating and developing particular categories. At the same time, the *episteme* of the day sets parameters for the way we classify things: "the conditions necessary if [an object] is to exist in relation to other objects, if it is to establish with them relations of resemblance, proximity, distance, difference, transformation—as we can see, these conditions are many and imposing" (44). In other words, classification is only ever one part of a much broader historical formation that creates the conditions of possibility for meaningful expert discourse.

In this way, Foucault helped lay the groundwork for a new sociology of classification. It became possible to see how classification shapes possibilities for thought and action without succumbing to the totalizing assumptions of structuralism. We can therefore study the tensions, possibilities for resistance, and historical ruptures in the way we classify things. This turn allowed Foucault and others who have followed in his footsteps to unpack the enormous, mostly overlooked power exercised by doctors, psychologists, criminologists, economists, market researchers, planners, public-health officials, and many other expert groups. At the same time, it helped us see how experts do not usually experience their classificatory work as an exercise of power per se, and how they only partly control the way systems of classification shift and churn. Foucault (2004) also showed how a major expansion of expert power—as when psychiatry was enrolled in the criminal justice system—can come at the cost of the scientific defensibility of their system of classification, rendering it nothing less than absurd (11–15, 34–41). In sum, Foucault pried open a sociological window onto the vast, dynamic terrain of expert classification and power.

Geoffrey Bowker and Susan Leigh Star put the finishing touches on our first conceptual pillar when they published their tour de force book on classification, *Sorting Things Out*. Building on Foucault and others, Bowker and Star (2000) showed how expert classification systems are not only pervasive, but also largely invisible. By hiding in plain sight, so to speak, systems of classification exert a far-reaching and almost uncontestable power. So, too, do the experts who design and control those systems. Expertise confers authority over the ways in which we categorize and measure things—over the very terms of experience, description, and negotiation. When these systems of classification seem given by nature or *apodictic*, it means that experts have succeeded in convincing us that theirs is the only conceivable way of grasping reality. That is a profound form of power. Bowker and Star (2000) put it very cogently: "Each standard and each category valorizes some point of view and silences another. This is not inherently a bad thing—indeed it is inescapable. But it *is* an ethical choice, and as such it is dangerous—not bad, but dangerous" (emphasis in original; 5–6).

We live in a world designed, in no small part, according to various standards and systems of classification. Bowker and Star explain how classifications are "operative": they "defin[e] the possibilities for action" (2000, 326). Their book therefore served as a sort of clarion call for greater scholarly attention to classification and its consequences. They point out that it is often only experts—be they plumbers, painters, electricians, civil servants, or doctors—who are aware of the role classification plays in any particular domain. Invisibility may be the norm, but "they may become more visible, especially when they break down or become objects of contention" (2000, 2–3). Suffice it to say that contention over classification can take many forms. To take two examples just from Bowker and Star, it can come from actors invested in a disruptive technology that does not conform to existing standards, or anti-Apartheid activists fighting against racist systems of human classification. The sociological study of classification therefore has liberatory potential. It can help us see how power masquerades as a neutral, expertise-driven way of ordering experience and practice. Just as classifications and standards serve as structures that constrain action, challenging them can expand the scope for agency. To quote Bowker and Star (2000, 3), classification creates an invisible "social and moral order . . . [whose] impact is indisputable, and as Foucault reminds us, inescapable."

So here we have our first and most fundamental conceptual pillar for a sociology of classification. Building on Durkheim, Foucault, Bowker and Star, and many others, sociologists of expertise have been able to peel back the veil on systems of classification that seem objective and inevitable to reveal their social origins and animating power dynamics. Indeed, they show how the privileged ability to classify sometimes grants experts an enormous amount of *unchallenged* power. For the most part, the experts are blind to this as well. They do not think of their practice as an exercise of power per se, even as they jealously guard their jurisdiction over certain dimensions of classification. In short, categories and systems of classification are always partial, prone to rupture, and power laden, even when they seem complete, timeless, and grounded in some kind of neutral truth. The more invisible the power dynamics of classification are, the more un-contested the power of experts.

Pillar Two: Performing Categories

The second conceptual pillar for the sociological study of classification also comes to us via philosophy: performativity. In his 1962 book *How to Do Things with Words*, J. L Austin broke with the prevailing analytic philosophers of the day to illustrate that language, rather than being a matter of mere description, can actually constitute a state of affairs—it can *make* something true. Sometimes, he argued, an utterance can usher in its own truth conditions, as when a person says, " 'I do (sc. take this woman to be my lawful wedded wife)'—as uttered in the course of the marriage ceremony" (1962, 5). Speech acts and written statements, in other words, can *perform* a new state of affairs. Language can change the world. The concept of performativity has been picked up by such major social theorists as Judith Butler (2006, 2010) and Karen Barad (2003) as well as by science studies scholars such as Andrew Pickering (1994), Donald MacKenzie (2006), and Michel Callon (1998, 2006). Callon pointedly distinguishes performativity from Merton's (1968, 475–490) notion of the self-fulfilling prophecy, where a claim or prediction like "there's going to be a run on the local bank!" leads people to act in ways that makes it so. Instead, the performative statements, theories, and models promulgated by experts *create their own truth conditions*. This way of thinking about performativity has been especially generative in economic sociology, where it has helped us understand how neoliberal theory was used to remake the world in its image, and how influential economic models only accounted for market behavior *after* actors adopted them as accurate (e.g., Aspers 2007; MacKenzie 2003, 2004, 2006; Mitchell 2005; Muniesa 2014).

The concept of performativity can help us understand the role and power of expert classification. Only a few previous works have seriously explored the idea of classification as a performative process (e.g., Waterton 2003; Greco 2012). And yet classification clearly creates the truth conditions for its own veracity. When experts classify an animal or crop breed a certain way, they are also taking part in the biological maintenance of those breeds as distinct from others. When we set out to write a piece of sociology, anthropology, history, biology, journalism, fiction, poetry, or what have you, we are helping to reproduce disciplinary distinctions with dubious histories. When we label one job blue collar and another one white collar, we help to perpetuate the inequalities in wealth and status, divisions between communities, and differences in bodies, manners, tastes etc., that make it so. Meanwhile, the built environment is made out of objects that are classified and standardized in any number of ways, from the residential neighborhoods and differentiated housing we live in to the streets and vehicles that allow us to move around. These distinctions all depend on the work of experts. They can be conceived of differently. They are all enforced by standards, laws, or norms—themselves crafted and/or enforced by experts—without which the categories in question would fall apart. In the way they simultaneously describe and thoroughly shape the world in their image, expert categories and systems of classification are quintessentially performative.

Pillar Three: The Dynamism of Human Classification

A final pillar for the sociological study of classification came directly from a philosopher, Ian Hacking (see 1995, 1998a, 1998b, 2006, 2007). As mentioned above, one major school in the philosophy of classification is nominalism. Its adherents argue that we use names, or *nomen* in Latin, to parcel up our experience of an irreducibly messy reality. Hence *nomin*alism holds that categories are applied to the world, not intrinsic to it. Drawing on Foucault, Hacking argues that the dominant debate between realism and nominalism in the philosophy of classification glosses over the dynamic nature of *human* classification. Building on this insight, Hacking's work on "dynamic nominalism" helped spur a new wave of research on the expert classification of human difference and its unforeseen cascading effects.

Hacking's point of departure is the inherently sociological point that classifying people is fundamentally different from classifying other sorts of objects. The static nominalist model does not quite fit when we are naming and labeling humans. Why? When we categorize chemicals, buildings, beer, stars, or any other nonsentient object, the act of classification itself has no direct impact on the thing to which it is applied. To be sure, we might use those things differently, make more or less of them, charge more for them, and so on. We also *make* them according to various standards, as discussed above. However, the sheer act of classification itself is inert. Saying that a bottle of wine is of this or that vintage and from such-and-such terroir does not change the biochemistry of the wine (though we know it changes how humans experience it, sommeliers included). Yet when we say that someone is White, or Brazilian, or female, or a refugee, or gifted, or bipolar, or any one of thousands of salient categories of human difference, it can have a profound impact on the person in question. It can change how they think about themselves. It can also change the way other people act toward them and, it follows, the social world they have to navigate. They might feel proud, or they might feel ashamed. They might seek out confrontation with other people who do not share the same identity. They might withdraw from social relations, or form new ones based on that identity—a point made and theorized decades ago by Erving Goffman (1986). As Howard Becker (1963) recognized when he developed "labelling theory" beginning in the 1950s, people sometimes start to behave in ways that conform to these categories even when they are socially undesirable. In short, when we are dealing with people, ascribing a classification can powerfully affect the thing being classified.

But Hacking took this insight two important steps further. First, if labeling theory is akin to a self-fulfilling prophecy, dynamic nominalism is more like performativity. Classifying people is not just a question of expectations, and it does not just work via our minds and personal identities. In Hacking's "looping" analytic framework, classifying people is far more than a question of labeling. A psychiatric diagnosis, for example, may indeed be a historically contingent category rather than a natural kind. Yet it is no less real as a result. It can bring with it a panoply diagnostic tools, literatures, therapies, drugs, communities, and other things that can shape a person far beyond the simple fact of a label. In this way, classifying a person subjects them to a world of tools and social forces that remake them in the image of the category in question. Classification can therefore "interpellate" people (Althusser [1970] 2014, 188–199) via a series of empirically tractable mechanisms.

Second, expert categories of human difference are not static, nor are they fully controlled by experts. Hacking and other have shown us how the "kinds of people" carved out by expert systems of classification often shape those who are so classified in unanticipated and even surprising ways. It may also lead to any number of unanticipated discoveries about them. In order to keep up, experts then must integrate these unexpected changes into a revised kind of person. Of course, that just starts the entire process anew. To top it all off, the classified themselves can decisively shape looping processes. Classifying people can lead to the formation of support groups, foundations, social clubs, activist organizations, and many other types of collectives that change our understanding of a kind of person. People might recognize things in themselves and their communities that the experts have missed. They might experiment with new treatments and therapies or develop new understandings of where their category comes from—what causes a disease, where an ethnicity originates from, and so on—and who is part of the category. Expert classification can also create oppositional resistance among the classified and their allies, who might seek to directly combat the prevailing expertise about the category they belong to, or to even wrest control of the category away from credentialed experts altogether.

Classifying human difference can therefore create looping processes that cause categories of human difference, expert practices, and the kinds of people who are classified to recursively change one another over time. This sort of approach has proven particularly useful to scholars in the social studies of science and medicine, whether or not they explicitly use the framework of dynamic nominalism. From autism and alcoholism (e.g., Eyal et al. 2010; Hacking 2006, 2007; Navon and Eyal 2016; Valverde 1998) to a host genetic disorders (e.g., Navon 2019; Wailoo 2001), to HIV/AIDS and myalgic encephalomyelitis/chronic fatigue syndrome (e.g., Aronowitz 1999; Epstein 1996), we have seen how these sorts of processes can radically remake the classification of human difference. The very power of human classification sets dynamic processes into motion that often result in deep changes to the original categories themselves.

For these reasons and more, expert classification is therefore especially consequential—but also singularly dynamic—when it is applied to humans. That is the topic to which we now turn.

Classifying People

Few things matter more than the way we classify one another. In different times and places, being categorized as one thing versus another can mean the difference between privilege and exclusion, freedom and subjugation, or even life and death. It is no coincidence that Foucault's work, as well as Bowker and Star's magnum opus on classification, dealt extensively with the expert classification of human diseases, psyches, races, and so on. This section will very briefly take stock of sociological work on diagnosis and medical expertise before moving on to other key dimensions of human classification.

Diagnosis and Medical Expertise

No topic brings together sociological work on classification and expertise more powerfully than *diagnosis*. Like other forms of classification, diagnostic systems try to make order out of a messy reality. They are indelibly bound up with medical expertise: nosology is nothing less than the way in which medicine scientifically describes the world, and the expertise of the doctor is to a large extent the ability to properly diagnose patients. When they are at their most powerful, these systems of medical classification are uncontested and taken for granted. As patients, we may not understand them, but we tend to accept them as correct in a sense that transcends their history. That is how classificatory systems can withstand the constant "effacement" or resistance discussed by Foucault (1973, 9; see also Armstrong 2011) when a doctor is dealing with an actual patient who can never quite fit the mold that has been cast for them.

While diagnosis has probably always been an important part of medical expertise, it has become an increasingly integral part of medicine over the past couple of centuries (Rosenberg 2002). It has also taken a very particular form. In *The Birth of the Clinic*, Foucault (1973) outlines the foundational shift in medical classification that unfolded in revolutionary France around the turn of the nineteenth century. Foucault shows how medical classification went from a typology of illnesses that were thought to enter the body from without and follow a certain course, to a new nosology grounded in the observation of patients' bodies and organs. This meant the expert work of diagnosis shifted from a focus on listening to a patient describe her symptoms to the study of bodily pathology. This new "anatamo-clinical gaze" sought to use sight, touch, laboratory techniques, and postmortem analysis to identify underlying organic lesions. Foucault described this shift as the "dissolution of the ontology of fever" (190), and nothing less than "a syntactical reorganization of disease in which the limits of the visible and invisible follow a new pattern" (195), Foucault also explained how the new spatialization of disease in bodily pathology was part and parcel of a new spatialization of medical practice in the hospital or clinic rather than the patient's home. As Keith Wailoo (2001) explains in his penetrating book on the history of sickle cell disease, a new medical classification requires the right social and clinical conditions of visibility, or what Foucault called its "surfaces of emergence" (41).

One essential element in the rise of clinical medicine, and the bevy of new disease categories that came with it, was a far-reaching shift in medical training and a newfound focus on the hospital and laboratory. This had huge implications for medical expertise. Doctors now have a legally sanctioned monopoly over medical classification. That medical monopoly is justified by roughly a decade of mandatory study and training. "Justified" in two senses. To be sure, doctors learn an enormous amount about human biology, health, illness, and disease over that time, and they (hopefully) develop a clinical acumen that goes beyond formal study. Yet the form, length, and specialization of modern medical training required in the United States was part of an organized professional campaign by allopathic doctors to drive out other medical traditions and control the supply of physicians (Starr 2008; Whooley 2013). Ever since this demanding system of training was established and consolidated by the American Medical Association and its allies in the early twentieth century, it has placed what many consider an undue premium on basic science and specialization. In turn, it has contributed to a severe shortage of primary-care physicians in the United States. In sum, the dual focus on clinical diagnosis and specialist training is indelibly bound up with modern medical expertise and its claims to authority, as well as important imbalances in the supply of doctors.

The issue of classification has unsurprisingly received considerable attention in medical sociology (see Armstrong 2011; Timmermans and Berg 1997, for two exemplary pieces), so much so that there is even an emerging subfield on the sociology of diagnosis (Brown 1990; Jutel 2009; Jutel and Nettleton 2011). The very bases for disease classification—symptoms, anatomical observation, psychiatric characteristics, or genetic test results, to name a few—have churned constantly throughout the history of medicine. Even today, as Armstrong (2011) has shown, primary-care doctors usually cannot make a diagnosis from the dominant International Classification of Diseases (ICD) system (though they may assign a residual category to facilitate insurance reimbursement). Theirs is still a mostly symptoms-oriented practice. Yet clinical nosology still reigns supreme: the ideal outcome of a medical encounter is a diagnosis rooted in some sort of bodily lesion or abnormality, regardless of how rare such a result is in practice. As Armstrong (2011) wrote, "underlying classificatory principles . . . both constitute and reflect the very nature of identity" (802). Other discrepancies in medical classification have to be negotiated as well. Even in a modern hospital, the same disease category is not quite the same thing across departments: as Annemarie Mol (2002) powerfully illustrated in her book *The Body Multiple*, a diagnosis like atherosclerosis partakes of different ontologies in different clinical settings.

Medical classification also sets the parameters for medicine's professional jurisdiction (see Abbott 1988), and therefore the scope of its expert practice. That is why sociologists have paid so much attention to "medicalization" over the past few decades. Beginning in the 1970s, especially with Peter Conrad's seminal 1975 article on the way moderate deviant behavior in children was recast as "hyperkenesis" (the forerunner to ADD and

ADHD), a range of studies have shown how human behaviors, traits, and problems can be rendered into new or expanded medical diagnoses. Examples range from border-line hypertension (van Dijk et al. 2016) and fibromyalgia (Barker 2002) to menopause (Bell 1987), pregnancy (Barker 1998), childbirth (Wertz and Wertz 1989), erectile dys-function (Tiefer 1994), homelessness (Snow et al. 1986), and various forms of so-called mental illness. Conrad and Barker (2010) explain how "we have a social predilection toward treating human problems as individual or clinical—whether it is obesity, sub-stance abuse, learning difficulties, aging, or alcoholism—rather than addressing the un-derlying causes for complex social problems and human suffering." Whether it is driven by imperious doctors, moralizing fearmongers, pharmaceutical interests, or patient ad-vocacy organizations (see Conrad 1975, 1992, 2005; Armstrong 1998), medicalization expands the reach of medical expertise into previously nonmedical forms of human dif-ference and experience.

Medicalization is especially rampant in psychiatry (see, e.g., Bandini 2015; Conrad and Slodden 2013; Horwitz 2002; Rapley, Moncrieff, and Dillon 2011). From ADHD and autism to anxiety and depression, the diagnostic criteria for many mental illnesses have been broadened to include vast swaths of the population. For example, the American Psychiatric Association's expert work group on mood disorders decided to remove the so-called "bereavement exclusion" from the diagnostic criteria for major depression in the DSM-V, leaving the grieving at risk of a major mental illness diagnosis just weeks after the death of a loved one (for a sociological critique and a careful defense of the move, see, respectively, Bandini 2015; Pies 2014). Recent estimates suggest that around one in five Americans has a mental illness at any given time,[2] and that nearly half of us will be diagnosable with a mental illness at some point in our lives (Kessler et al. 2005). This means that psychiatry, as a field of expert practice, can claim an astonishingly ex-pansive jurisdiction.

Yet medical classification in psychiatry is also especially fraught. As scholars from Foucault on have shown, psychiatry has always struggled to find a nosological footing as a field of modern medicine. Why? One key reason is that mental illness can almost never be plausibly traced back to pathological lesions in people's organs. As powerful as the "psy disciplines" often are (Rose 1998), the visibly subjective and mutable nature of psy-chiatric classification opens them to critique and resistance. It is hard to imagine another medical discipline confronting anything akin to the self-described antipsychiatry move-ment that came to the fore in the 1960s and 1970s. But activism can cut both ways. Take two targeted examples: homosexuality was demedicalized and removed from the DSM after resistance from gay rights activists; by contrast, activism played a key role in the diagnostic expansion of autism (Eyal et al. 2010), and the recent removal of Asperger's syndrome from DSM-V has been rejected by self-advocates for whom the category had become a core part of their identity. Hence, mental illness is one area where the vagaries of expert classification are highly visible and often hotly contested. As we will see below, recent moves to address the absence of a biological grounding is the source of major convulsions and controversies in contemporary psychiatry today.

In the face of so much potential resistance, how do psychiatric categories maintain such power? For one thing, the psy-disciplines have evolved into what Nikolas Rose (1992, 356) calls a "generous expertise": concepts and practices developed in psychiatry are regularly adopted by teachers, parents, human resources officers, counselors, and so on. That is very much the case for psychiatry's expert classifications. As Gil Eyal (2013, 868) cogently argues, the transformation of autism into the common condition and cause célèbre it is today happened because of a new network "that blurred the boundaries between parents, researchers, therapists, and activists." The power of psychiatric classifications, in short, cannot be understood by studying only psychiatrists; instead, we must analyze what Eyal calls the "networks of expertise" assembled around categories that "link together objects, actors, techniques, devices, and institutional and spatial arrangements" (864). In this way, we see the performative power of expert classification: medical categories *become* truly powerful when a whole infrastructure of tests, therapies, drugs, support groups, advocates, clinics, and so on, vivify them and change people in their names. Psychiatry does not just invent categories—it builds up networks and creates new kinds of people. However, that does not mean psychiatric experts control the networks of expertise that are built up around those kinds of people or even the way their diagnostic categories develop over time. Indeed, psychiatric classification is where we find looping processes at their most powerful—hence Hacking's two main examples of looping kinds of people are multiple personality disorder (now dissociative identity disorder) and autism (Hacking 1998b, 2007).

Race, Ethnicity and Nationalism; Class, Status, and Consumption

One the of the most powerful and extensively studied forms of human classification centers around race and ethnicity, and associated issues of caste, nation, and so on. W. E. B. Du Bois, in perhaps the first great sociological study of race in the United States, famously argued that the way we group each other into different races—and the racism that almost inevitably comes with it—creates enormous barriers to intersubjectivity and solidarity. He wrote about twofold "veil" that condemns Black people in the United States to a world of hostility and severely prescribed opportunity while simultaneously naturalizing racial oppression and inequality. Over the course of decades, social science scholars have built a huge body of work based on these sorts of insights about the impact of racism on both the oppressed and the oppressors. These scholars may disagree about many things, but they almost all adopt a nominalist approach to race and ethnicity. Many have forcefully argued that racism creates race, not the other way around. In other words, racist systems of classification—via the forms of domination, interpolation, and prohibitions against interbreeding they inspire—are what makes race itself real. While not everyone adopts such a radically constructivist position, you will not find a serious scholar who claims that how we classify race today represents a timeless or "correct" way of carving up human ancestral and phenotypic difference. Instead, scholars have shown how systems of racial classification develop and change and, above all, the way they create and perpetuate structures of domination. This is vital work: racism is even more dangerous when racial categories seem unimpeachably real; to whatever extent social science experts can deconstruct and diminish the givenness of racial classification, racism itself will be less powerful.

If you dig into the origins and history of racial classification, you are almost certain to encounter the work of experts. There is no doubt that we are still wrestling the awful legacy European race "science" left the world (see, e.g., Mamdani 2014; Washington 2008). Be it phrenology, archaeology, psychometrics, genealogy, or what have you, successive expert attempts to scientize race have usually resulted in calamity. Turning to notions of genetic inheritance has only made matters worse. From the eugenics experts of the early twentieth century (Kevles 1998; Paul 1995; Stern 2005; see also Duster 2003) to the infamous (and incessantly recurring) argument advanced in such work as Herrnstein and Murray's *The Bell Curve* (see Gould 1994 for an incisive critique), history has taught us to challenge expert claims about the genetic basis of racial difference. It is no coincidence that the most restrictive, racist immigration laws in US history were enacted during the heyday of eugenics. Racial categories are at their most dangerous when they appear to be timeless and rooted in biological expertise. Experts therefore have a vital role to play in the fight against racism and racial inequality: working to critique, *de*naturalize, and therefore undercut the power of race science and racial classification. As we will see, that is why so many critical social scientists have spoken up against new attempts to biologically vivify the old racial and ethnic categories that have wrought such misery ever since the rise of European imperialism. By showing how much racial categories change over time and place—for example, the way Irish and Jewish immigrants to the United States were not considered White in the early twentieth century—social scientists can help historicize and disarm expert claims about race (see Kahn et al. 2018 for an important recent example).

What about other key categories such as nation, class, status, and profession? Nationalism is another form of human classification that profoundly shapes our lives. Suffice it to say that there is an enormous literature on nationalism, its origins, and its consequences. Yet one thing otherwise opposed scholarly camps tend to agree on is the centrality of experts. Major figures who emphasize the role of state-building such as Ernest Gellner (1983), Charles Tilly (1994), and Eric Hobsbawm (1992) may disagree on many things, but one constantly encounters various sorts of experts in their work on the rise of nationalism. More culturalist scholars who follow Benedict Anderson's ([1983] 2006) casting of nations as "imagined communities" see things very differently, but they still carve out a huge role for experts. In Anderson's seminal book on the rise of nationalism, it took an army of middle-class experts churning out periodicals, novels, schools, censuses, museums, and maps to turn populations into imagined national communities. More recent work has gone even further, showing how expert groups like archaeologists, for example, are often instrumental in the development of national iconographies, identities, and historiographies (see Valiant 2017; and, especially, Abu El

Haj 2002). In this way, experts create the performative landscape that makes nations and nationalism possible. They inscribe the nation into the past via the museums we visit, the books we read, the school curricula we learn, and the monuments that populate our capital cities. Hence, even though the modern nation-state is barely more than a couple of centuries old, nations of people are often treated as though they transcend history. Far more than identity is at stake. The national groups we "belong to" are backed by laws and armies; they determine where we are allowed to live, who rules over us, and everything that goes along with that. Scratch the surface, and you find experts forging these seemingly timeless national bonds.

The quintessentially sociological question of class also raises a series of important questions about classification and expertise. It almost goes without saying that class distinctions are a pervasive feature of modern life. Marx famously argued that class was (or at least would eventually become) a function of a person's position with respect to the means of production. Beginning with Weber, however, a huge slice of sociology has been devoted to unpacking the complexity of the way class works in practice. Weber ([1921] 1978, 302–307, 926–939) built on Marx's straightforwardly materialist definition to develop the enduring concept of *social class*: a more nuanced set of class groupings between which social mobility is relatively difficult and rare. Social class encompasses not only access to capital, but also education and comportment, community and connections, race and caste, and many other things besides. In short, Weber pried open the concept of class, setting up an expansive field of research on the way wealth and status distinctions work in practice. Crucially for us, he showed how classification itself a key part of class dynamics.

Taking class categorization seriously therefore pushes us to reflect on our own expertise and practice as sociologists. Class is, after all, the most important dimension of social life where we regularly serve as the expert classifiers. But we cannot escape the fact that, when it comes to class, we are all inveterate classifiers looking at the world from a particular class position. No one made this point more forcefully than Pierre Bourdieu. Along with his legion of followers, Bourdieu showed us how class distinctions are seared onto the bodies, clothes, speech, manners, and minds of human subjects. Yet Bourdieu was adamant that "cultural capital" is not just a category that sociologists apply to people. Classification, Bourdieu (esp. 1984, 466–484) argued, is deeply embedded in social life itself. As he put it, "The social agents whom the sociologist classifies are producers not only of classifiable acts but also of acts of classification which are themselves classified." In short, people constantly classify one another in the real world, and this must be a key part of any sociological analysis of class dynamics. This sort of classification is ubiquitous, so much so that it hides in plain sight. The "primary forms of classification," Bourdieu argued, "owe their specific efficacy to the fact that they function below the level of consciousness and language, beyond the reach of introspective scrutiny or control by the will." Again, the invisibility of classification serves to make it all the more potent. At the same time, the dynamism of classification renders the sociology of class and stratification a moving target, and one where our own expertise contributes to the endless churning.

What's more, social class shapes who gets to be counted as an expert in the first place. Certain manners, styles of dress, and forms of comportment are often essential if one is going to be accepted as an expert. Thinking with Bourdieu, a particular *habitus* may be an integral part of what makes an expert an expert. Meanwhile, certain forms of cultural capital are often a prerequisite for entrée into a professional community. But what sort of cultural capital? As Michèle Lamont (1994) illustrated in *Money, Morals and Manners*, what it means to be part of the professional classes differs in the United States versus France. The forms of cultural capital that guide class differentiation vary by place and, undoubtedly, by time, profession, and institution. Still, social class can create closure with respect to expertise. This has sweeping implications. As long as many important communities of experts are skewed toward particular social classes—not to mention genders, races, etc.—expertise can never be exercised in a truly democratic way. Indeed, implicit bias has been extensively documented in medicine, law, academic, and many other expert fields. Conversely, expertise often serves to reify class distinctions. What could make someone seem more deserving of privilege than the long and arduous accumulation of legal, medical, engineering, or any other form of expertise?

Finally, the expert classification of professions, social classes, consumers, and voters is often overlooked, but it touches all of us in myriad ways. As Hacking (1990) provocatively asked, "Who had more effect on class consciousness, Marx or the authors of the official reports which created the classifications into which people came to recognize themselves?" (3). Not only do many countries have their own detailed classification of different professions and occupations, but the International Labor Organization publishes its International Standard Classification of Occupations (ISCO) as part of the United Nation's economic and social classifications. Market researchers play an even more pervasive role in our lives, categorizing us across various dimensions that affect our capacity and likelihood to spend and consume. This sort of classification helps determine the ads that appear on our screens and in our print media, the junk mail that is sent to our homes, and the way the stores we visit are organized. As we continue our march into an era of online working and living, portable and wearable devices, electronic transactions, and digital surveillance by companies and governments—all aided by big data analytics and algorithms—the expert classification of our habits and tendencies will become even more powerful. Market research even helped spawn related fields of expertise: perhaps most importantly, public-opinion research seeks to understand not only who is likely to vote for whom but also why; it also created the typology of political types and groups that we use to understand ourselves, and even the very idea of a "public" whose opinions and ideas could be classified and quantified (see Igo 2007).

All of these dimensions of human classification—class, race, nation, etc.—are bolstered by the work of experts, and they all have strong performative components. When we delineate, study, contrast, or intervene in these sorts of categories, we help to create the conditions for their existence and perpetuation. For example, we will see how long-standing modes of racial classification, and therefore racism itself, helped create the conditions for the new genetics of race. At the same time, experts often lose control of their categories and the people they were designed to capture. The working classes may demand more than the benevolent labor department bureaucrat had in mind; a subjugated people will rise up in resistance; as is all too apparent today, nationalism can lead to the sort of reactionary populism that has, at its core, a sweeping rejection of experts and their expertise. In short, classifications can change people in ways that experts did not recommend or foresee. Perhaps then, Hacking's concept of looping could be usefully extended beyond medicine and psychology into other domains of human classification.

Human Classification in the Age of Biomedicine

As many others have argued in one form or another, biology cannot resolve the intrinsically social, power-laden nature of human classification. Nevertheless, we are living through a resurgence of a powerful idea: that the only way to overcome subjectivity, or even arbitrariness, in the way we classify people is to get down to the biological bases of human difference. Whether it is contemporary neurobiology or genomics, the early biological psychiatry and criminology of Lombroso and Kraepelin, or the phrenology of the nineteenth and early twentieth centuries, we keep returning to the idea that biological markers represent the best way to classify people. From mental illness to race and ethnicity, there a growing push to identify the DNA or neurobiological underpinnings of different categories of people. In some cases, biological evidence can actually make and remake the categories themselves.

My argument here is *not* that biological evidence has no useful role to play in human classification. Far from it. It clearly holds great potential in medicine and in many other fields besides. But biology can never magically resolve disputes about the best way to classify illness, race, or anything else. Even when experts use sound biological data to rework our systems of classification, the categories they create remain contingent and power laden. We already saw how the turn to biology in the classification of human difference has often been nothing short of calamitous. Instead, we need to take stock of the performative component of biology in human classification, and the way that biological research can set new looping process in motion. Hacking (1995) himself recognized that biological explanations could have powerful looping effects. In one of his first pieces on looping, he gave the example of how "the scientific (biological) knowledge about alcoholics *produces a different kind of person*" (373; my emphasis). This section will take stock of the ways expert classification, biological research, and looping intersect and shape one another today.

Biologizing Mental Illness and Developmental Difference

Ever since the rise of clinical medicine, experts have tried to create a tight fit between disease classification and biological etiology. This biologizing mandate is so strong that even long-standing disease categories, when they cannot be reduced to a biological cause, often face contestation and elaborate processes of expert consensus building if they are to be taken seriously as medical conditions (Aronowitz 2001). The idealized model of medical classification is one and the same thing as biological classification, never mind that the practical reality is never so simple. In this sense, the turn to "biomedicalization" that social scientists have rightly paid so much attention to (see, esp., Clarke et al. 2003; Keating and Cambrosio 2006) builds on a much older mandate to unify pathology and medical classification.

When it comes to maladies of the mind, however, we saw how this mandate has always been especially problematic. The way we classify mental illness and developmental difference has never even come close to lining up with findings from biological research. It is not for lack of trying: psychiatric researchers and their allies have been on the search for etiological substrates for centuries now, be it in our brains, our genitals, our genomes, or what have you (see esp. Davidson 2004; Horwitz 2002; Whooley and Horwitz 2013). Ever since the late-1970s and the release of DSM-III, American psychiatry has been committed the "neo-Kraepelin" idea that the classification of mental disorders should be valid, that is, reliable, and that validity would one day give way to soundness, that is, a biologically grounded system of psychiatric classification (Horwitz 2002). Decades later, with that dream little closer to fruition, psychiatry finds itself in an increasingly precarious position as a medical field. Making matters worse, a growing number of people are now diagnosed with multiple forms of mental illness, rather than one underlying disease with shifting symptoms. This rise in comorbidity has heightened the sense of crisis around the prevailing system of psychiatric classification (Aragona 2009). In response, there are growing calls for a wholesale biologization of psychiatric classification. When the former director of the National Institute of Mental Health (NIMH) derisively noted "Biology never read [the DSM]" (quoted in Belluck and Carey 2013), he was making the point very clearly: biology is the real deal, and classification systems should be revised to correspond with that reality. Some in the field have even invoked the idea of Kuhnian crisis, with the only remedy being a revolutionary "paradigm shift" toward biomedical classification (Aragona 2009; Whooley 2014). In short, the very nature of psychiatric expertise is at stake in today's debate about the classification of mental illness.

Suffice it to say that there are reasons to be doubtful. For one thing, we simply do not know enough about the biology of mental illness to overhaul psychiatric classification in its image. Most of the people currently under some form of supervision by the various "psy-discipline" experts would be diagnostically orphaned, at great cost to the fields in question. Perhaps that is why the revolutionaries have now adopted a more future-oriented approach. Their new goal, headlined by the NIMH's Research Domain Criteria (RDoC), is designed to redirect psychiatric research so as to "transform diagnosis by incorporating genetics, imaging, cognitive science, and other levels of information to lay the foundation for a new classification system" (Insel 2013).

But there are also sociological grounds for skepticism. For one thing, biological reclassification will take a lot more than biological findings. Even if experts could point to faulty genes, abnormal brain functioning, or imbalanced hormones in everyone with signs of mental illness, that would just be the end of the beginning. It is abundantly clear that biology will not just refine existing categories. Instead, hormonal irregularities, brain defects, and so on tend to cut across many different categories of mental illness. Take the example of genomics—one of the most hyped areas of biological psychiatry. The same genetic mutation may be associated with several different forms of mental illness, even in the same patient, while other people may appear unaffected. We will not find a "gene-for" depression, schizophrenia, autism, or any other category of mental illness. Instead, we find many different mutations, each of which might account for a tiny fraction of this or that mental illness. But here is the rub: the communities of experts, advocates and patients built up around conditions like schizophrenia, ADHD, or autism are not going to rearrange themselves quickly and neatly into a series of rare but biologically specific disorders. The investments in resources and identity are too vast to simply abandon these more long-standing categories. Biological reclassification, if it is to happen at all, will take the form of a "trading zone" between common conditions like autism and rare disorders tied to genetic mutations and other biomarkers (Navon and Eyal 2014). In this way, both types of classification can thrive off one another even as the various experts and stakeholders involved maintain different goals and frameworks for understanding the relationship between illness and biology.

For another, biological classification does not magically resolve the far-reaching complexity of psychiatric classification. Nor does it put an end to looping processes. Experts have been discovering and delineating new conditions such as Triple X, 5p-, NGLY1, and 22q11.2 Deletion Syndrome strictly according to genetic mutations over the past sixty years. This practice, which I have called "genomic designation"—as clear an instance of biological reclassification as one could hope to find—quickly led to dozens of papers in leading medical and genetics journals (Navon 2019; see also Ledbetter 2008; Hogan 2016). And yet, it was decades before they gained traction as categories of medical practice or identity formation. It still took social mobilization and expert collaboration across fields to turn these mutation-based categories into robust kinds of people. Meanwhile, biological specificity did not put a halt to looping for the people and conditions in question—it just changes the looping dynamics at play. A genetic mutation may indeed be a more rigid scientific object than a psychiatric illness like depression or ADHD, but it does not follow that the population of people with that mutation is stable or straightforward. They are often beguilingly complex. Genomic designation is not a clean, timeless, or easily adopted way of carving up human difference at its joints. It still takes a many-varied network of expertise to make a mutation matter—no easy feat in a world geared toward clinical classification—unleashing new spirals of looping as a result.

Finally, biological research on well-established mental illnesses can have profound looping effects. This can happen because, to take an example from Hacking (1995, 373), "by and large, biology is exculpating," as when the idea that alcoholism is a biological condition reduces stigma or blame. Yet "geneticization" can also increase stigma (Phelan 2005; see Shostak, Conrad, and Horwitz 2008 for a more nuanced account). In fact, ideas and evidence about the biological cause of a condition can change it in even more fundamental ways. As Gil Eyal and I demonstrated, ideas and evidence about autism genetics played a direct role in recasting autism as a broad-spectrum disorder. "Geneticization" helped to destigmatize autism and spur an advocacy movement, but genetic evidence from twin studies also pointed toward a broader, more heritable version of autism. This led to diagnostic expansion and therefore rendered autism a far more common condition. In yet a further twist, those same changes in diagnostic practice also changed the genetic makeup of the autism population. They saw autism loop into a broad spectrum that is now associated with hundreds of genetic mutations. Most of these so-called "autism genes" would not have even been associated with autism prior to these looping processes (Navon and Eyal 2016). Evidence from biology can therefore play a dynamic role in the looping processes that make and remake kinds of people over time. In turn, looping may force biomedical experts to chase after a moving target, even as it helps create the conditions for future biological findings. Again, we see how performativity and looping are still very much at play when experts use biology to "refine" human classification.

Biologizing Race and Ethnicity

Let's turn to race and ethnicity. The standard position throughout most social and human sciences, as we saw above, is that racial and ethnic group distinctions are "socially constructed" rather than scientific categories. This does not (or should not) mean that there are no biological or genetic differences between human populations. For example, many genetic variants are *correlated* with racial and ethnic groups. But races are *not* biological categories. They are recent, social distinctions born largely of race "science" (that is, racism with a scientific veneer), European imperialism, nationalism, and the ongoing effects of racism in its many guises. There is more genetic and biological variation *within* racial and ethnic groups than *between* those groups—a famous fact that has led to intense debate ever since Lewontin's (1972) initial demonstration and argument that it invalidates racial taxonomy.

So, taking the most salient example today, what role does DNA testing have in helping us understand race and ethnicity? Experts have used genomics to shed new light on historical migration patters and the ubiquity of admixture, showing how ancestral groups are more complex and interbred than most would have it (e.g., Reich 2018, though we will see how his treatment of "race" itself left serious cause for concern). It has also been used to make claims to group membership. For example, DNA data has been used to validate ancestral links between the major Ashkenazi and Mizrahi Jewish populations and smaller Jewish groups from Ethopia, southern Africa, and northeast India—with important implications for their rights to immigrate to Israel (McGonigle and Herman 2015). Meanwhile, individuals have used genetic ancestry testing to claim membership of Native American groups and tribes, as well as some of the attendant rights, and genomics researarchers have even unsettled longstanding notions of indigeneity itself—often with troubling implications (TallBear 2013). Experts have used genetic testing to get at health disparities and pharmacogenomic differences between populations in the US, inadvertently helping to obfuscate the social determinants that we know to be far more powerful (see Duster 2003 for the classic critique). In recent years, direct-to-consumer genetic testing has been rolled out on a massive scale as a tool for people seeking to better understand their own race, ethnicity, and ancestry. Indeed, there is evidence that these tests can reshape identity and lead to visits, donations, and revised self-identification on census forms.

Scholars like Duana Fullwiley (2007) argue that genetics research and DNA testing may "re-inscribe" our belief in racial difference and groups (see also Abu El-Haj 2007; Duster 2005; Ossorio and Duster 2005). As she explained, a "back and forth between DNA and its seemingly natural organization by societal descriptors of race works to *molecularize* race itself" (p. 4). By using self-reported, census-based racial and ethnic classifications, genetics researchers are employing non-scientific variables and reifying existing social categories. Even though many experts appear to recognize how problematic these categories usually are—both scientifically and politically—their attempts to identify "pure" study participants end up re-inscribing racial and ethnic categories through the process of research itself. Fullwiley shows us how performative genetics research can be, and how we need to "get beyond the polemics of whether or not race is genetic—towards better understanding how it *becomes* genetic, or molecularized." (p. 23) Meanwhile, more recent research by Panofsky and Bliss (2017) shows how genetics experts often use incommensurate racial, ethnic, geographic, linguistic, national, and ancestral categories side by side in the same study. They use "population" as a sort of boundary object, rather than a hard and fast set of categories. In this way, classificatory ambiguity is conducive to scientific, that is, expert authority. They also rely on non-experts, mostly notably when they simply ask people which racial or ethnic group they identify with. So even here, where people turn to genomics to resolve outstanding questions about racial and ethnic identity, expert classification remains murky and ridden with the historical baggage of categories rooted in imperialism and racism. Reification and ambiguity frequently go hand in hand when it comes to the classification of human ancestral populations.

One area where we might expect to find the genetic re-inscription of race at its most powerful is direct-to-consumer (DTC) ancestry testing. After all, this is where experts purport to offer consumers genetic information about their own racial, ethnic, and national origins. As many others have pointed out, there are a whole host of things to take issue with here—not least the fact that these tests are not regulated, they rely on proprietary databases and algorithms, they do not adequately account for things like migration, selection or gene flow, they obfuscate their probabilistic status and the occurence of rare alleles in populations, and so on. There is also the manifest absurdity of using nations—political groups which are only decades or at most a few centuries old—as categories for genetics research and analysis. Above all, DTC ancestry tests rely on reference groups that are assumed to be "pure" in some meaningful sense, as though migration and admixture have not shaped their DNA. Yet, DTC ancestry testing unquestionably contributes to the biological/genetic re-inscription of race outlined by Fullwiley et al.

above. It has become an astonishingly cheap and easy way for people to access scientific expertise (however dubious) in their search for racial and ethnic identity.

Nevertheless, as Alondra Nelson (2008) argues, people often exercise considerable *autonomy* in their interpretation of DNA ancestry test results. Nelson showed how "test-takers can exercise latitude in determining the import of genetic ancestry analysis." While it is true that "root-seekers come to genetic genealogy with the expectation that it will supply definitive information about family history," the reality is that "a genetic 'match' is just the beginning of a process of identification" (p. 775). As Nelson neatly captures it, DTC customers often engage in "affiliative self-fashioning" whereby they integrate their DNA test results into a much broader understanding of their origins. They also often "display expertise through their command of jargon and recent genetics research" (762) as part of this active engagement with genomic meaning-making. In short, DNA testing shapes identity not because people mindlessly accept the word of genetics experts, but because they bring their own identities and lay expertise to bear when they interpret DTC genomic results. Genetics expertise can sometimes lead to ethnic reclassification, but it can also create new spirals of looping that experts did not envision or intend.

There is also a long and ignominious history of research on the genetics of behavior, intelligence, and ancestry—a history that has always been replete with racism. Even after the downfall of the openly prejudiced eugenics movement, genetics research on IQ never broke free of racist activism and ideology (Panofsky 2014). For the most part, the sort of scientific racism championed by Shockley and Jensen in the 1960s and 1970s and Charles Murray, James Watson, and Sam Harris today has been confined to the margins. Yet it is creeping back in more respectable guises. Take David Reich (2018), the Harvard geneticist whose book *Who We Are and How We Got Here* shows how extraordinarily complex, migratory, and admixed human populations have been for many thousands of years. Yet even Reich, in a piece for the *New York Times Sunday Review*, wrote: "Since all traits influenced by genetics are expected to differ across populations (because the frequencies of genetic variations are rarely exactly the same across populations), the genetic influences on behavior and cognition will differ across populations, too." The article provoked an incisive collective response from a group of researchers, including several of the critical social scientists cited above (Kahn et al. 2018), that tried to unpack the dangerous leaps of logic underlying Reich's startling claim. But it was also picked up and mobilized by right-wing ideologues who refuse to let go of the idea that genetics can explain away ongoing racial disparities. The dangers of expert-driven reification are always present in scientific research on intelligence, making it all the more important that there are voices with the critical expertise to unpack and disarm claims about biology, class, and race.

We need to take stock of the performative power of racial classification—brought to us via now-debunked race science and vivified through racism. It was racism and imperialism, after all, that helped *create* the very genetic facts that are now looping back to reify racial categories. Racism forbids the admixture that has been the norm throughout human history. It led to the forced migration of populations. Meanwhile, nationalism has constrained the freedom to migrate and therefore helped to stem population flows. As Troy Duster put it (2005, 1050), "There is a complex feedback loop and interaction effect between phenotype and social practices related to that phenotype." Hence today's genetics researchers and DTC ancestry companies are able to find variants that are more common in one of these populations than the others. But they are also engaging in performativity anew: when they assemble databases composed of samples from "pure" reference groups, they are creating new truth conditions for racial classification that, however flawed, can be applied to all of us. And yet, we saw how genetics research and DTC testing around race also produces reactions and surprising new forms of identity making. It can even create entirely new kinship relations and identity categories (like mitochondrial and Y-chromosome haplogroups) that can be pursued on online message boards and beyond. Meanwhile, even when people do use genetic ancestry information to reshape their identities, they may not do so just as the experts who created that data had in mind (Nelson 2008). In sum, biology will never resolve any of the enormous pitfalls of racial classification, but it can kick off a new a dangerous dance of performativity and looping effects.

CONCLUSION

Weber ([1921] 1978, 4–22) famously taught us to treat our categories of analysis as "ideal types": useful abstractions to guide sociological research, rather than distinct phenomena that are found in reality. When studying classification out there in the real world, however, we sociologists need to remember that most people are not Weberians. Nor are we most of the time. We *need* to take classification for granted as we go about our lives. To quote Marion Fourcade (2016): "This ability to classify . . . is both a product of human communication and an essential basis of social community" (175–176). Lakoff and Johnson (1999, 18) may have even been right to argue that categorization is nothing less than "an inescapable consequence of our biological makeup." We need to classify in order to navigate our daily lives. But the distinctions and categories we so depend on are indelibly social and historically fluid. As Jean and John Comaroff put it (cited in Fullwiley 2011, 18): "Categories are themselves just one of a series of available imaginative "implements." Whether they will be selected and how they will be used in any context is clearly a function of culture rather than nature." And yet, the systems of classification that surround us are very much real in their effects. They make the world in their image and therefore order reality in ways that are by no means reducible to our incessantly classifying minds.

In our modern world, no one has more control over classification than experts. Our three pillars for a sociology of classification help us understand what an enormous amount of power is therefore invested in various forms of expertise. First, categories are not given to us by nature, but they set the very terms of experience. Furthermore, systems of classification are often invisible, and this invisibility cloaks a vast reservoir of expert power that touches many different aspects of our lives. Second, categories are often performative: they help to create the conditions of their own truth. When it comes to kinds of people, expert classification and the practices that follow from it can even lead to biological findings that seem to bolster the validity of the category itself. Third, when it comes to kinds of people, credentialed experts almost never operate with total authority. It takes a much broader "network of expertise" (Eyal 2013) to make a powerful kind of person. People do not automatically conform to expert categories. Their transgressions, surprising findings, and unforeseen developments from many different quarters can loop back to change the categories themselves. When it comes to classifying humans, we therefore need to take stock of the dynamic relationship between experts, their categories, and the people who are classified.

Finally, we tackled the biologization of human classification. Whether it is race, national origin, traits, or diseases, biological expertise can never be more than a new element in a longer looping story. Trying to turn kinds of people into natural kinds is a hopeless and sometimes dangerous task. The classification of mental illness will never be rendered seamless or unproblematic, no matter how much we understand our brains, genes, or any other favored biological site. Likewise, biology will never deliver us from racism and bigotry. On the contrary, genetics can "re-inscribe" categories of racial difference and naturalize structures of racial inequality and oppression; pioneering scientists like James Watson can turn out to be odious racists just like any other sort of expert; as Panofsky and Donovan (2017) have shown, racists are also able to enroll serious lay genetics expertise in their activism and identity making. The biological classification of human difference—in psychiatry, population studies, or any other field—will only unleash new power dynamics and looping processes. When it comes to classifying people, sociologists of expertise should rigorously interrogate any new venture to carve nature at its joints.

Notes

1. See e.g., The United Nations Statistics Division (UNSD) and the many different classification systems and guides they publish: https://unstats.un.org/unsd/classifications/unsdclassifications.
2. See the National Institute of Mental Heath's main statistics page: https://www.nimh.nih.gov/health/statistics/mental-illness.shtml.

References

Abbott, Andrew. 1988. *System of Professions: Essay on the Division of Expert Labor*. Chicago: University of Chicago Press.

Abu El-Haj, Nadia. 2002. *Facts on the Ground: Archaeological Practice and Territorial Self-Fashioning in Israeli Society*. Chicago: University of Chicago Press.

Abu El-Haj, Nadia. 2007. "The Genetic Reinscription of Race." *Annual Review of Anthropology* 36 (1): 283–300.

Althusser, Louis. 2014. *On The Reproduction Of Capitalism: Ideology And Ideological State Apparatuses.* London, UK: Verso Books.

Anderson, Benedict. (1983) 2006. *Imagined Communities: Reflections on the Origin and Spread of Nationalism.* Rev. ed. London: Verso.

Aragona, Massimiliano. 2009. "The Role of Comorbidity in the Crisis of the Current Psychiatric Classification System." *Philosophy, Psychiatry, & Psychology* 16 (1): 1–11.

Armstrong, David. 2011. "Diagnosis and Nosology in Primary Care." *Social Science & Medicine* 73 (6): 801–807.

Armstrong, Elizabeth M. 1998. "Diagnosing Moral Disorder: The Discovery and Evolution of Fetal Alcohol Syndrome." *Social Science & Medicine* 47 (12): 2025–2042.

Aronowitz, Robert A. 1999. *Making Sense of Illness: Science, Society and Disease.* Cambridge, UK: Cambridge University Press.

Aronowitz, Robert A. 2001. "When Do Symptoms Become a Disease?" *Annals of Internal Medicine* 134 (Part 2): 803–808.

Aspers, Patrik. 2007. "Theory, Reality, and Performativity in Markets." *American Journal of Economics and Sociology* 66 (2): 379–398.

Austin, John Langshaw, and John L. Austin. 1962. *How to Do Things with Words.* Cambridge, MA: Harvard University Press.

Bandini, Julia. 2015. "The Medicalization of Bereavement: (Ab)normal Grief in the DSM-5." *Death Studies* 39 (6): 347–352.

Barad, Karen. 2003. "Posthumanist Performativity: Toward an Understanding of How Matter Comes to Matter." *Signs* 28 (3): 801–831.

Barker, K. K. 1998. "A Ship upon a Stormy Sea: The Medicalization of Pregnancy." *Social Science & Medicine* 47 (8): 1067–1076.

Barker, Kristin. 2002. "Self-Help Literature and the Making of an Illness Identity: The Case of Fibromyalgia Syndrome (FMS)." *Social Problems* 49 (3): 279–300.

Becker, Howard Saul. 1963. *Outsiders: Studies in the Sociology of Deviance.* London: Free Press of Glencoe.

Bell, Susan E. 1987. "Changing Ideas: The Medicalization of Menopause." *Social Science & Medicine* 24 (6): 535–42.

Belluck, Pam, and Benedict Carey. 2013. "Psychiatry's New Guide Falls Short, Experts Say." *New York Times,* May 6.

Bourdieu, Pierre. 1984. *Distinction: A Social Critique of the Judgement of Taste.* Cambridge, MA: Harvard University Press.

Bowker, Geoffrey C., and Susan Leigh Star. 2000. *Sorting Things Out: Classification and Its Consequences.* Cambridge, MA: MIT Press.

Brown, Phil. 1990. "The Name Game: Toward a Sociology of Diagnosis." *Journal of Mind and Behavior* 11 (3/4): 385–406.

Butler, Judith. 2006. *Gender Trouble: Feminism and the Subversion of Identity.* New York: Routledge.

Butler, Judith. 2010. "Performative Agency." *Journal of Cultural Economy* 3 (2): 147–161.

Callon, Michel. 1998. "Introduction: The Embeddedness of Economic Markets in Economics." *The Sociological Review* 46 (S1): 1–57.

Callon, Michel. 2006. "What Does It Mean to Say That Economics Is Performative?" CSI WORKING PAPERS SERIES 005. 2006. <halshs-00091596>

Clarke, Adele E., Janet K. Shim, Laura Mamo, Jennifer Ruth Fosket, and Jennifer R. Fishman. 2003. "Biomedicalization: Technoscientific Transformations of Health, Illness, and U.S. Biomedicine." *American Sociological Review* 68 (2): 161–194.

Conrad, Peter. 1975. "The Discovery of Hyperkinesis: Notes on the Medicalization of Deviant Behavior." *Social Problems* 23 (1): 12–21.

Conrad, Peter. 1992. "Medicalization and Social Control." *Annual Review of Sociology* 18:209–32.

Conrad, Peter. 2005. "The Shifting Engines of Medicalization." *Journal of Health and Social Behavior* 46 (1): 3–14.

Conrad, Peter, and Kristin K. Barker. 2010. "The Social Construction of Illness: Key Insights and Policy Implications." *Journal of Health and Social Behavior* 51 (1_suppl): S67–79.

Conrad, Peter, and Caitlin Slodden. 2013. "The Medicalization of Mental Disorder." In *Handbook of the Sociology of Mental Health*, edited by C. S. Aneshensel, J. C. Phelan and A. Bierman, 61–73. London, UK: Springer.

Davidson, Arnold I. 2004. *The Emergence of Sexuality: Historical Epistemology and the Formation of Concepts*. Rev. ed. Cambridge, MA: Harvard University Press.

Douglas, Mary. 1986. *How Institutions Think*. Syracuse, NY: Syracuse University Press.

Durkheim, Émile. 2001. *The Elementary Forms of Religious Life*. Oxford: Oxford University Press.

Durkheim, Emile, and Marcel Mauss. 1967. *Primitive Classification*. Chicago: University of Chicago Press.

Duster, Troy. 2003. *Backdoor to Eugenics*. 2nd ed. Routledge.

Duster, Troy. 2005. "Race and Reification in Science." *Science* 307 (5712): 1050–1051.

Epstein, Steven. 1996. *Impure Science: AIDS, Activism, and the Politics of Knowledge*. Berkeley: University of California Press.

Eyal, Gil. 2013. "For a Sociology of Expertise: The Social Origins of the Autism Epidemic." *American Journal of Sociology* 118 (4): 863–907.

Eyal, Gil, B. Hart, E. Onculer, N. Oren, and N. Rossi. 2010. *The Autism Matrix*. Cambridge, UK: Polity.

Foucault, Michel. 1954. *Maladie mentale et personnalité*. Paris: Presses Universitaires de France.

Foucault, Michel. 1973. *The Birth of the Clinic: An Archaeology of Medical Perception*. New York: Pantheon Books.

Foucault, Michel. 1982. *The Archaeology of Knowledge: And "The Discourse on Language."* New York: Vintage Books.

Foucault, Michel. 1988. *Madness and Civilization: A History of Insanity in the Age of Reason*. New York: Vintage.

Foucault, Michel. 2001. *Order of Things: An Archaeology of the Human Sciences*. 2nd ed. London: Routledge.

Foucault, Michel. 2004. *Abnormal: Lectures at the Collège de France, 1974–1975*. New York: Picador.

Fourcade, Marion. 2016. "Ordinalization: Lewis A. Coser Memorial Award for Theoretical Agenda Setting 2014." *Sociological Theory* 34 (3): 175–195.

Fullwiley, Duana. 2007. "The Molecularization of Race: Institutionalizing Human Difference in Pharmacogenetics Practice." *Science as Culture* 16 (1): 1–30.

Fullwiley, Duana. 2011. *The Encultured Gene: Sickle Cell Health Politics and Biological Difference in West Africa*. Princeton, NJ: Princeton University Press.

Gellner, Ernest. 1983. *Nations and Nationalism*. Ithaca, NY: Cornell University Press.

Goffman, Erving. 1986. *Stigma: Notes on the Management of Spoiled Identity*. New York: Touchstone.

Gould, Stephen Jay. 1994. "Curveball." *New Yorker*, November 28, 139–149.

Greco, Monica. 2012. "The Classification and Nomenclature of 'Medically Unexplained Symptoms': Conflict, Performativity and Critique." *Social Science & Medicine* 75 (12): 2362–2369.

Hacking, Ian. 1990. *The Taming of Chance*. Cambridge, UK: Cambridge University Press.

Hacking, Ian. 1995. "The Looping Effects of Human Kinds." In *Causal Cognition: A Multidisciplinary Debate, Symposia of the Fyssen Foundation*, edited by D. Sperber, D. Premack, and A. J. Premack, 351–394. New York: Oxford University Press.

Hacking, Ian. 1998a. *Mad Travelers: Reflections on the Reality of Transient Mental Illnesses*. Charlottesville: University of Virginia Press.

Hacking, Ian. 1998b. *Rewriting the Soul*. Princeton, NJ: Princeton University Press.

Hacking, Ian. 2006. "Making Up People." *London Review of Books*, August 17, 23–26.

Hacking, Ian. 2007. "Kinds of People: Moving Targets." *Proceedings of the British Academy* 51:285–318.

Hobsbawm, Eric J. 1992. *Nations and Nationalism Since 1780: Programme, Myth, Reality*. Cambridge UK: Cambridge University Press.

Hogan, Andrew J. 2016. *Life Histories of Genetic Disease: Patterns and Prevention in Postwar Medical Genetics*. Baltimore, MD: Johns Hopkins University Press.

Horwitz, Allan V. 2002. *Creating Mental Illness*. Chicago: University of Chicago Press.

Igo, Sarah Elizabeth. 2007. *The Averaged American*. Cambridge, MA: Harvard.

Insel, Thomas. 2013. "Transforming Diagnosis." NIMH Director's Blog, 29 April 2013. Retrieved https://web.archive.org/web/20130503094041/http://www.nimh.nih.gov/about/director/2013/transforming-diagnosis.shtml.

Jutel, Annemarie. 2009. "Sociology of Diagnosis: A Preliminary Review." *Sociology of Health & Illness* 31 (2): 278–299.

Jutel, Annemarie, and Sarah Nettleton. 2011. "Toward a Sociology of Diagnosis: Reflections and Opportunities." *Social Science & Medicine* 73 (6): 793–800.

Kahn, Jonathan, Alondra Nelson, Joseph L. Graves, Sarah Abel, Ruha Benjamin, Sarah Blacker, et al. 2018. "Opinion: How Not to Talk about Race and Genetics." BuzzFeed News. February 12, 2020. https://www.buzzfeednews.com/article/bfopinion/race-genetics-david-reich.

Kant, Immanuel. (1787) 2003. *Critique of Pure Reason*. Rev. ed. Translated by Norman Kemp Smith. Edited by Howard Caygill. Basingstoke, UK: Palgrave Macmillan.

Keating, Peter, and Alberto Cambrosio. 2006. *Biomedical Platforms: Realigning the Normal and the Pathological in Late-Twentieth-Century Medicine*. Cambridge, MA: MIT Press.

Kessler, Ronald C., Patricia Berglund, Olga Demler, Robert Jin, Kathleen R. Merikangas, and Ellen E. Walters. 2005. "Lifetime Prevalence and Age-of-Onset Distributions of DSM-IV Disorders in the National Comorbidity Survey Replication." *Archives of General Psychiatry* 62 (6): 593–602.

Kevles, Daniel J. 1998. *In the Name of Eugenics: Genetics and the Uses of Human Heredity*. Cambridge, MA: Harvard University Press.

Lakoff, George, and Mark Johnson. 1999. *Philosophy in the Flesh: The Embodied Mind and Its Challenge to Western Thought*. New York: Basic Books.

Lamont, Michèle. 1994. *Money, Morals, and Manners: The Culture of the French and the American Upper-Middle Class*. Chicago: University of Chicago Press.

Ledbetter, David H. 2008. "Cytogenetic Technology—Genotype and Phenotype." *New England Journal of Medicine* 359 (16): 1728–1730.

Lewontin, R. C. 1972. "The Apportionment of Human Diversity." In *Evolutionary Biology: Volume 6*, edited by T. Dobzhansky, M. K. Hecht, and W. C. Steere, 381–398. New York: Springer US.

MacKenzie, Donald. 2003. "An Equation and Its Worlds Bricolage, Exemplars, Disunity and Performativity in Financial Economics." *Social Studies of Science* 33 (6): 831–868.

MacKenzie, Donald. 2004. "The Big, Bad Wolf and the Rational Market: Portfolio Insurance, the 1987 Crash and the Performativity of Economics." *Economy and Society* 33 (3): 303–334.

MacKenzie, Donald. 2006. "Is Economics Performative? Option Theory and the Construction of Derivatives Markets." *Journal of the History of Economic Thought* 28 (1): 29–55.

Mamdani, Mahmood. 2014. *When Victims Become Killers: Colonialism, Nativism, and the Genocide in Rwanda*. Princeton, NJ: Princeton University Press.

McGonigle, Ian V., and Lauren W. Herman. 2015. "Genetic Citizenship: DNA Testing and the Israeli Law of Return." *Journal of Law and the Biosciences* 2 (2): 469–478.

Merton, Robert K. 1968. *Social Theory and Social Structure*. Enlarged ed. New York: Free Press.

Mitchell, Timothy. 2005. "The Work of Economics: How a Discipline Makes Its World." *European Journal of Sociology* 46 (02): 297–320.

Mol, Annemarie. 2002. *The Body Multiple: Ontology in Medical Practice*. Durham, NC: Duke University Press.

Muniesa, Fabian. 2014. *The Provoked Economy: Economic Reality and the Performative Turn*. London: Routledge.

Navon, Daniel. 2019. *Mobilizing Mutations: Human Genetics in the Age of Patient Advocacy*. Chicago: University of Chicago Press.

Navon, Daniel, and Gil Eyal. 2014. "The Trading Zone of Autism Genetics: Examining the Intersection of Genomic and Psychiatric Classification." *BioSocieties* 9 (3): 329–352.

Navon, Daniel, and Gil Eyal. 2016. "Looping Genomes: Diagnostic Change and the Genetic Makeup of the Autism Population." *American Journal of Sociology* 121 (5): 1416–1471.

Nelson, Alondra. 2008. "Bio Science: Genetic Genealogy Testing and the Pursuit of African Ancestry." *Social Studies of Science* 38 (5): 759–783.

Ossorio, Pilar, and Troy Duster. 2005. "Race and Genetics: Controversies in Biomedical, Behavioral, and Forensic Sciences." *American Psychologist* 60 (1): 115–128.

Panofsky, Aaron. 2014. *Misbehaving Science: Controversy and the Development of Behavior Genetics*. Chicago: University of Chicago Press.

Panofsky, Aaron, and Catherine Bliss. 2017. "Ambiguity and Scientific Authority: Population Classification in Genomic Science." *American Sociological Review* 82 (1): 59–87.

Panofsky, Aaron, and Joan Donovan. 2017. "Genetic Ancestry Testing among White Nationalists." *Social Studies of Science* 0306312719861434. doi: 10.1177/0306312719861434.

Paul, Diane B. 1995. *Controlling Human Heredity, 1865 to the Present*. Amherst, NY: Humanities Press.

Phelan, Jo C. 2005. "Geneticization of Deviant Behavior and Consequences for Stigma: The Case of Mental Illness." *Journal of Health and Social Behavior* 46(4):307–22. doi: 10.2307/4147660.

Pickering, Andy. 1994. "After Representation: Science Studies in the Performative Idiom." *PSA: Proceedings of the Biennial Meeting of the Philosophy of Science Association* 1994 (2): 413–419.

Pies, Ronald. 2014. "The Bereavement Exclusion and DSM-5: An Update and Commentary." *Innovations in Clinical Neuroscience* 11 (7–8): 19–22.

Plomin, Robert, and Sophie von Stumm. 2018. "The New Genetics of Intelligence." *Nature Reviews Genetics* 19 (3): 148–159.

Rapley, Mark, Joanna Moncrieff, and Jacqui Dillon. 2011. "Carving Nature at Its Joints? DSM and the Medicalization of Everyday Life." In *De-medicalizing Misery*, edited by M. Rapley, J. Moncrieff, and J. Dillon, 1–9. London: Palgrave Macmillan.

Reich, David. 2018. *Who We Are and How We Got Here: Ancient DNA and the New Science of the Human Past*. New York: Pantheon.

Rose, Nikolas. 1992. "Engineering the Human Soul: Analyzing Psychological Expertise." *Science in Context* 5(2):351–69. doi: 10.1017/S0269889700001228.

Rose, Nikolas. 1998. *Inventing Our Selves: Psychology, Power, and Personhood*. Cambridge, UK: Cambridge University Press.

Rosenberg, Charles. 2002. "The Tyranny of Diagnosis: Specific Entities and Individual Experience." *Milbank Quarterly* 80 (2): 237–260.

Scott, James C. 1999. *Seeing like a State: How Certain Schemes to Improve the Human Condition Have Failed*. New Haven, CT: Yale University Press.

Shostak, Sara, Peter Conrad, and Allan V. Horwitz. 2008. "Sequencing and Its Consequences: Path Dependence and the Relationships between Genetics and Medicalization." *American Journal of Sociology* 114(S1):S287–316. doi: 10.1086/595570.

Smith, Joseph Wayne. 1984. "Primitive Classification and the Sociology of Knowledge: A Response to Bloor." *Studies in History and Philosophy of Science Part A* 15 (3): 237–243.

Snow, David A., Susan G. Baker, Leon Anderson, and Michael Martin. 1986. "The Myth of Pervasive Mental Illness among the Homeless." *Social Problems* 33 (5): 407–423.

Starr, Paul. 2008. *The Social Transformation of American Medicine: The Rise of a Sovereign Profession and the Making of a Vast Industry*. New York: Basic Books.

Stern, Alexandra Minna. 2005. *Eugenic Nation: Faults and Frontiers of Better Breeding in Modern America*. Berkeley: University of California Press.

TallBear, Kim. 2013. *Native American DNA: Tribal Belonging and the False Promise of Genetic Science*. Minneapolis: University of Minnesota Press.

Tiefer, Leonore. 1994. "The Medicalization of Impotence: Normalizing Phallocentrism." *Gender & Society* 8 (3): 363–377.

Timmermans, Stefan, and Marc Berg. 1997. "Standardization in Action: Achieving Local Universality through Medical Protocols." *Social Studies of Science* 27 (2): 273–305.

Tilly, Charles. 1994. "States and Nationalism in Europe 1492–1992." *Theory and Society* 23 (1): 131–146.

Valiant, Seonaid. 2017. *Ornamental Nationalism: Archaeology and Antiquities in Mexico, 1876–1911*. Leiden, Netherlands: Brill.

Valverde, Mariana 1998. *Diseases of the Will*. Cambridge, UK: Cambridge University Press.

van Dijk, Wieteke, Marjan J. Faber, Marit A. C. Tanke, Patrick P. T. Jeurissen, and Gert P. Westert. 2016. "Medicalisation and Overdiagnosis: What Society Does to Medicine." *International Journal of Health Policy and Management* 5 (11): 619–622.

Wailoo, Keith. 2001. *Dying in the City of the Blues: Sickle Cell Anemia and the Politics of Race and Health*. Chapel Hill: University of North Carolina Press.

Washington, Harriet A. 2008. *Medical Apartheid: The Dark History of Medical Experimentation on Black Americans from Colonial Times to the Present*. New York: Anchor.

Waterton, Claire. 2003. "Performing the Classification of Nature." *The Sociological Review* 51 (2_suppl): 111–129.

Weber, Max. 1978. *Economy and Society*. Edited by G. Roth and C. Wittich. Berkeley CA: University of California Press.

Wertz, Richard W., and Dorothy C. Wertz. 1989. *Lying-In: A History of Childbirth in America*. Expanded ed. New Haven, CT: Yale University Press.

Whooley, Owen. 2013. *Knowledge in the Time of Cholera: The Struggle over American Medicine in the Nineteenth Century*. Chicago: University of Chicago Press.

Whooley, Owen. 2014. "Nosological Reflections: The Failure of DSM-5, the Emergence of RDoC, and the Decontextualization of Mental Distress." *Society and Mental Health* 4 (2): 92–110.

Whooley, Owen, and Allan V. Horwitz. 2013. "The Paradox of Professional Success: Grand Ambition, Furious Resistance, and the Derailment of the DSM-5 Revision Process." In *Making the DSM-5*, edited by Joel Paris and James Phillips, 75–92. New York: Springer.

PART IV

JURISDICTIONAL
STRUGGLES

15

BATTLE OF THE EXPERTS: THE STRANGE CAREER OF META-EXPERTISE

FRANK PASQUALE

INTRODUCTION

SOCIOLOGISTS, economists, and attorneys have often analogized expertise to a turf war: a concept defined by rivalries among experts (or between experts and laypeople) to establish epistemic, commercial, and political dominance in a sphere of human activity. Part of the success of a guild or professional association is asserting exclusive authority over a range of social problems, while developing methods of further formalizing, justifying, and refining this expertise. Criminal defendants do not seek out public relations (PR) experts or engineers when they plead their cases in a courtroom; they need an attorney for that (however much good PR may help outside that context). Similarly, even populist skeptics of medical expertise tend to see a doctor when their health problems are sufficiently advanced.

Sociologists and historians have explored the tactics used by professions to consolidate their jurisdiction over certain social phenomena. These struggles for recognition are politically controversial. Labor self-governance via professions tends to offend neoliberals, who object to the "interference" in labor markets; those who disdain the "professional-managerial class"; and some less-advantaged workers, who chafe at the relative privilege of others. To the extent that professions amount to an economic caste system, unfairly privileging some workers over others, their suspicions have some foundation. However, the independent evaluation of treatment methods, legal strategies, and other difficult and contextual judgments may be an epistemological foundation for the unbiased application of expertise—or, at least, a practice that is less biased than those dominated by market imperatives or state regulation can offer. Moreover, it is possible to soften stratification while promoting professions' higher aims.

Two strategies for doing so have increasingly sparked crises of expertise among professions. The first, recently analyzed by Gil Eyal, pits political authorities against experts, insisting on the subordination of the latter to the former.[1] It was exemplified in US law in the 2014 decision of the United States Supreme Court in *North Carolina Dental Association vs. Federal Trade Commission*. In that decision, a majority of the Court stated that dentists (and other professionals) could only set the rules of their profession if they were under "active supervision" by government officials.[2] In other words, state governments were not permitted to simply delegate authority over a market to boards of experts when those experts are competitors in that market. Governing professional boards of experts are, instead, required to report to political officials.[3]

North Carolina Dental is part of a widespread judicial and regulatory trend to bring professionals to heel in the United States. For example, the Federal Trade Commission has frequently intervened to attack occupational licensing schemes that it views as too protective of incumbents.[4] Yet many of the officials who should be actively supervising professions do not relish the burden of judgment. They instead wish to outsource it to consultants, economists, quantitative analysts, and others who promise to measure the performance and value of professional work. This entails a second strategy for limiting the power of experts: holding up their work to metrics, adapted from Taylorist methods of assessing productivity and refined to apply to more complex or contestable work. This metricization is part of a long line of social knowledge projects designed to rank, rate, and otherwise evaluate experts. It is "meta-expertise": the development of standardized and specialized algorithmic and quantitative methods that trans-substantively evaluate outcomes in particular experts' fields.[5]

The very concept of meta-expertise confounds traditional distinctions between elite power and democratic power. On the one hand, the meta-expert seems to suffer all the debilities of the traditional expert, only more so. Whereas a traditional expert at least has a bounded set of situations to claim to be knowledgeable about, the meta-expert asserts expansive intellectual authority. Suspicious of such authority, Will Davies has observed: "A profession that claimed jurisdiction over everything would no longer be a profession, but a form of epistemological tyranny."[6] Davies builds on Andrew Abbott's foundational observation that abstract and transcontextual knowledge offers professions a way to justify their existing power, and to try to expand it.[7] From Davies's perspective, the meta-experts in computer science and economics who aim to govern (or at least authoritatively appraise) other professions appear as overbearing, even autocratic figures. Skeptics of professions (as well as professional skeptics), however, claim that experts' authority must have some substantive (and not merely political and procedural) limits. These skeptics may style the meta-expert as a powerful tribune of "the people," capable of vindicating both common sense and counterintuitive findings in the face of guildish lethargy and incuriosity. Technocrats have embraced this emphasis on measurable results as a form of accountability.[8] So, too, have a collection of Silicon Valley cyberlibertarians, who aspire to recreate whole fields (finance, public health, literature, and more) based on their own commitments to rational argument, structured deliberation, and online voting to resolve disputes.[9]

Assertions of meta-expertise spark both ideological and material power struggles. In the next section, "Politics and/of Expertise," I describe the crises of expertise that have empowered meta-experts as potential agents of adjudication and resolution when the views of mere experts are contested. The section "Quality, Cost, and Governance in Health Care and Education" then examines particular applications of meta-expertise to the healthcare and education sectors, and their infirmities. The section "The Bounds of Meta-Expertise" concludes with reflections on the value and limits of meta-expertise.

POLITICS AND/OF EXPERTISE

There is a deepening chasm between politics and expertise, mass movements and bureaucratic acumen, popular will and elite reasoning. This congeries of semantic fields takes on more concrete meaning via comparison and contrast. Key terms have dictionary meanings, but also enjoy heft and resonance thanks to their frequent juxtapositions with other foundational concepts in a field. *Expertise* means something very different in physics, economics, public relations, and transit. *Politics* may have one meaning in a professional office setting (where it is usually frowned on), a course catalog (a field of study), or a party nominating convention.

Despite this diversity of meanings, we may gain a more solid sense of each term by comparing them. In law, such contrasts may be particularly instructive in not merely defining terms but also giving us a sense of their import and use. As Wittgenstein counsels, our goal here should less be scientific certainty about meaning than clarity about the use of the terms, to set forth a sense of which aspects of expertise are challenged by political actors, and which are affirmed.

The legitimacy of the modern administrative state rests on its ability to balance three sources of authority: legal regularity, politics, and expertise.[10] In the United States, for example, the Environmental Protection Agency (EPA) often must make decisions that implicate its attorneys' knowledge of law; its scientific staff's expertise in toxicology, ecology, and related fields; and the political preferences of the presidential administration that appointed its administrator and other political appointees. These political preferences may reflect little more than the coarseness of electoral binaries in two-party systems (such as more environmental protection or less). Sometimes a leader with a clear political agenda will try to radically change the agency's agenda, but if the agency is working well, a commitment to both legal regularity and scientific expertise will constrain the political leadership's will.

For example, in the EPA, the political leadership may wish to suspend certain air quality standards to promote pollution-heavy manufacturing. From a legal perspective, a sudden change in regulation has to be justified, and in some cases may only occur once proper procedures, as specified by the Administrative Procedure Act, are followed. When those procedures are followed, scientific and other experts are able to weigh in, challenging whether the proposed change is consistent with the agency's organic statute, the Constitution, and other legal authorities. Before finalizing the change, the agency must respond to the relevant comments, either changing its approach to recognize a comment's merits or explaining why its own combination of evidence and shifting political and policy commitments can support its chosen approach.

The same types of functional checks and balances would constrain an agency overtaken by particularly aggressive experts. If those experts try to change course too radically, there will be predictable legal challenges. If what they do is too unpopular, there may also be political consequences. These consequences may be, all things considered, tragic. For example, an EPA run by genuine experts on the likely effects of anthropogenic climate change would probably move much more aggressively to drastically reduce carbon emissions. However, a well-funded fossil fuel lobby can spend enormous sums to support its candidates for political office. They may also invest in extensive litigation to slow or stop science-driven regulation.

There is also a politics of expertise. Fossil fuel interests may buy their own researchers or research institutes, much as tobacco interests clouded the science of smoking for decades to avoid regulation. That is a clear subversion of science, an intrusion of politics in the raiments of objectivity. However, there are other ways of politicizing science— and especially the human sciences—that are entirely just and right. For example, the US psychiatric profession unjustly pathologized homosexuality for decades, until activists demanded that it change its position. The activists did not simply make a power play. Rather, they skillfully combined their own lived experience and the work of theretofore marginalized experts to demand that the psychiatric profession stop stigmatizing perfectly normal modes of life.

These fraught issues make the administrative balance between law, science/expertise, and politics both fragile and contestable. Commenting on such trends, Eyal argues that expertise is a way of talking about the "intersection, articulation, and friction between science and technology on the one hand, and law and democratic politics on the other."[11] This is, indeed, a venerable tension in administration, where bureaucrats must often make difficult decisions implicating both facts and values. For example, raising or reducing pollution limits is a decision with medical consequences (for the incidence of lung cancer), economic impact (on the profitability of enterprise), and even cultural significance (for the viability of, say, mining communities). Eyal's *The Crisis of Expertise* focuses on a democratic challenge to purely technocratic decision-making on that front.

Rather than the claim that experts are too removed from "the people," a rival challenge to their power is the claim that they are not expert enough. This amounts to a second crisis of expertise—or, more precisely, a clash of forms of expertise. Well-credentialed economists and computer scientists have asserted that their ways of knowing and ordering the world should take priority almost everywhere: from hospitals to schools and from central banks to war rooms. The general theme of many books on AI-driven automation and economic disruption is that the methods of economics and computer science are *primus inter pares* among other forms of expertise.

This is a form of knowledge backed by power. Managers often advance rhetorics of automation, artificial intelligence, and big data to devalue certain forms of labor by characterizing them either as routinizable or in need of rationalization via machine learning. For example, law firm partners and their consultants may deride legal research and writing as a task that, with enough data and computing power, will one day be accomplished by computers.[12] This convenient belief justifies paying current employees less, since they are modeled not as human capital to be invested in but, rather, as a fungible source of data generation to be replaced by software (or cheaper sources of data) once a critical mass of their daily tasks are computerizable.

Asserting meta-expertise over professions requires a long campaign to diminish the importance of intrinsic, internal goods relative to the type of external, instrumental ones that can be rendered as quantified data. Though the epistemological foundations of quantitative, economic, and computational meta-expertise are distinct, three common features fundamental to each motivate visions of algorithmic governmentality.[13] First, there is a drive to delimit the scope of analysis to situations where a limited set of data points matter, and then to rigorously analyze how a process should be affected by these data points (or how disputes should be settled with reference to such data). Second, there is an effort to replace human judgment with rules, and to find empirical reference points for the application of rules.[14] Third, there is a drive to replace the judgment with calculations ordinarily programmed by software coders or developed by economists, accountants, or similar quantitatively or algorithmically oriented professions.[15]

The normative vision behind these projects is to make accountability algorithmic, replacing the imprecision of words, language, and custom with the exacting and automatic logic of code and mathematics. Precision is supposed to banish, or at least diminish, the triple banes of indeterminacy, subjectivity, and bias. Quantitative and algorithmic meta-expertise also enjoys the pragmatic prestige of STEM fields, such as science and engineering. In an era of austerity, the promise of finding ways to maintain quality (as measured by some objective metrics) while cutting costs (measured by the obvious metric of money) is seductive.

Substitutive Automation as Professional Dispensability

From an individualistic, utilitarian perspective (dominant in mainstream economics), substitutive automation of machines to replace humans in many fields seems to be a foregone conclusion, thanks to a set of interlinked judgments and predictions.[16] Big data's boosters expect predictive analytics combine standardization and personalization that outstrips human skill. With the rise of machine learning, advocates of substitutive AI believe that machines can improve over time by scrutinizing past outcomes, abandoning unsuccessful strategies, and evolving toward optimization.[17] They see success as a series of improvements along clear, well-defined metrics. A mental health app might be evaluated by, *inter alia*, how often does a depressed patient using it register positive facial expressions. Similarly, AI education may be judged by the "degree premium" it results in, based on the starting salary of a graduate.

If such outward indicia of excellence are all that matter in professional-client interactions, then the path to the automation of professions is clear. With a large enough client population willing to be experimental subjects, experts in machine learning may try various strategies of mimicry to capture existing professionals' actions to determine which result in desired outcomes. Yet outcome measures account for only a small proportion of the skills, dispositions, and duties inculcated by a profession and the types of empathy, understanding, and open-ended conversation professionals can offer.

Professionals perform distinctive forms of work, and they owe certain ethical duties to their clients. For example, fiduciary duties require looking out for the best interests of clients, instead of simply advancing one's own commercial interests.[18] A psychiatrist, for instance, should only treat those who actually need her help, even if she could make far more money by recommending weekly analysis sessions, in perpetuity, for everyone. Contrast that duty with, say, the minimal commercial ethics of salespersons or marketers, who have no obligation to inquire whether the customers they solicit need (or can even afford) their wares.[19]

Professionals have been granted some degree of autonomy because they are charged with protecting distinct, noneconomic values that society has deemed desirable. As Talcott Parsons observed in his classic (and still relevant) "The Professions in Social Structure," the professional "is not thought of as engaged in the pursuit of his personal profit, but in performing services to his patients or clients, or to impersonal values like the advancement of science."[20] These services reflect, reproduce, and are enriched by those values when professions are functioning correctly in a well-ordered society. In professional spheres, knowledge, skill, and ethics are inextricably intertwined.[21] We cannot simply make a machine to "get the job done" because, frequently, dynamic and interactive task definition is a critical part of the job itself.[22]

Eliot Freidson once lamented the frequent failure of professionals to "spell out the principles underlying the institutions that organize and support the way they do their work."[23] One silver lining in the challenge of meta-expertise will be a renewed opportunity for professions to examine in more detail what their members accomplish beyond what AI and software can provide. One simple example of this "value-added" (and "values-added") approach is the ability of professionals to help their clients (and the public at large) distinguish among the varied AI products now vying for customers. Much as physicians are responsible for deciding the appropriateness of prescription drugs for their patients, therapists might take on a role deciding which mental health apps are actually worth using, or teachers may help students determine which online learning tools will most effectively assist them. In the face of automation, professions' optimal strategy for self-preservation would reaffirm and strengthen their own norms, highlight the importance of tacit skills and knowledge, and work to extend aspects of their status to other workers.

QUALITY, COST, AND GOVERNANCE IN HEALTH CARE AND EDUCATION

The professional bargain—workers granted autonomy in exchange for advanced education, a continued commitment to keep up with the cutting edge of their fields, and fiduciary duties to the clients they work for—has been critiqued for decades, by diverse academics and activists.[24] Critics have impugned the motives of the licensing boards that control access to certain types of jobs.[25] Occupational licensure requirements are frequently cast as a burden on growth and equity.[26]

Management theory at business schools has supported the economics- and engineering-based challenges to the professions that are now popular. Management experts embraced theories that could give straightforward, quantitative answers to pressing business dilemmas—including how to manage other experts.[27] A financialized mindset, stressing the quantification of risk and return in a world of uncertainty, became paramount. As McKenzie Wark has argued, this emphasis fit well with larger political trends:

> [There is] a link between a financialization of nonknowledge [uncertainty] and the state, attacks on expertise that accelerated under Reagan and Thatcher. They attacked the credibility of their own governing class. Knowledge no longer has an autonomous value. It has to show a return . . . [Thus f]inance became the manager of generalized risk...[28]

Managers of "generalized risk" (unlike those expert in some specific area, like medical or educational risk) claim the ability to arbitrate among varied claims to expertise in order to offer "objective" resolutions to social problems.

For a concrete example, consider the discourse about healthcare spending in the United States. There have long been debates over what the proper aggregate level of spending on healthcare is.[29] One way of answering the question about whether spending is excessive would be to consult public-health experts, who could assess whether the health system is adequately addressing current and potential needs. A far more influential group of experts in this debate in the United States has been health economists, who have tended to compare the percentage of the US gross domestic product (GDP) spent on healthcare with that spent in other industrialized nations.

There are many advantages to considering GDP percentages in the abstract. The public-health perspective would require difficult public conversations on such issues as the causes and consequences of the opioid crisis, the massive COVID death toll and whether better infrastructure could have prevented it, and the excessive costs imposed by private insurance paperwork, some forms of end-of-life care, and pharmaceutical firms. Market structures and concentration levels would be interrogated. The fairness of wage levels up and down the professional, paraprofessional, and nonprofessional healthcare labor force would be questioned as well. How much easier to simply point to a number that seems too high and then to use that observation to empower other meta-experts to set up incentive schemes (such as high-deductible, co-pay, and co-insurance health plans) to deter overspending.

These approaches advance a vision of consumer empowerment premised on straight-forward dashboards of quality and cost in services. Big data and other forms of popular assessment could empower consumers to make their own judgments of the trade-offs between price and quality, it is hoped. Nor are these assessment methods confined to healthcare. Teacher and doctor ratings, for example, could displace the extant licensing and certification processes in both professions, eventually providing a template for a more general outsourcing of quality measurement from expert boards to a larger on-line "crowd" of raters and rankers.[30] According to the usual economic logic here, such tiered rating of professionals (rather than all-or-nothing licensure, which excludes unli-censed practitioners from the market) would expand access, gifting the poor the chance to pay far less for, say, health or education by freely choosing the lowes-rated, cheapest institutions in both fields. If the cheapest provider is a robot, virtual charter school, or app, all the better, from this perspective.

Beyond these economic rationales, metrics also appeal to a common dream of someday being properly recognized for the value of our work. Sometimes this takes the form of hoping or demanding a ranking of one's work compared to peers—common in citation analyses for academics, and prevalent in other outcome measures for a wide range of professionals.[31] Managers recognize that they can take advantage of this altogether justifiable longing for recognition and direct it to their own purposes. The commensurating power of numbers, sweeping aside contestable narratives, promises a simple rank ordering of merit, whether in schools, hospitals, or beyond. As social theorist David G. Beer shows in his book *Metric Power*, measurements are not simply imposed top-down from above.[32] They also colonize our own understandings of merit—and at the limit, can count on self-interestedly rational support from the 49.9 percent of persons who are going to end up "above-average" on any percentile metric.

Metrics as Meta-Expertise

Despite quantitative analysis's claims to objectivity, it is often easy to game rating and ranking systems.[33] Firms with substantial marketing budgets can invest in search-engine optimization, review manipulation, and "astroturfed" recommendations (i.e., fake grassroots).[34] The choice of one set of data points for quantitative judgment excludes others. The more decision-makers try to account for the problems in the meta-expertise of metrics, via expedients like risk adjustment, the more they invite political battles over the proper scope and intensity of such adjustments.

Even those who perform well on metrics should be careful about promoting them because metrics so often distort the social practices they ostensibly merely measure. Journalism researchers have complained about a "chaos of data about online audiences."[35] Rated on their thirty-day mortality rates (i.e., the percentage of patients who are still living thirty days after an operation), surgeons may simply avoid operating on very sick patients.[36] Cheating scandals have rocked schools ranked and rated on test scores. Even when the schools play fair, they may drop physical education, art, music, and other classes in order to teach to tests dominated by quantitative and verbal measures. As sociologist Donald T. Campbell put it in the eponymous Campbell's law, "The more any quantitative social indicator is used for social decision-making, the more subject it will be to corruption pressures and the more apt it will be to distort and corrupt the social processes it is intended to monitor."[37]

Of course, the exposure of gaming itself needs to be practiced with critical discretion and humility. As the organizers of a conference on gamed metrics at the University of California, Davis asked, "Can we reliably draw a clear separation between gaming the metrics game and engaging in misconduct?"[38] Even if such distinctions are contestable, their very contestability illuminates what metrics so often hide: the political power and judgment necessary to prioritize allocation of resources and status.

Contestability also helps expose the vacuity of certain efforts to convert the necessary diversity of aesthetic and stylistic judgments into a single commensurating measure. Computer scientist Brian W. Kernighan (coauthor of the classic textbook *The C Programming Language*) mentions a classic challenge to this genre of metrics:

> In the 1980s, statisticians at Bell Laboratories studied the data from the 1985 "Places Rated Almanac," which ranked 329 American cities on how desirable they were as places to live. [Researchers] were able, by juggling the weights on the nine attributes of the original data, to move any one of 134 cities to first position, and (separately) to move any one of 150 cities to the bottom. Depending on the weights, 59 cities could rank either first or last.[39]

As anyone who has tried to decide whether to live in, say, Brooklyn or San Diego can tell, there is no plausible universal ranking of the two cities. The choice hinges on what is most important to the chooser. Perhaps at the outer extremes of habitability one can identify places in the United States that are clearly worse than others, all things considered. But that type of binary is a far cry from a meta-expertise that proposes to granularly assess the relative value of 329 cities.

Similar exercises could routinely expose the inevitably political dimensions of so many disputes over expertise, which "meta-expertise" attempts to paper over by gesturing to a higher level of knowledge. This "papering over" effect is particularly acute in the case of secret algorithms designed to rank and rate employees.[40] Rated individuals have a more difficult time gaming a metric when they cannot fully understand how it works.[41] But such measures tend to alienate knowledge workers and to confound consumers: How can they be assured a metric is truly meritorious if they (or trusted assessors and intermediaries) cannot inspect its component parts? As Cathy O'Neil shows in her book *Weapons of Math Destruction*, algorithmic assessments have unfairly denied critical opportunities for employment, career advancement, health, credit, and education, and they deserve far more scrutiny than they commonly receive.[42]

There is also a fair amount of hypocrisy in the deployment of such meta-expertise. High-level managers at firms now use algorithmic assessment tools to sort employees worldwide on criteria of cost-effectiveness but all too often spare themselves the same invasive surveillance and ranking.[43] Professionals beleaguered by quantitative metrics and reporting requirements may start demanding that administrators impose similar burdens on themselves. To the extent such a turnabout is impractical or rejected, meta-expertise may be exposed as being a matter of power more than knowledge.

Even important journals in health policy have acknowledged the fallibility of rankings. For example, an article in *Health Affairs* demonstrated that hospital rankings vary wildly, based on metrics like risk adjustment (e.g., how much an at-risk patient population should excuse poor outcome measures from a doctor or hospital).[44] New "risks" (and "benefits") are always being discovered as influencers of health outcomes. Consider the controversy over the "epidemiological paradox" of the higher-than-expected health status of Latinos in the southwestern United States: despite worse secondary indicators of health (such as blood pressure or obesity rates), this population appeared to live longer than many other groups with better numerical metrics.[45] A simple application of that fact to the metrics of hospital performance might require that we "risk adjust" for ethnicity—that is, that we carefully avoid giving too much credit to hospitals with a large Latino patient base because their results are being boosted by that demographic mix. However, there are many explanations for what some scholars have called the Hispanic Paradox.[46] Each of these prevails to varying degrees in the demographic mix at any given hospital. Do risk adjusters dive in to that granular level when assessing a hospital's patient mix? When do they stop the chain of risk adjustments (say, boosting the score of a hospital that takes on more patients with high blood pressure than other hospitals do) and of adjustments to risk adjustments (knocking the score back down a bit when it turns out the hospital has a high proportion of Latino patients)? Although the latter move may seem statistically justified, in practice it would penalize many institutions that serve largely minority populations. In a context of extensive and steep health disparities, such an outcome would be deeply troubling.

The risk adjustments necessary for rankings-driven meta-expertise are deeply political and philosophical—not just technological or statistical—questions. The authors of the *Health Affairs* study concluded that hospital rankings should be fine-tuned to be ever-better indicators of the true quality of the services provided. But what if a bad ranking decreases a hospital's number of privately insured patients (the most lucrative payers), reducing its resources, which in turn reduces its ability to do better in future rankings? A musical chairs logic of elimination might make sense for consumer goods that are discretionary purchases. But when it can lead to the closure or weakening of "failing" hospitals and schools that are concentrated in poorer areas (a designation that can easily become a self-fulfilling prophecy), those left behind are consigned to long commutes merely to meet basic needs. Thus, even well-meaning meta-experts may end up merely accelerating extant market forces toward stratified medicine.

THE BOUNDS OF META-EXPERTISE

A distinguished set of sociologists and philosophers have critically examined the interplay between professionalism and expertise through the twentieth century and into the twenty-first.[47] A skeptic may challenge my intervention so far, asking, What does a lawyer (even one with a taste for questions of political economy and social theory) have to add to the conversation? A threefold response is possible. First, lawmakers may contradict whatever jurisdictional claims experts or meta-experts may make over some a domain. Therefore, law is critical to the practical establishment of jurisdictional authority. Second, the field of administrative law has long addressed the proper balance of legal regularity, politics, and expertise in the proper functioning of agencies.[48] Third, and most specifically, as I noted in the chapter's introduction with respect to the *North Carolina Dental* case, antitrust law is a particularly potent way of unraveling some modes of professional self-organization and standards while promoting others.

Meta-expertise can mix in unexpected and toxic ways. For example, the metrics used to rank universities have pressured law schools to focus more on the numerical credentials of an entering class (GPA and LSAT scores), than on other equally or more important dimensions of merit (such as diversity in both the demographic and experiential sense). Outside the very top-ranked institutions, "enrollment managers" battle to use limited scholarship funds to attract applicants with top GPA and LSAT scores, instead of devoting those funds to need-based programs. This allocation of resources predictably disadvantages applicants from lower socioeconomic-status households.

A solution is possible: all schools could agree to hold in reserve, say, 30 percent of their scholarship funds for need-based aid. However, they have failed to do so because of their fears of antitrust law. In the 1990s, the US Department of Justice investigated many elite institutions for cooperating to structure merit-based aid. The ideal of the antitrust "meta-experts" was to preserve discount-based price competition, however disadvantageous it would be to many of the neediest applicants, who are also the most dependent on higher education as a route to social mobility.[49]

The lesson here is a complex one. The point of a critique of meta-expertise is not to encourage blind trust in experts. The Ivy League schools that were investigated for price-fixing their financial aid may well have had plenty of resources to bid for top talent and also to assist the needy. Statistical analyses of medical practices have revealed anomalies that harmed patients and drained Medicare and Medicaid coffers via fraud. No teacher can know everything, and all students are better off when AI, or even teaching robots, is developed to supplement lesson plans with topics ranging from foreign languages to physics. In each of these examples, "meta-experts" (on markets, mathematics, and machine learning) are of great use.

Problems emerge when the meta-expert tries to short-circuit properly political debate or judgment with an assertion of privileged access to higher or more rigorous knowledge. For example, the general question of financial aid in higher education is highly politicized. Cooperation among universities that is designed to husband scarce resources to serve broader societal goals should not be derailed by narrow readings of relevant antitrust laws, which are themselves buttressed by a narrow slice of the wide range of politico-economic expertise on offer.[50] When meta-experts say that their AI or robotic teachers can replace, rather than supplement, teachers, that claim almost invariably depends on a very narrow, outcome-oriented conception of the point of education (e.g., memorizing facts and applying principles, or job training, or achieving a salary boost due to a "degree premium"). Neither philosophers nor economists and computer scientists determine the purpose and goals of education—that is a consequence of decisions of polities, teachers, and parents. Nor can any simple statistical analysis conclusively demonstrate the mistreatment of any individual patient. Such determinations are highly dependent on the values of the relevant medical board, the deference accorded the board by the courts, and legislative interventions to either loosen or toughen standards.[51]

Promoting professionals' prerogatives to shape the adoption of technology in their fields is not to dismiss performance metrics, rankings, or meta-expertise altogether. Instead, policymakers should assure lasting and meaningful involvement of professionals in the processes meant to authoritatively judge professionals' value. Policymakers should think of ranking and rating systems, software, and robotics as technologies to be deployed symbiotically with the professionals they instruct and evaluate. Such an approach alleviates the hubris of expansive meta-expertise, while still empowering quantitative experts to advise and shape advances in service quality.

Ideally, professionals will play a role in helping to construct the ranking systems that measure their performance with an eye to improving their work. In the mid-2000s, doctors in New York and Connecticut found that insurers were rating them based on obscure "cost-effectiveness" metrics that often boiled down to how profitable their practice was for the insurer. The physicians sued, winning settlements that imposed a wide array of conditions on the rankings and ratings—including transparency about how they are calculated and the ability to contest scores and data.[52] This was not mere professional self-protectionism; the suits would not have worked as bare assertions of reputational integrity. Instead, they were based on consumer-protection rationales. Educators afflicted with similarly problematic rankings and ratings may want to alert the public to the troubling systemic implications of these forms of meta-expertise.[53]

The study of expertise and professionalism also must itself take responsibility for the alternative that stands to fill the vacuum of labor relations in the absence of strong professions (and their close kin, unions). Social-scientific critiques of institutions of expertise are not mere reflections of or statements about reality. They also feed into regulatory and legislative action to alter the labor market. When medical boards dominated by physicians irrationally limit scope of practice for other medical professionals, a hermeneutics of suspicion directed at such boards is in many respects emancipatory. When attacks on occupational licensure requirements effectively advance the interests of gig economy platforms or dominant middlemen that are set to profit from a sudden, wage-reducing, positive supply shock in labor, the political valence of critiques of professions is less clear.[54] A research agenda focused on democratizing, rather than discrediting, the professions is called for.

There is another, parallel reason to insist on a limitation of meta-expertise, a hedging of it away from areas requiring judgment, political contestation, or personal responsibility. The relative autonomy of doctors, journalists, teachers, and many other professionals reflects a hard-earned trust and a responsibility for governance. To the extent that persons are running and staffing institutions, there is always some residue of autonomy and power entrusted to them, locally—as opposed to the centralization of power into whatever mammoth firm is likely to be running the AI programs or cloud computing centers that meta-experts appeal to.[55]

For true believers in expansive meta-expertise, problems with existing metrics of assessment and algorithms of replication are simply a technical issue to be fixed, rather than a political problem to be negotiated and discussed. But such methods have their limits. Meta-expertise can complement local knowledge, but will always be dependent on the observation and dedication of persons charged with collecting and interpreting the data on which it depends. The development of proper guidelines for such collection and interpretation of data will be critical to the future development, recognition, and power of experts and meta-experts alike.

NOTES

1. Gil Eyal, *The Crisis of Expertise* (Cambridge, UK: Polity Press, 2019).
2. N.C. State Bd. of Dental Exam'rs v. Federal Trade Commission, 574 U.S. 494, 500 (2015).
3. *North Carolina Dental*, 574 U.S. 494, 500. The Court wrote: "The question is whether the State's review mechanisms provide 'realistic assurance' that a non-sovereign actor's anticompetitive conduct 'promotes state policy, rather than merely the party's individual interests." In other words, the only limit to market authority in dictating prices and the terms of service was to be explicit and direct political authority—not an indirect delegation of market power to market actors. The same rationale led the Federal Trade Commission to sue the city of Seattle and Uber drivers after the city passed legislation permitting the drivers to bargain as a group for better wages and working conditions. In the eyes of US antitrust authorities, the workers (as independent contractors) were forming an illicit cartel and thereby exploiting Uber. Sanjukta Paul, "Antitrust as Allocator of Coordination Rights," *U.C.L.A. Law Review* 67, no. 4 (May 2020): 380–431; Sanjukta Paul, "Uber as For-Profit Hiring Hall: A Price-Fixing Paradox and its Implications," *Berkeley Journal of Employment and Labor Law* 38 (2017): 233.
4. Sandeep Vaheesan, "Accommodating Capital and Policing Labor: Antitrust in the Two Gilded Ages," *Maryland Law Review* 78 (2019): 766–827.
5. This concept of meta-expertise is related to the meta-expertise discussed by Paul Warde and Sverker Sörlin. See Paul Warde and Sverker Sörlin, "Expertise for the Future: The Environment and the Emergence of Modern Prediction, 1920–1970," in *The Struggle for the*

Long Term in Transnational Science and Politics: Forging the Future, ed. Jenny Andersson and Egle Rindzeviciute (London: Routledge, 2015), 38–63. Jenny Andersson describes this meta-expertise as "a very particular form of expertise that was not based on the grasping of a particular subject matter, but rather, on the capacity to conjure synthetic and encompassing images of dramatic and threatening developments. In future[s] research, this expertise on world futures could encompass forms of world utopianism as well as new versions of global technocracy." Jenny Andersson, *The Future of the World* (Oxford: Oxford University Press, 2018), 8). This chapter re-purposes the concept of meta-expertise to describe the epistemic authority of experts in quantitative analysis, and AI—heirs of the technocratic vision Andersson describes.

6. Will Davies, "Elite Power under Advanced Neoliberalism," *Theory, Culture and Society* 34 (2017): 233.

7. Andrew Abbott, *The System of Professions: An Essay on the Division of Expert Labor* (Chicago: University of Chicago Press, 1988). Meta-expertise seems to be an extreme form of abstraction, particularly in the guise of machine learning, which would (at the most) watch, record, and process everything that everyone does, and then replicate it in silico. Abbott notes, however, that even among experts, abstraction needs to be "optimal," neither too little nor too much, to be credible. The same logic applies to meta-experts, who have lately been frustrated in their efforts to replicate an occupation as seemingly automatable as driving.

8. John Patrick Leary, *Keywords: The New Language of Capitalism* (Chicago: Haymarket Books, 2018), on the politics of "accountability."

9. Gideon Lewis-Kraus, "Slate Star Codex and Silicon Valley's War against the Media," *New Yorker*, July 9, 2020.

10. Peter H. Schuck, "Multi-culturalism Redux: Science, Law, and Politics," *Yale Law and Policy Review* 11, no. 1 (1993): 1–46.

11. Eyal, *Crisis of Expertise*, 20.

12. Frank Pasquale, "A Rule of Persons, Not Machines," *George Washington Law Review* 87 (2019): 1–55.

13. Antoinette Rouvroy & Thomas Berns, "Algorithmic governmentality: a passion for the real and the exhaustion of the virtual," (2015).

14. See, e.g., Cass Sunstein, "Algorithms, Correcting Biases," *Social Research* 86 (2019): 499–511.

15. Angéle Christin, "Predictive Algorithms and Criminal Sentencing," in *The Decisionist Imagination: Sovereignty, Social Science and Democracy in the 20th Century*, Daniel Bessner and Nicolas Guilhot ed. (Oxford: Berghahn Books, 2018):.

16. Amartya Sen and Bernard Williams, Introduction to *Utilitarianism and Beyond* (New York: Cambridge University Press, 1982), 4. ("Utilitarianism is thus a species of *welfarist consequentialism*—that particular form of it which requires simply *adding up* individual welfares or utilities to assess the consequences, a property that is sometimes called *sum-ranking*.")

17. Pedro Domingos, *The Master Algorithm* (New York: Basic Books, 2015).

18. Jack Balkin, "Information Fiduciaries and the First Amendment," *UC Davis Law Review* 49 (2016): 1183–1234.

19. Natasha Dow Schüll, *Addiction by Design: Machine Gambling in Las Vegas* (Princeton, NJ: Princeton University Press, 2012).

20. Talcott Parsons, "The Professions and Social Structure," *Social Forces* 17 (1939): 457–467, at 458.

21. For a concrete account of how this intertwining occurs in the legal profession, see Frank Pasquale, "Synergy and Tradition: The Unity of Research, Service, and Teaching in Legal Education," *Journal of the Legal Profession* 40 (2015): 25–48.

22. David Stark, *The Sense of Dissonance: Accounts of Worth in Economic Life* (Princeton, NJ: Princeton University Press, 2011).

23. Eliot Freidson, *Professionalism, The Third Logic: On the Practice of Knowledge* (Chicago: University of Chicago Press, 2001).

24. Parts of this section were originally published in the article "Professional Judgment in an Era of Artificial Intelligence and Machine Learning," in the journal *Boundary 2*. I wish to thank Duke University Press for permitting this text to be repurposed for the present article; it is used by permission of Duke University Press.

25. Walter Gellhorn, "The Abuse of Occupational Licensing," *University of Chicago Law Review* 44 (1976): 17–18. See also Magali Sarfatti Larson, *The Rise of Professionalism: A Sociological Analysis* (Berkeley: University of California Press, 1977); Keith Macdonald, *The Sociology of the Professions* (Thousand Oaks, CA: Sage, 1995), 5, describing left critics. Abbott helpfully summarizes these critics as the "power" or "monopoly" camp in the sociology of professions, to be distinguished from more functionalist work (like that of Parsons). See Abbott, *System of the Professions*.

26. Office of the White House Press Secretary, "Fact Sheet: New Steps to Reduce Unnecessary Occupation Licenses That Are Limiting Worker Mobility," press release, June 17, 2016, https://obamawhitehouse.archives.gov/the-press-office/2016/06/17/fact-sheet-new-steps-reduce-unnecessary-occupation-licenses-are-limiting.

27. Rakesh Khurana, *From Higher Aims to Hired Hands: The Social Transformation of American Business Schools and the Unfulfilled Promise of Management as a Profession* (Princeton, NJ: Princeton University Press, 2010); "Management Theory Is Becoming a Compendium of Dead Ideas," *The Economist*, December 17, 2016.

28. McKenzie Wark, *Sensoria* (New York: Verso, 2020).

29. Frank Pasquale, "The Hidden Costs of Health Care Cost-Cutting," *Law & Contemporary Problems* 77 (2015): 171–193.

30. Frank Pasquale, "Grand Bargains for Big Data: The Emerging Law of Health Information," *Maryland Law Review* 72 (2013): 682–772; Pasquale, "Reputation Regulation: Disclosure and the Challenge of Clandestinely Commensurating Computing," in *The Offensive Internet: Privacy, Speech, and Reputation*, ed. Saul Levmore and Martha C. Nussbaum (Cambridge, MA: Harvard University Press), 107–123.

31. Kieran Healy and Marion Fourcade, "Seeing like a Market," *Socio-Economic Review* 15 (2017): 9–29.

32. David Beer, *Metric Power* (London: Palgrave MacMillan, 2016). See also Wendy Nelson Espeland and Michael Sauder, *Engines of Anxiety: Academic Rankings, Reputation, and Accountability* (New York: Russell Sage Foundation, 2016). Michael Sauder and Wendy Nelson Espeland discuss how administrators are tempted to "game the system" by focusing resources on certain metrics. They "define gaming as cynical efforts to manipulate the rankings data without addressing the underlying condition that is the target of measurement. [For example,] some schools encourage underqualified applicants to apply to boost their selectivity statistics." Michael Sauder and Wendy Nelson Espeland, "The Discipline

of Rankings: Tight Coupling and Organizational Change," *American Sociological Review* 74 (2009): 63, 76–77. New methodologies may also be a kind of preemptive gaming. For example, Paul Caron has found that "in every alternative ranking of law schools, the ranker's school ranks higher than it does under U.S. News [the dominant ranking method]." Paul Caron, "Size Matters: Thomas Cooley's 2011 Law School Rankings," *TaxProf Blog*, February 9, 2011, http://taxprof.typepad.com/taxprof_blog/2011/02/size-matters-.html.

33. Frank Pasquale, "The Troubling Consequences of Trade Secret Protection of Search Engine Rankings," in *The Law and Theory of Trade Secrecy: A Handbook of Contemporary Research*, ed. Rochelle C. Dreyfuss and Katherine J. Strandburg (Northampton, MA: Edward Elgar, 2011), 381–405.

34. Joseph Reagle, *Reading the Comments* (Cambridge, MA: MIT Press, 2014).

35. Lucas Graves and John Kelly, "Confusion Online: Faulty Metrics and the Future of Digital Journalism," *Tow Center for Digital Journalism* (2010): [pages]. Certain dominant forms of audience measurement have addressed some of the problems Graves and Kelly decried, but they have contributed to new distortions, including a bias toward "clickbait," polarizing narratives, and authoritarian populist attention grabs. Frank Pasquale, *New Laws of Robotics: Defending Human Expertise in the Age of AI* (Cambridge, MA: Harvard University Press, 2020), chap. 4 (describing media distortions due to the automation of editorial judgment).

36. Sarah Knapton, "One in Three Heart Surgeons Refuse Difficult Operations to Avoid Poor Mortality Ratings, Survey Shows," *The Telegraph* (UK), June 3, 2016, http://www.telegraph.co.uk/science/2016/06/03/one-in-three-heart-surgeons-refuse-difficult-operations-to-avoid/?WT.mc_id=tmg_share_tw. A simple metric of comparison might be the "thirty-day mortality rate"—i.e., the number of patients who die within thirty days of surgery. But that number is manipulable. For example, a patient might be kept on mechanical ventilation postsurgery for thirty-one days to count as a survivor in the reporting period.

37. Donald T. Campbell, "Assessing the Impact of Planned Social Change," in *Social Research and Public Policies*, ed. Gene M. Lyons (Hanover, NH: University Press of New England, 1975), 35.

38. Innovating Communication in Scholarship, "Gaming Metrics: Innovation and Surveillance in Academic Misconduct," December 11, 2015, http://icis.ucdavis.edu/?p=826.

39. Brian Kernighan, "We're Number One!" *Daily Princetonian*, October 25, 2010.

40. Frank Pasquale, *The Black Box Society: The Secret Algorithms That Control Money and Information* (Cambridge, MA: Harvard University Press, 2015).

41. Frank Pasquale, "The Troubling Trend toward Trade Secrecy in Search Engine Results," in *Handbook of Trade Secret Research* (Northampton, MA: Edward Elgar Publishing), ed. Rochelle Dreyfuss and Katherine Strandburg (2011): 381–406.

42. Cathy O'Neil, *Weapons of Math Destruction: How Big Data Increases Inequality and Threatens Democracy* (New York: Crown, 2016).

43. Don Peck, "They're Watching You at Work," *The Atlantic*, December 2013, https://www.theatlantic.com/magazine/archive/2013/12/theyre-watching-you-at-work/354681/.

44. J. Matthew Austin, Ashish K. Jha, Patrick S. Romano, Sara J. Singer, Timothy J. Vogus, and Robert M. Watcher et al., "National Hospital Ratings Systems Share Few Common Scores And May Generate Confusion Instead Of Clarity," *Health Affairs* 34 (2015): 423–430.

45. Kyriakos S. Markides and Jeannine Coreil, "The Health of Hispanics in the Southwestern United States: An Epidemiological Paradox," *Public Health Reports* 101 (1986): 253–265. Works citing this paper put forward a surprising array of explanations for the paradox.

46. Ana F. Abraido-Lanza, Adria N. Armbrister, and Karen R. Florez, and Alejandra N. Aguirre, "Toward a Theory-Driven Model of Acculturation in Public Health Research," *American Journal of Public Health* 96 (2006): 1342–1346.

47. See, e.g., Harry M. Collins, *Artificial Experts: Social Knowledge and Intelligent Machines* (Cambridge, MA: MIT Press, 1990);

48. For more on the relationship between politics, expertise, and legal regularity, see Frank Pasquale, "Two Politicizations of U.S. Antitrust Law," *Brooklyn Journal of Corporate, Financial & Commercial Law* 15, no. 1 (2021): 97–130; Schuck, "Multi-culturalism Redux," 1–38.

49. Deborah Jones Merritt and Andrew Lloyd Merritt, "Agreements to Improve Student Aid: An Antitrust Perspective," *Journal of Legal Education* 67 (2017): 17–50.

50. For a broader view, see Zephyr Teachout, "Antitrust Law, Freedom, and Human Development," *Cardozo Law Review* 41 (2019): 1081–1140.

51. See, e.g., Hoover v. The Agency for Health Care Administration, 676 So.2d 1380 (Florida), 1986; *In re Williams*, 60 Ohio St.3d 85, 573 N.E.2d 638 (1991).

52. Kristin Madison, "The Law and Policy of Health Care Quality Reporting," *Campbell Law Review* 31 (2009): 215–255.

53. For an example of these distortions, see Timothy P. Glynn and Sarah E. Waldeck, "Penalizing Diversity: How School Rankings Mislead the Market," *Journal of Law & Education* 42 (2013): 417–457.

54. Sandeep Vaheesan and Frank Pasquale, "The Politics of Professionalism: Reappraising Occupational Licensure and Competition Policy," *Annual Review of Law and Social Science* 14 (2018): 309–327.

55. Brett Frischmann and Evan Selinger, "Utopia? A Technologically Determined World of Frictionless Transactions, Optimized Production, and Maximal Happiness," *UCLA Law Review Discourse* 64 (2016): 372–391.

16

GENDER AND ECONOMIC GOVERNANCE EXPERTISE

MARIA J. AZOCAR

INTRODUCTION

In this chapter, I map the contributions of gender scholars to the studies of experts and expertise in economic governance. These contributions come in three main forms: First, scholars have explored how state authorities and policymakers mobilize gendered assumptions to make expert claims intelligible and authoritative and render alternative claims unrecognizable. Second, by taking expertise as a series of practices, and not just a claim, gender scholars have explored the points of tension and conflict embedded in the work experts do to establish authority in economic policymaking. Third, gender scholars have studied expertise as institutional processes in which claims, people, and organizations are incorporated into networks that stabilize specific configurations of economic expertise over time. By analyzing gender at the level of claims, practices, and institutions, gender scholars have demonstrated that expertise is grounded in power relations that shape the construction, use, and dissemination of policy-relevant economic knowledge.

From this view, an affinity between the sociology of gender and the sociology of expertise becomes evident. In both cases, policy-relevant knowledge is said to be embedded in power relations. However, the sociology of gender as a knowledge project in itself has advanced a particular view of gender product of its own history of struggles. Different groups of gender activists and scholars, occupying different social locations, have promoted competing interpretations of the world, including those about the interpretation of gender. In this struggle, women of color made one of the most important contributions to feminist scholarship. For them, gender inequality never works alone, but in conjunction with other systems of oppression. Social categories such as gender, race, and class are products of dynamic, intersecting processes that gain meaning in and through their relationships with one another. As legal scholar Mari Matsuda (1991, 1189) explains: "The way I try to understand the interconnection of all forms of subordination is through a method I call "ask the other question." When I see something that looks racist, I ask, "Where is the patriarchy in this?" When I see something that looks sexist, I ask, "Where is the heterosexism in this?"" By "asking the other question," the sociology of gender offers a more complex and dynamic view of gender inequalities—one in which "gender knowledge" is understood as a never-finished project (Collins 2015).

This chapter highlights the benefits of an intersectional approach to expertise. As I will show, gender scholars have studied economic expertise in the context of development, pension, and finance, influencing theoretical and empirical explorations of the power dynamics shaping economic governance. But the answers proposed by gender scholars correspond to particular social contexts and specific interpretative communities. Thus, the chapter is an invitation to expand the reach of gender scholars' contributions in a dialogue that explores not only how expertise sustains social oppression, but also how expertise can be deployed as a tool for social justice.

GENDER IN EXPERT CLAIMS

Gender as an ideology separates the world into a binary of the masculine and the feminine, subordinating the latter to the former. In line with science and technologies studies (Harding 1986; Haraway 1988; Mol 1999; Fujimura 2006), gender scholars have demonstrated that, historically, the claims of mainstream economics have been sexist (that is, they have reproduced prejudice against women) and androcentric (they have reproduced the masculine as the gender-neutral standard). For example, scholars have shown that in mainstream economics textbooks and journals, the "economy" has often been linked to the gendered opposition between the public and private realms (Nelson 1992; Folbre and Hartman 1989 England 1993; Hewitson 1994; Robeyns 2000; Schonpflug and Behrens 2000). In particular, the economy came to be represented as a realm of unlimited wants, in which mostly White heterosexual men were authorized to behave in autonomous and selfish ways, while issues affecting women were linked to a private sphere, understood as being outside, and subordinate to, the economic realm. An iconic example of this conceptualization is care work. On its original definition, care work was understood as the terrain of "unproductive housewives" (Folbre 1991, 481). And although it was praised as being motivated by love and cooperation, it was linked to the realm of dependency, need, and biological vulnerability—a conceptualization that has had important implications for women, especially women of color (Folbre 2015; Parreñas 2001; Glenn 2010).

We do not need to trace explicitly gendered language to find out how gendered assumptions have shaped claims about the economy. In development policy, for example, scholars have studied the assumption that the austerity programs promoted in the 1980s by international organizations such as the World Bank were gender neutral. These programs framed the economic crises of those years as a matter of price distortions caused by the overproduction of nontradable goods and services (e.g., construction) and the underproduction of tradable goods (e.g., clothing). According to this diagnosis, countries in Asia, Latin America, and Africa had fewer goods to trade in the international market; as a result, they faced a shortage of foreign exchange that diminished their economic growth (Elson 1991, 167). Therefore, international organizations recommended the production of more tradable goods through export incentives. But as Elson (1991) points out, the problem with this proposal was that experts assumed that people change their behavior from producing nontradable to tradable goods as a "rational" response to economic incentives, when in practice, the issue is far more complex. Experts treated the production of goods as a given without considering the human investments needed to maintain the system of production itself.

For example, when governments from the global South implemented export-oriented policies in the 1980s, women, not men, became the primary source of cheap labor through low-paid employment (Beneria et al. 2015; Elson and Çağatay 2000 Çağatay and Ertuk 2004). Gender mattered here, not because women had a "natural" preference to do that sort of labor, but because that work was culturally defined as feminine. In the same way, since care work was defined as feminine work, women's work as caregivers intensified in those years. Thus, from a macroeconomic point of view, the policy proposals might have created more "efficiency" by encouraging women to participate in the production of export-oriented goods, but such efficiency was predicated on shifting costs from the paid economy to the unpaid economy.

This example shows, first, how mainstream expert claims ignored the gender dynamics in the process of reallocating labor from nontradable to tradable goods and dismissing the human investment needed to sustain people's lives. Second, this example shows the political nature of expert indicators measuring the reality of the economy. Indicators such as growth, productivity, and efficiency construct the economy as a matter of capital accumulation without considering that the economy also involves nonmonetary exchange. To put it differently, care work was simply omitted from national accounts based on the assumption that economic actors do not have needs or vulnerabilities, only wants to be satisfied through consumption (Perez-Orozco 2014). Thus, by assuming that these policies would benefit everyone, experts' claims in the 1980s penalized women as a group and constructed the economy in masculine terms.

Gender scholars have added nuance to the study of macroeconomic policies in a second way. Tinsman (2000, 2014), for example, shows that export-oriented policies in Chile during the 1980s impacted male agricultural workers' well-being by informalizing their jobs and lowering their salaries. Tinsman also argues that women's incorporation into the labor force as temporary workers increased their sexual vulnerability to male supervisors, but at the same time gave them greater agency within their families and local communities. Thus, the macroeconomic policy prescriptions promoted in Chile during the 1980s had contradictory effects: on the one hand, male dominance in the family eroded; at the same time, women suffered greater workplace abuse at the hands of their male coworkers and supervisors. On the other hand, women and men were subject to new forms of class segregation. This way of understanding the intersectional character of social inequalities demonstrates that gender scholars have not simply argued that expert policy prescriptions for the global South in the 1980s affected women "more" than men. For scholars such as Tinsman, the point of gender analysis has been to show what is distinctive about gender, the circumstances in which gender inequality gains salience and for whom, and how evidence that at first glance seems positive for some groups (e.g., women's increased agency through labor participation) implies other forms of oppression (e.g., women's increased sexual vulnerability in the workplace and men's and women's labor precariousness).

Another way to understand how gender scholars have contributed to our understanding of economic governance is in relation to their long-term view of the economy. Since the 1980s, the consensus among economic experts has been to implement deflationary policies to attract foreign capital (Krippner 2011). But as gender scholars have pointed out, this policy has favored a logic of short-term decision-making in finance and increasing volatility, which in the long run has disproportionately benefited rich Western White men at the expense of others, who have turned to credit (Elson and Çağatay 2000; Elson 2002; Albelda 2013; Seguino 2010). With this long-term view of financialization's effects, gender scholars have demonstrated the multifaceted impact of financial crises. For example, in the United States the 2007–2008 crisis hit men working in male-dominated jobs in the short-term, but it had greater effects on women (especially single mothers) and men of color in the long-term (Fukuda et al. 2013). In other regions and during other time periods, the patterns were different (Elson 2010). Thus, by analyzing financialization in relation to different structures of oppression (namely, patriarchy, racism, and capitalism), gender scholars have offered a more nuanced picture of financialization's contradictions.

Gender scholars have also raised concerns about policy experts' instrumentalization of gender knowledge. There are numerous examples of this phenomenon, including population-control initiatives (Ewig 2006), microfinance programs for women (Wada 2018), gender quotas in financial institutions (Elias 2016), and investments in girls' education designed to promote economic growth. Investment in girls' education has become popular in international organizations as part of so-called "smart economics" initiatives in the global South (Elias 2013, 156). It is based on the assumption that poor girls are more responsible, capable, and prudent than poor boys. In this way, policy experts have used the pretense of gender equality to give economic growth a "human-centered" appearance (153). But in such cases, gender equality becomes merely a vehicle for economic development rather than a goal in its own right. "Smart economics" policy prescriptions rely on gendered images (e.g., female prudence versus masculine risk-taking behavior) that not only suggest a problematic view of boys and adult women in the global South, but also overlook the educational barriers faced by girls in the global North (Prügl 2017).

In conclusion, the sociology of gender has made at least three contributions to the understanding of the relationship between gender and economic governance expertise. First, gender-neutral policy prescriptions often rely on gendered assumptions that reproduce sexist and androcentric views of the economy. Thus, when austerity measures were implemented in the 1980s in some countries of the global South, the intensification of women's care work remained concealed by macroeconomic indicators, even as women's participation as workers in export-oriented economies was celebrated as a measure of greater productivity and efficiency.

Second, to understand the differential impact of policy prescriptions, gender scholars have analyzed gender in the intersection with other social categories. For example, in the analysis of austerity measures, the point is not to say that poor women in the global South are always the passive victims of economic policies promoted in the global North, or that in comparison to men, they suffer more. Instead, scholars have made an effort to analytically distinguish gender, race, and class (and other categories) as different but interrelated hierarchies with heterogeneous and contradictory social consequences. As Tinsman (2000) demonstrated, macroeconomic policy prescriptions in Chile increased women's sexual vulnerability in the workplace during the 1980s and simultaneously empowered them at home and in their communities. Tinsman's conclusion is not that precarious employment in export-oriented economies was "good" for poor Chilean women. Instead, her aim is to show the specific saliency of regional, gender, and class power inequalities when women participate in the labor force. In the same way, by analyzing the impact of deflationary policies, scholars have demonstrated that, over the years, a small category of Western, mostly White, male elites have increased their power at the expense of others, particularly single mothers and people of color, who disproportionately bore the brunt of the financial crises (Albelda 2013; Seguino 2010; Fukuda et al. 2013). Again, the point is not that increased indebtedness is "good" for White people and "bad" for people of color; it is to show that the consequences of financialization depend on one's location within intersecting systems of power. Indeed, the sociology of gender's normative goal is to offer a more nuanced description of these consequences as a basis for proposing alternative ways to conceptualize and manage the economy.

Finally, the study of gender and expertise matters because gender-oriented knowledge always runs the risk of being co-opted by policy experts in ways that undermine social justice. In the post-2008 context, international organizations such as the World Bank have acknowledged long-standing feminist critiques of the sexist and androcentric biases of macroeconomic theories and have expressly attempted to include gender equality as a goal in their policy recommendations. However, gender equality remains subordinated to economic growth. As Elias (2013) demonstrates, policies promoting education for girls in the global South tend to reproduce the gender binary in ways that intersect with racism—for example, by assuming that it is not worthwhile to educate adult women and boys of the global South, and by implying that girls in the global North do not confront educational disadvantages. Because the sociology of gender is in itself a knowledge project, gender scholars have been particularly interested in self-reflection and in contesting established expertise, even if that means losing acceptability in the short term in order to attain radical transformations of the status quo in the long term (Ferree 2003).

GENDER IN EXPERTS' PRACTICES

Gender is not only an ideology; it is also a practice. In the study of expertise, this implies the need to explore experts' subjectivities and actions. Because we live in an androcentric society that confers status and authority on that which is masculine, male-bodied persons have advantages over female-bodied persons in attaining expert authority. At the same time, not all masculine performances are valued in the same way. In this section, I describe how the sociology of gender has contributed to understanding the differential values assigned to feminine and masculine performances of expertise. Ultimately, despite the presence of stable hierarchies—for example, of the masculine over the feminine, and of certain kinds of masculine performance over others—gender's effects are contingent on how experts mobilize authority in relation to other social categories (such as class, race, and age).

Scholars have demonstrated that, for Western economists, professional socialization often implies learning a form of arrogance predicated on the perception that economics is the profession that has the highest intellectual status in the social sciences (Markoff and Montecinos, 1993 Montecinos 2001; Fourcade et al. 2015). As Fourcade et al. (2015) have documented, in the Western world, economics tends to be a male-dominated field, insulated from other disciplines, highly lucrative compared to other social science disciplines, and hierarchically organized (with the top departments in the United States leading in university training and professional prestige). This social structure of the profession has given epistemic cohesion to the field as a whole and has fashioned a culture of male self-confidence, competitiveness, and transnational linkages. Moreover, with the increasing economization of the state and financialization of the economy, mathematical skills have become the profession's most valued asset, viewed as a symbol of the field's high complexity and international orientation because numbers transcend cultural barriers (Fourcade 2006). The recursive relationship between the social structure of the profession (male-dominated, insulated, hierarchical, lucrative, and internationally oriented) and its gendered cultural representations (male self-confident attitude, competitiveness, mathematical complexity) has contributed to the rise of specific masculine enactments in the economic profession. The election of Mark Carney as the governor of the Bank of England in 2013 illustrates this point (Clarke and Roberts 2016).

Carney, an economist and banker, began his career at Goldman Sachs before serving as the governor of the Bank of Canada. In 2013, he gained visibility as a candidate for the Bank of England governorship by embodying established forms of masculinity: the transnational business masculinity and the bourgeois masculinity.

The transnational business masculinity depends on the idea that men who enact a "can-do" attitude (Connell and Wood 2005, 350) dominate the world of global business. This means that they see themselves as confident, ambitious, and competitive managers who pursue cutting-edge, risky, and innovative business around the world. This form of doing gender interacts with the performance of age. Youth in the business world is often attached to the values of excitement, impulsiveness, dynamism, and fearless de-sire. It also gives the appearance of the physical strength necessary for overcoming the stress, travel, and long hours demanded by global finance. Thus, the link between masculinity and youth has facilitated the depiction of global business as the terrain of young, attractive, and virile men, who not only have the skills to manage the world but also to "self-master" their bodies (Connell and Wood 2005). Mark Carney embodied this form of ideal masculinity. He had thirteen years of experience in private banking, popularity as an attractive man who resembled actor George Clooney, and youth—all of which positioned him as a "young prince" compared to older policymakers (Clarke and Roberts 2016, 52). Moreover, several media stories reaffirmed this form of mascu-linity by describing how tough and combative he was in private meetings with bankers. Certainly, Carney's expert authority depended on his educational credentials, experi-ence, and knowledge, but it was the combination of his credentials and the power signi-fied by his enactment of a specific form of masculinity that made the difference for his popularity.

Second, Carney embodied a form of bourgeois masculinity (Clarke and Roberts 2016). As studied by McDowell (1997), this form of doing masculinity emphasizes a sober, calm, and clean-cut gentlemanly performance that is "cerebral, rather than corpo-real" (184). For state policymakers, bourgeois businessmen are seen as quasi-aristocrats who enact a conservative, dispassionate, and paternal masculinity. In the case of Mark Carney, the media depicted him as the ideal aristocratic father figure, a "good guy," not a "snake oil salesman" willing to do anything for profit (Clarke and Roberts 2016, 55). Furthermore, in the context of the post–2007–208 crisis, Carney represented the sober and rational man expected to control the excess and risky behavior of young and ambi-tious financial traders.

This example shows how gender, in conjunction with class, race, and age, confers vis-ibility on certain experts over others. Further, this masculinized image of economists has concrete effects on how claims gain leverage in policy debates. Because UK state authorities framed the financial crisis as a specific event caused by "testosterone-driven men behaving badly" (Clarke and Roberts 2016, 50), and not as a structural problem of increasing inequality and distributional conflict, Carney became a suitable candidate to run the bank. In other words, the combined effects of Carney's bourgeois masculinity and transnational business masculinity offered the promise of a return to normalcy: his enactment of a sober and calm masculinity offered rationality and credibility at a moment of disorder and crisis; his enactment of masculine self-confidence and ag-gressiveness promised resolution at a moment when unpopular decisions needed to be implemented.

Female-bodied people are at a disadvantage in enacting these forms of hegemonic masculine expertise. But that does not mean that they cannot perform masculinity. As gender scholars have argued, one strategy for maintaining professional credibility is to emphasize sameness with men and downplay femininity as much as possible. The other strategy is to enact a conventional femininity to avoid the exclusion or punish-ment that might result from "acting masculine" (Wade and Ferree 2015). Christine

Lagarde, the former chair and managing director of the International Monetary Fund, for example, used the latter strategy when, in the aftermath of the 2007–208 financial crisis, she declared that "when women are called to action in times of turbulence, it is often on account of their composure, sense of responsibility and great pragmatism in delicate situations" (Lagarde 2010). The problem with this strategy from the standpoint of critical gender theory, however, is that it normalized the financial crisis as a single event of risk-taking masculinity, as opposed to a structural feature of capitalism. This strategy also essentializes policymakers' expert skills and places female policymakers in a precarious position by subordinating them to men, who reserve the right to decide how much "women's work" is needed to solve the crisis. On this view, if moderation and composure do not offer a solution, men's supposedly natural aggressive skills might be required to impose an immediate resolution (Prügl 2012; Elias 2013; Griffin 2015; Clarke and Roberts 2016; True 2016).

Moreover, the effects of gender on the performance of expertise do not pertain only to women; they also create hierarchies among masculinities. As Wade and Ferree (2015) explain, male-bodied persons have a narrowed range of acceptable gender performances compared to female-bodied persons. Because of this constraint, specific groups of men confront significant gendered barriers in their search for expert recognition. For example, in the expertise struggles over pension policymaking in Chile, center-left economists constructed their expertise in a gendered manner to defend the privatization of pension administration (Azocar, 2020). They gendered their expertise by establishing a hierarchy vis-à-vis women and feminized professions (law and sociology), as well as vis-à-vis other men and masculinities (actuaries).

Actuarial science in Chile, like economics, is a male-dominated field that relies on mathematical abstraction as its most important professional skill (Azocar, 2020). However, economists, not actuaries, have obtained state recognition as pension policy experts. In contrast to economists, actuaries have performed a type of "nerd masculinity" (Kendall 1999; Cooper 2000; Ensmenger 2015) that is not aggressive or arrogant. Rather, it is a subordinated form of masculinity that signals excessive reserve and social isolation. As a result, economists have successfully depicted actuaries as lacking the necessary social skills to build alliances in pension policymaking and impose their views in the policy debate. As one actuary declared, "They [economists] often cross the line, they are opinionated, and they do things that. . . . I laugh because they do not know a lot of mathematics. But they give opinions about everything as if they have a position for everything. But at least they have that advantage. They have been able to impose their [opinions]" (Azocar, 2020, 658–659). By investing in their arrogant emotional subjectivity, economists have been able to claim that they are the experts who ask the "right questions" in the debate (659).

In conclusion, the study of gender points to the many barriers, insecurities, and tensions experts face in their pursuit of recognition from state authorities. In line with the contributions that scholars from the literature on the sociology of professions (Abbott 1988; Witz 1990) and epistemic communities have made (Haas 1992; Keck and Sikkink 1998), gender identities shape the opportunities and obstacles for expert groups trying to impose their views and gain recognition in jurisdictional struggles. In the case of economic policymaking, research has shown that to enact an ideal type of professionalism, economists had to carefully cultivate their masculine selves. However, as Mark Carney's case illustrates, to gain influence, it is not enough to master the elements of a single type of hegemonic masculinity. Rather, the combinatory effects of the power differentials that were embedded in transnational business masculinity, along with bourgeois masculinity, gave Carney leverage.

Moreover, even though male-bodied persons have advantages over female-bodied persons in attaining recognition as experts in economic policymaking, men do confront barriers. As the case of Chilean economists shows, economists played up the masculine nerd performance of actuaries to advance in their own positions as pension policy experts. Economists treated actuaries as lacking the social aptitudes of aggressive masculinity to build alliances and ask the right questions in the policy debate.

Finally, as the case of Christine Lagarde demonstrated, the situation is particularly difficult for economists who "do femininity." Theirs is often a lose-lose situation: if they downplay their femininity, they uphold the idea of masculine superiority; but if they emphasize their femininity, they subordinate themselves to male-bodied persons and the masculine. For this reason, the lack of diversity and the rampant culture of privilege within financial and economic organizations have been a major source of concern for gender scholars (McDowell 1997; Hooper 2001; Walby 2009; Schuberth and Young; Griffin 2013; Tsingou 2015; Cavaghan 2017). The presence of women and people of color in centers of power does not guarantee less biased policies, but research has shown that it does make a difference to which issues are put on the policy agenda (Wade and Ferree 2015). Because politics and expertise are mutually constitutive, when economic policymaking occurs behind the closed doors of the old boys' clubs, everything that deviates from the club's norms is regarded as inappropriate, which tends to reproduce masculine privilege.

GENDER IN THE INSTITUTIONALIZATION OF EXPERTISE NETWORKS

Gender is a claim, a practice, and an organizing principle of institutions. From an institutional perspective, gender shows how certain people, technologies, and claims are enrolled in an expertise network (Eyal 2013; Azocar and Ferree 2016). The analysis of gender highlights the contingency of the expertise network, how and why certain courses of actions were rejected in the past, and how expertise gets institutionalized over time; and from a normative point of view, it shows what could be done differently in the present. In this section, I take the current controversy around the financialization of pension funds to illustrate this point.

In the mid-1990s, the World Bank inaugurated a worldwide trend toward pension privatization (Madrid 2002; Weyland 2005; Kay and Sinha 2008). It recommended transforming the conventional defined-benefit plan of the pay-as-you-go-system into a defined-contribution plan managed by private financial companies. However, by the end of the 1990s, prominent economists were openly criticizing this policy. For example, Joseph Stiglitz, the World Bank's chief economist at the time, pointed out that the arguments in favor of pension privatization were "based on a set of myths that are often not substantiated in either theory or practice" (Orszag and Stiglitz 1999, 38). Later, the World Bank recognized that there was "no magic formula for success" (Gill et al. 2004, xviii) in pension policymaking, and suggested that each country should adopt its own policy approach. With no clear end to the controversy and increasing skepticism from financial markets, pension policymaking, and, more concretely, the financialization of pension funds, remain highly contested today (Barr and Diamond 2009; Béland and Waddan 2012; Orenstein 2013).

Historically, pension policy was conceived as a form of insurance sponsored by emerging welfare states in the West that were aiming to provide security for an uncertain future. But the link between state governance and insurance was possible only because of the prior existence of an insurance market and the social invention of risk and finance (Zelizer 1978; Ewald 1991; Ericson and Doyle 2004; O'Malley 2009). Pension-policy expertise was thus established in the spaces of the welfare, insurance, risk, and finance of the economy. Current disagreements on pension privatization, then, are connected to these four spaces and can be summarized in terms of two main controversies.

The first controversy in pension policy relates to the concept of responsibility. In the United States in the early twentieth century, the state and the insurance companies promoted insurance through a moral framework, which created the desire for a specific type of future security (Zelizer 1978, 1983; Gordo 1992; Fraser and Gordon 1994). As White male wage labor became increasingly tied to economic independence, the state and insurance companies conceptualized insurance as a form of poverty prevention. Poverty, in turn, was defined as form of dependency embodied by the "pauper," "the colonial native," "the slave" and "the housewife" (Fraser and Gordon 1994). Thus, the state and insurance companies framed the practice of mandatory contributions as the act of responsible men (and, in practice, mostly White, heterosexual men) who continued to provide security to dependents in old age. In other countries, such as France, state authorities specifically emphasized the redistributional component of welfare pension policy and employers' responsibility to provide security to their workers (Ewald 1999).

Notwithstanding the differences among countries (and within countries over time), in its original conceptualization, pension policymakers in the West normalized a gendered, raced, and class ideal of breadwinner responsibility that served to justify the need for pensions. As a result, current expert disagreements on pension policymaking often revolve around this ideal. In the United States, for example, critics have claimed that the universal provision of pensions causes people to be irresponsible (i.e., to avoid work), undermining the economic efficiency of the system as a whole (Somers 2017, 81). On the other hand, supporters of universal pension systems, including union activists from Canada, have argued that the privatization of pension administration is an instrument of class power and erodes solidarity and social equality among workers—that is, it excuses the rich from providing security (Skerrett and Gindin 2017). As this debate shows, the question of who is responsible for security in an uncertain future—individuals or the society—is linked to the androcentric assumption that security means economic independence in old age, and that the economy means the realm of formal employment. Framing the controversy in these terms excludes alternative conceptualizations of future security from the conversation. The rise of mass incarceration as a form of racialized social control, for example, shows how historically marginalized groups face insecurity in almost every aspect of their lives, not only in old age. Further, contemporary debates over pension policy separate the economy from nonmonetary exchanges that sustain people's well-being. In other words, pension governance, by excluding alternative conceptualizations of security and keeping production separate from reproduction, "feeds a hierarchical socioeconomic system in which the life of the hegemonic subject is the life worth living." (Perez-Orozco 2014, 24).

A second controversy that the study of gender power differentials in pension policy expertise reveals pertains to the legitimate sources of profit. As De Goede (2001) shows, until the nineteenth century, the commercialization of the future was considered an illegitimate activity. Credit, for example, was conceptualized as a "whore" (De Goede 2001, 27)—that is, as a terrain of chaos and madness, of emotional instability, corruption, and seductive temptations. Nevertheless, the increasing use of bookkeeping techniques provided an opportunity to master "lady credit" (De Goede, 2001 21). Accounting became legitimized as a scientific activity based on the gentlemanly virtues of rational calculation, punctual payment, and self-discipline, which were meant to control irresponsible speculation. More importantly, however, the creation of risk as a classification and measurement technique offered the "most durable defense of exchange trading" (202). This notion of risk created a distinction between future speculators, who could obtain easy profits by creating artificial risks (gambling), and speculators, who used mathematical knowledge to calculate natural market risks and took responsibility for the outcomes of their decisions (finance). Risk expertise, then, became an activity that was morally superior to gambling because it created wealth through masculine scientific work and a responsible ethos, not fraud. Over the years, finance increasingly came to be understood as the glamorous and heroic activity of the male Western global elite, conquering virgin territories around the world, self-confident in its scientific judgment, and willing to take risks at any opportunity, including speculating on deaths, ills, accidents, and old age (De Goede 2001).

Like the commercialization of future uncertainties, current controversies around the financialization of pension funds pertain to where the line between gambling and finance should be drawn, echoing past debates over the "legitimate grounds for making profits" (De Goede 2001, 81).

As discussed above, when a financial crisis is described as a problem of specific masculinities, supporters of pension financialization tend to advocate greater regulation of gambler masculinities (Prügl 2012). On the other hand, critics of pension financialization tend to call for keeping financialization to a minimum because of the "speculative mania" inherent in financial markets (Krippner 2011, 4). The problem of framing the controversy in these terms, however, is that finance and financial expertise remain necessary requirements for controlling fears about future uncertainties. After all, state policymakers assume that the regulators of idle gamblers are employing their expertise for noble ends, whereas frivolous gamblers are using their expertise for deviant and selfish purposes. As De Goede (2004) shows, constituting financial expertise as the exclusive purview of science and experts—something beyond public comprehension and outside the realm of politics—makes it impossible to discuss, in an open and democratic manner, what constitutes a risk for state authorities and experts. Nor is it even possible to hold experts responsible for their errors in decision-making because, ironically, financial risk management assumes the possibility of errors (De Goede 2004). Moreover, here again, the distinction between production and reproduction, or between the economy and politics, is reintroduced, keeping the former separated from nonmonetary exchanges that also define people's well-being and hopes for the future.

In conclusion, studying pension-policy expertise as a type of network exposes the tensions, silences, and political conflicts of the pension expertise assemblage. In line with social studies of the future (Medina 2011; Anderson 2007; Andersson 2012), politics heavily influence visions of the future and the enactment of those visions in the present. In the case of pension policymaking, gender power differentials have brought together several elements of the pension-policy expertise network to legitimize a specific future imaginary. Poverty in the future is seen as particularly degrading, the responsible provision of money from paterfamilias to their dependents is seen as normatively desirable, and masculine mathematical risk prediction is treated as the main tool for controlling anxieties about poverty in old age. Gender imaginaries, then, have organized the institutionalization of pension expertise, leaving unaddressed other relevant matters, such as the questions of how we wish to live in the future (De Goede 2004, 205) and which alternative imaginaries of security and insecurity should be considered in pension-policy debates.

CONCLUSION

Drawing on the examples of gender analyzes at the level of claims, practices, and institutions in economic policymaking, the chapter has highlighted two main points raised by gender scholars in the analysis of experts and expertise.

First, intersectional gender analyses add nuance to the study of power differentials in expertise. At the level of claims, for example, gender scholars, by exploring the gendered assumptions in economic knowledge, have demonstrated the complex and contradictory impacts of policy prescriptions. As the study of developmental policies in the global

South has shown, gender inequality does not increase automatically as class inequality rises. Rather, economic policies impact different groups both positively and negatively at the same time, both in the short and long terms.

At the level of practices, gender analyses have shown that experts gain influence and power when they successfully mobilize gender in interaction with other categories of difference, such as race, class, and age. Such strategic deployments of gender are both dynamic and contingent. For instance, gender, race, and class privilege can give candidates leverage as they run for office. But at moments of financial crisis, gender subordination might offer the opportunity to claim the distinctive skills necessary for returning the economy to normal. The performance of gender, then, interacts with other social categories, and the question of which circumstances favor which types of gender recognition in a given context is an empirical one.

Finally, at the level of institutions, gender scholars have shed light on the high stakes of pension policy. For example, the current controversy over pension privatization and financialization is usually understood as a matter of class power. It is framed as a debate around the question of who is financially responsible for pensions (the society or individuals) and which are the legitimate sources of profit (gambling or finance). By showing the collective and persistent efforts invested in supporting gendered distinctions between responsibility/irresponsibility and legitimate/illegitimate financial wealth, gender scholars have provided a fuller description of the issues obscured by the debate as it is currently framed, including the questions of how we wish to live (or die), and of which alternative imaginaries of security and insecurity should be considered in pension policy debates.

The second general contribution of gender scholars is to have explicitly promoted a normative discussion of experts and expertise. For example, by examining the gendered assumptions in economic knowledge prescriptions, gender scholars have denounced the many ways in which policy experts have subordinated gender equality to capital accumulation under the guise of "smart economics." At the level of expert practices, gender scholars have problematized the hierarchies in the economics profession and transnational policy organizations and made calls for greater diversity in these organizations. Finally, by analyzing gender at the level of institutions, gender scholars have pointed out that social justice is not simply obtained by adding women or other marginalized groups in economic policy considerations. What is needed is to reframe the meaning of the economy, welfare, finance, or security. For gender scholars, the point is to re-conceptualize economic governance as a matter of well-being that considers the economy as a world of monetary and nonmonetary exchanges, aiming to sustain a good life for all, not only for the few.

REFERENCES

Abbott, Andrew. 1988. *The System of Professions: An Essay on the Division of Expert Labor.* Chicago: University of Chicago Press.

Albelda, Randy. 2013. "Gender Impacts of the 'Great Recession' in the United States." In *Women and Austerity: The Economic Crisis and the Future for Gender Equality*, edited by Maria Karamessini and Jill Rubery, 104–123. Abingdon, UK: Routledge.

Anderson, Ben . 2007. "Hope for Nanotechnology: Anticipatory Knowledge and the Governance of Affect." *Area* 39 (2): 156–165.

Andersson, Jenny. 2012. "The Great Future Debate and the Struggle for the World." *American Historical Review* 117 (5): 1411–1430.

Azocar, Maria J., and M. M. Ferree. 2016. "Engendering the Sociology of Expertise." *Sociology Compass* 10 (12): 1079–1089.

Azocar, Maria J. 2020. "Policy Debates on Pension Reform in Chile: Economists, Masculinity and the Mobilization of Strategic Ignorance." In *Social Politics: International Studies in Gender, State and Society* 27(4): 648–669.

Barr, Nicholas., and Peter Diamond. 2009. "Reforming Pensions: Principles, Analytical Errors and Policy Directions." *International Social Security Review* 62 (2): 5–29.

Béland, Daniel and Alex Waddan. 2012. *The Politics of Policy Change: Welfare, Medicare, and Social Security Reform in the United States*. Washington, DC: Georgetown University Press.

Benería, Lourdes, Günseli Berik, and Maria M. Floro. 2015. *Gender, Development and Globalization: Economics as if All People Mattered*. New York: Routledge.

Çağatay, Nilufer, and Korkurt Ertuk. 2004. "Gender and Globalization: A Macroeconomic Perspective." Working Paper #19. Policy Integration Department. World Commission on the Social Dimension of Globalization. International Labour Office, Geneva.

Cavaghan, Rosalind. 2017. "Bridging Rhetoric and Practice: New Perspectives on Barriers to Gendered Change." *Journal of Women, Politics & Policy* 38 (1): 42–63.

Clarke, Chris., and Adrienne Roberts. 2016. "Mark Carney and the Gendered Political Economy of British Central Banking." *British Journal of Politics and International Relations* 18 (1): 49–71.

Collins, Patricia H. 2015. "Intersectionality's Definitional Dilemmas." *Annual Review of Sociology* 41:1–20.

Cooper, Marianne. 2000. "Being the 'Go-to Guy': Fatherhood, Masculinity, and the Organization of Work in Silicon Valley." *Qualitative Sociology* 23 (4): 379–405.

Connell, Robert W., and Julian Wood. 2005. "Globalization and Business Masculinities." *Men and Masculinities* 7 (4): 347–364.

De Goede, Marieke. 2001. *Virtue, Fortune, and Faith: A Geneaology of Finance*. Minneapolis: University of Minnesota Press.

De Goede, Marieke. 2004. "Repoliticizing Financial Risk." *Economy and Society* 33 (2): 197–217.

Elias, Juanita. 2013. "Davos Woman to the Rescue of Global Capitalism: Postfeminist Politics and Competitiveness Promotion at the World Economic Forum." *International Political Sociology* 7 (2): 152–169.

Elias, Juanita. 2016. "Whose Crisis? Whose Recovery? Lessons Learned (and Not) from the Asian Crisis." In *Scandalous Economics: Gender and the Politics of Financial Crises*, edited by Aida A. Hozic and Jacqui True, 109–125. New York: Oxford University Press.

Elson, Diane. 1991. "Male Bias in Macro-Economics: The Case of Structural Adjustment." In *Male Bias in the Development Process*, edited by Diane Elson, 164–190. Manchester, UK: Manchester University Press.

Elson, Diane. 2002. "International Financial Architecture: A View from the Kitchen." International Development Associates Ideas. https://www.networkideas.org/featured-articles/2004/01/international-financial-architecture/

Elson, Diane. 2010. "Gender and the Global Economic Crisis in Developing Countries: A Framework for Analysis." *Gender & Development* 18 (2): 201–212.

Elson, Diane, and Nilufer Çağatay. 2000. "The Social Content of Macroeconomic Policies." *World Development* 28 (7): 1347–1364.

England, Paula. 1993. "The Separative Self: Androcentric Bias in Neoclassical Assumptions." In *Beyond Economic Man: Feminist Theory and Economics*, edited by M. A. Ferber and J. A. Nelson. Chicago: University of Chicago Press.

Ensmenger, Nathan. 2015. "Beards, Sandals, and Other Signs of Rugged Individualism": Masculine Culture within the Computing Professions." *Osiris* 30 (1): 38–65.

Ericson, Richard. V., and Aaron. Doyle. 2004. *Uncertain Business: Risk, Insurance and the Limits of Knowledge*. Toronto: University of Toronto Press.

Eyal, Gil. 2013. "For a Sociology of Expertise: The Social Origins of the Autism Epidemic." *American Journal of Sociology* 118 (4): 863–907.

Ewald, François. 1991. "Insurance and Risk." In *The Foucault Effect: Studies in Governmentality*, edited by Graham Burchell, Colin Gordon, and Peter Miller, 197–210. Chicago: University of Chicago Press.

Ewald, François. 1999. "The Return of the Crafty Genius: An Outline of a Philosophy of Precaution." *Connecticut Insurance Law Journal* 6:47.

Ewig, Christina. 2006. "Hijacking Global Feminism: Feminists, the Catholic Church, and the Family Planning Debacle in Peru." *Feminist Studies* 32 (3): 633–659.

Ferree, Myra. M. 2003. "Resonance and Radicalism: Feminist Framing in the Abortion Debates of the United States and Germany." *American Journal of Sociology* 109 (2): 304–344.

Folbre, Nancy. 1991. "The Unproductive Housewife: Her Evolution in Nineteenth-Century Economic Thought." *Signs: Journal of Women in Culture and Society* 16 (3): 463–484.

Folbre, Nancy. 2015. "Accounting for Care: A Research and Survey Design Agenda." Paper prepared for the International Association for Research in Income and Wealth–OECD special conference "W(h)ither the SNA?," April 16–17. Paris. https://www. iariw.org.

Folbre, Nancy, and Heidi. Hartmann. 1989. "The Persistence of Patriarchal Capitalism Nancy Folbre." *Rethinking Marxism* 2 (4): 90–96.

Fourcade, Marion. 2006. "The Construction of a Global Profession: The Transnationalization of Economics." *American Journal of Sociology* 112 (1): 145–194.

Fourcade, Marion., Etienne. Ollion, and Yann. Algan. 2015. "The Superiority of Economists." *Journal of Economic Perspectives* 29 (1): 89–114.

Fraser, Nancy., and Linda. Gordon. 1994. "A Genealogy of Dependency: Tracing a Keyword of the US Welfare State." *Signs: Journal of Women in Culture and Society* 19 (2): 309–336.

Fujimura, Joan. H. 2006. "Sex Genes: A Critical Sociomaterial Approach to the Politics and Molecular Genetics of Sex Determination." *Signs Journal of Women in Culture and Society* 32:49–82.

Fukuda-Parr, Sakiko., James. Heintz, and Stephanie. Seguino. 2013. "Critical Perspectives on Financial and Economic Crises: Heterodox Macroeconomics Meets Feminist Economics." *Feminist Economics* 19 (3): 4–31.

Gill, Indermit Singh, Truman G. Packard, and Juan Yermo. 2004. *Keeping the Promise of Social Security in Latin America*. Washington, DC: World Bank.

Glenn, Evelyn. N. 2010. *Forced to Care: Coercion and Caregiving in America*. Cambridge MA: Harvard University Press.

Gordon, Linda. 1992. "Social Insurance and Public Assistance: The Influence of Gender in Welfare Thought in the United States, 1890–1935." *American Historical Review* 97 (1): 19–54.

Griffin, Penny. 2013. "Gendering Global Finance: Crisis, Masculinity, and Responsibility." *Men and Masculinities* 16 (1): 9–34.

Griffin, Penny. 2015. "Crisis, Austerity and Gendered Governance: A Feminist Perspective." *Feminist Review* 109 (1): 49–72.

Haas, Peter. M. 1992. "Introduction: Epistemic Communities and International Policy Coordination." *International Organization* 46 (1): 1–35.

Haraway, Donna. 1988. "Situated Knowledges: The Science Question in Feminism and the Privilege of Partial Perspective." *Feminist Studies* 14:575–599.

Harding, Sandra. G. 1986. *The Science Question in Feminism*. Ithaca, NY: Cornell University Press.

Hewitson, Gillian. 1994. "Deconstructing Robinson Crusoe: A Feminist Interrogation of "Rational Economic Man"." *Australian Feminist Studies* 9 (20): 131–149.

Hooper, Charlotte. 2001. *Manly States: Masculinities, International Relations, and Gender Politics*. New York: Columbia University Press.

Kay, Stephen J., and Tapen Sinha, eds. 2008. *Lessons from Pension Reform in the Americas*. Oxford: Oxford University Press.

Keck, Margaret. E., and Kathryn. Sikkink. 1998. *Activists beyond Borders: Advocacy Networks in International Politics*. Ithaca, NY: Cornell University Press.

Kendall, Lori. 1999. "'The Nerd Within': Mass Media and the Negotiation of Identity among Computer-Using Men." *Journal of Men's Studies* 7 (3): 353–369.

Krippner, Greta. R. 2011. *Capitalizing on Crisis*. Cambridge, MA: Harvard University Press.

Lagarde, Christine. 2010. "Women, Power and the Challenge of the Financial Crisis." *New York Times*, May 10. https://www.nytimes.com/2010/05/11/opinion/11iht-edlagarde.html.

Madrid, Raul. L. 2002. "The Politics and Economics of Pension Privatization in Latin America." *Latin American Research Review* 37 (2): 159–182.

Markoff, John., and Veronica. Montecinos. 1993. "The Ubiquitous Rise of Economists." *Journal of Public Policy* 13 (1): 37–68.

Matsuda, Mari. J. 1991. "Beside My Sister, Facing the Enemy: Legal Theory out of Coalition." *Stanford Law. Review* 43:1183–1192.

McDowell, Linda. 1997. *Capital Culture: Gender at Work in the City*. Massachusetts iNC: Blackwell Publishers Inc.

Medina, Eden. 2011. *Cybernetic Revolutionaries: Technology and Politics in Allende's Chile*. Cambridge, MA: MIT Press.

Mol, Annemarie. 1999. "'Ontological Politics': A Word and Some Questions." *Sociological Review* 47 (S1): 74–89.

Montecinos, Veronica. 2001. "Feminists and Technocrats in the Democratization of Latin America: A prolegomenon." *International Journal of Politics, Culture, and Society* 15 (1): 175–199.

Nelson, Julie. A. 1992. "Gender, Metaphor, and the Definition of Economics." *Economics and Philosophy* 8 (1): 103–125.

O'Malley, Pat. 2002. *Imagining insurance: Risk, Thrift, and Life Insurance in Britain*. Chicago, IL: University of Chicago Press,.

Orenstein, Mitchell. A. 2013. "Pension Privatization: Evolution of a Paradigm." *Governance* 26 (2): 259–281.

Orszag, Peter R., and Joseph E. Stiglitz. 1999. "Paper presented at the World Bank conference New Ideas About Old Age Security, September 14–15 ." Paper presented at the World Bank conference "New Ideas About Old Age Security." September 14–15.

Parreñas, Rhacel. 2001. *Servants of Globalization: Migration and Domestic Work*. Stanford, CA: Stanford University Press.

Perez-Orozco, Amaia. 2014. *Subversión feminista de la economía: Aportes para un debate sobre el conflicto capital-vida*. Madrid: Editorial Traficantes de sueños.

Prügl, Elisabeth. 2012. "'If Lehman Brothers Had Been Lehman Sisters . . .': Gender and Myth in the Aftermath of the Financial Crisis." *International Political Sociology* 6 (1): 21–35.

Prügl, Elisabeth. 2017. "Neoliberalism with a Feminist Face: Crafting a New Hegemony at the World Bank." *Feminist Economics* 23 (1): 30–53.

Robeyns, Ingrid. 2000. "Is There a Feminist Economics Methodology?." Paper. Academia.edu, October. https://uu.academia.edu/IngridRobeyns.

Schuberth, Helene., and Brigitte. Young. 2011. "The Role of Gender in Governance of the Financial Sector." In *Questioning Financial Governance from a Feminist Perspective*, edited by B. Young, I. Bakker, and D. Elson. Routledge.

Schönpflug, Karin, and Doris A. Behrens. 2000. "A Feminist Challenge to Paul A. Samuelson's Overlapping Generations Model." Conference Paper. 9th Conference of the International Association for Feminist Economics (IAFFE), 2000, Bogaziçi University, Istanbul, Turkey http://citeseerx.ist.psu.edu/viewdoc/download?doi=10.1.1.203.1783&rep=rep1&type=pdf.

Seguino, Stephanie. 2010. "The Global Economic Crisis, Its Gender and Ethnic Implications, and Policy Responses." *Gender & Development* 18 (2): 179–199.

Skerrett, Kevin. and Sam Gindin. 2017. "The Failure of Canada's Financialized Pension System." In *The Contradictions of Pension Fund Capitalism*, edited by Kevin Skerrett, Johanna. Weststar, Simon. Archer, and Chris. Roberts, 253–276. Ithaca: Cornell University Press.

Somers, Margaret. R. 2017. "How Grandpa Became a Welfare Queen: Social Insurance, the Economisation of Citizenship and a New Political Economy of Moral Worth." In *The Transformation of Citizenship*, edited by Jürgen Mackert and Bryan S. Turner, 76–98. London: Routledge.

Tinsman, Heidi. 2000. "Reviving Feminist Materialism: Gender and Neoliberalism in Pinochet's Chile." *Signs: Journal of Women in Culture and Society* 26 (1): 145–188.

Tinsman, Heidi. 2014. *Buying into the Regime: Grapes and Consumption in Cold War Chile and the United States*. Durham, NC: Duke University Press.

True, Jacqui. 2016. "The Global Financial Crisis's Silver Bullet: Women Leaders and 'Leaning In.'" In *Scandalous Economics: Gender and the Politics of Financial Crisis*, edited by Aida A. Hozic and Jacqui True, 41–56. New York: Oxford University Press.

Wade, Lisa., and Myra. M. Ferree. 2015. *Gender: Ideas, Interactions, Institutions*. New York: W. W. Norton.

Wada, Kenji. 2018. "18. Microfinance: Empowering Women and/or Depoliticizing Poverty?" In *Handbook on the International Political Economy of Gender*, edited by Juanita Elias and Adrienne Roberts, 252–264. Massachusetts: Edward Elgar.

Walby, Sylvia. 2009. "Gender and the Financial Crisis." Paper for UNESCO Project on Gender and the Financial Crisis. Lancaster University. https://www.lancaster.ac.uk/fass/doc_libr ary/sociology/Gender_and_financial_crisis_Sylvia_Walby.pdf

Weyland, Kurt. 2005. "Theories of Policy Diffusion Lessons from Latin American Pension Reform." *World Politics* 57 (2): 262–295.

Witz, Anne. 1990. "Patriarchy and Professions: The Gendered Politics of Occupational Closure." *Sociology* 24:675–690.

Zelizer, Viviana. A. 1978. "Human Values and the Market: The Case of Life Insurance and Death in 19th-Century America." *American Journal of Sociology* 84 (3): 591–610.

Zelizer, Viviana. 1983. *Markets and Morals*. Princeton, NJ: Princeton University.

17

FIELD THEORY AND EXPERTISE: ANALYTICAL APPROACHES AND THE QUESTION OF AUTONOMY

ZACHARY GRIFFEN AND AARON PANOFSKY

INTRODUCTION

EXPERTS and expertise are classic topics in the sociology of knowledge. In the sociology of professions tradition, the key objects of inquiry are expert groups: professions that certify members to carry out expert tasks in society. This literature has largely been concerned with the socialization processes through which people become validated as experts, and in particular, it has focused on how different professional groups compete with one another for jurisdiction over specific tasks (Abbott 1988; Whooley 2013; Starr 1982). More recently, sociologists inspired by science and technology studies have sought to shift focus from the study of *experts* to the study of *expertise*. Sociologists of expertise have emphasized "networks . . . linking together agents, devices, concepts, and institutional and spatial arrangements" (Eyal 2013a) or, as another group of scholars puts it, "movement, mediation, and materials" that enable expert intervention (Graizbord, Rodríguez-Muñiz, and Baiocchi 2017). This has allowed researchers to bring insights from science and technology studies to well-trod sociological terrain, and recent scholarship has sought to simultaneously analyze both the formation of jurisdictional boundaries and the accomplishment of expert tasks as codependent elements of a fully-fledged sociology of expertise (Eyal 2013a).

This chapter argues for sociologists to approach the study of expertise by drawing on insights from field theory. Field theory is "a more or less coherent approach in the social sciences whose essence is the explanation of regularities in individual action by recourse to position vis-à-vis others" (Martin 2003, 1). Although field is most associated with the work of Pierre Bourdieu, whose classic analyses of French society relied on the concepts of habitus, field, and capital, it has a history that both predates Bourdieu and has spilled over into other areas of inquiry within sociology. Among these is the sociology of science and expertise, about which Bourdieu wrote comparatively little (Bourdieu 1975, 2004, 1991), and making it a space in which field theory remained relatively underdeveloped until around 2010 or so.

In analyses of topics as diverse as terrorism (Stampnitzky 2013), behavior genetics (Panofsky 2014), think tanks (Medvetz 2012; McLevey 2015), economics (Fourcade 2011; Hirschman, n.d.), stream restoration (Lave 2012), and military intelligence (Eyal 2002), sociologists have recently demonstrated that the content of expertise cannot be disassociated from the fields in which experts are enmeshed. Studying the historical genesis of fields, as well as the ways in which boundaries are established and contested (both within and between fields), is an important part of understanding how expertise becomes mobilized and acts in the world. While our account is rooted in the type of field analysis advocated by Bourdieu (1996a, 1975, 2020), we draw on other field-theoretic work where appropriate and criticize Bourdieu on points that were not sufficiently developed in his account.[1] The overall aim is to provide some suggestions about how other sociologists might think of topics in the sociology of expertise in terms of field theory.

The chapter is organized around two issues that are crucial to the consideration of field theory and expertise, but that intersect the different strands of field theory in various ways. The first of these is a tension in discussions of field theory about whether it should be thought of as a heuristic approach for researching and explaining social action (expertise, for example) through certain relational and structurationist means, or as a substantive theory about the organization of modern societies structured by a differentiation of spheres and powers. This tension is deep, though rarely recognized, in Bourdieu's work (Martin and Gregg 2015), and we argue he did not try to resolve it but rather exploited it differently throughout his career. We continue by mapping problems in these approaches to this debate. In particular, we suggest that it is no accident that many recent analyses of expertise consider fields that are liminal or interstitial in nature; that is to say, social spaces that are not organized to facilitate the social closure that has traditionally made professional autonomy possible (Abbott 1988). Yet there is still something lacking in approaches that consider the "spaces between fields" (Eyal 2013b): a broader historical analysis that takes into account the political economy of contemporary capitalist social relations, which affect more autonomous scientific fields and interstitial fields alike. We argue that such an approach could transcend the limitations of both the heuristic and substantive modes of field analysis, and that this approach may illuminate broader structural crises that experts across different social spaces are faced with.

The second issue we tackle is the effect of field theory on how we think about normative issues and the politics of expertise. We explain how some scholars with strong normative concerns about expertise, Oreskes and Conway (2010) and Collins and Evans (2007), in particular, invoke field-like accounts of expertise: it is not just technical know-how that counts, but also participation and location with respect to expert groups structured in particular ways. Bourdieu also had explicitly normative concerns about expert fields that had historically achieved particular forms of institutionalization (Bourdieu 1975, 1989). Thus, we discuss different ways field scholars link the politics of expertise to the structure and dynamics of fields. In particular, we discuss Bourdieu's ideas about the collective intellectual and the defense of scientific field autonomy as the first and most authentic politics of experts (Bourdieu 1996a, 339–348), considering the relevance and dilemmas of this view for contemporary research agendas and our political moment. To illustrate the importance of thinking about scientific autonomy, not just as a normative ideal, but also as a collective accomplishment, we briefly consider three contemporary processes through which challenges to field autonomy can alter the organization of expertise: experts extending their work beyond their fields, nonexperts replacing experts within fields, and experts defending their individual rights instead of mounting a collective defense of the fields in which they are enmeshed.

We conclude with a discussion about how future research can heed these insights and be designed to tackle interesting new problems in the sociology of expertise. For example, how does neoliberalism and its focus on STEM fields at the expense of more humanistic forms of inquiry relate to various scientific "crises" (the "crisis of the humanities," the "replication crisis")? What do the increasing deprofessionalization of academic knowledge production (i.e., the large-scale conversion of tenure-track positions into adjunct and lecturer jobs) and the privatization of institutions mean for the viability of disciplinary fields as repositories of expertise? How does the digital age, which both accelerates the transnational circulation of knowledge and incentivizes private corporations to remove knowledge from circulation, affect the structure of these fields? We suggest that these developments are not cause to abandon Bourdieu's central insights into the organization of fields but, rather, are reasons to seriously grapple with them if we are to elucidate how expertise functions today.

PART ONE: HEURISTIC STRATEGY OR SUBSTANTIVE STRUCTURE?

What is field theory, and how is it used? Martin (2003) provides a general answer to this question, but here, we link it to the question of expertise. Field theories are accounts of mediated action: meso-level explanations of actions—those of experts, say—in terms of a mutual competition for authority and recognition in a domain. The evolving outcome of that competition constructs the identities and interests of the experts and establishes the parameters for both their micro interactions within and beyond the field and, on the macro level, their relations with forces and structures.

Bourdieu's version highlights particular features (habitus, capital, nomos, *illusio*, doxa, reflexivity, and homology), but field*ish* theories in the sociology of knowledge abound, from those that emphasize cognitive and conceptual spaces (Collins 1985;

Müller-Wille and Rheinberger 2012; Kuhn 1962) to social and spatial arrangements of institutional authority and competition (Abbott 1988; Fligstein and McAdam 2012). Field theories emphasize action at a distance (Martin 2003)—culture, norms, boundaries, identities, implicit rules—that pulls on field members. This is in contrast with the logic of networks, where links and associations are given ontological and explanatory primacy (Latour 2005). What is crucial in field theory is that the capacities and actions of experts cannot be understood without an account of the dynamics of the field itself.

A tension remains in this literature between the use of field as a heuristic for making sense of social action in bounded, relational spaces and a more substantive view that attempts to grasp how modern social life becomes differentiated into fields. Heuristic approaches to field theory are less concerned with broad historical narratives, and more interested in how we explain the interests of the actors who are seeking legitimacy and capital within fields—of expertise, and otherwise. By contrast, more substantive approaches focus on how society comes to be organized so that expertise and knowledge production have relative autonomy from the state, economic institutions, and even (particularly in earlier periods) religion. Rather than advocate for one of these approaches over the other, we propose instead that scholars of expertise focus their attention on another issue that might help to resolve this tension: the relationship between field differentiation and capitalism, or the political economy of fields.

The first approach we are interested in is field as heuristic strategy. In studies on various topics, including literary production (Bourdieu 1996a), cultural consumption (Bourdieu 1984), the market for single-family homes (Bourdieu 2005), academic success (Bourdieu 1988), and the status conferred by elite schooling (Bourdieu 1996b), Bourdieu uses a variety of methodological strategies to explain social action within fields that are relatively bounded and exhibit a degree of autonomy from external forces. In each of these case studies, the analytic approach Bourdieu (1998) adopted is a relational one "in that it accords primacy to relations" (vii), though there is some debate in the literature regarding how "relations" are best operationalized within a field (Emirbayer 1997; Mohr 2013). In addition, field theory is used primarily as a heuristic that, when combined with Bourdieu's other signature concepts (capital, habitus, symbolic power) provides a powerful theoretical apparatus for making sense of social relations between individuals or firms that exist in a common social space. While this is sometimes accompanied by a historical explanation for how the field in question came into being (this is done most successfully in *The Rules of Art* (Bourdieu 1996a), the emphasis is on the explanation of action within different domains of social life.

This mode of thinking gained traction in American sociology beginning in the late 1980s—in part to explain social reproduction in education (Wacquant 1993, 238–239)—and is prominently represented in the cultural sociology literature (Lamont and Lareau 1988; Mohr 1998), in which literature, the visual arts, elite education, philanthropy, and the like, are cast as organized social fields. Work in this vein has not always theorized what makes fields distinctive as a modern social form but, rather, has made strategic use of data to confirm or sharpen the field theoretic approach. In recent years, this has come to include increasingly large datasets and innovative computational methods (Rossman and Schilke 2014; Foster, Rzhetsky, and Evans 2015; Van Gunten, Martin, and Teplitskiy 2016; Mohr et al. 2020), which can be used to analyze how field structure relates to strategies for pursuing various forms of capital.

Key to deploying field theory as a heuristic is the idea of *homology*: that fielded spaces with similar logics of practice and comparable structures can develop across very different domains of social life and be analyzed with a general set of methodological principles (Bourdieu 2020). Perhaps the most prominent example of this mode is the general theory of fields advocated by Fligstein and McAdam (2012). Building on insights from economic sociology and social movement theory, as well as from Bourdieu, they redefine social fields as "strategic action fields" comprised of "incumbents, challengers, and governance units" (Fligstein and McAdam 2012, 8). In place of Bourdieu's theory of action, which is centered around the habitus and pursuit of capital, they propose that, on a phenomenological level, everyday practice revolves around the deployment of actors' "social skill," which, when combined with broader macro-level shifts in field environment, results in "episodes of contention" and eventual "settlements" (Fligstein and McAdam 2012, 8–9). Though Fligstein and McAdam do not explicitly draw on Bourdieu in proposing the notion of "social skill," it is worth noting that in analyzing his own intellectual trajectory, Bourdieu (2008) similarly indicated the importance of strategic positioning within fields. Fligstein and McAdam's theory is therefore notable for its generality and potentially broad applicability, making it similar to the ecological approach to social organization advocated by Abbott (2005b). Abbott is critical of what he sees as an overemphasis on stasis and conflict in Bourdieu's field theory (Abbott 2005a); nonetheless, it shares with the theory of strategic action fields a general analytical framework for understanding social organization in relatively bounded spaces (Liu and Emirbayer 2016).

As far as expertise is concerned, heuristic approaches to field theory are notable for their emphasis on how the structures of fields are constituted and maintained: that is to say, how struggles over forms of capital confer legitimacy within fields. By analyzing processes of boundary-making and social closure, scholars have demonstrated that a crucial function of fields is to demarcate the tasks experts have jurisdiction over, and where that jurisdiction ends (Gieryn 1983; Abbott 1988). While struggles over expert legitimacy are an obvious component of scientific fields (Frickel and Hess 2014; Frickel and Gross 2005), we know, from the work of Bourdieu, Abbott, and others, that these struggles drive the logic of practice in other fielded spaces as well. The presence of expert struggles to define legitimacy and establish boundaries across differentiated social fields leads us to the second mode of field theory we are interested in: a substantive approach that questions how expertise has become privileged as a site of authority in modern society.

Whereas the heuristic approach to fields focuses on expertise as a means of making boundaries and conferring legitimacy, the substantive approach seeks to uncover why expertise plays such an important role in the first place. What is it about *expertise* that gives it a distinctive authority in social fields? Bourdieu answers that the relatively dominant position of experts within fields is the result of a historically specific "interest in disinterestedness" tied to transformations in the political economy of the fields themselves (Bourdieu 1996a, 1993, 2017). Like work by the critical theorists of the Frankfurt School, Bourdieu's work on the historical genesis of artistic fields attempts to extend Marx's historicist understanding of capitalist social dynamics to differentiated societies within which various forms of capital can be accumulated.

In describing how Bourdieu's general sociological approach can be thought of as historical analysis, Craig Calhoun (2013) points out that Bourdieu "laid the basis for a general theory of fields as differentiated social microcosms . . . this became increasingly a theory of the distinctive nature of modern society, organized by the ways in which fields worked internally, related to each other, and mediated the influences of state and market" (49–50). Yet despite this, as Calhoun himself has pointed out, though Bourdieu's work successfully makes use of various notions of "capital," it fails to sufficiently lay out a broader theory of capital*ism* (Calhoun 1993, 2020; Desan 2013). Though Bourdieu himself might argue that this problem is resolved by referring to the overarching "field of power" that structures how value struggles in different fields are related to one another (Bourdieu 1998, 35–63; 2014), this is never systematically worked out. Despite protestations to the contrary (Lebaron 2003; Swedberg 2011), Bourdieu's theory of the "economic field" is less well-developed than his work on, say, culture or education (Desan 2013). Since Bourdieu frequently conceives of cultural or scientific fields as operating in opposition to economic logic (actors in these fields are motivated by an "interest in disinterest"), this has repercussions for how we understand expertise as well. Thus, the substantive approach to fields of expertise asks not just about how boundaries are created to police expert legitimacy, but also how the historical emergence of relatively autonomous fields confers social power on experts.

Comparative historical scholarship argues that relative field autonomy should not be taken for granted as a methodological principle but, rather, posed as a question of *degree* that can be verified empirically: how autonomous is this field, and why? Answers to this question can come at different levels: there are transnationally organized "global fields" that facilitate capital accumulation and valuation worldwide (Steinmetz 2007; Go 2011; Go and Krause 2016; Buchholz 2022); fields can result from the institutionalization of authority at the national level (Fourcade 2009; Ringer 1992; Bourdieu 1998); or, fields can emerge from internal struggles that create semiautonomous spaces within fields (Krause 2018; Abbott 2001). Regardless of level though, such accounts of field formation focus less on boundary-making, and more on the rejection of economic logic that makes the pursuit of other forms of capital "worth the candle"—that is to say, the historical emergence of habitus. Understanding how the relative autonomy of social fields is related to habitus is fundamentally a question about expertise: as Bourdieu would have it, how does one come to master the "logic of the game"? Scholars of expertise have found it most fruitful to not ask this question about fields existing in isolation but, rather, at the intersection of different fields.

Whereas treating field autonomy as a heuristic draws attention to boundary-making and social closure, and substantive approaches to individual fields trace the emergence of this autonomy, Gil Eyal's work demonstrates how experts derive authority by balancing competing interests between fields (Eyal 2002). This approach has two merits that have made it an attractive conceptual apparatus for contemporary sociologists interested in questions about expertise. On the one hand, it retains Bourdieu's penetrating insight that social action can be described neither as merely disinterested nor as motivated by a hidden pursuit of conventional forms of power, and that the pursuit of disinterestedness can be understood through historical analysis (Bourdieu 1987). On the other hand, the focus on expertise allows one to ask questions about social spaces that are populated by various fields of knowledge production. Studying the production of policy knowledge, for example, may require one to make sense of how various different academic fields relate to one another and how actors in those fields transgress boundaries and pursue goals that are seemingly contrary to the fields in which they have been trained (Medvetz 2012; Stampnitzky 2013; McLevey 2015). Even some seemingly well-defined academic fields have roots in multiple fields that came into contact for historical reasons and require the constant negotiation of competing interests and shifting boundaries (Panofsky 2014). Other topics are poised for a similar type of analysis, and sociologists will no doubt continue referring to Eyal's refinement of field theory as the literature on expertise continues to expand.

At the same time, even as scholarship incorporates the heuristic approach into an understanding of fields as emerging and evolving along with capitalist modernity (Gorski 2013), the work of Eyal and others increasingly points toward a common theme: expertise is in crisis (Eyal 2019). Despite the ubiquity of expertise across various fields, answering sociological questions about the politics of expert legitimacy and influence requires resorting to some kind of expert judgment (Eyal 2019, 104). This brings us to a normative question: how *should* the politics of experts relate to field autonomy? While much research has focused on how experts come to trust and relate to one another in common fields (Shapin 1994), in an increasingly skeptical society rife with concerns about "fake news" and "post-truth" (Sismondo 2017), field theory can also shed light on more foundational questions about the value of expertise being organized in particular ways.

PART TWO: EXPERTISE AND THE POLITICS OF FIELDS

A key issue undergirding field theories of expertise, regardless of the analytical approach, is a normative concern with how the autonomy of fields can be preserved in the context of the politics of expertise. In recent years, a combination of factors—skepticism about climate change, concerns about the advent of "fake news" and "alternative facts," concerns about how to safely navigate a global pandemic, and rising distrust of medical treatments such as vaccinations—has forced scientists to defend their expertise on topics over which they previously commanded greater authority. With his frequent invocation of science as requiring an "interest in disinterestedness" and a belief on the part of actors that the scientific endeavor is "worth the candle," Bourdieu was explicit about his normative commitment to science as a rational enterprise capable of promoting the common good. This section first examines how scholars evoke field-like accounts when analyzing expertise, even when they are not explicitly wedded to any particular version of field theory. We suggest that this is not accidental: to defend science on normative grounds usually requires either an antisociological approach that identifies something transhistorical and distinctive about science as a method or approach, or a defense of the field-like conditions that make scientific work and autonomy possible.[2] We then consider the link between the politics of expertise and the structure and dynamics of fields. Drawing on three examples, we argue that while experts have traditionally enjoyed relative autonomy over their work because of collective action that is engaged in during the process of field differentiation, today experts are being incentivized to act in ways that erode their hard-won autonomy.

Some of the most prominent recent interventions in the sociology and history of science have been normative defenses of scientific integrity. Oreskes and Conway (2010), for example, take a no-holds-barred approach in analyzing the history of climate change and tobacco research, arguing that corporations used their considerable financial resources to deliberately obfuscate how the findings about these topics were reported to the public. More recently, Collins and Evans (2017) have made an even more sweeping argument, advocating for a general defense of science as a moral good in democratic societies. Both accounts are similar in the normative claims they make about science as a rational endeavor and in their defense of open and democratic values. And for each, normative concerns are grounded in an implicit field that raises general questions for sociologists.

The vision of scientific activity put forward by Oreskes and Conway (2010) calls to mind the normative structure of science that Merton outlined back in the 1940s. Consider the following statement in the epilogue of *Merchants of Doubt*:

> Research produces evidence, which in time may settle the question . . . After that point, there are no "sides." There is simply accepted scientific knowledge. There may still be questions that remain unanswered—to which scientists then turn their attention—but for the question that has been answered, there is simply the consensus of expert opinion on that particular matter. That is what scientific knowledge *is*. (268)

In the next paragraph, Oreskes and Conway say, "Most people don't understand this," and then they develop a defense of scientific research that relies on an implicit field theory of expertise. "Often one side [in a scientific conflict] is represented only by a single 'expert,'" they write, which "leads to another important point: that modern science is a collective enterprise" (268). A few pages later, Oreskes and Conway explain how experts police the boundaries of science: "Because scientists are not (in most cases) licensed, we need to pay attention to who the experts actually are—by asking questions about their credentials, their past and current research, the venues in which they are subjecting their claims to scrutiny, and the sources of financial support they are receiving" (272). These are questions that any good field theory of scientific research should ask, though Oreskes and Conway present it with distinctly normative aims, a move that Oreskes repeats in a more recent treatment of similar issues (Oreskes 2019). Similar to Merton (1973), Oreskes and Conway share with field theory the idea that expertise works because it is enabled and protected by a cordoned off social space with semiautonomous logic and norms.

Meanwhile Collins and Evans, who have written extensively about what precisely constitutes "expertise," go one step further. In earlier work, Collins (1981) developed a field-like conception of scientific "core sets" and "peripheral sets," which involve actors with varying levels of expertise engaging in practical debates. More recently, due to the same concerns about the corporatization of science catalogued by Oreskes and Conway, Collins and Evans (2017) mount a defense of science, not merely as a means of producing objective knowledge, but also as "an institution that can provide moral leadership" to society as a whole (9). "*Good* actions are intrinsic to science's *raison d'être*," they write, and therefore "we need to make science's special nature clear, and show society what it stands for, before it is overwhelmed by the free-market tsunami like so much else" (9). Again, while they do not explicitly invoke the language of field theory, their defense of scientific autonomy as directly connected to the broader aims of modern societies is evocative of Bourdieu's argument in his most sustained treatment of the scientific field (Bourdieu 2004).

For much of his career, Bourdieu advocated for a field-theoretic approach to the study of science (as a paragon of expertise) for the same reasons he favored this approach to other topics: field theory captures the dual nature of action (science as a "field of forces" and a "field of struggles" to transform or conserve those forces), and it allows the analyst to break with preconceived notions of what constitutes any given social space (Bourdieu 1975). However, Bourdieu also tacitly developed a much more reflexive, and indeed normative, stance regarding scientific expertise that has been less explored by other scholars (Camic 2011). Perhaps more than for any other field, Bourdieu concerns himself with the ability of scientists to defend their autonomy and assert the primacy of their expertise when that is called for. If in Abbott's (1988) work, the exercise of expertise is related to credentialing and the ability of social groups to capture jurisdiction over particular "tasks and problems," for Bourdieu (1989), the autonomy afforded by jurisdictional claims is best defended by being explicit about material conditions. He explains that the authentic politics of experts is the "corporatism of the universal." This refers to experts' efforts to secure the autonomy and integrity their fields (via reflexivity driven by mutual competition), a form of politics that is sometimes misrecognized as a parochial defense of the comfortable prerogatives of the ivory tower at the expense of the democratization of knowledge. But Bourdieu argues that when experts fight for their own interests by fighting for their fields, they are actually fighting for the collective good of universal truth or, at least, for the greatest possibility of systematically producing or approaching universal truth. Experts' ostensibly parochial interest is in the service of a public good.

While the defense of field autonomy has historically been central to the politics of expertise, it is important to distinguish the politics of *expertise* from the politics of *individual experts*. Bourdieu's analysis of the politics of expertise is *pace* Gross and others who are primarily interested in the question of why scientific experts and professors are generally politically liberal (Gross 2013; Gross and Simmons 2014). Gross argues that the academy is on average a left-leaning field because of a self-selection process that results in fewer conservatives pursuing doctoral degrees. Yet other fields that have obtained relative autonomy from external forces also tend toward the political left (even in the corporate-friendly United States, fields of cultural production are still considered "the liberal elite"). The question that emerges here is: Are highly-educated, left-leaning people opting into careers in relatively autonomous fields—the so-called "professional-managerial class" (Ehrenreich and Ehrenreich 1977)—entirely due to self-selection, or is there a more direct relationship between the political field and the politics of experts? Is Bourdieu's account of the phenomenon (that intellectuals are the dominated fraction of the dominant class) sufficient to explain these dynamics?

To explore this question, we do not focus on the political beliefs of experts across fields of cultural production that have homologous relationships to the broader political field, but rather, on how the breakdown of this compact erodes the relative autonomy that fields had previously won. We briefly consider three examples: the extension of expertise to fields in which experts do not have jurisdictional claims (big tech); a field in which the traditionally valued expertise is being gradually eroded and replaced (the federal bureaucracy); and an emergent coalition of experts who defend individual rights over field autonomy (the "free speech" brigade).

The case of Silicon Valley and related big tech hubs engaged in "disruptive innovation" demonstrates how fields of expertise can be eroded and reorganized to prioritize the pursuit of economic capital over scientific or cultural capital. In this process, expertise is not devalued but, rather, *extended* beyond the confines of the industry, allowing a handful of increasingly large firms to claim jurisdiction over fields that were previously governed by their own logics of practice. The relative autonomy that enabled specific types of expertise to develop in the fields of education, science, urban planning, transportation, healthcare, and so on, is gradually eroded as the rules of the game are rewritten to encourage the pursuit of "übercapital": capital that is accrued algorithmically by valuing the accumulation of raw data (Fourcade and Healy 2017). These data can then be used to calculate, score, and classify people in various fields, leading to a reorganization of expertise that devalues the judgment of teachers, scientists, artists, civil servants, and others. The professional "data scientists" whose expertise is deployed in this process serve as a "dominated fraction of the dominant class" (Bourdieu 1984) within big tech, and their interests—and the interests of the experts whose fields their work encroaches on—are subordinated to the accumulation of data. If there is a form of relative autonomy being pursued here, it is not the autonomy of experts over their work; rather, it is autonomy of the owners of capital from state regulation that previously protected the jurisdiction of experts (Abbott 1988).

Another example of the eroding autonomy of experts is the US federal bureaucracy. The political history of the twentieth-century United States is largely a Weberian story about the institutionalization of a centralized regulatory apparatus that became involved, at some level, in the governance of nearly every facet of social and economic life (Orren and Skowronek 2017). This bureaucracy was long defined by its reliance on expertise: regardless of partisan affiliation, a professional pipeline ensured that civil servants across dozens of regulatory agencies possessed institutional knowledge that kept the federal bureaucracy running smoothly, and for the most part insulated it from external forces (Berman, 2022; Medvetz 2012; Bernstein 2001). In recent years however, increasing doubts about the efficacy of regulatory science have produced a "crisis of expertise" that has challenged the relative autonomy of these agencies and opened the door to other interested parties who can supplant them (Eyal 2019). Instead of continuing to rely on the entrenched institutional knowledge that has been key to operating the federal bureaucracy, the work of governance has increasingly been outsourced to entrepreneurial interests, such as management consulting (McKenna 2009). This process was especially pronounced during the Trump administration, as when the Jared Kushner–led "Slim Suit Crowd" of healthcare entrepreneurs attempted to contract out the government's coronavirus response to private-sector competition (Lahut 2020; Tashjian 2020). However, the federal bureaucracy's declining professional autonomy is not a strictly partisan affair, as evidenced by bipartisan efforts to outsource student-loan debt servicing, Medicare plans, and military equipment production to an ever-greater array of private-sector firms. As the various agencies making up the federal government have been hollowed out of civil servants over time, it has become increasingly difficult just to execute the nation's laws, regardless of political affiliation (Light 2008; Cassella and Ollstein 2020). The expertise of these agencies has historically been buttressed by their relative autonomy from political forces within the federal government, rather than the partisan beliefs of the civil servants themselves.

Finally, in the growing debates about "free speech" and "cancel culture," we see how the apparent defense of expertise can contribute to the erosion of field autonomy. Over the last several years, intellectuals from across various different academic fields have become increasingly vocal about the need to protect the free speech rights of scientific experts from nefarious sources: "mobs," "Social Justice Warriors," and "the Woke ideology" (Pluckrose and Lindsay 2020). An emergent field situated at the intersection of academia and journalism has cropped up to support this effort: organizations, such as the Heterodox Academy and the Foundation for Individual Rights in Education, and publications, including *Persuasion*, *American Affairs*, *New Discourses*, *Quillette*, and others, that claim to encourage "free thinking" in the face of "illiberalism." Those who contribute to the growth of this movement do not necessarily espouse the same political ideology or commitment to partisanship; rather, there is a common assertion that the foundational value underpinning all forms of expertise is the right to free speech and open debate. Contra Bourdieu's corporatism of the universal, this means that the individual rights of experts are valued above the relative autonomy of the fields in which they are enmeshed, eroding the cultural authority of various forms of expertise in general in favor of "specific intellectuals" (Foucault 2013). The further success of this movement could make it more difficult for intellectuals to intervene in public affairs by marshalling the symbolic capital accumulated by their field of expertise, instead privileging those who have succeeded in acquiring individual notoriety—by publishing a *New York Times* bestseller for a more popular audience perhaps.

In a recent essay, Gross and Robertson (2020) examine various calls to diversify the social sciences ideologically. Though they largely disagree with the idea that political diversification would improve the quality of social scientific fields, they also argue that future research should focus on "how a social scientist's political identity and commitments might affect scholarship via research practices that come to seem sensible in light of the deep philosophical assumptions that are often bundled together with politics" (Gross and Robertson 2020, 452). This might be useful for explaining the relationship between research and politics for individual experts, but it still presumes a short-circuiting of the dynamics of social fields by assuming a direct relationship between the political field and the politics of experts. When it comes to the politics of exper*tise*, we argue that a more pressing issue is whether fields encourage the defense of relative autonomy. The examples we briefly introduced—big tech, the US federal bureaucracy, and the "free speech brigade"—demonstrate how fields of expertise are eroded not because of the partisan beliefs of individual experts but, rather, because of the decoupling of expert practice from the defense of field autonomy.

CONCLUSION: THE TRANSFORMATION OF (FIELDS OF) EXPERTISE

In "The Corporatism of the Universal," Bourdieu (1989) wrote about the politics of expertise in a way that integrates the analytic, historical, and normative strands of field theory that we have discussed here. His article challenges two leading misconceptions about the politics of experts. On the one side, Bourdieu criticizes the idea that science and expertise occupy an apolitical zone of pure reason, and that politics are a corrupting social influence from without. Rather, scientists and other experts are clearly an interest group who advocate and lobby for political and cultural influence and resources. But on the other side, Bourdieu attacks the idea that scientific experts are merely junior members of the professional-managerial class whose political interests reflect nothing more than the class interests of their state capitalist paymasters. Avoiding both of these reductionistic accounts of expertise, Bourdieu instead argues that scientists, in defending their own professional interests (the set of social and cultural structures driving a mutual competition for scientific capital which produces an interest in disinterest), come to collectively embody a commitment to universal values of truth and knowledge for their own sake. Universalism becomes, literally, embodied in the expert collective.

This idea integrates the three themes in field theory—heuristic strategy, substantive account, and normative claim—covered in this chapter. As a heuristic strategy, field theory encourages us to understand fields as both relational fields of forces between experts as well as fields of struggles "to transform or preserve these fields of forces" (Bourdieu 1993, 30). As a substantive account, we use field theory to understand how societies differentiate into a set of domains, each dominated by a set of "experts" committed to a different universalist nomos—for example, artists and art for art's sake, lawyers and legal rationality, and scientists and the pursuit of objective knowledge. And as a normative account, Bourdieu's theory suggests that the authentic politics of experts is directed at securing for their field the autonomy, integrity, and structures that enable them to embody a commitment to the universal.

Here we conclude by suggesting future directions of research that might employ these three facets of field theory to understand ongoing transformations in the production and use of expertise by engaging three topics in particular: the emergence of various "crises" in knowledge production, the privatization and deprofessionalization of expertise, and the transnational circulation (or lack thereof) of knowledge.

Regarding the first issue, it is no secret that in the neoliberal era, education and science policy in the United States have encouraged a shift in emphasis for funding agencies and undergraduate degree seekers away from the humanities and toward the STEM fields. Along with this broader transformation, there have been moral panics within academia about two separate "crises" in knowledge production: the "crisis of the humanities" and the "replication crisis." The first is the result of concerns about declining enrollment in the humanities, particularly in traditionally popular liberal arts departments, such as English literature or history; whereas the second is about scientific researchers' inability to replicate a large percentage of experiments and statistical analyses. Both topics have received considerable attention in the press and are the subjects of constant discussion among academics, and there is little question that these supposed crises are in some way related to transformations in the way knowledge gets funded and produced in the United States.

Although the causes of these moral panics and the extent to which they accurately reflect the empirical reality in each case are interesting questions in themselves, for our purposes, they raise another interesting question: Are these problems reflective of problems within scientific fields, or do they represent a broader problem of science *as* a field? Bourdieu often wrote about "the scientific field," and his position in calling for a "corporatism of the universal" was that academics from different disciplinary backgrounds, working at different institutions, across different countries share common interests that should be defended collectively (Bourdieu 1989). However, thinking about these two supposed crises in knowledge production prompts tough questions about the possibility of a collective defense of intellectuals: over the same period in which disciplines like history experienced a significant decline in enrollment, entirely new fields such as Black studies emerged and became institutionalized (Rojas 2007). Similarly, the requirements for conducting scientific replications vary widely for different types of scholarship: while researchers who primarily perform statistical analysis can include their datasets and code in publications, it is much more difficult to replicate experimental conditions. The point here is not that these crises are manufactured or have no basis in material reality, but rather that science can be defined as a broad field of knowledge production or as an amalgamation of many smaller expert fields, and that making these analytical categories transparent will be important for diagnosing these issues. Sociologists of expertise who are interested in these questions might draw inspiration from theorists who have written about fields in terms of scale, such as Fligstein and McAdam (2012), Steinmetz (2016), and Krause (2018).

The second topic of potential interest for future scholarship is the deprofessionalization and privatization of knowledge production. Not only are these processes of great concern to many working academics, but they also are related to each other in ways that can be well addressed by the kind of relational thinking field theory provides. To take one obvious example, consider the academic discipline of economics. As with other fields, contemporary economics is dominated by a handful of elite departments that command outsized resources and attention, both within economics and in the public imagination (Fourcade, Ollion, and Algan 2015). On the whole though, economics departments across the United States are confronted with the same problems faced by other departments: the number of tenure-track jobs is not keeping pace with the number of new PhDs; undergraduate courses are increasingly being taught by lower-paid adjuncts and lecturers; and young people who previously might have considered a career in academia are instead getting professional degrees to work in industries with higher earning potential.

While one could imagine a variety of potential solutions to these transformations that would also reinforce the importance of having sound economic research to inform public policy, one of the biggest recent developments is the privatization of top-tier economic knowledge. In past decades, economists who were unable to find a tenure-track appointment might take a job at a policy school or in a business school's finance department, but recently, economists have been leaving academia in droves to take high-paying jobs in large tech corporations. A recent report from the Harvard Business School found that Amazon had hired some 150 economists within just the preceding five years (Holland 2018). In fact, in the United States, there may soon be more economists working in Silicon Valley than in the entire field of policy schools. This rapid transformation is particularly striking, given that the outsized presence of economists within policy schools is itself a relatively recent development (Berman, 2022). Sociologists of expertise would do well to think about how these dual processes—the deprofessionalization and the privatization of knowledge—are related phenomena across different academic fields. Academic departments that train a large percentage of PhDs knowing that they will ultimately be working in the private sector are empirical fodder for testing the analytical categories of field theory and reconceptualizing what the structure of expert fields looks like in the twenty-first century.

A final topic for scholars interested in fields of expertise is the transnationalization of knowledge production. As we discussed earlier in the chapter, field theorists have recently made some important advancements in reconceptualizing the global reach of fields, particularly in thinking about such topics as imperialism and the circulation of goods across national boundaries (Steinmetz 2007; Go and Krause 2016; Go 2011; Buchholz 2022). Bringing these concerns to the topic at hand, how are fields being remade in the digital age, as data and information become easier to store and transport at scale? This is not an entirely new question, as sociologists have previously demonstrated how ideas, such as the theoretical underpinnings of neoliberalism, were created through the construction of transnational fields of expertise (Bockman and Eyal 2002). Nevertheless, the variety of recent transformations in technology worldwide—such as the advancements in computing power and machine learning that power the "big data" movement—should prompt us to think about how the material infrastructure of data collection and knowledge transmission affects everyday practice within fields, as well as how these changes in practice alter the balance of power.

To take but one example, consider the explosion of "big data"–fueled initiatives that were spawned by the completion of the Human Genome Project. The initial project was spearheaded by the United States, but it was completed with the cooperation of some twenty research centers around the world. Despite the hope that the project would finally settle the debate over the biological basis of race, it led instead to "a discursive explosion, along with a mushrooming of technologies developed in the service of testing, manipulating, or capitalizing on race" (Bliss 2012, 2). This revolution in genomic sequencing resulted in a vast industry of personalized genetic testing and (soon to be) precision medicine initiatives that are paradoxical in nature: the fields of knowledge production in these domains are increasingly both transnationally oriented and privatized. While the global circulation of massive quantities of genetic data is made possible by these advancements, there is also huge financial incentive for corporations to commodify this data and frame the way it is interpreted by the public. Thinking about how private interests do or do not affect the circulation of data and the expertise required to make sense of these data is another challenge for field theory to make sense of because these issues are affected not just by everyday scientific practice but also the logics that make these practices possible.

These are just a handful among many topics that future research may address. While much of the research in the sociology and history of science has been conducted in opposition to field theory, we posit that both its analytic categories and its historicist approach make it a valuable resource for making sense of expertise. Furthermore, we believe that Bourdieu's normative approach to scientific knowledge, in particular his defense of a "corporatism of the universal," opens up a number of important questions about how "fields of expertise" may be conceptualized and mobilized for future research.

Notes

1. As Camic (2011) has noted, Bourdieu's sociology of science and expertise is less programmatic than his work on most of the other topics he tackled.
2. This is the "demarcation problem" that philosophers have never been able to solve in a satisfying way: their definitions either cut off activity commonly recognized as scientific or cannot exclude pseudoscientific activity (Gieryn 1983).

References

Abbott, Andrew. 1988. *The System of Professions: An Essay on the Division of Expert Labor.* Chicago: University of Chicago Press.

Abbott, Andrew. 2001. *Chaos of Disciplines.* Chicago: University of Chicago Press.

Abbott, Andrew. 2005a. "Ecologies and Fields." http://home.uchicago.edu/~aabbott/Papers/BOURD.pdf.

Abbott, Andrew. 2005b. "Linked Ecologies: States and Universities as Environments for Professions." *Sociological Theory* 23 (3): 245–274.

Berman, Elizabeth Popp. 2022. "Thinking like an Economist: How Economics Became the Language of U.S. Public Policy." Book. Princeton: Princeton University Press.

Bernstein, Michael A. 2001. *A Perilous Progress: Economists and Public Purpose in Twentieth-Century America.* Princeton, NJ: Princeton University Press.

Bliss, Catherine. 2012. *Race Decoded: The Genomic Fight for Social Justice.*

Bockman, Johanna, and Gil Eyal. 2002. "Eastern Europe as a Laboratory for Economic Knowledge: The Transnational Roots of Neoliberalism." *American Journal of Sociology* 108 (2): 310–352.

Bourdieu, Pierre. 1975. "The Specificity of the Scientific Field and the Social Conditions of the Progress of Reason." *Social Science Information* 14 (6): 19–47.

Bourdieu, Pierre. 1984. *Distinction: A Social Critique of the Judgement of Taste.* Cambridge, MA: Harvard University Press.

Bourdieu, Pierre. 1987. "Legitimation and Structured Interests in Weber's Sociology of Religion." In *Max Weber, Rationality and Modernity*, edited by Scott Lash and Sam Whimster, 119–136. London: Allen & Unwin.

Bourdieu, Pierre. 1988. *Homo Academicus.* Stanford, CA: Stanford University Press.

Bourdieu, Pierre. 1989. "The Corporatism of the Universal: The Role of Intellectuals in the Modern World." *Telos* 1989 (81): 99–110. https://doi.org/10.3817/0989081099.

Bourdieu, Pierre. 1991. "The Peculiar History of Scientific Reason." *Sociological Forum* 6 (1): 3–26. https://doi.org/10.1007/BF01112725.

Bourdieu, Pierre. 1993. *The Field of Cultural Production: Essays on Art and Literature.* New York: Columbia University Press.

Bourdieu, Pierre. 1996a. *The Rules of Art: Genesis and Structure of the Literary Field.* Stanford, CA: Stanford University Press.

Bourdieu, Pierre. 1996b. *The State Nobility: Elite Schools in the Field of Power.* Cambridge, UK: Polity Press.

Bourdieu, Pierre. 1998. *Practical Reason: On the Theory of Action.* Stanford, CA: Stanford University Press.

Bourdieu, Pierre. 2004. *Science of Science and Reflexivity.* Cambridge, UK: Polity.

Bourdieu, Pierre. 2005. *The Social Structures of the Economy.* Cambridge, UK: Polity.

Bourdieu, Pierre. 2008. *Sketch for a Self-Analysis.* Chicago: University of Chicago Press.

Bourdieu, Pierre. 2014. *On the State: Lectures at the Collège de France, 1989–1992.* Edited by Patrick Champagne, Rémi Lenoir, Franck Poupeau, and Marie-Christine Rivière. Translated by David Fernbach. Cambridge, UK: Polity Press.

Bourdieu, Pierre. 2017. *Manet: A Symbolic Revolution, Lectures at the Collège de France (1998–2000).* Medford, MA: Polity Press.

Bourdieu, Pierre. 2020. *Habitus and Field.* Cambridge, UK: Polity Press.

Buchholz, Larissa. 2013. *The Global Rules of Art: The Emergence and Divisions of a Cultural World Economy*. Princeton: Princeton University Press.

Calhoun, Craig. 1993. "Habitus, Field, and Capital: The Question of Historical Specificity." In *Bourdieu: Critical Perspectives*, edited by Craig Calhoun, Edward LiPuma, and Moishe Postone, 61–88. Chicago: University of Chicago Press.

Calhoun, Craig. 2013. "For the Social History of the Present: Bourdieu as Historical Sociologist." In *Bourdieu and Historical Analysis*, edited by Philip S. Gorski, 36–66. Durham, NC: Duke University Press.

Calhoun, Craig. 2020. "Moishe Postone and the Transcendence of Capitalism." *Critical Historical Studies* 7 (1): 145–165. https://doi.org/10.1086/708010.

Camic, Charles. 2011. "Bourdieu's Cleft Sociology of Science." *Minerva* 49 (3): 275–293.

Cassella, Megan, and Alice Miranda Ollstein. 2020. "Biden Confronts Staffing Crisis at Federal Agencies." Politico, November 12. https://www.politico.com/news/2020/11/12/shrinking-workforce-can-hurt-biden-436164.

Collins, Harry M. 1981. "The Place of the 'Core-Set' in Modern Science: Social Contingency with Methodological Propriety in Science." *History of Science* 19 (1): 6–19. https://doi.org/10.1177/007327538101900102.

Collins, H. M. 1985. *Changing Order: Replication and Induction in Scientific Practice*. London: Sage Publications.

Collins, Harry M., and Robert Evans. 2007. *Rethinking Expertise*. Chicago: University of Chicago Press.

Collins, Harry M., and Robert Evans. 2017. *Why Democracies Need Science*. New Jersey: Wiley.

Desan, Mathieu Hikaru. 2013. "Bourdieu, Marx, and Capital: A Critique of the Extension Model." *Sociological Theory* 31 (4): 318–342. https://doi.org/10.1177/0735275113513265.

Ehrenreich, Barbara, and John Ehrenreich. 1977. "The Professional-Managerial Class." *Radical America* 11 (2): 7–32.

Emirbayer, Mustafa. 1997. "Manifesto for a Relational Sociology." *American Journal of Sociology* 103 (2): 281–317. https://doi.org/10.1086/231209.

Eyal, Gil. 2002. "Dangerous Liaisons between Military Intelligence and Middle Eastern Studies in Israel." *Theory and Society* 31 (5): 653–693.

Eyal, Gil. 2013a. "For a Sociology of Expertise: The Social Origins of the Autism Epidemic." *American Journal of Sociology* 118 (4): 863–907.

Eyal, Gil. 2013b. "Spaces between Fields." In Gorski, *Bourdieu and Historical Analysis*, 158–182.

Eyal, Gil. 2019. *The Crisis of Expertise*. Cambridge, UK: Polity Press.

Fligstein, Neil, and Doug McAdam. 2012. *A Theory of Fields*. New York: Oxford University Press.

Foster, Jacob G., Andrey Rzhetsky, and James A. Evans. 2015. "Tradition and Innovation in Scientists' Research Strategies." *American Sociological Review* 80 (5): 875–908. https://doi.org/10.1177/0003122415601618.

Foucault, Michel. 2013. *Politics, Philosophy, Culture: Interviews and Other Writings, 1977–1984*. New York: Routledge.

Fourcade, Marion. 2009. *Economists and Societies: Discipline and Profession in the United States, Britain, and France, 1890s to 1990s*. Princeton, NJ: Princeton University Press.

Fourcade, Marion. 2011. "Cents and Sensibility: Economic Valuation and the Nature of 'Nature.'" *American Journal of Sociology* 116 (6): 1721–1777. https://doi.org/10.1086/659640.

Fourcade, Marion, and Kieran Healy. 2017. "Seeing like a Market." *Socio-Economic Review* 15 (1): 9–29.

Fourcade, Marion, Etienne Ollion, and Yann Algan. 2015. "The Superiority of Economists." *Journal of Economic Perspectives* 29 (1): 89–114. https://doi.org/10.1257/jep.29.1.89.

Frickel, Scott, and Neil Gross. 2005. "A General Theory of Scientific/Intellectual Movements." *American Sociological Review* 70 (2): 204–232. https://doi.org/10.1177/000312240507000202.

Frickel, Scott, and David J. Hess. 2014. *Fields of Knowledge: Science, Politics and Publics in the Neoliberal Age*. Political Power and Social Theory 27. Bingley, UK: Emerald Group. https://doi.org/10.1108/S0198-871920140000027000.

Gieryn, Thomas F. 1983. "Boundary-Work and the Demarcation of Science from Non-science: Strains and Interests in Professional Ideologies of Scientists." *American Sociological Review* 48 (6): 781–795.

Go, Julian. 2011. *Patterns of Empire: The British and American Empires, 1688 to the Present*. New York: Cambridge University Press.

Go, Julian, and Monika Krause. 2016. *Fielding Transnationalism*. Malden, MA: Wiley Blackwell.

Gorski, Philip S. 2013. *Bourdieu and Historical Analysis*. Durham, NC: Duke University Press.

Graizbord, Diana, Michael Rodríguez-Muñiz, and Gianpaolo Baiocchi. 2017. "Expert for a Day: Theory and the Tailored Craft of Ethnography." *Ethnography* 18 (3): 322–344. https://doi.org/10.1177/1466138116680007.

Gross, Neil. 2013. *Why Are Professors Liberal and Why Do Conservatives Care?* Cambridge, MA: Harvard University Press.

Gross, Neil, and Christopher Robertson. 2020. "Ideological Diversity." In *The Production of Knowledge*, edited by Colin Elman, John Gerring, and James Mahoney, 432–456. Cambridge, UK: Cambridge University Press. https://doi.org/10.1017/9781108762519.017.

Gross, Neil, and Solon Simmons. 2014. *Professors and Their Politics*. Baltimore, MD: Johns Hopkins University Press.

Hirschman, Daniel. n.d. "Inventing the Economy: Or, How We Learned to Stop Worrying and Love the GDP." PhD diss., University of Michigan.

Holland, Roberta. 2018. "Hunting for a Hot Job in High Tech? Try 'Digitization Economist.'" Harvard Business School Working Knowledge, October 29. http://hbswk.hbs.edu/item/looking-for-a-hot-job-in-high-tech-try-digitization-economist.

Krause, Monika. 2018. "How Fields Vary." *British Journal of Sociology* 69 (1): 3–22. https://doi.org/10.1111/1468-4446.12258.

Kuhn, Thomas S. 1962. *The Structure of Scientific Revolutions*. Chicago: University of Chicago Press.

Lahut, Jake. 2020. "Jared Kushner's Coronavirus 'Impact Team' Mocked as the 'Slim Suit Crowd' and a 'Frat Party' Descended from a UFO." Business Insider. https://www.businessinsider.com/coronavirus-kushner-impact-team-mocked-slim-suit-crowd-frat-party-2020-4.

Lamont, Michele, and Annette Lareau. 1988. "Cultural Capital: Allusions, Gaps and Glissandos in Recent Theoretical Developments." *Sociological Theory* 6 (2): 153–168. https://doi.org/10.2307/202113.

Lave, Rebecca. 2012. *Fields and Streams: Stream Restoration, Neoliberalism, and the Future of Environmental Science*. Athens: University of Georgia Press. http://public.eblib.com/choice/publicfullrecord.aspx?p=1222471.

Lebaron, Frédéric. 2003. "Pierre Bourdieu: Economic Models against Economism." *Theory and Society* 32 (5/6): 551–565.

Light, Paul Charles. 2008. *A Government Ill Executed: The Decline of the Federal Service and How to Reverse It*. Cambridge, MA: Harvard University Press. http://catdir.loc.gov/catdir/toc/ecip083/2007044648.html.

Liu, Sida, and Mustafa Emirbayer. 2016. "Field and Ecology." *Sociological Theory* 34 (1): 62–79. https://doi.org/10.1177/0735275116632556.

Martin, John Levi. 2003. "What Is Field Theory?" *American Journal of Sociology* 109 (1): 1–49. https://doi.org/10.1086/375201.

Martin, John Levi, and Forest Gregg. 2015. "Was Bourdieu a Field Theorist?" In *Bourdieu's Theory of Social Fields*, edited by Mathieu Hilgers and Eric Mangez, 39–61. New York: Routledge.

McKenna, Christopher D. 2009. *The World's Newest Profession*. Cambridge, UK: Cambridge University Press.

McLevey, J. 2015. "Understanding Policy Research in Liminal Spaces: Think Tank Responses to Diverging Principles of Legitimacy." *Social Studies of Science* 45 (2): 270–293. https://doi.org/10.1177/0306312715575054.

Medvetz, Thomas. 2012. *Think Tanks in America*. Chicago: University of Chicago Press.

Merton, Robert King. 1973. *The Sociology of Science: Theoretical and Empirical Investigations*. Chicago: University of Chicago Press.

Mohr, John W. 1998. "Measuring Meaning Structures." *Annual Review of Sociology* 24 (1): 345–370. https://doi.org/10.1146/annurev.soc.24.1.345.

Mohr, John W. 2013. "Bourdieu's Relational Method in Theory and in Practice: From Fields and Capitals to Networks and Institutions (and Back Again)." In *Applying Relational Sociology: Relations, Networks, and Society*, edited by François Dépelteau and Christopher Powell, 101–135. New York: Palgrave Macmillan. https://doi.org/10.1057/9781137407009_5.

Mohr, John, Christopher Bail, Margaret Frye, Jennifer C. Lena, Omar Lizardo, Terrence McDonnell, et al. 2020. *Measuring Culture*. New York: Columbia University Press.

Müller-Wille, Staffan, and Hans-Jörg Rheinberger. 2012. *A Cultural History of Heredity*. Chicago, IL: University of Chicago Press.

Oreskes, Naomi. 2019. *Why Trust Science?* Princeton, NJ: Princeton University Press.

Oreskes, Naomi, and Erik M. Conway. 2010. *Merchants of Doubt: How a Handful of Scientists Obscured the Truth on Issues from Tobacco Smoke to Global Warming*. New York: Bloomsbury Press.

Orren, Karen, and Stephen Skowronek. 2017. *The Policy State*. Cambridge, MA: Harvard University Press.

Panofsky, Aaron. 2014. *Misbehaving Science: Controversy and the Development of Behavior Genetics*. Chicago: University of Chicago Press.

Pluckrose, Helen, and James Lindsay. 2020. *Cynical Theories: How Activist Scholarship Made Everything about Race, Gender, and Identity—and Why This Harms Everybody*. Durham, NC: Pitchstone.

Ringer, Fritz K. 1992. *Fields of Knowledge: French Academic Culture in Comparative Perspective, 1890–1920*. Cambridge, UK: Cambridge University Press.

Rojas, Fabio. 2007. *From Black Power to Black Studies: How a Radical Social Movement Became an Academic Discipline*. Baltimore, MD: Johns Hopkins University Press.

Rossman, Gabriel, and Oliver Schilke. 2014. "Close, but No Cigar: The Bimodal Rewards to Prize-Seeking." *American Sociological Review* 79 (1): 86–108. https://doi.org/10.1177/0003122413516342.

Shapin, Steven. 1994. *A Social History of Truth: Civility and Science in Seventeenth-Century England*. Chicago: University of Chicago Press.

Sismondo, Sergio. 2017. "Post-Truth?" *Social Studies of Science* 47 (1): 3–6. https://doi.org/10.1177/0306312717692076.

Stampnitzky, Lisa. 2013. *Disciplining Terror: How Experts Invented "Terrorism."* Cambridge, UK: Cambridge University Press.

Starr, Paul. 1982. *The Social Transformation of American Medicine.* New York: Basic Books.

Steinmetz, George. 2007. *The Devil's Handwriting: Precoloniality and the German Colonial State in Qingdao, Samoa, and Southwest Africa.* Chicago: University of Chicago Press.

Steinmetz, George. 2016. "Social Fields, Subfields and Social Spaces at the Scale of Empires: Explaining the Colonial State and Colonial Sociology." *Sociological Review* 64 (2 suppl): 98–123. https://doi.org/10.1111/2059-7932.12004.

Swedberg, Richard. 2011. "The Economic Sociologies of Pierre Bourdieu." *Cultural Sociology* 5 (1): 67–82. https://doi.org/10.1177/1749975510389712.

Tashjian, Rachel. 2020. "Jared Kushner Brings an End to the Era of the Skinny Suit." *GQ*, April 7. https://www.gq.com/story/jared-kushner-skinny-suit-over.

Van Gunten, Tod S., John Levi Martin, and Misha Teplitskiy. 2016. "Consensus, Polarization, and Alignment in the Economics Profession." *Sociological Science* 3 (December): 1028–1052. https://doi.org/10.15195/v3.a45.

Wacquant, Loïc. 1993. "Bourdieu in America: Notes on the Transatlantic Importation of Social Theory." In Calhoun, LiPuma, and Postone, *Bourdieu: Critical Perspectives,* 234–262.

Whooley, Owen. 2013. *Knowledge in the Time of Cholera: The Struggle over American Medicine in the Nineteenth Century.* Chicago, IL: University of Chicago Press.

PART V

MAKING THE FUTURE PRESENT

18

ADDRESSING THE RISK PARADOX: EXPLORING THE DEMAND REQUIREMENTS AROUND RISK AND UNCERTAINTY AND THE SUPPLY SIDE LIMITATIONS OF CALCULATIVE PRACTICES

DENIS FISCHBACHER-SMITH

INTRODUCTION

> There is a view that the very *raison d'être* for management resides in the fact that both the process and function of managing are required to deal with uncertainty. If there were no uncertainty within and around organizations, then there would be no need to make decisions and therefore no need for managers. In other words, *the principal task of management should be to deal with risk.*
>
> —Smith and Irwin (2006, 221).

The opening quotation raises a number of issues in relation to the nature of risk as a construct; the demand for calculative practices in support of risk management; and the relationships that exist between risk and uncertainty and, especially, around the predictive validity associated with risk analysis. The management function within organisations has a principal role in dealing with the uncertainty that ultimately requires decisions to be made. The ways in which that uncertainty is expressed and quantified and its consequences, considered over various time frames, all contribute to the challenges around dealing with risk as measurable uncertainty. However, each of these elements also brings problems around the accuracy of predictions, the role played by expert (and nonexpert) judgments about hazards, and the ways in which emergent conditions confound those judgments in terms of cause-and-effect relationships. Put another way, there is an argument that states: the *requirements* from decision-makers for tools and techniques that allow for the effective prediction of hazardous events will almost invariably outstrip the *abilities* of those calculative practices to supply robust and appropriate analytical processes and practices, especially, those that have the required level of predictive validity needed to inform those decisions. This is the paradox that sits at the core of the risk management process.

There is an implication in the phrase "the management of risk" that those who are involved in the activity are able to: identify and quantify the likelihood of a hazard occurring; determine its likely consequences and the damage pathways through which it can cause harm; intervene to mitigate those "risks,"; and develop plans to respond to any residual hazards that may remain. By any reasonable benchmark, those are challenging tasks, and they can be seen to represent the demand side of risk management. These elements of the risk management process are challenging largely as a function of the nature of sociotechnical systems and because of the complexity inherent in many risk-based problems.

In addition, the implicit assumption that risk can be adequately calculated and managed is impacted by the potential for emergence that exists within complex sociotechnical systems (Erikson 1994; Holland 1998; Tenner 1996). This is especially the case when we are dealing with "radical uncertainty"—the class of events that are rare, unforeseen, and that in many cases, lie outside the capabilities of organizations to fully predict their onset (Kay and King 2020b; Taleb 2007; Weick and Sutcliffe 2015). These are often termed "extreme events"—that is, low-probability, high-consequence events—which often have high destructive energy and are difficult to control (Fischbacher-Smith 2010; Smolka 2006). The Covid-19 pandemic serves as an example of this kind of extreme event because of the scale of its impact, the emergent nature of the virus, and the challenges associated with its mitigation and control.

According to Knight ([1957] 2006), risk should be seen as measurable uncertainty: that is, the calculation of the probability (and consequence) of uncertain future events relies on an a priori or statistical basis and, where that is not feasible, then on the views of experts in the field. Knight, however, sees the latter as the weakest of these calculative practices. It is the relationships between the likelihood of a hazard being realized, the consequences associated with that hazard, and the potential for mitigation that risk management seeks to address. It is the ambiguities associated with the meaning of risk in practice which generates many of the problems in terms of delivering robust risk estimations into the policy and practice domains.

The aim of this chapter is to consider the range of tensions that exist between the *demand* for the effective prediction of damaging events and the abilities of risk analysis to *supply* a high degree of calculated certainty in the face of radical uncertainty.

The relationships between these supply-and-demand processes also bring into question the nature and role of expertise in the processes of risk management. This is especially the case when uncertainty is high, where the diagnosis of vulnerability—rather than the expression of certainty—is the most likely outcome, and where emergence within the system generates conditions that are often unknowable until the harm is caused. These tensions drive the paradox at the core of risk management—namely, that the abilities of calculative practices to provide an accurate prediction of risk (with an appropriate level of predictive validity) will always be outstripped by the demand for such calculations.

The COVID-19 pandemic provides an opportunity for discussing both the nature of risk as a construct and its implications for expert judgment, along with the extent of the predictive validity that is associated with the use of calculative practices. The chapter considers the management of risk within sociotechnical systems[1] and the role played by expertise in that context, and it explores this range of issues in the broader setting of the supply and demand relationships for calculative practices that are together labeled "risk analysis." Finally, the chapter considers the ways in which information around the uncertainty associated with hazards becomes codified, with one of the potential outcomes being the masking of the uncertainty that is inherent in the assessment process.

ESTIMATE-BASED EVALUATIONS OF UNCERTAINTY

> Knowledge is a big subject. Ignorance is bigger. And it is more interesting.
> —Firestein (2012, 10)

As stated earlier, the notion of risk as measurable uncertainty can be traced back to the work of Frank H. Knight ([1957] 2006), who highlights the distinction between unmeasurable forms of uncertainty and those that are deemed to be measurable: that is, those phenomena that are subject to effective statistically based calculative processes or *a priori*[2] forms of reasoning. Knight also outlined a third form of probability measure that is associated with "estimates", and he sees the latter as both having "no valid basis of any kind for classifying instances" and that they have "the greatest logical difficulties of all" (225). The reasons for this view are that such estimates of probability have weak predictive validity and can be seen to be open to influence by a range of social and psychological factors. Knight argues that estimates of uncertainty in decision-making can be seen to

> deal with situations which are far too unique, generally speaking, for any sort of statistical tabulation to have any value for guidance. The conception of an objectively measurable probability or chance is simply inapplicable. (231)

For Knight ([1957] 2006, 233), the distinction between risk and uncertainty is therefore between measurable and unmeasurable uncertainty. The former allows for the calculation of a distribution of outcomes that is both known and understood; and he uses the term "uncertainty" for phenomena where it is not possible to calculate the distribution of outcomes with any predictive validity and where uncertainty remains high.

Decisions that involve emergent, unique, or relatively rare situations are particularly challenging in this regard due to the cognitive processes and assumptions of those who are involved in shaping the analysis. There is an additional problem in that many of the failures in those systems are not random. The random nature of failure is an important element in determining the probability of an outcome, although it is invariably shaped by the situational context in which that failure occurs, as well as by the role both human actors and emergent conditions played in precipitating that failure. Because of the challenges associated with predicting emergence, as well as the actions of human actors, decision-makers invariably make assumptions about the role that both elements play in the failure process.

A number of factors shape the ways in which both experts and nonexperts make judgments about uncertainty. The role of cognitive bias in shaping estimates of uncertainty has been a subject of considerable debate within the academic literature (Camilleri et al. 2019; Curley et al. 2020; Tversky and Kahneman 1973, 1974). Kahneman (2011) highlights the distinction between our rapid decision-making processes (referring to them as System I) and more deliberate analytical processes (System II). Along with Tversky, Kahneman identified a series of cognitive shortcuts (heuristics) that allow us to function in time-constrained contexts but can also lead us to make mistakes in relation to judgments we make under conditions of uncertainty (Tversky and Kahneman 1973, 1974). These heuristics can be defined as "a strategy that ignores part of the information, with the goal of making decisions more quickly, frugally, and/or accurately than more complex methods" (Gigerenzer and Gaissmaier 2011, 454).

From the perspective of an estimates-based assessment of risk, it could be argued that the impacts of heuristics are likely to prove particularly challenging in relation to such judgments, especially so for those rare events for which there is little prior experience. These extreme events can challenge the assumptions of those who design and manage sociotechnical systems, because such events invariably sit outside the experience base for the operation of that system. The sinking of the *Titanic* on its maiden voyage, for example—a ship previously considered unsinkable by some—illustrates the problem of trying to assess the probability of failure when there is no effective a priori knowledge or statistical data available to make effective calculative judgments. After all, the *Titanic* only sank once!

Risk analysis can be seen as a process of measuring uncertainty around failure modes and effects, one that is based on a priori reasoning or statistical evidence. The expectation would be that failures assessed in this way would be random in nature (thereby allowing for a statistical basis of determining failures) and would not involve human actors owing, primarily, to their largely unpredictable nature. In addition, the ways in which data are collected and analyzed can also add additional uncertainty into the data. This clearly has implications for the management of risk, particularly, in situations where the evidence base in support of the analysis is limited.

A further problem arises from the fact that many of the hazards and uncertainties facing organizations are both multidisciplinary and multidimensional. This serves to add to the potential uncertainties that exist in the assessment of risk, especially for sociotechnical systems. The need for a multidisciplinary approach to risk analysis adds to the complicated nature of the issues and also has implications for the role that expertise plays in the generation of estimates. This can be challenging because of the "transscientific" nature of the problems being investigated (Weinberg 1972, 1977, 1985)—that is, they go beyond the ability of science to prove—and it highlights the role uncertainty can play in the scientific understanding underpinning the hazards being assessed. Similarly, the complex, multilayered nature of organizations and the interconnected nature of their processes generates the potential for emergent conditions, which also impacts on the role played by technical expertise in the assessment of hazards (Smith 2005). It is in this context that expert judgments, and their relationships with the knowledge that is available to decision-makers, are important, and where the core of many of the issues associated with the risk paradox can be found.

FRAMING THE RISK PARADOX

We may view the risk paradox from several perspectives. At one level, it might simply be impossible to calculate with precision the probability and consequences associated with certain hazards, and so organizations are forced to work with estimates of the potential probabilities of those hazards (Besner 2012; Pauchant and Mitroff 1990; Smith 1990). From Knight's perspective, these estimates would be weak predictors of risk. This aspect of the paradox also highlights the issue of knowledge generation within highly uncertain environments and the difficulties of making accurate decisions under such conditions (Jasimuddin, Klein, and Connell 2005; Murphy and Pauleen 2007; Snowden 2002). There are also questions around the provision of governance under conditions of radical uncertainty, especially in terms of the need for a precautionary approach when the potential consequences of the hazard are high. This highlights the role played by expert judgments in that precautionary process (Calman and Smith 2001; Evans 2012; Streatfield 2001).

In a related governance issue, key elements in the process of building transparency around decision-making relate to questions around the nature of what makes an expert, the validation (and accreditation) of that expertise, and the domain of knowledge in which an individual is deemed to be an expert. Expertise is invariably considered to be specific to a knowledge domain and does not readily transfer from one specialism to another without additional training and knowledge acquisition (and, arguably, validation). The potential problems generated by "instant experts" can be significant when we are dealing with complex technical issues and there is a need to ensure the validation of such expertise within policy debates. This is a also problematic issue in dealing with low-probability, high-consequence (extreme) events, for which there is little, if any, prior experience that allows for effective predictions; or where emergence within the system generates new, often unforeseen, outcomes (Holland 1998; Morowitz 2002). In such cases, it may be more logical to discuss vulnerability within systems and its implications for processes of control rather than risk, as vulnerability should consider the potential impact of failure on the overall performance of the system instead of focusing on the probability of that failure.

Spiegelhalter (2019) highlights the various forms that uncertainty can take, which range from "aleatory uncertainty," which represents the inevitable unpredictability about future systems states, to "epistemic uncertainty," where there is a lack of knowledge and information available on which to make a meaningful prediction. Put another way, there is the potential for uncertainty to exist in the data (direct uncertainty) and also in the underlying science used to interpret that data (indirect uncertainty. As a consequence, those involved in management and those who make and implement policy should embrace the various dimensions of uncertainty in their decision practices and do so in a transparent manner that recognizes the imprecision that can exist within calculative practices.

Disagreements between groups of experts are also important here, and the challenge for policymakers is related to the networked nature of that expertise and the reiterative nature of changing estimates, as these reassessments also become open to questions concerning their validity (Eyal 2013, 2019; Oppenheimer et al. 2019). This can result in endless technical debate around the scientific determination of risk (Collingridge and Reeve 1986a, 1986b), especially when it takes place in the context of an environment dominated by radical uncertainty. These debates and conflicts invariably have the potential to erode the public's trust of expert judgment, further contributing to the risk paradox by generating more confusion around risk estimates and eroding trust in expert groups.

An issue at the core of discussions around uncertainty, therefore, concerns the nature and extent of the information available to decision-makers in terms of dealing with hazards, the ability to extract meaning from that information, and the role of expertise in codifying and framing the meaning derived from the information, such that others in the organization can act on it (Boisot 1995, 1998; Hidalgo 2015). Here, a challenge also arises from the political and institutional barriers to revising estimates of risk as new information becomes available. This was evident in many of the debates around Covid-19.

Taken together, these issues also require that decision-makers recognize the role their own worldviews can play in constraining their willingness to accept and act on new information or to recognize the challenges generated in terms of their core assumptions that any new information could provide (Fischbacher-Smith 2012; Fischbacher-Smith and Fischbacher-Smith 2009). As Kunreuther and Useem (2018) observe, the ability to overcome the experts' biases and assumptions is an important component in the recognition and management of uncertainty.

Quantification can be a powerful element in shaping the decision-making process. Starr (1991), for example, commented: "Quantification is very persuasive to a decision maker when all else is vague" (3). Starr had previously highlighted the need to balance the calculation of uncertainty with the societal acceptability of the hazards, especially when they are expressed as a challenge to the perceived likelihood and potential consequences associated with those hazards (Starr 1969). Again, this involves balancing statistically determined (and predictive) calculations of failure modes and effects with the perceptions of a system's vulnerability, which are difficult to quantify. Emergent conditions also generate a problem in terms of the acquisition of knowledge about hazards because those conditions can generate additional forms of uncertainty or impact the ability of the organization to communicate the nature of the hazards and the uncertainty surrounding them. Others have also commented on the knowledge-based challenges that such uncertainty generates. Kenneth Arrow (1992), for example, observes that our "knowledge of the way things work, in society or in Nature, comes trailing clouds of vagueness. Vast ills have followed a belief in certainty" (46).

It is the extraction of meaning from that information that is often challenging for decision-makers, and it can occur on a number of levels. Firstly, the information about a phenomenon may be tacit—that is, it is held by some within the organization but not communicated to others. This tacit knowledge may contradict the decision-makers' assumptions about the performance of the system (Wynne 1989, 1996). Secondly, when the knowledge about a phenomenon is highly codified, it often masks much of the uncertainty that is associated with it (see, among others, Beer 1985; Boisot 1995). Thirdly, the verification of information around systems performance is often constrained because of the scale of the information flows that take place within the system, which requires taking much of that information on trust (Brookfield and Smith 2007; Collingridge 1992; Fischbacher-Smith and Fischbacher-Smith 2014).

Thus, the search for certainty in an environment of ambiguity caused by radical uncertainty becomes the context in which the supply of risk analysis (expressed in terms of measurable uncertainty) cannot meet the demand for it from both decision-makers and those who make policy. It is here that many risk debates have centered on the role of expert judgment in shaping calculations of risk, and these debates are often set against the unwillingness to accept those calculations by those who are exposed to the hazards.

Kay and King (2020b) observe that, irrespective of the sophistication of the modeling tools used, if the underpinning knowledge is flawed or does not exist, then good decisions are not likely. The drive toward ever more sophisticated modeling can be seen to relate to the increased societal demands for risks to be managed (both in terms of the probability of the hazards causing harms and the nature and extent of those harms). However, it does so at the same time that the complexity within sociotechnical systems often makes that modeling more difficult to carry out. At the same time, the complex nature of those systems has the potential to generate new forms of hazard and vulnerability—through the process around "emergence" (Erikson 1994; Holland 1998; Morowitz 2002; Tenner 1996) or "overflowing" (Callon, Lascoumes, and Barthe 2009). This serves to undermine still further the effectiveness of those attempts at prediction, control, and mitigation. Also, in some cases, there is little in the way of a statistical basis for determining the likelihood and consequences of failures, and the result is that much of what passes for quantified risk analysis can be seen to be driven by the judgments of experts (and, often, of nonexperts within organizations) instead of being grounded in either an a priori or a statistical basis for prediction. Extreme events add to the complexity around this issue, as do the threats to system security generated by both accidental and intentional human threat actors, which are often difficult, if not impossible, to predict with a high degree of accuracy.

We can add to these challenges around the risk paradox the very ambiguities that surround the use of the term *risk* itself; and there are multiple, often contradictory, definitions, which adds to the confusion (Aven and Renn 2009; Kay and King 2020b). As a consequence, there has been criticism of the use of the term *risk* in public discourse because of the ambiguities that are associated with it (Dowie 1999). Thus, the core definition of risk used within discussions around uncertainty also serves to play a role in shaping the risk paradox. Risk management implies that the probabilities and consequences of a particular hazard can be identified and assessed in a way that has both a robust and a reliable degree of predictive validity. This is not possible in many cases, and the result is that the expert estimates of the probabilities and consequences of risk are often open to debate and dispute (Collingridge and Reeve 1986a, 1986ab). Thus, the ambiguities around the nature of risk and its relationship with uncertainty are a central factor in the role expertise plays expertise in the management of hazards and, especially, within sociotechnical systems.

There is, therefore, a balance to be struck among the provision of calculations of uncertainty, the assumptions that decision-makers hold about the ways in which that uncertainty is quantified, and the potential consequences based on a failure of those assumptions. Against this background, there has been an erosion of the trust of expert judgments around the issues of uncertainty, even though those with expertise are invariably better placed to make informed judgments than nonexperts are. This adds to the challenges around the risk paradox, where one of the biggest challenges has to do with the ambiguities around the use of the term *risk*.

MANAGING THE RISK CHIMERA: THE NATURE OF RISK ASSESSMENT

"Risk"—including all cognates such as "risks" and "risky"—is a sort of conceptual pollutant. Being common to discourses of all kinds and levels, it encourages people to assume that they know what they are talking about when they use it—but, much worse and much more significant, to assume that they know what others are talking about when they hear or see it used. It is a highly dangerous chimera which can be dispatched without loss.

—Dowie (1999, 42)

For Jack Dowie, the ambiguity inherent in the use of the term "risk" is a central component of many of the issues and conflicts associated with the management of uncertainty.
Dowie's framing of risk as a conceptual pollutant can also be seen in Callon et al.'s (2009)
labeling of risk as a "false friend." Thus, the uncertainties in the definition of risk itself
compound the problems associated with the risk paradox by generating ambiguities
of meaning within the discourse around hazards. Douglas (1990), for example, argues
that more general interpretations of risk frame the concept in terms of danger. In other
contexts, the term *risk* implies that the potential threats of harm that are inherent in hazardous activities and processes can be calculated with a reasonable (and acceptable) degree of accuracy, and that such calculations will have an associated predictive capability.
In essence, when we discuss the nature of risk, we are dealing with the part of uncertainty that can be measured, and the clarity this measurement brings should be based on
a robust articulation of the concepts used. Kay and King (2020a) extend this argument:

> Discourse about uncertainty has fallen victim to a pseudo-science. When no mean-
> ingful quantification is possible, algebra can provide only spurious precision, while
> at the same time the language becomes casual and sloppy. The terms risk, uncertainty
> and volatility are treated as equivalent; the words likelihood, confidence and proba-
> bility are also used as if they have the same meaning. But risk is not the same as un-
> certainty, although it arises from it.

There is, therefore, a degree of consensus around the ambiguities that are present in the
use of the term risk within public discourse, and this has implications for way we see risk
management as a process. Kay and King (2020b) argue that calculations of risk are possible where the underlying processes are understood to be close to immutable—that is,
they are stationary processes that are unaffected by human actions. In contrast, human
behaviors are more challenging as an individual's intent to undertake a particular action
can be seen to effectively generate a probability of 1, unless that intent and its associated actions can be identified and then mitigated by organizational controls. Thus, when
discussing risk, there is a need to ensure that the uncertainties surrounding the reliability of the processes around risk analysis are also acknowledged.

In the context of our present discussion, risk is seen to have two main components:
the probability of a hazard occurring (within a particular period of time) and the
consequences associated with that hazard (which also has a spatial and temporal dimension in terms of latent or immediate effects and the distances over which its impacts
occur; see, for example, Griffiths 1980; Hutter 2010; Warner 1992). If either of these two
components is missing or unknown, then the notion of risk can degrade to the level
of the conceptual pollutant that Dowie identifies, especially because ambiguities in
meaning can lead to assumptions being made about the reliability of any underpinning calculations that form the basis of a risk estimation. If the probabilities are unknown (or unknowable), then the discussion should be about the nature and extent of
the residual uncertainty, and consideration should also be given to the range of potential
vulnerabilities that can generate harm. This shifts the nature of the discourse away from

the *probabilities*—which may be indeterminate—toward the range of *possibilities* (as a function of vulnerability) and their associated consequences. By doing so, it can bring to the surface the assumptions of the decision-makers, and this can lead to a wider consideration of the potential causal processes for hazardous events. To contextualize the relationships between the various elements of risk assessment and the potential points of intervention by the expert community, we need to outline a framework for considering the processes involved.

RISK, UNCERTAINTY, AND THE CHALLENGES FOR EXPERT JUDGMENT

> The trouble with technocrats is because they believe they're smart, expert indeed, they don't do what all humans should—and all politicians must—acknowledge when they've made mistakes, learn from errors and adjust their assumptions . . . Because to do so would be to challenge their conception of themselves as bearers of superior insights who are not as susceptible to error as the rest of us.
>
> —Mr. Michael Gove (2016, 27)

This comment by Michael Gove,[3] a minister in the UK Government at the time of this writing, was made during the campaign around the United Kingdom's June 2016 referendum on whether to leave the European Union. Brexit[4] was a policy decision for which there was no prior experience, and where the consequences of the decision were subject to considerable uncertainty. Conventional approaches to the analysis of the "risks" associated with Brexit were therefore fraught with problems around prior experience, predictive capability, and the burden of proof. Gove's comments highlight some important policy-related issues that are relevant to any discussion of the management of uncertainty.

First, Gove raises the issue of expert assessments of uncertainty and the potential for errors that exists within those estimates. Perhaps more significantly, he points to the need to acknowledge the nature and extent of the errors that are made in expert judgments and states that policymakers should similarly acknowledge their own mistakes. Although it is expected that experts will have more insight into their areas of technical specialism than nonexperts, Gove can be seen to be echoing the arguments put forward by Knight about the weaknesses of expert assessments of uncertainty. Gove does not, however, offer an alternative to expert judgment that would provide the predictive validity associated with more robust forms of measuring that uncertainty.

Secondly, Gove points to the need to adjust expert estimates over time, especially as new information becomes available. In this respect, he can be seen to be supporting elements of a Bayesian view, which sees estimates of probability being revised based on a range of information and evidence related to a hazard (see, for example, Sheldon and

Smith 1992). This information can include a range of inputs to the process, including those that are a priori and statistically based, along with a range of probability estimates that recognize the perceptual dynamics of such estimates.

Thirdly, but perhaps more subtly, Gove highlights the need for transparency and adjustment in the policymaking process, especially where expert judgment is involved; again, this has echoes of a Bayesian perspective. Of course, there is also the question of the validity of any insights specialists might have regarding an issue, especially relative to individuals who do not have expertise in a relevant field. There have been several instances where policymakers, often with no technical background in an area, have been content to express strong views on a subject, and sometimes even to contradict those with expertise. Of course, the irony here is that Gove had no effective empirical basis for making his judgments about the costs and benefits associated with the Brexit decision, and therefore could be seen as guilty of the same form of "paradigm blindness" (Fischbacher-Smith 2012, 2013) that he accused others of displaying. It is the politicization of such views and the power that key influencers can bring to bear on debates that becomes critical in shaping policy the discussions around potentially harmful events (Collingridge 1984, 1992).

Finally, the potential for ideological bias to shape discussions around uncertainty is also considerable. An implicit issue here concerns the question of trust and the role that ideological views can play in the sifting and prioritizing of the evidence used in attempts to determine risk. It is a lack of transparency, combined with the role of highly technocratic language in discourse and the associated use of calculative practices, which is often seen to lie at the core of the conflicts over expert judgments in risk management.

An additional problem concerns the extent of the residual uncertainty that remains in any risk analysis (where the probabilities and consequences of a hazard are not easily measurable or the determinates of risk have insufficient predictive validity). Organizations often overlook this issue when making judgments about the nature and acceptability of the risk. For example, the UK Government's mantra during the Covid-19 pandemic was that the advice it was giving and its policy were being led by the science. But as many researchers have observed, science is invariably driven by uncertainty (see, for example, Firestein 2012), and so policymakers should, within the parameters of Gove's comments, recognize and acknowledge the uncertainty in their policy decisions. Against that argument, there is invariably an assumption on the part of many that those making policy decisions do so based on robust expert assessments of the uncertainty associated with policy issues. This is despite the uncertainty in policies where emergent problems are prevalent. These are often seen as wicked problems that defy easy policy solutions (Rittel and Webber 1973), and they are often typified by the challenges associated with the risk paradox (Fischbacher-Smith 2016a).

The complexities within sociotechnical systems and of the associated emergent conditions arising from them often combine to generate situations where the ability of expert judgment to calculate risk is constrained, but the demand for robust leading-edge scientific advice is high. Such conditions invariably create challenges around the burden of proof associated with the expert opinions and, especially, concerning the role of professional and organizational cultures and processes in shaping such estimates (Collingridge and Reeve 1986b). This has led to concerns about the objectivity of expertise, the role powerful interests can play in shaping the use of science in decision- and policymaking, and the imbalances in power that often exist between those who generate (and benefit from) the hazardous activity and those who are the potential victims of that activity (Adekola et al. 2017; Smith 1991). The outcome of these debates has often been an erosion of the value accorded expert judgment—perhaps more apparent in what some have labeled the "post-truth" era (BBC News 2016; D'Ancona 2017; Mann 2018; Nichols 2017), although the use of the term *post-truth* clearly has it important caveats attached.

It is apparent, though, that the way in which the questioning of evidence, and the interpretation of meaning that is associated with the evidence, has led to tensions around the role of expert judgment in decision-making. There have been associated debates around the use of a range of calculative practices to support formal risk-assessment processes and the extent of their predictive capabilities (Smith 1990; Wynne 1996). The paradox, of course, is that these calculative practices are often called into question at times when the need to identify and manage uncertainty is at its highest, a phenomenon illustrated by the Covid-19 crisis. Policymakers' dismissing evidence and reasoned analysis as "fake" simply adds to the problems associated with managing the uncertainty within public discourse (Mann 2018; Roozenbeek and van der Linden 2019; Wynne 1989). And there is an additional issue regarding the ways that risk is defined and operationalized. It is that ambiguity adds to the challenges associated with the use of risk as a construct in policymaking.

RISK ASSESSMENT: CALCULATIVE PRACTICES AND THEIR ACCEPTABILITY

Figure 18.1 illustrates the main elements of risk assessment as they were originally conceptualized by Rowe (1975). This risk assessment has two primary components—risk analysis and risk acceptability. *Risk analysis* relates to the range of calculative practices and expert judgments used in identifying hazards, estimating the probability of their occurrence, and determining the range of potential consequences associated with those hazards. *Risk acceptability* concerns the acceptability (or otherwise) of those calculated risks, and ideally, it will be based on a full consideration of the extent of the uncertainty surrounding the calculations. While there is an argument that risk analysis should be seen as an empirical and expert-driven process, there are those who argue that the process is invariably more normative that that, owing to a range of factors that can influence the role played by empirical and scientific evidence (Fischer 1980, 1990; Wynne 1996). There are also arguments suggesting that there are uncertainties in the theoretical frameworks we use to analyze risk and in the potential impact that cognitive biases can

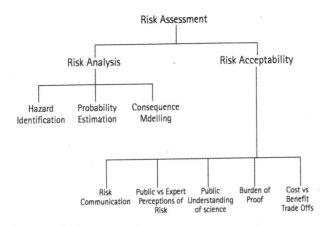

FIGURE 18.1. Elements of risk assessment.

Source: Fischbacher-Smith, Irwin, and Fischbacher-Smith (2010). Adapted from Rowe (1975).

have on the determination of the boundaries of the data to be quantified (Kahneman 2011; Porter 1995).

The process of risk analysis consists primarily of a range of calculative practices that allow for the effective identification and determination of both the probability and the consequences associated with particular hazards. In contrast, risk acceptability is invariably portrayed as a process of social construction in which a range of social and political processes underpin the debates around the acceptability (or otherwise) of those calculated "uncertainties." There has been, however, considerable debate around the socially constructed nature of the risk analysis process itself (Beck 1986, 1992; Giddens 1990), in which the rational nature of the scientific basis of those calculative processes has been called into question, especially because of the potential influence that is brought to bear on the process by powerful political and economic interests (Collingridge and Reeve 1986a, 1986b; Smith 1990). This is illustrated by the conflicts associated with linking smoking (and more recently, vaping) to health impacts, as well as in the anti-vaccination lobby (see Adekola, Fischbacher-Smith, and Fischbacher-Smith 2019; Berridge 2006; Blume 2006).

In the absence of a priori and statistically based data in sociotechnical systems, where much of the calculated risk is based on expert judgments, the argument for a degree of social construction in risk analysis has some merit. In addition, the calculative power of risk analysis is stronger for engineered systems, where failures at the component level are random and do not involve the actions of human operators. Once humans are involved in the failure process, their unpredictable nature can serve to increase the uncertainty in the risk analysis process. Such criticism, however, does not invalidate the experts' insights on the nature of hazards. Instead, it points to the need for discussions of vulnerability, where the probabilities of failure are relegated to lesser status in importance and the emphasis shifts to a discussion of the weaknesses in controls, as well as of the failure modes and the effects associated with those failures.

Of course, it is also possible that certain elements of society will see a potential hazard as more problematic than the scientific evidence would suggest (see Adekola, Fischbacher-Smith, and Fischbacher-Smith 2019; Berridge 2006); there are two dimensions to this. On the one hand, there are inputs from individuals who are not traditionally considered to be experts, but who have direct experience of the phenomena being assessed—this is often termed "citizen science" (Irwin 1995, 2001). One of the most-cited examples of this is concerned with the exposure of sheep in the England's Lake District to the radioactive fallout from the Chernobyl nuclear accident (Wynne 1996). In studying this case, Brian Wynne found that the experts' assessment of the level of exposure was refuted by the local farmers, who were drawing on their contextual knowledge of the sheep's grazing patterns and other local factors (see also Wynne 1989, 2008). At the same time, there have also been cases when attempts to refute a scientific risk assessment were based on a less robust evidence base. One example here was the suggestion that the measles, mumps, rubella (MMR) vaccine may play a role in the development of autism in children (Wakefield 1999). Andrew Wakefield's research in this area was discredited, and he was found to have conducted his research in an unethical manner by the United Kingdom's General Medical Council in terms of having a conflict of interest, resulting in his paper being withdrawn by the journal that had published it (Dyer 2010; Eggertson 2010; Flaherty 2011; Godlee, Smith, and Marcovitch 2011). Yet despite the unequivocal rejection of his findings, Wakefield's research, the web-based spread of disinformation, and celebrity endorsements of the link between vaccination and autism took hold with some of the public and combined to shape an antivaccination debates among some social groupings (Kata 2010, 2012; Ołpiński 2012). More recently, the antivaccination movement has been implicated in controversies associated with governments' Covid-19 responses, not least for promulgating the conspiratorial claim that the vaccine was developed by the "global elite" as a means of controlling society (Burki 2020; Hotez 2020; Jolley and Lamberty 2020). The conflict highlight the erosion of the traditional role played by science and expertise in debates around risk and uncertainty (Mann 2018; Nichols 2017). Thus uncertainty proves to be a multilayered construct in discussions around hazards in which the ambiguities that exist serve to generate spaces for conflict in public discourse.

Firstly, there is the question of what risk means in practical terms and, especially, in ways that take account of the technical limitations that are inherent within it. In particular, the relationships between risk (as a process of measuring the uncertainty associated with the likelihood of a hazard being realized, along with its associated consequences) and the residual uncertainty around those hazards are important. These relationships are often misunderstood and misrepresented in practice, and calculations of risk are often portrayed as predictive and reliable when they are not.

Secondly, in managing complex sociotechnical systems, the emergent conditions arising from the interactions among elements of the systems will invariably generate challenges to reliable forms of prediction. This is often a function of the novel nature of those interactions, whose outcomes will not have been foreseen because of the emergence they generate. Emergence has the potential to negate or undermine quantitative assessments of uncertainty because it generates such novel characteristics.

Thirdly, there are challenges associated with the knowledge base that underpins the role of expert judgment in risk analysis, particularly around areas that involve innovative processes and technologies. Innovative processes almost inevitably generate new forms of failure potential, and there is often insufficient operational experience to develop an effective statistical basis for considering failure modes and effects that provide robust predictive validity. The evidence that emerged in 2018 and 2019 about the problems with the Boeing 737 Max jet airliner highlights this issue and points to the difficulties of addressing early warnings about potential safety problems[5] and to long-standing issues around the regulation of such safety-critical technologies (see, for example, Heimann 2005; Hoppe, Pranger, and Besseling 1990; Latham 2011; Vaughan 1989). Some of these innovations can also be framed in terms of new working practices that arise when operators adapt existing processes and operational protocols. These emergent forms of working (which are sometimes seen as necessary violations to get the job done) can become problematic when they are not incorporated into formal organizational protocols and procedures. The result is a dislocation between what is happening in practice and what managers think is happening based on the established formal protocols and procedures.

Fourthly, many of the calculative practices that are embedded in risk analysis can break down when anticipating threats associated with human actors (Fischbacher-Smith 2016a). This is especially problematic in cases where the intent underpinning the behaviors is a fundamental driver in the generation of harm. These actions can involve acts of commission—that is, intentional acts or violations of process that generate accidents—and acts of omission, where human operators neglect to carry out a task or fail to respond to early warnings and near-miss events (Reason 1990, 1997). Threats from human actors can be immediate or delayed in effect and may emanate from the managerial or operational levels of the organization. They are ubiquitous across a range of organizations, and even the most highly regulated environments, such as aviation and healthcare, have witnessed the potential harm that can be caused by hostile threat actors who have the ability to bypass multiple layers of control to cause catastrophic harm (Fischbacher-Smith 2015; Smith 2002).

Finally, the global nature of organizational activities adds a further layer of complexity to all the issues that have just been raised because extended supply and value chains, along with the highly interconnected nature of production systems, transect different organizational and national cultures. There are also challenges in ensuring the reliability of products and, in some cases, of services in the global setting, because any supply chain is inevitably only as robust as its weakest link. An organization's culture then becomes an important but often difficult to measure element in ensuring effective compliance with regulatory requirements across a diverse range of organizations and national characteristics. This adds to the uncertainty already present within the system and provides a context in which expertise is used in risk analysis.

EXPERTISE AND UNCERTAINTY: KNOWLEDGE AND THE MANAGEMENT OF RISK

A key element in the risk management process relates to the ways in which we make sense of the information that we have about the uncertainty in the system; and the extraction of meaning from this information can have both positive and negative consequences. This is dependent, in part, on the effectiveness of the analytical lens through which information is assessed and the manner in which it is codified. The complexity associated with sociotechnical systems and the generation of emergent conditions can also present challenges to the successful extraction of that meaning. Emergence—or as Stewart (2019) frames it, the "Law of Unintended Consequences" (3)—is a critical element in the management of risk and uncertainty and it is shaped by the knowledge the organization holds about the nature of those emergent conditions. The core issue here concerns the knowledge base that is used within the processes of making decisions under uncertainty, and it is possible to add to Knight's categorization around risk by integrating the classification of what is known and unknown that was outlined by Donald Rumsfeld (2002, 2011).

Within Knight's definition of risk as measurable uncertainty, we can argue that it requires that the decision-makers both know and understand the phenomena being assessed and are also aware of the ambiguities in the information they have in hand, the problems associated with extracting meaning from that information, and the limits of understanding within the whole process. In the case of Rumsfeld's two forms of existing knowledge—the knowns and the unknown knowns—the information concerning a potential failure can be seen to be available somewhere inside the organization, but it may not always be made available in an explicit and usable format to senior decision-makers. These unknown knowns would include the early warnings and near-miss information that is known to some as "tacit knowledge," but that has not been codified and disseminated to others. Codification of that information can, in certain cases, lead to the masking of any ambiguity that exists within the data, and this will potentially to impact any decisions taken. Such early warning or weak-signal information can be seen to be a function of both the information-gathering capabilities of the organization and the cognitive and social filters that can prevent the significance of such signals from being recognized (Fischbacher-Smith 2012; Mack and Rock 2000). Codification may well mask any uncertainties that exist around a phenomenon and generate the impression of certainty around issues that does not exist in reality.

These unknown knowns can also be a function of tacit knowledge that is lost through restructuring and staff departures. This can serve to shape a particular paradigmatic view of the world, resulting in a form of "paradigm blindness" (Fischbacher-Smith 2012). A similar process was termed "subjugated knowledges" by Foucault (1997). In essence, relevant information is available within the system but is, essentially, not recognized (because of the assumptions made about systems performance) or seen as significant by decision-makers. Foucault makes the distinction between two forms of such knowledge.

The first occurs where that knowledge becomes masked, or hidden, over time within the formally accepted worldviews of the organization. As a result, anything that runs counter to the dominant worldview is likely to be rejected, and this will affect the organization's ability to recognize the information generated by early warnings and near-miss events. These worldviews can shape the ways in which organizations approach the collection of information around systems' performance. Seidl (2007), for example, argues that a "duality of structure" occurs where accepted knowledge becomes a function of what is observed and measured, and the resultant established knowledge and insight then serves to shape the range of the parameters that organizations seek to observe and measure. While organizations invariably measure the things that are deemed to be important, they also tend to focus on phenomena that lend themselves to measurement. The result is that some organizations tend to measure what is possible and then to manage what can be measured. Although those elements of performance can be important, they may serve to prevent more complex and less tangible, elements from being included in the monitoring process.

The second distinction identified by Foucault arises out of the view that knowledge can be undermined or, as he puts it, "disqualified." This is done on the basis of a shift in the prevailing underpinning theoretical frameworks. The result is that certain forms of knowledge are downgraded in their relative status, and this might, in turn, subsequently affect the data-collection process. This latter form of subjugated knowledge can be seen to have much in common with the arguments set out by Collingridge and Reeve (1986a, 1986b), who suggested that powerful interests are able to effectively undermine the legitimacy of certain forms of evidence that do not fit their worldviews. In doing so, they generate a faux sense of consensus within the accepted scientific evidence. Collingridge and Reeve term this process the "under-critical model of science," and it has been shown to have saliency in a number of cases where particular forms of scientific evidence have been undermined in public debates by powerful economic and political interests (Adekola, Fischbacher-Smith, and Fischbacher-Smith 2019; Irwin 1995; Smith 1990). This also highlights the issue of indirect forms of uncertainty that are present in the underpinning scientific knowledge base or the established views of systems performance.

As we move into the area of the unknowns seen in Figure 18.2 (both known unknowns and unknown unknowns), the knowledge around systems performance does not exist within the organization or its networks, and so the challenges of prediction increase considerably. It is here that issues around information provision can increase the problems around uncertainty. The extent of these unknowns ensures that any attempts at risk analysis will be constrained by the nature of the uncertainty in the underlying knowledge base—both in terms of the probabilities of the hazard being realized and the consequences associated with it. This problem can be compounded when unpredictable human actors are involved in the failure process. Individuals—both benign and hostile—can generate uncertainty and emergence through both their actions and inactions and this will impact the determination of the vulnerabilities within a system

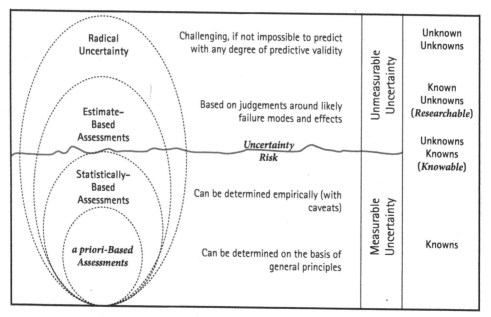

FIGURE 18.2. Risk, uncertainty, and the nature of knowledge.

(Fischbacher-Smith 2015; Smith 2002). Thus the issue of structure becomes important in shaping those information flows, because a failure to collect, codify, and disseminate information or to make assumptions on the basis of incomplete information are likely to contribute to the generation of failure (Fischbacher-Smith 2016b). The case of Covid-19 illustrates many of the issues around the risk paradox and it serves to highlight the role played by expertise within the risk analytical process.

COVID-19: THE RISK PARADOX IN PRACTICE

Given the emergent nature of the SARS-CoV-2 virus, it is perhaps not surprising that governments found it difficult to manage, despite some having been warned of the potential for an emergent pandemic (King 2020, 15). There were significant challenges surrounding Covid-19 as an emergent problem, especially in terms of the underlying characteristics of the hazard, its transmission characteristics, and the population that is potentially at risk. The Covid-19 pandemic has been described as an example of radical uncertainty because it is an example of a dynamic situation where there is some understanding of the problem, but the knowledge base is insufficient for decision-makers to be confident in the robustness of their actions. As Kay and King (2020a) noted:

A global pandemic is not a "black swan," an unknown unknown. Nor is it a low probability event, an extreme observation from a known probability distribution . . . A global pandemic was a likely event at some point, a known unknown in that sense. But the occurrence of such a pandemic was not a very likely event, and we could not in advance do anything more than guess at what form it would take, and even then our guesswork was likely to be limited by mixing and matching between what we know about more familiar pathogens. We could acknowledge the possibility of something new and different, outside the range of past experience, but have only a limited ability to imagine what this might be, still less reckon with the probability of it coming to pass. (Kay and King 2020a)

For Kay and King, the probabilities associated with Covid-19 could not be effectively determined using the normal approaches to risk management because the phenomena in question are not produced by the "stationary processes" that allow for a determination of probability (Kay and King 2020a). The Covid-19 pandemic illustrates the problems of dealing with the radical uncertainty associated with extreme events.

Firstly, there are challenges associated with the emergent nature of the virus itself and the lack of effective contingency planning for dealing with such an emergent outbreak at scale. For example, Yamey and Wenham (2020) refer to the Global Health Security Index (GHS Index 2020), which before the pandemic had rated both the United States and the United Kingdom the top two countries in terms of pandemic preparation. In commenting on the relatively poor responses of both countries in dealing with the pandemic, Yamey and Wenham (2020) observed:

The two countries that *on paper* were the best prepared to deal with a pandemic turned out by June 2020 to be two of the world's biggest failures in tackling COVID-19. . . . There's a reason the scorecard got it so wrong: It did not account for the political context in which a national policy response to a pandemic is formulated and implemented.

The role of the policy response in shaping the consequences associated with the pandemic was, therefore, critical to how it was managed. The Global Health Security Index report highlights the challenges associated with attempts to manage radical uncertainty and the role policy actors can play in the generation of hazards and the effectiveness of mitigation strategies. Again, this was illustrated throughout the pandemic and this was compounded by the problems associated with medical populism (Lasco and Curato 2019) and what has become known as "vaccine nationalism" (Bollyky and Bown 2020).

Secondly, its emergent and uncertain nature made the initial analysis of the characteristics and origins of the SARS-CoV-2 virus challenging and especially problematic from an information-sharing perspective. Given the emergent nature of the virus and the associated deficits of the underlying data, attempts to quantify the probabilities of infection and death have proven challenging, especially in the early stages of the pandemic (Lai et al. 2020; Petropoulos and Makridakis 2020). Denworth (2020), for example, highlights the importance of the characteristics of the virus in shaping the nature of the pandemic and the challenges for mitigation:

> This coronavirus is unprecedented in the combination of its easy transmissibility, a range of symptoms going from none at all to deadly, and the extent that it has disrupted the world. A highly susceptible population led to near exponential growth in cases. (38)

Covid-19's potential impact on sections of the human population was initially also shrouded in uncertainty, and it wasn't clear at the start of the pandemic which groups would be most vulnerable to the virus, beyond those with underlying health conditions. This information was generated in real time as the numbers of those infected increased, and the groups that were most affected became clearer (Platt and Warwick 2020; The Lancet 2020). While Coronaviruses are not new (SARS and MERS are part of the same family), Covid-19, which is the respiratory disease caused by the underlying SARS-CoV-2 virus (Andersen et al. 2020; Shereen et al. 2020), has proved challenging to manage in a number of countries. This is especially so in the absence of effective test-and-trace policies, a lack of population immunity, and the early lack of an available vaccine (Rajan, Cylus, and McKee 2020; Schmidt 2020). The issues around the global supply chain for vaccines, contractual obligations, and the supporting materials and services needed to deliver those vaccines exacerbated the problems of crisis preparation (BBC News 2021; Boffey and Savage 2021). Farrar for example, argues that there are issues associated with the wider global supply chain that underpins the production, distribution, and deployment of a vaccine (cited in Rusbridger 2020). He highlights the nature of these challenges, observing:

> I think that a vaccine has a very good chance of working, but there's a glass shortage in the world at the moment, there isn't enough glass to put a vaccine into glass vials. There's a syringe shortage, so if we had to inject the vaccine, we wouldn't have enough syringes in the world. And then finally, you've got a horrible geopolitical structure at the moment which means you're in grave danger of going into something akin to vaccine nationalism, where each country will have to look after itself in national stupidity, really, without thinking of the need to take a global perspective. (quoted in Rusbridger 2020)

A global pandemic requires a global response if it is to be effective. However, politicians have not always embraced global cooperation, especially in countries with a more populist agenda or where politicians initially downplayed the impact of the virus (Bennett 2020; Du 2020; Yamey and Jamison 2020). A just-in-time process can, under conditions of intense pressure, be seen as a tightly coupled and interactively complex system (Perrow 1984) in which the speed of a failure in the system can expose vulnerabilities elsewhere in the globalized setting. Just-in-time can very quickly become just-too-late; and there was considerable evidence of a failure to adopt an integrated approach to dealing with the pandemic, especially in the early stages. As the virus mutated, the challenges re-emerged as governments attempted to contain the spread of the mutated strain (Roberts 2021).

Thirdly, there is a related issue concerning the communicating the problems to the various public groups. In some cases, this arises from the uncertainty that exists in the problem space itself. There is also the range of virus conspiracy theories promulgated by the anti-vaxxer movement (Argentino 2020; Jolley and Lamberty 2020), which has added to the complexity around the politization of the pandemic. There is also a challenge around the paradox of preventative action, where decisions can be perceived as taking too long or the responses as too quick and overzealous. This is inevitable in emergent forms of crisis. However, some communication problems were a function of structural problems in governmental procedures and practices and the lack of trust between some political leaders and the scientific communities. This was perhaps most evident in former president Trump's response to the World Health Organisation. His comments about using sunlight and disinfectant to kill the virus also caused controversy (Kreuz 2020). In Brazil, there is concern about President Bolsonaro's approach to the threat from Covid-19:

> With the debatable exception of Donald Trump, Jair Bolsonaro has taken the pandemic less seriously than any other world leader. At every level he has downplayed the threat, calling it "merely a flu." He pointedly broke lockdown both personally, disregarding social distancing guidelines, and politically, trying to force governors to reopen their states. He has fired not one—but two successive health ministers. (Blunck 2020, 18)

Such political responses are sometimes enabled by the problems generated by radical uncertainty, where the burden of proof is not clearly defined and the codification of uncertainty can mask the cause-and-effect relationships around hazards. The question of whether policy in the broadest sense is being led by the science or by political interests clearly remains open for debate.

Fourthly, there are the quite profound problems around the role played by science and expertise in the communication of risk. In the United Kingdom, the government the mantra that it is being led by the science in making decisions about the control measures in place to deal with the pandemic. However, that approach has not been without its critics, including some in the scientific community that advises the government (Grundmann 2020; Wickham and Baker 2020). Farrar, who has been a member of the government advisory body Scientific Advisory Group for Emergencies, or SAGE, has commented on the challenges associated with policymakers' the use of science:

> When you come to put science and uncertainty with policy, you actually have to make decisions. This is a very, almost unholy alliance in some ways, because you can't just base policy on hard science, especially when that science is uncertain. Yet you can't wait until the science is certain just to make policy. In that grey zone between the unholy alliance, you've got some really tough things to do. (quoted in Rusbridger 2020)

Farrar also highlighted the importance of transparency in the provision of advice, as well as in terms of providing the underlying rationale for the decisions that are made. If the underpinning science is uncertain, and if the discourse around that uncertainty is not transparent, then governments could be accused of simply legitimizing their own policy decisions through the selective use of scientific advice and comment, but without the expressions of the uncertainty and associated caveats that come with that advice.

Finally, Denworth (2020) highlights the potential to learn lessons from previous pandemics (Influenza A) and the more limited outbreaks of SARS and MERS. At the core of many of these concerns is the issue of anticipatory contingency planning for a pandemic, the failure to learn lessons from previous outbreaks, the capabilities of health services to respond to the task demands of such hazards, and the perceived risk of overreacting (Clift 2020; Devakumar, Bhopal, and Shannon 2020; Peeri et al. 2020). In addition to the learning that takes place within the expert and the policy communities, there is also a need to ensure that the lessons are also communicated to public groups to prepare them for the actions that will be taken in the event of an outbreak. There are, of course, barriers to the effective learning that takes place in the aftermath of crises (Fischbacher-Smith and Fischbacher-Smith 2009; Smith 2001; Smith and Elliott 2007). Gouldner (1954, 1984) has argued that there is also the potential for generating a "mock bureaucracy" that provides the veneer of a response to catastrophic events but is not especially effective in making changes to the core operational and cultural conditions that generated the crisis (see, for example, Elliott and Smith 2006). In the case of the Covid-19 pandemic, the UK Government was criticized for its failure to learn from previous exercises. A previous pandemic planning exercise had highlighted the potential for problems with providing personal protective equipment (PPE) to key workers, and the government was criticized for not acted upon this learning (Abbasi 2020; Clift 2020).

The questions that arise from the discussions of the uncertainty around Covid-19 concern the relationships between evidence, the determination of fact (where possible), the role of established (and verifiable) expert opinion, and the ideological lenses through which the issues around determining risk are viewed and interpreted. The management (or otherwise) of these elements has the potential to generate a perfect storm around risk management, especially under crisis conditions, and in some cases, they can allow for the emergence of disinformation and conspiracy theories that distort the public's understanding of the issues. As Wallis (2020) has observed: "Fear and fraud often travel together. As coronavirus anxiety began to spread across the land, so did bogus nostrums promising protection from this modern-day plague" (17).

Wallis's comment highlights the challenges associated with the management of emergent forms of hazard, where the problem is not fully understood and where the potential for mitigating the effects of the hazard is also framed by uncertainty. The result is that claims about the nature of the risks are made that are not supported by evidence and do not have the predictive validity that effective risk management normally requires. Yet despite the challenges, managers and policymakers alike have to attempt to determine the likelihood and consequences associated with certain forms of threat as a function of their governance roles. And so, the demand for effective forms of risk management will remain. The questions are whether the tools that are available to decision-makers have the predictive capability that is often assumed they have, and whether the supporting evidence and the knowledge base for evaluating that evidence are robust enough to support such calculative process. Ultimately, while the quantification of uncertainty is clearly a desirable goal, our abilities to deliver on that goal may be somewhat constrained.

CONCLUSIONS

This chapter has argued that there is a problem facing the demand side of risk analysis—that is, the provision of appropriate calculative practices that allow for the effective quantification of uncertain events and do so in a way that provides a robust degree of predictive validity. Such analyses are required for events with potentially significant consequences; yet the extent of the uncertainty within many of those hazardous activities negates the effectiveness of attempts to quantify them. Much of the discussion around risk in organizational and societal contexts is based on a definition of risk that does not conform to the Knightian notion of "measurable uncertainty." The risks being referred to are often expert (or, in some cases, nonexpert) estimates of failure, rather than being grounded in either the a priori or statistically based evidential processes required by Knight for an effective determination of risk. These estimates often have little in the way of predictive validity, especially for extreme events, and invariably, they fail to outline and make transparent the extent of the uncertainty that exists within those estimates. As argued earlier, this generates a paradox at the core of managing uncertainty, especially within complex sociotechnical systems. On the one hand, there is increasing demand for calculative practices that provide both decision-makers and those who might be affected by the consequences of a decision with a clear sense of the likelihood and consequences associated with a particular set of hazards. On the other hand, the complex nature of sociotechnical systems often makes such calculative practices problematic due to the lack of effective a priori or statistical evidence needed to generate the required predictive validity that would, in turn, allow those "risks" to be effectively managed. The role played by human actors in the failure process adds a further level of uncertainty to those calculative practices.

The relationships between the range of calculative practices used in organizations and the management of risk and uncertainty can be contextualized in terms of a fractured and, at times, a confused landscape. Managers often talk about risk when they mean uncertainty, while other groups may talk about risk when they mean harm. Either way, it could be argued that both of these determinations of "risk" can be taken to suggest that groups do not have sufficient knowledge about the uncertainties associated with particular hazards to measure the uncertainty associated with them. At the same time, the responses to risk and uncertainty are central elements of the management function and, despite the populist rejection of expert judgment, they require the use of technical expertise to frame the contours of uncertainty around a diverse range of potentially hazardous and damaging events. However, these judgments also clearly need to articulate the uncertainties within assessments and the underlying assumptions of experts that form the basis of the analysis. Within organizations, the processes by which information about hazards is codified and attenuated often mask the uncertainty that is inherent in attempts to quantify uncertainty. What an effective governance approach to risk management therefore requires is a clear articulation of the nature of the uncertainty inherent in the calculative processes. This extends to the advice provided by the expert community and any weaknesses in their evidence and insights about the nature and likelihood of those hazards.

Organizational leaders and policymakers must be circumspect when talking about risk because it is often the uncertainty, vulnerability, and harm that are the more accurate constructs that should be used in public discourse. This does not require a new vocabulary for describing the relevant elements, but rather, a more structured, nuanced, and consistent use of the existing terms, perhaps in line with Knight's original definitions. In recognizing that much of the discussion of risk is, in fact, about vulnerability, there is the potential for more meaningful and nuanced discourse about the acceptability of those hazards, the effectiveness of those management controls that are in place to deal with them, and the overarching acceptability of the uncertainty within the analysis.

NOTES

1. A *sociotechnical system* involves activities where human actors and the technical components of the system are highly interconnected and cannot be considered in isolation.
2. There are some challenges around the interpretation of a priori forms of reasoning, as indicated by the range of definitions of the term that are used in practice. For our present purposes, *a priori reasoning* is seen as the elements of a system that are fully understood and for which there is no debate about their nature or significance. As a result, their failure modes and effects can be determined on a logical basis.
3. Mr. Gove's comments were directed at the then-governor of the Bank of England, Mark Carney, who had warned of Brexit's consequences for the UK economy. Gove was a major supporter of Brexit.
4. The United Kingdom left the European Union in January 2020, but there was a transition period; it ended on the December 31, 2020, at which point the UK left formally.
5. Boeing staff raised concerns about 737 Max issues in text messages in 2016. See "Boeing Staff Texted about 737 Max Issue in 2016," BBC News, October 18, 2019. https://www.bbc.co.uk/news/business-50101766.

REFERENCES

Abbasi, K. 2020. "COVID-19: A Public Inquiry in Hard Times?" *Journal of the Royal Society of Medicine* 113 (6): 203.

Adekola, J., Denis Fischbacher-Smith, and Moira Fischbacher-Smith. 2019. "Light Me Up: Power and Expertise in Risk Communication and Policy-Making in the E-Cigarette Health Debates." *Journal of Risk Research* 22 (10): 1294–1308.

Adekola, J., Moira Fischbacher-Smith, Denis Fischbacher-Smith, and O. Adekola. 2017. "Health Risks from Environmental Degradation in the Niger Delta, Nigeria." *Environment and Planning C: Politics and Space* 35 (2): 334–354.

Andersen, K. G., Andrew. Rambaut, W. Ian. Lipkin, Edward. C. Holmes, and Robert. F. Garry. 2020. "The Proximal Origin of SARS-CoV-2." *Nature Medicine* 26 (4): 450–452.

Argentino, Marc-André 2020. "QAnon Conspiracy Theories about the Coronavirus Pandemic Are a Public Health Threat." *The Conversation*, April 8. https://theconversation.com/qanon-conspiracy-theories-about-the-coronavirus-pandemic-are-a-public-health-threat-135515.

Arrow, Kenneth J. 1992. "I Know a Hawk from a Handsaw." In *Eminent Economists: Their Life and Philosophies*, edited by M. Szenberg, 42–50. Cambridge, UK: Cambridge University Press.

Aven, Terje and Otway. Renn. 2009. "On Risk Defined as an Event Where the Outcome Is Uncertain." *Journal of Risk Research* 12 (1): 1–11.

BBC News. 2016. "'Post-Truth' Declared Word of the Year by Oxford Dictionaries." BBC News, November 16. http://www.bbc.co.uk/news/uk-37995600.

BBC News. 2021. "Covid: EU and AstraZeneca in 'Step Forward' on Vaccines." BBC News, January 31. https://www.bbc.co.uk/news/world-europe-55879345.

Beck, Ulrich. 1986. *Risikogesellschaft: Auf dem Weg in eine andere Moderne*. Frankfurt: Suhrkamp Verlag.

Beck, Ulrich. 1992. *Risk Society: Towards a New Modernity*. Translated by M. Ritter. London: SAGE.

Beer, Stafford 1985. *Diagnosing the System for Organisations*. Chichester, UK: John Wiley & Sons.

Bennett, Brian. 2020. "Trump Is Waging a Losing War against the Bad News of COVID-19." Time.com, July 15. https://time.com/5867511/trump-coronavirus-bad-news/.

Berridge, Virginia. 2006. "The Policy Response to the Smoking and Lung Cancer Connection in the 1950s and 1960s." *Historical Journal* 49 (4): 1185–1209.

Besner, Claude. 2012. "The Paradox of Risk Management: A Project Management Practice Perspective." *International Journal of Managing Projects in Business* 5 (2): 230–247.

Blume, Stuart. 2006. "Anti-vaccination Movements and Their Interpretations." *Social Science & Medicine* 62 (3): 628–642.

Blunck, Julia. 2020. "A Stadium of the Dead." *Prospect* September/October (290): 18.

Boffey, Daniel., and Michael. Savage. 2021. "How the EU's Floundering Vaccine Effort Hit a Fresh Crisis with Exports Row." *The Guardian*, January 31. https://www.theguardian.com/world/2021/jan/31/how-eus-floundering-vaccine-effort-hit-a-fresh-crisis-with-exports-row.

Boisot, Max. H. 1995. *Information Space: A Framework for Learning in Organizations, Institutions and Culture*. London: Thompson Business Press.

Boisot, Max. H. 1998. *Knowledge Assets: Securing Competitive Advantage in the Information Economy*. Oxford: Oxford University Press.

Bollyky, Thomas. J., and Chad P. Bown. 2020. "The Tragedy of Vaccine Nationalism: Only Cooperation Can End the Pandemic." *Foreign Affairs* 99 (5): 96–108.

Brookfield, David, and Denis Smith. 2007. "Managerial Intervention and Instability in Healthcare Organisations: The Role of Complexity in Explaining the Scope of Effective Management." *Risk Management: An International Journal* 8 (4): 268–293.

Burki, Talha. 2020. "The Online Anti-vaccine Movement in the Age of COVID-19." *Lancet Digital Health* 2 (10): e504–e505.

Callon, Michel., Pierre Lascoumes, and Yannick Barthe. 2009. *Acting in an Uncertain World: An Essay on Technical Democracy.* Translated by Graham Burchell. Cambridge, MA: MIT Press.

Calman, Kenneth, and Denis Fischbacher-Smith. 2001. "Works in Theory but Not in Practice? Some Notes on the Precautionary Principle." *Public Administration* 79 (1): 185–204.

Camilleri, Andrew, Damien Abarno, Carolyne Bird, Anne. Coxon, Natasha Mitchell, Kahlee Redman, Nicol Sly, Stephen Willis, Edmund Silenieks, Ellie Simpson, Heather Linsay 2019. "A Risk-Based Approach to Cognitive Bias in Forensic Science." *Science & Justice* 59 (5): 533–543.

Clift, Ashley Kieran 2020. "Anatomising Failure: There Should Be a Statutory Public Inquiry into the UK Government's Handling of COVID-19." *Journal of the Royal Society of Medicine* 113 (6): 230–231.

Collingridge, David. 1984. "Lessons of Nuclear Power US and UK History." *Energy Policy* 12 (1): 46–67.

Collingridge, David. 1992. *The Management of Scale: Big Organizations, Big Decisions, Big Mistakes.* London: Routledge.

Collingridge, David, and Colin Reeve. 1986a. "Science and Policy—Why the Marriage Is So Unhappy." *Bulletin of Science, Technology and Society* 6 (4): 356–372.

Collingridge, David, and Colin Reeve. 1986b. *Science Speaks to Power: The Role of Experts in Policy-Making.* London: Francis Pinter.

Curley, Lee J., James Munro, Martin Lages, Rory MacLean, and Jennifer Murray. 2020. "Assessing Cognitive Bias in Forensic Decisions: A Review and Outlook." *Journal of Forensic Sciences* 65 (2): 354–360.

D'Ancona, Matthew 2017. *Post Truth: The New War on Truth and How to Fight Back.* London: Ebury Press.

Denworth, Lydia 2020. "What Comes Next: Large Outbreaks of Disease in the Past Suggest How COVID-19 Could Play Out." *Scientific American* 322 (6): 38–39.

Devakumar, Delan, Sunil S. Bhopal, and Geordan Shannon. 2020. "COVID-19: The Great Unequaliser." *Journal of the Royal Society of Medicine* 113 (6): 234–235.

Douglas, Mary 1990. "Risk as a Forensic Resource." *Daedalus* 119 (4): 1–16.

Dowie, Jack. 1999. "Communication for Better Decisions: Not about 'Risk.'" *Health, Risk & Society* 1 (1): 41–53.

Du, Lisa. 2020 ."India Has Cut Off Half the Supply of a Potential Coronavirus Treatment Touted by Trump." Time.com, April 6. https://time.com/5816105/coronavirus-treatment-cut-off-india/.

Dyer, Clare 2010. "Lancet Retracts Wakefield's MMR Paper." *BMJ.*

Eggertson, Laura. 2010. "Lancet Retracts 12-Year-Old Article Linking Autism to MMR Vaccines." *Canadian Medical Association Journal* 182 (4): E199–200.

Elliott, Dominic, and Denis Smith. 2006. "Active Learning from Crisis: Regulation, Precaution and the UK Football Industry's Response to Disaster." *Journal of Management Studies* 43 (2): 289–317.

Erikson, Kai 1994. *A New Species of Trouble: Explorations in Disaster, Trauma, and Community.* New York: W. W. Norton.

Evans, Mark 2012. "Beyond the Integrity Paradox—toward 'Good Enough' Governance? *Policy Studies* 33 (1): 97–113.

Eyal, Gil. 2013. "For a Sociology of Expertise: The Social Origins of the Autism Epidemic." *American Journal of Sociology* 118 (4): 863–907.

Eyal, Gil. 2019. *The Crisis of Expertise*. Cambridge, UK: Polity Press.

Firestein, Stuart 2012. *Ignorance: How It Drives Science*. Oxford: Oxford University Press.

Fischbacher-Smith, Denis. 2010. "Beyond the Worse Case Scenario: 'Managing' the Risks of Extreme Events." *Risk Management: An International Journal* 12 (1): 1–8.

Fischbacher-Smith, Denis. 2012. "Getting Pandas to Breed: Paradigm Blindness and the Policy Space for Risk Prevention, Mitigation and Management." *Risk Management* 14 (3): 177–201.

Fischbacher-Smith, Denis. 2013. "Paradigm Blindness." In *Encyclopedia of Crisis Management*, edited by K. Penuel, M. Statler, and R. Hagen, 716–720. Thousand Oaks, CA: SAGE Publications.

Fischbacher-Smith, Denis. 2015. "The Enemy Has Passed through the Gate: Insider Threats, the Dark Triad, and the Challenges around Security." *Journal of Organizational Effectiveness: People and Performance* 2 (2): 134–156.

Fischbacher-Smith, Denis. 2016a. "Framing the UK's Counter Terrorism Policy as a Wicked Problem." *Public Money and Management* 36 (6): 399–408.

Fischbacher-Smith, Denis. 2016b. "Leadership and Crises: Incubation, Emergence, and Transitions." In *Leadership in Organizations: Current Issues and Key Trends*, 3rd ed., edited by J. Storey, 70–95. London: Routledge.

Fischbacher-Smith, Denis, and Moira Fischbacher-Smith. 2009. "We May Remember but What Did We Learn? Dealing with Errors, Crimes and Misdemeanours around Adverse Events in Healthcare." *Financial Accountability and Management* 25 (4): 451–474.

Fischbacher-Smith, Denis, and Moira Fischbacher-Smith. 2014. "What Lies Beneath? The Role of Informal and Hidden Networks in the Management of Crises." *Financial Accountability & Management* 30 (3): 259–278.

Fischbacher-Smith, Denis, G. Alan Irwin, and Moira Fischbacher-Smith. 2010. "Bringing Light to the Shadows: Risk, Risk Management and Risk Communication." In *Risk Communication and Public Health*, edited by Peter Bennett, Kenneth Calman, Sarah Curtis, and Denis Fischbacher-Smith, 23–38. Oxford: Oxford University Press.

Fischer, Frank. 1980. *Politics, Values, and Public Policy: The Problem of Methodology*. Boulder, CO: Westview Press.

Fischer, Frank. 1990. *Technocracy and the Politics of Expertise*. Newbury Park, CA: Sage Publications.

Flaherty, Dennis K. 2011. "The Vaccine-Autism Connection: A Public Health Crisis Caused by Unethical Medical Practices and Fraudulent Science." *Annals of Pharmacotherapy* 45 (10): 1302–1304.

Foucault, Michel. 1997. *"Society Must Be Defended": Lectures at the Collège de France*. Translated by David Macey. London: Penguin Books.

GHS Index. 2020. *Global Health Security Index: Building Collective Action and Accountability*. Nuclear Threat Initiative. https://www.ghsindex.org/wp-content/uploads/2020/04/2019-Global-Health-Security-Index.pdf.

Giddens, Anthony. 1990. *The Consequences of Modernity*. Cambridge, UK: Polity Press.

Gigerenzer, Gerd, and Wolfgang Gaissmaier. 2011. "Heuristic Decision Making." *Annual Review of Psychology* 62 (1): 451–482.

Godlee, Fiona, Jane Smith, and Harvey Marcovitch. 2011. "Wakefield's Article Linking MMR Vaccine and Autism Was Fraudulent." *BMJ* 342:c7452.

Gouldner, Alvin Ward 1954. *Patterns of Industrial Bureaucracy*. New York: Free Press.

Gouldner, Alvin Ward 1984. "Three Patterns of Bureaucracy." In *Critical Studies in Organization and Bureaucracy*, rev. ed., edited by Frank Fischer and Carmen Sirianni, 96–106. Philadelphia: Temple University Press.

Gove, Michael. 2016. "'Experts' like Carney Must Curb Their Arrogance." *The Times*, October 21, 27.

Griffiths, Richard F. 1980. "Acceptability and Estimation in Risk Management." *Science and Public Policy* 7 (3): 154–161.

Grundmann, Reiner 2020. "Coronavirus: Do Governments Ever Truly Listen to 'the Science'?" *The Conversation*, April 3. https://theconversation.com/coronavirus-do-governments-ever-truly-listen-to-the-science-134308.

Heimann, Larry. 2005. "Repeated Failures in the Management of High Risk Technologies." *European Management Journal* 23 (1): 105–117.

Hidalgo, César. 2015. *Why Information Grows: The Evolution of Order, from Atoms to Economics.* London: Penguin Books.

Holland, John H. 1998. *Emergence: From Order to Chaos.* New York: Oxford University Press.

Hoppe, Rob, Rob Pranger, and Erik Besseling. 1990. "Policy Belief Systems and Risky Technologies: The Dutch Debate on Regulating LPG-Related Activities." *Industrial Crisis Quarterly* 4 (2): 121–140.

Hotez, Peter J. 2020. "Anti-science Extremism in America: Escalating and Globalizing." *Microbes and Infection* 22 (10): 505–507.

Hutter, Bridget M. 2010. "Anticipating Risks and Organising Risk Regulation: Current Dilemmas." In *Anticipating Risks and Organising Risk Regulation*, edited by Bridget M. Hutter, 3–22. Cambridge, UK: Cambridge University Press.

Irwin, Alan 1995. *Citizen Science: A Study of People, Expertise and Sustainable Development.* London: Routledge.

Irwin, Alan 2001. "Constructing the Scientific Citizen: Science and Democracy in the Biosciences." *Public Understanding of Science* 10 (1): 1–18.

Jasimuddin, Sajjad M., Jonathan H. Klein, and Con Connell. 2005. "The Paradox of Using Tacit and Explicit Knowledge: Strategies to Face Dilemmas." *Management Decision* 43 (1): 102–112.

Jolley, Daniel, and Pia Lamberty. 2020. "Coronavirus Is a Breeding Ground for Conspiracy Theories—Here's Why That's a Serious Problem." *The Conversation*, February 28. https://theconversation.com/coronavirus-is-a-breeding-ground-for-conspiracy-theories-heres-why-thats-a-serious-problem-132489.

Kahneman, Daniel 2011. *Thinking, Fast and Slow.* London: Macmillan.

Kata, Anna 2010. "A Postmodern Pandora's Box: Anti-vaccination Misinformation on the Internet." *Vaccine* 28 (7): 1709–1716.

Kata, Anna 2012. "Anti-vaccine Activists, Web 2.0, and the Postmodern Paradigm—an Overview of Tactics and Tropes Used Online by the Anti-vaccination Movement." *Vaccine* 30 (25): 3778–3789.

Kay, John, and Mervyn King. 2020a. "The Radical Uncertainties of Coronavirus." *Prospect* (277), May. https://www.prospectmagazine.co.uk/magazine/coronavirus-model-uncertainty-kay-king.

Kay, John, and Mervyn King. 2020b. *Radical Uncertainty: Decision-Making for an Unknowable Future.* London: Bridge Street Press.

King, David 2020. "Heed the Expert Voice." *Prospect* (290): 15.

Knight, Frank H. (1957) 2006. *Risk, Uncertainty and Profit.* Mineola, NY: Dover Publications.

Kreuz, Roger J. 2020. "Why 'I Was Just Being Sarcastic' Can Be Such a Convenient Excuse." *The Conversation*, July 2. https://theconversation.com/why-i-was-just-being-sarcastic-can-be-such-a-convenient-excuse-141764.

Kunreuther, Howard, and Michael Useem. 2018. *Mastering Catastrophic Risk: How Companies Are Coping with Disruption*. New York: Oxford University Press.

Lai, Chih-Cheng, Tzu-Ping Shih, Wen-Chien Ko, Hung-Jen Tang, and Po-Ren Hsueh. 2020. "Severe Acute Respiratory Syndrome Coronavirus 2 (SARS-CoV-2) and Corona Virus Disease-2019 (COVID-19): The Epidemic and the Challenges." *International Journal of Antimicrobial Agents*: 105924.

Lasco, Gideon, and Nicole Curato. 2019. "Medical Populism." *Social Science & Medicine* 221: 1–8.

Latham, Mark A. 2011. "Five Thousand Feet and Below: The Failure to Adequately Regulate Deepwater Oil Production Technology." *Boston College Environmental Affairs Law Review* 38 (2): 343–367.

Mack, Arien, and Irvin Rock. 2000. *Inattentional Blindness*. Cambridge, MA: MIT Press.

Mann, Douglas L. 2018. "Fake News, Alternative Facts, and Things That Just Are Not True: Can Science Survive the Post-Truth Era?" *JACC. Basic to Translational Science* 3 (4): 573–574.

Morowitz, Harold J. 2002. *The Emergence of Everything: How The World Became Complex*. New York: Oxford University Press.

Murphy, Peter, and David Pauleen. 2007. "Managing Paradox in a World of Knowledge." *Management Decision* 45 (6): 1008–1022.

Nichols, Tom 2017. *The Death of Expertise*. New York: Oxford University Press.

Ołpiński, Marian 2012. "Anti-vaccination Movement and Parental Refusals of Immunization of Children in USA." *Pediatria Polska* 87 (4): 381–385.

Oppenheimer, Michael, Naomi Oreskes, Dale Jamieson, Keynyn Brysse, Jessica O'Reilly, Matthew Shindell, Milena Wazeck 2019. *Discerning Experts: The Practices of Scientific Assessment for Environmental Policy*. Chicago: University of Chicago Press.

Pauchant, Thierry. C., and Iain I. Mitroff. 1990. "Crisis Management: Managing Paradox in a Chaotic World." *Technological Forecasting and Social Change* 38 (2): 117–134.

Peeri, Noah C., Nistha Shrestha, Md Siddikur Rahman, Rafdzah Zaki, Zhengqi Tan, Saana Bibi, Mahdi Baghbanzadeh, Nasrin Aghamohammadi, Wenyi Zhang, Ubydul Haque 2020. "The SARS, MERS and Novel Coronavirus (COVID-19) Epidemics, the Newest and Biggest Global Health Threats: What Lessons Have We Learned?" *International Journal of Epidemiology* 49 (3): 717–726.

Perrow, Charles 1984. *Normal Accidents*. New York: Basic Books.

Petropoulos Fotios, and Spyros Makridakis. 2020. "Forecasting the Novel Coronavirus COVID-19." *PLoS One* 15 (3): Article e0231236. https://doi.org/10.1371/journal.pone.0231236.

Platt, Lucinda, and Ross Warwick. 2020. *Are Some Ethnic Groups More Vulnerable to COVID-19 Than Others?* IFS Nuffield Foundation report. London: Institute for Fiscal Studies.

Porter, Theodore M. 1995. *Trust in Numbers: The Pursuit of Objectivity in Science and Public Life*. Princeton, NJ: Princeton University Press.

Rajan, Selina, Jonathan D. Cylus, and Martin McKee. 2020. "What Do Countries Need to Do to Implement Effective 'Find, Test, Trace, Isolate and Support' Systems?" *Journal of the Royal Society of Medicine* 113 (7): 245–250.

Reason, James T. 1990. *Human Error*. Oxford: Oxford University Press.

Reason, James T. 1997. *Managing the Risks of Organizational Accidents*. Aldershot, UK: Ashgate.

Rittel, Horst W. J., and Melvin M. Webber. 1973. "Dilemmas in a General Theory of Planning." *Policy Sciences* 4 (2): 155–169.

Roberts, Michelle 2021. "South Africa Coronavirus Variant: What Is the Risk?" BBC News, February 8. https://www.bbc.co.uk/news/health-55534727.

Roozenbeek, Jon, and Sander van der Linden. 2019. "The Fake News Game: Actively Inoculating against the Risk of Misinformation." *Journal of Risk Research* 22 (5): 570–580.

Rowe, William D. 1975. *An "Anatomy" of Risk*. Washington, DC: Environmental Protection Agency.

Rumsfeld, Donald. 2002. "DoD News Briefing—Secretary Rumsfeld and Gen. Myers. News Transcript." US Department of Defense, Office of the Assistant Secretary of Defense Public Affairs. Accessed August 17, 2011. http://www.defense.gov/Transcripts/Transcript.aspx?TranscriptID=2636.

Rumsfeld, Donald. 2011. *Known and Unknown: A Memoir*. New York: Sentinel.

Rusbridger, Alan. 2020. "SAGE Coronavirus Expert: We've Had an Epidemic That to Some Degree Could Have Been Avoided." *Prospect* https://www.prospectmagazine.co.uk/science-and-technology/alan-rusbridger-sage-jeremy-farrar-covid-19-coronavirus-dominic-cummings-herd-immunity.

Schmidt, Charles 2020. "The Vaccine Quest: Only Genetic Engineering Can Create a Protective Serum in Months Rather Than Years." *Scientific American* 322 (6): 34–37.

Seidl, David 2007. "The Dark Side of Knowledge." *Emergence: Complexity and Organizations* 9: 13–26.

Sheldon, Trevor A., and Denis Smith. 1992. "Assessing the Health Effects of Waste Disposal Sites: Issues in Risk Analysis and Some Baysian Conclusions." In *Waste Location: Spatial Aspects of Waste Management, Hazards and Disposal*, edited by Clark, Michael, Denis Smith, and Andrew Blowers, 158–186. London: Routledge.

Shereen, Muhammad. A., Sulimn Khan, Abeer Kazmi, Nadia Bashir, and Rabeea Siddique. 2020. "COVID-19 Infection: Origin, Transmission, And Characteristics of Human Coronaviruses." *Journal of Advanced Research* 24: 91–98.

Smith, Denis 1990. "Corporate Power and the Politics of Uncertainty: Risk Management at the Canvey Island Complex." *Industrial Crisis Quarterly* 4 (1): 1–26.

Smith, Denis 1991. "Beyond the Boundary Fence: Decision-Making and Chemical Hazards." In *Energy, Resources and the Environment*, edited by John Blunden, and Alan Reddish, 267–291. London: Hodder and Stoughton.

Smith, Denis 2001. "Crisis as a Catalyst for Change: Issues in the Management of Uncertainty and Organizational Vulnerability." In *E-risk: Business as Usual?*, 81–88. London: British Bankers Association and Deloitte and Touche.

Smith, Denis. 2002. "Not by Error, but by Design—Harold Shipman and the Regulatory Crisis for Health Care." *Public Policy and Administration* 17 (4): 55–74.

Smith, Denis . 2005. "Dancing with the Mysterious Forces of Chaos: Issues around Complexity, Knowledge and the Management of Uncertainty." *Clinician in Management* 13 (3/4): 15–123.

Smith, Denis, and Dominic Elliott. 2007. "Exploring the Barriers to Learning from Crisis: Organizational Learning and Crisis." *Management Learning* 38 (5): 519–538.

Smith, Denis, and A. Irwin. 2006. "Complexity, Risk and Emergence: Elements of a 'Management' Dilemma." *Risk Management* 8 (4): 221–226.

Smolka, Anselm 2006. "Natural Disasters and the Challenge of Extreme Events: Risk Management from an Insurance Perspective." *Philosophical Transactions of the Royal Society A: Mathematical, Physical and Engineering Sciences* 364 (1845): 2147–2165.

Snowden, David 2002. "Complex Acts of Knowing: Paradox and Descriptive Self-Awareness." *Journal of Knowledge Management* 6 (2): 100–111.

Spiegelhalter, David 2019. *The Art of Statistics: Learning from Data*. London: Pelican Books.

Starr, Chauncey 1969. "Social Benefit versus Technological Risk." *Science* 165 (3899): 1232–1238.

Starr, Chauncey 1991. "Plenary: Twenty-Year Retrospective on 1969 Science Paper of C. Starr, 'Social Benefit vs Technological Risk.'" In *Risk Analysis: Prospects and Opportunities*, edited by Constantine Zervos, 1–5. New York: Plenum Press.

Stewart, Ian 2019. *Do Dice Play God? The Mathematics of Uncertainty*. London: Profile Books.

Streatfield, Phillip J. 2001. *The Paradox of Control in Organizations*. London: Routledge.

Taleb, Nassim Nicholas. 2007. *The Black Swan: The Impact of the Highly Improbable*. London: Penguin Books.

Tenner, Edward 1996. *Why Things Bite Back: Technology and the Revenge Effect*. London: Fourth Estate.

The Lancet. 2020. "Redefining Vulnerability in the Era of COVID-19." Editorial. Lancet.com, 395: 1089–1089.

Tversky, A., and D. Kahneman. 1973. "Availability: A Heuristic for Judging Frequency and Probability." *Cognitive Psychology* 5 (2): 207–232.

Tversky, Amos, and Daniel Kahneman. 1974. "Judgment under Uncertainty: Heuristics and Biases." *Science* 185 (4157): 1124–1131.

Vaughan, Diane. 1989. "Regulating Risk: Implications of the Challenger Accident." *Law & Policy* 11 (3): 330–349.

Wakefield, Andrew J. 1999. "MMR Vaccination and Autism." *The Lancet* 354 (9182): 949–950.

Wallis, Claudia 2020. "How to Boost Your Immunity." *Scientific American* 323, no. 1 (July): 17.

Warner, Fredrick 1992. *Risk: Analysis, Perception and Management*. London: Royal Society.

Weick, Karl E., and Kathleen M. Sutcliffe. 2015. *Managing the Unexpected: Sustained Performance in a Complex World*. Hoboken, NJ: Wiley.

Weinberg, Alvin M. 1972. "Science and Trans-Science." *Minerva* 10 (2): 209–222.

Weinberg, Alvin M. 1977. "The Limits of Science and Trans-Science." *Interdisciplinary Science Reviews* 2 (4): 337–342.

Weinberg, Alvin M. 1985. "Science and Its Limits: The Regulator's Dilemma." *Issues in Science and Technology* 2 (1): 59–72.

Wickham, Alex, and Katie J. M. Baker. 2020. "Scientists Advising the UK Government on the Coronavirus Fear Boris Johnson's Team Is Using Them as 'Human Shields.'" BuzzFeed News, April 22. Updated April 23. https://www.buzzfeed.com/alexwickham/coronavirus-uk-scientists-human-shields.

Wynne, Brian. 1989. "Sheepfarming after Chernobyl: A Case Study in Communicating Scientific Information." *Environment: Science and Policy for Sustainable Development* 31 (2): 10–39.

Wynne, Brian. 1996. "May the Sheep Safely Graze? A Reflexive View of the Expert-Lay Knowledge Divide." In *Risk, Environment and Modernity: Towards a New Ecology*, edited by Scott Lash, Bronislaw Szerszynski, and Brian Wynne, 44–83. London: SAGE Publications.

Wynne, Brian. 2008. "Elephants in the Rooms Where Publics Encounter 'Science'? A Response to Darrin Durant, 'Accounting for Expertise: Wynne and the Autonomy of the Lay Public.'" *Public Understanding of Science* 17 (1): 21–33.

Yamey, Gavin, and Dean T. Jamison. 2020. "U.S. Response to COVID-19 Is Worse Than China's. 100 Times Worse." Time.com, June 10. https://time.com/5850680/u-s-response-covid-19-worse-than-chinas.

Yamey, Gavin, and Clare Wenham. 2020. "The U.S. and U.K. Were the Two Best Prepared Nations to Tackle a Pandemic—What Went Wrong?" Time.com, July 1. https://time.com/5861697/us-uk-failed-coronavirus-response/.

19

EXPERTISE AND THE STATE: FROM PLANNING TO FUTURE RESEARCH

JENNY ANDERSSON

INTRODUCTION

EXPERTISE has increasingly been studied not in terms of the knowledge it offers to some receiving entity, but in terms of its role as a form of social intervention (Eyal 2019, Eyal and Buchholz 2010; Sending 2015). As a social intervention, expertise contributes to the constitution of objects so that they appear governable and open to regulation and control. A range of studies have shown that the objects of expertise can vary widely, ranging from colonial territories to possible future terror attacks. Some studies have also noted that some objects are somehow more reliant on expertise than others and suggested that we consider the notion of *meta-expertise* (Warde and Sörlin 2015; Poskanzer 2019). The objects of meta-expertise appear to share some properties—they are somehow in themselves indiscernible and unknowable without particular synthetic, encompassing, or conjuring forms of analysis. This, in turn, seems to rely on a certain notion of "thinking about thinking"—in other words, an act of synthesizing numbers, merging data of various sorts, and oftentimes combining this with elements of subjectivity, imagination, and narrative. What is produced is a new image of coming realities, in which facticity plays a role but is not necessarily the central element of expertise. It has been argued that meta-expertise has been directly involved in, for instance, the expert production of the environment, which in contrast to nature is a socially mediated, constructed, and regulated arena in which expertise contributes in decisive ways to rendering interrelationships between natural elements and human activity visible over time. Meta-expertise is also crucial for the constitution of the category of climate, which is a complex construct of systemic interplay between the atmosphere, global data, and technological systems, all mediated through synthetic acts of visualization and narration

(Edwards 2010). And meta-expertise is also crucially involved, as will be argued here, in the constitution of the category of the future (Andersson and Rindzevičiūtė 2015). The objects of meta-expertise appear to have certain things in common. They are deeply intertwined with spatial and temporal representations of a system that is often, or at least was from the 1960s on, thought to be a global or planetary world system. In that sense they are *global categories*; in other words, they defy the authority of the nation-state as it is conventionally understood, and instead, they affect a space that is beyond national boundaries in both space and time (Andersson 2018). As global categories, they draw on global, globalistic, or globalizing expertise. Such expertise is often anchored in transnational arenas and constituted through important processes of world circulation (Clavin 2005; Lorenzini 2019), contrary to how the sovereignty of nation-states also drew on national arenas of social science and planning. Globalistic expertise tends to rest on universalizing claims about the validity of certain causalities or tendencies on the world level, indeed, on the level of world order of the world system (Slobodian 2018; and for another perspective, Rosenboim 2017).

Warde and Sörlin (2015) suggest that *future*, quite like *environment*, is a category of knowledge that demands a particular kind of epistemic engagement, one in which the dramatic and radical consequences of the present are depicted in aggregate and synthetic representations of catastrophic or apocalyptic ends of humanity. Historians have referred to this as a *crisis concept* and argued that in the constitution of such a crisis concept, expertise plays the role of projecting representations of future urgency and decline that push for forms of present action (Koselleck 2006). It can be suggested that this catastrophic charge and the call to urgency are what lends authority to particular forms of future expertise and to future experts, in ways that might be compared to how, for instance, financial forecasters or terror experts juggle images of risk and uncertainty and make promises about the future (compare Stampnitzky 2013; Holmes 2014). The idea of uncertainty figures prominently in futuristic expertise, and can become, as Christina Garsten and Adrienne Sörbom suggest, a strange source of capitalization when uncertainty becomes a resource based on which one can make authoritative claims and perhaps even build lucrative advice and consultancy businesses (Garsten and Sörbom 2016; Wedel 2009; Zuboff 2018). In what might be called the "future industry," the idea that the future is deeply unknowable and quintessentially uncertain in itself becomes a legitimization of expertise, because it allows experts to present contrasting scenarios as if they are equally plausible or possible. To enable choice between different future images, in ways that reflect specific orders of preference, and to then coordinate forms of action around this strategy, becomes in itself part of the expertise provided. This gives expertise a direct bearing on the future that it claims to portray. An element of self-fulfilling prophecy is arguably central to any kind of prediction—but it can, in fact, be argued that what futurists or forecasters do is not so much create new forms of knowledge about the future but pave the way for distinct forms of action. This pushes the argument that expertise is a performative intervention, and not a knowledge-creating function per se.

The future becomes an object of intervention precisely through references to its intangible state, its quintessential status of uncertainty (Aradau 2014; Aradau and Munster 2007; Amoore 2013; Krahmann 2018). By preaching uncertainty or emphasizing the epistemic character of the future as a "black box" or as something that is by definition "open", the future paradoxically becomes acted upon as an object of expert knowledge. This is a treacherous expertise strategy, because many things can be known about the future, whether our examples are in climate change, financial markets, or epidemics. The future is not a black box, but rather the result of manifold forms of action across time and space, and rare are the futures that are in reality not foreseen by at least some knowledge community. In fact, most "black swans" were foreseen but ignored because the future they throw up is too far from the dominant lines of the present (compare Taleb 2007). Problems of the future are thus not problems of knowledge but problems of the constitution of knowledge and of the social role of expertise in advanced capitalist societies. That future expertise often shies away from things that are actually known about the future to privilege what is unknown is a power strategy; it should therefore be considered in light of the power structures of the present and the question of whose needs and interests are being expressed. Expert verdicts on coming time are defined not so much by their capacity to conjure the coming end of the world as by their capacity to draw up synthetic images of a future that, more often than not, resembles the present and therefore serves the status quo. The very need for a kind of futuristic expertise in foresight, forecasts, scenarios, and simulations seems to be inherently about a stabilization of the present through which the future itself is essentially evacuated. Futurists are, indeed, often involved in activities that would appear problematic if they were, for instance, concerned with future challenges such as the climate crisis or the erosion of democracy —they advise fossil industries, manipulate images of stability in risk-prone financial markets, and "empower" local communities by helping them to "accept" future challenges, such as when the melting of the Arctic ice cap paves the way for new mining and extraction industries, or when environmental groups become mobilized for future scenarios that have in fact been scripted by industry lobbyists (Andersson and Westholm 2019). Although there are examples of futurists working for social movements, future expertise very rarely seems to be about how to imagine radical, or even tangential, system change. Rather, it seems quintessentially to be involved in a management of expectation, by presenting judgments on how to preserve capitalist structures and management logics in the face of what appear to be disturbing evolutions. As such, it plays a role in stabilizing a deeply unstable present. This can, as Lynsey McGoey and Will Davies have suggested, include a fair dose of active nonknowledge production, in other words, a production of ignorance that we do not commonly associate with expertise (Davies and McGoey 2012), but which come through clearly when futurists speak for instance of "thinking outside of the box." It is a common presumption in the literature that expertise helps mediate social conflicts and is therefore a link between the governing and the governed with a view to a better future. Future expertise can, however, also serve a deeply conservative function, one that does not solve the conflicts of the present but postpones them and pushes their solution onto coming time. Expertise based on manifold forms of knowledge in a complex mix of data and technology (computer models, scenarios, forecasts) that depicts global images of coming developments is, properly speaking, futuristic in the sense that it construes visions and images of things not yet materialized, and also uses this immanent materiality to conjure authority. It does not follow from this that it expresses an ambition to solve future problems. To manage and stabilize expectations about the future seems to be of utmost importance in highly globalized and capitalized societies, and the chapter will put this in the context of the relative decline of the nation-state and its capacity to plan and steer. Contemporary structures of governance in capitalist societies include transnational polities such as the European Union, international organizations, and multinational corporations. Future experts seem to have a facility for moving between the different fields that constitute such networked structures and using this circulation to constitute a future as intervention. If we understand, as I do here, future expertise to be involved in a quintessential governance of the present, we might ask the question of what such future expertise contributes to the governance of contemporary societies and what kind of authority it contributes. The dominant purpose of such authority, it will be argued, is not to provide future knowledge, but rather, to manage expectations and solve social struggles over temporality by displacing them from the present to coming time (where somehow, they are pacified and removed from collective action). In this pacification, a specific image of the future is part of the intervention into the present and of a stabilizing function. It is from this perspective that I propose to understand the shifts in the relationship between expertise and state-like structures after 1973 that future research seems to illustrate.

This chapter will be devoted to so-called forecasting expertise, or expertise grounded in methods such as forecasts, Delphis, scenarios, and simulations of future developments. The first section argues that such methods have a particular history as interventions into complex time and space relations, and that they play a crucial role in contemporary governmentalities as political technologies for a deeply uncertain "present future" (Adam and Groves 2007). They have to be considered in the context of a relationship to the state or, more correctly, governing authority since states have also gone through significant forms of transformation in the second part of the postwar period. I propose that future-oriented political technologies gained much of their power from a changed relationship between states and expertise, in several important ways. First, the historically anchored suture between nation-states and social science expertise imploded in the late 1960s, as the social sciences fragmented and also began to prize a new and critical relationship to state power (Wagner, Weiss, and Wittrock 1991). Second, and partly related to this, planning structures in much of the Western world entered into a period of crisis in the late 1960s and early 1970s. Planning structures were confronted with problems that challenged prevailing conceptions of linear developments, and introduced a new measure of feedback relationships, negative consequences, and overlap. Oftentimes, as in environmental planning, this was directly related to new time and space relationships that challenged forms of steering having the national territory as its base. The same period saw the delegitimization of economic and conjectural planning, replaced in the years after 1973 with long-term forecasting and scenario planning. As new means of planning, forecasts and scenarios permitted state elites to save or reinvent a form of statist control over the temporalities of territory, albeit in a different guise from the legacies of planning from the interwar period on. As such forms of future planning went hand in hand with a fragmentation of the modern state, its turn to neoliberal forms of governance, and its outsourcing of authority to many other entities. The second section of the chapter discusses what kind of performative act such future-oriented expertise in fact performs, and the distinct notion of knowledge as intervention that it seems to rely on.

States and Future Planning

A central proposition in the literature on expertise has been that expertise constitutes a missing link between states and forms of knowledge, and that this mediation of knowledge allows states to govern territory and population. While political scientists and international relations scholars pinpointed so-called epistemic communities (Haas 1992) and saw them as supplying something in response to demands from public powers, other perspectives have put to the side the "supply and demand" dimension and focused instead precisely on the role of expertise as a mediator of social struggles and as a governmental intervention in temporal and spatial relations. In a seminal paper, Timothy Mitchell urged state scholars to pay attention to the forms of knowledge, expertise, and technologies that states use to produce authority and sovereignty over territory. Mitchell's argument was directed against a unilateral use of the concept of "state" in political science, and against the idea that state power somehow exists and is unproblematically tied to a given state body. States are, Mitchell argued, performative agents, and use artefacts of knowledge and expertise to produce what he famously referred to as the "state effect" (Mitchell 1991, 2002; Steinmetz and Mitchell 1991). It was important to the argument on the colonial state in Egypt that its future was uncertain and hinged on the domestication of both space and time. Maps of the future of colonial territory mattered in Mitchell's argument, and scenarios can be thought of as maps of time in contemporary state structures. Mitchell opened up a wider scholarly interest in the problem of states and knowledge. Following in Foucault's footsteps, this literature, reaching over STS studies to anthropology and history, emphasized the complex links between state-produced ontologies and state authority (Scott 1998). It brought attention to the manifold forms of expertise that states make use of to construct objects of governance—population, territory, economy—nature, climate, future. A side effect of this literature was to deconstruct the state itself—and show that governmental authority can be exercised by a multitude of social actors, not all of which are in the contemporary period, immediately identifiable with the state (see King and Legales 2017). In the second part of the postwar period, not only states but also international and transnational organizations are governmental actors. Multinational corporations, in the past, as well as in the present, perform statist functions and identify with governmental power (Chandler and Mazlish 2005).

Planning—which originated in early forms of double bookkeeping in the medieval period and grew to encompass the cameral sciences and political economy during the rise of the mercantilist state in the seventeenth and eighteenth centuries, before becoming expressively concerned with the expansion of the economy that followed the breakthrough of Keynesian thinking in the 1930s—had always included an element of futurity. For the larger part of the twentieth century this element of futurity was based on the idea of linearity, and consisted of representations of developments that grew in linear and exponential fashion and that essentially followed the growth curve (Schmelzer 2016; Armatte 1992). As such, planning did not foresee plural future developments, or, indeed, either open-ended futures or feedback effects, but attempted to extrapolate trends, usually within a time frame of three to five years. National five-year plans and budgets were the main products of this thinking. The late 1960s and early 1970s saw a decisive shift in epistemologies of planning. In most countries of the Western world (and the Socialist Bloc), states complemented their existing planning bodies with new units that were explicitly devoted to a new time frame beyond the present, usually referred to as the "long term" and encompassing a 5-, 15-, or 25-year horizon. The meaning of the notion of "long term" was simply derived from what was beyond the temporal horizon of planning in an effort to complement plans with new forms of strategic thinking for the future. As this took place during the turbulent period in contemporary history between 1967 and 1973, the category of the long term came to encompass very different things. A first rationale of the new long-term units was to improve planning by increasing the scope of choice over time, in other words, to point to the different possible overlap and side effects of decision-making in different areas, pinpoint negative effects and feedback loops of policy, and compensate for consequences of industrial growth in terms of the human and ecological costs. In many places, these new bodies produced debates and documents that were central to an emerging argument about the negative effects of growth on the environment, and informed by notions of a new value revolution in so-called postindustrial societies. In this debate, liberals and social democrats could participate in a new dialogue with planners, experts, and intellectuals around welfare and quality of life. A few years later, however, long- term bodies had become central spaces for a reflection that paved the way for the neoliberal critique of the state. The French and the Belgian Long-Term Division produced so-called *scenarios de l'impossible*, "scenarios of disaster," which showcased the devastating cost explosion that would follow from an end to growth and a continued expansion of public sectors. The American year-2000 commission introduced a theme of ungovernability that years later resurfaced in the Trilateral Commission. These themes arguably depended on a forecaster with a new kind of future expertise, who was no longer an expert in financial markets or demographics but, rather, a kind of qualitative thinker on crisis and change.

Long-term units such as the Scientific Council of Government in the Netherlands (*Vetenschapplijke Raat het Regierungsbeleid*), the Commission on the Year 2000 in the United States, the Secretariat for Futures Studies in Sweden, or the Long-Term Division of the French Plan, which all appeared between 1967 and 1973, were distinct from planning units of old in both their setup and the nature of the expertise they provided.

They were devised as public think-tank structures and situated in direct proximity to policymaking structures (presidential or prime ministerial offices), but outside the planning structures. Their independence, and their public role as "future thinkers," was often stressed. In several places there were major controversies over how long-term planning should be positioned in relation to public power (Andersson and Keizer 2014; Andersson and Prat 2015). These debates reiterated debates conducted in economic planning, where macroeconomic forecasting and modeling had been concentrated in units like the National Bureau of Economic Research in the United States, at a kind of arm's-length distance from political power due to the perceived power of prophecy (Fourcade 2009; Seefried 2014). In several places, debates about the proper constitutional place of forecasting units led to advanced reasoning on the philosophy and epistemological status of planning and its relationship to academic expertise, policy, and public participation. In some countries, long-term planning bodies themselves participated in a critique of technocracy and expertise, and hence, positioned themselves as a possible solution to a legitimation problem that by the late 1960s had affected decision-making structures in the Western world. Representation gave way to participation, and the top-down role of planning gave way to scenarios about the year 2000, oftentimes published for a large audience (as was the case with the year report published by the Commission on the Year 2000 (Bell and Graubard 1967). There were strikingly different answers to the problem of representation and participation in different geographic contexts and political cultures: in Sweden, the Secretariat for Futures Studies was set up to conduct a new dialogue between social science expertise and public participation in future debates that involved whole communities and a range of new techniques from visual future maps to cartoons; in the Netherlands, the Scientific Council was an unashamedly technocratic structure devised to complement (and counteract) the so-called pillarization of the Dutch model (by which religious communities and trade unions were represented in the making of plans) and in the United States, the Commission on the Year 2000 became a virtual battlefield between the leftovers of a Cold War intelligentsia, the New Left, and a budding neoconservative elite (Andersson and Keizer 2014, Andersson 2021).

Importantly, these future units also incorporated a new kind of planner, different from the planners of old, who were often economists, demographers, or sociologists and, generally, bureaucrats and public servants. Whereas the planners of old were statisticians or economists, the new future units often employed noted professors, journalists, or leading public intellectuals, including such figures such as Daniel Bell of the American Commission on the Year 2000; Bertrand de Jouvenel, Jacques Delors, or Jacques Lesourne in France; environmental philosopher Carl Friedrich von Weiszäcker in West Germany; and Nobel Prize laureate Alva Myrdal in Sweden. Compared to Warde and Sörlin's notion of the meta-expert—a conjurer of grand images of the future from forms of synthetic observation—these experts also incarnated the role of "expertise on expertise," the meta reflection on the future, drawing on imagination, subjective opinion, intellectual judgment, and a certain sense of being with the spirit of the time. The philosopher Paul Ricoeur, for instance, participated in the French Long-Term Commission. In several places, the United States not least, it is clear that the role of the public intellectual in these inquiries on the future was to mediate a difficult transition from one time to another and soothe turbulent decades with a new and promising image of the future— consider the role of Daniel Bell as the president of a future commission that began in 1964 as the Great Society was being rolled out and concluded ten years later with several commission members leading the neoconservative revolution. In Sweden, Alva Myrdal chaired a commission on the future whose central role was to consider how the future of a small social-democrat model would live up to new challenges of a globalized and radicalized world (Andersson 2006).

While one function of these new future hubs was thus to perform a kind of public inquiry into the long term, another function was to reinvent the idea of planning by incorporating a new set of sciences into the *sciences de gouvernement*. The new governmental science par excellence in the 1970s was systems analysis, a way of synthesizing and modeling complex time and space relations on a global or planetary scale. Systems analysis developed out of so-called operations of research and engineering during World War II (Hughes and Hughes 2000). Systems analysts were often also metaplanners or philosophers of planning—concerned with the "image" or overarching goal of the system. This applies, for instance, to planners who set up new future-oriented bodies or developed modeling tools; Andrew Schonfield in the United Kingdom, Bernard Cazes in France, Lars Ingelstam in Sweden, Jan Tinbergen in the Netherlands, or Hazan Ozbekhan in the United States (the latter went from RAND Corporation to IBM to design the first model for the Club of Rome). Systems analysts could straddle a new and strange position between the inherent technocracy of modeling and a distinct and almost utopian will to world improvement. Ozbekhan, for instance, believed that the world system could be reengineered so that all the world's problems (starvation, war) disappeared. Systems analysts were also profoundly inscribed in an emerging global space, strongly marked by new transnational and global institutions such as the OECD, the emerging European Community, the World Bank, and the United Nations system (Rindzevičiūtė 2016). This global space, in turn, gave birth in the same period, from about 1967 to 1973, to a new set of futuristic hubs that were directly concerned with producing images and representations of world futures. Examples include the Club of Rome, which produced the *Limits to Growth* report in 1972, and the International Institute for Advanced Systems Analysis (IIASA), which was set up as a metaphorical bridge over the Iron Curtain. These spaces were platforms for thinking about problems that could not be dealt with on the national level and required new forms of transnational collaboration between experts, for instance, in data sharing, but also new tools for envisioning problems pertaining to the long-term horizon. The meta-experts of the 1960s and 1970s had a new capacity for transnational networking, and thus they were both enabled by and constitutive of a new global space. They also contributed to the widening of the planners' gaze, in not only time but also space, because the very meaning of the "long term" came to refer not simply to an extended temporal gaze, but also to developments that encompassed the world, or planetary, system. Spatially, long-term developments were about developments understood as global and common, or "shared," and that thus outreached the nation-state level and referred explicitly to a new global space that in itself required new forms of expertise (Sylvest and Van Munster 2016, Djelic and Quack 2010).

The shift toward future-oriented planning technologies by the late 1960s and early 1970s, which were carried by systems analysis and a new mode of planning, can also be clearly related to a new form of circulation, not simply between national planning units and new global spaces, but between the planning bodies of states and those of large companies. This was not, as such, new; expertise and governmental knowledge had circulated between public planning bodies and the research departments big firms since the late nineteenth century (Graber 2011). Oftentimes, this took place through common interests in large projects and large-scale changes, for instance, in energy, communication, or finance. By the late 1960s, the multinational corporation was a major producer of planning technologies and expertise oriented to anticipation and strategy. The research departments of IBM, Kodak, Kaiser Aluminum, and Bell Industries were key providers of future-oriented forms of planning, including forecasts, scenarios, and strategy gaming. In the United States, these corporations were directly involved in discussions about strengthening the role of research and development and state planning in the 1960s. In Europe, a public-corporate and also military "complex" was part of the development of the nineteenth-century welfare state but was hybridized in the 1960s and 1970s around commerciable applications of planning in fields such as defense systems, telecom, and energy markets (Stenlås et al. 2010). In France, it is clear that public companies such as the railroads (SNCF) or electricity (EDF) were a central site for the interest in long-term planning, and that these were also spaces for training high-level public servants who would later serve as part of the French planning apparatus, as well as in the building of the European Community in areas of energy and nuclear security (Mallard 2009, Mallard and Lakoff 2011). When scenarios, Delphis, and forecasts were first discussed in France, it was as mentioned through a discussion group that brought managers of the large French companies together with managers and planners of public administration around the interest in new so-called decision technologies. Many of these technologies had first been experimented with in French companies after 1945. By the late 1960s and early 1970s, they were now considered potent for solving problems of public policy and, indeed, of cost explosion, bureaucratization, and lack of foresight.

The period from the mid-1960s on was also when multinational corporations began perceiving themselves as state-like structures and as performing a governmental, even welfarist, function that was more or less comparable to that of nation-states (perhaps they had always done so, as histories of the East India companies, for instance, would suggest). This explains why multinationals such as Kodak, IBM, or Royal Dutch Shell invested heavily in systems analysis and scenario planning they thought would help them manage increasingly complex time and space relations across the globe. By the mid-1960s, these corporations had become central sites for the development of foresight expertise and predictive technologies. The history of the Shell scenarios is a case in point. In 1967, the nuclear strategist Herman Kahn, who had written scenarios for the Commission on the Year 2000 and funded the neoconservative think-tank the Hudson Institute in the United States, developed the Corporate Scenario Project at Hudson

(Williams 2016). The Corporate Scenarios involved a group of the world's largest multinationals in a scenario-scripting exercise, in which the 1970s world was presented as a choice between two scenarios: a new "Belle Epoque" of deregulation, market relations, and corporate power or a "World of Internal Contradictions" scenario in which sclerosis triggered a vicious circle of inflation, trade-union demands, and government regulation. All the major oil companies participated in the exercise, and the scenario technique was imported to Shell's own research department by the French strategist Pierre Wack (Andersson 2020). Interestingly, Kahn's scenarios were also discussed in the French Long-Term Division by planners Pierre Massé, Jean Monnet, and Jacques Delors—all of whom would be centrally involved in developing planning structures for the emerging European Community and the Euratom program.

This corporate dimension of the new and future-oriented planning technologies was important, because in the mid-1960s, when future research began migrating into public sectors as an extension of public planning, it transferred a managerial logic that had, in fact, been developed for large corporations, and drew on a notion of decisionist rationality that was directly related to strategic notions of utility and optimal preference. Scenarios and foresight were thus devised with an aim to identify the "rational decision"—*decision rationelle*—in a larger field of possible decisions and consequences. As this was applied to problems of sclerosis and rising costs in European welfare states, scenario planning and long-term forecasts thus brought a new element into economic planning, which was no longer meant planning for production factors or gauging inflation versus unemployment but setting a long-term objective of economic stability and growth. As stated by the OECD's so-called Interfutures group in 1975, achieving a new stability and harmony in Western societies demanded the creation and diffusion of new and positive images of the market (Andersson 2019).

THE AUTHORITY OF FUTURE EXPERTISE

As future-shaping tools such as scenarios started being used in planning and expertise in both the corporate and the public environments, these tools were motivated by their capacity to govern uncertainty and unpredictability over time and space. The solution to uncertainty was to set out an image of the future around which actors could cohere. In 1970s scenarios, the stress on the need to assert a positive image of the market and to project an economic future beyond wage restraints, spending cuts, and the loss of state protection was absolutely central. At this point, the promise of scenarios was clearly that of a governmental tool that allowed for the creation of positive future images for a crisis-ridden present, with the hope that such images would have an effect on social turmoil and help pacify new social demands.

It makes sense to pause here in our discussion of uncertainty to underscore the importance of a new set of factors that by the mid-1960s and early-1970s were understood to be causing a new phenomenon of unpredictability in global market relations and in the governability of Western welfare states. Uncertainty is not a mere starting point for expertise; rather, expertise constructs uncertainty, and uncertainty is also a historically specific, not universal, phenomenon. The 1970s notion of uncertainty, which informed other notions, not least that of ungovernability, referred to a massive shake up in value relations, both between the Western world and the global South and between Western governments and their populations. By the late 1960s—and culminating with the oil crisis in 1973—an essentially colonial and Fordist world system of commodity relations was being shaken to the core by an unprecedented mobilization of the Third World and by demands for a radically different economic world order (Garavini 2012, 2019). This was reflected in world commodity prices that saw new patterns of fluctuation, in sharp contrast to a long postwar period of essentially stable prices. This was true not least of oil, which was the object of some of the most important scenario exercises. In the scenario tool used by Royal Shell in 1972 and 1973, the price of oil was linked to a value revolution in the Third World due to a rejection of "Western" images of the future. At the same time, Western countries experienced a domestic value revolution, triggered by trade union demands for wage increases and by a new set of environmental and antinuclear protests. Scenarios were designed to meet these two challenges, which both were central elements in the notion of ungovernability and constituted notions of a global value revolution that threatened the growth contract of the Fordist world. In the years between 1973 and 1978, Western governments and international organizations invested heavily in scenario units and future research, with the clear hope that this would be a new way of managing global uncertainty.

Forms of scenario planning, therefore, marked a shift in governmental technologies in the 1970s, as linear and conjectural planning entered into a state of profound crisis, and a new need for long-term harmonization became of the essence. Because the same period marks the beginning of debates about the rollback and erosion of state capacity, it is important to stress that scenario planning hardly represented a weaker form of governmental control on population and territory, it simply represented a conversion of the statist gaze onto a new set of problems. Like conventional means of planning, the purpose of future-oriented methodologies was to govern population, territory, and the economy; but unlike other means of planning, they sought to do so, not by setting out key quantitative objectives but by crafting *images* of coming developments, by which persuasive accounts of desirable forms of change could be performed. The power of future image was not underestimated, and it is arguably this that explains the transformations in future expertise in the 1970s. One of the first uses of Kahn's scenario method, before the Corporate Scenario project at Hudson, was in race relations and concerned the future of the American Black population. This was in the papers Daniel Bell commissioned Kahn to write for the Commission on the Year 2000 and concerned the very future of the American polity. In France, scenarios were introduced by the Long-Term Division in the immediate post-1968 context, and were used not only as a speculation on the future, but as political technologies in the sense of narrative devices that could be used to set out convincing and appealing images of the future of France to the French public at a time of youth revolt and protest. Again, the intellectual played a key role here—as the provider of input to the scenarios and as the writer of narrative scripts (in the years to come the Long-Term Division would solicit both Paul Ricoeur and Raymond Aron to think about the future of France in the year 2000, see *France face au choc du futur*, 1972). Within the American Commission on the Year 2000, not only did Kahn write scenarios, but so did the anthropologist Margaret Mead, who adapted her earlier theories on the continuous transfers of values from generation to generation into the more ominous idea that radical value change in the United States risked turning the future generation of Americans into a different continent. The need for future reflection was thus directly motivated by feelings of uncertainty having to do with pervasive changes in the values and social fabric of Western populations.

The shift from linear forms of planning to forms of future-oriented steering that had taken place by the late 1960s and early 1970s did not represent a weakening of governmental ambitions, but rather an extension of these into hitherto not considered horizons of time and space. An extension of governmental ambition was also enabled through the diffusion or outsourcing of steering capacities to a much larger group of actors, including experts and consultants from the large consultancy and corporate world. This argument is essential for understanding the changing notions of expertise in these decades. Scenarios, forecasts, and simulations are hard to understand as forms of knowledge production, if they are not understood precisely as a reconversion of political technologies—now for an era dominated by widespread perceptions of uncertainty in time and space. On the axis of time, uncertainty referred to ideas of unforeseen consequences of economic growth and technological developments, particularly in terms of value revolutions in Western populations. On the spatial level, uncertainty linked up with ideas of global interdependence and a new world system in which forms of expertise also had to leave the framework of the nation. From this period on, transnational entities such as the intergovernmental organization, the UN system, the global think-tank, or, indeed, the multinational corporation become central providers of expertise, and the new transnational movements of expertise also increasingly demonstrate a decoupling from the national space.

By way of conclusion, it might be proposed that both historians and political scientists have been a little too quick in identifying a crisis of planning and predictability and a weakening of expertise, or even an end to the "problem solving" approach to government in the 1970s and on (Wagner 2002). Clearly, states have morphed from top-down structures into larger network forms in which the act of governing is also transformed into a diffusion process among different societal actors on a variety of levels (King and Le Galès 2017). The history of future research offered in these pages illustrates, however, Mitchell Dean's point that states that outsource power to a new constellation of actors do not necessarily lose power or reduce their governing ambitions; rather, they draw a larger set of social actors into the act of governing. Expertise can be a form of outsourcing by which state authority is delegated (Dean 2007). In the process, there is not necessarily less statist power, rather, subjects are drawn into what Foucault originally defined as le *souci de soi*, the governance of conduct. From this perspective, the forging of a future image and the aim of using this image to steer social relations and forms of collective and individual behavior across a range of social arenas, is a distinct act of statist power (Foucault 2010). The literature clearly shows that states did not go weak in a sudden abandonment of state institutions in favor of the market in the long period of "neoliberalization" that began the 1970s on; rather, states began to exercise power differently (King and Le Galès 2017). The transformation of planning from linear or conjectural approaches to more open-ended, strategic, or future-oriented forms is absolutely central to this development. In many places, transformations of planning did not immediately mean replacing welfare statist notions of the well-being of populations with acute forms of marketization; rather, it meant new styles of governing and new programs of intervention into the social and economic world where market and corporate forms of rationality were applied. As shown, future research was an important carrier of ideas of the rational decision, but future research is also indicative of the changing use of expertise toward the model of a performative intervention. In the process, the role of expertise changed to what Trentmann, Sum, and Rivera (2018, 29) have referred to as a discursive process, or a process in which "the expert is a person whose predominant feature, while still knowledge based, is to mediate, reason, and connect with public debate." Future-oriented tools of planning enacted exactly this shift in expertise toward discourse, narration, and persuasion. As political technologies, scenarios are not important for the knowledge of the future they provide; rather, their role is to act as communicative devices, with which specific images of coming developments can be forged and diffused. The expert played a key role in this process, not only by providing input to the scenario in question, but also by diffusing it to a range of social actors, and here, the capacity of expert movement and circulation between different fields of expertise is a fundamental resource.

The role of the multinational corporation here is interesting, because of its role as a site of circulation and global reflection, but also as a de facto producer of governmental authority in the period from the 1970s on. Shell's scenarios are today truly global exercises that involve a wide range of experts and publics in the search for what Shell defines as the global "common good". Meanwhile scenarios have been used by a wide range of other arenas to grasp developments of population, territory, and economy and set in place forms of dialogue between policy experts and publics about future change. The European Union, deeply uncertain of its future, is an example in point. The EU championed anticipatory forms of governance since its beginning in the EC. Over time, this activity developed from one directly concerned with commodity and energy markets, to one concerned with territory, population, values, and even governance structures themselves, reflecting an ever deeper identity crisis in the European project since the 2000s. European foresight developed into a formidable consultancy driven industry, where advice was taken from think-tanks, planning units, and private research bodies across Europe. Since the financial crisis, such expert-driven forecasts have also been increasingly complemented with algorithmic foresight. Many nation-states have held widely observed scenario processes at times of uncertainty: Finland at the end of the Cold War in 1989, South Africa at the end of Apartheid, Germany during reunification, Malaysia and South Korea at the height of the Asian miracle, and several Arabic states after the Arab spring. In all of these, expertise is the link between the governing and the governed, the state and publics. As such, expertise performs a different function from that of simply providing knowledge and enters deeply into the governing of the social. Expertise becomes an intervention into social life by communicating a shared, or at least intended to be shared, set of expectations, aspirations, and finalities for social developments (Eyal and Buchholz 2010; compare Beckert 2016). Such a perspective underscores the role of expertise again as part of state action, and not as an autonomous action field (Fligstein and McAdam 2011) or as epistemic communities somehow in an outside demand and supply position to the state (Haas 1992; Hall 1993), but rather, as constituted by state power and as enacting state power (see Vauchez and Mudge 2012)—including in cases where the states concerned are not actually states but statelike structures. In this way, it can be argued, foresight does not debunk state authority but, rather, concentrates it in the expert.

References

Adam, B., and C. Groves. 2007. *Future Matters, Marking, Making and Minding Futures for the 21st Century*. Amsterdam: Brill.

Amoore, L. 2013. *The Politics of Possibility: Risk and Security beyond Probability*. Durham, NC: Duke University Press.

Andersson, Jenny. 2006. "Choosing Futures: Alva Myrdal and the Construction of Swedish Futures Studies, 1967–1972." *International Review of Social History* 51 (2): 277–295.

Andersson, Jenny. 2018. *The Future of the World: Futurology, Futurists, and the Struggle for the Post Cold War Imagination*. Oxford: Oxford University Press.

Andersson, Jenny. 2019. "The Future of the Western World: The OECD and the Interfutures Project." *Journal of Global History* 14 (1): 126–144.

Andersson, Jenny, and A. G. Keizer. 2014. "Governing the Future: Science, Policy and Public Participation in the Construction of the Long Term in the Netherlands and Sweden." *History and Technology* 30 (1–2): 104–122.

Andersson, Jenny, and Pauline Prat. 2015. "Gouverner le 'long terme.'" *Gouvernement et Action Publique* 4 (3): 9–29.

Andersson, Jenny, and Eglė Rindzevičiūtė, eds. 2015. *The Struggle for the Long-Term in Transnational Science and Politics: Forging the Future*. New York: Routledge.

Andersson, Jenny, and Erik Westholm. 2019. "Closing the Future: Environmental Research and the Management of Conflicting Future Value Orders." *Science, Technology, & Human Values* 44 (2): 237–262.

Andersson, Jenny, 2020. "Ghost in a Shell: the Scenario Tool and the World Making of Royal Dutch Shell, *Business History Review*, 94 (4): 729–751.

Aradau, Claudia. 2014. "The Promise of Security: Resilience, Surprise and Epistemic Politics." *Resilience* 2 (2): 73–87.

Aradau, Claudia, and Rens Van Munster. 2007. "Governing Terrorism through Risk: Taking Precautions, (Un)Knowing the Future." *European Journal of International Relations* 13 (1): 89–115.

Armatte, M. 1992. "Conjonctions, conjoncture et conjecture: Les baromètres économiques (1885–1930)." *Histoire et mesure* 7 (1–2): 99–149.

Beckert, J. 2016. *Imagined Futures: Fictional Expectations and Capitalist Dynamics*. Cambridge, MA: Harvard University Press.

Bell, Daniel, and Stephen Graubard, eds. 1997. *Toward the Year 2000: Work in Progress*. Cambridge MA: MIT Press.

Chandler, A. D., and B. Mazlish, eds. 2005. *Leviathans: Multinational Corporations and the New Global History*. Cambridge, UK: Cambridge University Press.

Clavin, P. 2005. "Defining Transnationalism." *Contemporary European History* 14 (4): 421–439.

Commissariat Général au Plan, 1972. *1985, La France face au choc du futur*. Paris: Commissariat Général au Plan.

Davies, William, and Linsey McGoey. 2012. "Rationalities of Ignorance: On Financial Crisis and the Ambivalence of Neo-liberal Epistemology." *Economy and Society* 41 (1): 64–83.

Dean, Mitchell. 2007. *Governing Societies: Political Perspectives on Domestic and International Rule*. Maidenhead UK: Open University Press, McGraw-Hill Education.

Djelic, M. L., and S. Quack, eds. 2010. *Transnational Communities: Shaping Global Economic Governance*. Cambridge, UK: Cambridge University Press.

Edwards, P. N. 2010. *A Vast Machine: Computer Models, Climate Data, and the Politics of Global Warming*. Cambridge, MA: MIT Press.

Eyal, Gil, and L. Buchholz. 2010. "From the Sociology of Intellectuals to the Sociology of Interventions." *Annual Review of Sociology* 36:117–137.

Eyal, Gil. 2019. *The Crisis of Expertise*. Cambridge MA: Polity Press.

Fligstein, N., and D. McAdam. 2011. "Toward a General Theory of Strategic Action Fields." *Sociological Theory* 29 (1): 1–26.

Foucault, Michel, A. I. Davidson, and G. Burchell. 2010. *The Government of Self and Others: Lectures at the Collège de France 1982–1983*. London: Palgrave MacMillan.

Fourcade, Marion. 2009. *Economists and Societies: Discipline and Profession in the United States, Britain and Germany*. Princeton: Princeton University Press.

Garavini, Giuliano. 2012. *After Empires: European Integration, Decolonization, and the Challenge from the Global South 1957–1986*. Oxford: Oxford University Press.

Garavini, Giuliano. 2019. *The Rise and Fall of OPEC in the Twentieth Century*. New York: Oxford University Press.

Garsten, Christina, and Sörbom, Adrienne. 2016. "Magical Formulae for Market Futures: Tales from the World Economic Forum Meeting in Davos". *Anthropology Today* 32 (6): 18–21.

Graber, Frédéric, 2011. "Du faiseur de projet au projet régulier dans les Traveaux Publics (XVIIIe-XIX siècles): pour une histoire des projets". *Révue d'histoire moderne et contemporaine*, 58 (3): 7–33.

Haas, P. M. 1992. "Introduction: Epistemic Communities and International Policy Coordination." *International Organization* 46 (1): 1–35.

Hall, P. A. 1993. "Policy Paradigms, Social Learning, and the State: The Case of Economic Policymaking in Britain." *Comparative Politics*, 25 (3): 275–296.

Holmes, D. R. 2014. *Economy of Words: Communicative Imperatives in Central Banks*. Chicago: University of Chicago Press.

Hughes, A. C., and T. P. Hughes. 2000. *Systems, Experts, and Computers: The Systems Approach in Management and Engineering, World War II and After*. Cambridge, MA: MIT Press.

King, Desmond, and Patrick Le Galès. 2017. *Reconfiguring European States in Crisis*. Oxford: Oxford University Press.

Koselleck, R., and M. W. Richter. 2006. "Crisis." *Journal of the History of Ideas* 67 (2): 357–400.

Krahmann, E. 2018. "The Market for Ontological Security." *European Security* 27 (3): 356–373.

Lorenzini, S. 2019. *Global Development: A Cold War History*. Princeton, NJ: University Press.

Mallard, Grégoire. 2009. "L'Europe puissance nucléaire, cet obscur objet du désir." *Critique Internationale*, 42 (1): 141–163.

Mallard, Grégoire, and Andrew Lakoff. 2011. "How Claims to Know the Future Are Used to Understand the Present." In Michel Lamont, Charles Camic, Neil Gross, eds. *Social Knowledge in the Making*. Chicago: Chicago University Press, 339–359.

Mitchell, Timothy. 1991. "The Limits of the State: Beyond Statist Approaches and Their Critics." *American Political Science Review* 85, no. 1. (March): 77–96.

Mitchell, Timothy. 2002. *Rule of Experts: Egypt, Techno-Politics, Modernity*. Berkeley: University of California Press.

Mudge, S. L., and A. Vauchez. 2012. "Building Europe on a Weak Field: Law, Economics, and Scholarly Avatars in Transnational Politics." *American Journal of Sociology* 118 (2): 449–492.

Poskanzer, D. 2019. "A Planet-Changing Idea." *Issues in Science and Technology* 35 (4): 92–94.

Rindzevičiūtė, Eglė. 2016. *The Power of Systems: How Policy Sciences Opened up the Cold War World*. Ithaca, NY: Cornell University Press.

Rosenboim, O. 2017. *The Emergence of Globalism: Visions of World Order in Britain and the United States, 1939–1950*. Princeton, NJ: Princeton University Press.

Schmelzer, M. 2016. *The Hegemony of Growth: The OECD and the Making of the Economic Growth Paradigm*. Cambridge, UK: Cambridge University Press.

Scott, J. C. 1998. *Seeing like a State: How Certain Schemes to Improve the Human Condition Have Failed*. New Haven, CT: Yale University Press.

Seefried, E. 2014. "Steering the Future. The Emergence of 'Western' Futures Research and Its Production of Expertise, 1950s to early 1970s." *European Journal of Futures Research* 2 (1): 1–12.

Sending, Ole J. 2015. *The Politics of Expertise: Competing for Authority in Global Governance*. Ann Arbor: University of Michigan Press.

Slobodian, Quinn. *Globalists*. Cambridge MA: Harvard University Press.

Stampnitzky, L. 2013. *Disciplining Terror: How Experts Invented "Terrorism."* Cambridge, UK: Cambridge University Press.

Stenlås, N., P. Lundin, and J. Gribbe. 2010. *Science for Welfare and Warfare: Technology and Initiative in Cold War Sweden*. Sagamore Beach: Watson Publishing Science History Publications.

Taleb, Nassim Nicholas. 2007. "Black Swans and the Domains of Statistics." *American Statistician* 61 (3): 198–200.

Trentmann, Frank, Anna Barbara Sum, and Manuel Riviera, eds. 2018. *Work in Progress. Economy and Environment in the Hands of Experts*. Munich: Oekom Verlag.

Van Munster, Rens, and Caspar Sylvest, eds. (2016). *The Politics of Globality Since 1945: Assembling the Planet*. London: Routledge.

Wagner, P. 2002. *A Sociology of Modernity: Liberty and Discipline*. London: Routledge.

Wagner, Peter, C. H. Weiss, B. Wittrock, and H. Wollman, eds. 1991. *Social Sciences and Modern States: National Experiences and Theoretical Crossroads*. Cambridge, UK: Cambridge University Press.

Warde, Paul, and Sverker Sörlin. 2015. "Expertise for the Future: The Emergence of Environmental Prediction c. 1920–1970." In *The Struggle for the Long-Term in Transnational Science and Politics*, edited by Jenny Andersson and Eglė Rindzevičiūtė, 38–62. New York: Routledge.

Wedel, Janine R. 2009. *Shadow Elite: How the World's New Power Brokers Undermine Democracy, Government, and the Free Market.* New York: Basic Books.

Williams, R. J. 2016. "World Futures." *Critical Inquiry* 42 (3): 473–546.

Zuboff, Shoshana. 2018. *The Age of Surveillance Capitalism: The Fight for a Human Future at the New Frontier of Power.* New York: Public Affairs.

PART VI

THE TRANSFORMATION AND PERSISTENCE OF PROFESSIONS

20

PROFESSIONAL AUTHORITY

RUTHANNE HUISING

The professions dominate our world. They heal our bodies, measure our profits, save our souls.

—Andrew Abbott (1988[1])

THUS began the book that created an inflection point in the study of professions. Abbott (1988) argued that professions claim jurisdiction—a body of work related to a social problem—and maintain control over this work—the right to diagnose and treat the problem—via expertise. This diverged from the then dominant view of professions and professional jurisdiction as institutionally claimed and legally defined.[1] Critiquing structural analyses, often of single professions, Abbott shifted attention away from the institutional markers of a profession and toward the grounded duels of expertise and expert practice through which professions struggle to control a body of work and through which labor related to social problems (health, money, information, etc.) is divided among expert groups.

Abbott's ideas have shaped how many of us conceptualize and study professions. Yet thirty years later, the epigraph that began this chapter no longer seems accurate. At my fingertips lie information, tools, and services that augment, minimize, or replace my reliance on various professions. Accompanying this is a newfound confidence, overconfidence really, that I can diagnosis my child's rash, answer my international tax questions, and design my kitchen without consulting members of professions. I wonder when I will be replaced by algorithms that can synthesize and draw insights from a body of work and by digital forms of teaching. I sense that the dominance and security experienced by the modern professions is slipping away. We—as researchers and members of a profession—may want to revisit the status of professions and the role of expertise in producing professional authority.

In doing so, we might consider that Abbott (1988) studied professions because of his broader interest in how "societies structure expertise" and that he understood professions as "the main way of institutionalizing expertise in industrialized societies" (323). He argued that expertise was institutionalized in people who were selected, educated, and socialized into relatively homogenous, closed, self-governing groups of full-time practitioners. Expertise, in the context of professions, is knowledge—more or less abstract, proprietary, and tethered to a set of techniques and tools—that provides the basis for the diagnosis and treatment of a class of social problems.

Reading Abbott through the professions lens highlights foreclosed questions about the institutionalization of expertise, perpetuating the idea that expertise remains the fundamental resource through which professions claim and maintain control of a task jurisdiction. Reading Abbott through an expertise lens allows reflection on whether professions continue to be the main way that expertise is institutionalized and whether expertise remains a fundamental resource for professions. Such reflection also opens questions about whether societal conceptions of expertise and its value have changed. If expertise has migrated from closed groups and their members to, for example, networks of heterogeneous rules, technologies, human actors, and organizations, what does this mean for the dominance of professions? If expertise is less valued in society, can it be relied on as a means of producing authority? If conceptions of expertise have shifted away from those Abbott described, do professions face competition beyond commensurable experts?

In this chapter, I grapple with the uncertain efficacy of expertise in producing professional authority and the alternative means that are used to generate professional authority in contemporary workplaces. In doing so, I heed one of Abbott's central warnings: time is not a constant, abstract background for the phenomenon we study. With time, organizing principles change, altering the orders and institutions built on such principles. Across eras, values shift, disrupting the established significance and legitimacy of signs and symbols. Changing conditions bring new constraints and opportunities. Resources whose value has been steady may fluctuate in worth. In the thirty years since Abbott wrote, we have experienced—from the fall of the Berlin Wall to the rise of Amazon.com Inc.— a continuous stream of economic, political, technological, and social change. It would be extraordinary if the resources that professions draw on to claim and maintain authority over their work had not changed as well.

My read across recent studies of professions suggests that the role of expertise in producing professional authority has shifted in at least a few ways. For one, traditional notions of expertise are being supplemented with new forms of knowledge and practice that are generated through interactions with adjacent professions and clients. Through these interactions, members of professions learn how to leverage traditional expertise to diagnose and treat problems in situ, and to influence how those around them understand their work and the outcomes of their work. The interactional nature of this new supplemental expertise suggests that it resides or is institutionalized in the transaction rather than in the member of the profession or the profession. It is produced relationally in particular situations and in concrete interactions. This expertise is important in generating authority because it influences diagnosis, treatment, and compliance with requests. Given this, it produces valued ends for the profession, and it influences how others—the client, the employer, the adjacent profession—assess and evaluate the profession's advice and treatment. Further, this expertise seems not to produce authority because it gives the member of the profession a priori the means or the right to issue commands and the expectation that they will be considered; it produces authority because of the expected or experienced ends of the profession's work. This relates to the more recent ways in which expertise is evaluated and valued through bureaucratic (managerial evaluations in organizations) and technological means (client evaluations on social media).

I examine how professional authority is produced via interdependence, contextual expertise, interactive expertise, and the ethos or the moral character of how work is done to create outcomes that are valued by those who seek or depend on professional advice. Beyond substantive outcomes (winning a legal case, removing a tumor, designing a new product), competence includes accomplishing outcomes in ways that reflect clients' interests, including saving them time, money, and discomfort.

There are a few ways to make sense of the altered place of expertise in producing authority. First, , professions continue to be employed and apply their expertise in bureaucratic organizations. Having worked in these contexts for several decades now (Abbott 1991; Barley and Tolbert 1991), professions have grown accustomed to managerial and entrepreneurial logics that shape how professions claim authority and challenge alternative or complementary means of institutionalizing expertise. Second, many would argue that the values of scientific rationality and evidence-based treatment—the cultural basis of expertise—can no longer be assumed to be a legitimate or preferred foundation for action (Ball 2017). As such, expertise should not be expected to induce respect and compliance, at least not automatically. This source of professional authority seems to be out of vogue in the post-truth era. Third, those who seek professional advice—patients, clients, colleagues—seem more organized, informed, and agentic than in the past. Activists, interest groups, and well-educated, demanding clients are guiding how professions understand and treat problems (e.g., Epstein 1995; Eyal 2013). These changes contribute to making sense of the changing place of expertise in the study of professions. I discuss the implications for conceptualizing and studying professions, professional dominance, and future studies of workplace authority. I begin with a short synthesis of the concept of authority, in general, and professional authority, in particular.

PROFESSIONAL AUTHORITY AND EXPERTISE

The dominance of professions can be broken down into two components—authority and autonomy. *Authority* is the right to command and the reasonable expectation that others will listen. Professional authority allows a group of practitioners to diagnose and treat a class of problems. *Autonomy* is the right to work without external interference. Professional autonomy allows a group of practitioners to conduct themselves with minimal external interference. In the case of the professions, this has largely meant self-governance and control over all aspects of their work, including the selection and preparation of new members, the evaluation of the work, and the disciplining of members. The distinctions between professional authority and professional autonomy are rarely made; however, they become important when observing professional dominance in organizations and society. For example, physicians may retain the authority to make decisions about patients; but in many parts of the world, physicians' autonomy has been significantly weakened. In free-market systems, insurance companies and large employing organizations have made significant incursions into the timing, range, and availability of the treatments physicians can use. In public systems, new public management has done much the same via new management systems—layers of bureaucracy and management that are meant to control physicians' decision-making. Reflecting on professional autonomy raises questions about the degree to which professions control their work and self-govern; whereas reflecting on professional authority raises questions about whether professions still dominate the work of healing our bodies, measuring our profits, and saving our souls.

Authority, a form of power, is often described as the right to command and the inducement to obey based on the *source* of the command, that is, on the perceived status, resources, or attributes of those issuing the commands, rather than the *content* of the command (e.g., Wrong 1979). The source of the command is sufficient grounds for assessing whether to obey. Two sources of command—formal role and expertise—have long been considered the bases of professional authority. In the context of professions, authority is the right to issue commands related to a set of tasks. It signifies the right of a group of practitioners, often their sole right, to work on a class of problems, and their warrant to decide how to do that work and evaluate the results of their efforts. Members of the profession claim authority, and audiences grant authority, based on the understanding that the profession has the institutional right or most appropriate expertise to address a social problem.

Professional authority is sometimes understood to stem primarily and directly from a formal role or status (employed in the position of legal counsel or being board certified), which gives one the right to issue commands and suggests to others that there is good reason for them to consider these commands. Authority, in this case, is structurally derived. It is the institutionally sanctioned right, enabled by credentialing and licensing systems, to diagnose and treat problems in a domain. This authority depends on an institutional infrastructure that generates, certifies, and licenses practitioners, for example, professional associations, universities, and government agencies. There is a long line of scholarship within sociology and institutional theory that examines the creation and evolution of such institutional infrastructures (e.g., Carr-Saunders and Wilson 1933; Larson 1979; Wilensky 1964). Expertise is evidenced by advanced university degrees complemented by some form of apprenticeship, as found in medicine, law, accounting, and architecture. However, expertise contributes indirectly to the achievement of formal authority.

This early, dominant lens examined professions as an institutional product and institutional force (Greenwood, Suddaby, and Hinings 2002; Scott 2008). However, traditionally very few occupational communities (Van Maanen and Barley 1984) have journeyed toward or crossed into the land of "true" professions, with the marks of credentialing, licensing, and state-approved monopoly. This threshold perspective implies that professional authority is an all-or-nothing achievement bestowed on very few (e.g., doctors, lawyers, accountants, architects). At the same time, this threshold has become almost meaningless, as most occupation communities—including psychics, manicurists, and plumbers—have the institutional markers typically indicating a "profession" (Redbird 2017).

Abbott considered these structural signals, including training and credentialing, to be epiphenomenal or perhaps even irrelevant to analyses of professional authority. His examination of professions as the dominant means of institutionalizing expertise argued that expertise, not institutional signals such as licensing and credentialing, were the primary means through which professions claimed a body of work as their jurisdiction—a task space in which they alone have the authority to issue commands and in which they would expect these commands to be acknowledged as legitimate. To say that authority emanates from expertise means that the directives of a profession are heeded out of the belief in their superior knowledge to decide which courses of action best accomplish an outcome, be it treating a disease, increasing returns on a pension fund, or latching a newborn baby onto her mother's breast. Authority is claimed in relation to how the work of solving problems in a domain is done. It is granted depending on whether the basis and the logic of procedures mesh with broader societal values.

The expertise that a profession uses to diagnose, theorize, and treat cases is based, more or less, on an abstract knowledge system. This knowledge system is produced, recorded, and curated by academic practitioners, who nurture its growth while preserving its logic and rigor. In general, abstract knowledge systems are argued to fuel expert authority claims and to legitimize these claims because they reflect the cultural values of modernity—rationality, logic, objective method, and evidential rigor. It is important to understand that expertise generates authority based, not on the content of the advice (e.g., an evaluation of the quality of the advice or its utility in addressing a problem), but on the source of the advice. Professional advice is granted legitimacy because there is societal trust in the procedures or method underlying the advice. The assumed scientific basis of professional advice and discretion also implies that it is impartial and given independently of individual and group interests.

It is through abstraction that a profession defines its problems and tasks and generates related practical techniques. A theoretical knowledge base is used by professions to define social problems and to shape the public's understanding of the problem in relation to their professional knowledge system, claiming that their abstract knowledge, relative to those of other professions, is best suited to address those problems. The abstract knowledge system at the base of professional expertise is theorized to shape the degree of professional authority possible and the resilience of the authority in the face of challenge. The higher the degree of abstraction available to the profession, the more flexible and resilient it is in responding to changing conditions and threats. This is how Abbott explained variance in professional control and authority.

Professions use this abstract knowledge and related objects—texts, dictionaries, tables, tools, forms of dress, and techniques—to shape outsiders' understandings of a class of problems and their own experience of those problems (Starr 1982). From these understandings, the profession and its methods are deemed socially appropriate and desirable to solve problems. While it is true that professional expertise is difficult for outsiders to evaluate or imitate, this opacity is not the basis for authority. However, it does facilitate the ability of professions to shape the clients' interpretations of their work, further fostering the conditions under which their approaches are accepted as legitimate. Abstractness and opacity discourage clients from questioning professionals, keeping "all serious [assessments and] judgments of competence within the circle of recognized colleagues" (Hughes 1958, 141). Performances of expertise (Collins and Evans 2008), demonstrations of rare capacities, may also increase the clients' belief in professionals' prescriptions, thereby conditioning obedience and securing dominance.

When reflecting on expertise as the basis of professional authority, it is helpful to consider the more general point that "behind the world of professional work lies a rationalizing, ordering system that justifies it with general cultural values" (Abbott 1988, 58). The alignment between the principles underlying professional claims of authority and the general cultural values accounts for the success of these claims. This suggests that expertise is not an essential source of authority. As cultural values shift, what justifies professional authority over work would also need to shift. The implication is that we may need to take stock of how the forces shaping the system of professions have changed and—in the process—rethink how we conceptualize the production of professional authority.

In the slow buildup to a postindustrial knowledge-based economy, the scientific values of logic; objective, disinterested methods of making knowledge claims; and evidential rigor rose in esteem (e.g., Bell 1976). Over the past decades, these values have been eroding in the face of questions about the "value" of higher education, the rise of alternative forms of accreditation (massive open online courses, or MOOCs; coding bootcamps; for-profit educational firms); the worship of college-dropout entrepreneurs; the endless unpaid internships; and the decline of long-term, full-time white-collar employment (Nichols 2017). Add to this the recent rise of populism, post-truth everything, efforts to democratize expertise, and the celebration of amateurs (d'Ancona 2017). At the same time, information and knowledge that used to be more or less monopolized by professions or organizations are increasingly available to all. This availability has meant that those with time and some learning capacity may develop significant insight into the knowledge and practices of professions. As a consequence of these widespread phenomena, we might expect slippage between our theoretical ideas about expertise as a source of authority and the place of expertise in the empirical world.

The means that I describe—interdependence, contextual expertise, interactive expertise, and ethos—suggest that professional authority is increasingly granted based on competence or—as Eyal (2013) discussed—the accomplishment of tasks. Professions seem to be maintaining authority by demonstrating that they are able, perhaps best able, to accomplish an outcome on behalf of those they treat and in relation to the broader ecosystem in which they work. Further, professions continue to claim—independent of expertise—that this accomplishment is pursued and achieved in relation to the interest of the client and is void of self-interest. Competence and objectivity are claimed not in relation to an abstract knowledge system but through a consistency with the values and interests of those the profession treats or of the broader system of treatment. This pragmatic, problem-solving approach to authority reflects the appreciation and worth of creativity, competence, and achievement. As managerial and entrepreneurial logics expand into most realms of the social world, the value of expertise may be in decline and the value of getting things done may be on the rise. Below I describe how professions get things done—and maintain their authority—through interdependence, contextual expertise, interactive expertise, and ethos.

Authority through Interdependence

Traditionally the literature on professions has not recognized expertise, its generation, performance, and effect, as an interdependent process. In the system of professions, the specialized division of tasks created boundaries based on distinct expertise and a clear separation of responsibilities. The maintenance of these boundaries—and thus professional authority over a domain of work—occurred by emphasizing differences among and keeping distance from adjacent experts.

Recent work, however, highlights the interdependence among professions and the benefits of this for strengthening professional authority by embedding professions in networks, contexts, and relationships. Acknowledging the ways in which professions develop and maintain control over their work via interdependence suggests that abstract expertise in isolation is not sufficient for producing professional authority. Overall, a profession's legitimacy to treat, ability to infer, and effectiveness in practice relies, in no small part, on the interactions with and the responses of those they treat and surrounding allies. For example, through a comparative historical analysis of two occupational associations—systems men and production planners—Kahl, King, and Liegel (2016) showed how interdependent responses to the introduction of computing in the workplace allowed a profession to survive this change. The systems men worked to differentiate their role and expertise, ultimately losing their place in the production process. The production planners emphasized their interdependence with related occupations and reached out to those occupations to demonstrate task interdependence and their willingness to work together. This historical analysis reveals that our focus on specialized expertise and knowledge has been misplaced. Interdependencies increase the demand for a profession and their continued performance in the larger collective.

One important implication of these findings is that expertise might be better understood as generated and mobilized in relation to a network or assemblage that includes a range of actors (Eyal and Buchholz 2010), rather than as institutionalized in individuals or groups of practitioners. For example, Eyal (2013) reveals the network of parents, researchers, and therapists that came together, their distinctions waning, as they worked to understand the collection of health and social issues that became known as autism. Expertise was located in a "new actor-network, composed of arrangements that blurred the boundaries between parents, researchers, therapists, and activists . . . [that] was finally able to 'solve' the problem" (868). Authority within a task domain is claimed through a profession's contribution within this network, so it becomes a contribution to addressing the problem. In this light, professional authority is not granted based on how abstract knowledge is leveraged in connection and relation to others in the service of a broader problem. Expertise generates authority through an integration and application challenge. While Eyal's larger point is that we should examine expertise as distributed rather than embodied, there remains the question of how those who claim to embody expertise claim authority.

These studies raise questions about the basis on which authority is granted. Instead of appreciating the esoteric foundation of the source of commands, the embeddedness of the source in a broader ecosystem that works to treat problems seems to generate authority. The boundaries between professions have traditionally been seen as fueling authority by preventing encroachment and buttressing autonomy. However, these boundaries may prevent a profession from offering adequate solutions or efficacious responses to problems. By understanding and leveraging interdependencies, a profession may be able to appear more relevant and effective in contributing to a valued collective goal. In doing so, the profession signals its focus on competence and its contribution to a domain of problems that extends beyond its boundaries. Interdependence generates the potential for authority because it facilitates the competent application of expertise.

AUTHORITY THROUGH CONTEXTUAL EXPERTISE

Barley (1996) distinguishes between "substantive professional expertise," which is "abstract and principled," and relational expertise, which is "situated" and "contextual" (429). This relational or contextual expertise stems from an understanding of the web of interactions through which work is accomplished and a recognition of one's role in this web. It means understanding who knows what and whom, the bounds of each actor's role, and how the interlinking actors and action are coordinated to, more or less, produce an outcome to which the profession contributes in part. Apprehension of one's work in the context of a broader system such as an organizational bureaucracy or a system-level bureaucracy (e.g., the legal system) is an important resource because it can be mobilized to achieve client goals beyond what expertise distilled from abstract expertise systems can do. For example, Sandefur (2015) finds that lawyers create significant value for their clients, influencing case outcomes, not because of their substantive understandings of the law but through their expertise about how courts work: the procedures, spaces, rituals, and routines. They use this expertise to navigate through the justice system, and it is this familiarity that brings better outcomes for their clients.

Knowledge and skills produced via abstract knowledge systems tend to be universal, independent of the particular context in which they are employed. Understanding the relational system in which one is embedded produces practical know-how about how to get things accomplished. In cases like Sandefur's (2015) lawyers, contextual expertise may complement abstract expertise. Contextual expertise allows professions to leverage their unique expertise more efficiently and successfully. This bundling of expertise may discourage clients from doing the work themselves or relying on commoditized expertise. In both mundane legal cases (traffic violations, misdemeanors, small claims disputes) and personal tax filing, it is technically possible for the average citizen to do the work themselves. However, because these transactions are embedded in large, complex bureaucratic systems whose functioning is unfamiliar to most citizens, we may hire an expert who regularly deals with these systems. We expect our lawyers and accountants to leverage their contextual expertise to serve our interests, decrease our stress, and save us time.

Contextual expertise can also become the primary means through which a group of practitioners controls a task domain. Within professional bureaucracies, new occupational groups have emerged that stake their claims via their contextual expertise, in particular, their ability to buffer elite professions from administrative work (Huising and Silbey 2011, 2013; Kellogg 2014). Process expertise, competence at managing communication and information flow across and within realms, is also increasingly valued and needed within contemporary workplaces (Treem and Barley 2016, 2). Contextual expertise is fundamental to such work.

Leveraging contextual expertise requires an understanding of its value and a willingness to rely on it. Such an understanding may be particularly important when a profession faces threats to its abstract expertise. Librarians, for example, initially dismissed the possibilities of Internet searches, disregarding the implications for their role (Nelson and Irwin 2014). They considered themselves the masters of search and did not anticipate the tolerance we would all develop for long lists of potentially, but often not, relevant information. With time, librarians reframed their profession from being "masters of search" to being "connectors of people and information." They transformed themselves into guides, helping searchers through the complexities of information sources and structures and facilitating their searching.

Those who are used to relying on their professional expertise may not recognize contextual expertise may as a means of generating authority. Or they may see it as an inferior resource because it does not depend on unique, specialized knowledge and skills. However, for experts working with large complex organizations and systems, contextual expertise appears to be a resource that should not beignored. Indirectly, contextual expertise contributes to professional authority by facilitating the application of the profession's specialized knowledge and skills. Contextual expertise may also contribute to professional authority in its own right. Outsiders may grant the profession the right to do or to continue to do a body of work because they demonstrate that they can broker and buffer. In this sense, the profession has the ability, beyond the technical, to protect their clients from any pitfalls of the system and to bestow the benefits of moving efficiently through the system. The values here are not the rationality of science and logic but the rationality of efficiency and effectiveness. Expertise that facilitates the diagnosis and treatment of a problem in a time- and cost-conscious manner is likely to be valued by clients. There are several unknowns related to this source of authority, including its durability and longevity, beyond giving human expertise a distinct advantage over competing commodities and technologies.

Authority through Interactive Expertise

Beyond deep contextual knowledge of the system in which they work, practitioners may be better able to enact and leverage their expertise through their understanding of and relationships with the individuals and groups they treat. Interactive expertise, though it appears similar to contextual expertise, is generated in interaction with clients, requiring that practitioners adjust the way they interact with clients and, potentially, their work practices. As with contextual expertise, such adjustments depend on practitioners acknowledging and appreciating this form of expertise. Developing interactive expertise involves working in ways that do not emphasize the specialized knowledge and skills of a profession. One example comes from the work of psychotherapists, who report relying on their emotions and intuitions, experienced while working with a patient, to help them—in addition to the knowledge and skills of their profession—in their diagnosis, inference, and treatment work (Craciun 2018). Observing psychotherapists working with their patients, Craciun (2018) finds that emotions are additional "epistemic tools" that help therapists gain insight into the patient's situation, allowing for better diagnosis and increasing the likelihood that treatments will be accepted and thus more likely to be heeded. Emotions give the psychotherapists access to their patients' realms of struggle.

In a similar way, scut work gives health physicists—responsible for radiation control in scientific laboratories—access to scientists' realm of daily work (Huising 2015). By doing menial tasks on a regular basis in laboratories, health physicists develop knowledge of scientists' challenges with and objections to following their counsel and requirements. Health physicists also develop a deep familiarity with the habits, language, and logics of the labs. They leverage this knowledge to tailor and more effectively enforce their treatment. Using this interactive knowledge, in addition to their specialized knowledge and skills, they are able to induce scientists to accept and largely defer to their requirements. They maintain their authority through a mix of expert and interactive expertise.

The degree to which a practitioner can perform expertise depends on influencing the patient's or client's affective response, on increasing their willingness to open up to diagnostic questions and motivation to follow treatment. Given this, a sense or interpretation of the focus of treatment is invaluable in the diagnosis-inference-treatment process. This is also likely for the professions of coach (Chambliss 1988) and nurse (Anspach and Halpern 1993; Chambliss 1996). It is particularly true when the relationship is of longer duration, creating a string of observable responses to treatment.

Interactive expertise may also be more relevant to members of professions who work in bureaucratic organizations, and whose clients reside within the same organization. In such cases, clients, who may not want or value the advice of the profession, are assigned to the profession. Applying one's expertise in an indifferent or hostile environment is likely to be challenging, yet members of the profession depend on clients or patients granting them authority to do their work by taking up their advice. The profession achieves its mandate in the organization via the client's consent. Compounding this challenge is that the achievement of the mandate is likely to be monitored and evaluated by management. When clients do not comply and professionals do not achieve their professional mandate, managers may use their formal authority to intervene in how the professionals work, undermining their professional autonomy. Beyond those they apply their expertise to (i.e., clients and patients), professions that are embedded in large, complex bureaucracies need to influence the managers through whom their work opportunities are made possible. For example, mental health professionals in the US Army must gain the consent and trust of commanding officers to be able to treat their soldiers in the way they deem appropriate. This requires gaining the rapid trust and commitment of these officers (DiBenigno 2019).

Interactive expertise allows members of the profession to better understand and anticipate the behavior of clients and develop advice that is more likely to correct problems and be adopted by the client. Operating as a supplement or complement to "expert resources," it is leverage to increase the efficacy of the advice. However, generating such expertise requires that professions work in ways that may not emphasize or leverage their hard-earned expertise and the related privileges of remaining detached, in control, objective, or—even—clean. Working in these ways requires that the professional embed themselves in relations in their work setting in ways that distract from or downplay their expert source of authority. In exchange, the professional generates important information that increases the efficacy of their advice and interpretations of their competence.

Authority through Ethos

Ethos—values and moral character—may be drawn on to attain legitimacy and thus professional authority when expertise is perceived to be lacking or ineffectual, or when the work of the profession is contested on moral grounds. Ethos, a shared understanding of "the proper conduct with respect to the matters that concern their work" (Hughes

1958, 287), has long been understood to be the basis of occupational work. These appropriate "modes of thinking and belief" (Hughes 1958, 287)—embodied by those doing the work—are the basis of the group's mandate to claim a domain of tasks. The conduct of members is guided and constrained based on moral or normative notions of how the work ought to be done. The moral character of the group of practitioners most often articulates ways of working that serve the needs of clients, protecting their dignity, and are socially oriented rather than self-serving (e.g., Nelsen and Barley 1997). In the same way that abstract expertise, rooted in evidence and rationality, is thought to create "objective" constraints on professional conduct and to minimize opportunities for self-serving conduct, an ethos constrains professional conduct, guiding it toward the broader social good and client needs. Both expertise and ethos have the potential to control how work is done, and in whose interests, inducing external audiences to evaluate a profession as valuable and trustworthy, and thus conferring legitimacy and authority.

Given this, a profession can draw on its ethos as a resource to claim or maintain authority when its expertise does not distinguish it from competing professions. For example, the jurisdictional battle between gynecologic oncologists and gynecologic pelvic surgeons was fought and won, not on the basis of expertise and skills, but on the basis of ethos (Zetka 2011). The oncologists' holistic, patient-centric treatment ethos was preferred over the surgeons' narrower mechanical surgery ethos. Where both sufficient skills and expertise existed, the profession with a patient-centered ethos was better able to claim authority over the set of tasks. In another case, service designers were able to claim and control design work in relation to competing occupations, including traditional designers, management consultants, and marketing experts, not through distinct expertise and skills, but via the values that informed how they worked (Fayard, Stigliani, and Bechky 2017). The values—holistic, empathetic, co-creating—were made manifest in the daily actions of the service designers. These studies demonstrate that where skills and knowledge are similar, the moral character of the work may, as a complement to expertise, generate authority. In particular, an ethos emphasizing the profession's dedication to patient or client service appears to maintain professional authority.

However, ethos and expertise may also have a roughly inverse relationship. For example, when a profession becomes embroiled in controversy over the social value of its practices and conduct, it may become necessary to abandon—at least temporarily—expertise as a means of generating legitimacy and to turn to "loftier ideals and practices" (Fourcade and Healy 2007, 305) as a means to restore or shore up legitimacy. Following the financial crisis of 2008, the accounting profession stressed its commitment to the social and environmental aspects of financial reporting (Campbell-Verduyn 2017). Alternatively, where audiences consider the content of a daily professional practice to be morally questionable, professions are likely to take extra steps to control and communicate their practices as moral and in service of the broader good (Anteby 2010; Cohen and Dromi 2018). Making the moral character of the work, conduct, and membership of a profession known and acceptable to external audiences is a means to generate or restore authority. New and competing professions may gain advantage by promoting character over or in addition to expertise.

CONCLUSION

For Abbott (1988), professional authority stemmed from justifying practices and prescriptions in relation to the "central values of the larger culture" (187). This justification, like Starr's (1982), centers on how professions do their work—the logic, principles, methods, and evidence that underlie how they diagnose and treat clients. Abbott argued that the expected achievements of professions—to treat a category of social problems—are constant but that expectations about *how* problem-solving is achieved—the legitimate basis—are evaluated in relation to dominant values. Members of professions were called on to treat problems based on the perceived relevance of their expertise in treating the problem, not on the efficacy of their solution. Of course, effective treatment is always helpful for a profession, but the evaluation of treatment is something professionals also worked to control. A focus on the link between the expert bases of professional work and cultural values (means) limited the examination of what is expected and achieved by professions (ends). What if the dominant values of achievement shift? What if those seeking treatment expect professions to contribute to a problem that spans categories (e.g., autism)? What if those relying on professions expect their work process to meet particular metrics for time, cost, and satisfaction? What if cultural values suggest that authority should be granted based on the outcomes of professional practice rather than on the expertise informing and underlying them?

It seems time to look beyond expertise derived from proprietary abstract knowledge systems as the primary source of professional authority. Professions and those who study them cannot count on appeals to rationality and scientific logic to enable survival in workplaces and labor markets that continue to be structured according to bureaucratic and market logics. It seems likely that professions will continue to reproduce themselves and emerge anew in relation to domains of tasks. However, I argue that the source of their legitimacy and authority will be increasingly based on evaluations of the outcomes of their commands. In other words, authority will be derived from an assessment of collective competence potential by those without relevant expertise and in relation to metrics set by large organizations or the most organized or networked paying customer.

Although the outcomes of professional advice have always been subject to discussion, controversy, and evaluation, much of this has resided within the profession itself. The expert bases of commands limited who could practically and legitimately evaluate these outcomes. However, consumers, patients, and clients now have the means to communicate and organize across their particular cases and experiences. They also have access to the data, information, and knowledge drawn on by the profession. At the same time, the organizations that professions work in and for increasingly measure and monitor the costs, timing, and results of their work. Professions that can pragmatically solve problems and produce results—results valued by clients, organizations, and markets—may be more likely to maintain their authority. The values underlying competence include efficiency, efficacy, timeliness, and customer service.

What are the implications of these emerging empirical patterns? The fundamental implication relates to this pesky distinction between professions and occupations that haunts those who study work. The never-ending, dull conversation about whether a group of practitioners should be considered a profession, a "true" profession, or an occupation, might cease as we increasingly focus on the array of resources that groups of practitioners draw on to claim and maintain authority over a set of tasks. For those who, like Abbott, view authority over a work jurisdiction as stemming from resources beyond institutional markers, the distinctions have always been false. For those who view authority stemming from abstract expertise systems to be different from authority stemming from collective know-how, the distinction should be weakening. Expertise based on abstract knowledge systems is but one source of authority that appears, increasingly, to require fortification by the alternative means described here. Those professions that continue to rest on their expertise, understanding themselves as a protected species, may not grasp the changing circumstances in which their descendants will compete to survive. Instead, professions and occupations that focus on accomplishing valued outcomes are more likely to be granted authority to continue issuing commands.

This suggests that Abbott's (1988) precept that "we must stop studying single professions . . . and start studying work" (325) continues to be relevant. To understand how groups of practitioners claim, generate, or lose authority, we would be wise to drop ex ante ideas about professions, occupations, experts, amateurs, managers, clients, laypeople, citizens, and so on. The relevant questions become: Who is granted authority to perform domains of work? On what basis? And what are the societal implications? Established ideas about the building and maintaining of jurisdiction will also need to be revisited. How might the role of boundaries be changing? How are relationships and work across these boundaries being remade? How is expertise generated and maintained across these boundaries? How is the role of those who seek and receive expert advice changing? These are some of the questions we might follow.

I doubt that these changes have been lost on professions working in the wild. Physicians are well aware of the managerial, market, and customer service logics that are increasingly intertwined in the diagnosis and treatment of patients, just as management consultants understand routes into capturing aspects of the work of architects, economists, and accountants, by leveraging contextual and interactive expertise. However, those of us who study these processes may be missing or misunderstanding the character and significance of these changes, caught up in an aging conceptual apparatus. The slippage between the theoretical and empirical worlds needs to be addressed.

As we do this work, I hope that we continue to read *The System of Professions*. In particular, I hope that we continue to remind ourselves of Abbott's critiques of the work that came before: change is not unidirectional, change to individual professions must be understood within the system of professions, the work and interactions of professions must be understood in tandem with their social structure, professions are not homogenous units, and time is not a constant background for changes in professions and their work.

NOTE

1. Note that this approach is distinct from that of institutional theorists in sociology and organizational theory (e.g., Muzio, Brock, and Suddaby 2013; Scott 2008). The distinction is important to understanding why two main bodies of literature on the professions have emerged in relative independence from each other. Finding ways to bring empirical patterns identified in both streams together in ways that shed light on the focal phenomenon is important but neglected work.

REFERENCES

Abbott, Andrew. 1988. *The System of Professions: An Essay on the Division of Expert Labor.* Chicago: University of Chicago Press.

Abbott, Andrew. 1991. "The Future of Professions: Occupation and Expertise in the Age of Organization." *Research in the Sociology of Organizations* 8 (1): 17–42.

Halpern, S., and R. R. Anspach. 1993. "The Study of Medical Institutions: Eliot Freidson's Legacy." *Work and Occupations* 20 (3): 279–295.

Anteby, Michel. 2010. "Markets, Morals, and Practices of Trade: Jurisdictional Disputes in the US Commerce in Cadavers." *Administrative Science Quarterly* 55 (4): 606–638.

Ball, J. 2017. *Post-truth: How Bullshit Conquered the World.* London: Biteback.

Barley, Stephan. R. 1996. "Technicians in the Workplace: Ethnographic Evidence for Bringing Work into Organizational Studies." *Administrative Science Quarterly* 41 (3): 404–441.

Barley, Stephan. R., and P. S. Tolbert. 1991. "Introduction: At the Intersection of Organizations and Occupations." In *Research in the Sociology of Organizations*, vol. 8, edited by P. S. Tolbert and S. R. Barley, 1–13. Greenwich, CT: Jai Press.

Bell, D. 1976. "The Coming of the Post-industrial Society." *Educational Forum* 40 (4): 574–579.

Campbell-Verduyn, M. 2017. *Professional Authority after the Global Financial Crisis: Defending Mammon in Anglo-America.* Cham, Switzerland: Springer.

Carr-Saunders, A. M., and A. P. Wilson. 1933. *The Professions.* Oxford: Clarendon Press.

Chambliss, D. F. 1988. *Champions: The Making of Olympic Swimmers.* New York: William Morrow and Co.

Chambliss, D. F. 1996. *Beyond Caring: Hospitals, Nurses, and the Social Organization of Ethics.* Chicago: University of Chicago Press.

Cohen, A. C., and S. M. Dromi. 2018. "Advertising Morality: Maintaining Moral Worth in a Stigmatized Profession." *Theory and Society* 47 (2): 175–206.

Collins, Harry, and Robert Evans. 2008. *Rethinking Expertise.* Chicago: University of Chicago Press.

Craciun, M. 2018. "Emotions and Knowledge in Expert Work: A Comparison of Two Psychotherapies." *American Journal of Sociology* 123 (4): 959–1003.

d'Ancona, M. 2017. *Post-truth: The New War on Truth and How to Fight Back.* London: Random House.

DiBenigno, Julia. 2019. "Rapid Relationality: How Peripheral Experts Build a Foundation for Influence with Line Managers." *Administrative Science Quarterly* 65 (1): 20-60. https://doi.org/10.1177/0001839219827006.

Epstein, Stephen. 1995. "The Construction of Lay Expertise: AIDS Activism and the Forging of Credibility in the Reform of Clinical Trials." *Science, Technology, & Human Values* 20 (4): 408–437.

Eyal, Gil. 2013. "For a Sociology of Expertise: The Social Origins of the Autism Epidemic." *American Journal of Sociology* 118 (4): 863–907.

Eyal, Gil, and L. Buchholz. 2010. "From the Sociology of Intellectuals to the Sociology of Interventions." *Annual Review of Sociology* 36:117–137.

Fayard, A. L., I. Stigliani, and B. A. Bechky. 2017. "How Nascent Occupations Construct a Mandate: The Case of Service Designers' Ethos." *Administrative Science Quarterly* 62 (2): 270–303.

Fourcade, Marion, and K. Healy. 2007. "Moral Views of Market Society." *Annual Review of Sociology* 33:285–311.

Greenwood, R., R. Suddaby, and C. R. Hinings. 2002. "Theorizing Change: The Role of Professional Associations in the Transformation of Institutionalized Fields." *Academy of Management Journal* 45 (1): 58–80.

Hughes, E. C. 1958. *Men and Their Work*. Glencoe, IL: Free Press.

Huising, Ruthanne. 2015. "To Hive or to Hold? Producing Professional Authority through Scut Work." *Administrative Science Quarterly* 60 (2): 263–299.

Huising, Ruthanne, and Susan S. Silbey. 2011. "Governing the Gap: Forging Safe Science through Relational Regulation." *Regulation & Governance* 5 (1): 14–42.

Huising, Ruthanne, and Susan S. Silbey. 2013. "Constructing Consequences for Noncompliance: The Case of Academic Laboratories." *ANNALS of the American Academy of Political and Social Science* 649 (1): 157–177.

Kahl, S. J., B. G. King, and G. Liegel. 2016. "Occupational Survival through Field-Level Task Integration: Systems Men, Production Planners, and the Computer, 1940s–1990s." *Organization Science* 27 (5): 1084–1107.

Kellogg, K. C. 2014. "Brokerage Professions and Implementing Reform in an Age of Experts." *American Sociological Review* 79 (5): 912–941.

Larson, M. 1979. *The Rise of Professionalism: A Sociological Analysis*. Berkeley: University of California Press.

Muzio, D., D. M. Brock, and R. Suddaby. 2013. "Professions and Institutional Change: Towards an Institutionalist Sociology of the Professions." *Journal of Management Studies* 50 (5): 699–721.

Nelsen, B. J., and S. R. Barley. 1997. "For Love or Money? Commodification and the Construction of an Occupational Mandate." *Administrative Science Quarterly* 42 (2): 619–653.

Nelson, A. J., and J. Irwin. 2014. "'Defining What We Do—All Over Again': Occupational Identity, Technological Change, and the Librarian/Internet-Search Relationship." *Academy of Management Journal* 57 (3): 892–928.

Nichols, Tom. 2017. *The Death of Expertise: The Campaign against Established Knowledge and Why It Matters*. Oxford: Oxford University Press.

Redbird, B. 2017. "The New Closed Shop? The Economic and Structural Effects of Occupational Licensure." *American Sociological Review* 82 (3): 600–624.

Sandefur, R. L. 2015. "Elements of Professional Expertise: Understanding Relational and Substantive Expertise through Lawyers' Impact." *American Sociological Review* 80 (5): 909–933.

Scott, W. R. 2008. "Lords of the Dance: Professionals as Institutional Agents." *Organization Studies* 29 (2): 219–238.

Starr, Paul. 1982. *The Social Transformation of American Medicine: The Rise of a Sovereign Profession and the Making of a Vast Industry*. New York: Basic Books.

Treem, J. W., and W. C. Barley. 2016. "Explaining the (De)valuation of Process Experts in Contemporary Organizations." In *Expertise, Communication, and Organizing*, edited by J. W. Treem and P. M. Leonardi, 213–231. Oxford: Oxford University Press.

Van Maanen, J., and S. R. Barley. 1984. "Occupational Communities: Culture and Control in Organizations." *Research in Organizational Behavior* 6:287–365.

Wilensky, H. L. 1964. "The Professionalization of Everyone?" *American Journal of Sociology* 70 (2): 137–158.

Wrong, D. 1979. *Power: Its Forms, Bases and Uses*. New York: Harper Colophon.

Zetka, J. R., Jr. 2011. "Establishing Specialty Jurisdictions in Medicine: The Case of American Obstetrics and Gynaecology." *Sociology of Health & Illness* 33 (6): 837–852.

21

THE POSTINDUSTRIAL LIMITS OF PROFESSIONALIZATION

PAUL STARR

SINCE the 1990s some sociologists have called for a conceptual shift from "professionalism" to "expertise" or "expert labor." Gil Eyal (2013) proposes that we "replace the sociology of professions with the more comprehensive and timely sociology of expertise" (863). The two, however, are not mutually exclusive; each highlights questions that are outside the frame of the other. The sociology of professions calls attention to modes of occupational organization, the control of markets, and aspects of social structure that are not well addressed from the standpoint of a sociology of expertise.

Professionalism in its formal institutional sense varies widely among professional and technical occupations. Professional schools, associations, and licensing are ubiquitous in some fields but less developed in others. Census Bureau data on licensing highlight just how wide those variations are in the United States. In 2021, 45.3 percent of those employed in the broad category of "professional and related occupations" reported that they were licensed. The proportion with a license, however, stood at a high of 76.4 percent for "health care practitioners and technical occupations" but was only 12.9 percent for "computer and mathematical occupations" (US Bureau of Labor Statistics 2021). That gap clearly does not stem from a difference in the abstraction or difficulty of the knowledge base in these fields or the expertise they require. The computer and mathematical occupations are no less intellectually complex than those in healthcare, nor are they so esoteric that the difficulty of mastering them effectively restricts entry and makes licensing superfluous.

The low professionalization of high-tech points to a theoretical question: Why do some institutional fields see little professionalization even though they demand levels of expertise comparable to fields where professional institutions have been established? Social theorists in the mid-twentieth century anticipated that the professions would become increasingly central to a postindustrial or information society (Bell

1973). Professional and technical workers have indeed increased sharply as a share of the labor force. Although union membership has declined from a peak of 35 percent in 1954 to about 7 percent today, membership in professional associations has grown. The proportion of workers in the United States reporting they hold a certification or license increased from 5 percent in the 1950s to between 20 percent and 29 percent in the 2010s (Kleiner and Krueger 2013). Although not all of this increase was in occupations that are recognized as professions, the social and economic footprint of professionalization continues to grow. But if there is a direct relationship between postindustrialism and professionalism, it ought to show up in the heart of the information economy, and that is not the case—that is, if we understand professionalism as involving institutions that draw boundaries between the qualified and unqualified or, at least, between those with and without credentials.

Specialized training programs, professional organizations, and systems of certification and licensing serve as means of occupational closure by limiting economic competition (Weeden 2002). Professional institutions establish exclusive jurisdictions for professional practice; on Andrew Abbott's (1988) account, "Jurisdiction is the defining relation in professional life" (3). Abbott's conception of jurisdiction emphasizes interprofessional relations and the content of work rather than economic relations and rents, but the ideas of a monopolized jurisdiction and monopolized market are fundamentally the same: Professions are organized means of making claims to exclusive competence.

The variations in the contemporary development of professionalism may result from one or more social processes. First, as a result of earlier historical developments, professionalization may become entrenched in some institutional fields but not others, and then vary directly in growth rates according to those earlier patterns as new occupational groups imitate established ones—*the entrenchment hypothesis* (Starr 2019). Conversely, in a field of competition already dominated by a powerful profession, new groups may consider it fruitless to compete on the same terms and try instead to blur the boundaries between jurisdictions and contest the criteria for expertise—*the counter-entrenchment hypothesis*.

Third, professionalization may vary because of the differential receptivity or resistance of organizations that employ expert labor. To the extent they are successful, professions introduce a constraint on organizations, limiting whom they can employ to do different kinds of tasks. Many organizations have accommodated themselves to professional jurisdictions. But in the fields that have emerged as central in the knowledge economy, flexibility and adaptability are highly prized, while licensed jurisdictions are anathema—*the organizational flexibility hypothesis*. In this respect, there is a tension between postindustrialism and professionalization that early theories of postindustrialism failed to anticipate.

Fourth, professionalization may vary because of political or ideological resistance to an expanded role for the state through the extension of licensing to new occupations. The past half century has seen not only a postindustrial shift in the structure of the economy, but also a neoliberal shift in many areas of public policy as governments have rolled back certain forms of economic regulation—*the neoliberal policy hypothesis.*

Finally, in a variant of the two preceding interpretations, the practitioners in some occupations may oppose state regulation, seeking to preserve flexibility for themselves as agents in the market. Instead of pursuing professionalization, they may have adopted an individualistic, entrepreneurial, market-oriented ideology and therefore be disinclined to invest in collective organization to restrict occupational entry—*the entrepreneurial ideology hypothesis.*

These hypotheses are not mutually exclusive; they describe social processes that may or may not take place simultaneously. To explore the sources of variation in professional institutions, I begin with a reconsideration of earlier theoretical perspectives and then turn to an analysis of the low professionalization of high-tech compared to the hyper-professionalization of healthcare. Finally, I return to the question of whether the sociology of professions is dispensable in view of Eyal's formulation of an alternative sociology of expertise.

TOWARD A THEORY OF NON-PROFESSIONALIZATION

One step toward clarity in thinking about the professions is to distinguish between professionalism as a status and as an institution (Freidson 1994, 15–16). As a status, professionalism is a basis of personal identity and social recognition, involving subjective orientations to work and cultural understandings of its meaning and value. In its institutional sense, professionalism is a way of organizing and controlling an occupation (Johnson 1972). Professional institutions constitute the professional community, and they regulate it by setting and enforcing technical and ethical standards and denying outsiders entry into the market. Professionalism in the status sense does not necessarily depend on professionalism in the institutional sense; members of an occupation may self-identify as professionals and be recognized as holding that status without the benefit of formal professional institutions.

In this chapter, I use the term *professionalization* exclusively in the institutional sense, referring to the development of occupational institutions that create boundaries between professionals and non-professionals. Although some sociologists once saw professionalization as a linear process with determinate stages, the use of the concept does not imply any such assumptions; under different conditions, professional institutions of various kinds may advance or retreat, gain in centrality or become marginalized. My interest here is precisely in those variations across institutional fields. To understand professionalization, in other words, we also need a theory of non-professionalization.

As the sociology of the professions took shape in the twentieth century, theories of professionalization fell into two broad traditions. In the functionalist view, the professions could be defined as self-regulating occupations with a service orienta-tion that apply systematic knowledge to problems related to central social values; the professions grew because they answered social needs. For Émile Durkheim (1957), pro-fessional communities answered the need for moral cohesion and stability. In a sim-ilar vein, Talcott Parsons saw the professions as embodying a "collectivity orientation," elevating the importance of "cognitive rationality," thereby promoting both morality and modernity. Parsons (1968) was not just talking about labor force statistics when he wrote that "the development and increasing strategic importance of the professions probably constitute the most important change that has occurred in the occupational system of modern societies." (536) The professions, as Parsons saw them, were not only functional for society as a whole but also for their individual clients: They brought ra-tional knowledge to bear on the problems clients faced and observed moral rules that protected clients from exploitation. Drawing on Parsons, Kenneth Arrow (1963) argued that professionalism in medicine was one of several institutional responses to infor-mation asymmetries that otherwise put patients at a disadvantage. These theories were warmly embraced in the professions themselves.

In polar opposite fashion, the critical alternative to the functionalist account has viewed professionalization as a collective project aimed at exploiting control of knowledge and markets (Larson 1979). To those working in this vein, professions are occupations that enjoy market power and high status by monopolizing valued knowledge. The monopoly view of professions has had a long lineage, going back to nineteenth-century opponents of monopoly power in all its forms. In economics, the monopoly perspective was particularly associated with advocates of the free market such as Milton Friedman, but in sociology in the 1970s, it came more from work on the left questioning contemporary forms of social inequality. Randall Collins's (1979) book *The Credential Society* offers a sophisticated Weberian account of this type. The develop-ment of the professions in America, Collins argued, was "only a new variant on the fa-miliar process of stratification through monopolization of opportunities" (131–132). As Collins saw it, the extension of schooling in the nineteenth and twentieth centuries did not reflect the practical vocational value of book learning but, rather, its usefulness to elites in monopolizing remunerative occupations. Professionalization is a form of status group closure. Collins saw that process as depending on cultural influences affecting the unity of occupational groups and on political struggles over the structure of education and enactment of licensing protection. For Collins, variations in political resources ulti-mately explain which occupations succeed in professionalization.

An additional strain of work has emphasized cultural changes in the nineteenth and twentieth centuries that elevated the authority of science, technical knowledge, and ra-tional organization, and thereby lent support to claims by professionalizing occupations (Bledstein 1976; Haskell 1977). That support was reflected, for example, in the enact-ment of licensing protections, investments in professional education, and reliance on professional judgment in judicial proceedings and regulatory agencies. The significance of changes in the cultural authority of science and the professions may be integrated into either of the two dominant traditions. In the functionalist tradition, the changes in cultural authority reflected the advance of knowledge and the demands of modernity. In the monopoly tradition, the rising cultural receptivity to claims based on scientific and technical knowledge provided a basis on which members of professionalizing occupations could win support for institutional recognition and occupational closure.

What about explanations for non-professionalization? Of course, one could argue—and some did—that many occupations were just in an earlier stage of development and would eventually achieve recognition as professions. Taking issue with that idea in his article, "The Professionalization of Everyone?" Harold Wilensky (1964) insisted on what he called a "traditional model of professionalism which emphasizes autonomous expertise and the service ideal" and argued that professionalism in this traditional sense would not spread far beyond the already-established professions. Would-be professions, according to Wilensky, faced two kinds of barriers: bureaucratic organizations, which threatened the service ideal even more than they threatened autonomy, and knowledge bases that were either too general or too specific to sustain an exclusive jurisdiction. Wilensky failed to explain, however, why bureaucracy would prove fatal to some occupational aspirations even though many professions coexist with bureaucracies. Nor did he specify what kind of knowledge met his Goldilocks criterion of being neither too general nor too specific, but just right for professionalization. Occupations' organizational relationships and knowledge bases may be related to non-professionalization, but Wilensky's account did not convincingly show the connections.

From the monopoly perspective, non-professionalization is chiefly a political story, involving the factors that affect the collective organization of members of an occupation, the role of the state, and sources of receptivity or resistance to monopolization. Collins (1979), for example, explained the "failure of the engineers" to establish a strong, unified profession in the United States on the basis of "conflicts among rival status groups within engineering . . . [that] have kept a strong occupational community from emerging to monopolize practice and control the routes to organizational power." (169) In Europe and America, engineering had diverse origins ranging from skilled manual labor (millwrights, stonemasons, clockmakers) to supervisors of large construction projects (military officers, government officials). In some societies, notably France, state-led efforts to upgrade education for engineering led to the emergence of an elite engineering profession; but in other societies, notably England, engineering remained divided between its manual-labor and managerial elements. The United States developed a pattern all its own. Although civil engineering became highly professionalized, the engineering fields associated with industrialization—mechanical, metallurgical, chemical, and electrical engineering—remained caught in an in-between position. The more management-oriented engineers, reflecting the interests of employers, resisted calls for lengthened engineering training and licensing protection (see Layton 1971).

To be sure, the non-professionalization of an occupation in one historical period does not guarantee that the pattern will persist indefinitely. In the United States, physicians in the early through mid-nineteenth century lost control of the market for medical services as licensing laws were repealed and proprietary medical schools and medical sects proliferated. But in the late nineteenth century and the early twentieth century, the profession became more unified and found more external support for upgrading and limiting medical education and strengthening licensing protection. Changes in the organization of healthcare enhanced professional unity; for example, having access to hospitals became crucial for professional practice, and elite physicians succeeded in making membership on a hospital staff conditional on membership in the local medical society. Moreover, the shift toward greater trust in scientific judgment in the late nineteenth century and the Progressive era boosted the cultural authority of physicians, enabling them to secure public support for licensing protection and a critical gatekeeping role in relation to hospital care, prescription drugs, and, later, insurance coverage—all of which contributed to their income and status (Starr [1983] 2017). In this account, cultural and political changes in society at large interact with specific institutional configurations to produce the conditions that allow members in an occupation to overcome collective action problems and secure regulatory protection.

Although the outcome of struggles over professionalization is never settled once and for all, there are, nonetheless, strong tendencies toward distinct patterns in different institutional fields. Constitutive choices in periods of institutional change often have durable effects. Professional and technical occupations exhibit varying levels of formal professionalization in part because of historically evolved norms in institutional fields that become the basis for isomorphic patterns of occupational group organization (DiMaggio and Powell 1983). The low level of professionalization in the high-tech sector compared to healthcare illustrates those patterns.

The Low Professionalization of High-Tech

No field better illustrates the phenomenon of isomorphic professionalism than healthcare. After physicians established the template and succeeded spectacularly at raising their status and income, other healthcare occupations sought to organize themselves along the same lines. The pattern became deeply entrenched. Medical work has changed drastically, but the professional paradigm has continually been extended. Other healthcare occupations mimic the structure of the medical profession; regulatory agencies then reinforce the pattern, which extends to specialties and subspecialties within occupations, each marking out its territory. With its pervasive scope-of-practice rules, healthcare has become a warren of exclusive jurisdictions.

But the high-tech sector and new media have been highly resistant to being carved up this way. As I noted at the outset, the "computer and mathematical"—or information-technology (IT)—occupations are characterized by extremely low levels of licensure. They also do not have standardized educational requirements, strong professional associations, or other occupationally based regulatory institutions, even though much of the work in those fields requires a high level of expertise and is accorded professional status. The same is true in new media, where there is also little standardized education, licensing, or any other form of occupational regulation.

Novelty is not the explanation for these patterns. As new technologies have emerged in healthcare, the occupations associated with them have followed the usual course of professionalization. Although groups have challenged physicians' monopoly of expertise, they have not changed the dominant mode of occupational development. The pattern fits the entrenchment hypothesis, not the counter-entrenchment hypothesis. The low professionalization of high-tech is also a case of institutional continuity: The occupations that have come together in the high-tech sector were not highly professionalized to begin with. Professionalization in engineering, as Collins argues, was kept in check by internal divisions and opposition by employers. The media field, including journalism and the arts, has also historically resisted the development of exclusive jurisdictions and limits on non-professional practice. In the case of media, the legal principles of free expression are incompatible with forms of occupational regulation that would bar the unlicensed from the market.

Postindustrialism would have had to generate new pressures toward professionalization to overcome the established patterns in these fields. Yet the pressures have gone in the opposite direction. The prevailing organization and ideological tendencies in high-tech have been incompatible with exclusive jurisdictions and protected markets for professional services.

The organizational forms that have flourished in the high-tech sector do not rely on specialized jurisdictions protected by state regulation. More flexible and collaborative forms of organization dominate. Instead of assigning employees to narrowly defined jobs, organizations often expect them to apply their skills across broad areas and to adapt to new demands. The problem facing companies "at the leading edge of production," according to Charles Heckscher (2007), is to "combine knowledge and skills flexibly around changing tasks" (1). To increase their flexibility, organizations often outsource work, develop strategic alliances, and make use of temporarily assembled project teams. In their efforts to foster peer production, postbureaucratic organizations are entirely compatible with professionalism as an orientation to work and a claim to status (Heckscher and Donnellon 1994). But the opposition to any scope-of-practice rules separates the postbureaucratic forms from the types of organization that match up with professionalism in an institutional sense.

Studies of contracting professionals reveal the conflict between postindustrial organizational forms and strong professional institutions. Professionals who work on contract, often as part of time-limited projects, have no choice but to be entrepreneurial and adaptable, continually investing in their own skills and developing their social networks. In their analysis of independent contractors in the high-tech industry, Stephen Barley and Gideon Kunda (2004) identify a distinctive type of "itinerant professionalism": contractors move from firm to firm, continually trying to anticipate which new technologies or products will be in high demand so as to be at the optimal point for getting paid at a premium rate. As part of the trade-off, as Debra Osnowitz (2010) puts it in another study of professional contractors, "Employers offer fewer promises and demand less adherence to formal rules. Individuals exercise greater latitude and decision making." (8)

While the shift to nonstandard forms of employment has put many workers in precarious economic circumstances, some professional workers seek out opportunities to be "free agents" in the market. In a study of the new media and fashion industries, Gina Neff, Elizabeth Wissinger, and Sharon Zukin (2005) describe a form of "entrepreneurial labor"—workers who are willing to accept increased risk and insecurity in the hope of getting "cool jobs" in "hot industries." They write: "The new economy's cutting edge—and its true social innovation—is the production of a new labor force that is more 'entrepreneurial' than previous generations of workers." (309) Even though only a few are lucky enough to work for start-ups that go public and give them stock options, many have relatively high earnings and, perhaps most important, identify with the entrepreneurial vision that dominates the field.

These studies are consistent with what I called earlier the organizational flexibility and entrepreneurial ideology hypotheses about low professionalization in high-tech. The rise of "entrepreneurial labor" also accords with the tech-industry leadership's widespread opposition to government regulation. But there is little to bear out the neoliberal policy hypothesis—that is, to indicate any specific effect on professional licensing and organization from the ideological movement to roll back the state. To be sure, some free-market economists have updated long-standing arguments against professional licensing; for example, Tyler Cowen and Alex Taborrak (2015) claim that consumers' easy and cheap access to online information has so reduced information asymmetries as to make state regulation of the professions obsolete. But professional licensing has not, in fact, been rolled back. As mentioned earlier, the proportion of workers holding a license or certification has risen sharply over the past half century. Much of this growth reflects the expansion of healthcare and related fields where professional institutions were already established, even as professionalization remains weak in the new industries of the information economy.

These developments put non-professionalization in a different light from the way in which analysts of the professions used to conceptualize it. Sociologists, as well as economists, generally assumed that members of an occupation would seek occupational closure as a route to collective mobility. Wilensky set out a "natural history" of professionalization, which suggested a determinate set of stages. In this view, what prevented occupations from ascending through the stages were "barriers" to professionalization having to do with bureaucracy and the knowledge required to sustain a jurisdiction. In the more political analysis associated with the monopoly perspective, the barriers involve not only bureaucracy (employers) but also internal conflicts within occupations and the role of the state.

Several limitations of these approaches are now apparent. Members of occupations demanding high levels of expertise may not, in fact, seek occupational closure—they may have other ideas about advancing their interests or enhancing their status. Professionalism may matter in another way to workers in both technical and professional occupations. They may see professionalism as a measure of the value of their work, even when they have no interest in professionalism as a means of institutionally restricting entry into their fields. For technicians, as Stephen Barley, Beth Bechky, and Bonalyn Nelsen (2016) show in a synthesis of ethnographic accounts, "being professional is not a plea for status or power but rather an indicator of what they believe constitutes successful performance and an acceptable orientation to one's work." Professionalism, in this context, is about respect and dignity.

The potential for professionalization in the institutional sense may also be limited, not by bureaucracy, but by postbureaucratic organizations that break down professional jurisdictions. There is more than one way to organize expertise, and dividing it into fixed jurisdictions does not appear to be functionally superior to more flexible approaches. The functionalist perspective mistakenly assumed that professionalism had singular advantages for the organization of expert work. The monopoly perspective underestimated the potential for the emergence of competing ideologies of entrepreneurial labor and collaborative enterprise.

The entrenchment of alternative logics in different institutional fields provides a set of baseline expectations about professionalization. According to the entrenchment hypothesis, professionalism tends to grow where it has already been planted. Postindustrialism, in other words, has industrial (and even preindustrial) hangovers. But the entrenchment hypothesis cannot resolve the question of which logic will prevail in institutional fields where the professional and entrepreneurial (or other) models overlap and collide. Health informatics, for example, is an area that in principle belongs equally to the high-tech and healthcare fields, but its leaders have attempted to configure it after other "board-certified" occupations in healthcare. The explanation may be the large number of health informatics professionals who are employed by healthcare organizations that are accustomed to rewarding professional credentials and respecting professional jurisdictions. The emergence of new occupations that overlap institutional fields creates test cases for assessing the factors that affect which historical patterns conflict.

These questions about the scope of professionalization in the postindustrial economy return us to my original question about the field of sociology itself: Do we need a sociology of the professions at all?

Professionalism and Expertise as Sociological Frames

The growth of the high-tech and new-media industries without any accompanying professionalization is just one of several developments that may appear to suggest that a focus on professionalism is out of date. In a variety of areas, including healthcare, lay groups have become more assertive in contesting professional claims. Online platforms afford consumers alternative means of acquiring information instead of depending on professionals. Professionals may also become dispensable for some tasks as their work is automated and carried out through algorithms. Algorithmic decision-making may drastically reconfigure the jurisdictions that professions claim as their own. In these and other ways, mid-twentieth-century postindustrial theory failed to appreciate that technological innovation might be turned against professionalism, eroding the autonomy and authority of professionals.

So is it time to ditch the sociology of professions in favor of what Eyal (2013) refers to as a "more comprehensive and timely" sociology of expertise? Eyal makes this claim in connection with a fascinating case study in which he demonstrates the significance of lay expertise and influence in the adoption and diffusion of the diagnosis of autism and, consequently, the inadequacy of an analysis that is narrowly focused on professional jurisdiction. The case of autism resembles other instances in healthcare when popular movements and increased organization among people with shared health interests, often in conjunction with dissenting professionals, have disrupted the dominant medical monopoly on expertise (Brown 2004). Eyal (2013) is right that the social consequences of expertise are not the same as social consequences of experts, and that "experts and expertise are not reducible to one another" (899). But his approach does not address other important questions about occupational institutions in expert work and their relationship to markets, social inequality, and political power.

The professions' relationship to markets and social structure is every bit as important a question now as it was in the twentieth century. The "credential society" has not disappeared. What complicates any general analysis is that developments supporting professionalism and eroding it have been occurring at the same time. Although a postindustrial economy favors an increase in the organized professions in some fields, it obstructs professionalization in others. The historically evolved norms and structures in different institutions help to explain those variations, but a more complete explanation has to take into account organizational and ideological changes. We do not just need to understand professionalism in the areas where it is fully developed; we also need to understand the forces at work in areas where professional institutions have been stymied or undercut. In fields without institutionalized professionalism, many people nonetheless think of themselves as professionals and hold to standards and ideals they derive from the worldview of professionalism. As long as the institutions of professionalism and the status of professionalism continue to shape social life in significant ways, the sociology of professions will have plenty of work to do.

References

Abbott, Andrew. 1988. *The System of Professions*. Chicago: University of Chicago Press.

Arrow, Kenneth. 1963. "Uncertainty and the Welfare Economics of Medical Care." *American Economic Review* 53:942–973.

Barley, Stephen R., and Gideon Kunda. 2004. *Gurus, Hired Guns, and Warm Bodies: Itinerant Experts in a Knowledge Economy*. Princeton, NJ: Princeton University Press.

Barley, Stephen R., Beth A. Bechky, and Bonalyn J. Nelsen. 2016. "What Do Technicians Mean When They Talk about Professionalism? An Ethnography of Speaking." *Research in the Sociology of Organizations* 47:125–161.

Bell, Daniel. 1973. *The Coming of Post-industrial Society*. New York: Basic Books.

Bledstein, Burton J. 1976. *The Culture of Professionalism: The Middle Class and the Development of Higher Education in America*. New York: Norton.

Brown, Phil, Stephen Zavestoski, Sabrina McCormick, Brian Mayer, Rachel Morello-Frosch, Rebecca Gasior Altman. 2004. "Embodied Health Movements: New Approaches to Social Movements in Health." *Sociology of Health and Illness* 26:50–80.

Collins, Randall. 1979. *The Credential Society: An Historical Sociology of Education and Stratification*. New York: Academic Press.

Cowen, Tyler, and Alex Tabarrok. 2015. "The End of Asymmetric Information." Cato Unbound, April 6. http://www.cato-unbound.org/2015/04/06/alex-tabarrok-tyler-cowen/end-asymmetric-information.

DiMaggio, Paul J., and Walter Powell. 1983. "The Iron Cage Revisited: Institutional Isomorphism and Collective Rationality in Organizational Fields." *American Sociological Review* 48: 47–160.

Durkheim, Émile. 1957. *Professional Ethics and Civic Morals*. London: Routledge & Paul.

Eyal, Gil. 2013. "For a Sociology of Expertise: The Social Origins of the Autism Epidemic." *American Journal of Sociology* 118:863–907.

Freidson, Eliot. 1994. *Professionalism Reborn: Theory, Prophecy, and Policy*. Chicago: University of Chicago Press.

Haskell, Thomas L. 1977. *The Emergence of Professional Social Science: The American Social Science Association and the Nineteenth-Century Crisis of Authority*. Urbana: University of Illinois Press.

Heckscher, Charles. 2007. *The Collaborative Enterprise: Managing Speed and Complexity in Knowledge-Based Businesses*. New Haven, CT: Yale University Press.

Heckscher, Charles, and Anne Donnellon. 1994. *The Post-bureaucratic Organization: New Perspectives on Organizational Change*. Thousand Oaks, CA: SAGE Publications.

Johnson, Terence J. 1972. *Professions and Power*. London: Macmillan

Kleiner, Morris M., and Alan B. Krueger. 2013. "Analyzing the Extent and Influence of Occupational Licensing on the Labor Market." *Journal of Labor Economics* 31:S173–S202.

Larson, Magali Sarfatti. 1979. *The Rise of Professionalism*. Berkeley: University of California Press.

Layton, Edwin. 1971. *The Revolt of the Engineers*. Baltimore, MD: Johns Hopkins University Press.

Neff, Gina, Elizabeth Wissinger, and Sharon Zukin. 2005. "Entrepreneurial Labor among Cultural Producers: 'Cool' Jobs in 'Hot' Industries." *Social Semiotics* 15:307–334.

Osnowitz, Deborah. 2010. *Freelancing Professionals in the New Economy*. Ithaca, NY: Cornell University Press.

Parsons, Talcott. 1968. "Professions." 536-546 In *International Encyclopedia of the Social Sciences*, edited by David Sills. New York: Macmillan.

Starr, Paul. (1983) 2017. *The Social Transformation of American Medicine*. Updated ed. New York: Basic Books.

Starr, Paul. 2019. *Entrenchment: Wealth, Power, and the Constitution of Democratic Societies*. New Haven, CT: Yale University Press.

US Bureau of Labor Statistics. 2021. "53. Certification and licensing status of the employed by occupation, 2021 annual averages." https://www.bls.gov/cps/cpsaat53.htm.

Weeden, Kim A. 2002. "Why Do Some Occupations Pay More than Others? Social Closure and Earnings Inequality in the United States." *American Journal of Sociology* 108 (1): 55–101.

Wilensky, Harold L. 1964. "The Professionalization of Everyone?" *American Journal of Sociology* 70:137–158.

22

(IN)EXPERTISE AND THE PARADOX OF THERAPEUTIC GOVERNANCE

E. SUMMERSON CARR

IT was the summer of 2009, and I was in a mid-size, postindustrial, Midwestern American city, where I had been invited to gather with ten helping professionals.[1] Most of them were paying out-of-pocket for ongoing training in motivational interviewing (MI)—a behavioral intervention designed to "address the common problem of ambivalence about change" (Miller and Rollnick 2013, 29, 410). Introduced as a method to engage problem drinkers in the early 1980s, MI has spread dramatically across professional fields, including counseling psychology, child welfare, corrections, dentistry, nursing, nutrition and weight control, primary-care medicine, safe-water interventions, and social work, thanks to scores of published MI-specific books and several thousand research articles on the method, and a virtual army of devoted trainers. Across these varied domains, MI trainers promise their growing professional audiences something almost irresistible: a set of rhetorical techniques and sensibilities that, when properly combined in the motivational interview, impel ambivalent clients to "talk *themselves* into change" (159).

The helping professionals gathered in the room that summer day had discerned that, besides potentially helping their clients, MI would help advance their own careers, perhaps even catapult them into a more widely recognized expert status. Indeed, aside from wanting to deepen their skills in and knowledge of the increasingly popular method, about half of the trainees aspired to become MI trainers themselves, whether in their own agencies or as contractual entrepreneurs—like their local MI trainer, Norman. Norman had long since quit his job as a parole officer to travel the country and the world to train others in MI. This included criss-crossing the United States to conduct MI coding, traveling to Singapore to train doctors, and holding regular Skype coaching sessions with a psychologist in Bulgaria. The ever-affable, globetrotting Norman was living proof that if one were to devote themselves to the rigorous, extensive, and, indeed, ongoing MI training, one could escape the frustrations of direct-care work and become a full-time MI trainer.

Norman was also sign that there was nothing at odds about being "an old guy," who is "slow" and "apologizes for everything," as one trainee affectionately described him, and being a recognized expert in MI. At time of the training, knowing that Norman is a pioneer of developing MI in corrections and had authored books and papers on the topic, I was deeply puzzled by Norman's dramatic fumbling, near constant hedging, and regular acts of self-deprecation. Along with his trainees, I would eventually learn that the enactment of expertise in MI resembles its generic antithesis: displaying uncertainty, disavowing the authority and credentials bestowed by relevant institutions, and forecasting a readiness to take direction from the (lay)people—whether clients or trainees—whom one is ostensibly charged with directing.

I would also grow to understand that like expertise, (in)expertise requires continuous, sometimes dramatic enactment (Carr 2010). Throughout the day, Norman regularly questioned himself aloud, asking the trainees how he was doing or whether they needed something he hadn't managed to give them. When his PowerPoint slides included technical points, he readily attributed them to others, at one point even saying that he "didn't really understand it all." When I returned home to Chicago, I was greeted with a message from Norman reiterating his request that I send him my tapes of all the training and coaching sessions I had recorded, explaining, that he was "uncertain" about so many aspects of his practice and that "there's always so much to learn."[2]

As my fieldwork continued and I observed two dozen MI trainers and scores of trainees in action, I learned that (in)expertise is evident at the very "top" or—as MI proponents would surely prefer, the "center"—of the MI training community. Consider my observations of and interactions with Dr. William R. Miller—Professor Emeritus of Psychology and Psychiatry at the University of New Mexico; founder and lead developer of MI; coauthor of its foundational text, *Motivational Interviewing*;[3] and one of the world's most-cited social scientists according to the Institute for Scientific Information (ISI). At a university-sponsored lecture I attended, along with 240 others, Miller—sporting his signature bolo tie—casually leaned against the podium throughout his talk and fumbled with the remote for his PowerPoint presentation, almost as if he were at home, clicking through stations to find the local evening news. During the lecture, Miller fluidly shifted between explanations of information-packed slides displaying the latest findings from research on MI—which now boasts almost 2000 randomized controlled trials—and stories about the method's origins, beginning with his fledgling experience as an ill-prepared intern at a Midwestern VA hospital.

The next day, during an MI training session that Miller was conducting at the university, a highly educated audience of professionals eager to advance their MI skills and knowledge were satiated by the founder's signature (in)expertise. He greeted new trainees as soon-to-be old friends, his hands in his pockets, head cocked and nodding, eyes glistening as he listened intently to their questions and comments, all the while modeling his method.

141 PowerPoint slides and several application exercises later, Miller leaned back in his chair and whimsically broke into a folk song about the dangers of motorcycle riding, a topic that an apprentice had minutes earlier broached as topical fodder for a demonstrated (or "role-played") MI session. As the audience marveled at how effortlessly Miller eased the motorcycle rider into taking certain safety precautions, Miller pointed out several ways his modeled interview could be improved.

Miller not only refuses to accept the moniker "expert" himself, but also warns his professional audience against enacting expert hubris in their interactions with clients. In his writings, published interviews, and lectures, and in recorded discussions with me, he repeatedly suggests that motivational interviewing requires the professional relinquishing of a definitive knowledge base. He condemns the "diagnostic method" by which clinical knowledge is typically accrued, suggesting that "question-answer routines" are not just ineffective, failing to ascertain the complexities of behavioral change, but also unethical, further instantiating the authority of the party who directs the inquiry and decides what counts as knowledge. By contrast, Miller frames MI as a "collaborative conversation style" that is "simple, but not easy" to learn, necessitating ongoing specialized training, *and* a "way of being with people" that involves enacting the professional self as a receptive, nonjudgmental listener.

MI's foundational textbook, *Motivational Interviewing*, first published in 1992 and now in its third edition, underscores these points, asserting that the rejection of expertise is fundamental to the method. For instance, Miller and Rollnick (2013) write: "Many professionals during post-graduate education were taught and expected to come up with the right answer and provide it promptly. Willing suspension of this reflex to dispense expertise is a key element in the collaborative spirit of MI" (16). Expertise is also repeatedly framed as a "trap," ensnaring because its "most common effect is to edge [clients] into a passive role, which is inconsistent with the basic goals of motivational interviewing" (Miller and Rollnick 2002, 60). And in case readers somehow missed the prominent warnings scattered throughout the text (i.e., Miller and Rollnick 2013, 42, 136, 142), the book's glossary of MI-specific terms includes: "Expert Trap: The clinical error of assuming and communicating that the counselor has the best answers to the client's problems" (Miller and Rollnick 2013, 409). Instead, Miller and Rollnick (2002) insist, "within motivational interviewing, in a real sense it is the client who is expert" (60).

Such public projections and pronouncements of (in)expertise are striking. For while projections of uncertainty can be an effective way glean necessary knowledge from the patient or client in an expert interaction (see, esp., Bergmann 1992), the coproduction of knowledge is often retroactively black-boxed, allowing would-be experts to claim coproduced knowledge as their own (Eyal 2013; Latour 1988, 1999). But if MI differs from more familiar ways of constituting expertise, I argue here that the MI brand of (in)expertise not only has a precedent in other American clinical traditions, but also reveals deep tensions in American democratic governance.

Specifically, the "expert trap" is not simply a warning against a "clinical error," as the glossary entry defines it. It is a caution against *political error* as well. I will show how established cultural concerns about directiveness and authority render the expression of expert knowledge in the dyadic interaction between clinical professional and client—in a kind of scaled-down version of political authoritarianism—especially problematic. Instead, as we will see, MI proponents aspire to make the motivational interview a quintessentially democratic interaction, one that invites the participation of and recognizes the client as equal party, with equally valid knowledge, who feels free to choose and pursue her own ends.

Freedom, equality, participation, recognition, autonomy are powerful keywords in MI precisely because they are what Nancy Fraser (2003) calls "folk paradigms of justice"[4]— that is, powerful, influential ways in which social relations are imagined, understood, and evaluated *as* democratic relations. In the United States, these folk paradigms enjoy a diverse range of advocates, animators, and institutional hosts, who, in evoking their constituitive terms transform putatively apolitical arrangements into potential events of democratic expression and reflection. MI training turns these democratic paradigms into a disciplined set of professional practices that circumvents the public mistrust of authority, particularly, the authority of expertise. Repeatedly, MI presents itself almost as if it were a dyadic form of participatory democracy: a method that equalizes the interactional terms of engagement in a (once) hierarchical relationship, presenting itself as concertedly nondirective.[5]

However, these democratic aspirations are complicated by the fact that motivational interviewers are also *intent on directing* the client toward specific normative, professionally supported behavioral change goals—whether quitting smoking, sanitizing water,[6] losing weight, or taking prescribed medications—a seeming contradiction that often puzzles professionals when they are first learning the method. MI training involves translating these ostensibly contradictory aims—to recognize clients as equal participants and to direct them—into a recipe for professional action. In this sense, MI training enlightens a paradox with which American experts and American democrats alike have long grappled—that is, how to (non)authoritatively direct subjects who are recognized to be self-governing.

To be sure, MI proponents and practitioners are hardly alone in addressing the pressing questions: how to square the force of authoritative rhetoric with the demand that individual speech be free; how to exert influence without appearing to wield authority; and how to recognize others as equal actors and speakers without a demonstrably equitable redistribution of knowledge and power. By designing a method that soothes these long-standing tensions, MI also provides a chance to critically examine what it takes to act—at once—as an American expert and democrat, or what I gloss here as "the paradox of (in)expertise."

THE POLITICAL HISTORY OF (THERAPEUTIC) (IN)EXPERTISE

In the late summer of 2010, I made my first trip to Albuquerque to visit and record a series of conversations with the founder and lead developer of MI, William R. Miller. I was taking him up on an unprompted email invitation he had sent a year earlier, when I was just beginning to consider doing an ethnographic study of MI. Miller had heard about my still nascent interest in MI from a local trainer, with whom I had spoken just a few days before. Imagine my surprise when I received an email, with no subject line, from one of the world's most cited scientists:

> My friend told me that you may be interested in ethnographic study of how motivational interviewing is disseminating. If I can be helpful to you in this regard, feel free to contact me. When I wrote the original article in 1983 *I certainly had no idea* how it was going to flower (emphasis added).

By the time I came face to face with Miller—first in an office at University of New Mexico and then in his modest ranch home in an Albuquerque suburb—I was nine months into my study of a yearlong MI training conducted by one of Miller's former apprentices, whom I call "Ki." I had also spent over a year poring over the MI literature, including interviews others had conducted with Miller. Given this reading, I understood that "I had no idea" was not just a throwaway line in an email missive; it is, instead, a common refrain in Miller's framings of MI when he marvels at how far the method has come from its, and his, professional origins.

Miller began his postgraduate career counseling alcoholics in the early 1970s at Veterans Affairs (VA) hospital, a thousand-bed facility in Milwaukee that I visited one fall afternoon when I was first contemplating a study of MI. I had become fascinated with Miller's reformulations of mainstream American ideas about addiction, having just completed a book on the subject. Yet by his own account, when Miller first took the position at the VA hospital, he knew next to nothing about the field he would soon revolutionize. He once told a historian of addiction treatment, William White, who characterized Miller as "one of the most influential voices in the modern treatment of alcohol and other drug problems":

> [When] I went on internship to Milwaukee, I mainly just put on my Carl Rogers hat and with reflective listening essentially asked these people—mostly men—to teach me about their experience: "How did you get to this place in your life?" "What's been happening in your life?" and "Where are going from here?" I didn't have any therapeutic advice for them, so I just listened, and they seemed to appreciate that, to respond well. I learned an awful lot from these folk's own stories . . . I have always loved stories. And there was chemistry also. Then I began to read the literature and it said, "Alcoholics are liars and they have this immature personality that is so defended that you can never get through it. You've just got to hit them with a brick to get anywhere, and you can't trust them." It puzzled me, because those weren't the same people I'd been talking to. It didn't seem right.[7]

Here Miller explicitly disavows expertise, claiming that he "didn't have any therapeutic advice" for the men at the VA and therefore "just listened" to them—at least, after asking them a series of open questions. He portrays his approach as concertedly narrative and humanistic, circumventing attempts to diagnose problems or provide prescriptive advice. And in saying that he "learned an awful lot from these folk's own stories," Miller retrospectively positions his clients as knowledgeable subjects, if not experts in their own right, in an early iteration of what would become a mantra, repeated in MI texts and trainings alike: "We learn from our clients."

In characterizing his approach as a fledgling practitioner, Miller underscores that he *recognized* the men that so many others misrecognized. Confronted with the pathological characterizations of alcoholics that were indeed rife in addiction scholarship and practice at the time—that is, alcoholics are untrustworthy, immature liars and should be approached as such—the defiant young Miller (as animated by the older and wiser, if ever humble Miller) states his opposition to the authority of the literature: "Those weren't the same people I'd been talking to. It didn't seem right." Whereas clinical authorities caricatured "alcoholics" in a way that justified and perpetuated their lack of engagement with them, Miller enjoyed conversations with "people," finding them to be a source of learning. MI's founder makes clear that scientific and institutional authorities—or experts—had not fully recognized alcoholics as people from the start.

A strikingly similar focus on recognition was at the very center of Carl Rogers's highly influential mid-twentieth-century therapeutic program, which he had staked against behaviorist psychology, the tradition in which Miller was trained.[8] It is therefore particularly telling that (the young) Miller (as narrated by the older Miller) entered his first postgraduate clinical position wearing a "Carl Rogers hat." His wardrobe metaphor suggests that, despite his own behaviorist training, Miller appreciates that since the mid-twentieth century, many Americans have considered Rogerian therapy—otherwise known as "humanist" or "client-centered" therapy—virtually synonymous with ethically sound and politically progressive psychotherapeutic practice.[9]

Rogers based his therapeutic program on the premise that clients will "self-actualize" as long as professionals abstain from overtly evaluating and directing them—the excesses of expertise (e.g., Rogers 1946, 1951, 1961). "Unconditional positive regard" for those in the process of self-actualization, despite interim behavior that may be destructive or dysfunctional, became the centerpiece of Rogers's highly influential approach to psychotherapy. Its central technology was "reflective listening"—an ostensibly passive process of verbally echoing the client's statements, which effectively casts the client-centered therapist as supportive witness to the client who is so centered. Much as Miller would do a few decades later, Rogers cast diagnosis as profoundly antidemocratic, claiming that it simultaneously props up expert authority and fails to recognize its subject.

Developing his approach in postwar America, Rogers was originally interested in creating the therapeutic conditions that allowed clients to see themselves as free and to act accordingly. By the late fifties and early sixties, in line with growing antiauthoritarian sentiment, he sought opportunities to frame this project in overtly political, as well as clinical terms. For instance, on a public stage, in 1962, he boldly asserted:

Man has long felt himself to be a puppet in life, molded by world forces, by economic forces. He has been enslaved by persons, by institutions, and, more recently, by aspects of modern science. But he is firmly setting for a new declaration of independence. He is discarding the alibis of "unfreedom." He is choosing himself, endeavoring to become himself: not a puppet, not a slave, not a copy of some model, but his own unique self. I find myself very sympathetic to this trend because it is so deeply in line with the experience I have had working with clients in therapy (Kirschenbaum and Henderson, 1989, 83).

According to Rogers, "man" has been enslaved by persons, institutions, and modern science, uniformly cast as "alibis of unfreedom." Notably, the critique is scaled from the clinical to the political by way of recognizably democratic ideals. The neo-Hegelian—and by prominent extension, paradigmatically democratic—premise of Rogers's antidote is unmistakable: once clients' natural struggle to self-realize is recognized and regarded in a positive way, they can be set free. No longer "slaves" or "puppets," these purportedly "unique selves" emerge from the Rogerian therapeutic encounter psychically prepared to newly declare their independence as autonomous Americans.

This portrait of the therapeutic encounter as democracy writ small reappears in official framings of MI. Following Rogers, Miller repeatedly portrays MI as a method that equips professionals to recognize the individual clients they engage as equal and autonomous parties, just as he once recognized the men at the Milwaukee VA hospital. In the preface of the third edition of *Motivational Interviewing*, for instance, the authors write: "We continue to emphasize that MI involves a collaborative partnership with clients, a respectful evoking of their own motivation and wisdom, and a radical acceptance recognizing that ultimately whatever change happens is each person's own choice, an autonomy that cannot be taken away no matter how much one might wish to at times" (Miller and Rollnick 2013, viii).

In turn, thousands of American professionals—across a wide range of fields—have embraced MI as an exemplary means of recognizing and engaging otherwise overlooked clients as autonomous equals. Strikingly, MI's democratic discourse finds its way into such sites and situations as corrections and child welfare that are arguably especially poorly equipped to realize the aforementioned promises. This suggests that in MI, clients are recognized as experts to the extent that professional interviewers afford them unconditional positive regard and, more particularly, regard them as equal parties no matter their actual ability to freely participate or collaborate.

This was one of the many puzzles I had come to discuss with Miller, who later that evening, extended a more phenomenological account of recognition-by-MI into an explicit political framing of his method as antidote to totalitarianism, a point to which I return in the conclusion. The next section turns to what makes this framing all the more interesting and so indicative of deeper ideological tensions—that Miller's method is as *directive* as it is client-centered, integrating central elements of behavioral psychology that Rogers himself publicly attacked as profoundly antidemocratic.

COLD THERAPIES, MI REMEDIES

The opposition between Carl Rogers and B. F. Skinner loomed large for Americans who, like Miller, had trained in psychology in the 1960s, and the tensions that Miller sought to synthetize and overcome in developing MI were not simply disciplinary ones. In mid-twentieth-century America, political questions were commonly couched in psychological terms; many Americans viewed the Cold War as a battle between the safeguarding of freedom of thought and the active suppression of it (Cohen-Cole 2014). Skinner's radical behaviorism was widely associated with the latter tendency, and not just by the FBI, who assembled an ample file on the social scientist (see Wyatt 2000), but also by his scholarly colleagues, who, in an academy that equated interdisciplinary research with the enactment of "open minds," regarded Skinner's scholarly program as narrow and rigid (Cohen-Cole 2014, 124–125; see also Hull 2010, 258). Rogers was one of Skinner's most vociferous critics, staunchly opposed to Skinner's focus on the environmental correlates of human behavior, his attendant rejection of mentalist explanations, and his unapologetic insistence that therapeutic interventions should stimulate and reinforce ethical, socially adaptive behavior.

Although American historians argue that skepticism of experts reached new heights in the postwar period, the public's critique of expert authority was in fact quite selective. At the same time that readers were lapping up Dr. Benjamin Spock's now infamous child-rearing advice, they chafed at the *Ladies Home Journal* article in which Skinner described the "air crib" that he designed for his baby daughter.[10] Skinner's 1948 utopian novel *Walden Two*, in which he imagined a world where punishment had no place and positive reinforcement reigned, was met with similar reactions. By the time he published *Beyond Freedom and Dignity* in 1971, which summarized his scientific work and philosophy for a popular audience, some prominent critics cast Skinner's unapologetic behaviorism not just as antidemocratic, but as distinctly un-American as well (Nye 1992; Richelle 1993; Rutherford 2009). More particularly, Skinner's central thesis of *operant conditioning*, which he defined as the ongoing shaping of behavior relative to its environmental consequences (see, e.g., Skinner 1953, 65–67; 1971, 26), was translated by critics as "another word for Nazism" (M. Lancelot, quoted in Richelle 1993, 4) and publicly received as attack on the cherished ideal that American individuals are the authors of their own acts and that participation in public life is unmediated by external authorities.[11]

Indeed, a tellingly broad range of prominent political figures expressed outrage over Skinner's rejection of the ideal of the sovereign will and the free-thinking subject, as well as his interest in designing environments to stimulate and direct ethical, prosocial human behavior. For instance, within months of Noam Chomsky's (1971) scathing review of Skinner's work in the *New York Review of Books*, which compared a Skinnerian world to "a well-run [if punishment free] concentration camp" (22), the then vice president, Spiro Agnew (1972), issued a warning to the American public: "Skinner attacks the very precepts on which our society is based" and seeks to perform "radical surgery on the national psyche" (84)—a psyche that the Cold War American public all the more adamantly insisted should be recognized, not directed.[12] Skinner came face to face with one of his fiercest and most vociferous critics when he joined Carl Rogers in the first of two public debates in 1962. The debate was charged, in large part because neither man was shy in embracing the practical and political implications of their disciplinary concerns.[13] Claiming that his brand of therapeutic encounter hosted and even facilitated Americans who were ready to reassert their independence, Rogers—whose therapeutic approach was on the rise at the same time that criticism of Skinner's behaviorism was mounting—did nothing less than suggest that the very survival of American democracy was at stake in the choice between client-centered therapy and the behaviorism of his opponent. Take, for instance, this unsparing charge:

> Here are some of the words and concepts that I have used which are almost totally without meaning in the behaviorist frame of reference: freedom is a term with no meaning; choice, in the sense I have used it, has no meaning . . . . Purpose, self-direction, value or value choice—none of these has any meaning; personal responsibility as a concept has no meaning (quoted in Kirschenbaum and Henderson 1989: 86).

In his appeal the university audience, Rogers underscored that clinical direction *is* political direction, and that behaviorism is totalitarianism, if on a smaller scale. Homing in on Skinner's foundational premise that "man . . . [is] the product of past elements and forces and the determined cause of future events and behaviors" (Kirschenbaum and Henderson 1989, 85)—a notion Rogers associated with Freud as much as with Skinner— a highly animated Rogers went on to offer a familiar formula positing that the realization of participatory democratic ideals hinges on the self-actualization of the individual, unfettered by external control. As he put it:

> In summary, to the extent that the behaviorist point of view in psychology is leading us toward a disregard of the person . . . toward the control of the person by shaping his behavior without his participant choice, or toward minimizing the significance of the subjective . . . I question it very deeply. My experience leads me to say that such a point of view is going against one of the strongest undercurrents in modern life, and is taking us down a pathway with destructive consequences. (quoted in Kirschenbaum and Henderson 1989, 86).

Throughout the debate, Rogers repeatedly returned to the idea that "minimizing the significance of the subjective" is as much of an anathema in politics as it is in psychotherapy. Rogers's therapeutic program, after all, depended on the idea that people should be authors of their own acts, and that their behavior is traceable to sources within themselves. Therefore, to offer explicit expert direction is to interfere with the process of self-actualization and, by extension, to violate the principle of individual freedom. By contrast, for Skinner and those he inspired, "the inner events which seem so important to us are not essential to action and probably do not, in any important case, precede action" (as quoted in Kirschenbaum and Henderson 1989, 101). Whereas Rogers (1946) insisted that therapists accept the "principle that the individual is basically responsible for himself" (416), for Skinner, the goal of interventions is precisely to direct, or positively "condition," people to act in responsible ways (see, e.g., Skinner, 1953, 382–383). Thus for Skinner, the pressing political question was not *whether* to direct people but how to do so in positive, productive, and nonpunitive ways.

At an especially critical juncture of the debate, the ever-genteel Skinner emphasized his conviction that no human intervention—whether directive or client centered—should have surreptitious elements. Skinner also subtly raised the question of what his opponent might be hiding, suggesting—as Rogers's own students did a few years later[14]—that even the most putatively unmediated "ways of being with people" have directive elements, whether the practitioner recognizes it or not. Indeed, transcripts of Rogers's psychotherapy sessions show the subtle ways in which he selectively reinforced some client statements, for instance, with verbal affirmations, but remained silent in the face of others (Traux, 1966; see also Smith 2005).

Given these germinal debates about psychological approaches and their political correlates, one can imagine why a young Miller donned a Rogerian hat rather than a Skinnerian lab coat upon entering an urban VA hospital, especially having just registered with his local draft board as a conscientious objector. Nevertheless, Miller's doctoral training in behavioral psychology has arguably been central to the formulation and development of motivational interviewing, if less prominent in MI's self-description than its Rogerian roots. Indeed, if Rogers (1980) reasonably concluded late in his career that the "basic difference between a behaviorist and a humanistic approach to human beings is a philosophical choice" (56), William R. Miller seized upon that very disjuncture as an opportunity for professional innovation.

In fact, in the very first book-length descriptions of the method, MI is presented as "client-centered" and "directive" at the same time (Miller and Rollnick 1992). Sixteen years later, Miller and another coauthor more colloquially referred to their method as "client-centered . . . with a twist" (Arkowitz and Miller 2008, 4)—"the twist" being that the motivational interviewer is always working *to direct* the client toward a specific behavioral-change goal, whether quitting smoking, sanitizing water, losing weight, or taking prescribed medications. MI training involves translating these ostensibly contradictory aims into a recipe for professional intervention.

Consider the article, "Eight Stages in Learning Motivational Interviewing" (Miller and Moyers, 2006), which is compulsory reading in almost all the MI training programs I've studied. In it, MI apprentices learn that their first task is to develop "an openness to collaboration with clients' own expertise" (3). A few paragraphs later, professionals are reminded that they are to be "consciously and strategically goal-directed" (7) and steer the client to some behavioral-change goal while keeping the initial charge in mind. Although these instructions may, understandably, befuddle outsiders and are a tall order for apprentices, Miller and the thousands of MI trainers maintain that the motivational interview is simultaneously a site where clients can freely express and direct themselves in accordance with their "own expertise" and an opportunity for professionals to "strategically goal-direct" clients to change what they say and do.

Though avowedly Rogerian, Miller and those who train others in the method he developed make it clear to their immediate interlocutors that MI is not primarily concerned with clients' self-actualization. The behaviorist in Miller sees people in terms of their acts rather than their essences. As he once put it to me, "My training was behavioral, and so it's natural for me to think in terms of what people do and not who they *are*." In particular, MI trainers refuse to allow their apprentices to explain clients' behavior by way of presumed internal states, and they concertedly resist intervention agendas that are not behaviorally targeted. In lieu of the mentalist explanations that Rogers favored, MI training refocuses professional attention on the environmental correlates of why clients act the way they do, with particular attention to the context of the interview itself. More specifically, and as we will see later, MI trainers provide guidelines for how to set up communicative events to produce speech from clients, speech that—significantly— is understood as behavior in its own right.

Indeed, nowhere is MI more saturated with behaviorism than in its working understanding of language. A careful read of MI's foundational text reveals the influence of psychologist Daryl Bem (1967, 1972), who is widely credited for applying Skinner's ideas about verbal behavior to self-perception theory, and who insisted that meaning is contained neither in an utterance nor in the person who emits that utterance but, rather, emerges in act of the utterance in the context of interaction (cf. Wright, 1987, 86).[15] From Bem, Miller and Rollnick derive their central thesis that *people believe what they hear themselves say*, which understands verbal expression as a kind of behavior in its own right that precipitates more behavior of other sorts. Since "generally what people say during counseling about the possibility of change is related to whether it will actually occur" (Miller and Rollnick 2002, 9), motivational interviews are designed to coproduce behavioral "change statements" that *shape* rather than *derive from* what the client thinks, believes, or feels. This is a far cry from Rogers (1947) who, deeply committed to a referentialist language ideology, once averred that the "[verbal] material from client centered interviews comes closer to being a 'pure' expression of attitude than has yet been achieved by other means" (358). For Rogers, the role of the therapist is to evoke and witness the self in speech rather than to shape that speech and self in any way.

Although Miller rarely misses an opportunity to publicly mark his indebtedness to Rogers, he tends to be less publicly forthcoming about MI's behaviorism. And while MI proponents occasionally use behaviorist terms in their writings, as in Miller's statement that "from an operant perspective, the MI counselor responds to client speech in a way that differentially reinforces change talk" (Miller and Moyers 2006, 7),[16] Miller more frequently translates his behaviorist take on verbal behavior in terms of American folk heroes. For instance, in popular writings, he and his coauthors cite Benjamin Franklin's use of the written word to produce rather than simply express a decision (Miller and Rollnick 2013; Miller and Rose 2015). In a training I observed, Miller explained MI's behaviorist understanding of verbal behavior by way of writer and *Prairie Home*

Companion host Garrison Keillor, who purportedly commented: "You do not know what you yourself think until you hear yourself say it." And if this figures audible speech as if no one is co-present, in MI, professionals pour much conversational labor into the production of such efficacious statements—not just as coparticipants but as "guides" of the interview. Indeed, as the avowedly Rogerian Miller once told an audience of professionals in an advanced MI training I observed, "You only know [MI is] working when you know what *your* direction is."

"An Interesting Dialogue": Rebinding the Paradox of (In)expertise

As we have seen, the directive and client-centered schools of American psychotherapy hold opposing ethical stances, clinical practices, and political programs stemming from starkly divergent epistemologies. Yet what outsiders and newcomers might see as contradictions in MI, Miller embraces as *paradox*: that which makes the method both unique and uniquely productive.

That said, the ties that bind paradox tend to loosen over the course of its social and institutional travels, requiring new glue (See Carr, in press). And so, as MI has spread into new fields and encountered new practitioners who are wedded to their own disciplines and institutionalized modes of practice, the method has had to find new ways of framing and forging connections across felt contradictions. As noted, MI is now increasingly used in fields like corrections, where clients are mandated to interact with professionals, raising serious practical challenges to MI's "client-centered" promise to "partner" and "collaborate" with clients, notwithstanding the intentions of individual practitioners. MI is also increasingly used as a "brief intervention," which sometimes consists of a single encounter, making it exceedingly difficult to afford full recognition of clients in practice. But even as some worry that MI is sacrificing its "client centeredness" in these relatively new fields of practice, others suggest that it is not nearly directive enough.

As MI has spread, it has also encountered stark differences in the institutional power and professional authority of its trainees. For instance, bald directiveness is generally acceptable, and even expected, from male doctors but tends to be more fraught for female social workers, meaning that MI entails differential risks for stratified practitioners. More generally, although some helping professionals are accorded expert status by their clients and the general public, others never have had the opportunity—let alone the inclination—to become ensnared in the "expert trap" (Miller and Rollnick 2013, 409). Yet such sociological exigencies were apparently not the primary reason for reaffirming MI's client-centered directiveness, one of the goals in releasing the third edition of *Motivational Interviewing* (which was being copy-edited at the time of my first visit). Instead, Miller framed the matter as an ethical one, with familiar demands coming from two opposing parties, each of whom had valid points that could nevertheless be reconciled. He and Rollnick, after all, had long devoted themselves to working the difference (see Carr, in press).

WRM: We had thought more and written more about the ethics of motivational interviewing in relation to questions that were coming up in workshops of, "Isn't this just manipulating people?" from one side, and from the other side, "Shouldn't you be doing something? You're just kind of sitting there." And so, we had both extremes of concern. To the very directive person this looks pretty slow.
ESC: Right.
WRM: Or, on the other hand, "Are you doing something to people without really being honest with them about what you're doing?" So . . .
ESC: Hmm.
WRM: So that continues to be an interesting dialogue.

Here, Miller frames the paradox as ethical rather than epistemological in nature, resolutely avoiding the temptation to take sides. Positioning himself between the behaviorists, who demand speedier solutions to pressing client problems, and those in the client-centered tradition concerned about expert authority and "manipulation," Miller insists on "an interesting dialogue."

Various attempts to do just that appear throughout the third edition of *Motivational Interviewing*. Some of this work had to do with finding new ways to poetically package the paradox of client-centered directiveness. Consider, for instance, the use of new metaphor of "guiding" to explain what the professional does during a motivational interview. As the Miller and Rollnick (2013) explain in the opening pages of the new edition, "It is possible to think about helping conversations as lying along a continuum. At one end is a directing style, in which the helper is providing information, instruction and advice . . . . At the opposite end of this continuum is a following style. . . . In the middle is the guiding style. MI lives in this middle ground between directing and following incorporating aspects of each" (4–5).

In this description MI is both a middle ground, which implies that other helping conversations are outlier extremes, and an amalgam that incorporates aspects of these oppositional styles. Extending the metaphor, Miller and Rollnick (2013) ask readers to imagine traveling abroad and hiring a guide. "It is not the guide's job to order you when to arrive, where to go, and what to see or do. Neither does a good guide simply follow you around wherever you happen to wander" (4–5). According to this rendering, the tour guide directs, not only because she knows a terrain, but because she intuits where those she is guiding want to go. In case readers remain unconvinced, the authors provide a list titled, "Some Verbs Associated with Each Communication Style," a reminder that to be an MI guide is, among other things, to "awaken . . . encourage . . . enlighten . . . inspire . . . kindle" (5).

Though Miller and Rollnick cast both *directing* and *following* as undesirable extremes, the former is far more unpalatable than the latter. To therapeutically direct is to "command . . . determine . . . govern . . . order . . . prescribe . . . preside" and even to "rule" (Miller and Rollnick, 2013, 5). But if this nomenclature is normatively offensive, directiveness is commonplace in many of the institutional settings in which MI is actually practiced, whether because clients are mandated or are thought to pose extreme threats to themselves or others, and/or professionals are working under performance quotas and time constraints, which demand the rapid production of behavioral change. In this light, we might understand that the directive elements of MI have been refined and euphemized over the method's life course. Note, for instance, how the changes of professional direction are differentially signaled in the subtitles of each edition of *Motivational Interviewing*, MI's foundational text:

Preparing People to Change Addictive Behaviors (1st ed., 1992)
Preparing People for Change (2nd ed., 2002)
Helping People Change (3rd ed., 2013)

Thus, in reading *Motivational Interviewing's* most recent packaging, a newcomer would reasonably conclude that professionals are trained to "help" rather than "prepare," to "guide" rather than "direct," and to hold authoritative prescriptions for behavior change at bay. And readers of the third edition text would find that the method is no longer "directive" but "directional," suggesting a softening of professional aims. These euphemisms suggest that MI proponents are highly attentive to a familiar pressure: that is, to assure their growing audience that they recognize the client, as a fully actualizable democratic subject free to speak and therefore choose her own ends without interference from expert authority.

The management of the competing demands on the method, and how they are interpreted by would-be practitioners, is not just a matter of packaging and repackaging. MI training centrally entails teaching professionals how to create the dialogical conditions for clients to (a) talk themselves into behavioral change, and (b) *feel that they have done so without professional prodding*. By design, MI clients work with relatively sparse understanding of the terms of engagement— not only or even primarily raising questions about the equitable distribution of knowledge and power in the motivational interview, but also about how *transparent* that distribution is. If the motivational interview is performed properly, it shrouds its directive elements, allowing practitioners to steer the conversation while appearing to simply respond to the client whom they have "centered." Ironically, projecting (in)expertise in this way requires ongoing rigorous practice.

For professionals who are new to MI, the most pressing question is not necessarily about directiveness per se; it is about the lack of transparency with which the MI practitioner directs clients (or as Miller himself put it, "Are you doing something to people without really being honest with them about what you're doing?") The next section explores this aspect of the "interesting dialogue" by examining an advanced training in which Miller and a co-trainer manage professionals' concerns that the method they are learning might not only direct but also manipulate, posing new challenges to MI's "both and" framing. And if this dialogue sounds familiar, it is because—far beyond the walls of an MI training room—Americans' efforts to persuade and direct others frequently must contend with the democratic ideal of autonomy and its actualization in "free" speech. One prominent way to hold these conflicting goals together is to be less than forthcoming about where one is going, putting at risk yet another democratic ideal: *transparency*. After all, transparency is also a "folk theory of justice," and as we will see, this is where MI's democratic aspirations meet their most profound challenges. The ways proponents and practitioners address them have broader implications for the constitution of American (in)expertise.

DIRECTION, DETECTION, AND EXPERT DEFLECTION

When Miller arrived on an ivy-covered, urban campus in the summer of 2014 to conduct an advanced training with his former apprentice Ki, MI had just celebrated its thirty-first birthday. Miller had received dozens of applications for the daylong training session, from which he selected seventy highly educated participants, including clinical researchers from the university, clinicians of various stripes, and social service providers from organizations all over the city.[17] These professionals had paid $250 apiece and relinquished a full workday to brush up on their MI knowledge and skills, and to do so in Miller's presence.

Unbeknownst to some of the university's training participants, Miller and Rollnick had just released that third edition of *Motivational Interviewing*, launching what is now known by insiders as *MI-3*. Most of the day was, accordingly, devoted to what was new in *MI-3*, which Miller framed as a response to the most recent research findings about the method's clinical efficacy, as well as to professional critiques and training impasses (as he had suggested in his interview with me).[18]

Early in the morning on the day of the training, Ki was working hard to make sure that participants' folders were in order, double checking the AV set-up, and periodically pausing to greet the arriving participants with his characteristic warmth. I had observed Ki train MI apprentices for nine months in another setting, and along with his warm greeting, I received his admission that training alongside Miller was especially nerve-wracking, a pinnacle moment of his career to date. Miller had also already settled in the training room, and in contrast, appeared completely relaxed; his crossed hands rested on one knee, and he had somehow managed to drape his slender frame on an notoriously uncomfortable institutional stacking chair, as if reclining. Then the training commenced with the chime of a replica Tibetan bell, which would be used throughout the day to mark transitions between the practice exercises and didactic presentations. Ki welcomed the group, who had picked up flavorless Danishes and bitter coffee, and were now seated at one of ten preset tables, turned toward the front of the room with what appeared to be great expectations.

As if demonstrating MI's readiness to, professionally and democratically, level the playing field for master and apprentice, Ki went first, introducing the definitional changes in the method's key terms with the help of an elaborate PowerPoint presentation. In describing the "evolution of MI from MI-2 to MI-3," Ki began—not surprisingly—with the evolution of MI's paradigm of recognition. He focused primarily on the "the new language of *partnership*, which is sort of the notion of the evolution of *collaboration*." Audience members, in line with the second edition (2002, 34), had long used the latter term to indicate their "client-centered" readiness to abdicate professional authority and recognize their clients as equally (in)expert. Yet, as Miller relayed and I had previously seen, MI trainees often found the call to collaborate with clients to be at odds with the directive nature of the method. In response, Ki glossed MI's *client-centered directiveness* in a new way:

> There really is a *shared* expertise when we are working with those we serve. Really recognizing that while I certainly have expertise to bring to bear, that ultimately the person or the people with whom I am working are *truly* the experts in their own experience, and acknowledging that not only further *engages* people in their process of change, but in fact can save a lot of time. If we find out what people already know, we can include that right up front in the process of change.

Here, we see that professional expertise is neither entirely negated nor framed as a "trap," but rather redistributed ("shared") with clients, whom the therapist has recognized and nominated as experts in their own right. This unusually bald reclamation of expertise may have been a response to the highly professionalized audience and the elite academic setting. Nevertheless, Ki's remarks are at once a marked contrast to the retrospective black-boxing of laypeople's contributions to the production of expertise (see Latour 1999; Eyal 2013) and an echo of the democratic ideals of participation, equality, and recognition found in Rogerian therapy.

One might also note that MI's client-centeredness has been framed in rather utilitarian terms. By stressing "partnership," the recognition of client expertise stays true to MI's humanism and at the same time responds to demands for efficient behavioral results. Recognizing a partner, Ki insists, can "save a lot of time." In this way, partnership *economizes* recognition, presenting it as a more efficient version of "collaboration," not only "doing something," as behaviorists insist on, but also (at least implicitly) saving time, labor, and money along the way.

Ki's account of efficient recognition appeared to satisfy his attentive audience, who raised no immediate questions or challenges. However, he as proceeded through the presentation, he soon encountered another familiar ideological threat. Ki's next task was to explain why *MI-3* had abandoned the term *directive*—which had coded the method's behaviorist elements for over thirty years—in favor of *directional*. The typically eloquent Ki stumbled as he tried to explain this terminological shift and its implications: "I will give this a try and then I may, so . . . so there is *direction* and there is *directing*, and there is *being directional* . . . and, versus *being directive.*" Flashing a self-deprecating smile as the audience began to giggle, Ki continued: "And [by] that I mean there, there was a time when being directive was a part of the MI definition. Right? It was a *directive* style. I think there is an effort to move a bit away from that because it can, there is, it's, it's not too far from being directive to, 'Here's what you need to do; here's what you are going to do.'"

Although he struggled to parse the updated terms, Ki's concern about the method's reception relative to its apparent directive/directional qualities was all too clear. Voicing the commands of a highly "directive" professional, he addresses how authoritarian the method might appear to others, including potential practitioners and clients.[19]

As if to acknowledge the risks, Ki warned the apprentices: "It has been said that MI is negative reinforcement." So, as he explained the new approach in *MI-3* to "being directional," he emphasized "that there is something *aspirational* potentially" in MI's brand of behaviorism. Evoking the image of the "guide," Ki added that when it comes to behavioral change: "We are moving away from something, and ideally, we are always moving toward something."

Despite Ki's efforts, there were questions from some puzzled members of the audience. Whether they were doctors encountering chronically overweight patients, psychologists dealing with functional alcoholics, or social workers struggling to engage self-harming teens, those gathered before Ki understood that clients seldom share professionals' behavioral goals and commitments from the start, significantly complicating attempts to serve as guide. A skeptical psychologist in the room raised such an example, referencing those who have been court-mandated to submit to treatment. She questioned Ki's reframing of "direction" as "aspiration," implying that there might be something disingenuous at play, a point that seemed to have traction judging from the half-dozen nodding heads around the room. At stake in this discussion was not only (or even primarily) the more-or-less directive nature of *MI-3*, but, as noted earlier, how transparent the method is about its direction/aspiration.

Before the now flustered Ki could respond at any length, Miller rose from his sideline repose to take center stage. Rather than sidestep the question of transparency, he shared a secret with the soon-to-be recaptivated audience, underscoring the need to keep it under wraps:

> I say sometimes about 80% of what we do comes right out of Carl Rogers . . . but having a direction in which to move in motivational interviewing, you need to know where you are trying to go, otherwise you are doing just client-centered counseling, which is fine. But MI is *directional.* "I want to get over *there, that* is where we are going."

It is significant that the pronouns Miller employs index the aspirations of the motivational interviewer rather than the client interviewee. Departing rather radically from

Ki's proposed "ideal" of client-provided direction, Miller's explanation underscores that direction is provided by the professional "I," who steers the interview. Significantly, Miller animates the professional "I" as having a conversation *with herself*, rather than with her client, about which way the intervention is headed. Placing the interviewer in the driver's seat, Miller reminded the apprentices that their vehicle is language, as he continued: "The way you get over there is with the evoking process of using *particular forms of language* . . . to have clients give you the motivations and reasons and ideas for change and movement and direction."

Here, Miller makes a striking pedagogical U-turn. In addition to assuming that the interviewer *evokes* the "motivations and reasons and ideas for change" from the client, as Ki had earlier implied when he said that client speech *is free*, Miller advised apprentices that they can "influence the amount of change talk that you are going to hear rather dramatically" through a highly conscious, strategic directing of the interview as a kind of conversation (see also Miller and Moyers, 2006).[20] Perhaps in a canny read of his diverse professional audience, Miller promptly stripped away any impression that his method—in practice—had become any less directive, whatever the change in terminology. In emphasizing the directive side of motivational interviewing over the client-centered side, Miller demonstrates yet another productive pleasure of paradox: in those moments when one can't have it both ways at once, there is always a well-established side in which to take temporary shelter.

With the central rhetorical principle of MI effectively underscored, Miller and Ki began preparing apprentices for their first practice exercise, providing a pithy reminder of the interview's constituent speech acts—open questions, reflections, affirmations, and summaries—all borrowed from client-centered therapy. Yet as Miller reminded his apprentices, motivational interviews only succeed to the extent that they make "*selective use of Rogerian tools to create direction*":

> Motivational interviewing gets directional [because] we ask particular questions and not others; there is guidance about which things to reflect. *Where* you ask for elaboration. There are particular guidelines [in MI] that I never ran across in client-centered counseling that are kind of *nudging* people in certain direction.

Implied in Miller's explanation is that the "certain" direction in which clients are "nudged" generally is toward the cultural and professional norms of healthy behavior, if not a more specific set of institutional mandates. In so suggesting, Miller had both answered and, arguably, set aside the audience member's earlier question about the ethics of explicit direction. For here, according to Miller, it is not that the content of professional directives is necessarily ethically misguided; nor is directing problematic in and of itself. It is, rather, that transparent attempts to persuade or direct are *practically* ineffective, because, as he warned the apprentices, "the truth is you can't tell somebody what to do." As his apprentices would continue to learn, effective MI practitioners are effective rhetoricians, who can influence or "nudge" people to do certain things as long as their efforts are under their clients' radar (See Carr, in press).[21]

This is not to say that this training, or the others that I studied, completely circumvented the ethical aspects of directing clients' behavior. Quite the contrary, the co-trainers spent significant time talking with apprentices about the kinds of situations when maintaining a neutral stance on behavioral change, such as a client's drunk driving or suicidal ideation, could be considered socially and professionally irresponsible, and other situations, such as divorcing a spouse or taking a new job, when direction could unnecessarily impinge on client autonomy. So even as Miller and Ki reminded the apprentices that "MI was developed to . . . strategically guide behavior in a particular direction," unsurprisingly, they offered no prescriptions across cases. Instead, they highlighted the idea of "equipoise"—defined as a "conscious clinical decision" about whether and when to remain neutral (see also Miller and Rollnick 2013, 232–237).

To be sure, motivational interviewers are trained to be highly conscious about their clinical decisions and rigorously reflexive about the ways they seek to realize them in their interviews (Carr, 2021). It is all the more striking, then, that their professional decisions and directions are designed to be opaque to client interviewees, who are "nudged" rather than baldly directed toward particular behavioral goals. Indeed, there is one glaring ethical quandary that was never explicitly raised by the co-trainers or their trainees: that is, what to make of the surreptitious quality of the motivational interview? For if MI proponents are dedicated to recognizing clients, whether as collaborators or as partners whose knowledge and expertise generally equals that of the professional, their intervention generates a radically *unequal* distribution of knowledge about the terms and dynamics of professional-client engagement.

MI proponents are sensitive to this critique and would certainly not like to read it here. In an article titled "Ten Things That MI Is Not," which is commonly cited and distributed at MI trainings, Miller and Rollnick (2009) are adamant that "MI is not a way of tricking people into doing things they don't want to do" (131). Of course, the *point* is not to trick the client. Rather, from the perspective of MI proponents, professional directions are disguised *in order to* generate the client's experience of being recognized as an equal coparticipant. More specifically, the motivational interview is designed so that clients actually articulate professional objectives and in turn hear *themselves* as experts and feel recognized as such (see Carr, in press).

In this way, MI simply enlightens a particularly stubborn problem with which American democrats have long grappled—that is, how to authoritatively direct subjects recognized to be self-governing and who feel they participate on their own terms. It also offers telling resolution by rhetorically masking rather than abolishing expert authority and disguising rather than avoiding professional direction, alerting us that expertise in democracies, more generally, may rely on subterfuge. Indeed, if some adherents see in MI a recipe for participatory democracy writ small, it may be precisely because, as Miller put it to that room full of captivated apprentices, "Motivational interviewing is a kind of nonauthoritarian way of trying to move in a particular direction where you [the professional] want to go."

***

As ideal types, American expertise and American democracy have some rather profound differences, suggesting why the latter often appears to be the more attractive choice for framing one's practices. Expertise objectifies and specifies; democracy subjectifies, individuates, and accommodates difference.[22] Expertise discriminates by way of its own categories, deciding what qualifies as the kind of thing it can know from the start, before it sets about making further qualifications (Carr 2010). Democracy claims to be radically nondiscriminatory and able to accommodate anyone within its borders. Expertise unabashedly divides expert and layperson, claiming ownership over some domain of knowledge and the responsibility to wield that knowledge wisely relative to those who do not share it. Democracy disavows meaningful difference between what (in)experts and their interlocutors know, as if unequally weighted ways of knowing, which are reinforced by any number of social institutions and ideologies, can simply be equalized in individuals' face-to-face encounters. It is for all of these reasons that Miller, his colleagues, and his apprentices choose to recognize clients as individuals and equal partners and to disavow rather than assert expertise.

Yet if, for all these reasons, democracy is a more appealing way to frame professional practice, we would do well to recognize that, whereas expertise tends to acknowledge its authority, democrats are inclined to deny and obscure it—rendering the enactment of democratic expertise something of a conundrum. In closing, and with this in mind, and, I want to circle back to Norman, the MI trainer we met at the beginning of the chapter. Norman's apprentices were collectively reflecting on the lessons of what is known as a "real play"—a common derivative of the role play, wherein apprentices present dilemmas from their own lives as practice—when the following exchange occurred:

INTERVIEWEE: And the thing is, is that when [the role-played interviewer was] goin'
    there, that was what really made me want to resist a lot.
TRAINER: You could kind of *feel* that direction.
INTERVIEWEE: Yeah. Like [the interviewer] was saying, when it comes down to it, I
    have to just suck it up, do it, and quit whining.
TRAINER: But in the end, she didn't say it to you.
INTERVIEWEE: No, she did *not* say it to me.
TRAINER: Right. In the end, *you* said it.
INTERVIEWEE: I did.
TRAINER: *That's* motivational interviewing.

As the trainer points out, even though the interviewer errs by allowing the interviewee to "feel the direction" at the outset of the practice interview, she recovers in the end, achieving her professional goals without ever betraying them as her own. In other words, the engagement can only falter to the extent that professional authority allows itself to be seen, opening itself up to an array of responses and interventions (shutting down, refusing to respond or participate, or—as I've described in other work—*flipping the script*). That, the trainer underscores, is *not* MI.

In beginning to decipher just what MI *is*—that is, a recognizably democratic, American mode of exchange, let us first recall Skinner's insistence that the *surreptitious* control of behavior is inherently problematic. Whereas Rogers insisted that the American client be free from expert direction, Skinner underscored that people should be able to *know and see* how they are being directed, not simply so that they can blindly comply, but so they can determine how to respond. In other words, transparency was the democratic ideal on which Skinner insisted. In both traditions, democratic principles are weighed and negotiated against each other, indexing the difficulties and establishing and projecting (in)expertise. As I've argued in this chapter, operationalizing the democratic paradigms of recognition, autonomy, and equality in MI means sacrificing transparency and rhetorically driving professional authority underground. For, as we have seen, "in the end" the professional goals "to suck it up, do it, and quit whining" are articulated by the interviewee as if they were her own, as if she were the expert, and as if the interviewer recognized her all along. As the MI trainer triumphantly declared in response to his apprentices post-real-play report: "*That's* motivational interviewing."

CONCLUSIONS: (IN)EXPERTISE AND THE AUTHORITY OF AMERICAN DEMOCRACY

When Miller returned from his kitchen, having apparently done some dinner menu planning with his wife, and immediately broached a new theory of MI's spread, it seemed to me as if the idea had just occurred to him. But as he went on to explain his theory—a patently political one—it became clear that it was one that he had considered before. Signaling to me to turn on my recorder, he offered:

WRM: I've wondered sometimes if there's something about the state of the culture where [MI] is a complementary idea whose time has come.
ESC: Hm, mm, hm.
WRM: I mean America's become a very polarized, binary, authoritarian place in a way. And [MI] is the— [it is] radically different from that. You know, radically different from trying to figure out who are the good guys and who are the bad guys and who's gonna make somebody else do what, you know. And it's not unique to this country, I mean. This is— but it may be that you know [MI] particularly takes in countries that have swung a little bit far in the expert authoritarian direction.
ESC: hm!
WRM: And it's kind of a complement that people recognize, say, "Yeah, there's another there's a different way to do this," you know, "than the way we're living."

At the time of our conversation, I couldn't help but wonder how a man who had lived through the height of the Cold War would pick 2010 as the year to make the claim that

MI had spread the way it has precisely because it is an antidote to that authoritarianism. Later in my research, I came to understand that the explicitly anti-expert stance is what renders MI—in the eyes of its proponents and practitioners—a quintessentially democratic practice, as well as an especially effective clinical one. Thus, by the time I was studying MI's official training for trainers in October of 2015, I was unsurprised by the sentiments of a sixty-something, White male New Zealander, who explained to me that MI is the only just way of intervening in indigenous communities, which he—as a public health specialist—had been doing for the bulk of his career. "We don't buy into that expertise rubbish," he said, "We see people for who they are."

  If it is true—as Miller told me—that the rise of American authoritarianism is contemporaneous with the spread of MI, it is also true that folk paradigms of democracy are culturally authoritative. For instance, the ideal of recognition as antidote or "salve" (Markell, 2003, 167) has grown so prominent that many scholars have productively worried about the fate of other ways of understanding and addressing contemporary democratic challenges. And although the genealogy of recognition-by-MI clearly leads back to Carl Rogers, it is no wonder that a method that embraces recognition so prominently in its self-description has spread so rapidly over the last thirty years that it almost appears to "flow" (Miller 2009, 890).

  The case of MI, in turn, suggests that democratic paradigms can function as modes of expert vision—that is, as interpretive frameworks that provide professionals a specific and, indeed, *authoritative* way of understanding and responding in some field of practice (see Goodwin, 1994).[23] At the same time, as MI also illustrates, expert vision can disavow its own authority, understanding itself as *(in)expertise*. As Miller continued to explain what he called the "sweep" of MI, he substantiated his theory by providing evidence that his method had been adopted with particular zeal in professional fields with particularly pronounced authoritarian tendencies. He specified that practitioners in addiction treatment, corrections, and healthcare—where "doctors have a long history of godlikeness"—were especially eager to disengage from the "expert trap" and did so by way of MI.

  Motivational interviewers—like other Americans who have been elected to lead—face a formidable paradox: how to direct people recognized as equally knowledgeable, self-determining subjects. Not surprisingly, when they first begin their training, MI apprentices idealize their newly recognized clients' speech as being *free*—that is, unfettered by the influence and authority of others, including their own expertise. Yet over the course of their training, they are taught how to subtly steer the interview so that professionally desirable, normative behavioral goals are articulated by clients as if those goals were always already clients' own.

  As Jamie Cohen-Cole (2014) has persuasively argued, a wide range of American experts have long faced public scrutiny and suspicion to the extent that they appear to challenge democratic ideals. My argument here is certainly not that expertise *essentially* challenges democracy, but rather than the enactment of American expertise involves certain challenges.[24] Furthermore, in a society that envisions people to be (properly) autonomous, self-knowing, and equal relative to others, expertise that takes the human subject as its object is especially risky business. Nicholas Rose (1998, 1999) has written about how American psychology, more specifically, has historically struggled to produce counseling styles consistent with the production of free, democratic subjects. And, indeed, many if not all psychotherapeutic interventions rely on the participation of reflexive knowledgeable subjects, which places even more critical scrutiny on questions of transparency, as well as autonomy.

That said, how MI explains itself, whether in textual representations or during in vivo training, reflects how it understands the ideological proclivities of its audience, including the widespread and long-standing distrust of, if continual reliance on, experts in the United States. Might it be, then, that (in)expertise is a form of democratic governance that far exceeds the motivational interview, even if it finds exquisite expression there?

NOTES

1. "Helping professional" is a term of art, which rather euphemistically refers to those—such as social workers, counseling psychologists, nurses, teachers, and dieticians—whose jobs are devoted, by definition, to "helping" others and typically involve a complex choreography of care and control. Although I have elaborated on this professional habitus elsewhere (Carr, 2021; in press), here it is pertinent to note that American helping professionals, including those with extensive training and graduate degrees, do not tend to enjoy the same status or expert authority as other professionals, such as lawyers or medical doctors.

2. This is also indicative of the vernacular pragmatism of MI, in which the possibility of definitive and generalizable conclusions is eschewed for the delight of knowing that there is always more to be learned from every interaction (see Carr, 2021). Although this aspect of MI certainly relevant to the cultivation of (in)expertise, I focus here on questions of clinical and democratic governance.

3. *Motivational Interviewing* is undoubtedly the most influential of Dr. Miller's massive body of written work. Coauthored with UK-based clinical psychologist Stephen Rollnick, the book is written for a broad, nonspecialist, professional audience. In more than twenty-eight chapters, the authors lay out MI-specific principles of practice and the accompanying terminology, avoiding theoretical propositions about psychology or pathology that may inhibit the method's spread. To date, its three editions have been translated into over twenty languages. Since its publication in January 2013, and as of this writing, the third edition alone has been cited 26,761 times.

4. Fraser (2003) writes: "Folk paradigms of justice do not express the perspective of any determinate set of social subjects. Nor do they belong exclusively to any one societal domain. Rather they are transpersonal normative discourses that are widely diffused throughout democratic societies, permeating not only political public spheres, but also workplaces, households, and civil-society associations. Thus, they constitute a moral grammar that social actors can (and do) draw on in any sphere to evaluate social arrangements" (208).

5. In this sense, *recognition* appears to be the antidote to expertise. Unlike expertise, which specifies, authorizes, and erects institutional boundaries, recognition provides MI with a way to scale across institutional and professional borders, particularly in a time when the politics of recognition have taken on renewed charge. The disavowal of expertise in MI,

then, signals the *recognition of* others as equally knowing subjects, vivifying a key principle of American democracy.

6. One of the most frequently cited examples of MI's international and interdisciplinary reach is Angelica Thevos et al (2002) MI intervention research with Zambian public-health workers, who were trained to use MI in their efforts to get villagers to sanitize their drinking water.

7. The full interview is posted on Miller's website, http://casaa.unm.edu/AddictionInterv iew/. For an excerpt, see Miller (2009), "Conversation with William R. Miller," *Addiction* 104 (6): 883–893. No individual is identified as the interviewer.

8. Miller's emphasis on the recognition of clients *as people* also resonates with the mid-century work of Franz Fanon (1952), who famously explored the wounded self-perception of colo-nial subjects, whose very humanity was left unrecognized by White colonizers—a theme picked up by Charles Taylor's defense of recognition decades later. Yet while many scholars periodize recognition relative to identitarian social movements (e.g., Taylor 1994; Young 1990; cf. Honneth 2003, 122–124) or the rise of the multicultural state (e.g., Povinelli 1998, 2002), very few recognize Rogers's, therapeutic approach in genealogies of recognition.

9. To be sure, the third-wave behavioral therapies have enjoyed tremendous economic suc-cess, having been widely institutionalized and trained in, though notably, they do much to restore the willful interiority—"cognitively" or otherwise—that radical behaviorists were criticized for largely evacuating. On this and other grounds, adherents and many clients of cognitive behavioral therapy (CBT), for instance, would argue that it is ethically preferable to Rogerian therapy.

10. The air crib was enclosed with three opaque sides and a glass front that allowed the baby visual stimulation but also provided light, temperature, and sound control. It was also equipped with a rotating linen-like plastic sheet; the crib also diminished the amount of laundry generated and therefore the maternal labor required (Nye 1992). Although critics charged that the "baby box" (as the title of the *Ladies Home Journal* article dubbed it) was simply a larger version of the box Skinner had created for his pigeons (see Bjork 1997), the air crib was undoubtedly also controversial for drawing attention to existing conventions of infant control, implicitly questioning their efficacy, and easing maternal labor. See Skinner (1945). Skinner's use of the word "experiment" in the article drew especially vit-riolic commentary, because it suggested that he had turned his own daughter into an ob-ject of his expertise and even that human babies, like those of any other animal, could be positively "conditioned" given an ideal environment. Because the vaguely understood nature of Skinner's scientific program of behaviorism coalesced with the public focus on the externally uninhibited cultivation of open American minds, the explicitly directive na-ture of Skinner's child-rearing, labor-saving device was considered problematic, while Dr. Spock's pointers on child-rearing remained implicit and normatively acceptable.

11. As historian of psychology, Alexandra Rutherford (2006; 2009) adroitly explains, this criticism coexisted with the remarkable applications of Skinnerian ideas about beha-vior modification in many fields. And while third-wave behavioral therapies—like CBT or DBT—have enjoyed tremendous success, in part because of their relative efficiency and cost-effectiveness, they have been cleansed of the most politically problematic implications of Skinner's radicalism, most centrally, his displacement of an internal will as the motor of human action (i.e., autonomy).

12. Rutherford (2006) notes that Agnew's speech was originally delivered at the Farm Bureau of Chicago and later reprinted in *Psychology* Today. See Agnew (1972).

13. Both Rogers and Skinner ran active research labs and did not hesitate to generalize their findings to actual practice (see Kirschenbaum and Henderson 1989). Skinner—unlike Rogers—was not a practicing psychotherapist; he nevertheless was keenly interested in the practical implications of his theory of behavior, especially in the field of education. As with the psychotherapist in therapy, Skinner argued, the teacher's job is "to implant or shape behavior—to build it up and strengthen it, rather than to find it already in the student and draw it out [as Rogers claims]" (quoted in Kirschenbaum and Henderson 1989, 118).

14. Using transcripts of Rogers's sessions, Traux (1966) and Traux and Carkhuff (1967) examined the "directive" elements of their former teacher's work. William Miller, with the apparent aim of supporting his own melding of client-centered and directive approaches (see the next section, "'An Interesting Dialogue': Rebinding the Paradox of (In)expertise"), frequently cites this research, and underscored in my interviews with him that "Rogers was not happy with that finding."

15. Chomsky's disgust with Skinner was likely spawned in large part by their competing theories of language, and well before his attempt to take down Skinner's *Beyond Freedom and Dignity*, Chomsky (1959) wrote a scathing review of the behaviorist's 1957 book, *Verbal Behavior*. After all, Skinner's refusal to accept mentalist explanations of language not only challenged Chomsky's cognitivist theory of universal grammar, but also the portrait of the (political) subject on which that theory relied.

16. Despite this distinctly behaviorist approach, MI proponents maintain that the direction of client speech, and, by extension, client behavior, does not prevent the very same professional from recognizing and centering the client as "the expert" (Miller and Rollnick 2002, 60). Indeed, in the same article on the "differential reinforcement" of change talk, Miller and Moyers (2006) refer to the motivational interview as a process of "evoking [clients'] own intrinsic motivations for change" (7). In so saying, they appear to muddy both terms in the method's very moniker, as if *motivation* and *interviewing* can be understood—at one and the same time—from behaviorist and Rogerian perspectives.

17. Of the seventy participants in the university training, almost 67% had earned master's degrees, and 22% held PhDs, PsyDs, or MDs.

18. Regardless of the impetus, it is clear that developments in the already popular method, once branded as such, are economically lucrative for authors, publishers, and trainers of MI. After all, each new edition of *Motivational Interviewing* means new definitions, mnemonic devices, and practical understandings that those already familiar with the previous edition will need to learn; the second edition, which now stands in the implicit shadow of its successor, is considered less effective, if not entirely outmoded.

19. Accordingly, *MI-3* has developed different definitions of itself for different audiences, using a particularly client-centered framing of the method for "laypeople": "Motivational interviewing is a collaborative conversation style for strengthening a person's own motivation and commitment to change" (Miller and Rollnick 2013, 29).

20. Miller may well have provided an explanation that contradicted Ki's no matter what the latter man said—a performance of paradox that is not unusual in co-led MI trainings and coauthored texts.

21. Consider the oddly parallel "nudge" of Thaler and Sunstein's (2009) "libertarian paternalism"—another paradoxical formulation—where the goal is to influence and restrict choice while respecting the freedom to choose. This suggests that MI is simply one version of a much broader strategy of expertise, which has thriving contemporaries as well as long-standing roots in American democratic thought.

22. It is for this reason, Cohen-Cole (2014) suggests, that Americans have so frequently associated expertise, not just with elitism, but with myopia as well.

23. As Charles Goodwin (1994) incisively notes, "Discursive practices are used by members of a profession to shape events in the domains subject to their professional scrutiny. The shaping process creates objects of knowledge that become the insignia of a profession's craft: The theories, artifacts, and bodies of expertise that distinguish it from other professions" (606). His analysis suggests that institutional contexts (such as courtrooms) and professional affiliations (such as "doctor" and "lawyer") do not automatically confer expert statuses onto their inhabitants, and it is only when we rigorously attend to real-time semiotic interaction—where struggles between law, science, magic, and medicine play out in improvisational and contingent, if always already conventionally controlled, ways—that we can also discern just what role institutions have in the organization, authorization, and enactment of expertise (see also Carr 2010; Silverstein 2004, 2006).

24. Arguably, some experts play the especially important roles of "checking and balancing" in democracy (see Collins et al., chapter 3, this volume).

References

Agnew, Spiro T. 1972. "Agnew's Blast at Behaviorism." *Psychology Today* pp. 4, 84, 87.

Arkowitz, Hal, and William R. Miller. 2008. "Learning, Applying, and Extending Motivational Interviewing." In *Motivational Interviewing in the Treatment of Psychological Problems*, edited by Hal Arkowitz, Henny A. Westra, William R. Miller, and Stephen Rollnick, 1–25. New York: Guilford Press.

Bem, Daryl J. 1967. "Self-Perception: An Alternative Interpretation of Cognitive Dissonance Phenomena." *Psychological Review* 74 (3): 183–200.

Bem, Daryl J. 1972. *Self-Perception Theory*. New York: Academic Press.

Bergmann, J. R. 1992. "Veiled Morality: Notes on Discretion in Psychiatry." *Talk at Work: Interaction in Institutional Settings*, edited by Paul Drew and John Heritage, 137–162. Cambridge UK: Cambridge University Press.

Bjork, Daniel W. 1997. *B. F. Skinner: A Life*. Washington, DC: American Psychological Association.

Carr, E. Summerson. 2010. "Enactments of Expertise." *Annual Review of Anthropology* 39:17–32.

Carr, E. Summerson. 2021. "Learning How Not to Know: Pragmatism, (In)expertise, and the Training of American Helping Professionals." *American Anthropologist*. 123 (3): 526–538.

Carr, E. Summerson. In Press. *Working the Difference: Science, Spirit and the Spread of Motivational Interviewing*. Chicago: University of Chicago Press.

Chomsky, Noam. 1959. A Review of B. F. Skinner's *Verbal Behavior*. *Language* 35 (1): 26–58.

Chomsky, Noam. 1971. "The Case against B. F. Skinner." *New York Review of Books*, January 30: 18–24.

Cohen-Cole, Jamie. 2014. *The Open Mind: Cold War Politics and the Sciences of Human Nature*. Chicago: University of Chicago.

Eyal, Gil. 2013. "For a Sociology of Expertise: The Social Origins of the Autism Epidemic." *American Journal of Sociology* 118 (4): 863–907.

Fanon, Franz. 1952. *Black Skin, White Masks*. New York: Grove Press.

Fraser, Nancy, and Alex Honneth. 2003. *Redistribution or Recognition? A Philosophical Exchange*. Translated by Joel Golb, James Ingram, and Christiane Wilke. London: Verso Books.

Goodwin, Charles. 1994. "Professional Vision." *American Anthropologist* 96 (3): 606–633.

Honneth, Axel. 2003. "Redistribution as Recognition: A Response to Nancy Fraser." In *Redistribution or Recognition? A Philosophical Exchange*, by Nancy Fraser and Axel Honneth. Translated by Joel Golb, James Ingram, and Christiane Wilke. London: Verso Books. 110–160.

Hull, Matthew. 2010. "Democratic Technologies of Speech: From WWII America to Postcolonial Delhi." *Journal of Linguistic Anthropology* 20:257–282.

Kirschenbaum, Howard, and Valerie Land Henderson, eds. 1989. *Carl Rogers Dialogues: Conversations with Martin Buber, Paul Tillich, B. F. Skinner, Gregory Bateson, Michael Polanyi, Rollo May and Others*. Boston: Houghton, Mifflin.

Latour, Bruno. 1988. *Science in Action*. Cambridge, MA: Harvard University Press.

Latour, Bruno. 1999. *Pandora's Hope: Essays on the Reality of Science Studies*. Cambridge, MA: Harvard University Press.

Markell, Patchen. 2003. *Bound by Recognition*. Princeton, NJ: Princeton University Press.

Miller, William R. 2009, "Conversation with William R. Miller," *Addiction* 104 (6): 883–893.

Miller, William R., and Theresa B. Moyers. 2006. "Eight Stages in Learning Motivational Interviewing." *Journal of Teaching in the Addictions* 5 (1): 3–17.

Miller, William R., and Stephen Rollnick. 1992. *Motivational Interviewing: Preparing People to Change Addictive Behaviors*. New York: Guilford Press.

Miller, William R., and Stephen Rollnick. 2002. *Motivational Interviewing: Preparing People for Change*. 2nd ed. New York: Guilford Press.

Miller, William R., and Stephen Rollnick. 2009. "Ten Things That MI Is Not." *Behavioural and Cognitive Psychotherapy* 37 (2): 129–140.

Miller, William R., and Stephen Rollnick. 2013. *Motivational Interviewing: Helping People Change*. 3rd ed. New York: Guilford.

Miller, William R., and Gary Rose. 2015. "Motivational Interviewing and the Decisional Balance: Contrasting Responses to Client Ambivalence." *Behavioural and Cognitive Psychotherapy* 43 (2): 129–141.

Nye, Robert D. 1992. *The Legacy of B. F. Skinner*. New York: Thomas Brooks / Cole Publishing.

Povinelli, Elizabeth A. 1998. "The State of Shame: Australian Multiculturalism and the Crisis of Indigenous Citizenship." *Critical Inquiry* 24 (2): 575–610.

Povinelli, Elizabeth A. 2002. *The Cunning of Recognition: Indigenous Alterities and the Making of Australian Multiculturalism*. Durham, NC: Duke University Press.

Richelle, Marc N. 1993. *B. F. Skinner: A Reappraisal*. Hillsdale, NJ: Erlbaum.

Rogers, Carl. 1946. "Significant Aspects of Client-Centered Therapy." *American Psychologist* 1: 415–422.

Rogers, Carl. 1947. "Some Observations on the Organization of Personality." *American Psychologist* 2: 358–368.

Rogers, Carl. 1951. *Client-Centered Therapy: Its Current Practice, Implications, and Theory*. London: Constable.

Rogers, Carl. 1961. *On Becoming a Person: A Therapist's View of Psychotherapy*. London: Constable.

Rogers, Carl. 1980. *A Way of Being*. New York: Houghton Mifflin Company.

Rose, Nikolas. 1998. *Inventing Our Selves: Psychology, Power, and Personhood*. New York: Cambridge University Press.

Rose, Nikolas. 1999. *Governing the Soul*. New York: Free Association Books.

Rutherford, Alexandra. 2006. "The Social Control of Behavior Control: Behavior Modification, Individual Rights, and Research Ethics in America, 1971–1979." *Journal of the History of the Behavioral Sciences* 42 (3): 203–220.

Rutherford, Alexandra. 2009. *Beyond the Box: B. F. Skinner's Technology of Behaviour from the Laboratory to Life, 1950s–1970s*. Toronto: University of Toronto Press.

Silverstein, Michael. 2004. "'Cultural' Concepts and the Language-Culture Nexus." *Current Anthropology* 45 (5): 621–652.

Silverstein, Michael. 2006. "Old Wine, New Ethnographic Lexicography." *Annual Review of Anthropology* 35:481–496.

Skinner, B. F. 1945. "Baby in a Box—Introduction to the mechanical Baby Tender." *Ladies Home Journal*, 62, 30–31, 135–136, 138.

Skinner, B. F. 1953. *Science and Human Behavior*. New York: MacMillan.

Skinner, B. F. 1971. *Beyond Freedom and Dignity*. New York: A. A. Knopf.

Smith, Benjamin. 2005. "Ideologies of the Speaking Subject in the Psychotherapeutic Theory and Practice of Carl Rogers." *Journal of Linguistic Anthropology* 15 (20): 258–272.

Taylor, Charles. 1994. "The Politics of Recognition." In *Multiculturalism: Examining the Politics of Recognition*, edited by Amy Gutmann. Princeton, NJ: Princeton University Press, 25–73.

Thaler, Richard H., and Sunstein, Cass R. 2009. *Nudge: Improving Decisions about Health, Wealth, and Happiness*. London: Penguin Books.

Thevos, Angelica K., Sonja J. Olsen, Josefa M. Rangel, Fred A. Kaona, Mathias Tembo, and Robert E. Quick. 2002. "Social Marketing and Motivational Interviewing as Community Interventions for Safe Water Behaviors: Follow-up Surveys in Zambia." *International Quarterly of Community Health Education* 21 (1): 51–65.

Traux, Charles B. 1966. "Reinforcement and Non-reinforcement in Rogerian Psychotherapy." *Journal of Abnormal Psychology* 71: 1–9.

Traux, Charles B., and Robert R. Carkhuff. 1967. *Toward Effective Counseling and Psychotherapy*. Chicago: Aldine.

Wyatt, W. Joseph. 2000. "Behavioral Science in the Crosshairs: The FBI File on B.F. Skinner." *Social and Behavioral Issues* 10: 101–109.

Wright, James. 1987. "B. F. Skinner: The Pragmatist Humanist." In *B.F. Skinner: Consensus and Controversy*, edited by Sohan Modgil and Celia Modgil, 85–92. New York: Routledge.

Young, Iris Marion. 1990. "The Ideal of Community and the Politics of Difference." In *Feminism/Postmodernism*, edited by Linda Nicholson, 300–323. New York: Routledge.

PART VII

NEW MEDIA AND
EXPERTISE

23

THE SOCIAL DISTRIBUTION OF THE PUBLIC RECOGNITION OF EXPERTISE

JAKOB ARNOLDI

INTRODUCTION

THE notion of a post-truth era has gained significant traction in recent years (Brown 2016; Hopkin and Rosamond 2018; Manjoo and Johnston 2008; Ylä-Anttila 2018), especially after political events such as the election of Donald Trump in the United States and Brexit in the United Kingdom. In both cases, political debates and media coverage seemingly abandoned many criteria (and ideals) of truth and truthfulness. Famously, one of the key Brexit campaigners, Michael Gove, stated that people in Britain had had enough of experts. Echoing this, former president Trump swept aside scientific reports about climate change, saying that he did not believe them. Similar issues have emerged in relation to issues such as vaccination, where stories about the health risks of vaccination are promulgated in social and even some mainstream media and sustained by various "facts" and forms of expertise. Quite obviously, the dynamics underlying the discussion of a post-truth era are related to expertise and the changing role of experts, both in public debate and government decision-making. The fact that very conflicting (if not alternative) expert accounts of politics, technology, climate, medicine, and so on, can exist in the public sphere arguably hints at a relativism in which very different types of knowledge have equal worth and equal standing—and at a fragmentation in which separate communities subscribe to different definitions of expertise and believe in the expertise of very different persons. That fragmentation seems related to a development in the news media and the public sphere in which news sources have multiplied and the political framing of news has become polarized (Newman et al. 2017), from Breitbart to BuzzFeed.

This chapter will to some extent embrace the notions of relativism and fragmentation implied in the discussions about a post-truth era. It will also take as its point of departure an attributionist or relativist definition of expertise. It will not, however, ultimately subscribe to relativist notions that truth has been abandoned, or to attributionist notions that expertise can be randomly assigned to any persons or any professions. Rather, it will argue that the attribution or recognition of expertise is currently undergoing changes that stem from transformations in the technological and institutional frameworks through which expertise is legitimized and recognized as such. Broadly speaking, these transformations happen because institutions that previously enjoyed monopoly positions in terms of respectively *having* and *publicly recognizing* expertise are being disrupted by political and technological changes. Key among these institutions are universities and the news media. Again, broadly speaking, universities once held close to a monopolistic position as expert "hubs," while the news media enjoyed a close to monopolist position in attributing public recognition to single individuals and professions as experts and expertise. Both of these monopolistic positions have been undermined by social and technological changes in, I suggest, a process that has had two discernable stages of development in the last fifty or so years. The first stage entailed two things: a social distribution of knowledge production into sectors such as think-tanks and knowledge-intensive private industries *and* the emergence of a new public concern with science and the negative side effects of technology (Gibbons et al. 1994; Leydesdorff and Etzkowitz 2001; Nowotny 2000a; Nowotny, Scott, and Gibbons 2001). The second, more recent, stage entails a disruption of news media (primarily due to social media) and, with it, the public sphere, whereby the news media lose their monopoly on news and information. With that change, expertise clearly becomes vulnerable to accusations of bias and alignment with various (vilified) groups, such as "elites." More importantly, the public recognition of expertise becomes fragmented, leading to more conflicting claims of expertise and more conflicting expert accounts.

The result of this development is a double loss of monopoly: the first is the universities' loss of their monopoly on the types of knowledge most often publicly recognized as expertise, and the second is the traditional news media's loss of its monopoly on publicly recognizing expertise. This double loss of monopoly will be described through the concept of "social distribution," which entails a social distribution *both* of knowledge production and the public recognition of knowledge as expertise. The chapter embraces relativism insofar as it assumes that definitions of expertise are historically contingent (Arnoldi 2007; MacLeod 2003); but it will also voice concern over the increasingly loose coupling of professional status and the recognition acquired from peers within small professional communities, on the one side, and the public recognition of being an expert on the other, which is a result of this development.

What an expert is; which kinds of persons are experts; what experts do; and not least, how many different types, roles, and functions of expertise exist are complex questions (Turner 2001). Because the chapter's main interest is the *legitimization* of knowledge as expertise, and not expertise per se, the chapter allows itself to sidestep discussions about the intrinsic nature of expertise. Instead, it simply defines public expertise as any type of professional knowledge or experience to which the public attributes value and legitimizes as expertise. The disadvantage of such a broad definition is that it risks conflating different kinds of persons, professions, and societal roles. It may conflate the roles played in public and the political discourse of, say, a natural scientist specializing in climate change and a person with a political background who is now working as a media pundit. What unites the different roles is that a certain degree of authority is attributed to the statements of both the scientist and the pundit in the public discourse because they possess professional knowledge that, in turn, is recognized and enjoys some degree of legitimacy. Because the chapter is concerned with the public recognition of expertise, it is preoccupied with the use of expertise in public domains, and primarily the public domain(s) created in and by various types of media. However, the demarcation between mediated public domains and other domains is purely analytical. One of the arguments in fact is that expertise is being legitimized—and thus, if not "created," then at least reaffirmed—through public discourse in media. The resulting reaffirmed expertise may then be used in other public domains, such as in court hearings or government testimony.

THE ARENAS IN WHICH PUBLIC EXPERTS APPEAR

Public discourse in news media is a highly complex and diverse phenomenon. Yet, what we broadly call news media (newspapers, magazines, radio, and TV broadcasts) produce news that despite its diversity also follows a set of standard formats, and is highly routinized, professionalized, and, indeed, institutionalized. Most news producers, for example, subscribe to some common criteria and standards of reporting, which include conventions regarding objectivity and the use of sources (Schudson 2000). For that reason, news is (or at least was historically) commonly separated into different formats so that commentary, debate, and opinion are kept clearly separate from traditional news reporting (Jacobs and Townsley 2011). The news stories themselves follow routinized narrative and discursive structures. Many new stories, for example, are presented in an "inverted pyramid" format (Vos 2002), where the core of the story is presented first, after which background, causes, implications, explanations, and underlying political conflicts may be presented.

Public experts may appear both in traditional news stories and in more opinion-based kinds of news typically found in the op-ed section. The former, traditional news stories, where journalists use experts as sources, has two variants. In the first, expert sources are often used to provide background in a news story, typically in the part of the news story that seeks to explain the causes or the likely consequences of a given event (Arnoldi 2003). For example, an economist may be used in the background part of a news story on a damaging hurricane, where the lead would be the catastrophic events as they have unfolded, but part of the story also concerns the long-term economic consequences of the disaster. In the second variant, expert sources feature because the news item itself is, or directly related to, science. For example, an economist might warn about the danger of an imminent recession, or a medical doctor might warn about health effects of vaping. The two variants are not different in kind; rather, they differ in the degree to which expert sources feature in the story. However, there are some qualitative differences that often, but not always, spring from that initial difference. In the first type of news story, in which experts are used to assess the causes or consequences—or otherwise provide context and perspective—the expert source often stands alone and is not contradicted or countered by any opposing views. This is in contrast to the way journalists normally cover political affairs, which typically report on conflicting views (although often with different emphasis or length). A news story of the second variant, that covers, say, a potential recession or health risk of vaping may in contrast quote multiple and disagreeing expert sources. But even in these cases, expert sources are rarely, if ever, interrogated critically by journalists in the way, say, politicians would be.

Public experts may also appear in the op-ed sections of newspapers or on commentary programs on radio and TV. Here, academics, think-tankers, and other professions possessing knowledge or experience that is recognized as valuable may make more subjective statements, in what has been aptly named the "space of opinion" (Jacobs and Townsley 2011). The role of public expert here is more complex. This is, first, because the space of opinion is also occupied by journalists and other media professions, and second, because it exhibits significant variety in terms of specific news formats, which may have different levels of authority and subjectivity. The statements of newspaper columnists may, for example, be less contested than statements made on commentary programs on TV, where more than one pundit may be in the studio.

The commentary types of news overlap to some degree with more objective forms of journalism and share some commonalities. Some public experts may appear as expert sources in objective news stories and as opinion-makers in commentaries. Economist and *New York Times* columnist Paul Krugman is one example. Both the use of expert sources in objective news and the volume of commentary in news media have increased dramatically since the 1970s (Alterman 1999; Arnoldi 2003, 2007; Jacobs and Townsley 2011). News stories have become more complex, providing more background and analysis of the individual news items, creating more space for expert sources. Moreover, topics such as health and technology's side effects receive much more coverage in today's news media than before. At the same time, as commentary-type news has increased in the last thirty to forty years, the commentary is increasingly (but far from exclusively) delivered by academics (Jacobs and Townsley 2011). Again using Paul Krugman as an example, one should see him as a combined example of both developments, where both expert sources and pundits and commentators have come to feature more prominently in news media discourse.

The notion of the public expert developed here extends to both expert sources and columnists or pundits. In both cases, the public expert attains a privileged illocutionary role (albeit of different types), and a certain social status or prestige comes with this.

And, public experts actually accumulate prestige and status through their appearances as public experts. One can, of course, object that there are simultaneous and continuous attempts to question or degrade these public experts by populist news media organs that question their legitimacy. Yet few news media do not use public experts, and the hostility toward public experts can and should be considered as much, if not more, a token of the competition over who gets to have this privileged role rather than a rejection of the role per se. That said, it should also be remembered that roles are subject to change. Indeed, the changes in news formats are intrinsically linked with some of the larger changes with which this chapter is concerned.

PUBLIC EXPERTISE AS SYMBOLIC CAPITAL

Not every type of professional knowledge, and not any kind of person, can become a public expert. There are informal yet institutionalized rules that, by and large, determine from which professions public experts are recruited. The role of public expert is therefore attributed to certain professions (for example, academics and scientists) with a high degree of regularity. Yet, while relatively stable, the roles and recruitment of public experts nevertheless shift historically (MacLeod 2003) in the way that any institutional order can change over time, especially in periods of technological, social, and economic change. Crucially, the role of the public expert is also subject to change because it is a privileged position for which different actors in different professions vie.

To better understand the dynamics underlying both the recognition of public experts and the changing dynamics of that role, we can draw on Pierre Bourdieu's relational praxeology (Bourdieu 1977, 1984, 1986, 1988, 1990), in combination with strands of new institutionalist theory (Powell and Dimaggio 1991). Bourdieu's work is particularly useful because publicly recognized expertise of the type discussed here can be defined as "symbolic capital," which Bourdieu defines as a generic type of capital that is recognized outside specific professional "fields." Fields, for their part, are relatively autonomous hierarchical social networks constituted by groups of actors vying for recognition by their peers (Bourdieu and Wacquant 1992). As such, fields can be equated with professions and the institutionalized roles and norms that are associated with, surround, and sustain them. Through Bourdieu's theoretical lens, an academic field, for example, exists as a subfield of a larger field of cultural production, and is itself divisible into several subfields, equal to academic disciplines, in which different actors compete for academic capital in the shape of academic titles, awards, publications, citations, etc. Attaining a dominant position in a field such as the academic field entails possessing *capital*, which can be noneconomic yet is, nevertheless, a resource, generated through labor and accumulated through investment (Bourdieu 1986). The various fields (economic, political, legal, academic, etc.) are themselves embedded in a (historically contingent) hierarchical structure (in Bourdieu's terminology, a *social space*), in which some fields are dominant, and others subordinate. Any capital held by an individual is field-specific, yet some form of exchange—with the "exchange rate" reflecting the hierarchical relationship between fields—constantly occurs.

Symbolic capital is in this regard, according to Bourdieu, a unique type of capital because it transcends specific fields (as does one other form of capital, namely, social capital). This means that, for example, an academic scholar can be recognized within the academic field and thus hold *academic capital* but also be recognized as an expert by the general public and thus hold *symbolic capital*. The degree to which that happens hinges, crucially, on the status of the academic field relative to other fields. Thus, the higher the position of the academic field in social space, the more likely it is that academic capital will be recognized as a form of symbolic capital by the general public. Or, put more simply, and in terms directly related to our topic: The higher the status of the academic profession, the higher the likelihood that an academic will be recognized as a (public) expert. Based on this short exegesis, we can now define *public expertise*, as it will be used in this chapter, as public recognition of a person's professional knowledge and/or authority that entails a privileged role or position in public discourse. That recognition is a function of *both* the professional achievements (capital) of a person and the status and legitimacy of the professional field to which the person belongs. This means in turn that people with high professional status (capital) within fields that occupy a (relatively) dominant position in social space are the most likely to be recognized as experts. Even so, cultural capital varies by individual; some people may hold high status in less-established (subordinate) fields; others have lower status in more dominant fields. In any case, it is when the capital is recognized outside the field that public expertise emerges. That emergence may have further recursive effects. Once symbolic capital has been generated (i.e., once someone is recognized as a public expert), this may itself produce more recognition. A public expert may thus gain legitimacy from the symbolic capital accumulated through continuing appearances as a public expert, as opposed to field-specific capital per se. And symbolic capital may help generate more field-specific capital, which is to say that being a publicly recognized expert may, at least to some extent and in some fields, boost one's position within a field. Counterexamples of this, however, also exist. Academics, for example, may risk losing position in their field if they appear too frequently, or in too many contexts, outside the field.

THE SOCIAL DISTRIBUTION OF THE ACADEMIC FIELD AND THE MEDIATED LEGITIMATION OF PUBLIC EXPERTISE

It has been argued that universities during the last thirty to forty years have lost a monopoly on knowledge production and with it a monopoly on expertise (Delanty 2001). This has happened as knowledge production increasingly takes place in what have been referred to as "Mode 2" organizations, such as think-tanks and knowledge-intensive private corporations (Nowotny et al. 2001; Nowotny, Scott, and Gibbons 2003). At the same time, the very status of scientific expertise has also changed somewhat. At least since the publication of Rachel Carson's book *Silent Spring* in 1962, both the general public and governments have been faced with doubts and concerns over unintended side effects of technological advancements. What has followed is a new politicization of science and expertise and a new degree of public scrutiny of science (Nowotny 2000b). Arguably, the growing concern about science and technology has to some degree deflated the myth of expertise. Although expertise still is sought after, it has become more questioned—and perhaps "secularized" in the sense that it is critically interrogated by a general public that no longer is in awe of, and no longer blindly submits to, the authority of expertise. That does not mean that expertise is less used or sought after; on the contrary, any uncertainty voiced has to be based on scientific knowledge (Arnoldi 2009, chap. 5; Yearly 2005). For that reason, scientific and academic knowledge is, if anything, more sought after, and more used. But that usage also means it is increasingly subject to critical interrogation. Therefore, we can summarize this discussion by saying that expertise has been *socially distributed*, both in the sense that production of research-based knowledge has dissipated to fields outside the academic field and in the sense that the general public is more concerned with, more exposed to, and more critical of scientific and academic knowledge (Nowotny 2000b).

As part of the social distribution of knowledge, traditional academia has arguably lost some status relative to other knowledge-producing professional fields. This development means that people from other professions are more likely to be endowed with symbolic capital and thus recognized as experts. Reflecting this development, new competitors to the established experts (university academics) have emerged in the public sphere, in that consultants, think-tank researchers, media pundits, and other professionals are increasingly testifying and commenting as experts in government hearings and used as expert sources in new stories (Medvetz 2012; Rich 2001). This is a strong indication of a shift in the hierarchical relationship between the academic field and other subfields of cultural production.

At the same time as the social distribution of knowledge has happened, the importance of the mass media has increased. Bourdieu notes in his analyses of the academic field that historically it has enjoyed a dominant position in the general field of cultural production. But, he suggests, this dominant position has eroded as new, more commercial forms of cultural production have gained status (Benson 1998; Bourdieu 1998). One particular element of this process is that the mass media have attained greater symbolic power simply because most people get information and knowledge from and through mass media and because much political discourse is "mediatized" (Blumler and Kavanagh 1999). That dominance also, at least in the development's early stages, resulted in greater power and status for the journalistic profession, or the journalistic field, in Bourdieu's terminology (Coenen-Huther 1998). Reflecting this increased symbolic power, it has been suggested that the mass media possess a kind of symbolic "meta-capital" in that mass media, and specifically the news media, are able to influence which types of capital are recognized in the public sphere (Couldry 2003).

The notion of symbolic meta-capital is obviously important to our argument. It extends to public expertise in that people used as expert sources (and the professions from which they are typically chosen) are bestowed with symbolic capital (as public experts) through media exposure (Arnoldi 2007). The media's ability to bestow symbolic capital is rooted and reflected in several things. First, the mass media, and particularly electronic media, have become increasingly important in framing and defining the everyday experiences and worldviews of the public (Schulz 1997; Thompson 1995). Second, professions within the media industry (and this includes journalists, at least in the process's earlier stages) have gained status and influence. Indeed, throughout the twentieth century, journalism as a profession has built up a strong professional ethos based on the idea of the "fourth estate" and the notion that journalists, as public watchdogs, uphold democracy and social justice (Alexander 2016; Ryfe 2012). This professional ethos is the premise for a powerful and coherent (meta)field; journalists must strive for professional recognition, the value of which ultimately hinges on rational myths manifested by the field's *doxa* and professional ethos. And that ethos has only been nourished by evidence that journalists have a real impact and can speak truth to power, something that was no doubt epitomized by the Watergate scandal and the subsequent resignation of President Nixon. Importantly, journalism as a field or profession had both external status and internal coherence. Internally, among news media professionals, there were clear professional status hierarchies, with the big broadsheets and, especially, the large national TV networks being at the apex.

The increased status of the field of journalism is also reflected in, and arguably also created by, developments in news discourse itself. Journalists' news reports, as mentioned above, changed over the course of the twentieth century from being mere factual accounts of events to include analyses, assessments, and reflections on events (Arnoldi 2003; Schudson 1982). This has not necessarily made news reporting more subjective, though. As Broersma (2013) noted, the "key to journalism's authority is that it successfully conveys that it has developed reporting techniques and discursive strategies to discover truth and mirror this in a comprehensible way to a general audience" (32). It is important to note that one of the ways journalists insert current factual events into a larger discursive framework of past causes and future effects is by quoting, or conveying statements by, experts. In such a discursive framework, the expert role is a privileged role because in the discursive structure of a news story, it stands largely unchallenged and is attributed with great weight (Arnoldi 2003).

Thus, we are dealing with the combination of a high-status profession (journalism) and an authoritative discursive style of mass communication, which legitimizes both the expert sources used in the news discourse as public expertise and itself as an authoritative account of the truth. Of course, the degree to which news discourse legitimizes expertise hinges on the type and subject of a given news story. In some news stories, scientific expertise is questioned in terms of the unintended consequences of a given technology. Articles of that type diminish the status and authority of some types of expertise and simultaneously create a new demand for (alternative) scientific expertise, simply be-cause the concerns need to be voiced, analyzed, and debated by actors with authoritative knowledge about the matters of concern. Expert knowledge has therefore come to play a more visible public role than ever before, which nonetheless brings greater scrutiny. And as mentioned above, this has happened at the same time as sophisticated know-ledge production increasingly happens in many more sectors, meaning that experts be-come more diverse (Rich 2001).

The critical interrogation of scientific expertise and the voicing of concerns about science and technology have happened primarily in a mediatized public sphere, with journalists acting as representatives of the general public. In that process, the recogni-tion by journalists of specific people and professions as holders of public expertise has not only reflected societal conceptions of what expertise is; it has also reproduced, sus-tained, and even changed these conceptions. That mass media have the power to define the world, including defining expertise, is a frequently made argument (Curran 2000; Dijk 1999; Luhmann 2000; Schulz 1997). One consequence of the media's increasing symbolic power has been a tendency among journalists themselves to emerge as, if not public experts per se, then at least as pundits. Journalism, as a profession, has changed from being exclusively about reporting to being about interpreting and reflecting crit-ically on the news. That journalists emerge as a category of expert, or at least pundit, is a reflection of the strengthened positions of the field of journalism vis-à-vis other (sub) fields within the field of cultural production. It is also a reflection of the (meta)sym-bolic capital of mass media. And it reflects a perhaps worrying tendency for public ex-pertise to become more self-referential. To gain media exposure as a public expert is to increase one's credentials *as a public expert*, which makes it easier to gain access to the mass media later, and to be recognized again as a public expert. Or, put differently, public expertise can increasingly legitimize itself so that the underlying field-specific cultural capital (such as scientific credentials) comes to matter less. This development is, by the way, furthered by a tendency among journalists to search for expert sources in news archives, meaning that previously cited experts are more likely to be selected again as expert sources.

WEB 2.0 AND THE SOCIAL DISTRIBUTION OF THE FIELD OF JOURNALISM

So far, the account given here has been one of a knowledge or information society in which expert knowledge has become more socially distributed and the mass media and, with them, the journalistic profession, have become more important. But the developments of the information society have continued into a more recent phase in which the trajectories, in terms of status and influence, of mass media, on the one hand, and the journalistic field, on the other, have bifurcated. With Web 2.0 (largely, a term used to describe online media that facilitate peer-to-peer communication), electronic media have entered into a new stage in which news increasingly is distributed online and news content is shared and even created in (online) peer networks and social media platforms (Mazali 2011; Shirky 2011). This has, of course, not made mass news media less important, but it has disrupted traditional news media—especially newspapers but also TV networks. And, clearly, it has had severe implications for the journalistic profession. However, the impact also extends to the public sphere and to the symbolic recognition and legitimization of expertise as described here.

The talk of a second stage of the information society, or of the implications of Web 2.0, should not mask the fact that some changes in the news media and the public sphere related to the public recognition of expertise began long before Web 2.0. Already in the 1980s, there was a fragmentation of the media landscape with the proliferation of radio and TV networks, and thus of news outlets (Gorman and Mclean 2003). In the United States, the Federal Communication Commission in 1987 abandoned the Fairness Doctrine, which until then had stipulated that news broadcasters should ensure some degree of political evenness in their reporting. The result of these developments has been an increasing political and informational fragmentation. That fragmentation has only continued in the new mediascapes dominated by Web 2.0. The social media peer-content provision has, somewhat paradoxically, created more homophily in that people—especially due to the filtering mechanisms of social media—tend to cluster with, and receive information from those with similar values and demographic profiles (Anspach and Carlson 2018; Dijk 1999).

The consequences of this development are many. Due to new online providers of news content, but also due to the content no longer being delivered only by professional journalists working for news outlets but also laypeople on Facebook, Twitter, etc., the traditional news outlets have lost their monopoly on news creation. This has had consequences for the journalistic profession.

> Big media . . . treated the news as a lecture. We told you what the news was . . . It was a world that bred complacency and arrogance on our part. Tomorrow's news reporting and production will be more of a conversation. The lines will blur between producers and consumers . . . The communication network itself will be a medium for everyone's voice, not just the few who can afford to buy multimillion-dollar printing presses, launch satellites, or win the government's permission to squat on the public's airwaves. (Gillmor 2004, quoted in Alexander 2016, 5)

The quote predicts, firstly, a change in both news style and content as the news becomes more peer-to-peer oriented. It also hints at a change in power relations, as the media lose their gatekeeper positions, and a lower status of journalism as a profession, or to adopt the theoretical vocabulary used in this chapter, at a diminishing position in social space for the journalistic field. Finally, but not least importantly, it illustrates how the traditional news media, along with the journalistic field, are also becoming socially distributed: Just as academia has lost its monopoly on knowledge production, so the traditional news media have lost their monopoly on news production.

For the field of journalism, the effects are severe, both in terms of people losing their jobs and in regard to the profession's ethos and self-image, as indicated by the growing number of pessimistic prophesies about the future of the profession (Broersma 2013). This pessimism corresponds with the public's perception of the news media, and thus with the profession of journalism, in that public trust in the media and the press has decreased in many Western countries (not least the United States) during the last twenty years (Daniller et al. 2017; Hanitzsch, Van Dalen, and Steindl 2018). Exactly what this is a reflection of is subject to some discussion (Daniller et al. 2017), but the downward trend is certainly another indicator of a diminishing professional status of journalists and the legitimacy and authority of (traditional) news accounts.

The Legitimization of Expertise in the Age of Web 2.0

The recent transformations in the news media strongly indicate that the mass media have become fragmented and that the field of journalism has lost status and perhaps even coherence. To grasp the consequences of this development, a helpful starting point is the proposition contained in the notion of social distribution: even though scientific knowledge and now also the news are created in many different sites, and not just by academia and the traditional news media, neither scientific knowledge nor news reporting are losing their importance. If anything, the opposite is true. However, the inevitable consequence seems to be a pluralization and fragmentation, which, insofar as public expertise is concerned, means that more types of knowledge, legitimized by more types of media, can form the basis for public expertise. But it is still not a random free-for-all. Special public expert status and legitimacy are still attributed to certain professions (and individuals), just as certain professions (and individuals) still play a decisive role in determining which professions should be accorded that status and legitimacy. However, with socially distributed public recognition, the recognition happens in more and other fora than just traditional news media, and more and other professions than journalists instigate the recognition. Who, then, are the new "public recognizers"? The most obvious place to look for them is on social media, which has spawned new types of public figures—for example, "influencers," an indication that the public recognition of expertise is still media borne. The difference now is that this recognition no longer happens solely or even predominantly within the field of journalism but much more broadly (i.e., in more socially distributed fashion) among social media content creators. The implication is that mass media still have symbolic metacapital. It is primarily the journalistic field that has lost position relative to other fields within the larger field of cultural production. The argument is not (at least, not in the first place) that individuals with high social media profiles are themselves acting as experts. Rather, they can help legitimize certain people as experts and certain knowledge as expertise. The anti-vax movement is a good example; it has sustained itself first and foremost via social media but also by having various celebrities and "influencers" act both as mouthpieces and as legitimizers of various kinds of (faux) public expertise.

The social distribution of public recognition has other implications. First, even though one may consider the criteria journalists use to select expert sources to be arbitrary or superficial, traditional news organs (and journalism as a profession) were nevertheless governed by a set of professional norms and conventions that were—though mostly informal—highly institutionalized: Journalists generally produced news adhering to specific news formats and news criteria, which among many other things entails norms about who can function as expert sources and how these sources can be used in news discourse. This, at least at the current stage of development, does seem to be the case for the new socially distributed forms of news production, where a lack of such criteria add to the pluralization and fragmentation. Second, the increasing self-reference of symbolic capital—in our case, the self-reference of the public recognition of (public) expertise—may well continue or even intensify. The ultimate form of this intensification will be social media providers and creators acting as pundits or experts, influencers providing knowledge about diet regimes and health, or making authoritative statements about, say, finance. This is, in fact, not far from already being reality, but watch out for the day when, say, a prominent YouTuber is employed as a media pundit by one of the larger TV networks. Once new kinds of media professionals gain entry into traditional media, the transformation has definitely occurred. Third, this chapter has used a rather fuzzy definition of public experts and public expertise, which can be seen in the conflation of, for example, media pundits with public experts. Yet despite its weaknesses, this fuzzy definition is arguably becoming more relevant as more kinds of media are legitimizing more kinds of (public) expertise. Fragmentation of the type described here simply makes absolute definitions of public expertise all the more difficult.

Conclusion

The information society is a one in which information abounds, but certainty is a precious commodity. In other words, there is an abundance of data but a shortage of wisdom (Nowotny et al. 2001, 12). The abundance of information and data is created precisely by the increasingly diverse (socially distributed) sites of *knowledge production* in the information society and now—the chapter has argued—increasingly the numerous and diverse sites of *legitimization of knowledge*. Maybe there is a great and tragic paradox embedded in this. The more there are different and conflicting types of knowledge, creating uncertainty about expertise, the greater the demand for authoritative syntheses provided by experts. This paradox is very much at the heart of modern technological society. The next question, then, is where, if at all, such authoritative syntheses are found and who is offering them in the public sphere?

The answer centers on the notion of the social distribution of the public recognition of expertise, something which has happened because of changes in the relations among professional fields in social space, which, in turn, are the result of technological and social changes, especially changes in communication technology. Particularly salient are changes in the mass media whereby the field of journalism has lost status due to the rise of new, peer-based forms of news creation. A potential problem that springs from the social distribution of the public recognition of expertise is that that it may not be those with the most valid expert knowledge who are promoted as public experts. This was already a problem that attended the legitimization of expertise through traditional news media. Already, the coupling between field-specific expertise (field-specific capital, in Bourdieu's terminology) and the general public's recognition of expertise (symbolic capital) was loose. This is both because journalists had (and have) people with different professional backgrounds available to them as potential expert sources (due to the social distribution of expertise), and because the journalists' choice of expert sources would (and can) hinge as much on journalistic criteria as on questions of relevance or validity. With the social distribution of the public recognition of expertise, the coupling becomes even looser. This is not least because the newer kinds of mediated recognition of public experts are less professionalized and institutionalized, and therefore also more diverse, if not entirely random. In other words, it may have been a problem that journalists would (and will) choose expert sources based on journalistic criteria and conventions, but at least they were guided by conventions. Now, the public recognition of expertise may not be based on any journalistic conventions at all. One implication of this is that the idea of an authoritative synthesis of the news, and of a united coherent public sphere, becomes incommensurable with our current reality. In the first stage of the information society, expertise was socially distributed in the sense that people from several different professional fields could be recognized as experts. Today, not only expertise but also the recognition of expertise is socially distributed, with new types of media, and not only professional journalists, instigating the recognition. This constitutes a second-order pluralization of public expertise.

Theorizing expertise in this way may lead to criticism, for being both too relativistic and too pessimistic and dismissive of the more open and democratic definitions of expertise that have emerged with social media. But though it may be relativistic, it seems undeniable that the definitions, roles, and functions of experts in political and public life have historically always changed and been subject to power struggles (MacLeod 2003). An essentialist approach to expertise—especially public expertise, where one is dealing with expertise outside specific professional realms—therefore seems futile. Although the tone of the chapter seems somewhat skeptical and pessimistic because it links social distribution with populist politics and celebrity endorsements of *faux* science, this pessimism is not all-encompassing. The truly pessimistic diagnosis would be the one that describes social institutions in general—politics, media, academia, etc.—as in a state of crisis owing to massive social distrust and the abandonment of facts and the ideals of truth. While there may be an element of truth to this, in that traditional institutions are under pressure, it is not the whole truth, for at least two reasons. First, as noted earlier, expertise may well be questioned, doubted, and criticized to an increasingly high degree, but that does not mean that the demand for expertise has diminished; if anything, it is the other way around. Second, drawing on Bourdieu's theory, one should assume that even though there may be changes, and declines, in the status and authority of various types of knowledge and professions, *some* kinds of knowledge, and some professions for that matter, will always have more authority than others. From that perspective, the diagnosis is not that legitimate (public) expert knowledge no longer exists. Instead, what constitutes legitimate and publicly recognized expert knowledge is changing and being pluralized. That, admittedly, does bring us back to the accusation of relativism, but social institutions do change over time. Discussion about whether these changes are for the better or worse should recognize this—and should realize that the social recognition of any type of knowledge is subject to professional contestation.

Another criticism of the arguments made here could be that we are not really witnessing a social distribution of the recognition of expertise; instead, there has just been a shift in which the power to recognize expertise is being transferred from one profession (journalism) to another, which perhaps should be called the profession (or field) of social media influencers. This would require us to focus on the new media professions that have emerged with social media and on the knowledge production done by these new professionals. This is a noteworthy and valid critique, not least because much of social media content is a mix of entertainment, politics, and expert knowledge. And certainly, there is reason to see social media as creating new fields in Bourdieu's sense. However, I argue that the shift in question also entails a social distribution of the recognition of expertise, or a looser coupling between field-specific credentials and general public recognition.

Without a doubt, the social distribution of the recognition of expertise creates new possibilities for manipulation and politicization. Both have only been made easier by the fragmentation of the public sphere due to social media filtering, which has made debate among people with conflicting views less common. There is also little doubt that the balance of power between the political system and the news media has shifted in favor of the former, which has allowed for an increased politicization of expertise. The politicization of expertise also shows that the political system cannot be a guarantor of a tighter coupling between field-specific and symbolic capital.

Finally, any kind of professional knowledge can enjoy legitimacy only if social actors bestow legitimacy on it. Thus, some of the criticism, and the loss of status, of professional fields such as academia or journalism may reflect a diminished social contribution and relevance. In that light, while this chapter may have set a pessimistic tone, it also contains the simple proposition that a legitimacy crisis can happen for perfectly valid reasons.

REFERENCES

Alexander, Jeffrey. C. 2016. "Introduction: Journalism, Democratic Culture, and Creative Reconstruction." In *The Crisis of Journalism Reconsidered: Democratic Culture, Professional Codes, Digital Future*, edited by E. B. Breese, J. C. Alexander, and M. Luengo, 1–28. Cambridge, UK: Cambridge University Press.

Alterman, Eric. 1999. *Sound and the Fury: The Making of the Punditocracy*. Ithaca, NY: Cornell University Press.

Anspach, Nicolas. M., and Taylor. N. Carlson. 2018. "What to Believe? Social Media Commentary and Belief in Misinformation." *Political Behavior* 42 (3): 1–22.

Arnoldi, Jakob. 2003. "Making Sense of Causation." *Soziale Welt* 54 (4): 405–427.

Arnoldi, Jakob. 2007. "Universities and the Public Recognition of Expertise." *Minerva* 45: 49–61.

Arnoldi, Jakob. 2009. *Risk: An Introduction*. Cambridge, UK: Polity Press.

Benson, Rodney. 1998. "Field Theory in Comparative Context: A New Paradigm for Media Studies." *Theory and Society* 28: 463–498.

Blumler, Jay G. and Dennis Kavanagh. 1999. "The Third Age of Political Communication: Influences and Features." *Political Communication* 16: 209–230.

Bourdieu, Pierre. 1977. *Outline of a Theory of Practice*. Cambridge, UK: Cambridge University Press.

Bourdieu, Pierre. 1984. *Distinction: A Social Critique of the Judgment of Taste*. Cambridge, MA: Harvard University Press.

Bourdieu, Pierre. 1986. "The Forms of Capital." In *Handbook of Theory and Research for the Sociology of Education*, edited by J. G. Richardson, 241–258. New York: Greenwood Press.

Bourdieu, Pierre. 1988. *Homo Academicus*. Cambridge, UK: Polity Press.

Bourdieu, Pierre. 1990. *The Logic of Practice*. Cambridge, UK: Polity Press.

Bourdieu, Pierre. 1998. *On Television*. New York: New Press.

Bourdieu, Pierre., and Loic. J. D. Wacquant. 1992. *An Invitation to Reflexive Sociology*. Cambridge: Polity.

Broersma, Marcel. 2013. "A Refractured Paradigm: Journalism, Hoaxes and the Challenge of Trust. In *Rethinking Journalism*, edited by Chris Peters and Marcel Broersma, 40–56. Abingdon, UK, and New York: Routledge.

Brown, Tracey. 2016. "Evidence, Expertise, and Facts in a 'Post-truth' Society." *BMJ 2016*: 355:i6467.

Coenen-Huther, Jacques. 1998. "The Paths of Recognition: Bourdon, Bourdieu and the 'Second Market' of Intellectuals." *International Journal of Contemporary Sociology* 35 (2): 208–216.

Couldry, Nick. 2003. "Media Meta-Capital: Extending the Range of Bourdieu's Field Theory." *Theory and Society* 32: 653–677.

Curran, James. 2000. "Rethinking Media and Democracy." In *Mass Media and Society*, edited by J. Curran and M. Gurevitch, 120–154. London: Arnold.

Daniller, Andrew., D. Allen, A. Tallevi, and D. C. Mutz. 2017. "Measuring Trust in the Press in a Changing Media Environment." *Communication Methods and Measures* 11 (1): 76–85.

Delanty, Gerard. 2001. *Challenging Knowledge*. Buckingham, UK: Society for Research into Higher Education.

Van Dijk, Jan. 1999. *The Network Society*. London: Sage.

Newman, Nic, Richard Fletcher, Antonis Kalogeropoulos, David. Levy, and Rasmus Nielsen. 2017. *Reuters Institute Digital News Report 2017*. Reuters Institute for the Study of Journalism.

Department of Politics and International Relations, University of Oxford. https://reutersin stitute.politics.ox.ac.uk/sites/default/files/Digital%20News%20Report%202017%20web_ o.pdf.

Gibbons, Michael, Camilla Limoges, Helga Nowotny, Simon Schwartzman, Peter Scott, and Martin Trow. 1994. *The New Production of Knowledge*. London: Sage.

Gillmor, Dan. 2004. *We the Media: Grassroots Journalism by the People, for the People*. Cambridge: O'Reilly.

Gorman, Lyn, and David Mclean. 2003. *Media and Society in the Twentieth Century*. Malden, MA: Blackwell.

Hanitzsch, Thomas, Arjen Van Dalen, and Nina Steindl. 2018. "Caught in the Nexus: A Comparative and Longitudinal Analysis of Public Trust in the Press." *International Journal of Press/Politics* 23 (1): 3–23..

Hopkin, Jonathan, and Ben Rosamond. 2018. "Post-truth Politics, Bullshit and Bad Ideas: 'Deficit Fetishism' in the UK." *New Political Economy* 23 (6): 641–655.

Jacobs, Ronald and Eleanor Townsley, 2011. *The Space of Opinion*. New York: Oxford University Press.

Leydesdorff, Loet and Henry Etzkowitz. 2001. "The Transformation of University-Industry-Government Relations." *Electronic Journal of Sociology* 5 (4): 1–31.

Luhmann, Niklas. 2000. *The Reality of the Mass Media*. Cambridge, UK: Polity Press.

MacLeod, Roy. 2003. *Government and Expertise: Specialists, Administrators and Professionals, 1860–1919*. Cambridge, UK: Cambridge University Press.

Manjoo, Farhad, 2008. *True Enough: Learning to Live in a Post-fact Society*. Hoboken, NJ: John Wiley & Sons.

Mazali, Tatiana. 2011. "Social Media as a New Public Sphere." *Leonardo* 44 (3): 290–291.

Medvetz, Thomas. 2012. *Think Tanks in America*. Chicago: University of Chicago Press.

Nowotny, Helga. 2000a. "The Production of Knowledge beyond the Academy and the Market: A Reply to Dominique Pestre." *Science, Technology and Society* 5 (2): 183–194.

Nowotny, Helgae. 2000b. "Transgressive Competence." *European Journal of Social Theory* 3 (1): 5–21.

Nowotny, Helga, Peter Scott, and Michael Gibbons. 2001. *Re-thinking Science: Knowledge and the Public in an Age of Uncertainty*. Cambridge, UK: Polity Press.

Nowotny, H., P. Scott, and M. Gibbons. 2003. "Introduction: 'Mode 2' Revisited: The New Production of Knowledge." *Minerva* 41 (3): 179–194.

Powell, Walther W., and Paul J. Dimaggio, eds. 1991. *The New Institutionalism in Organizational Analysis*. Chicago: Chicago University Press.

Rich, Andrew. 2001. "The Politics of Expertise in Congress and the News Media." *Social Science Quarterly* 82 (3): 583–601.

Ryfe, David M. 2012. *Can Journalism Survive? An Inside Look at American Newsrooms*. Cambridge, UK: Polity Press.

Schudson, Michael. 1982. "The Politics of Narrative Form: The Emergence of News Conventions in Print and Television." *Daedalus* 11 (4): 97–112.

Schudson, Michael. 2000. "The Sociology of News Production Revisited." In *Mass Media and Society*, edited by J. Curran and M. Gurevitch, pp. 141–159. London: Arnold.

Schulz, Winfried. 1997. "Changes of the Mass Media and the Public Sphere." *Javnost–The Public* 4 (2): 57–69.

Shirky, Clay 2011. "The Political Power of Social Media: Technology, the Public Sphere, and Political Change." *Foreign Affairs*, 90 (1): 28–41.

Thompson, John. B. 1995. *Media and Modernity*. Cambridge, UK: Polity Press.

Turner, Stephen. 2001. "What Is the Problem with Experts?" *Social Studies of Science* 31 (1): 123–149.

Vos, Tim. 2002. "News Writing Structure and Style." In *American Journalism*, edited by William David Sloan and L. M. Parcell, 296–305. Jefferson, NC: McFarland and Company.

Yearly, Steven. 2005. *Making Sense of Science*. London: Sage.

Ylä-Anttila, Tuukka. 2018. "Populist Knowledge: 'Post-truth' Repertoires of Contesting Epistemic Authorities." *European Journal of Cultural and Political Sociology*, 5 (4): 1–33.

24

MEDIA METACOMMENTARY, MEDIATIZATION, AND THE INSTABILITY OF EXPERTISE

ELEANOR TOWNSLEY

JOHN Oliver has been called "the most trusted man in America."[1] His late-night cable comedy show *Last Week Tonight with John Oliver* has won multiple Emmy and Peabody awards, even though Oliver eschews journalism and mocks its pretensions. Despite this, what Oliver says—his descriptions of the world, his social diagnoses, his identification of heroes and villains—is taken seriously. The stories on *Last Week Tonight* are analyzed widely in other news media, and the show has massive online audiences in the United States and around the world. Oliver's 2016 analysis of then-presidential candidate Donald Trump, for example, was the most viewed content on YouTube at the time, and now has over 40 million views. How does Oliver create the social trust to act as an authoritative cultural critic and media expert? What is the nature of his criticism and his expertise? And what do his performances suggest about the nature of expertise more generally?

These questions are pressing in late modern societies, where trust in the institutions that authorize expertise has eroded, and any expert claim is difficult to evaluate. Broad fields of information and new communities of understanding mean that anyone with a connection to the internet can evaluate expert claims made by government agencies, businesses, scientists, and journalists. Elites do not appear to agree about the authority of facts, nor do wider publics. Multiple complex media logics reinforce the social flux, reshaping and subordinating other social institutions, including family, state, school, and leisure institutions, as well as the organization of intellectual life and everyday knowledge. There are few expert claims that can resist the leveling effects of our epistemologically fragmented, profoundly mediated culture.

My contention is that the success of *Last Week Tonight* is connected to John Oliver's skill at media metacommentary—a historically specific form of media criticism that uses the comparison of media formats and media texts as the basis for critical judgment (Jacobs and Townsley 2015; Townsley 2015). As media metacommentary developed, it undermined traditional performances of expertise in journalism and politics, and it also accelerated the erosion of expertise in other institutional domains. Like others before him, Oliver uses media metacommentary to claim expert media authority while destabilizing other forms of expertise. He combines methods of juxtaposition, intertextual referencing, spoofing, and other forms of visual and media play to create entertaining performances, capture audience attention, and make social criticisms. Despite the satirical postmodern style, however, Oliver manages to establish sincere political and cultural positions. The resulting performances stitch together the attention of varying audiences and craft authentic collective narratives that represent large democratic publics.

In what follows, I consider the erosion of traditional expertise in the context of increasingly complex media environments for social performance. I sketch the dual origins of media metacommentary in the tradition of social criticism and in the cultures of the authorized social expert, and I trace the development of metacommentary to the media formats of the late twentieth century and the rise of new media. The second half of the chapter focuses on John Oliver and *Last Week Tonight*, which has innovated the genre of media metacommentary in distinctive ways. Oliver's use of media metacommentary produces authentic performances and social influence by using expert media knowledge about *mediatization*—that is, the dense interconnection of media logics and formats that permeate the institutional life of the contemporary societies (Hepp and Krotz 2014; Hjarvard 2008; Livingstone 2009; Couldry and Hepp 2013; Barnard 2018). This enables him to construct critical transmedia narratives with effects that go well beyond journalism or entertainment.

EXPERTISE AS A CHALLENGE OF PERFORMANCE

If expertise links specialized knowledge with wider social concerns—connecting tools, expert communities, clients, and institutional arrangements (Eyal 2013)—then the cultural performances that create these links are at the heart of expertise and cannot be taken for granted. As Alexander (2004) has argued, a successful performance is a contingent action that requires the *fusion* of the actor/creator, the performance and its objects, and the audience. In symbolic performances in early societies, Alexander shows that "ritualized social actions fuse the various components of performance—actors, audiences, representations, means of symbolic production, social power, and mise-en-scène" (536), but in complex, postritual societies, where the elements of performance have become disconnected, or *de-fused*, successful performances that are natural, authentic, and compelling are far more difficult.

Alexander's analysis traces the historical development of secular cultural performances as they developed from earlier ritual forms. Written texts separated social scripts from background collective representations; the means of symbolic production were removed from the mass of social performers into the hands of the few; and elites became separated from the social audiences they sought to represent (Alexander 2004, 539–544). As modern societies developed further, the differentiation and disconnection between elements of performance widened. Cities grew in importance, literacy expanded, and institutional complexity deepened. Secular cultural performances developed, becoming autonomous from religious and political authorities. In areas like theater and literature, autonomous institutions were established, and had their own principles of distinction that were defined against the powers of money and against established authorities (see also Bourdieu 2005, 1991). Nurtured in artistic and literary fields, social criticism emerged as a way to express collective meaning in and for the wider society. New secular narratives included stories of scientific discovery and social exploration, tales of heroic political action in voting or revolutionary resistance, as well as stories of romance and domestic life that informed the development of private selves and public identities (Habermas [1962] 1989; Calhoun 1992; Taylor 1992). These kinds of stories and the performances through which they are conveyed continue to represent and define modern social relationships.

If we extend Alexander's analysis, it becomes apparent that specific claims to expertise were also based on wider public narratives, as different groups struggled to gain jurisdiction over particular social problems. To be sure, expert claims were justified by reference to special knowledge and skill, and they were addressed to particular clients. In this respect, expert performances drew on principles of autonomy, similarly to those made in the artistic and literary fields. But they were different in important ways: they were more likely to be made on behalf of some defined social purpose, to draw on discourses of science and reason, and to be secured through legally mandated scientific, educational and professional institutions (Abbott 1988; Starr [1982] 2017; Rose 2007). Despite these differences, both critics and experts performed their roles as representatives of social interests, either by invoking established authority or by speaking on behalf of wider publics to hold power to account.

As these various cultural performances circulated out into society and back again, they shaped the underlying values, collective representations and communicative institutions of modern publics (and counterpublics; Fraser 1990, Habermas [1962] 1989, 1992, 1996). Collective representations and public narratives circulated in a diverse and overlapping array of media, including art, books, plays, scientific treatises, pamphlets and newspapers, radio, television, and, eventually, the internet and social media (Eley 1992; Keane 1991; Barkin 2015; Webster 2014). These media are an essential part of the story of modern societies: both because they provide the infrastructure and symbolic resources that make large-scale public discourse possible and because they facilitate the governance of diverse communities and complex divisions of labor that enable large groups of people to coordinate social action (Habermas 1996; Jacobs and Townsley 2011; Jacobson 2017). If the current crisis of expertise is part of the "recursive legitimation crisis" of late modern society (Weingart 2003), then media are central to the crisis.

MEDIA EXPERTS AND MEDIA EXPERTISE

Since the nineteenth century, media such as newspapers, magazines, radio, television, and film have served as repositories of collective representations. Media are a source of social scripts and the means through which those scripts are circulated among wide publics. Media also provide the vehicles and platforms through which experts and social critics have conveyed their performances. Media expertise consists in knowledge of and the ability to use media to create successful expert performances. On the one hand, media experts are a special class of experts who use their knowledge of the media field to participate in and shape public debates and wider social life. These include journalists, critics, and editors; figures such as publicists, marketing and public relations experts; and more recently, hackers, trolls, and gaslighters. On the other hand, media also represent and support other performances of expertise. If experts seek to participate in the public sphere, they need to master some level of media expertise. They will need to understand how media operate and to develop communicative skill in media performance. Moreover, whereas media intellectuals once needed to master the techniques of print culture, now they need to understand television and a wide array of new online media formats.

NEW MEDIA AND EXPERTISE

By the end of the twentieth century, mass media had been transformed again by a "digital revolution" that connected digital formats on computational devices to form the Internet (Chun and Keenan 2005). Social media comprised diffuse and ever-expanding communicative networks, and media expertise began to diffuse out into society. A broad range of actors participate in new media spaces as consumers and citizens, and in the process, they become more aware of the dynamics of media performances and media institutions. Expertise and criticism have diffused online among regular users, on fan accounts, in comment sections, and on major platforms like Facebook, Twitter, YouTube, and TikTok with a subsequent decline in larger public narratives in favor of microcommunities, niche audiences, and experiments in targeted marketing (Turow 1997). Under new media conditions, expert claims are subject to the flattening effects of diffuse social criticism (Kurasawa 2017). These changes also raise democratic concerns about audience fragmentation and political polarization (Webster 2014).

From the point of view of a sociology of expertise, new media have accelerated the erosion of the distinction between expert and amateur across social fields. More than a "pluralization of expertise" (Rhomberg and Stehr 2013), new media provide wider contexts in which citizens, consumers, and others are able to assess the claims of traditional experts, making available more diverse, global and critical sources than in the past. DIYers can now find and use technologies that once only experts controlled, and they can offer their own competing ideas. This has enabled new forms of critical expertise to flourish. At the same time, new media spaces also provide resources for those excluded from traditional positions of institutional power. Those with less mainstream political, educational, or religious identities or those marginalized on the basis of race, ethnicity, gender, sexuality, or ability can now participate in wider communities of knowledge, and they can do so on their own terms. For example, new media spaces enable the political and moral critique that putatively neutral expert performances are not being representative or responsive to wider publics. Using social media, people can find each other, build alternative communities, challenge the symbolic domination of the established authorities, and make competing knowledge claims (e.g., Epstein 1995; Wynne 2001; Perlman 2004; Cook and Robbins 2004; Suryanarayanan and Kleinman 2012). New media have also enabled social-movement mobilization in new ways, including nationalist populist movements (Tufecki 2017; Moffitt 2016). The result of all these changes has been to accelerate the decentralization and deinstitutionalization of authoritative expert claims to knowledge.

Problematically, with the diffusion of performative styles within new media spaces, it is not always easy to distinguish the products of traditional experts from those of less qualified competitors who draw on the stagecraft and symbolic frames of older expert performances (Collins and Evans 2007). Kurasawa's (2017) analysis of climate change discourse on social media reveals, for example, that climate change denial websites often draw on scientific language. Many climate change deniers online offer performances grounded in evidence-based logic similar to that associated with peer-reviewed science, even though the actual data and arguments they publish are fabricated or have been widely dismissed by established scientists.

The ability to undermine expert authority by using the stagecraft and styles of traditional expert performance in new media spaces has also been particularly challenging for journalistic forms of expertise. Journalists have been beset by fake news crises including serious charges that the 2016 US presidential election was manipulated by hackers publishing targeted fake news to sway voters and the crisis generated by what is termed "The Big Lie" that the 2020 Presidential election was stolen. In this context, journalists struggle to maintain symbolic boundaries about what constitutes journalism and the journalistic field (Jacobs 2017; Barnard 2017, 2018). This is fundamentally a challenge of performing journalistic expertise. Under conditions where information, "breaking news," and reporting are seemingly up for grabs in the (socially networked) public domain, journalists, just like Kurasawa's climate scientists, have difficulty sustaining traditional performances of neutrality, fairness, and balance. The authority of journalistic performances is deflated by critics who claim the "mainstream media" are liberal and elitist; they are deflated when they are mocked in comedic parodies of earnest media styles on cable television; and they are diminished when successful competitors in newer, shorter, more entertaining, or better networked formats disrupt the distinctions of the journalistic field on YouTube or Twitter. By 2022, this is no longer a novel observation. It is clear that in the new media environment, it is difficult to craft authentic public narratives that can connect a multitude of smaller audiences and provide enough common meaning for large publics to form at all.

This question has special valence if we consider that the media field is weakly autonomous—more subject to the influence of money and state authority than other cultural fields. As Bourdieu has argued, this threatens to replace the deep reflection and serious thinking that defines fields like science and art with that fast-talk and a shallow concern with appearances that are more common in media spaces (Bourdieu 2005). Bourdieu was undoubtedly correct that media logics are more influential in intellectual life—indeed, wider social life—than they once were. This is especially true for new media styles, which affect all expert performances and are required to be shorter, faster, more entertaining, and more convenient to hold the attention of audiences. These changes impact performances both within the media field, for figures like journalists, as well as for experts who are formally outside the media field in other institutions, such as academics, scientists, and artists.

Scientists and academics may possess high autonomy relative to the market and the state, but compared to an earlier era, these intellectuals now have far less autonomy *relative to media*. Although experts continue to provide specialist knowledge and information to journalists, their performances are circumscribed by journalistic formats that require sharp, simple, brief language to inform general publics. This was true for the "public intellectual" of the 1980s and 1990s, who was often an academic hoping to offer broad opinions to wider publics by speaking in the journalistic field (Jacoby 1987; Collini 2006; Townsley 2006). More recently, the "thought leader" is an expert who speaks on a single topic (Drezner 2017) and is very much a creation of the media field.

That said, it is important that the negative narrative of media influence does not censor our analysis of the current operation or the future possibilities of the digital, socially networked media environment. Moreover, in making a distinction in favor of the cultural fields of art and science against the media field that views it as less autonomous or intellectually worthy, we run the risk of not valuing the autonomy the media field, in fact, possesses—that is, the autonomy the media field can marshal on behalf of democratic publics. Media are differentiated, after all, in highly varied media spaces for expert performances, critical performances, and a range of counterperformances (Jacobs and Townsley 2011, 2014). If we only focus on the damage done to traditional critical and expert formats by changes in the organization and power of the media field, then we fail to fully comprehend the changes that are occurring or to consider what strategies and formats can create spaces for effective critical, expert, or critical-expert performances. One such innovation that leverages the opportunities of the new media spaces is media metacommentary, where media intellectuals use expert knowledge of the media field to de-authorize the traditional performances of other journalistic, political, and cultural experts (Jacobs and Townsley 2018).

Media Metacommentary as Critical Expertise

Media metacommentary is, first, a criticism of the techniques of stagecraft and communication that are common in media spaces. Most concretely, it is a criticism of other actors' media expertise, and it typically challenges and redefines the established distinctions in the media field, such as those between serious and trivial, earnest and comedic, and news and entertainment. In this respect, media metacommentary draws on the legacy of the independent cultural critic, which arose within the larger aesthetic discourse of modernity (Alexander 2004, 2009; Bourdieu 2005, 1992, 1993, [1988] 1996; Jennings and Kemp-Welch 1997; Eyerman 1994, 2011; see also Baumann 1987).

Critics have been important for modern societies because they pushed the boundaries of representation in different cultural forms. Historically, critics defined the principles of distinction within the literary, artistic, and, later, the journalistic fields, and they carved out independent positions for themselves as gatekeepers who could evaluate the effectiveness and quality of different actor's performances within those fields (Bourdieu 1993, 2005; Alexander 2004; Jacobs 2012; Baumann 2007). Over the course of the twentieth century, the idea of the critical intellectual also developed as a distinct social role, and eventually came to include the revolutionary intellectual, the movement intellectual, and, more recently, the public intellectual (Eyerman 2011; Jacoby 1987; Townsley 2006). These intellectual roles all emphasized deep learning and experience; the application of independent criteria for the evaluation of cultural performances; and courage in the face of opposition from entrenched interests, captured in the idea of speaking truth to power. When John Oliver criticizes the media performances of politicians, other journalists, or entertainers as inauthentic, then, he is very much a part of the tradition of modern criticism.

More specifically, Oliver is heir to a tradition of autonomous intellectual criticism within twentieth-century journalism, as it developed within the space of opinion located at the intersection of the journalistic, political, and academic fields (Jacobs and Townsley 2011). Similarly to opinion intellectuals, such as columnists and media commentators, Oliver analyzes the substance of ideas and policy proposals. And like these earlier critics, he also bases his critical analyses on an examination of the mechanics and style of public speech and action, understood primarily as *performance*. To be sure, critics are themselves engaged in performances to establish their own bona fides to speak as critics. This gives rise to a dynamic of performance and counterperformance as different kinds of critical intellectuals vie to establish their collective narratives, their understanding of the problems and challenges of the day, and their decisions and policies for addressing those challenges. With media metacommentary, this dynamic becomes pronounced, so that the critical, comparative analysis of media performances is a major vehicle for telling stories.

The second tradition that media metacommentary draws from is journalism, specifically, political journalism as a form of expertise. This includes the research methods that define investigative journalism, as well as analysis and opinion writing. Importantly, traditional journalism is also organized around a commitment to objectivity, which is understood to be created by methodical approaches to establishing facts (Schudson 1978), and is also believed to be central to journalism's higher social purpose to inform and represent democratic publics (Habermas 1996; Jacobson 2017). In other words, the traditional model of objective journalism orients itself to an institutional landscape that is defined by a particular relationship between political and journalistic institutions—a landscape that has experienced massive changes in the last thirty years.

Oliver and his colleagues who work in spaces defined by traditional journalistic expertise, extend the journalistic tradition by commenting on and reflecting the much broader media ecology that now exists. This is a media ecology that interweaves massive, differentiated yet overlapping intertextual, networked social relationships. It is also a media ecology in which older distinctions between serious and trivial and news and entertainment are far more porous than they once were (Williams and Delli Carpini 2011). This observation is typically made in the form of the criticism that entertainment values have come to influence news in ways that conflict with the sober legacy of the traditional journalistic expert (see, for example, Postman 1985). Oliver and his cohorts recognize this, but they also go beyond it. Their entertaining news performances acknowledge that the collective representations and social scripts that matter to people have always cut across fictional and nonfictional genres. There is a parallel tradition in modern criticism, where serious ideas are embedded in playful styles (Tucker 2010; Glas et al. 2019). The playfulness on a show like *Last Week Tonight* is a way of winking at the audience, acknowledging that news formats are performances; indeed, that entertainment genres have always informed news performances.

Entertainment genres are an important element of media metacommentary, and they are also important because they inform historical understandings of expertise. In the first place, entertainment media offer collective representations of the social world as a world where knowledge is organized by science, experts, and truth. Crime dramas, for example, showcase ballistics and DNA experts, who make conclusive claims about legal evidence; talk shows unpack psychological research for mass audiences; and advertising relies on a range of scientific claims to sell everything from pharmaceuticals to laundry detergent. More than in news formats, entertainment media represent the institutional contexts and cultures of expertise in great detail with well-known representations of law firms, police stations, law courts, hospitals, and scientific and educational institutions forming the backdrop of popular stories. These representations circulate widely, becoming available as shared cultural understandings of what these institutions *should* look like. In the same moment, however, because they are fictional performances of expertise, they reveal the performative quality of all expert claims.

The different sources that inform the practice of media metacommentary create significant levels of evaluative instability within the media field, and they create a serious challenge for mediated forms of expertise. Because the media field requires that all actions be overtly performed, there is always a possibility of a *de-fusion* of the performance—that is, of the performance not "coming off," to use Goffman's terms. Thus, while media metacommentary relies on the history of journalistic expertise, and while it borrows authority from expert sources by relying on a broad cultural understanding of expertise, as well as the authority of the academic, artistic, and scientific institutions to construct stories, it always, at the same time, reveals that expertise is a performance. This has significant consequences for those whose performances of expertise have long been premised on the idea that they are somehow standing outside the performance itself, in a purer, more abstract, and independent space of truth and reason. A performance of detached objectivity is less problematic in social conditions where established institutions enjoy high levels of social trust. In conditions of pervasive social challenges to expertise, however, the constructed quality of media performances accelerates the unraveling of all expert performances (Jacobs and Townsley 2018; Townsley 2015).[2] The deflationary effect of criticism is to reduce public trust in all performances, an effect seen clearly in the development of media metacommentary, which began to evolve as a news format in the 1980s, during the Reagan administration.

Media Metacommentary since the 1980s

A distinctive feature of neoliberal policies in the United States in the 1980s was the deregulation of news media and the abolition of the Fairness Doctrine, which had prescribed fairness and balance in news reporting. Conservative commentators and radio shock jocks parlayed these changes in the regulatory environment into an opportunity to develop more partisan media formats. Building on existing forms of political satire and opinion,[3] figures like Rush Limbaugh developed styles that mocked the presentations of other media intellectuals and questioned the professional motives of journalists, critics, and politicians in traditional formats (Berry and Sobieraj 2014; Jacobs and Townsley 2014). The effect was to make traditional news performances seem inauthentic, self-interested, and out of touch.

Partisan formats also developed quickly on cable television, where news styles became more sensational, entertaining, faster, and repetitive (PEW Research Center 1998; Jurkowitz et al. 2013; Barkin 2015). The amount of news content that was available mushroomed, as multiple news and news-related outlets aired new opinion formats and comedy styles (Williams and Delli Carpini 2011). The distinction between news and entertainment eroded quickly. As Wild (2019) recounts, not only did this period mark a turning point for journalism but also for politics, which increasingly pervaded entertainment, comedy, and other media fields. As traditional journalists were trapped in the criticism that news was becoming like entertainment, they were slower to realize the possibilities and challenges of the new media landscape, which was quickly becoming connected to multiple other institutional domains through shared platforms, media logics, and talent networks. As with radio, the critical strategy on cable television was to reveal the artifice and hypocrisy of the mainstream media by deconstructing its biases. Conservative programs (as well as the more liberal and progressive cable television programs that followed) presented their opinions and their political positions clearly, while denouncing the technique of "balance" and deconstructing it as a form of ideology (Jacobs and Townsley 2014). These formats shifted the relationship between the journalistic and political fields. Unlike traditional news media that were committed to autonomy *from* politics, which was performed through signs of neutrality, balance, and fairness in representation, these new formats sought to maintain autonomy and influence *in* politics by refining ever more partisan positions (Jacobs and Townsley 2014). In the process, *both* entertainment and news became far more political.

Innovations in media criticism continued to proliferate, as each new format took aim at the performance styles and the stagecraft of the format that preceded it. By the turn of the century, media metacommentary had become a distinctive and peculiar form of expert discourse, which legitimated the act of criticism while also relativizing it. *The Daily Show with Jon Stewart,* which first appeared on The Comedy Channel in 1999, was in large part an extended critique of the opinion programs that had appeared on cable television, most notably, those on CNN and Fox News. A spin-off from that show, *The Colbert Report,* was a parody of the Fox News Channel's most popular program *The O'Reilly Factor* (Jacobs and Wild 2013; Wild 2019). John Oliver's *Last Week Tonight* is currently dominant in this oeuvre, and is central to discussions of political events in formal public spaces and in informal conversations throughout civil society.

LAST WEEK TONIGHT

Like the comedy news formats it builds on, *Last Week Tonight* uses media metacommentary as the basis for criticism, but it innovates in significant ways. Unlike *The Daily Show* or *The Colbert Report,* for example, the show does not include guests as commentators or experts, nor does it enact symbolic dialogues with powerful figures from government or business, such as happens on Fox's *Hannity* and MSNBC's *The Rachel Maddow Show* (Jacobs and Townsley 2011; Clayman and Heritage 2002). There is also no intention to report about the entire news landscape or to respond immediately to breaking news, as there is in traditional news formats. The show airs weekly and centers on Oliver, who presents narratives on a single topic that last from ten to twenty minutes. The length of the show is more similar to a news magazine than a live news broadcast, but unlike magazines or other long-form news shows, Oliver typically performs alone as a sole critical narrator in front of a live studio audience (although this changed during the pandemic when live events were halted).

As a part of his shtick, Oliver claims he is not a journalist, a claim he repeats despite the fact that the show deploys traditional methods of investigative journalism, and employs a dedicated team of writers who perform verification and fact-checking.[4] Analysts who assert that Oliver is a journalist observe, for example, that the category has been deflated in recent years; "it's a stupid word" James Poniewozik says in *Time* magazine, "used to lend an air of professional respectability to jobs that we should just describe directly: writing, reporting, analysis, criticism, opinion and so on." Oliver's show not only shares this deflationary intent; it is based upon it. Key to his successful performance is a form of media expertise that both depends on traditional performances of journalistic, academic, and policy expertise and uses them as a foil to elevate his own more critical media performance. In Alexander's terms, Oliver offers a successful, fused media performance that combines diverse elements, and at the same time, he successfully de-fuses the performances of others.

Disclaiming a journalistic vantage point also means that *Last Week Tonight* can follow the newer partisan formats by taking unambiguous moral positions in its stories. This also differentiates the show from its postmodern styling, as it pivots to represent publics and define particular positions. Reminiscent of the New Sincerity style, associated with the writer David Foster Wallace in literature or with the "awesomeness" of Jesse Thorn on International Public Radio, *Last Week Tonight* pokes serious fun and defines agendas. And though *Last Week Tonight* is not culturally or politically conservative, it is not strictly aligned with party politics either. Offering broader cultural stories as part of the mix, it takes aim at many different kinds of powerholders, from politicians to the World Wrestling Federation, and it takes up topics from drone technology to health insurance. The denial of a journalistic purpose also means that Oliver is not bound by the rules of journalism. He can rely on a wide range of different media formats, including entertainment styles. He can make offensive, even defamatory statements, without being held accountable in the same way a traditional news anchor might, and he can engage in direct social action in a way that has been traditionally disavowed by journalists. In short, Oliver (and his show) can act in the public interest—as he defines it—without being held accountable to established authorities in media or politics.

Like Stewart's and Colbert's shows before him, *Last Week Tonight* is, above all, a comedy news show. In contrast to modes of news criticism that rely heavily on standards of rationality and truth (Wild 2019; Alexander 2004), media metacommentary is playful, funny, and self-consciously performative. It draws on the devices of an extended stand-up comedy routine, performed by a single voice, albeit sitting behind a multimedia news desk. The narrative works at the level of comedy, using jokes and gags to hold the different narrative elements together, juxtaposing photographs and verbal elements in a rapid, intertextual, cross-referential array. The show is relentlessly self-referential too, with long-term running gags that refresh earlier comedic elements.

One major effect of this style of media metacommentary is to render an image of a dense and institutionally varied media ecology in which stories, data, people, and scripts circulate constantly. This is a successful collective representation of a networked mass public. If people's daily experience in media suggests that they live in polarized media microcommunities defined by friends and enemies, Oliver's presentation suggests how these communities might all really be connected together in a broader media landscape in which they have a shared interest. This is an important method through which *Last Week Tonight* sets agendas for mass publics.

NET NEUTRALITY

A good example of Oliver's expert media performance is the thirteen-minute story on Net neutrality he aired in the fifth episode of *Last Week Tonight*, in June 2014. Oliver went on to update this story several times in the following years, and he created a second long-form narrative on the same topic in 2017, but the first story in 2014 is exemplary of Oliver's innovation of media metacommentary. As Table 24.1 shows, Oliver uses a wide range of media elements to frame the narrative about net neutrality. In a rapid comedic sequence, he makes jokes about Coyote urine, connects this to multiple popular culture references, including widely known memes and a pop star. Viewers may not be familiar with every reference, but they know some of them and are connected to others through Oliver's narrative. This strategy offers a collective representation of different media spaces and different media audiences. It recognizes the porous boundaries between audience member, consumer, user, client, citizen, and beneficiary, and between public and private. It stitches these fragments together to evoke a wider, collective internet space and a public that inhabits it which has a common cause in resisting proposed changes to the internet.

Table 24.1 Opening sequence, Net Neutrality I, John Oliver, June 1, 2014

0:00–0:12	A definition of the Internet as a cat database (with a photo of grumpy cats, an Internet meme).
0:013–0:23	The statement that the Internet is a fabulous place (with a stock photo of the google search bar), described as good because it is a place you can do things like file taxes, apply for jobs, and buy Coyote urine (with a photo of Coyote urine for sale online).
0:24–0:35	An extended joke about how hard it was to get Coyote urine prior to the Internet (with a photo of a man feeding a coyote Gatorade).
0:36–0:42	The story switches gears with the statement that the Internet is being changed.
0:43–0:51	Cut to a traditional newscaster reporting that the federal government is considering policies to change net neutrality.
0:51–0:56	Cut to different newscasters saying, "net neutrality." Cut back to Oliver repeating the term "net neutrality" in the same tone as the other journalists.
0:57–1:10	Oliver makes the point that Net neutrality sounds boring and then makes a joke about Sting being boring (with a photo of Sting playing guitar).
1.11–1:18	Cut to a video of a federal official discussing the net neutrality policy changes aired by C-Span.
1:19–1:25	Oliver, gesticulating about how boring the public hearings are, says, "Even by C-Span standards."

As an example of media metacommentary, Oliver's performance not only demonstrates expert knowledge of a range of media performances but also particularizes and relativizes those other performances. His first move is to decontextualize other media performances and juxtapose them against each other. By comparing different media platforms, media styles, and media personalities, he illuminates the stagecraft that underpins other media performances. This undermines the authority of these performances by arraying them as a set of competing possible interpretations or references to the main story. Importantly, these decontextualized performances are still used to support Oliver's own narrative by establishing facts and evidence about the proposed change to federal communications policy. Paradoxically then, he relies on and borrows the expert authority of other media performances in the same moment that he destabilizes the authority of these other expert media performances. This might be understood as a critical, antiprofessional mode of expertise.

Oliver also collapses a major distinction in the media field between news and entertainment styles by suggesting that news is often like entertainment, and that entertainment has news value. For example, the dramatic tension of the narrative opening in the net neutrality story opposes the fun, useful Internet, which we all use, with the sober political modes of reporting about the Internet that rely on government sources, best exemplified by C-SPAN. Oliver does not only demonstrate that he can use the popular content to help tell a serious story; by using less effective traditional formats as a foil, he elevates his own performance as more authentic than the performances of staid, cookie-cutter newscasters, who do not really understand the stakes of the issue or the audiences they are addressing.

Oliver's substantive argument is that "we" the users/viewers/audience members are being intentionally misdirected by boredom, so that we fail to notice policy changes that will affect our lives. This government misdirection is amplified by media reporting that uncritically reports information from official sources. For Oliver, this is a failure of mainstream news reporting, which is letting the government and cable companies get away with massive changes without being held accountable to the Internet-using public. In the remaining twelve minutes of the story, Oliver uses similar methods of juxtaposition, jokes, spoofing, and intertextual and historical references, to explain the complex context of the proposed changes to policies that regulate cable companies. He describes key stakeholders, legal precedents, lobbying activities of cable companies, and the likely consequences of the changes. In the process, he joins a tradition of news analysis historically performed by opinion columnists such as Walter Lippmann and other gatekeepers in the space of opinion (Jacobs and Townsley 2011).

Unlike traditional gatekeepers, however, in Oliver's performance the comedy format works to frame an otherwise fairly traditional intervention in the policy debate. In this, his performance is similar to performances by Jon Stewart and Trevor Noah on *The Daily Show* and Stephen Colbert of *The Colbert Report*. What Oliver adds, however, and in contrast to Jon Stewart, Trevor Noah, and Stephen Colbert, is a much sharper focus on setting an agenda in this case about policies that regulate cable companies. It is not that traditional media outlets failed to report the proposed changes to regulation of cable providers. They did, and they did so on major news platforms, as Oliver acknowledges. It is more that the standard reporting of routine government performances is less effective than it once was in setting a public agenda around a complex policy issue. The issue requires dedicated contextualization, which works against the trends in news media to deliver shorter, sharper, faster soundbites. Providing enough context requires time, and these days, all performers are competing for attention in a crowded and entertaining media environment. These are challenges of the new media environment that Oliver navigates particularly well.

Critical to Oliver's performance is the representation of the new media environment itself as a central element in the story. The media comparisons and intertextual references that litter the narrative provide light relief from the news narrative, which largely relies on official sources. Together, they set a mood, capture attention, and create the time and space to tell a complex story. Referring to the C-SPAN coverage of the FCC hearings on policy, Oliver says: "I would rather read a book by Thomas Freidman than sit through that hearing," a reference to the respected media intellectual Thomas Friedman, a former foreign correspondent and now an opinion columnist for the *New York Times*. "I would rather sit down with my niece and watch *Caillou*," which is a reference to a character on a Canadian children's show that Oliver mocks as boring and unsophisticated. Activists and big media corporations are on the same side of the issue Oliver argues, which is like Lex Luthor and Superman getting together to complain about a noisy neighbor. In rapid succession, Oliver connects data and stories about federal lobbying by Comcast with references to cable television shows like Lizard Lick Towing, and jokes about social life on social media. This is a virtuoso display of media knowledge, and as such, it is a performance of critical media expertise. At the center of Oliver's media metacommentary on *Last Week Tonight*, then, is expert knowledge of the diversity of the media field, with its different styles, epistemologies, aesthetics, and subcultures. It is this performance of expert knowledge that authorizes Oliver's analysis and commentary.

Multimedia Expertise as Transmedia Performance

For the 2014 net neutrality story, an additional layer is that it is also a story about the conditions of media production and media performance. Oliver positions himself as the representative and leader of an Internet-using public against the proposed government policy of deregulating cable provision. He acknowledges the multiple characteristics of audiences as bad, good, citizen, consumer, beneficiary etc., and argues they have a common cause. Allowing cable companies to set differential prices and speeds for Internet service will be problematic for all, Oliver argues. It is here that Oliver's performance introduces a new element to media metacommentary by marshaling

Internet-using publics to shape political policy about the means of symbolic production themselves. In a long closing call to action, Oliver makes the appeal to Internet audiences directly.

> There might actually be something that you can still do. . . . The FCC are literally inviting internet comments at this address [screen shot of address]. And at this point and I can't believe I'm about to do this but I would like to address the internet commenters out there directly. [he sighs] Good evening monsters. This may be the moment you've spent your whole life training for."

Oliver then provides multiple examples of Internet trolls, tweeting outrageous statements about children, Disney movies, and his own show. This is a rich, detailed performance that again maps a wide media landscape. He concludes,

> We need you to channel that anger, that badly spelled bile . . . for once in your lives focus your indiscriminate rage in a useful direction. Seize your moment my lovely trolls . . . and fly my pretties.

This is a call to action that leverages the fact that government processes rely on the Internet to solicit public participation. Oliver effectively encouraged his audience to go online and comment on net neutrality. His audience did this in huge numbers. The FCC website crashed shortly following the show, and the FCC reported receiving 3.7 million comments on the proposed changes, the most it had ever received in its history. The *New York Times* and other media outlets picked up the story, suggesting that as a result of the Oliver show, the FCC seemed to be moving to a tougher stance on Internet regulation.

Two weeks later, Oliver aired a follow-up story that revisited a joke about Tom Wheeler, the FCC chairman, having a conflict of interest. Oliver had said in the original broadcast that appointing Wheeler FCC chairman was equivalent to hiring a dingo to babysit. This was another popular culture reference, this time to a famous Australian tragedy, later a movie starring Meryl Streep. Oliver then aired a video clip of a C-Span reporter asking the FCC chairman whether or not he had seen John Oliver's story on net neutrality and what he thought about it. Wheeler responds slowly at first, and then opens up and cracks a joke that responds to Oliver, saying, "For the record, I am not a dingo." The point is that the story on Oliver's comedy news show unfolds in time well beyond the original episode and included millions of Internet users acting online to shape the public process of policy review at the Federal Communication Commission. This is then elaborated in other news sources on television and online, and then returns to Oliver's show for a comedic recap that engages the FCC commissioner. At the same time, the story illuminates that we are all living in a transmedia environment that is a far more complex, connected, and integrated social space than that imagined by the traditional models of journalism and politics.

If we define a transmedia narrative as "a multimedia product which communicates its narrative through a multitude of integrated media channels" (Kalinov and Markova, quoted in Kalinov 2017) then the net neutrality story is a transmedia performance. Oliver uses intertextual references, television, YouTube, and Twitter to tell the story. What he adds to this is a dedicated strategy to manipulate other social processes and institutions that are now connected through social networks on the Internet. That is, Oliver uses the features of the densely networked media environment—content, platforms, actors, and audience members—to shape a news story in real time. It is a successful critical expert media performance in which active audience members participate as actors in media spaces to shape the conclusion *as it unfolds*. Like the conservative critics of the liberal media and the comedy critics of conservative cable news, Oliver critiques earnest news styles. But more than this, by the end of Oliver's story C-SPAN reporters and political principals are both referencing his jokes to frame their discussion of policy and political participation, and this, too, is reported widely in news and entertainment media.[5] Oliver has altered the media performances of other actors by drawing them into his transmedia performance.

Similar in some ways to earlier journalistic ideals of providing information so that citizens can vote for the best candidate who supports their policy preferences, Oliver's performance is different from traditional journalism because it takes a particular policy position and makes a direct call to social action. The performance critiques government policy and corporate action in a traditional muckraking style, but it then creates the conditions for large-scale social action within and against the administrative power of the state *using the media*. By marshaling large publics as user-citizens, Oliver's performance effectively crosses the boundary from communication media to direct political action, leveraging a state institutional process. Importantly, that state process is part of the social network because it is connected through the Internet. Although this tactic is heir to strategies from an earlier era of political action, such as flooding the helplines of phone banks, in the case of the net neutrality story, the media action occurs on a much larger, more public scale that reverberates in real time as it is happening.

HACKING THE MEDIATIZED SOCIAL WORLD: AN ALTERNATIVE MEDIA REPRESENTATION

The awareness and use of the full media ecology is a marked feature of *Last Week Tonight*, and reflects the wider conditions of mediatization that define social relations and institutional fields. Mediatization creates a situation in which traditional performances of expertise are repositioned so that they come to undermine the principles that inform the performance. In this case, Oliver legitimizes some media performances by relying on them, but he also destabilizes their institutional claim to authority by relativizing and criticizing them *as performances*. Similarly, he reveals that though the FCC has called for public comment on proposed policy changes, it may not really take that process seriously. Oliver implies that it might be an insincere call for public participation. As a challenge to the expert performances of others in their institutional context, this is a highly successful strategy.

To be sure, Oliver is not the first well-situated media personality to manipulate the mediatized environment to affect changes in important public narratives, institutional arrangements, or public actions. Another well-known example is the extraordinarily successful 2015 presidential campaign of Donald Trump, whom David Karpf (2016) called the "clickbait candidate." Trump's behavior on the campaign trail was good for television news ratings, which had just for the first time become measurable in real time using online news metrics. The metricized environment fueled a twenty-four-hour news cycle as Trump's statements ensured a steady drip of entertaining, and at times outrageous news stories. Ladd (2016) observes that Trump also used shock tactics and He lied brazenly to manipulate the media into covering his statements, regardless of whether those statements were true. Journalists' commitments to fairness and balance ensured that Trump's statements would be reported alongside other more traditional and reasonable statements. This is the sense in which the Trump campaign hacked the culture of the news media to attract media attention and dominate the political narrative throughout the campaign. Following his loss of the Presidency in 2020, the storming of the Capitol on January 6, 2021, and his continuing refusal to concede his loss, Trump's ability to hack the traditional news media directly has been somewhat diminished. Nonetheless, Trump's influence in politics and political news media, remains substantial.

Data & Society's danah boyd (2017) defines hacking as "leveraging skills to push the boundaries of systems." In her recounting, hacking has a long history of "goofy teenagers," trolls, and gamers who played with the incentive structure of old and new media to create effects, typically to prove they could do it and be amusing. Later, social media marketers, political groups, and hate groups developed similar strategies for less humorous, more harmful purposes. By tracking the overlapping networks and subcultures in which hacking techniques were developed, boyd's analysis reveals how media expertise came to rest in the ability to manipulate the entire attention economy of mainstream media and, later, the social media ecology. This has now been extended to other social institutions that are increasingly connected through the Internet, including government, business, and cultural institutions.

Not inherently good or bad, the conditions of mediatization create a complex, connected social space that requires media expertise for any exercise of authority. It underlines the fact that media spaces have never been simple vehicles or technical platforms for social action. They are deeply embedded elements of social action. It is not that media are hacked because a hacker manipulates the technical functioning of the system (although that certainly occurs). Rather, mediatized social relationships are hijacked when hackers manipulate the norms and behaviors of the people using the media. A good example of this is boyd's critical analysis of the uncritical way journalists reported the term *incel* after a terrorist attack in Canada. As a sensational element of the story, journalists amplified a fringe term from rape culture and gave it enormous public currency. Mainstream news readers then googled the term in large numbers, creating a trending effect across media platforms, which took it from a position of marginal curiosity to a more legitimate and central position in public discourse. The point boyd makes is that traditional media performances need to be more critically aware of how the densely interconnected media environment shapes social action. A new form of media expertise is required to navigate this environment, one that understands that the mediatized nature of society and, in particular, the role of powerful legacy media—both in their dominance as platforms, and in their production of particular news cultures and behaviors—are subject to manipulation.

Oliver's analysis of the net neutrality issue is an example of this new media expertise. Like older journalistic models, Oliver's stories have an agenda-setting function and represent large democratic publics. Like entertainment genres, Oliver's stories capture and keep the audience's attention, which is an accomplishment for a news format in the current news and entertainment environment. Like partisan media, Oliver's stories make effective calls to action. Innovatively, Oliver uses transmedia storytelling strategies to unfold the story over time, and in the case of net neutrality, he effectively constrained other actors to alter their own performances. Importantly, the story made use of transmedia methods and a deep knowledge of how media logics shape wider social relationships. This is a key to Oliver's innovation of media metacommentary—his critical media-based interventions that rely on the fact that media logics pervade the institutional infrastructure of business, politics, and everyday life.

There are many other examples of this from *Last Week Tonight*. In one story about medical debt (June 5, 2016), Oliver hacks real institutional structures by creating a debt collection company online, purchasing $15 million worth of medical debt for $60,000, and then forgiving the medical bills of 9,000 people on live television.[6] Relying on the Internet-enabled ease of manipulating the existing system, Oliver is able to carry the story beyond the moment of the show itself while also illuminating the complexity and inhumanity of the current system, where most medical debt is never recovered, but still the healthcare, legal, and financial systems continue to harass sick and poor people about their unpaid medical bills.

Similarly, an investigative report (September 21, 2014) into the claims made by the Miss America Pageant that they are "the world's largest provider of scholarships for women" ends with Oliver providing the web addresses of other scholarship organizations for women. He concludes by suggesting making donations to these other organizations "if you want to change the fact that currently the biggest scholarship program exclusively for women in America requires you to be unmarried with a mint-condition uterus and also rewards a working knowledge of buttock adhesive technology." Other women's scholarship organizations, such as the Society of Women Engineers, reported an uptick in donations following the story.[7]

Another episode (August 16, 2015) illuminated the lack of government oversight of predatory televangelists who exploit vulnerable, often disadvantaged people. In a series of episodes, Oliver established a church "to test the legal and financial limits of what religious entities are able to do," and then asked his audience to "profess their belief" in his church. In two follow-up broadcasts, Oliver publicized the response, reporting on the tens of thousands of dollars that were sent in, "mostly in single dollar bills." Then after dissolving the church, he redirected the funds to Doctors Without Borders.[8]

In each of these examples, Oliver combines standard journalistic practices with entertainment styles to tell complex institutional stories. He characterizes the heroes and the villains, and identifies courses of social action to take that respond to the story. He also extends the analysis over time and across platforms when he includes his audience and wider publics in the story—forgiving medical debt, encouraging contributions to scholarly women's organizations, and soliciting donations to a fake church to illuminate the exploitative practices of televangelists.

Oliver also engages in seemingly more outré cultural criticism, as in one show where he forms a relationship with a "rogue" Japanese anime mascot named Chiitan, who is known for making silly, sometimes edgy and violent videos with puppets. As a part of the story, Oliver creates his own anime mascot, called Chiijohn, who travels to Japan to steal Chiitan's former best friend, Shinjo-kun, who is the official mascot of the city prefecture of Susaki.[9] The story played out across popular media, as Japanese citizens complained about the Chiitan videos to the prefecture government and also directed tax dollars to Susaki to support the city. More recently, Chiitan's Twitter accounts in Japan, and in Korea, Brazil, and Turkey, were suspended. Chiitan's team set up a Change.org petition to help them win back the Twitter accounts. And all this occurred amid news that "TV Tokyo suspended a Fairy Chiitan cartoon anime show because of the dispute, while the SEGA Game company also canceled plans to collaborate with Chiitan in an online game."[10] Chiitan challenged John Oliver to a wrestling match, and all of this was chronicled in traditional and specialist media, and now in this published essay! Since then, the mascot Chiitan has continued to make videos and participate in the public sphere.

This story also illuminates the broader media environment in which media metacommentary operates as a critical form of media expertise. Not only has the Chiitan story been reported in the *New York Times* and the *Washington Post,* but even in these traditional outlets, the boundary between the real world and the fictional world of online media is quite unclear. To be sure, this has always been true of fictional stories and fictional characters, but it has been far less common for fictional characters to be treated as real actors in the news media, where there is still an attempt to keep the world of serious facts segregated from the fictional worlds of entertainment. The story of Chiitan may be dismissed as entertainment news or even an empty public relations stunt as Oliver and his team attempt to create wider effects for their stories, but I want to suggest that this might miss the critical point. What Oliver's Chiitan story provides is a collective representation of a global world connected through the Internet across multiple media platforms as well as legacy media; in short, he represents a mediated global public that can share stories and common concerns. This is a media performance that both illuminates and pushes the boundaries of the media system as it operates "in real life," and as it comes to dominate more and more of what is called "real life." Oliver is aware of this, saying:

You might be wanting to ask: How does an umbrella-wielding coked up otter being assaulted in a windowless room encourage tourism to the small Japanese port city of Susaki? Well, I'm on TV and I'm talking about the small Japanese city of Susaki so that should answer your stupid question. (Oliver April 28, 2019)

Learning from John Oliver

If Oliver is a critical media expert, then what does his success suggest for other expert performances? Like other comedy news anchors, Oliver collapses any easy distinction between news and entertainment, expert and amateur. As he deflates the performances of the powerful and their serious, earnest styles, he unmasks the privilege of unquestioned authority that accompanies established cultural power. This is one way the expansion of the new political satire associated with figures like Oliver has the potential to increase media reflexivity (McBeth and Clemons 2011); that is, Oliver illuminates the crisis of expertise. He reveals that authority must be claimed and does not simply come with the law degree, the PhD, or the fancy title. It suggests, further, that all experts should become more aware of their positions of privilege in relation to clients, audiences, and wider publics. This is especially true if the expert position maps other forms of privilege, such as race, class, or gender privilege.

Second and connected to this, Oliver illuminates the crucial importance of media skill in performing expertise. He never wavers in observing that what he is doing is a performance. He is performing, others are performing, and the conditions of performance are a critical, political question.

Third, Oliver's hackeresque style demonstrates the instability of institutional conditions of expertise. No one who is connected through the Internet is ever unavailable to criticism, it seems, and everyone, everywhere is connected to the Internet. Oliver uses this fact to hold a range of actors to account, in government, business, and media institutions.

Fourth, unlike the exclusive worlds of hackers, Oliver includes his audience in his critical, broad-based transmedia performance. The user-audience is a key element of his performative fusion, as the performance extends out past each individual show and has consequences for people "in real life." This relationship to the audience is a key to Oliver's credibility and authenticity, and it is also why Oliver has been able to marshal networked publics to act collectively. His performances recognize the multiple identities and relationships of his audiences and then connect them to invoke a public. This stitching together of networked publics through collective representations of the social are also shown to exist only in and through the media.

Finally, Oliver's performances illuminate a mediatized social world that requires a form of expert media knowledge that encompasses the entire operation of the media ecology. Couldry's (2003, 2012, 2014) idea of "media meta-capital," which is defined as a form of power in the media field that allows one to exercise power over other forms of media, encapsulates this idea. To be sure, Oliver exercises media metacapital as the host of a popular, well-financed, and well-publicized show on HBO. That said, the key to his success lies in his innovation of media metacommentary, which allows him to elevate his own performance of critical media expertise while relativizing and destabilizing the performances of others.

Media metacommentary is important because it resolves the underlying tensions between epistemological uncertainty, the challenges of performing expert authority, and the demand for authentic collective narratives that can inform contemporary public spheres. Importantly though, the history of media metacommentary shows that it is neither inherently progressive nor inherently critical. Although it offers some clues for effectively managing the epistemological uncertainty of late modern societies, there is no guarantee that media metacommentary improves social reflexivity, or that it can resist the influence of money and power. Whatever the future of media metacommentary as a particular performance of expertise, it is clear that the performance of all kinds of expertise is tied up with an ability to marshal media expertise rooted in an understanding of our profoundly mediatized social world.

As a case study then, Oliver's media metacommentary traces one thread in the social reorganization of expertise that has occurred in and through the media, and it also underscores the centrality of media knowledge for expert performances as they become increasingly unstable under conditions of mediatization. This is true both for media intellectuals and for experts who do not consider themselves primarily oriented to media. This suggests the fundamental importance of autonomy for media institutions, media actors and media processes. Under conditions of mediatization, the autonomy of a critic like Oliver relies on the overall media ecology being able to preserve a space of autonomy in which he can perform. This is also why the story about net neutrality and the policies that shape access to the media is important. The autonomy of the media space is increasingly relevant to the ability of *all* experts to perform their knowledge, for *all* critics to engage in criticism, and, arguably, also for the constitution of democratic publics.

NOTES

1. Oliver's successes are closely chronicled in the news media and his Wikipedia page is meticulously curated. It relates multiple instances of the impact of stories aired by *Last Week Tonight* as reported in other news sources. For a sampling of the coverage, see Jon Dekel, "The John Oliver Effect: How the Daily Show Alum Became the Most Trusted Man in America," *National Post*, February 18, 2015; Victor Luckerson, "How the 'John Oliver Effect' Is Having a Real-Life Impact," *Time*, January 20, 2015; "Elizabeth Biernan—John Oliver, the 100 Most Influential People," *Time*, April 17, 2019; Brian Stelter, "Even John Oliver Enjoys a Drumpf Bump," *CNNMoney*, accessed April 17, 2019.
2. Media metacommentary is steeped in social media practices like blogs that connect different sources through reposting and commentary. It is also connected to practices of news

aggregators that collect sources, sometimes with a preference for particular political or cultural positions. The format of *Last Week Tonight* follows this pattern in a television broadcast format that goes out to very large audiences. My thanks to reviewers and editors for drawing out this point.

3. News satire has a long history. In the United States, it is associated with articles by Mark Twain, fictitious news segments on long-running shows like *Saturday Night Live*, and enormously varied online offerings, such as *Citizen Kate*, *Faking News*, and, most prominently, *The Onion*, which was founded as a collegiate newspaper in 1988 and began publishing online in the 1990s. Some of these outlets are less overtly political than the partisan formats on cable television, which were more closely tied to party politics. What they all have in common is a form of media criticism that has contributed to the changing and challenging environment for traditional performances of expertise, and especially journalistic expertise.

4. There is a small journalistic cottage industry that writes about John Oliver and journalism. See Asawin Suebsaeng, "'Last Week Tonight' Does Real Journalism, No Matter What John Oliver Says," *The Daily Beast*, September 29, 2014; David Bauder, "Oliver Adds Journalism to His Comedy," *Associated Press*, September 26, 2014; James Poniewozik "Unfortunately, John Oliver, You Are a Journalist," *Time*, November 17, 2014.

5. The official YouTube video of Oliver's net neutrality segment had been viewed over 14 million times as of May 2019. Media coverage of the net neutrality story and its effects include Jacob Kastrenakes, "FCC Received a Total of 3.7 Million Comments on Net Neutrality," *The Verge*, September 16, 2014, https://www.theverge.com/2014/9/16/6257887/fcc-net-neutrality-3-7-million-comments-made; Colin Lecher, "Read the FCC's Internal Emails about John Oliver's Net Neutrality Segment," *The Verge*, November 13, 2014, https://www.theverge.com/2014/11/13/7205817/fcc-john-oliver-net-neutrality-emails; Steve Lohr, "FCC Plans Strong Hand to Regulate the Internet," *New York Times*, February 4, 2015, https://www.nytimes. com/2015/02/05/technology/fcc-wheeler-net-neutrality.html; Tom Risen, "FCC Chairman Tom Wheeler: 'I Am Not a Dingo,'" *U.S. News & World Report*, June 13, 2014, https://www.usnews.com/news/blogs/washington-whispers/2014/06/13/fcc-chairman-tom-wheeler-i-am-not-a-dingo; Michael Roppolo, "John Oliver's Rant about Net Neutrality Crashes FCC Site," *CBS News*, June 3, 2014, https://www.cbsnews.com /news/fcc-comment-page-crashes-after-john-olivers-rant-about-net-neutrality/; Rebecca R. Ruiz and Steve Lohr, "FCC Approves Net Neutrality Rules, Classifying Broadband Internet Service as a Utility," *New York Times*, February 26, 2015, https://www.nytimes.com/2015/02/27/ technology/net-neutrality-fcc-vote-internet-utility.html; Edward Wyatt, "FCC, in a Shift, Backs Fast Lanes for Web Traffic," *New York Times*, April 23, 2014, https://www.nytimes.com/2014/04/24/technology/fcc-new-net-neutrality-rules.html.

6. Leslie Salzillo, "John Oliver Buys Up $15 Million in Medical Debt, Then Pays Off the Debt for 9,000 People in Hardship," *Daily Kos*, June 6, 2016, https://www.dailykos.com/stories/2016/6/6/1535091/-John-Oliver-buys-up-15-million-in-medical-debt-then-pays-off-the-debt-for-9-000-people-in-hardship.

7. Barbara Herman, "John Oliver Takes On Miss America Pageant's 'Unbelievable' Scholarship Claims," *International Business Times*, September 22, 2014, https://www.ibtimes.com/john-oliver-takes-miss-america-pageants-unbelievable-scholarship-claims-1692908; Ted Gregory, "'John Oliver Bounce' Benefits Chicago-based Women's Engineering Group," *Chicago Tribune*, September 24, 2014, https://www.chicagotribune.com/entertainment/tv/ct-pageant-engineer-scholarships-20140923-story.html.

8. For media coverage of the online church story, see Lisa Respers France, "John Oliver Forms His Own Church and Just Keeps on Winning," *CNN*, August 17, 2015, https://www.cnn.com/2015/08/17/ entertainment /john-oliver-last-week-tonight-feat/; "John Oliver Starts His Own Church to Expose 'Predatory' Televangelists," *Hollywood Reporter*, August 17, 2015, https://www.hollywoodreporter.com/ news/john-oliver-exposes-televangelists-by-815767; Chris Mandle, "John Oliver Inundated with Donations after Setting Up Fake Church to Make a Point about Tax-Dodging Televangelists," *The Independent*, August 24, 2015, https://www.independent.co.uk/news/people/john-oliver-inundated-with-donations-after-setting-up-fake-church-to-make-a-point-about-tax-dodging-10469577.html.

9. Oona McGee, "Chiitan Needs Your Help! Japanese Mascot Suspended on Twitter after John Oliver Feud," *SoraNews24*, May 15, 2019, https://soranews24. com/2019/05/15/chiitan-needs-your-help-japanese-mascot-suspended-on-twitter-after-john-oliver-feud/.

10. Simon Denye, "The Feud between a Giant Japanese Otter Mascot and John Oliver, Explained," *Washington Post*, May 3, 2019, https://www.washingtonpost.com/world/2019/05/03/subversive-japanese-otter-mascot-ready-take-john oliver/.

References

Abbott, Andrew. 1988. *The System of Professions: An Essay on the Division of Expert Labor.* Chicago: University of Chicago Press.

Alexander, Jeffrey C. 2004. "Cultural Pragmatics: Social Performance between Ritual and Strategy." *Sociological Theory* 22:527–573.

Alexander, Jeffrey C. 2009. "Public Intellectuals and Civil Society." In *Intellectuals and Their Publics*, edited by Andreas Hess, Christian Fleck and E. Stina Lyon, 19–28. Farnham, UK: Ashgate Books.

Barkin, Steve M. 2015. *American Television News: The Media Marketplace and the Public Interest.* London: Routledge. (Original work published in 2003 by M. E. Sharpe).

Barnard, Stephen R. 2017. *Citizens at the Gates: Twitter, Networked Publics, and the Transformation of American Journalism.* Palgrave Macmillan.

Barnard, Stephen R. 2018. "Tweeting #Ferguson: Mediatized Fields and the New Activist Journalist." *New Media & Society* 20 (7): 2252–2271.

"The Journalistic Field in a Time of Mediatization." SocArXiv. February 25. doi:10.31235/osf.io/r9bbm

Baumann, Shyon. 2007. *Hollywood Highbrow: From Entertainment to Art.* Princeton, NJ: Princeton University Press.

Bauman, Zygmunt. 1987. *Legislators and Interpreters.* Oxford: Polity Press.

Berry, Jeffrey, and Sarah Sobieraj. 2014. *The Outrage Industry.* Oxford: Oxford University Press.

Bourdieu, Pierre. (1988) 1996. *On Television.* New York: New Press.

Bourdieu, Pierre. 1991. "Universal Corporatism: The Role of Intellectuals in the Modern World." *Poetics Today* 12:655–669.

Bourdieu, Pierre. 1992. *The Logic of Practice.* Stanford, CA: Stanford University Press.

Bourdieu, Pierre. 1993. *The Field of Cultural Production.* New York: Columbia University Press.

Bourdieu, Pierre. 2005. "Political, Social Science, and Journalistic Fields." In *Bourdieu and the Journalistic Field*, edited by R. Benson and E. Neveu, 29–47. Cambridge, UK: Polity Press.

Calhoun, Craig, ed. 1992. *Habermas and the Public Sphere.* Cambridge, MA: MIT Press.

Chun, Wendy Hui Kyong, and Thomas Keenan. 2005. *New Media, Old Media: A History and Theory Reader*. New York: Routledge.

Clayman, Steven E., and John Heritage. 2002. *The News Interview: Journalists and Public Figures on the Air*. Cambridge, UK: Cambridge University Press.

Collini, Stefan. 2006. *Absent Minds: Intellectuals in Britain*. Oxford: Oxford University Press.

Collins, H. M., and Robert Evans. 2007. *Rethinking Expertise*. Chicago: University of Chicago Press.

Cook, Guy, Elisa Pieri, and Peter T. Robbins. 2004. " 'The Scientists Think and the Public Feels': Expert Perceptions of the Discourse of GM Food." *Discourse & Society* 15 (4): 433–449.

Couldry, Nick. 2003. "Media Meta-Capital: Extending the Range of Bourdieu's Field Theory." *Theory and Society* 32 (5/6): 653–677.

Couldry, Nick. 2012. *Media, Society, World*. Cambridge, UK: Polity Press.

Couldry, Nick. 2014. 'When Mediatization Hits the Ground." In *Mediatized Worlds: Culture and Society in a Media Age*, edited by Andreas Hepp and Friedrich Krotz, 54–71. New York: Palgrave Macmillan.

Couldry, Nick, and Andreas Hepp. 2013. "Conceptualising Mediatization: Contexts, Traditions, Arguments." *Communication Theory* 23 (3): 191–202.

Drezner, Daniel W. 2017. *The Ideas Industry*. Oxford: Oxford University Press.

Eley, Geoff. 1992. "Nations, Publics, and Political Cultures: Placing Habermas in the Nineteenth Century." In *Habermas and the Public Sphere*, edited by Craig Calhoun, 289–339. Cambridge, MA: MIT Press.

Epstein, Steven. 1995. "The Construction of Lay Expertise: AIDS Activism and the Forging of Credibility in the Reform of Clinical Trials." *Science, Technology, & Human Values* 20 (4): 408–347.

Eyal, Gil. 2013. "For a Sociology of Expertise: The Social Origins of the Autism Epidemic." *American Journal of Sociology* 118 (4): 863–907.

Eyerman, Ron. 1994. *Between Culture and Politics: Intellectuals in Modern Society*. Cambridge, UK: Polity.

Eyerman, Ron, 2011. "Intellectuals and Cultural Trauma. *European Journal of Social Theory* 14:453–467.

Fraser, Nancy. 1990. "Rethinking the Public Sphere: A Contribution to the Critique of Actually Existing Democracy." *Social Text*, 25/26, 56–80. doi:10.2307/466240.

Glas, René, Sybille Lammes, Michiel de Lange, Joost Raessens, and Imar de Vries. 2019. "Introduction to Part III." In *The Playful Citizen: Civic Engagement in a Mediatized Culture*, edited by René Glas, Sybille Lammes, Michiel de Lange, Joost Raessens, and Imar de Vries, 275–278. Amsterdam: Amsterdam University Press. http://www.jstor.org/stable/j.ctvcmx pds.18.

Habermas, Jürgen. (1962) 1989. *The Structural Transformation of the Public Sphere*. Translated by Thomas Burger. Cambridge MA: MIT Press.

Habermas, Jürgen. 1992. "Further Reflections on the Public Sphere and Concluding Remarks." In Calhoun, *Habermas and the Public Sphere*, 421–480.

Habermas, Jürgen. 1996. *Between Facts and Norms: Contributions to a Discourse Theory of Law and Democracy*. Cambridge MA: MIT Press.

Hepp, Andreas. 2013. "The Communicative Figurations of Mediatized Worlds: Mediatization Research in Times of the 'Mediation of Everything." ' *European Journal of Communication* 28 (6): 615–629.

Hepp, Andreas, and Friedrich Krotz, eds. 2014. *Mediatized Worlds: Culture and Society in a Media Age*. New York: Palgrave Macmillan.

Hjarvard, Stig. 2008. *The Mediatization of Culture and Society*. New York: Routledge.

Jacobs, Ronald N. 2012. "Entertainment Media and the Aesthetic Public Sphere." In *The Oxford Handbook of Cultural Sociology*, edited by J. Alexander, R. Jacobs, and P. Smith, 318–342. New York: Oxford University Press.

Jacobs, Ronald N. 2017. "Journalism after Trump." *American Journal of Cultural Sociology* 5 (3): 409–425.

Jacobs, Ronald N., and Eleanor Townsley. 2014. "The Hermeneutics of Hannity: Format Innovation in the Space of Opinion after September 11." *Cultural Sociology* 1:1–18.

Jacobs, Ronald N., and Eleanor Townsley. 2011. *The Space of Opinion: Media Intellectuals and the Public Sphere*. Oxford University Press.

Jacobs, Ronald N., and Eleanor Townsley. 2018. "Media Meta-Commentary and the Performance of Expertise." *European Journal of Social Theory* 21, no. 3 (August): 340–356.

Jacobs, Ronald N., and Nicole Michaud Wild, 2013. "A Cultural Sociology of *The Colbert Report* and *The Daily Show*." *American Journal of Cultural Sociology* 1:69–95.

Jacobson, Thomas. 2017. "Trending Theory of the Public Sphere." *Annals of the International Communication Association* 41 (1): 70–82.

Jacoby, Russell. 1987. *The Last Intellectuals: American Culture in an Age of Academe*. New York: Basic Books.

Jennings, Jeremy, and Anthony Kemp-Welch, eds. 1997. *Intellectuals in Politics: From the Dreyfus Affair to Salman Rushdie*. London: Routledge.

Jurkowitz, Mark, Amy Mitchell, Laura Santhanam Houston, Steve Adams, Monica Anderson, and Nancy Vogt. 2013. "The Changing TV News Landscape." PEW Research Center, March 17. Accessed May 28, 2019. https://www.journalism.org/2013/03/17/the-changing-tv-news-landscape/#fn-37405-1.

Kalinov, Kalin. 2017. "Transmedia Narratives: Definition and Social Transformations in the Consumption of Media Content in the Globalized World." *Postmodernism Problems* 7:60–68.

Karpf, David. "The Clickbait Candidate" *The Chronicle of Higher Education* June 19, 2016 https://www.chronicle.com/article/the-clickbait-candidate/ Accessed December 7, 2022

Keane, John. 1991. *The Media and Democracy*. Cambridge, UK: Polity.

Kurasawa, Fuyuki. 2018. "Climategate, or, the Birth of the Digital Culture of Climate Change Denialism." Digital Citizenship Lab..

Ladd, Jonathan. "Trump's only significant campaign skill is manipulating the media. But he's great at it." *Vox* September 26, 2016. https://www.vox.com/mischiefs-of-faction/2016/9/26/13061494/trump-media-manipulation Accessed December 7, 2022

Livingstone, Sonia. 2009. "On the Mediation of Everything." *Journal of Communication* 59 (1): 1–18.

McBeth, Mark, and Randy Clemons. 2011. "Is Fake News the Real News? The Significance of Stewart and Colbert for Democratic Discourse, Politics, and Policy." In *The Stewart / Colbert Effect: Essays on the Real Impacts of Fake News*, edited by A. Amarasingam and R. McChesney, 79–98. Jefferson, NC: McFarland.

Moffitt, Benjamin. 2016. *The Global Rise of Populism: Performances, Political Style and Representation*. Stanford, CA: Stanford University Press.

PEW Research Center. 1998. "Changing Definitions of News," March 6. Accessed May 28, 2019. https://www.journalism.org/numbers/changing-definitions-of-news/.

Perlman, Marc. 2004. "Golden Ears and Meter Readers: The Contest for Epistemic Authority in Audiophilia." *Social Studies of Science* 34 (5): 783–807.

Postman, Neil. 1985. *Amusing Ourselves to Death*. New York: Penguin.

Rhomberg, Markus, and Nico Stehr. 2013. "Experts." In *Blackwell Encyclopedia of Sociology Online*, edited by George Ritzer. Malden, MA: Blackwell Publishing Ltd.

Rose, Nikolas. 2007. "Beyond Medicalisation." *The Lancet* 369 (February 24): 700–702.

Schudson, Michael. 1978. *Discovering the News*. New York: Basic Books.

Starr, Paul. (1982) 2017. *The Social Transformation of American Medicine: The Rise of a Sovereign Profession and the Making of a Vast Industry*. Updated ed. New York: Basic Books.

Suryanarayanan, Sainath, and Daniel L. Kleinman. 2012. "Be(e)coming Experts: The Controversy over Insecticides in the Honey Bee Colony Collapse Disorder." *Social Studies of Science* 43 (2): 215–240.

Taylor, Charles. 1992. *Sources of the Self: The Making of Modern Identity*. Cambridge, MA: Harvard University Press.

Townsley, Eleanor. 2006. "The Public Intellectual Trope in the United States." *American Sociologist* 37:39–66.

Townsley, Eleanor. 2015. "Science, Expertise and Profession in the Post-normal Discipline." *American Sociologist* 46 (1): 18–28.

Tucker, Kenneth. 2010. *Workers of the World, Enjoy! Aesthetic Politics from Revolutionary Syndicalism to the Global Justice Movement*. Philadelphia: Temple University Press.

Tufecki, Zeynep. 2017. *Twitter and Tear Gas: The Power and Fragility of Networked Protest*. New Haven, CT: Yale University Press.

Turow, Joseph. 1997. *Breaking Up America: Advertisers and the New Media World*. Chicago: University of Chicago Press.

Webster, James G. 2014. "The Marketplace of Attention." In *The Marketplace of Attention: How Audiences Take Shape in a Digital Age*, 1–22. Cambridge, MA: MIT Press. http://www.jstor.org/stable/j.ctt9qf9qj.4.

Weingart, Peter. 2003. "Paradoxes of Scientific Advising." In *Expertise and Its Interfaces*, edited by Gotthard Bechmann and Imre Hronszky, 53–89. Berlin: Edition Sigma.

Wild, Nicole Michaud. 2019. *Dubious Pundits: Presidential Politics, Late-Night Comedy, and the Public Sphere*. New York: Lexington Books.

Williams, Bruce A., and Michael X. Delli Carpini. 2011. *After Broadcast News: Media Regimes, Democracy, and the New Information Environment*. Cambridge, MA: Cambridge University Press.

Wynne, Brian. 2001. "Creating Public Alienation: Expert Cultures of Risk and Ethics on GMOs." *Science as Culture* 10 (4): 445–481.

Index

For the benefit of digital users, indexed terms that span two pages (e.g., 52–53) may, on occasion, appear on only one of those pages.

Figures are indicated by *f* following the page number